Modern Public Finance
The Study of Public Sector Economics

The Irwin Series in Economics

Consulting Editor
LLOYD G. REYNOLDS   *Yale University*

Modern Public Finance
The Study of Public Sector Economics

BERNARD P. HERBER

Professor of Economics
University of Arizona

Third Edition   1975

RICHARD D. IRWIN, INC.   Homewood, Illinois   60430
Irwin-Dorsey International, London, England   WC2H 9NJ
Irwin-Dorsey Limited, Georgetown, Ontario   L7G 4B3

Third Edition

First Printing, January 1975

ISBN 0-256-01621-6
Library of Congress Catalog Card No. 74–82924
Printed in the United States of America

To Jean

Preface

The author attempts in this third edition of *Modern Public Finance,* as he did in the first two editions, to provide a comprehensive framework for analyzing the influence of governmental revenue-gathering and expenditure activities in all functional areas of economic activity. In general, this encompasses a study of "public sector economics" but, more specifically, it constitutes a study in "public fiscal economics." That is, the framework of the book focuses upon the nonneutral effects, both positive and negative, exerted by public sector fiscal decisions on the allocation, distribution, stabilization, and economic growth goals of the society. Thus, even though the subject matter at times is concerned tangentially with nonfiscal aspects of public sector economics such as monetary policy, its primary content relates to the manner in which the public sector budget affects the basic functioning of a "mixed economy" through various taxation, debt-creation, user-pricing, and expenditure policies. The "mixed" American economy, of course, is characterized by a private sector dominance, but nonetheless by a significant public sector presence, in its overall economic performance. Moreover, this public sector presence is economically justified due to partial market failure in its performance of the allocational, distributional, stabilization, and economic growth functions.

In the preparation of this edition, the entire book has been appraised for possible improvement. Hence, the revision effort may be viewed as comprehensive, not partial. This policy has led to several varieties of change. Among these are the inclusion of recent contributions to the literature of public fiscal economics; the updating of tables and other statistical data; an effort to improve the written clarity of the discussion and, in addition, a rearrangement in certain places of the sequence of chapters and subject content so as to yield a more meaningful interrelationship between topics.

This reorganization results in the deletion of Part Five of the second edition, a section which analyzed several specific fiscal problem areas. However, important material from this section has been retained and transferred to other relevant parts of the book. The discussion of environmental externalities, for example, is moved to the analysis of *public goods* in Part One. Moreover, the overall public goods discussion is revised and expanded. Relatedly, new material on political-interaction costs is introduced into the public choice theory discussion of Chapter 5.

A considerably expanded treatment of the income elasticity of taxation concept is provided in Chapter 6 which is devoted to the subject of fiscal rationality criteria. This chapter introduces Part Two and is the first of ten chapters dealing with *public sector revenues.* Chapter 7 discusses the principles of equity in the distribution of tax burdens and Chapter 8 analyzes tax shifting and incidence principles. The seven following chapters provide detailed economic analyses of the major types of taxes. Among the changes in these chapters are an expanded appraisal of the value-added tax, a description of the net wealth tax, and empirical evidence concerning the income elasticity coefficients of major American taxes. Moreover, the discussion of the economic effects of federal social security taxes has been enlarged. The order of the taxation chapters has been rearranged to correspond with the primary objects or bases of taxation, namely, income, wealth, and transactions or sales.

The poverty chapter, after substantial revision and additions, has been moved to Part Three where it joins six other chapters in analyzing the overall *public sector budget,* its characteristics, and its economic effects. Meanwhile, the discussion of urban economic problems is transferred from the deleted Part Five to the discussion of intergovernmental fiscal relations in Part Three. Moreover, the evaluation of the public sector in other nations is now included in the public sector budget section. Furthermore, the coverage of benefit-cost analysis in Part Three has been enlarged and rewritten. The same is true of the intergovernmental fiscal relations (fiscal federalism) analysis which, in addition, has been divided into separate "problems" and "techniques" chapters due to the overall length of the discussion. In Part Four on the subject of *aggregate fiscal policy,* revisions and additions occur at a number of locations including the "inflation-recession paradox" discussion as well as the theoretical analysis of "governmental debt burdens." In all, the author has considered each and every component of the previous edition in an effort to improve the overall composition of the book.

Appreciation is expressed to all who have assisted in the preparation of this edition of *Modern Public Finance*. This list includes Darwin W. Daicoff, Lloyd G. Reynolds, Paul U. Pawlik, Gerald J. Swanson, J. S. H. Hunter, and Brooke F. Cadwallader. However, the author alone is responsible for any inadequacies which may remain. My appreciation is expressed also to my wife, Jean, for her assistance on the manuscript. To all of those mentioned above, and to others not mentioned who have provided assistance on this or earlier editions, I extend a sincere "thank you."

Tucson, Arizona   BERNARD P. HERBER
December 1974

Contents

part two

Public Sector Revenues

the United States: *Historical Development of Selective Sales Taxes. Present Status of Selective Sales Taxes.* General Retail Sales Taxation in the United States: *Historical Development of General Sales Taxes. Present Status of State and Local General Sales Taxes.* Fiscal Rationality Criteria Applied to Sales Taxes: *Allocational Effects. Distributional Effects. Stabilization-Growth, Revenue Productivity, and Intergoal Performance.* The Proposed Substitution of a Federal Value-Added Tax for the Federal Corporation Income Tax: *Background. Different Types of Value-Added Tax. The Economic Effects of an "Unshifted" Corporation Income Tax versus a Value-Added Tax. The Economic Effects of a "Shifted" Corporation Income Tax versus a Value-Added Tax. Intergoal Conflict.* A Variety of Other Taxes: *Severance Taxes. Capital Stock Taxes. The Lump-Sum Tax.*

Alternative Techniques for the Financing of Quasi-Public Goods. Earmarked Taxes and Trust Funds: *Federal Social Security Programs. Interstate Highway and Other Trust Funds. Economic Analysis of Earmarked Taxes and Trust Funds.* The Commercial Principle and User Prices: *The Extent of Commercial Activity by American Government. Fiscal Rationality and Government Commercial Activity.* Administrative Revenues.

part three
The Public Sector Budget: Trends, Techniques,
and Issues

Expenditure Patterns: *Prior to 1900. Twentieth-Century Expenditure Trends.* Revenue Patterns: *Prior to 1900. Twentieth-Century Revenue Trends. Functional Analysis of Twentieth-Century Expenditure and Revenue Trends.* Theoretical Analysis of Public Sector Growth: *Wagner's Hypothesis of Increasing Governmental Activity. The Displacement, Inspection, and Concentration Effects. The Critical-Limit Hypothesis.*

Constitutional Division of Fiscal Powers: *Fiscal Limitations on the Federal Government. Fiscal Limitations on State Governments. The Taxation of Governmental "Instrumentalities." Fiscal Limitations Imposed by State Government Constitutions.* The Development of Formal Public Sector Budgeting in the United States. Federal Budgetary Procedure: *Executive Preparation and Submission of the Budget. Legislative Review and Enactment of the Budget. Executive Implementation of the Budget. Auditing of the Budget by the General Accounting Office.* Types of Government Budgets: *The Unified Federal Budget. The Federal Tax Expenditures Budget. The Full-Employment Budget. The Capital Budget. Other Budget*

the United States: *Overall Comparisons. Fiscal Comparisons. Income Tax Reform in Canada.* The Public Sector in an Open System: *International Tax Coordination. Financing and Regulating International Collective Consumption.*

part four

**The Public Sector and Aggregate
Economic Performance**

The Performance of a Pure Market Economy: *The Classical Theory of Aggregate Economic Performance—Say's Law. The Keynesian Theory of Aggregate Economic Performance. Deflationary and Inflationary Gaps. The Problem of Economic Growth.* The Employment Act of 1946—A Legislative Mandate for Fiscal Policy: *Nature of the Employment Act. Defining and Measuring Employment Act Goals.*

Automatic Fiscal Stabilizers. Discretionary Fiscal Stabilizers: *The Tax Multiplier. The Transfer Expenditures Multiplier. The Exhaustive Expenditures Multiplier. The Balanced Budget Multiplier.* The Application of Discretionary Fiscal Stabilizers to Economic Stabilization Goals: *Fiscal Policy Applied to Deflationary Gap Conditions. Fiscal Policy Applied to Inflationary Gap Conditions. The Balanced Budget Multiplier and Fiscal Policy. The Balance of International Payments and Fiscal Techniques.*

Fiscal Techniques for Economic Growth. Interaction between Fiscal Policy Goals: *Full Employment versus Inflation. Full Employment versus the Allocation, Distribution, and Balance-of-Payments Goals. Government Fiscal Policy and Interrelated Growth-Cycle Objectives. Fiscal Policy and Regional Economic Activity.* Techniques of Deficit Financing and Surplus Disposal: *The Deficit Budget. The Surplus Budget.*

Rules or Norms of Fiscal Policy: *The Annually Balanced Budget Fiscal Norm. The Functional Finance Fiscal Norm. A Comparison of the Annually Balanced Budget and Functional Finance Norms. The Cyclically Balanced Budget Fiscal Norm. The High-Employment Budget Fiscal Norm.* The Full-Employment Budget Surplus Concept and Fiscal Drag. A Further Discussion of Automatic Fiscal Stabilizers. Monetary Policy as a Norm for Rational Economic Policy. The Need for Comprehensive and Flexible Economic Policy.

History of Public Sector Debt in the United States: *Federal Government Debt. State Government Debt. Local Government Debt. Intergovernmen-*

part one

Public Goods and Public Sector Decision Making

1

Resource Scarcity and
Intersector Allocation

THE ECONOMIC FUNCTIONS AND GOALS OF
THE PUBLIC SECTOR

The basic economic problem of *scarcity* provides a logical departure
point for the study of public finance. The resources available to any
society are "limited" in their ability to produce economic goods by both
quantitative and qualitative constraints.[1] *Land,* which may be defined
generally as natural resources, is limited in quantity by the geographical
area of the nation and by the magnitude of raw material deposits within
this land area. Moreover, natural resources vary in quality among nations. *Labor* faces quantitative constraints as a productive resource
through the numerical size and age distribution of the society's population and qualitative limitations through such determinants as the prevailing ethical, health, and educational standards of the society. *Capital,*
in turn, is limited in quantity by the society's past capital formation
behavior and in quality by the relationship of its capital stock to the
prevailing state of technology.

This limited supply of the productive resources available to a society
leads to the *allocation* function of economics. The "unlimited" scope

---

[1] Although the traditional classification of productive resources into land, labor, and
capital components will be used in this book, it should be recognized that many economists prefer an alternative classification arrangement whereby all resources are classified
as *capital* in the form of either "material" or "human" capital. However, since resource
scarcity exists under either system of classification, the particular system selected will not
affect the validity of the present discussion.

of aggregate human wants, alongside the "limited" resources which produce the economic goods (including intangible services) capable of satisfying these wants, makes necessary the allocation of scarce resources among alternative uses. An infinite or unlimited quantity of economic goods cannot be produced. When some goods are produced with the scarce resources, the opportunities to produce other goods are forgone (assuming full employment of resources). Thus, an *economic system* must exist to determine the pattern of production, that is, to answer the questions (1) which economic goods shall be produced? and (2) in what quantities shall they be produced? Moreover, the allocation function possesses an additional important dimension in that it must be concerned with the *institutional means* through which the allocation decisions are processed. Herein, the link between the basic economic problem of scarcity and the study of public finance is established.

Modern society offers two institutions through which the decisions of the allocation branch of economics are made. These are the *market* and *government* means of resource allocation.[2] Alternatively, the market allocational institution may be designated the *private sector* and the government allocational institution the *public sector*. The forces of demand and supply and the price mechanism, as determined by consumer sovereignty and producer profit motives, characterize private sector allocation. Public sector allocation, on the other hand, is accomplished through the revenue and expenditure activities of governmental budgeting. In reality, of course, no economic society allocates all of its resources through a single allocational institution. Instead, each economy in the world is "mixed," to one degree or another, between market-determined and government-determined resource allocation. Accordingly, a given national economy may typically be referred to as "capitalist" or "socialist" depending upon the degree to which it stresses the market or government means of allocation.

In the pages which follow, the analysis will consider resource allocation in a society characterized by a preference for the private sector approach. More specifically, it will emphasize the allocation behavior of a public sector operating within a mixed, though market-oriented, economic system.

Besides directing the allocation function, both the private and public

---

[2] It may be argued that a third allocational institution exists in the form of the *nonprofit sector* which is exemplified by such organizations as those engaged in religious and philanthropic work. Nonprofit organizations, however, are a much less important source of resource allocation in American society than are the market and government institutions. Moreover, though operating from a base somewhat analogous to private property, these organizations ordinarily do not pursue profits as a primary objective, but instead emphasize social goals. Thus, because of both their "relative unimportance" in the United States and also their "hybrid" motivation, the nonprofit institution is not considered in this textbook to constitute a separate and basic allocational institution. Rather, the choice between market- and government-determined resource allocation will be emphasized.

sectors of a mixed economy also determine the performance of the other major branches of economic activity. These consist of the distribution, stabilization, and economic growth functions. Hence, the present textbook will be concerned not only with the influence of the public sector on resource allocation, it will consider also the impact of the public sector in these other economic areas. The *distribution* function (branch) relates to the manner in which the "effective demand" over economic goods is divided among the various individual and family spending units of the society. More specifically, this effective demand, which determines the distribution of "real output" among the population, stems from the pattern of income and wealth distribution in the private sector and the pattern of political voting influence in the public sector. The *stabilization* function (branch) concerns itself with the attainment by the economy of full- or high-level employment of labor and utilization of capital, price stability, and a "satisfactory" balance of international payments. The *economic growth* function (branch) pertains to the rate of increase in a society's productive resource base, and a related "satisfactory" rate of growth in its real per capita output, over a period of time.[3] Since the public sector inevitably will influence the performance of the national economy in terms of these four economic functions, it is reasonable to assume that society will wish to consciously formulate *fiscal policies* so as to attain given allocation, distribution, stabilization, and economic growth *goals*. Hence, the four functions or branches of economics may be viewed also as the "goals," "targets," or "objectives" of public sector economic activity. These goals cannot always be separated in a precise manner. Thus, a given budgetary act usually will exert an influence on more than one goal. The resulting complexity with which public finance becomes involved is evident throughout the book and will be more comprehensively analyzed in Chapter 6 in the discussion of "intergoal nonneutrality."

Finally, it should be observed that the term *public finance* is somewhat of a misnomer for the content of this book. "Finance," as such, suggests "monetary flows" as represented by the revenue-gathering and expenditure activities of the governmental budgetary (fiscal) process. Indeed, these monetary flows are a relevant component of the analysis which follows. Nonetheless, the "basic" economic functions of the public sector are those which influence resource allocation, the distribution of effective demand and real output among the population, aggregate economic performance, and the rate of economic growth. These are the "direct" results of public sector economic activity. Hence, the term *public sector economics* is a more accurate representa-

---

[3] Many economists include the *economic growth* function as part of the stabilization function.

tion of the content of the book than is the term *public finance*.[4] Yet, out of respect to the orthodox nature and well-engrained popularity of the latter term, a bit of semantical quality will be compromised and the terms will be used interchangeably in the chapters which follow.

INTERSECTOR RESOURCE ALLOCATION

Optimal and Suboptimal Intersector Allocation

As observed above, an economic system must determine the "mix" of its resource allocation between the private and public sectors.[5] An *actual* allocation division between the two sectors will exist at any one point of time. Moreover, it is possible to conceptualize the existence of an *optimal* allocation mix, known also as *social balance*, given the preference patterns and "effective" demand of the members of the society.[6] The points of actual and optimal intersector allocation may or may not coincide. If they do not coincide, it may be said that intersector resource allocation is *suboptimal*, or alternately, that *social imbalance* or *intersector misallocation* exists.

The relationship between optimal and suboptimal intersector resource allocation is demonstrated in Figure 1–1. In this graph, private sector output as a percentage of total national output is measured on the horizontal axis and public sector output as a percentage of total national output on the vertical axis. It is *assumed* that point *A* represents an optimal division of national output between the private and public sectors with the private sector controlling 75 percent of resource allocation and the public sector controlling 25 percent. In a conceptual sense, this social balance point would thus be assumed to reflect the true preferences of the people of the society for private and public goods as made "effective" by the *distribution* of income, wealth, and political voting power among the people.[7]

If point *A* represents *optimal* intersector allocation, and the *actual* mix of resources between private and public goods in the society is at point *A*, then the "optimal" and "actual" points of intersector resource

---

[4] Since the term "public sector economics" could be said to relate to the functional economic effects of both governmental *budgetary (fiscal) activities* and to the effects of money supply control as in *monetary economics,* a still more precise term for the present subject matter would be *public fiscal economics.*

[5] It will be demonstrated in Chapter 3 that allocational activities need not be provided "exclusively" by a single sector. For example, the public sector may finance part of the costs of a privately produced good.

[6] The question as to the "proper" role of government in a market-oriented economy has been in the minds of economists since at least the time of Adam Smith (1723–90). More recently, the term "social balance" has been applied to this concept by John Kenneth Galbraith in his *The Affluent Society* (Boston: Houghton Mifflin Co., 1958).

[7] The significant relationship between the "existing state of distribution" and "effective demand" or "actual allocation" will be developed further in the pages which follow.

FIGURE 1–1

Intersector Resource Allocation: Optimal and Suboptimal Points

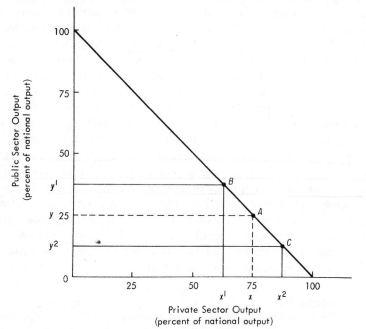

A = Point of *optimal* intersector resource allocation (assumed)
B, C = Points of *suboptimal* intersector resource allocation

allocation coincide. In this instance, no social imbalance is present. Given the preference patterns of the individuals of the society, no welfare improvement would result from any reallocation between private and public goods. On the other hand, if point A represents *optimal* intersector allocation, and the *actual* allocation is at point B, or at point C, then suboptimal allocation or social imbalance does exist. In this instance, reallocation between the two sectors is required if societal welfare is to be maximized. The imbalance gap between points A and B represents an underallocation of resources to the private sector and an overallocation of resources to the public sector by the "percentage" amounts xx^1 and yy^1, respectively. The imbalance gap between points A and C, on the other hand, represents an overallocation of resources to the private sector and an underallocation of resources to the public sector by the "percentage" amounts xx^2 and yy^2, respectively.

The Indifference Approach to Optimal Intersector Resource Allocation

The application of indifference analysis to the concept of intersector resource allocation allows the point of "optimal" intersector allocation to be *logically derived* instead of merely assumed as above. The indifference approach to intersector allocation is demonstrated in Figures 1–2, 1–3, and 1–4. In each graph, private sector output is shown along the horizontal axis and public sector output along the vertical axis. In Figure 1–2, the *production-possibility curve* of the society, designated as *P*, relates the "marginal rates of transformation" between the production of private and public goods with the scarce productive resources available to the society. That is, it shows the various combinations of private and public goods that can be produced with the *full employment* of the "quantitatively" and "qualitatively" limited land, labor, and capital resources available to the society at a given point of time. The higher the position of the production-possibility curve on the graph, the greater the production potential of the society due to the greater quantity and/or quality of its productive resources. At point *B*, all of society's resources would be allocated to the private sector. At point *A*, all of the resources would be allocated to the public sector.

The society's production-possibility curve *P* is *concave* to the origin of the graph. This reflects the fact that scarce resources cannot be substituted with equal efficiency between the production of public and

FIGURE 1–2
The Production-Possibility Curve for a Society

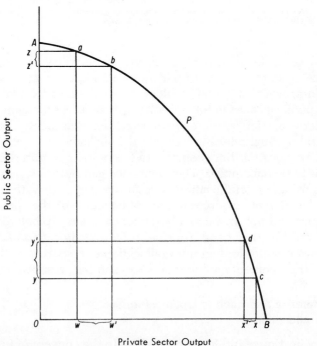

Private Sector Output

FIGURE 1–3
Social Indifference Curves

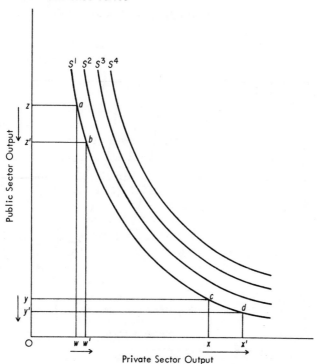

private goods. Thus, in Figure 1–2, a reallocation of resources along the upper part of the P curve, as from a to b, would add more in private sector output, the distance ww^1, than is sacrificed in public sector output, the distance zz^1. This would be due to "decreasing returns" in the production of public goods. To the contrary, a movement along the lower portion of the P curve, as from c to d, will add more in public sector output than is sacrificed in private sector output. This would be due to "decreasing returns" in the production of private goods. A comparison of the distances yy^1 and xx^1, respectively, reveals this phenomenon.

This unequal tradeoff in the output of private and public goods, as resources are reallocated in production between the two sectors, may be explained by the following reasons: *First,* some economic goods by their very nature are produced more efficiently, with less real input costs per unit of output, by one sector than by the other. Thus, if the private sector were allocating most resources, as would be true toward the lower part of the P curve, it likely would be providing goods such

FIGURE 1–4

Intersector Resource Allocation: Optimal and Suboptimal Points

INDIFFERENCE APPROACH

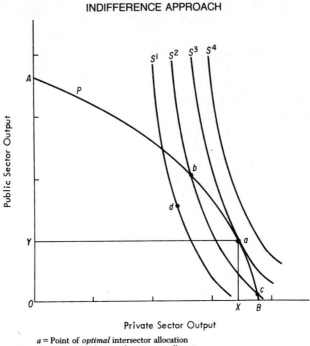

Private Sector Output

a = Point of *optimal* intersector allocation
b, c, d = Points of *suboptimal* intersector allocation

as national defense. Yet, if the national defense function were transferred from federal government control to market control, production efficiency in defense would doubtless decline with a greater loss in public sector output than is added in private sector output. This may be viewed in Figure 1–2 toward the lower end of the *P* curve with the distance y^1y representing a greater loss from the public sector *not* producing national defense than the value of defense production, x^1x gained with private sector production of defense. *Second,* but equally important, increasing costs tend to occur when too many goods are produced by one sector due to the principles of diminishing returns and decreasing returns to scale coming into operation.[8] These principles of

[8] The short-run principle of *diminishing returns* states that as successive units of a variable productive resource (assume labor) are added in production to a resource constant in quantity (assume capital), real input costs per unit of output will eventually increase. The long-run principle of *decreasing returns to scale* states that as the quantities of all resources are increased by equal proportions in a production situation, real input costs per unit of output will eventually increase. Both principles may be classified as *increasing cost* principles.

increasing costs are applied ordinarily to the analysis of private sector production, but they may also be applied validly to public sector production. Thus, toward the upper end of the *P* curve, the society would be incurring increasing costs in the production of public goods and toward the lower end it would be incurring increasing costs in the production of private goods. In either situation, the reallocation of a given bloc of resources from one sector to the other would yield greater output results in the second sector than if the same resources were retained for use in the original sector.

Having defined the production-possibility curve for the society, the next step in the derivation of the point of optimal intersector resource allocation involves the use of *social indifference curves*. In Figure 1–3, each of the social indifference curves S^1, S^2, S^3, and S^4 relates the "marginal rates of substitution" in the society's consumption of private and public goods in providing a *given level of satisfaction* (utility) along each curve. That is, each curve shows the various combinations of private and public goods which will provide a constant level of welfare to the society. Moreover, the higher the position of the social indifference curve, the greater the level of societal welfare that it represents since a greater aggregate output is being consumed.

The "family" of social indifference curves, only four of which are displayed in Figure 1–3 for reasons of simplicity, are related in a significant manner to the state of "market" and "political" *distribution* in the society.[9] In other words, they reflect the aggregate preferences of the individual members of the society for private and public goods *as made effective* by the distribution of income and wealth in the private sector and political representation in the public sector.[10] Individual preferences for public and private goods are meaningless, of course, unless made "effective" by purchasing power in the private sector and by voting power or related political representation in the public sector. Clearly, an individual with a superior income and wealth base in the market can command a higher level of consumption than can a consumer of lesser means. Similarly, not all individuals are represented equally in the consumption of public goods. In the United States, for

---

[9] The important relationship between the *state of distribution* in the society and *optimal intersector resource allocation* will also be treated in Chapters 4 and 5 under the discussion of "welfare economics" and "welfare politics" or "public choice theory" respectively.

[10] Even though an "individual" consumer indifference curve is independent of the level of income, it is possible to aggregate individual indifference curves to obtain an "aggregate" indifference curve under the following assumptions: If all utility functions are homogeneous of any degree (but the degree of homogeneity is the same for *all* individual utility functions), or if the utility functions are *homothetic* (not homogeneous but still giving rise to parallel indifference curves), it is possible to construct "social indifference curves" by aggregation. These indifference curves would change in shape as income distribution changes.

example, some individuals are more adequately represented before the public sector by lobbies, pressure groups, elective officials, and appointive officials than are others. Thus, importantly, the pattern and shape of the social indifference curves do not represent mere preferences, but instead represent the "effective demand" of the individual members of the society for private and public goods as this demand *can* be made "operational" by the state of income, wealth, and political voting distribution in the society. The extent to which such preferences *do* become operational and thus become precise allocational realities will be determined by the ability of the market and political processes to accurately reveal these effective preferences in an efficient manner.

The social indifference curves S^1, S^2, S^3, and S^4 are *convex* to the origin of the graph. This reflects the fact that along each curve there is a *diminishing marginal rate of substitution* between private and public goods in providing a given level of societal welfare. Thus, toward the upper end of social indifference curve S^1 in Figure 1–3, the quantity of public goods that the society would be willing to sacrifice to gain an additional unit of private goods is greater than it is toward the lower end of the curve. Stated alternately, it may be said that the society in Figure 1–3 is willing to give up a more than proportionate amount of public goods to get a smaller quantity of private goods toward the upper end of curve S^1, and vice versa toward the lower end. For example, a movement from a to b yields the greater loss in public goods zz^1 for the smaller gain in private goods ww^1. To the contrary, as the society is consuming mostly private goods toward the lower end of the curve, it would be willing to give up a less than proportionate amount of public goods to obtain a larger quantity of private goods. This is represented by a movement from c to d along curve S^1 which yields the smaller loss in public goods yy^1 for the larger gain of private goods xx^1, with the same overall level of societal welfare being maintained.

This declining marginal rate of substitution between the consumption of private and public goods in providing a constant level of welfare may be explained by the following reasons: First, the *more scarce a good* becomes, the greater is the tendency for its "relative substitution value" in relationship to another good to increase. That is, its marginal utility increases relative to the marginal utility of the other good that now is relatively more plentiful. For example, toward the lower end of a social indifference curve, such as those presented in Figure 1–3, the marginal utility of public goods would tend to be *high*. Thus, society would be willing to give up a more than proportionate amount of private goods to obtain a smaller quantity of the now relatively more scarce public goods. By contrast, toward the upper end of a social indifference curve, the marginal utility per unit of public goods is *low* as society has a relative oversupply of such goods. Thus, it would be willing to give up

a larger amount of public goods to obtain a smaller quantity of the now
relatively more scarce private goods, while maintaining the same level
of total utility. More generally, it may be said that when society's consumption approaches either extreme, the marginal increments of societal welfare or satisfaction diminish as the society consumes mostly
private or mostly public goods. A *second* reason for the convexity of a
social indifference curve is that significant losses of both "political" and
"economic" freedom are incurred as government allocation becomes
dominant near the upper end of the curve.[11] Thus, a society would
likely choose to give up a more than proportionate quantity of public
goods in order to attain a smaller quantity of private goods if, as a result,
additional political and economic freedom can be gained. On the other
hand, the convexity toward the lower (private sector) end of the social
indifference curve may be explained by the fact that an extreme degree
of market allocation would likely create an undesirable state of anarchy
where basic law and order does not prevail. Thus, society would be
willing to give up a more than proportionate quantity of private goods
in order to obtain government-provided law and order.

The final step in deriving the point of *optimal intersector resource
allocation* through the indifference approach involves the placing of
the societal production-possibility curve and its social indifference
curves on the same graph. Thus, in Figure 1–4 both relevant parts of
the above analysis are combined. The production potential of the society, as determined by its resources and technology, is brought into
a "relevant relationship" to the society's preferences for public and
private goods, as made effective by the state of income, wealth, and
political voting distribution. This results in optimal intersector resource
allocation being established at point *a* in Figure 1–4 where the
production-possibility curve *P* is *tangent* to the social indifference curve
S^3, providing *OX* in private sector output and *OY* in the public sector
output.[12]

It should be observed that the production-possibility curve *P* and
social indifference curve S^3 have the *same slope* at this point. This
means that at point *a* the *marginal rate of transformation* in the pro-

---

[11] *Political freedom* refers to such conditions as representative government, free
speech, and the free practice of religion. *Economic freedom* includes the right to own
and use the property factors of production, land, and capital, and one's own labor resource, without "undue restraint" from government.

[12] The point of tangency reflects not only optimal intersector *allocation efficiency,* but
also represents optimal *technical efficiency* in an input-output and production cost sense,
since the latter has been assumed to be present along any production-possibility curve
in order to reflect the full production potential of a society's resources. To distinguish,
allocation efficiency implies the selection of those economic goods which the society
prefers to consume as provided by the appropriate sector in keeping with "effective"
consumer preferences. *Technical efficiency* implies the least cost combinations of productive resources in providing these economic goods given a prevailing level of technology.

duction of private and public goods is equal to the *marginal rate of substitution* by the society in the consumption of these goods. Effective social preferences for economic goods have been brought into equilibrium with the production capabilities of the society. Maximum welfare or satisfaction from the consumption of economic goods is attained for the society at point *a*. Moreover, this point of tangency also represents what is known in welfare economics as the condition of *Pareto optimality*.[13] In other words, at point *a* every reallocation of resources will have been undertaken which would make one individual better off without reducing the welfare of any other individual. Also, it should be noted that there would be a different optimal intersector resource allocation point for every different state of income-wealth and political voting distribution in the society.

It is possible, of course, that the *actual* intersector division of resources in a society may not be at the point of optimal allocation. The deviation of actual from optimal allocation would result from "institutional defects" such as the difficulty encountered in revealing preferences for public goods in the political process and from imperfect market structure distortions in the production and allocation of private goods in the market sector. The point of *actual* intersector resource allocation could be anywhere along the production-possibility curve, *P*, or at any point inside *P* toward the origin of the graph. Thus, points *b*, *c*, and *d* in Figure 1–4 represent selected examples of points of actual allocation which deviate from the point of optimal allocation. Each of these reflects a condition of *suboptimal (nonoptimal) intersector resource allocation* or, in short, a condition of *social imbalance*. That is, effective societal preferences for economic goods are not being accurately revealed by the market and government institutions of allocation.

At point *b*, there is an overallocation of resources to the public sector. At point *c*, there is an overallocation of resources to the private sector. Yet at each of these allocation points, there exists an optimal condition of *full resource employment* because both points rest on the production-possibility curve *P* which represents full employment along its entire length. Intersector resource allocation, however, is suboptimal because Points *b* and *c* provide a level of societal welfare represented by social indifference curve S^2 instead of S^3. Thus, points *b* and *c* represent "full resource utilization," but *not* "efficient resource utiliza-

---

[13] The welfare economics concept of "Pareto optimality," named after the Italian economist Vilfredo Pareto (1848–1923), will be developed more fully in Chapters 2 and 4. Moreover, it should be stipulated here that, strictly speaking, attainment of optimal intersector resource allocation at point *a* would require (1) perfect competition in the private sector, (2) the absence of consumption and production externalities [defined in Chapter 2], and (3) a complete [100 percent] voting approval rule in the public sector [explained in Chapter 5].

tion" in the allocational sense, the latter yielding a higher level of attainable welfare as attained at point *a*. It should be observed, accordingly, that full resource employment is a *necessary, but not a sufficient,* condition for optimal intersector allocation. Finally, if allocation is at point *d* along social indifference curve S^1, the society is experiencing both social imbalance and an underemployment of productive resources—the latter because output is occurring at a point "inside" the production-possibility curve *P*.

CHANGES IN INTERSECTOR RESOURCE ALLOCATION OVER TIME

The foregoing discussion of intersector resource allocation is static in the sense that it considers the conditions of optimal and actual allocation as they would exist at a "given point of time." It is useful, however, to add also a "time dimension" to the discussion which allows for *changes* in the points of optimal and actual allocation over time. The possibilities of intersector allocation change over time include various "types of change." These may be summarized under two primary classifications: (1) changes in actual intersector allocation with optimal intersector allocation constant, and (2) changes in both actual and optimal intersector allocation. The changes are discussed in reference to Figure 1–4.

Changes in Actual Intersector Allocation with Optimal Intersector Allocation Constant

1. The society can move from an actual allocation point which is optimal to a suboptimal point, such as from point *a* to points *b, c,* or *d.*
2. The society can move from an actual allocation point which is suboptimal to an optimal allocation point, such as from points *b, c,* or *d* to point *a.*
3. The society can change the "degree" of suboptimal allocation; that is, points *b, c,* or *d* could move closer to or further from point *a.*
4. The society can change the "direction" of suboptimal allocation. For example, it can move from point *b* to point *c,* or from point *c* to point *b,* or between points *b* and *c* and *d.*
5. The society can move from a point of "full resource employment," such as points *a, b,* or *c,* to a point of "under-full employment" such as point *d.* Or, it can move from "under-full employment" at point *d* to "full employment" at points *a, b,* or *c.*

The changes described under (1) through (4) above would result largely from changes in the *institutional efficiency* of the "market" and the "political process" as these allocational institutions interpret individual preferences for economic goods.

Changes in Both Actual and Optimal Intersector Allocation

1. The production potential of the society can change as the quantity and/or quality of its productive resources increase or decrease. Thus, economic growth can move the societal production-possibility curve P to the right so that it will become tangent to a higher social indifference curve, thus increasing aggregrate societal welfare, or a catastrophe such as war can move P to the left where it will become tangent to a lower social indifference curve thus yielding a lower level of societal welfare. In either case, the point of optimal intersector resource allocation will have changed.

2. A change in societal preferences for public and private goods, or a change in the state of income, wealth, or political voting distribution which converts these preferences into "effective demand," may cause the family of social indifference curves to change their position and slope (though they would remain convex to the origin). Hence, they would become tangent to a "given" production-possibility curve, such as P, at a different point of optimal allocation between private and public goods.

3. Both the P and S curves could change for the above reasons with the very likely establishment of a new point of optimal intersector allocation.

4. The points of actual allocation can change in various degrees and directions as optimal allocation changes with a multiple number of possible results.

The final section of this chapter will place the intersector allocation concept in the perspective of contemporary discussion in American society.

THE CONTEMPORARY DISCUSSION OF INTERSECTOR RESOURCE ALLOCATION

American history has been characterized by a continuing discussion regarding the "proper size" of the public sector in the economy. The intensity of this controversy tends to ebb and flow during different periods of time. The latest period of peak interest emerged during the latter part of the 1950s and carried through the 1960s to the present time. However, the main discussion now encompasses a disaggregation into *types of economic goods* (social priorities) and *alternative alloca-*

tional techniques rather than a singular emphasis on the optimal overall size of the public sector relative to that of the private sector.

A brief summary of the contemporary discussion seems in order at this point since it provides the reader with a current dimension to the theoretical intersector allocation analysis introduced in this chapter and to be developed in greater detail in subsequent chapters. Moreover, the popular discussion of optimal intersector allocation is relevant in the important sense that the concepts of "optimal" and "actual" intersector allocation are *realities* even though the precise measurement of each is impossible. Society does make collective judgments and institutes *actual* policies in reference to these concepts. As Galbraith has commented, the inability to find the precise point of social balance (optimal intersector allocation) "will be of comfort only to those who believe that any failure of definition can be made to score decisively against a larger idea."[14]

The contemporary discussion of optimal intersector resource allocation may be traced to books written by Hansen and Galbraith.[15] Hansen contends that the public sector should be used to promote the educational and cultural development of Americans. This is related, in turn, to the desirability of raising the living standard of the bottom decile (10 percent) of the American population, called the "submerged tenth" by Hansen.[16] Poverty conditions in the United States have not improved appreciably since Hansen's book was written in 1957. By the official federal government definition of poverty, there are nearly 26 million Americans living in poverty at the present time. Many of these people live in economically depressed environments incapable of providing adequate educational and other public services for their citizens. Thus, a "vicious circle" is created whereby "poverty begets poverty." According to Hansen, the public sector must break this circle if the living standards of the "submerged tenth" are to be improved. He believes that economics in a mature society should emphasize *social priorities* such as better education and the elimination of poverty rather than the goal of *maximum national output.* He designates the public sector as the institution best able to serve this reallocation of scarce resources.

Galbraith, like Hansen, believes that *inter*sector resource misallocation (social imbalance) exists in the form of an underallocation of resources through the public sector. In addition, he contends that complex technical forces in an industrial society tend also to distort *intra-*

---

[14] Galbraith, *The Affluent Society,* pp. 254–55.

[15] See Alvin H. Hansen, *The American Economy* (New York: McGraw-Hill Book Co., 1957); and Galbraith, *The Affluent Society.*

[16] Chapter 21 will be devoted fully to the problem of American poverty and an analysis of the alternative solutions to the problem.

sector allocation between different types of economic goods within the public sector.[17] "Intersector" misallocation with too small a public sector is traced to two sources: (1) a "historical bias" against governmental resource allocation, and (2) a "dependence effect" whereby the demand for private goods is inordinately reinforced by advertising. "Intrasector" misallocation, on the other hand, is attributed to the operational nature of decision making in a highly technical industrial society.

First, regarding *inter*sector misallocation, Galbraith observes that until the Industrial Revolution allowed nations to achieve economic maturity, mankind was "oppressed" by scarce resources to the extent that all his wants were basic to survival. These "high urgency" wants, for the most part, were produced by the private sector. Hence, the market tended to provide food, clothing, and shelter. Only one high urgency want—an orderly environment in which the other basic wants could be enjoyed—was provided by the government. Significantly, the government was largely unstable and unreliable in pre-industrial and early-industrial revolution days and frequently did not perform this "environmental function" very well. Hence, it is alleged that an irrational bias was built up in favor of private sector goods and against those of the government. "Alcohol, comic books, and mouthwash all bask under the superior reputation of the market. Schools, judges, and municipal swimming pools lie under the evil reputation of bad kings."[18] Thus, according to Galbraith, social priorities are sacrificed and too few economic goods are provided through the public sector.

Galbraith contends that the above imbalance is further widened through the efforts of modern advertising in behalf of market-produced goods. He suggests that wants are of "low urgency" if they must be contrived for man by businesses which create the wants through advertising. A man need not be told by advertising media that he is hungry and needs food. In a world of independently determined consumer wants, the consumer as a voter can make fairly rational independent choices between public and private goods. However, given the *dependence effect*—that consumer wants are created by the production process which satisfies the wants—the consumer does not make rational choices. Thus, according to Galbraith, the consumer is subject to the advertising and emulation by which "production creates its own demand." Social priorities, once again, are sacrificed as public goods are undersupplied.

Second, regarding *intra*sector misallocation, Galbraith argues that

---

[17] Galbraith's *inter*sector misallocation contention appears in his *The Affluent Society,* cited above, while his *intra*sector misallocation contention appears in his more recently written *The New Industrial State* (Boston: Houghton Mifflin Co., 1967).

[18] Galbraith, *Affluent Society,* p. 135.

the "industrial state" inherently attempts to control its own economic environment (product market, factor market, etc.) and, in so doing, ignores or holds unimportant those public sector goods which are not "closely related" to the needs of the industrial system.[19] Thus, while national defense, the subsidization of research and technological development, and highways are *not* neglected because they serve the "industrial state," health services, parks and recreation areas, and pollution control represent areas of inadequate governmental influence.[20] Accordingly, Galbraith has added the issue of "*intra*public sector" misallocation to his earlier citation of alleged intersector imbalance in the direction of an undersupply of economic goods provided through the public sector.

Hayek opposes the viewpoints of Galbraith and Hansen.[21] In particular, he objects to Galbraith's dependence-effect concept. He argues that all wants except the innate wants—which he defines as food, shelter, and sex—arise through emulation, that is, because we see others enjoying them. "To say that a desire is not important because it is not innate is to say that the whole cultural achievement of man is not important."[22] Hayek asserts that very few needs are "absolute" in the sense that they are independent of social environment and indispensable for survival.

He believes that the *non sequitur* (illogic) of Galbraith's argument is best indicated when the dependence effect is applied to the arts, such as music, painting, or literature. "Surely an individual's want for literature is not original with himself in the sense that he would experience it if literature were not produced. Does this mean that the production of literature cannot be defended as satisfying a want because it is only the production which provokes the demand?"[23] Furthermore, he argues that public education instills a taste for literature in the young and it employs producers of literature (teachers) for that purpose. Hayek observes, in this analogy to Galbraith's "dependence effect," that the utility of cultural wants should not be assumed to be zero

---

[19] In his *The New Industrial State*, Galbraith contends that advanced technology has changed the entire operational behavior of American industry so that "individual decision makers" become unimportant and are displaced by "system decision making." The large enterprises comprising such an industrial system thus work through an elaborate decision-making "technostructure" which requires *control* over production resources, selling prices, and all other relevant economic conditions if profits are to be earned in the face of huge, long-term investment commitments.

[20] However, the intervention of government in matters of pollution has increased considerably since Galbraith's *The New Industrial State* was published in 1967.

[21] F. A. Hayek, "The *Non Sequitur* of the 'Dependence Effect,' " *Southern Economic Journal*, April 1961, p. 346.

[22] Ibid., p. 346.

[23] Ibid., p. 347.

simply because they do not arise spontaneously through innate human needs.[24]

Wallich agrees in substance with the Hansen-Galbraith conclusion that too many of the "wrong wants" are being satisfied.[25] He argues, however, that such misallocation does not imply that improved allocation can result only from a higher proportion of total resources being allocated through the public sector. That is, one should not conclude that the only alternative to foolish private spending is public spending since better private spending is just as much of a possibility.[26] According to Wallich, the choice between public and private financing (resource allocation) is a choice between *means* while those dissatisfied with present market allocation should be concentrating upon changing the *ends* or *objectives* of private sector allocation. Thus, Wallich adds the dimension of "intraprivate sector" misallocation to the discussion.

Furthermore, he observes that the bulk of both undersatisfied needs and new needs are in a competitive area that might be provided with reasonable efficiency by either the market or government sectors. These include such items as services for the aged, health services, college education, housing, and natural resource development. He contends that where the needs can be provided with comparable efficiency by either sector, the private sector should be allowed to meet them because of costs in the form of reduced freedom and lost incentives which may accompany the displacement of private resource allocation by public sector allocation.[27] It should be observed, however, that the question still remains whether the private sector, acting alone, will have the inducement to allocate these desirable goods in sufficient quantities. This important issue will be examined more thoroughly in Chapter 2 when the nature of public goods, private goods, and quasi-public (private) goods is discussed. In any event, the fact that either sector can provide many important goods suggests the probability that "joint allocational techniques" involving the cooperative effort of both sectors often may be utilized.

In concluding this summary of the contemporary optimal intersector resource allocation (social balance) discussion, it may be observed that

---

[24] An essential point of contention between the Galbraith and Hayek viewpoints involves the necessity of distinguishing between goods with "zero" marginal utility as opposed to those with "low" marginal utility. Galbraith's general argument suggests that the public sector, due to present social imbalance, can allocate goods with higher marginal utility than can the private sector. The Galbraith argument thus does *not* appear to require that private goods have "zero" marginal utility, only that some of them provide lower marginal utility than alternately produced public goods could provide.

[25] Henry C. Wallich, *The Cost of Freedom* (New York: Harper & Row, Publishers, 1960).

[26] Ibid.

[27] See footnote 11 for a distinction between "political freedom" and "economic freedom."

the ingredients of the discussion have been broadened beyond an emphasis on the alleged underallocation of resources through the public sector. In addition, the discussion now reflects (1) a serious inquiry into *intra*sector misallocation, especially intrapublic sector misallocation, and (2) a new appreciation of the ability of the public and private sectors to "jointly" attack major economic and social problems through a cooperative approach to these problems. Hence, the latest discussion reduces, though it does *not* eliminate, the consideration of a "proper" intersector allocation balance. It emphasizes, instead, the consideration of possible *intra*sector "tradeoffs" which, for example, might reduce the amount of public sector resources utilized in such areas as defense and space and increase those employed for domestic law and order, rehabilitation of urban areas, control of pollution, the elimination of poverty, and other domestic social problems. Furthermore, many of the recently proposed solutions to these problems involve techniques which are inclusive of significant participation by both the public and private sectors. Chapter 3 will demonstrate a number of these "joint" allocation techniques.

THE PLAN FOR THE BOOK

While it is impossible to completely separate the allocation, distribution, stabilization, and economic growth functions (branches) of public sector economics, certain sections of this book nonetheless do stress particular functional areas. Thus, allocation receives the major attention in Part One (Chapters 1 through 5). Part Two is concerned mainly with the distribution branch while Part Three discusses, to a considerable extent, both allocational and distributional issues. Part Four, in turn, deals mostly with aggregate economic performance in terms of the stabilization and economic growth goals.

2

The Concept of Public Goods

The previous chapter considered the conditions required for optimal resource allocation between the private and public sectors of the economy. The present chapter will provide an analysis of the nature of those economic goods which are typically provided by the public sector. In so doing, it will provide an economic argument for the existence of a public sector for resource allocation purposes in a market-oriented society.

Conceivably, all economic allocation could be provided by the market except for the governmental function of providing minimal law and order to prevent anarchy in the society. Moreover, the market approximates more closely the political nature of democratic government which is so popular among Western nations. Why, then, do substantial public sectors exist for resource allocation purposes in *all* democratic nations of the West? This question will be answered in the pages which follow.

HISTORICAL EVOLUTION OF PUBLIC SECTOR ARGUMENTS

In *The Wealth of Nations* (written in 1776), Adam Smith, the father of modern capitalism, enumerated four "justifiable" categories of governmental allocation activity.[1] These were:

[1] Adam Smith, *The Wealth of Nations* (London: Routledge, 1913), Book 5, pp. 541–644.

1. The duty of protecting the society from violence and invasion by other independent societies which, of course, is the function of national defense.
2. The duty of protecting every member of a society from the injustice or oppression of every other member of the society. This reflects the obligation of establishing an "administration of justice" which provides law and order within the society so that the market economy may function.
3. The duty of establishing and maintaining those highly beneficial public institutions and public works which are of such a nature that the profit they earn could never repay the expense to any individual or small number of individuals to provide them and which, therefore, it cannot be expected that they would be supplied in adequate quantities.
4. The duty of meeting expenses necessary for support of the sovereign, an expense which varies depending upon the form of political structure.

Though Smith often has been described as a bold advocate of minimal governmental activity, his writings fail to indicate significant opposition to a public sector for allocative purposes in the society. To the contrary, the four functions of government described above would require a level of public sector resource allocation substantially greater than a laissez-faire economic system would advocate.[2] The most relevant of Smith's four functions of government are the first and the third, namely, the national defense or external security and public works functions. The second function, that of providing domestic stability in the form of law and order and the protection of property, and the fourth, that of maintaining the sovereign or executive level of government, could be logically opposed only by an avowed anarchist. Since these are *not* controversial functions of government, they do not require a lengthy analysis in the effort to construct an economic case for the existence of a public sector for resource allocation purposes in a market-oriented economy.

The national defense and the public works functions, however, are less intrinsic to governmental provision than the justice and sovereign-support functions. For example, defense need not be so comprehensively a "collective" undertaking in a primitive society as it is in modern society. Smith observed, quite accurately, that government becomes involved increasingly in the defense function as a society "advances in civilization."[3] He recognized the change introduced into the art of war

---

[2] Laissez-faire, in this context, refers to private sector resource determination in *all* areas of economic activity except for the use of resources by government to provide minimal law and order and private property rights protection in the society.

[3] Smith, *Wealth of Nations*, p. 555.

by the invention of firearms as a significant cost-increasing factor. Indeed, history since the time of Smith has experienced an enormous growth in the complexity of weaponry and, consequently, in the absolute resource cost and the relative importance of the national defense function of government. Thus, little controversy exists in modern nations regarding the role of government in the allocation of national defense though society, in an "*intra*public sector" sense, may question the "relative emphasis" placed on national defense as opposed to other areas of governmental expenditure.

Probably, the most significant of the four governmental functions introduced by Smith is that relating to "public works." Smith observed that certain social capital items like roads, bridges, canals, and harbors would not be allocated without the influence of government because they could not be provided by private enterprise on a profitable basis. Similarly, John Stuart Mill, in his *Principles of Political Economy* (1848), argued that in the particular conditions of a given age or nation "there is scarcely anything really important to the general interest, which it may not be desirable, or even necessary, that the government should take upon itself, not because private individuals cannot effectively perform it, but *because they will not.*"(Italics provided.)[4] Mill thus believed that at certain times and places the public sector would be required to provide roads, docks, harbors, canals, irrigation works, hospitals, schools, colleges, printing presses, and other public works. He thought that government should enhance the happiness of its subjects "by doing the things which are made incumbent on it by the helplessness of the public, in such a manner as shall tend not to increase and perpetuate, but to correct that helplessness."[5] He favored, to the extent possible, the attainment of these publicly provided goods through means relating to the voluntary activity of individuals.

Many years later John Maynard Keynes reiterated the viewpoints of Smith, Mill, and others on the importance of public works allocation by government. Keynes commented: "Government is not to do things which individuals are doing already, and to do them a little better or a little worse; but to do those things which at the present are not done at all."[6] The position by Smith, Mill, and Keynes on public works will be developed later in this chapter as part of the "decreasing cost" characteristic of public goods.

The economic case for substantial public sector resource allocation was "supplemented" by the theoretical development of marginal con-

---

[4] John Stuart Mill, *Principles of Political Economy* (London: Longmans, Green, 1926), p. 978.

[5] Ibid.

[6] John Maynard Keynes, "The End of Laissez-faire," in *Laissez-faire and Communism* (New York: New Republic, Inc., 1926), p. 67.

cepts which occurred during the 1870s and 1880s. William Stanley Jevons (England), Léon Walras (France), and Eugen Böhm-Bawerk (Austria) were the men most responsible for applying marginal utility analysis to private sector demand while Alfred Marshall (England) was most responsible for applying marginal analysis to private sector supply as well as to reconciling both sides of the market mechanism.[7] Subsequently, marginal analysis was incorporated expertly into public finance theory by A. C. Pigou in his *A Study in Public Finance* (1928).[8] The analysis by Pigou takes the form of the marginal utility theory of public goods allocation which is described in Chapter 4. In defining this theoretical point of optimal intersector allocation, Pigou implicitly recognizes the need for a public sector. The same implication may be drawn from the voluntary-exchange approach to optimal intersector resource allocation of Erik Lindahl and Howard Bowen et. al., also discussed in Chapter 4, and to the political process insight of Knut Wicksell regarding public goods allocation.[9]

Thus, it has been observed that the development of economic theory in the Western world has shown an appreciation of the need for governmental resource allocation in a system characterized by a basic preference for market or private sector economic activity. The remainder of this chapter will develop a comprehensive economic argument for the existence of a public sector for allocative purposes in a market-oriented culture. This approach will rest upon the "failure of the market" to optimally allocate all of society's resources. Yet, for reasons to be demonstrated below, this argument must be qualified as a *necessary*, but not in all cases a *sufficient*, condition for public sector allocational intervention. Moreover, in developing the argument, the inherent characteristics of public goods will be demonstrated.

THE CASE FOR A PUBLIC SECTOR TO ALLOCATE RESOURCES

The economic arguments for a public sector which follow are presented in the context of the *allocation* branch of economics. Though other economic arguments for the existence of government may be developed in terms of the distribution and aggregate economic performance functions of an economic system, these will *not* be an important part of the analysis in the present chapter. The "allocative case" for a public sector (beyond that which would supply minimal law and

---

[7] See Alfred Marshall, *Principles of Economics* (8th ed.; London: Macmillan and Co., 1930).

[8] A. C. Pigou, *A Study in Public Finance* (London: Macmillan and Co., 1928).

[9] See Chapter 5.

order and the protection of property rights) will now be presented. It will focus upon the phenomena of:

1. Decreasing production costs.
2. Zero production costs—the polar extreme of decreasing production costs.
3. Collective consumption and nonexclusion.
4. Significant economic effects [externalities] not captured by the price system.
5. A variety of special supply phenomena.

Decreasing Costs of Production[10]

A significant allocational complication arises under conditions of *imperfect market structure* (pure monopoly, oligopoly, monopolistic competition) if "marginal cost equals average revenue" (price) at a point of output where the average cost of production is *decreasing*. Moreover, these types of market structure are prevalent in the American economy. Importantly, such markets do *not* have a "coincidence" of the *best profit point of production* for the firm—marginal cost equal to marginal revenue—with the *optimal social allocation* point for the society—marginal cost equal to average revenue (price). On the other hand, these points do coincide under conditions of perfect competition where many sellers and buyers are present in the market and where the product is homogeneous.

The contrast between perfect and imperfect markets in this allocative matter is demonstrated in Figure 2–1ab. In Figure 2–1a, the perfectly competitive firm producing at its best profit point, quantity *OA*, where marginal cost equals marginal revenue at point *a*, is also producing where marginal cost equals average revenue (price) at point *b*. Thus, output is carried up to the point where the additional cost of the marginal unit just equals the price that people are willing to pay for it. In this instance, consumer sovereignty determines output in a social optimum manner. Moreover, as the firm produces at the output where price (average revenue) is equal to marginal cost, in the long-run, it is certain that the total costs of the firm will not exceed total revenues as the firm produces the social optimum output.

On the other hand, it may be seen in Figure 2–1b that in an imperfect market (as exemplified here by a pure monopoly) the *best-profit output OA*, as determined by the intersection of marginal cost and

---

[10] This concept has been developed over the years with significant contributions made by Smith, Mill, Walras, Marshall, Pigou, Bergson, Hotelling, Samuelson, Bator, and others. A thorough presentation of this concept may be found in Francis M. Bator, *The Question of Government Spending* (New York: Harper & Row, Publishers, 1960).

FIGURE 2–1
Pricing and Output under "Perfectly Competitive" and "Imperfectly Competitive" Conditions

a. Pricing and Output for Firm in Perfect Competition

b. Pricing and Output for Imperfectly Competitive Firm as Compared to Perfectly Competitive Firm

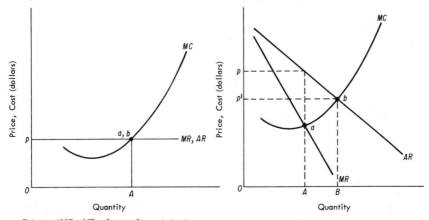

Point *a*—(*MC* = *MR*)—*firm profit-maximization*
Point *b*—(*MC* = *AR*)—*optimal social allocation* under conditions of "consumer sovereignty"
Note: Points *a* and *b* "coincide" in the perfectly competitive market. Points *a* and *b* "diverge" in the imperfectly competitive market.

marginal revenue at point *a,* does *not* also yield the *optimal social output OB,* as determined at point *b* where marginal cost is equal to average revenue. Hence, the firm in an imperfect market (monopolistic competition, oligopoly, and pure monopoly), in fixing its profit-maximizing output, selects necessarily a price-quantity combination where marginal cost is less than average revenue because of individual firm monopoly power (control over price). Thus, efficient social allocation in conformance with consumer sovereignty is *not* attained.

The misallocation of output in Figure 2–1b, if the firm maximizes its profits, is represented by the reduced output *AB.* In other words, *OA* is the best-profit output, *OB* is the optimal social output, and *AB* is the amount of misallocated (reduced) output. In particular, if the economic good in question is deemed socially necessary or desirable by a collective consensus of the society, an argument may be established for possible public sector influence on the allocation of the good in quantities closer to, if not actually at, the social optimum output *OB.* Moreover, the *social optimum 'quantity OB cannot be produced at a profit* if the firm faces "decreasing production costs" at that output point. Inevitably, total costs would exceed total revenues under these conditions. Furthermore, this inability to operate profitably may occur under either short-run or long-run conditions, though it is potentially more serious in the long-run since a firm in the short run could continue to operate with losses as long as the variable costs of production were covered.

Thus, in Figure 2–2 the firm could produce social optimum output *OB* only at a *loss*. This is true because under "decreasing average cost" conditions, marginal cost must be below average cost causing the intersection of marginal cost and average revenue (price) to be where average revenue is less than average cost. Consequently, total losses are *wxyz* when optimal social output *OB* is produced. Loss per unit is the vertical amount (distance) *CP*, *wx*, or *zy*. There could be no output of the good in the long run since the losses could not be sustained during this time period by a private firm. This situation bears a close resemblance to the traditional historical arguments cited earlier in the chapter that the public sector should influence the provision of those "desirable" economic goods which the private sector does not provide in adequate quantities, if at all, because of the inability to produce them profitably.

Thus, since losses cannot be sustained in the long run by a private firm, public sector allocational influence such as governmental produc-

FIGURE 2–2

Loss at Point of Optimal Social Allocation under Decreasing Production Costs in an Imperfect Market

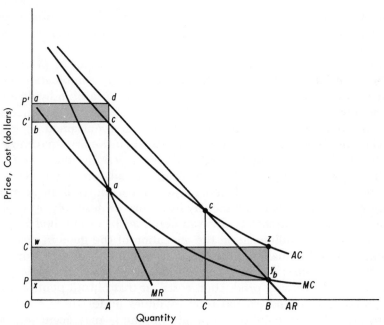

Point *a*—(*MC* = *MR*)—firm profit-maximization
Point *b*—(*MC* = *AR*)—optimal social allocation
Point *c*—(*AC* = *AR*)—point of "normal" economic profits

tion of the good, or subsidization of the private firm losses, would be required if the good is to be provided in the social optimal quantity *OB*. Alternately, the public sector could require through "public utility regulation" that the firm produce output *OC* as determined by the intersection of average cost and average revenue at point *c*. At this point, the firm would be earning a "normal" economic profit and would be producing an output, *OC*, which is closer to the social optimum output, *OB*, than is the profit-maximizing output for the firm, *OA*. In any event, the combined presence of "imperfect market" and "decreasing production cost" conditions for an important economic good, especially if the decreasing cost conditions prevail over the *entire range of feasible* outputs, represents a degree of allocational failure in the market which strengthens the case for possible governmental allocative influence.[11]

Zero Marginal Cost

A polar or extreme case of the above phenomenon exists for those economic goods whose marginal costs are zero. Thus, in Figure 2–3, the marginal cost curve (*MC*) coincides with the horizontal axis. At the social optimum output *OB*, which is determined by the intersection of marginal cost (*MC*) and average revenue (*AR*) at point *a*, the attainment of allocational efficiency requires that the price of the good be zero since the marginal cost is zero. In other words, this extreme variation of the decreasing cost phenomenon requires that the good be provided *free of charge* since the good can be consumed by additional individuals without an increase in production costs.

Bator refers to this polar case of decreasing costs as involving "public goods," that is, a "collectively-consumed" good whose consumption by Consumer *X* would lead to no subtraction from what is left over for consumption by Consumers *Y* and *Z*.[12] Thus, another radio listener,

---

[11] However, this is not to suggest that a mandate exists for the public sector to compel output to be at the *MC* = *AR* level for *all* goods produced in imperfect markets. Since the very existence of imperfect markets constitutes a "suboptimal" allocative situation, any solution must be "second best" in nature. Yet, it is argued here that the case for governmental influence is strengthened when imperfect markets and decreasing production cost conditions exist. However, it is *not* argued that production at or near the *MC* = *AR* points is to be sought in every case.

[12] Bator, *Question of Government Spending*, p. 94. Some economists refer to the "marginal cost equal to zero" phenomenon as a "special case" of *joint supply*. For example, see J. G. Head, "Public Goods and Public Policy," *Public Finance* (No. 3, 1962), pp. 197–219. However, these economists readily point out that a basic difference exists between "joint supply," in this sense, and "joint supply" in the Marshallian sense as developed by the great British economist, Alfred Marshall. The term in the Marshallian context follows the market mechanism more closely. For example, jointly supplied mutton and wool are divisible economic goods that can be exchanged through the price system. On the other hand, jointly supplied public goods are usually intangible services which are collectively consumed and impossible to resell.

FIGURE 2–3

The Polar Case of Zero Marginal Cost
(note that MC = 0 at the optimal social output point, point *a*,
where *MC = AR*)

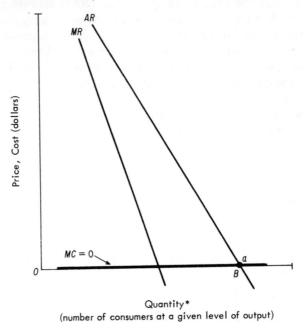

Quantity*
(number of consumers at a given level of output)

* For an explicit description of "Quantity," as used here, see the discussion
of Figure 2–3 in the text.

another television viewer, or another citizen protected by national
defense activities need not subtract from the consumption of these
activities by someone else. For example, if the marginal cost of an
additional person tuning in a television program is zero, the consumption of the television program can be increased without decreasing the
consumption of any other good by drawing scarce resources away from
the production of the other good. Thus, any price charged for television
reception, whether a uniform price or a "variable" price imposed in
a discriminatory manner between consumers, would misallocate resources since consumption would be reduced below the "quantity" that
would be consumed at the social optimum point where price equals
marginal cost. That is, if the marginal cost of an additional unit of
consumption is zero, price must be zero if resources are to be allocated
in accordance with the social optimum rule. Significantly, private profit
would be impossible with a zero price.

It is extremely important in relation to the above discussion to distinguish between *quantity* in the sense of "additional units of consumption" and *quantity* in terms of a "higher level of production." Thus, in

Figure 2–3, the marginal cost is zero ($MC = 0$) for supplying a given level of television transmission to "additional viewers" who, within the geographical range of the transmission, may tune in the program that is being transmitted. However, the marginal cost would be greater than zero ($MC > 0$) for the "production" of a higher level of television transmission which would widen the geographical area within which potential viewers may tune in the programs. Realistically, the latter may be viewed as the "expansion of capacity" in a *long-run* time period while the former may be viewed as a *short-run* phenomenon within a "fixed capacity."

Thus, with a fixed transmission range capable of reaching (say) 25,000 potential viewers, the marginal cost of the second viewer, on up to viewer number 25,000, is zero. However, an increase in the transmission capacity so that 50,000 potential consumers instead of 25,000 may watch the program obviously requires additional production costs. Consequently, it may be said that additional consumption of the *service*, within the present short-run scale or capacity to produce the *service*, may be enjoyed at a "zero marginal cost." Alternatively, a long-run expansion in the scale or capacity to provide the *service* would be attained only with a "positive marginal cost" since, assuming full resource employment, additional resources must be withdrawn from alternative productive uses in order to attain the expanded capacity.

The italicizing of the word "service" in the above paragraph is intended to draw attention to the fact that an economic good which can be consumed within a given production level by one individual, without reducing the quantity available to someone else, is likely to be an intangible service.[13] Such an intangible service could be "consumed" at a marginal "supply" cost of zero (in the short-run cost sense) by two or more individuals. Hence, the *other dimension* of the "supply" characteristic of zero marginal cost is, indeed, the "demand" characteristic of "joint consumption" whereby the benefits of an economic good are *indivisible* among two or more consumers. That is, the additional consumption of an economic good at zero marginal cost involves the important "demand" phenomenon of *joint* or *collective consumption*—a concept which will be discussed next.

The Phenomenon of Collective Consumption

Proceeding from the above discussion, a further important aspect of the allocative argument for the existence of a public sector in a market-oriented society can now be developed. This is the concept of *collective*

---

[13] However, *all* services are not subject to the unique characteristics of "joint" and "equal" consumption. The labor services of a doctor, dentist, attorney, or tax accountant, for example, are normally specialized for the private benefits of a particular consumer.

or *joint consumption* with *nonexclusion*. The primary characteristic of collective consumption with nonexclusion is the fact that the "jointly consumed" economic goods are *indivisible* in the important sense that their benefits cannot be priced in the market. In the extreme case of *all* benefits being indivisible, the good is normally called a "pure public good." If such a good is supplied in the economy, it is consumed in an *equal* amount by all consumers.[14] Moreover, no one can be "excluded" from its consumption by a failure to voluntarily pay for it.[15]

On the other hand, a *divisible* "pure private good" *is* subject to the exclusion principle. That is, an individual can be "excluded" or "prevented" from consuming the good because he does not voluntarily pay for it. Such a good is completely subject to the pricing mechanism. *All* of the benefits are "private" to its purchaser. *None* are "collectively" consumed.

Thus, if W reflects the total market quantity of a pure private good, such as bread, and the society has two consumers, A and B, and if W_a and W_b represent the quantities of the private good consumed by A and B, respectively, then W must equal the *summation* of W_a and W_b. If Consumer A uses more of good W, consumer B must use less under conditions of full resource employment. There exists a *rivalness in consumption* between Consumers A and B. For example, if the market supplies 20 units of Good W (bread), and Consumer A consumes 15 units, 5 units remain for consumption by Consumer B. Moreover, if a consumer does not pay the price, he does not consume the bread.

To the contrary, a collectively consumed economic good (service) such as national defense is *not divisible* among consumers. Instead, once supplied at a particular level or scale, it is "jointly" consumed on an "equal" basis by all consumers in the society. Here there exists a *nonrivalness in consumption* between Consumers A and B. Thus, let Z reflect the total quantity of the pure public good (national defense) and let Z_a and Z_b refer to consumer A's and consumer B's consumption of the good. Since the consumption of the total cannot be divided between A and B, the relevant equations are: $(Z = Z_a)$ and $(Z = Z_b)$, respectively. There is no way by which Consumer A can cause Consumer B to consume less if he consumes more, which is not true for the divisible private good, bread, described above. If the public good is supplied to one of the consumers, it must also be supplied at the same level (say 20 units of national defense) to the other consumer regardless of any financial contribution. Hence, the exclusion principle does not

---

[14] Consumption in an *equal* amount applies to *pure* public goods, not to *quasi-public* goods, as will be explained in Chapter 3.

[15] "Technically," exclusion may be possible for virtually every economic good, but only at such "prohibitive cost" in some cases that it can practically be said that "exclusion is impossible." This topic will be discussed further below.

apply to the collectively consumed good, and A and B *each* individually consume the total quantity of the economic good. The difference between a "pure private good" whose benefits *are subject* to the exclusion principle, and a good of the "pure public" variety whose benefits *are not subject* to the principle, may be demonstrated as follows:

Assuming that the total production of each good (bread and national defense) is equal to 20 units,

$$W = W_a + W_b$$
$$20 = 15 + 5$$

The *exclusion principle does* apply to the *pure private good* in the above equation, but it *does not* apply to the *pure public good* in the equation below.

$$Z = Z_a \qquad Z = Z_b$$
$$20 = 20 \qquad 20 = 20$$

Graphically, Figure 2–4 demonstrates the conventional "horizontal" summation of *individual* demands to obtain *market* demand under conditions where the exclusion principle applies with a divisible "pure private good." Thus, a summation of the 15 units (loaves) of bread demanded by Consumer A and the 5 units demanded by Consumer B at a price of 50 cents per unit results in a total market demand for bread of 20 units.

FIGURE 2–4
Demand Summation for a Pure Private Good (exclusion principle *does* apply)

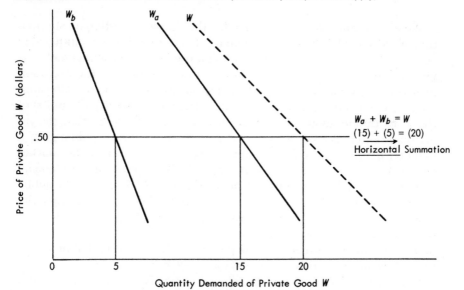

FIGURE 2–5

Demand Summation for a Pure Public Good (exclusion principle *does not* apply)

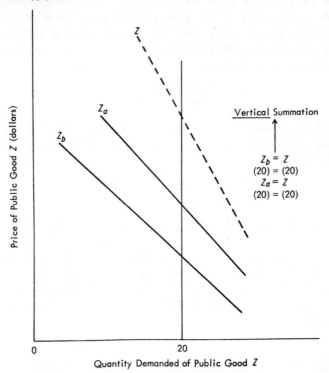

Now, in Figure 2–5 let us consider the "nonconventional" summation of individual demands to obtain market demand with an indivisible "pure public good" such as national defense. This economic good (service) is "indivisible" among consumers in the sense that the exclusion principle cannot be applied to the consumption of its benefits. Consumers *A* and *B* each individually consume the total quantity (20 units) of the pure public good. Thus, it is important to recognize that the individual demands by Consumers *A* and *B* for the "pure public good," national defense, have been summed *vertically* to obtain the market demand instead of *horizontally* as with the "pure private good." Hence, the "collective consumption" of the "indivisible" pure public good precludes the opportunity of an individual consumer to vary the quantities of the good which he would purchase at a particular market price. Instead, he must consume an equal amount of the good with all other consumers regardless of the particular price (if any) that he might be willing to pay for that quantity of the good.

Still another example may be offered to clarify the applicability and inapplicability of the exclusion principle: If an individual is allowed to make his own decision about the expenditure of $500, he might decide to spend it for new clothes knowing that he cannot acquire these clothes unless he pays for them. He can be excluded from consuming the clothes by not voluntarily exchanging money for them. On the other hand, he would not "volunteer" a $500 contribution to the federal government to help finance national defense since he can consume just as much defense as others in the society while allowing others to pay for it. He will be motivated to be a "free rider" since he cannot be excluded from consuming the benefits of defense by a failure to voluntarily pay for it. Since all consumers would desire to follow similar behavior to avoid payment, the jointly consumed economic good will not be financed by voluntary market-type payments if the size of the group is sufficiently large that each individual feels that his inaction will not affect those of the other members of the group. Collectively consumed goods ordinarily will not be provided unless the public sector exists and finances the goods through compulsory or coercive means.

It is important to distinguish further between the concepts of (1) zero marginal cost, and (2) collective consumption. The presence of conditions whereby an additional consumer can enjoy an intangible good (service) at no additional short run cost must necessarily involve the joint consumption of that good by two or more individuals. However, this condition of zero marginal cost does *not* necessarily mean that the good must "ultimately" be collectively consumed. Instead, it may be possible to incur additional costs and, by so doing, supply the good on an exclusion (pricing) basis to the individual consumers.

The ability to convert a "zero marginal cost—joint consumption" arrangement to a pricing or exclusion situation will be a function of such determinants as (*a*) the "technical" ability to exclude consumption of the good from nonpaying individuals and (*b*) the relative size of the consuming group. The success of *free rider efforts*, which are a natural outgrowth of joint consumption, will be dependent upon the *ability to exclude*. Such efforts will fail if exclusion is successful. The ability to exclude, as noted, will depend upon the technical feasibility of exclusion and, subsequently, upon the costs of exclusion. These costs will tend to become greater as the consuming group becomes larger. A pure public good such as national defense represents an example of a good for which the technical feasibility of exclusion is lacking and the costs of exclusion due to large group size are prohibitive. This might be contrasted to the transmission of a television program for which a "technologically-available" scrambling device can exclude consumption if payment is not made.[16]

---

[16] Though technical *exclusion* is possible in this case, the question of the cost of such exclusion as well as other economic considerations of its desirability would still need to be considered.

The supplying of national defense necessarily involves *both* zero marginal cost for protecting an additional citizen *and,* also, long-run joint consumption since an individual *cannot be excluded* from consuming national security in an equal amount with other individuals in the society. In this case, the requisite "combined" presence of zero marginal cost and collective consumption conditions with nonexclusion provides a stronger argument for public sector allocational influence than does either condition alone. The resulting economic good is the polar case of a "pure public good." Moreover, since the "large size" of the consumption group in the national defense example provides a firm basis for the "free rider" motivation whereby voluntary financing of defense from the private sector will *not* be forthcoming, the case for significant governmental allocational influence is further strengthened.

The Concept of Externalities

Many economic actions undertaken by producers and consumers exert "external economic effects" on other producers and/or consumers which "escape the price mechanism." Such "nonprice effects" are commonly known as *externalities,* but at times the terms *spillovers* or *neighborhood effects* are also used to refer to the same phenomenon. Specifically, an *externality* may be viewed as either an economic gain or loss accruing to one or more "recipient" economic agents as the result of an economic action "initiated" by another economic agent —with the gain or loss *not* being reflected in price. Either the "initiating" or the "recipient" economic agent may be either a "producer" or a "consumer."

The initiating agent, in the producer sense, will be motivated by a *profit* goal. The initiating agent, in the consumer sense, will be motivated by a *utility (satisfaction, welfare)* goal. If the recipient of an externality is a producer, an external "gain" or "benefit" will take the form of an improved profit position while, on the other hand, an external "loss" or "cost" will take the form of reduced profits or increased losses. If the recipient of an externality is a consumer, an external "gain" or "benefit" will take the form of increased utility (satisfaction, welfare) while, on the other hand, an external "loss" or "cost" will take the form of reduced utility (dissatisfaction, loss of welfare). Thus, "an external gain," whether of production or consumption, may be referred to as a *positive externality* or *external economy* and an "external loss," whether of production or consumption, may be designated a *negative externality* or *external diseconomy.*

It is significant to observe that most economic actions initiated by an economic agent yield at least some economic effects which escape the price mechanism. Thus, externalities are rather commonplace, but often are not economically signigicant. Table 2–1 summarizes the primary characteristics of externalities as discussed in this section. There are a number of possible externality combinations. For example: (1) A consumption action may yield external production effects; (2) a production action may yield external consumption effects; (3) a consumption action may yield external consumption effects; and (4) a production action may yield external production effects. The possible combinations increase in number and complexity when the consideration of both positive externalities (gains) and negative externalities (losses) are added. Moreover, an action undertaken by a given economic agent —such as a producer—may exert nonmarket effects on *both* "other" producers and consumers.

TABLE 2–1
Some Characteristics of Externalities

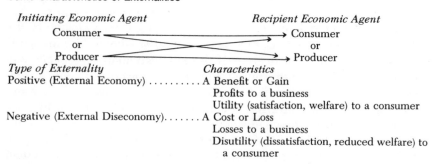

Initiating Economic Agent	Recipient Economic Agent
Consumer	Consumer
or	or
Producer	Producer

Type of Externality	Characteristics
Positive (External Economy)	A Benefit or Gain
	Profits to a business
	Utility (satisfaction, welfare) to a consumer
Negative (External Diseconomy).......	A Cost or Loss
	Losses to a business
	Disutility (dissatisfaction, reduced welfare) to a consumer

For example, a firm manufacturing steel may install new blast furnaces which increase the technical efficiency of its production. The *explicit* costs of acquiring this new productive capital is easily demonstrated by the price mechanism (assume a cost of $1 million). Now assume that the new blast furnaces significantly increase air pollution in the surrounding area—a result which both diminishes the profit positions of producers (assume by $200,000) in a nearby recreational industry and residential consumers who have their welfare diminished by breathing the polluted air. Both the producers and consumers would incur *nonmarket costs* ($200,000 plus the welfare loss to the consumers), but since these are not explicit market costs which the steel firm must calculate when assessing its profit position, there will be a tendency to "oversupply" the steel and, thus, to create the negative externalities due to the underpricing of the scarce resource "air."

Alternately, suppose that an individual who has a great liking for jungle animals decides to convert his residential backyard into a home zoo. His individual welfare or satisfaction increases as he spends $10,-

000 to purchase the animals so that he can enjoy their presence. Yet, the private consumption gains to the owner of the menagerie of jungle animals result in negative externalities of consumption to his neighbors in the form of noise, unpleasant odors, and lowered property values. The private expenditure of $10,000 has not been required to consider the nonmarket diminishment in welfare of the neighbors.

Externalities are elusive, though real, and "potential" public interest derives from the very nature of these externalities. There is no self-correcting market mechanism at work since externalities, whether positive or negative, are not measured in price values. Moreover, it is difficult to convert many externalities to control through the market. Yet, as will be demonstrated below, the mere presence of an externality does *not* provide a prima facie case for public sector allocative intervention.

The Relationship Between Externalities and Public Sector Allocation.
The discussion of the relationship between externalities and governmental allocative policy will be introduced in the terminology of the late British economist A. C. Pigou, as developed several decades ago.[17] Then, subsequent sophistication of the Pigovian analysis, especially in "policy" terms, will be presented. Pigou distinguishes between *private* benefits and costs and *social* benefits and costs. *Private* benefits and costs represent those internal effects of an economic action which do not escape the price mechanism and which, thus, are retained within the economic calculus of the initiating agent. *Social* benefits and costs, on the other hand, represent both these internal private effects as well as external effects which do escape the price mechanism and, thus, go beyond the motivational calculus of the initiating agent. The latter benefits and costs are essentially "nonmarket" in character.

If social effects of a benefit variety exceed private benefits, it is said in Pigovian terms that an *external economy* (positive externality) exists. In this instance, a private firm is likely to produce less than the social optimum amount of an economic good because the firm is adding benefits to society greater than the quantity of benefits for which it is being compensated in the market. The typical "policy" prescription to correct this undersupply was a governmental *subsidy* to the private producer to encourage production of the *economic good* which yields the benefit. On the other hand, if social costs exceed private costs, it is said in Pigovian terms that an *external diseconomy* (negative externality) is present. In this instance, there would be a tendency to provide an oversupply of the economic bad since the total cost of allocation is being absorbed, in part, by individuals other than the initiating economic agent. The typical "policy" prescription in this case was the imposition of a *tax* to discourage the allocation of the *economic bad*.

---

[17] A. C. Pigou, *The Economics of Welfare* (London: Macmillan and Co., 1920).

Thus, in economic circumstances where only partial exclusion occurs, and externalities result, there is a tendency for *economic goods* to be "undersupplied" and, where negative externalities result, for *economic bads* to be "oversupplied." If "social benefits exceed private benefits," there is a free rider motivation inducing those receiving the excess benefits *not* to voluntarily pay for them. Even more importantly, as observed in the preceding paragraph, there is a motivation for the producer of the benefits *not* to supply that excess of social benefits over private benefits for which payment is not received under the operation of the exclusion principle.

If "social costs exceed private costs," the initiating economic agent does not have to bear that excess cost which escapes the price mechanism. Hence, the economic bads may be oversupplied. Moreover, the recipient(s) of the economic bads (diseconomies, negative externalities) cannot "reject" them. Such "nonrejectability" occurs because the price mechanism does not control the costs and the recipient thus cannot voluntarily *not acquire* them. Of course, the supplier of the external *costs* will not voluntarily eliminate them since they are not part of his economic maximizing calculations. This is analagous to the free rider problem in the external *benefits* case in which the recipient of the benefits will not voluntarily offer payment. Meanwhile, the "supplier" of the benefits is reluctant to supply what is not paid for.

More recently, and especially during the decade of the 1960s, subsequent analysis has added sophistication to the Pigovian analysis concerning the "conceptual" and "public policy" aspects of externalities.[18] Thus, it should be recognized that the mere existence of an externality does not in itself merit corrective action. It may be that a greater loss in welfare will occur from "internalizing" ("correcting for") an externality through a resource reallocation than the gain in welfare deriving from such an action. For example, the cost of "internalizing" a *positive externality*, where social benefits exceed private benefits, may be greater than the welfare gains of the externality itself.[19] Or, the cost of "internalizing" a *negative externality*, where social costs exceed private costs, may be greater than the "reduced" welfare costs (welfare

---

[18] See the contributions of R. H. Coase, "The Problem of Social Cost," *The Journal of Law and Economics,* October 1960, pp. 1–44; James M. Buchanan and William C. Stubblebine, "Externality," *Economica,* November 1962, pp. 371–79; and Otto Davis and Andrew Whinston, "Externalities, Welfare and the Theory of Games," *Journal of Political Economy,* June 1962, pp. 241–62. For excellent summaries of these contributions, see Ralph Turvey, "On Divergences between Social Cost and Private Cost," *Economica,* August 1963, pp. 309–13; and William J. Baumol, *Welfare Economics* (2d ed.; Cambridge: Harvard University Press, 1965), pp. 24–36.

[19] In a "strict" sense, an externality is said to be "internalized" only if it is converted back into the price system. However, since conversion of this sort will not always be possible, other corrective action may be undertaken. The use of the term "internalization" in this book will follow the latter "broad" interpretation inclusive of nonprice conversion.

benefits obtained through the elimination of the externality). In either case, the welfare position of the society would have been made worse by the policy adjustment for the externality. Moreover, in some instances the externally damaged (benefited) party may not even be motivated to seek corrective action. In this instance, the externality is not related to marginal costs and an attempt to internalize it, such as through a governmental subsidy or tax, would have no economic influence whatsoever on its production.

On the other hand, the cost of internalizing an externality through a resource reallocation, in many cases, may warrant a policy adjustment. This would be true if the cost of internalization is less than the gain in welfare deriving from such an action. Yet, it should also be observed that the *public sector* alone does not represent the only possible means of corrective policy. Moreover, even public sector policy may involve "regulation" and not "actual governmental production." In addition, *private* contractual negotiation, legal action, or other privately-initiated means outside the direct allocative intervention of government may constitute plausible alternatives. That is, such market-oriented techniques may be capable of "internalizing the externality" more efficiently than can be accomplished through the direct action of government. The opportunity for such privately-attained improvements in welfare will be enhanced when the externalities are technologically capable of divisibility under the price system. Importantly, such divisibility at any one point of time will also reflect the "ability" and "willingness" of the society to define *property rights* in such a manner that the economic goods (benefits) or bads (costs) will be "salable" and thus adaptable to the exchange process.

Although the definition of property rights will help to determine the limits of product divisibility, and thus the possibility of exchange, there remains a significant presence of economic goods and bads under present technological constraints which are not conducive to such divisibility. This is especially true if the externality occurs in a *large group* situation in which the motivation is not strong for a single individual to initiate corrective action. Under such conditions, the market or private sector exchange techniques may be incapable of exerting corrective action and such action, if it is to occur, must result from the policy of the public sector.

Finally, it should be noted that the discussion above concerning the establishment of an economic argument for the existence of a public sector in a market-oriented society rests upon the goal of "allocational efficiency." *Distributional* considerations are only incidentally treated. However, it must be recognized that both private and public sector efforts to "internalize externalities," an allocational goal, are likely to yield significant distributional side effects. For example, if the steel firm which installs the "polluting" blast furnaces (see the above example) is legally required to install "pollution-control" devices to protect the businesses and consumers in the surrounding area, the distribution of the burden of pollution control will fall "initially" upon the steel firm and, perhaps, "ultimately" upon the consumers of the firm's products who may pay higher prices for steel products. Importantly, the internalization of the pollution externality—an *allocational* consideration—would have been attained only with accompanying *redistributional* side effects favorable, in this case, to the pollution-affected firms and consumers in the surrounding area, but economically unfavorable, initially at least, to the steel firm. The legal requirement that the steel firm is responsible for those harmed by the pollution, which constitutes a specific definition of *property rights,* is the basis for these redistributional effects. Indeed, *property rights* are a strategic link between "allocational" and "distributional" activities.

In conclusion, it may be said that the presence of externalities creates a necessary, but *not in all cases* a sufficient, condition for public sector allocative action. The public sector, of course, does exist as *one* of the "primary" institutions which may apply corrective action in order to improve resource allocation and societal welfare. Yet, it is not the only possible means of corrective action and, moreover, "no action" by either the public or private sector will sometimes be the best policy. Furthermore, institutional arrangements can change over time and thus provide additional techniques for welfare improvement. This is especially true to the extent that technological change may allow a changing ability to "define property rights." Thus, even though the public sector must exist to influence resource allocation to an extent greater than that required to provide minimal law and order, each individual case for potential governmental action should be evaluated upon its own merits. No conclusive generalization can be made for governmental action in the case of *all* externalities.

A "Variety" of Supply Causes of Market Failure

To this point in the chapter, the analysis has focused upon several primary determinants of market failure leading to an economic role for government in a market-oriented society. However, there remain several additional, though generally less important, causes of partial market failure which merit brief discussion. Essentially, these additional phenomena are of a "supply" nature.

The *lack of adequate market knowledge* by a firm is more severe in some cases than in others. At times, this lack of knowledge can prevent the attainment of sufficient output levels of an important economic good by the market. For example, risk probabilities were assessed incorrectly by the market regarding the supply costs and the demand for electricity in rural areas of the United States prior to 1936. In that year, a series of federal government loans and subsidies were initiated through the Rural Electrification Administration (REA). This program demonstrated that rural electrification was feasible on a profit basis in many parts of the United States since a significant demand existed for this economic good. Presently, almost all American farmers use electricity as provided today by both the public and private sectors.

Other examples of a long-run payoff from "collective risk taking" may be drawn from such occurrences as development of atomic energy by the Atomic Energy Commission (AEC), development of communications satellites under the substantial (though not complete) public sector influence of the National Aeronautics and Space Administration (NASA), and the development of public power through the Tennessee Valley Authority (TVA). In the latter case, the extensive development of public power during the 1930s proved to privately owned electric utilities that the demand for electricity was not as inelastic as they had believed it to be. Hence, improvements in market knowledge, as attained through "collective risk taking," may well enhance the long-run profits of private firms and, in so doing, increase the supply of desirable economic goods.

Secondly, the *immobility of productive resources* can help to prevent the attainment of efficient resource allocation results. The nature of plant and equipment makes the geographical mobility of real capital very difficult, if not completely impossible. However, labor resources may also be immobile due to such forces as the nature of pension plans, seniority provisions, and entry restrictions into new job markets. In any case, when resources are not free to move to their most efficient points of usage, as indicated by market forces, the conditions of long-run general equilibrium are not attained and a subsequent retardation of the ability of the private sector to allocate resources in an efficient manner results. Indeed, both capital and labor resources reflect the lack of perfect mobility under market conditions in the United States. Yet, various public sector programs may be designed to enhance resource mobility, particularly labor mobility, and thus improve resource allocation. An example of this in the federal personal income tax law is the allowability of deductions for "moving expenses" between job locations.

Thirdly, the *conservation of certain resources* is sometimes necessary when the resources are uniquely scarce and/or unique in character. While society considers the full employment (as reasonably defined) of most labor and capital resources to be desirable, it cannot consider the "short-run" full employment of natural resources (the land factor of production) to be desirable. Thus, when short-run profit considerations would lead to overutilization of uniquely scarce or important natural resources, such as the radio wave spectrum or the cutting of 2,000-year old redwood trees, long-run societal welfare may require the practice of "governmentally-directed" resource conservation. Moreover, society needs to conserve clean water and clean air as natural resources. Among the techniques which can be employed for the conservation of natural resources are government ownership of the resources, public utility regulation, severance taxes, nonutilization subsidies, and water-air pollution standards.

Hence, the risk which accompanies imperfect market knowledge, inadequate resource mobility, and the unique characteristics of certain resources each may suggest the desirability, as indicated by a "societal consensus," of allocative intervention by the public sector.

Finally, a distinction should be made between those economic goods allocated under governmental influence which are *intermediate* as opposed to *final* in nature.[20] For example, government may provide a direct consumption item or *final* good such as national or internal security. On the other hand, it may produce an *intermediate* good, typically capital in nature, which will lead to the ultimate production and consumption of a final consumer good. This final consumer good may be either privately- or publicly-produced. Thus, public sector provision of an irrigation project may increase the ability of a private agricultural industry to produce food. Or, governmental provision of a hydroelectric project may lead to the production of electricity by either a government- or privately-owned utility. Another example would entail public sector production of roads, a capital good, which helps to improve the production of a final consumer good such as bus transportation—which again may be produced by either the private or public sector. Hence, either final or intermediate economic goods may be allocated under public sector influence.

SUMMARY

In all, this chapter has demonstrated several causes of market failure. These include:

1. Decreasing production costs over an entire range of feasible outputs in imperfectly competitive industries
2. The polar case of decreasing costs known as "zero marginal costs"
3. The phenomenon of collective consumption

---

[20] For a discussion of this distinction, including its relevance in relation to cost-benefit analysis as discussed in Chapter 18 of this book, see Richard A. Musgrave, "Cost-Benefit Analysis and the Theory of Public Finance," *Journal of Economic Literature*, September 1969, pp. 799–801.

4. The phenomenon of externalities
5. A variety of special supply conditions.

The market failure which derives from the above phenomena constitutes a *general* economic argument for the existence of a public sector for allocational purposes in a market-oriented system. Nonetheless, *specific* case-by-case analysis is still required. For example, it cannot be said a priori that the existence of a condition of market failure provides both a *necessary* and *sufficient* condition for governmental allocational intervention. It may be that private sector allocational efforts can better improve the situation. Or, it may even be better not to initiate any effort to rectify the market failure.

In the final sense, an economy must follow the "effective demand" directives of its given state of income, wealth, and political voting distribution in order to determine the allocation of its resources among private sector and public sector activities. "Noneconomic" considerations such as the degree of political and economic freedom desired by the people of the society may also play an important role. Relatedly, as will be observed in the following chapter, a variety of allocative techniques characterized by both market and collective traits may be employed. That is, there exist many "hybrid" allocational devices which allow varying mixtures of both private and public sector "direction" in the allocation process.

3

Techniques of Public Sector Resource Allocation

ECONOMIC GOODS AND ALLOCATIONAL TECHNIQUES

In the previous chapter, an economic argument was established for the existence of a public sector to influence resource allocation in a market-oriented system. It was observed, for example, that certain economic goods are characterized by the joint or collective consumption of their benefits, that is, their benefits are *indivisible* among two or more consumers. Thus, individuals in a large group are motivated to become "free riders" and avoid voluntary payment for such goods. At the other extreme, it was recognized that certain other economic goods possess benefits which are primarily, if not totally, *divisible* to the individual thus making these goods subject to pricing through the application of the exclusion principle. Moreover, other demand or supply characteristics may help place a particular economic good at the "public" or "private" extreme. However, the majority of economic goods are *neither* "purely public" *nor* "purely private" in nature. These "intermediate" goods may be classified as *quasi-goods* and, more specifically, they may be classified as *quasi-public* or *quasi-private* goods depending upon whether their allocation is determined primarily by the public sector or by the private sector of the economy. Unlike *pure public goods* where such a condition as the free rider problem may be present, there often is no compelling reason why the public sector should dominate the allocation of the "quasi-good."

A wide variety of allocational techniques exist whereby quasi-economic goods can be allocated. Broadly speaking, where allocational influence by the public sector is deemed desirable, government may, at one extreme, produce the economic good itself or, at the other extreme, it may loosely regulate the private production of the good, or it may adopt any of a variety of "in-between" techniques. These "in-between" or "hybrid" techniques may be either essentially "governmental" or essentially "market" in nature, or they may be somewhat evenly divided between governmental and market characteristics. Thus, efficient resource allocation requires not only the optimal intersector solution, discussed in Chapter 1, but it requires also the selection of the specific *techniques of allocation.*

Relatedly, a clear distinction should be made between public sector *organization of supply* and actual public sector *production* of an economic good. The former might well consist primarily of governmental financing of the good with the good being essentially produced by, and purchased from, the private sector. The latter, on the other hand, suggests both outright governmental financing and production of the good.

The selection of a particular technique for influencing the allocation of quasi-goods is often decided on "noneconomic" grounds. Considerations of freedom, along with other related social and cultural criteria, become highly relevant to the selection of an allocation technique. Prevailing American culture and tastes prefer minimal public sector influence on resource allocation. American society continually weighs through the political process the relative economic efficiencies of direct or indirect, complete or partial, public sector allocation influence against the existing social, cultural, and political values. Heller comments that "one would be naïve to think that efficiency alone dictates the choice," and further, "the role of both economic and noneconomic constraints must be given full weight" in policy decisions as to the method of allocation.[1] As discussed in Chapter 1, Wallich argues that unless the public sector has a decided edge in the technical efficiency of combining productive resources to produce the optimal output, the community may prefer indirect and partial allocation influence—and this *only* when circumstances require any governmental influence at all.[2]

A typical example of the argument in behalf of partial and indirect public sector allocation influence is found in Friedman's suggestion that subsidies in the form of transfer payments be paid to individuals to be used to purchase education services from schools.[3] Specifically, Fried-

---

[1] Walter W. Heller, "Economics and the Applied Theory of Public Expenditures," *Federal Expenditure Policy for Economic Growth and Stability,* Joint Economic Committee, 85th Cong., 1st sess. (Washington, D.C.: U.S. Government Printing Office, 1957), pp. 106–7.

[2] Henry C. Wallich, *The Cost of Freedom* (New York: Harper & Row, Publishers, 1960).

[3] Milton Friedman, *Capitalism and Freedom* (Chicago: University of Chicago Press, 1962), chap. 6.

man suggests a system of both public and private schools, at least for primary and secondary education, whereby parents who choose to send their children to private schools would be paid a sum equal to the estimated cost of educating a child in a public school, provided that at least this amount will be spent on education in an approved school.[4] Via this technique, a quasi-public good (education) would be supplied in adequate quantities through public sector influence even though the good could be produced largely in the market. Thus, it is argued that "economic" gains specifically accrue from the increased education and from the competition between the schools while both "economic" and "noneconomic" gains result from the greater freedom of choice regarding the selection of a school.

TECHNIQUES VERSUS ISMS

Most resource allocation decisions do not involve a sharp distinction between socialistic planning and market decentralization. The majority of allocation decisions, to the contrary, are concerned with selection between a variety of "mixed techniques" which contain elements of both market and government allocation. Dahl and Lindblom comment:

> . . . techniques and not "isms" are the kernel of rational social action in the Western world. Both socialism and capitalism are dead. The politico-economic systems of the United States and of Britain differ in important respects, to be sure; yet both major parties in both countries are attacking their economic problems with fundamentally the same kinds of techniques. Ideological differences between the parties in each country and between the countries themselves are significant in affecting the choice of techniques; but policy in any case is technique-minded, and it is becoming increasingly difficult in both countries to argue policy in terms of the mythical grand alternatives.[5]

Economic planning, for example, occurs under *governmental* influence both in socialist Russia and in (largely) capitalistic France. Furthermore, the management of large private American firms such as the American Telephone and Telegraph Company and General Motors involves extensive planning operations. Planning per se is neither socialistic nor capitalistic, though the initial incentive for planning may be "social welfare" in the one case and "profits" in the other. Nonetheless, planning is a technique for improving administrative efficiency in either a governmental or a market situation.

It also may be observed that the number of alternative allocational

---

[4] Ibid.

[5] Robert A. Dahl and Charles E. Lindblom, *Politics, Economics and Welfare* (New York: Harper, 1953), p. 16.

techniques is continually increasing through discovery and innovation. Innovation is not confined to technology in the physical sciences. The social structure also may benefit from innovation in social techniques. Lend-lease, scientific management, old age and survivors insurance, workmen's compensation, collective bargaining, full-employment policy, urban renewal, and the Peace Corps are a few of many available testimonies to this fact. Thus, many of the techniques through which the public sector may influence resource allocation need not be confined to a static "either-or choice" between socialism and capitalism. Instead, they may be efficient and dynamic "compromises" between the two "isms." Similarly, intersector resource allocation, as discussed in Chapter 1, need not be an "either-or choice" between pure public sector and pure private sector resource allocation. Techniques may be selected which will commit the society to neither extreme.

CONTINUUM OF ALTERNATIVE ALLOCATIONAL TECHNIQUES

Table 3–1 presents a continuum showing some of the major alternative techniques which the public sector can use to influence resource allocation. These techniques range from those which are applied directly and completely by government to those where the public sector's influence is very indirect and incomplete. In the former case, government power and compulsion prevail. In the latter, the techniques more closely resemble market power and individualism. At point 1 on the continuum, governmental allocational influence is direct and complete. The public sector both finances and produces the economic good, whether it be a *final* consumption good like national defense or an *intermediate* item of social capital like a water reclamation project which only only "indirectly" relates to the ultimate production of a final consumer good. Moreover, it produces the component parts of the good and owns or "directly" controls all resources used in the production of these components.

Even national defense is not governmentally-supplied to this extreme degree in the United States. Most intermediate components (missiles, planes, ships) of the final good (national defense) are produced in the market and purchased by the federal government. Furthermore, now that the draft has ended, members of the armed forces (the labor element of national defense) serve on a voluntary rather than on a compulsory basis. Though provision of national defense in the United States cannot be strictly located at the polar extreme of governmental allocative intervention, the federal government nonetheless possesses considerable financial power and authority to divert resources toward defense production. Thus, point 2 on the continuum represents the

TABLE 3–1
Continuum of Some Alternative Techniques of Public Sector Resource Allocation

Degree of Influence*	Description of Technique
100%	1. The public sector finances and produces a *final* or an *intermediate* economic good. In addition, it produces all components of the good and it owns or "directly" controls all productive resources used in producing these components.
	2. The public sector finances and produces a *final* or an *intermediate* economic good, but purchases some or all of the components and/or productive resources, including labor, in the market.
	3. Monetary system owned or basically controlled by the public sector.
	4. Substantial subsidy plus direct (public utility) regulation of an economic good produced by private enterprise in the market.
	5. Combined public-private ownership of a firm, or publicly- and privately owned firms coexisting in the same industry.
50%	6. Substantial subsidy of a market-produced good.
	7. Direct regulation of a market-produced good.
	8. Tax penalty or fee to ration consumption of a good.
	9. Public sector licensing of private enterprise in the form of charters, franchises, and licenses.
	10. Transfer-type operations and other fiscal acts which "directly" redistribute income, wealth, and political voting power and thus "indirectly" change the pattern of allocation.
	11. General antitrust regulation.
0	

* Positioning of numbered techniques shows percentage ranking as to approximate degree of "directness" and "completeness" of public sector allocation influence.

approximate directness and completeness of public sector defense influence in the United States. At this position on the continuum, the public sector finances and produces the final good but buys some or all of the intermediate components and/or productive resources from the market.

In the United States, the federal government influences the performance of the money and banking system in a significant manner. The monetary tools of the Federal Reserve System control the money supply (including demand deposits) through the behavior of a fractional reserve, commercial banking system. The Federal Reserve System and the Treasury Department, moreover, issue all circulating currency and coins. The Federal Reserve is, in a sense, a quasi-governmental body. The 12 regional banks are owned by the commercial banks of their respective areas and, in addition, are partially managed by business and banking representatives of the regions which they serve. Thus, point

3 on the continuum is used to denote the approximate influence of the federal government on the allocation of money and banking services in the economy. Indeed, it is a substantial influence. Yet, it is not a direct and complete one in the polar sense.

The public sector may influence resource allocation by combining the techniques of subsidy and direct (public utility) regulation. Each of these means, of course, may also be used separately. The combined subsidy-direct regulation technique of allocation may be located approximately at point 4 on the continuum diagram if the subsidies and regulation are substantial.

Subsidies may take a variety of forms. A subsidy, for example, can be derived from the spending side of a government budget in the form of an outright monetary payment to a private economic agent or as a productive resource or economic good provided to the private agent. The above-market-price purchases of farm products by the Commodity Credit Corporation is representative of the expenditure type of subsidy. Partial expenditure subsidies occur when government provides a productive resource or an economic good to a private economic unit at a price beneath the cost of providing the resource or good. Long-term, low-interest loans and commercial mailing privileges are examples of this type of subsidy. On the revenue side of the government budget, subsidies may take the subtle and disguised form of tax preferences (loopholes) designed to reduce the tax burdens of certain groups or occupations. Regardless of its obscurity, such a subsidy may nonetheless be of significant monetary importance to the recipient. Basically, the primary subsidy alternatives reduce to the broad categories of private gains resulting from either of the following: (1) the receipt of public expenditures, or (2) reduced tax obligations on the revenue side of the budget.

Direct regulation is best exemplified by public utility regulation in the United States. The first comprehensive and effective application of this technique in the United States was on the railroads during the 1870s and 1880s through the state "granger laws" and the federal "Act to Regulate Commerce." All states presently possess public utility commissions. In addition, many municipalities have regulatory bureaus while the federal government sponsors such powerful regulatory agencies as the Interstate Commerce Commission, Civil Aeronautics Board, Federal Power Commission, Federal Communications Commission, and the Securities and Exchange Commission. Public utility regulation provides direct control over private business firms in such economic facets as (1) the conditions of entry into the industry, (2) price of service, (3) quantity of service, and (4) quality of service.

A historic example of combined subsidies and direct regulation is provided by the development of the western railroads in the United

States. These railroads received substantial land grant subsidies constituting 242,000 square miles of land—much of which was rich in terms of soil, minerals, and timber. The subsidies helped to promote the rapid development of a highly effective transcontinental railroad network during the last half of the 19th century. Substantial services were provided and the various positive externalities emanating from improved transportation benefited the entire economy. Furthermore, as observed above, the state governments of Iowa, Illinois, Minnesota, and Wisconsin introduced the "granger laws" to directly regulate railroads during this era. The era witnessed, moreover, the beginning of direct federal regulation of interstate railroad services through the creation of the Interstate Commerce Commission in 1887. The railroads thus received substantial subsidies, but they also faced substantial regulation. Although the "combined" subsidization and public utility regulation of privately owned enterprises does *not* constitute the polar extreme of direct and complete public sector allocation, it does constitute a substantial influence by the public sector on the allocation of scarce resources.

An allocation technique which may be located on the continuum at approximately the same point as the "combined subsidy-direct regulation" technique is the "combined public-private ownership" means of allocation. It may be applied either to a firm or to an industry. Examples of this technique being applied to "firms" include public corporations with tripartite control such as those employed in the French electricty and railroad industries. In the United States, the Communications Satellite Corporation (Comsat), as endorsed by Congress, contains many features of joint government-market ownership and control of a firm. Furthermore, the development of nuclear energy under the direction of the Atomic Energy Commission (AEC), and the cooperation of the AEC with private enterprise, constitutes another example of the partnership means. In addition, the research-oriented Sandia Corporation is owned by the Atomic Energy Commission and operated by the American Telephone and Telegraph Company. An "industrywide" application of this technique is found in Canada's transcontinental railroad service where two companies, one government owned and the other private, provide virtually parallel routes. A similar arrangement is found in the domestic airline industry of Australia. In the United States, the Tennessee Valley Authority provides a "yardstick" of competition to privately owned utilities in the Tennessee Valley region. The partnership or coexisting firms technique serves as a compromise between the extremes of direct and complete public sector influence and no public sector allocational influence at all.

It was observed above that "combined" subsidies and direct public utility regulation provide substantial allocation influence. It should be remembered, however, that subsidies and direct regulation often exist on a separate basis in the American economy. When this occurs, the degree of public sector allocation influence is necessarily less than when the two techniques are jointly used. It is estimated in Table 3–1 that separate usage of either the subsidy technique or of the direct regulation technique would fall at points 6 and 7, respectively, along the continuum. The subsidy or direct regulation would need to be substantial, of course, in order to provide even this degree of allocation influence. Slight or unimportant subsidies and weak regulation would fall much further down on the continuum.

Point 8 on the continuum represents an estimate of the relative importance of tax penalties or fees as an instrument of allocational influence by the public sector. Sometimes the most rational governmental allocation technique, given the nature of community preferences, is one which "discourages" instead of encourages production or consumption. Prevailing community feelings regarding the consumption of liquor and tobacco products, for example, may result in the classification of these economic goods as "vices" which need to be discouraged. Given such community preferences, the public sector may impose substantial excise taxes, known as "sumptuary" taxes, on the consumption of liquor and tobacco products, or it may control their marketing as in the case of government-operated liquor stores. In other instances, government may charge a price (fee, toll) for the use of some economic good or resource in order to ration its use within available supply or capacity. Heavy bridge or road traffic, for example, may necessitate the charging of a substantial toll in order to regulate traffic usage within the capacity of the bridge or road. A further usage of tax penalties or prices to discourage consumption occurs on an aggregate basis during the inflationary pressure conditions of a wartime economy as during World War II. The desire, in this case, is to restrain aggregate demand by imposing new taxes, or by raising present tax rates, in order to reduce the allocation of private goods relative to war goods.

The public sector can restrict entry to professions and industries via the issuance of charters, franchises, or licenses. However, such policies frequently worsen allocational efficiency rather than improve it because they increase monopoly power and thus cause a greater deviation between the profit-maximization point of output (marginal cost equals marginal revenue) and the optimal social allocation point (marginal cost equals average revenue). At times, however, they can improve allocation by conserving uniquely scarce or important productive resources. The issuance of charters, franchises, or licenses are located at point 9 on the continuum. Charters, franchises, and licenses do not directly involve the expenditure and tax sides of the budget in an important manner. They involve no "direct" *price* or *quantity* controls.[6] Instead, they are incomplete and indirect means of public sector influence over resource allocation.

A subtle and "indirect" technique whereby government may influence resource usage is by redistributing private sector income and wealth and public sector political voting power so that a different pattern of community allocation decisions occurs. Examples of this technique include: (1) government transfer payments (which do not directly absorb resources), (2) the pattern in which tax burdens are distributed, (3) the manner in which an asymmetrical (unequally distributed) public debt is maintained in terms of taxes collected and interest payments made on the debt. In general, the public sector budget can be employed to change a given distributional structure and, in so doing, change the pattern of resource allocation in the society. In any event, since this technique only "indirectly" influences allocation while working "directly" on the distributional objective of public sector economics, it is classified as an indirect and incomplete governmental allocation technique. It is located at point 10 on the continuum.

General antitrust regulation is the final allocation alternative to be considered. In the United States it is a very indirect and incomplete technique, in terms of its allocational influence, and is classified toward the bottom of the continuum at point 11 in Table 3–1. Just as with the policy of issuing franchises, this technique may worsen allocation if it is used improperly, that is, to enhance a monopoly position. For purposes of this book, general antitrust regulation and public licensing will not be considered as important public sector allocation techniques. Transfer-type operations will be considered "important" only because of their relationship to the distribution branch of public sector economics. In addition, due to the "specialized" importance of money in an economic system, the influence of the "monetary" system will be excluded from the basic "fiscal" considerations of this book except as it relates to the stabilization, growth, and debt policies of the public sector.

ECONOMIC GOODS, ALLOCATIONAL TECHNIQUES, AND ALLOCATING SECTORS: A SUMMARY

It was observed in the previous chapter that the presence of such phenomena as decreasing production costs in the range of socially-feasible outputs, collective consumption, and externalities do not in

---

[6] However, they may involve "direct" *quality* controls such as government-imposed health and sanitary standards for the operation of a restaurant or a barber shop.

themselves constitute an a priori (conclusive) argument in behalf of governmental allocative intervention in market economic activity. In the case of *externalities,* this is true because (1) the externality may not enter into marginal cost considerations, which would mean a lack of motivation to internalize the externality; (2) even with a desire to correct for the externality, it may be that the societal welfare gained from correction may be less than the cost of such internalization, or (3) even if internalization is warranted by a gain in societal welfare, means other than governmental, that is, private sector arrangements, may provide a more efficient solution to the externality problem than can be provided by the public sector. However, it should be emphasized that the "presence" or "absence" of strong traits of "publicness," whether deriving from externalities or from some other source, does provide a logical "tie-in" with the institutional sector, public or private, which is likely to be the more efficient in influencing the allocation of a particular economic good. Nonetheless, a "case-by-case" approach is still required.

The discussion of Figure 3–1 hopefully will enlighten this point as well as further develop the relationship between the various types of economic goods, the alternative allocational techniques, and the institutional sectors of allocation. This discussion will focus, in particular, upon

FIGURE 3–1
Spectrum of Economic Goods Based on "Mix" of Private or Public Characteristics

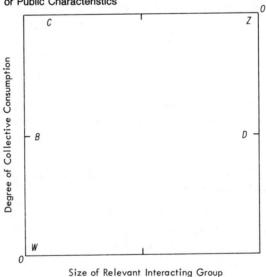

Size of Relevant Interacting Group

Source: This figure is adapted from James M. Buchanan, *The Demand and Supply of Public Goods* (© 1968 by Rand McNally & Company, Chicago, Figure 9–1, p. 175. Reprinted by permission of Rand McNally College Publishing Company).

the *collective consumption* characteristic of public-type goods and the *private consumption* characteristic of market-type goods.

In Figure 3–1, the size of the *relevant interacting group* is measured along the horizontal axis. The term "relevant" here suggests the connotation of "interdependent" consumption. Essentially, it asks this question: Is the group small enough to reach a market-type agreement without encountering a serious "free rider" problem? For purposes of discussion, the total U.S. population is represented on the horizontal axis while the smallest "subpart" of this total, a single consumer, is located at the extreme southwest corner. The degree of collective consumption (product indivisibility), whether "partial" or "complete," is measured along the vertical axis. For a given economic good, the degree of indivisibility will be influenced by such factors as the prevailing definition of property rights (to be discussed below).

At *O* (southwest corner of the diagram), the exclusion principle would apply perfectly to *pure private good "W"* ($W = W_a + W_b$). This means that the benefits of the good are "completely divisible "in that none escape the price mechanism. A candy bar may be offered as an example of such a good. On the other hand, the exclusion principle would *not* apply at O^1 (northeast corner of the diagram) to *pure public good "Z"* ($Z = Z_a$; $Z = Z_b$). The benefits here are "completely indivisible," that is, they are jointly and equally consumed at the same level of output by all American consumers. National defense may be offered as an example of such a good.

An economic good of the *"B"* variety, by contrast with goods *"W"* and *"Z"* above, possesses partial traits of both "privateness" and "publicness" since some of the benefits are "divisible" and some are "indivisible." It is jointly, but *not* equally, consumed since the exclusion principle applies to only part of the total benefits. Yet, the number of persons concerned with the good is small enough that negotiated agreements on its allocation can be reached. For example, two individuals may live as neighbors in houses on adjoining properties. They may agree that one large "police dog" will provide protection from burglary and vandalism to both of them, though perhaps more to the individual who actually will keep the dog on his property. The "protective" benefits of the dog are thus partly divisible and partly jointly consumed by the two neighbors. Yet, even though some benefits are "jointly consumed," the total benefits are *not* "equally consumed." Instead, the neighbor on whose property the dog resides receives the superior protection due to a *locational* factor. Yet, a "market-type solution" without governmental allocative intervention is feasible since the relevant consuming group is small enough to negotiate the financing of the arrangement.

An economic good of the *"C"* category, on the other hand, is represented by the characteristics of both "joint consumption" and "equal consumption." The degree of product indivisibility is complete within the group. Relatedly, the short-run marginal cost of supplying consumption to an additional individual is zero. Yet, if the size of the group is small enough, some market-type arrangement for allocating the good can be achieved through the negotiating efforts of the individuals who are involved. This might be exemplified by a private club which through some established decision-making procedure decides to build a new indoor swimming pool for the exclusive use of its members. The services of the pool are available (once it is constructed) at a short-run marginal cost of zero to the members of the club. Moreover, its benefits are completely indivisible to its members who will use it as a "free good" and not pay for it on an exclusion principle basis. Importantly, this economic good, though it contains important traits of "publicness," is subject to a nongovernmental allocational solution. This is because the size of the relevant group, as indicated along the horizontal axis, is small enough to avoid a significant "free rider" problem. That is, there is no meaningful motivation among the club members to let another club member pay for the good.

In the case of economic goods *W*, *B*, and *C* the size of the interacting consuming group is "small enough"[7] to avoid the need for "direct" governmental intervention. Market-type procedures can essentially perform the allocational function. Government need provide only "indirect" allocational influence such as the protection of property rights including the enforcement of contracts, the deterrence of fraud, and overall antitrust (market structure) policies.

The above conditions change significantly when the size of the relevant interacting group becomes large enough that the "free rider" motivation prevails. This is true for economic goods in both the *"D"* and *"Z"* categories. Economic goods of the *"D"* classification contain both divisible and indivisible benefits—the latter occurring under conditions of *large-group consumption*. University education may be offered as an example of this type of good. The fact that part of the benefits are indivisible throughout the entire society leads to a "free rider" motivation since the group is large enough to reduce the likelihood that efficient market-type pricing can be applied. Hence, the practice of governmental financing of universities is commonplace. Yet, the consumption, though "joint," is not "equal." He who receives the university education receives greater total benefits than he who does not, though both receive some general benefits which are derived by the community as a whole from a more educated populace. In any event, the "probable" need for significant public sector allocative influence is considerably greater for goods in the *"D"* category than for

---

[7] With Good *W*, only one consumer receives all of the benefits.

goods in the *"W," "B,"* and *"C"* categories where allocation ordinarily can be influenced more efficiently by the private sector of the "mixed" economy. Indeed, the technical feasibility and costs of exclusion become a very relevant factor in determining whether the public or private sector should supply a particular economic good.

Finally, an economic good located in category *"Z",* as observed above, represents the polar opposite of a pure private good (category *"W"*), namely, a *pure public good.* All "in-between" caterogies (*"B," "C,"* and *"D"*) represent *quasi goods* (impure goods) and, more specifically, goods *"B"* and *"C"* may be designated *quasi-private goods,* since market allocation influence prevails, and good *"D"* as a *quasi-public good* since governmental allocation influence would tend to be substantial. A pure public good such as national defense is both "jointly consumed" and "equally consumed" by the members of the national society. The relevant or interacting group is very large, exclusion is impossible, and voluntary payments to finance its production will not be forthcoming. The free rider dilemma is acutely present. The probability that national defense can be allocated more efficiently by the public sector rather than by the private sector is considerable. Moreover, since the short-run marginal cost equals zero for one additional citizen "protected," the *organization of supply* through government, for still another reason, will likely be more efficient than through the market.[8] Indeed, the strongest argument for the public sector to serve as the primary allocating institution using comprehensive allocational techniques is when an economic good is characterized by conditions of zero marginal cost, joint and equal consumption, and large group interaction with the impossibility of exclusion.

Thus, it may be said that a certain logical thread of relationship tends to exist between the nature of an economic good, the allocational techniques employed to provide the good, and the institutional sector of allocation. Yet, this general thread of logical relationship, it once again must be advised, *does not* provide a conclusive a priori argument for governmental allocation whenever significant traits of "publicness" such as zero marginal cost, joint and equal consumption, and large group interaction are present. However, it *does* suggest that government may often be called upon to intervene in a significant manner under such circumstances in order to promote the allocational goals of the society.

Table 3–2 summarizes the major conceptual points of Chapters 2 and 3 as they relate to the nature of economic goods, allocational techniques, and allocating sectors. Although *economic* considerations play

---

[8] This does not suggest, of course, the government *financing or organization of supply* excludes all private sector participation in the actual production of national defense as an economic good.

TABLE 3–2
Economic Goods, Allocational Techniques, and Allocating Sectors: A Summary

Economic Sector	Economic Goods		Allocational		Mathematical Equations
	Type	Characteristics*	Techniques	Criteria	
Public Sector	Pure Public Goods	1. Joint and equal consumption 2. Large-group interaction 3. Exclusion impossible 4. Zero short-run marginal cost 5. Decreasing production costs at optimal social allocation point ($MC = AR$) 6. High risk due to very imperfect market knowledge 7. Unique resource conditions	Tendency toward "direct" and "complete" Public Sector allocational techniques	*Economic* criteria prevail in determining allocating sector and allocational technique(s)	$Z = Za$ $Z = Zb$
Tendency toward Public Sector allocational involvement	Quasi-Public (Impure-Public) Goods	*Mixed* "public" and "private" characteristics	*Mixed* allocational techniques inclusive of both Public Sector and Private Sector traits	*Noneconomic* criteria assume greater importance in determining allocating sector(s) and allocational technique(s)	
Tendency toward Private Sector allocational involvement	Quasi-Private (Impure-Private) Goods				
Private Sector	Pure Private Goods	1. Nonjoint private consumption 2. Two-person exchange 3. Exclusion possible 4. Short-run marginal cost greater than zero 5. Constant or increasing production costs at optimal social allocation point ($MC = AR$) 6. Moderate or little risk due to adequate market knowledge 7. No unique resource conditions	Tendency toward Private Sector allocational techniques with no appreciable Public Sector influence	*Economic* criteria prevail in determining allocating sector and allocational technique(s)	$W = Wa + Wb$

* Not all of these characteristics need be simultaneously present to affect a good's classification. Moreover, characteristics (1) through (5) are the most basic characteristics.

a major role in the allocation of *quasi-goods* (*quasi-public* and *quasi-private goods*), the role is not as strong as it is in the polar positions of pure private and pure public goods. The relative diminishment of the economic role is supplemented, in turn, by the increased importance of *noneconomic* considerations in the allocation of these goods. Among the most prominent of these noneconomic considerations in the United States is the strong cultural preference for *individual freedom* of action which sometimes will "tip the balance" toward the market in the determination of the primary "allocating sector" and, if governmental allocational influence is called for, the selection of less direct and less comprehensive "allocational techniques" such as those shown toward the bottom of Table 3–1 above.

CONSUMPTION OF THE VARIOUS TYPES OF ECONOMIC GOODS IN THE AMERICAN ECONOMY

Though precise measurement of the consumption of pure public, pure private, quasi-public, and quasi-private goods in the American economy is impossible from existing data, useful approximations of the consumption of each type of economic good can still be provided. Table 3–3 presents estimates of such consumption for the years 1952 and 1963.[9] In order to be consistent with the available data, *pure public* goods are classified as those goods provided by government to which the "exclusion principle" cannot be applied and *quasi-public* goods are considered as government expenditures for other than pure public goods. Furthermore, *quasi-private* goods are defined as those goods provided by the market which are judged to possess significant externalities or indivisibilities while the remaining category, *pure private* goods, consists of those consumption items acquired from the private sector which do not have important external effects or indivisibilities.

In 1963, some 75 percent of the economic goods consumed were produced by the private sector. Most of these market goods were pure private goods (by the above definition for this study), though quasi-private goods such as utilities, communications, transportation, and medical care constituted more than one fifth of the private sector total. Total public sector output constituted nearly 25 percent of total economic goods. More than one half of the public sector total was in the

---

[9] The present discussion is based upon an unpublished manuscript by Harold M. Stults entitled "Economic Wants: A Quantitative Classification." Department of Commerce data are used in this study. In particular, "government expenditures by type of function" and "personal consumption expenditures by type of product" are employed. Government transfer payments are excluded from the governmental expenditure data in order to emphasize exhaustive expenditures. Since consumption is the direct purpose of the study, business acquisition of capital goods is also excluded.

TABLE 3–3
Economic Goods by Type of Good, in Both Dollar and Percentage Terms,
for 1952 and 1963

Type of Good	Dollar Terms (Billions)		Percentage Terms		
	1952	1963	1952	1963	
Pure Private	186.5	306.0	62.0	61.3	Total Private = 75.3 Sector
Quasi Private..........	33.2	69.8	11.0	14.0	
Pure Public	53.1	69.6	17.7	13.9	Total Public = 24.7 Sector
Quasi Public...........	28.0	53.8	9.3	10.8	

Source: An unpublished manuscript by Harold M. Stults entitled "Economic Wants: A Quantitative Classification."

form of pure public goods (as defined for this study) inclusive of such items as national defense, international affairs and finance, and general government.

The allocation of economic goods by the private sector constituted a higher percentage of total economic goods in 1963 than in 1952. This difference, however, may be explained by the abnormal impact of the Korean War on the pure public goods category of the public sector in 1952. The most pronounced trend indicated by the data is the relative expansion in the importance of quasi or impure goods, both quasi-private and quasi-public, during the period. This trend may be significant in the sense that increasing attention is being directed today in the United States toward "joint" governmental and private sector efforts to achieve social goals.

THE ENVIRONMENTAL CRISIS—A PROBLEM OF RESOURCE SCARCITY AND NEGATIVE EXTERNALITIES

Ecology is defined as "a branch of science concerned with the interrelationship of organisms and their environments."[10] When the decade of the 1960s began, this term meant little to the average American. Ten years later it had become a prominent topic of conversation in the United States and other industrial nations. It is inevitable that the economic activity of man will affect the environment in which he lives by affecting the balance of nature. Moreover, this natural balance must be viewed as *finite* or *limited* in the extent to which it may be altered without adversely affecting mankind and his environment. Alternately, it may be said that the basic economic problem of *scarcity* applies also

---

[10] *Webster's New Collegiate Dictionary* (Springfield, Mass.: G. & C. Merriam Co., 1973), p. 360.

to man's environment. That is, man's environment is not an "unlimited resource."[11]

The American economy uses some 1.5 billion tons of fuel annually.[12] In addition, it uses another 1 billion tons of minerals, food, and forest products each year. The ultimate result of such resource usage is *waste* which, whether it be in the form of a gaseous oxide or an empty beer bottle, must be classified as a *negative externality.* Moreover, the American economy in recent times has been experiencing an economic growth rate of approximately 4.5 percent per year in real GNP terms. Quite clearly, the greater the output of economic goods, the greater will be the potential volume of waste materials that the environment must absorb. Thus, if the annual growth rate of 4.5 percent is projected 50 years into the future, GNP will be 10 times greater in the year 2020 than it is in 1970. Frighteningly, the amount of waste may also reflect a 10-fold increase unless changes occur in the composition of output or in technology. The latter, for example, could provide better techniques for "recycling" materials so as to reduce the volume of pollutants remaining in the environment. Though resource scarcity has not prevented American economic growth during the past century, nor is it likely to do so in the foreseeable future, a new type of scarcity—*nature's limited capacity to absorb wastes*—is emerging as a distinct reality. Hence, the environmental crisis involves a *tradeoff* between the traditional emphasis on conventional economic growth and the quality of life for mankind within his environment.

The environmental problem of waste, as discussed above, may also be termed the *pollution* crisis. Pollution may take a variety of forms. Wastes released into the atmosphere, for example, constitute *air* pollution. Moreover, *water* is often used as a receptacle for waste or the *land* itself may be the recipient. Junk cars or a slag pile at a copper mine serve as examples of land pollution. Furthermore, excessive *noise* may pollute the environment as residents living near large jet airports have sadly learned. Finally, *congestion* such as a freeway traffic jam may be considered a form of pollution.

In each of these cases of pollution, there is an element of "common consumption." Air, water, land, and noise pollution, or a traffic jam, involve circumstances in which one agent is attempting to share an economic good which is not available on an earmarked basis to each user.[13] Thus, beyond some threshold or capacity level, the presence of other users affects adversely the consumption quality of a given user.

---

[11] In this section of the chapter, the terms "resource" and "good" will be used interchangeably in discussing the environmental crisis.

[12] See the discussion in *Toward a Social Report*, U.S. Department of Health, Education, and Welfare (Washington, D.C.: U.S. Government Printing Office, 1969), chap. 3.

[13] See the discussion in Jerome Rothenberg, "The Economics of Congestion and Pollution: An Integrated View," *American Economic Review*, May 1970, pp. 114–16.

Once again, evidence of the economic problem of scarcity comes to the fore. The environment and space (in the case of the traffic jam) are not unlimited.

Let us stop for a moment to construct an "interim summary" of the fundamental issues involved in the current environmental crisis as these issues have been discussed to this point. *First*, the environment is a "scarce" resource. Its limited capacity to absorb waste and to avoid congestion gives proof of this fact. As an example, air was formerly classified by most economists as a "free" good. That is, it was considered to be unlimited in quantity. In effect, this led to an underpricing of its value and to its subsequent overuse. The result has been air pollution. The social cost of air, in Pigovian terms as developed in Chapter 2, has exceeded the private cost of air thus creating an external diseconomy (negative externality). *Secondly,* environmental resources tend to be "consumed jointly." This "public good" ("public bad") characteristic of environmental resources is a crucial element in the environmental crisis facing the world today. An elaboration of this important point will now be undertaken.

Essentially, the crowding or using up of environmental resources introduces *negative externalities* among their users. The "nonmarket" nature of these externalities tends to make them "nonrejectable" by their recipients. That is, they rest largely outside the price mechanism (see Chapter 2). These *negative externalities,* which also are known as *public bads,* may be initiated by either a producer or consumer in the private sector or, in an analogous sense, by a unit of government in the public sector. Who can deny, for example, that an air force jet plane is equally capable with a commercial jet of producing noise pollution for a community?

Importantly, the joint consumption of public bads—frequently by a large number of individuals—produces a "free rider" problem in reverse. That is, just as joint consumption of a "public good" by a large number of individuals gives each individual the incentive to avoid voluntary payment for the good, so also does the joint consumption of a "public bad" by a large number of individuals provide each individual with an incentive *not* to voluntarily withdraw from the creation of the bad. For example, one person will likely not voluntarily install a smog control device on his automobile unless he knows that all other car owners will do the same. He cannot be expected to voluntarily do so himself because of the small effect his action will have on total air pollution. Yet, if the public sector requires all automobiles to have such a device, then "compulsion" will force him to purchase the device along with the other consumers. Hence, the public bad will be reduced or eliminated by a "joint" effort enforced by compulsion. The analogy with the "compulsory nature of a tax" is apparent.

Thus, it has been observed that the environmental crisis is based upon the misallocation of scarce resources. This misallocation results in negative externalities of the joint consumption variety. Due to their nonmarket characteristics, these externalities cannot easily be rejected. Relatedly, individuals do not have the incentive to voluntarily pay for an internalization of the externality.

The question may now be asked: How should society meet the environmental crisis? It is beyond the scope of this book to provide a comprehensive answer to this question. Nonetheless, certain general reference points based on the principles of public sector economics can be stipulated as guidelines for the adoption of a corrective program. These are listed below:

1. No a priori case can be made to the effect that *all* negative externalities of an environmental variety should be removed. The cost of internalizing (removing) a negative externality, for example, may be greater than the welfare gained in its elimination. Moreover, both the allocational and distributional effects of "internalization" should be considered.

2. Since the major environmental resource problems—such as clean air—contain substantial traits of "publicness," it is likely that the public sector must play a major role in many internalization efforts. This is supported by the fact that public bads generally are jointly consumed by a large number of persons and are nonrejectable by the individual consumer. The division of governmental authority over policies may be guided by the "national," "quasi-national," or "nonnational" nature, in a geographical sense, of the public bad in question. Hence, the federal government would tend to play the dominant role in the internalization of a negative externality in the first instance and a minimal role for nonnational public bads. In the case of a quasi-national public bad, it is likely that both the federal government and state-local governments would play an important role in corrective policy.

3. The public sector may use a variety of techniques to deal with negative externalities. These may range between direct and comprehensive policies to those which are indirect and undertaken largely in the private sector under loose governmental guidelines. Thus, just as a continuum of techniques is available for allocating public and quasi-public goods through governmental influence, as noted earlier in the chapter, there exists also a continuum of alternative techniques for the removal of public bads whether they be of the national, quasi-national, or non-national variety.

4. Some of the major techniques which are available for the internalization of negative externalities (public bads) are the following: (*a*) the direct prohibition of certain types of environmental pollution; (*b*) the establishment of a system of governmental coordinated prices or

charges on wastes dumped into the environment; (c) the allowance of special tax provisions to firms to encourage the installation of pollution control devices or, on the expenditure side of the budget, the payment of direct subsidies to firms for such installation; (d) the sponsorship by government of research for the development of pollution reduction devices such as the development of a low-pollution automobile engine; (e) further efforts to redefine "common resource ownership" into "private property rights," to the extent that it is feasible; and (f) the public sector taking on itself the primary expense and direct responsibility to "clean up" major effluent situations.

5. One of the techniques mentioned under (4) above appears to "stand out" above the rest in terms of its economic efficiency characteristics. Namely, the establishment of a governmentally coordinated system of user prices or charges on the emission of wastes into the environment has the advantage of relying extensively upon the *price system* to achieve its pollution control results. In so doing, it recognizes the environment as a "scarce resource" which should carry a price when it is "used up" in the productive process. If effluents thus were included in the cost considerations of profit-motivated firms—just as the costs of labor and other inputs are included—the firms producing the wastes would be motivated to reduce these costs by acquiring the most efficient emission controls possible. In fact, there would likely be a greater incentive to develop new, more efficient, pollution control devices than under a tax incentive or direct prohibition approach where the acquisition of "presently available" devices would suffice. Moreover, if a tax provision such as a tax credit were less than a 100 percent credit against tax liability, the firm would still bear some of the costs of installing the pollution control equipment and thus might decide not to install it.

Despite these advantages cited in behalf of the "effluent price" technique, it is not suggested here that other control techniques are without merit. Indeed, it would appear that a problem as complex as environmental pollution must be attacked on a multitechnique basis. Thus, an eclectic (many-sided) approach seems necessary if successful results are to be attained. Nevertheless, it should generally be noted that the greater the extent to which the price system is employed in the effort to control environmental pollution, the more consistent the overall pollution control policy will be with the market orientation nature of American society.

6. Finally, it should be observed that since the environment is a limited resource, economic in nature, any improvement of the environmental crisis will necessarily involve the economic concept of "opportunity cost." This may take the "general" form of the *tradeoff* between a reduced emphasis on economic growth as a goal and an increased emphasis on the quality of the environment. Stated alternately, Ameri-

can society may need to deemphasize the attainment of "maximum" aggregate output as a primary economic goal and emphasize, instead, the "composition" of aggregate output. Or, in terms of a "specific" example, an opportunity cost may be incurred (within a full-employment economy) when resources are withdrawn from alternative consumptive uses in order to produce such environment-oriented goods as pollution control devices. Relatedly, a need appears to exist for the improvement of social accounting techniques so as to avoid an overemphasis on monetary magnitudes and, at the same time, to increase emphasis on the welfare, either positive or negative, provided by nonmarket consumption. Unquestionably, solving the environmental crisis will increase the overall welfare of all members of the society whether it shows up in traditional national income and product figures or not.

4

Welfare Economics and Public Sector Decision Making

Chapter 1 considered the issue of optimal resource allocation between the private and public sectors of a mixed economy. This earlier discussion, however, dealt with the problem in a general fashion. The present chapter, on the other hand, will develop the concept of optimal intersector resource allocation in a more comprehensive and sophisticated manner now that (a) an "allocative" argument has been established for the existence of a public sector [Chapter 2], (b) the nature of public goods has been analyzed [Chapters 2 and 3], and (c) the alternative techniques of allocation have been considered [Chapter 3]. In an overall sense, the chapter will be concerned with both the allocation and distribution branches of public sector economics. Particular emphasis, however, will be placed on the former. Distribution, in turn, will be stressed only when the interrelationship between allocation and distribution becomes relevant.

As discussed in Chapter 1, an economic system must solve the following allocative issues: Which economic goods shall be produced? Which economic sector, public or private, shall provide the economic goods? Which levels and units of government within the public sector, and which firms within the private sector, shall provide the goods? Relatedly, what is the "optimal" division of economic output between the public and private sectors? Moreover, a highly significant consideration arises concerning the ability of the economic decision-making process to "detect" and to "implement" the resource allocation preferences of the society regarding these questions. Hence, the analysis to follow here and in Chapter 5 will fall into two major categories. This chapter will consider the conditions required for optimal intersector resource allocation with particular emphasis on the specific economic problems which arise in the allocation of economic goods with substantial traits of "publicness." In other words, an attempt is made to develop a "beginning" theory of the demand and supply of public goods.[1] Much of this analysis rests in the analytical area of *welfare economics*.[2] Then, in Chapter 5, a discussion will be provided concerning the emerging area of knowledge known as *welfare politics* or *public choice* theory. Here the direct concern is with the revelation of societal preferences for public-type economic goods within a democratic political framework.

Three approaches will be presented relevant to the first of these issues. They are: (1) the marginal utility approach (2) the voluntary-exchange approach and (3) the Samuelson "pure public goods" model. The latter two of these three approaches are the more significant for a sophisticated understanding of the conditions required for optimal intersector resource allocation. Moreover, the voluntary-exchange approach, in particular, helps to conceptually "open the door" to the public choice discussion of the following chapter.

The marginal utility and voluntary-exchange approaches derive from two orthodox public finance concepts of equity in the distribution of tax burdens, namely, the *ability-to-pay* and *benefit* theories, respectively.[3] These two distributional theories have been "converted" into optimal allocation theories. The primary architect of this refinement for the ability-to-pay approach, which may te termed the *marginal utility theory of public goods allocation,* was the British economist, A. C. Pigou. The major contributors to the conversion of the *voluntary-exchange theory of public goods allocation* from the benefits-received principle of distribution were Knut Wicksell, Erik Lindahl, Howard Bowen, plus a number of Italian politico-economists.

---

[1] For an excellent discussion, in detail, of the economic issues involved in the provision and consumption of public goods, see James M. Buchanan, *The Demand and Supply of Public Goods* (Chicago: Rand McNally & Co., 1968).

[2] *Welfare economics* considers the performance of the economy in terms of its ability to achieve certain "desirable" goals. It is "normative" in nature. It says what ought to be. *Positive economics,* on the other hand, relates to the performance of the economy in a "functional" and "predictive" sense without direct interest in the desirability of economic results in terms of value-judgment determined goals. It attempts to observe "what is."

[3] The full depth of the ability-to-pay and benefit principles of distribution, which historically may be traced back to Adam Smith, will be presented in Chapter 7.

THE MARGINAL UTILITY THEORY OF PUBLIC GOODS ALLOCATION

Traditional marginal utility analysis may be used to provide further insight to the concept of optimal public goods allocation and the attainment of maximal welfare for the society.[4] The *marginal utility theory of public goods allocation* thus relates the "marginal utility" derived by individuals in a society from the consumption of public goods to the "marginal disutility" incurred by these individuals in the payment of taxes to the public sector for the financing of the goods. The disutility or "negative" utility of tax payments is determined by the "positive" utility sacrificed in the form of private goods consumption in order to pay the taxes. Optimal intersector resource allocation, and thus the optimal supply of both "public" and "private" goods, occurs at the point where the *marginal utility of public goods* (MU_{pg}) is *equal* to the *marginal disutility of tax payments* (MD_t). Moreover, intersector optimality in resource allocation under this approach requires that the marginal utilities of the various economic goods allocated by each sector be *equal* within that sector. In addition, optimality requires, in a strict sense, the *full employment* of productive resources.[5]

In Figure 4–1, which may be used to demonstrate this theory, the *marginal utility of public goods* and the *marginal disutility of tax payments* are measured on the "vertical" axis while the *government budget,* inclusive of both spending and taxes, is measured on the "horizontal" axis. Both the MU_{pg} and the MD_t curves reflect the *law of diminishing marginal utility.* That is, as the consumption of public goods increases along the horizontal axis, the marginal satisfaction derived by society from the additional consumption of public goods diminishes. Thus, the MU_{pg} curve possesses a downward slope (see the upper half of the diagram). Relatedly, the MD_t curve also slopes downward (see the lower half of the diagram) because the marginal disutility of tax payments becomes greater as public goods consumption increases. This occurs because, with limited societal resources, the greater production of public goods means that the quantities of private goods foregone at the margin through tax payments represent relatively higher marginal utility values since fewer private goods are being produced.

Point *E* represents the optimal supply of public goods since at output *OE* of public goods, the marginal utility of public goods (vertical dis-

---

[4] See A. C. Pigou, *A Study in Public Finance* (London: Macmillan & Co., 1928), especially Part 1, chap. 7.

[5] For example, the disutility of a tax dollar, as established by the "opportunity costs" of the private goods foregone, would not exist when there are unemployed resources which could be used to supply incremental public goods without a reduction in the level of private goods production.

FIGURE 4–1

Public Goods Allocation: Optimal and Suboptimal Points (marginal utility approach)

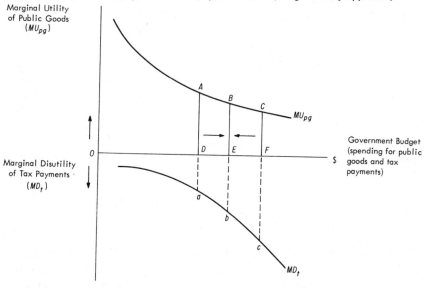

At point D	$MU_{pg} > MD_t$	Underallocation of public goods and overallocation of private goods
At point F	$MU_{pg} < MD_t$	Overallocation of public goods and underallocation of private goods
At point E	$MU_{pg} = MD_t$	Optimal intersector allocation of public and private goods

tance BE) is *equal* to the marginal disutility of tax payments (vertical distance Eb). At any point to the left of point E, however, there is an "underallocation" of resources to the public sector. At point D, for example, the marginal utility of public goods exceeds the marginal disutility of tax payments by the excess of vertical distance AD over Da. Thus, an expansion of public sector allocation toward point E is desirable. On the other hand, if public goods allocation is at a point to the right of point E, there is an "overallocation" of resources to the public sector. At point F, for example, the marginal utility of public goods (vertical distance CF) is less than the marginal disutility of tax payments (vertical distance Fc). Thus, greater societal welfare can be attained by a movement back toward point E with a resulting decrease in the consumption of public goods and an increase in the consumption of private goods.

Two problems related to the marginal utility approach should be noted. *First,* no effective means exists whereby utility and disutility can be quantified. Hence, the point of optimal intersector allocation cannot be precisely detected in a cardinal (absolute) measurement sense. *Second,* the equating of the marginal utility of public goods to the marginal disutility of tax payments for "society as a whole," rather than on an "individual member" basis, means that some individuals may derive either "more" or "less" marginal utility than the marginal disutility which they incur in the payment of taxes. Thus, a critical distributional question of equity arises: How should the marginal utilities and disutilities be divided among the people of the society? The distribution of income, wealth, and political voting representation bears importantly upon this question and will be developed further in this chapter and in Chapter 5.

THE VOLUNTARY-EXCHANGE THEORY OF PUBLIC GOODS ALLOCATION

The allocation of public goods may also be viewed from the perspective of the *voluntary-exchange approach.*[6] This approach suggests that resources should be allocated to the public sector in a manner analogous to their allocation in the market with its price system. In other words, an individual should buy public goods through taxes just as he elects to purchase private goods through market prices—with the standard consumer equilibrium principle of "satisfaction-maximization" applying. He becomes a *taxpayer-buyer* who "pays taxes" for public goods in accordance with the "benefits received" from them, that is, he would equate the marginal ratios of tax prices to public good benefits *within* the public sector. Similarly, he would equate the cost-benefit ratios, on an intersector basis, between public goods and private goods. In this manner, the logical derivation of a point of optimal intersector allocation would also be attained.

Figure 4–2 demonstrates the voluntary-exchange approach to optimal intersector resource allocation. The quantities demanded and supplied of public good Z are measured on the horizontal axis while its demand prices and supply costs are measured on the vertical axis. Assumptions, for the purpose of simplicity, are: (1) constant production or supply costs for the public good, as indicated by the horizontal shape of the supply curve *FS,* (2) a society consisting of only three consumers or taxpayers—X, Y, and Z, and (3) only one type of public good—here

---

[6] For presentations of the "voluntary-exchange" approach, see Erik Lindahl, *Die Gerechtigkeit der Besteuerung* (Sweden: Lund, 1919). Relevant portions of this are printed in English in Richard A. Musgrave and Alan T. Peacock (eds.), *Classics in the Theory of Public Finance* (London: Macmillan & Co., 1958). Also, see Howard R. Bowen, *Toward Social Economy* (New York: Rinehart, 1948).

FIGURE 4–2

Public Goods Allocation: Optimal and Suboptimal Points (voluntary-exchange approach)

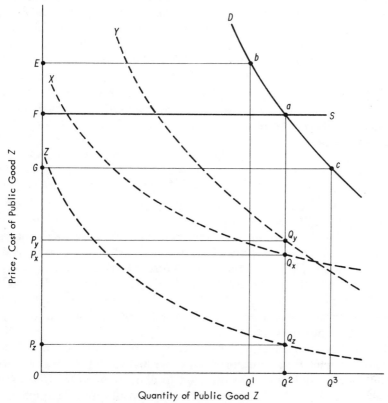

At point b, an underallocation of Public Good Z by the amount $Q^1 - Q^2$
At point c, an overallocation of Public Good Z by the amount $Q^2 - Q^3$
At point a, optimal allocation of Public Good Z with amount Q^2

Source: Adapted from Howard R. Bowen, *Toward Social Economy* (New York: Rinehart, 1948), Figure 2, p. 177.

a "pure public good" designated as public good Z—is demanded by the three consumer-taxpayers.

Curve X represents the demand by Consumer X for Public Good Z. Curve Y indicates the demand by Consumer Y for the good, and curve Z shows the demand for the good by Consumer Z. Each of these individual demand curves reflect the prices that X, Y, and Z would be willing to pay for various quantities of Public Good Z. Curve D represents the *total demand* for the good by these three consumer-taxpayers (taxpayer-buyers). Importantly, the "summation" of the individual demand curves to obtain the total societal demand curve for Public Good

Z is *vertical* rather than horizontal, as it would be for a private good.[7] For example, the *total quantity* demanded, Q^2, as indicated at point *a* on the *total demand curve*, is the "same amount" as demanded by each consumer-taxpayer on his *individual demand curve*. That is, Q^2 is the same quantity as Q_x, Q_y, and Q_z. This means that the amount consumed by *each* individual is exactly the same as the total amount consumed. There is both "joint" and "equal" consumption of the good.

The *optimal* equilibrium output for Public Good Z is at point *a* with quantity Q^2. This is determined by the intersection of the total demand curve D and the supply curve FS. At any quantity less than Q^2, for example—quantity Q^1 at point b on the total demand curve, the demand price per unit exceeds the supply cost per unit (here by the amount EF). This represents suboptimal allocation in the sense of an undersupply of the public good. Thus, output should be expanded toward the optimal quantity Q^2. On the other hand, at any quantity greater than Q^2, for example—quantity Q^3 at point c on the total demand curve, the supply cost per unit exceeds the demand price per unit (here by the amount FG). This represents suboptimal allocation in the sense of an oversupply of the public good. Thus, output should be contracted back toward the optimal quantity Q^2. At optimal output Q^2, consumer X will pay price per unit OP_x, Consumer Y will pay OP_y, and Consumer Z will pay OP_z. The combined payment, OF, of the three taxpayer-consumers is equal to the cost per unit, also OF, as measured along the vertical axis.

The voluntary-exchange approach is useful in many ways. These include the fact that it provides an exposure to the nature of public goods and the difficulty encountered in allocating them in a market manner due to the "collective" or "joint" consumption characteristic. In particular, when "joint" consumption is also "equal" consumption, as it would be in the case of a "pure public good," the competitive market benchmark must fail. This is so because a competitive firm must charge the *same price* for the *same quantity* to *each individual consumer*. That is, it cannot reflect the *differential marginal evaluations* placed on Public Good Z by the three consumer-taxpayers in the form of charging the differential prices P_x, P_y, and P_z.

Yet, in addition to exposing such a dilemma, the voluntary-exchange approach also provides a vehicle for considering the conceptual issues involved in rationalizing public sector decision-making.[8] It is, indeed, a fact that both private and public choice involve the same group of consumer decision makers whose welfare is provided by economic

---

[7] This important characteristic of a public good was also observed in Chapter 2.

[8] See James M. Buchanan, *Demand and Supply of Public Goods*, and Donald R. Escarraz, *The Price Theory of Value in Public Finance* (Gainesville, Fla.: University of Florida Press, 1966).

goods from both the private and public sectors of the economy. Stated alternately, an analysis of the supply and demand of both private and public goods starts at the same point. The "taxpayer-buyer" is a "tax-payer-voter" who must "reveal his preferences" for public and quasi-public goods through the political process. Yet, he is also the same consumer who must "reveal his preferences" for private and quasi-private goods through the market process. Hence, the consideration of *fiscal institutions* through which the preferences for public and quasi-public goods may be revealed becomes as relevant as the *price system* is for the allocation of private and quasi-private goods. Welfare politics or public choice theory, the subject of the next chapter, is a natural adjunct to a theory of public goods and the voluntary-exchange approach to public goods allocation helps "open the door" to this discussion.

THE SAMUELSON MODEL OF PUBLIC GOODS ALLOCATION

Samuelson provides a sophisticated and widely accepted approach to efficiency in the allocation of public goods.[9] The Samuelson model will demonstrate the fundamental differences that exist between the allocation of public and private goods when traditional microeconomic principles are applied. Then, it will be recognized, as was suggested both in the analysis of Chapter 2 as well as in the voluntary-exchange discussion of the present chapter, that the conditions required for efficient public goods allocation are inapplicable through market means when the economic good is "jointly" and "equally" consumed. Moreover, this situation is accentuated if consumption entails a large group of consumers. In addition, discussion of the model will help to emphasize the importance of the distributional value judgment which is prerequisite to the determination of optimal intersector resource allocation.

The Samuelson model constitutes a polar case in its treatment of the allocation of a public good. It may be viewed as the extreme opposite of the private goods situation represented by the "Walrasian" general equilibrium case of perfect competition.[10] The polar case for public goods may be approached from the standpoint of either an "authoritarian" or a "democratic" political environment. The former inter-

---

[9] See Paul A. Samuelson, "The Pure Theory of Public Expenditure," *Review of Economics and Statistics,* November 1954, pp. 387–89; "Diagrammatic Exposition of a Theory of Public Expenditure," *Review of Economics and Statistics,* November 1955, pp. 350–56, and "Aspects of Public Expenditure Theories," *Review of Economics and Statistics,* November 1958, pp. 332–38.

[10] "Walrasian" refers to the theoretical contributions of the French economist, Leon Walras.

pretation may be termed the "group mind" approach. It is virtually devoid of economic implications and requires political value judgments about an authoritarian role for government that cannot be challenged in economic terms. The latter approach, on the other hand, is consistent with "individualism" which is, of course, the focal point of democratic political societies such as those existing in Western Europe and North America.

The "individualistic" approach, which is adopted in the Samuelson model, may be divided further into (1) the rejection of interpersonal comparisons of utility, or (2) the acceptance of such comparisons.[11] If interpersonal comparisons cannot be made, then the social welfare of the community is merely a heterogenous collection of individual welfares. This analysis leads to the condition of *Pareto optimality* whereby social welfare is said to increase "only" if one person can gain utility or satisfaction through an allocative readjustment without another person losing welfare. This is a restrictive approach in the sense that no judgment can be made concerning social welfare when one person loses as another gains. Pareto optimum conditions, of course, basically reflect the fundamental problem of "scarcity" in economics since one individual would not lose welfare while another gains if all economic goods were in infinite supply. The second individualistic group noted above accepts interpersonal utility comparisons in the sense that ethical or value judgments may be used concerning the aggregation of individual welfares to acquire societal welfare. The Samuelson model essentially follows the individualistic approach in this latter context, that is, the acceptance of interpersonal utility comparisons based on distributional value judgments. These ethical judgments are then applied to an economic efficiency norm—the same *Pareto-optimum norm* mentioned above—in the form of a *social welfare function*. An explicit description of the Samuelson model and related concepts follows:

Figure 4–3 (a,b,c,d) demonstrates the Samuelson model as such. In each graph, the quantity of the "collectively consumed" *Pure Public Good Z* is measured on the horizontal axis and the quantity of the "privately consumed" *Pure Private Good W* on the vertical axis. In Figure 4–5a, the relative preference pattern of Consumer A for Public Good Z and Private Good W is shown along indifference curves I_a^1, I_a^2, I_a^3. In Figure 4–5b, the relative preference pattern of Consumer B for Public Good Z and Private Good W is indicated by indifference curves I_b^1, I_b^2, and I_b^3. Figure 4–3c demonstrates the society's production possibility (transformation) curve P-P'. This curve reflects the various combinations of Public Good Z and Private Good W that can be

---

[11] *Interpersonal comparisons of utility* would require cardinal (absolute) measurement of the pleasure and displeasure (utility and disutility) derived from consumption by the various members of a society.

FIGURE 4-3

Optimal Allocation of a Pure Public Good: Samuelson Approach

a. Consumer A's Indifference Schedule between Private Good W and Public Good Z

b. Consumer B's Indifference Schedule between Private Good W and Public Good Z

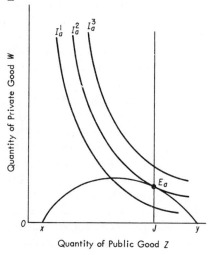

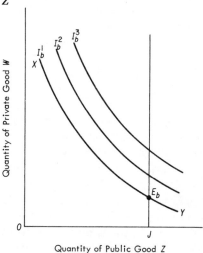

c. Production-Possibility (Transformation) Schedule of the Society for Private Good W and Public Good Z

d. Optimal Intersector Allocation between Private Good W and Public Good Z as Determined by the Tangency of Social Welfare Function S^2 and the utility frontier line fg at Point H

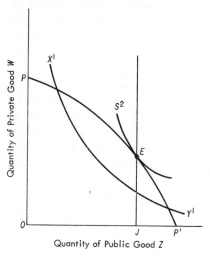

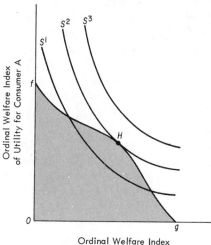

fg = Utility Frontier or Horizon of Pareto-Optimal Points
S^1, S^2, S^3 = Alternative Social Welfare Functions
Source: Adapted from Paul A. Samuelson, "Diagrammatic Exposition of a Theory of Public Expenditure," *Review of Economics and Statistics* (November, 1955), Charts 1, 2, 3, and 4, pp. 351-2.

produced with the limited productive resources available to the society.[12]

It is important to note in Figures 4–3a, 4–3b, and 4–3c that the quantity of Public Good Z is the same, OJ, on each graph. As observed earlier, a pure public good characterized by joint and equal consumption must possess the same quantity scale value on each graph since an increase in the total quantity of the public good (like a move to the right of J on Figure 4–3c) would increase the quantity available to both Consumers A and B by an amount *equal* to the total increase in quantity.

The discussion of the Samuelson model to this point has indicated (1) the individual preferences by the two consumers in the society for the public and private good (Figures 4–3a and 4–3b) and (2) the constraint imposed by scarce resources as shown by the societal production-possibility curve (Figure 4–3c). What, then, is the optimal allocation point between Public Good Z and Private Good W in the society? In other words, what is the allocation division which will maximize welfare according to the preferences of A and B—the two individuals in the society? Or, in terms of collective consumption as the focal point, what is the optimal social allocation of the pure public good?

Assuming the *Pareto-optimum* social welfare norm whereby aggregate societal welfare is increased if one individual moves to a higher indifference curve *without* another individual's satisfaction level being moved to a lower indifference curve, points of allocation efficiency can be established in Figures 4–3a, 4–3b, and 4–3c.[13] In order to apply this norm, assume that one consumer is at a *specified* level of indifference so that his satisfaction level will not be changed. The problem, then, of optimal social allocation becomes one of moving the second consumer of this two-consumer society to his highest possible indifference curve (satisfaction or welfare level).

Thus, in Figure 4–3b, set Consumer B on the *specified* indifference curve I_b^1, which will now be designated XY. Keeping in mind the "output constraint" of the production-possibility line $P\text{-}P'$ in Figure 4–3c, what is the highest level of satisfaction (the highest indifference curve) that consumer A can attain? The answer is shown by tangency point E_a in Figure 4–3a. The corresponding equilibrium points are at E_b in Figure 4–3b and E in Figure 4–3c.

This equilibrium is derived by placing indifference curve XY from Figure 4–3b on Figure 4–3c and designating it $X^1 Y^1$. Then, subtract

---

[12] See Chapter 1 for an additional discussion of the societal production-possibility curve.

[13] As indicated above, the Pareto-optimum criterion of welfare holds that any change which makes some people better off (in their own estimation), while making no one else worse off, is an *improvement*.

$X^1 Y^1$ "vertically" from production-possibility line P-P', the residual or difference being the quantities of the public good and the private good which are available to Consumer A. This amount may be placed on Figure 4–3a and designated xy. Consumer A thus reaches his highest attainable satisfaction level at tangency point E_a where xy touches the highest attainable indifference curve $I_a{}^2$. Thus, xy provides the constraint of resource scarcity in the society, based on the "given" consumption level of Consumer B, and indifference curve $I_a{}^2$ reflects the relative preferences of Consumer A between the public and private goods. This Pareto-optimum point means that there is no movement away from point E_a, in terms of a reallocation of resources, that would not make one of the consumers worse off than before in terms of welfare.

An "infinite number" of such Pareto-optimum points may be said to exist. That is, for every "given" indifference curve along which Consumer B might consume, a different optimal tangency point of welfare would occur for Consumer A. In other words, E_a in Figure 4–3a would *not* be the optimal allocation point if Consumer B were consuming along any indifference curve other than $I_b{}^1$ (XY) in Figure 4–3b. These infinite Pareto-optimum points, which are represented along line fg in Figure 4–3d, cannot be compared "without" a normative *social welfare function*. Such a social welfare function would be arrived at through ethical or value judgments, which render interpersonal comparisons of utility, and thus establish a state of "effective" distribution.

In Figure 4–3d, these "welfare possibilities" for Consumers A and B, who comprise the total consumption of the society for the public and private goods, are presented in "ordinal measurement" terms. Since the "utility frontier" of Pareto-optimum welfare points is indicated by line fg, any point within (to the southwest) of this line, as designated by the shaded area, represents a "less than" Pareto-optimum position. The Pareto-optimum line slopes to the southeast to reflect the conflicting consumption interests between Consumers A and B in the face of resource constraint. This inverse relationship means, of course, that reallocation would improve one consumer's position (putting him on a "higher" indifference curve) while making the other consumer's position worse (putting him on a "lower" indifference curve). Since society cannot maximize its welfare from any of the "non-Pareto-optimum" points within the utility frontier, it is obvious that any movement from within the frontier to the frontier line fg will be a "welfare improvement" for the society because such a movement will allow one person to improve his welfare position without reducing the welfare of anyone else by putting the latter on a "lower" indifference curve.

However, the critical question which arises is: Where along the utility frontier fg in Figure 4–3d is the point of optimal social allocation for the society? The answer, in terms of Figure 4–3d, is at point *H* where the utility frontier *fg* is tangent to the highest attainable social indifference curve S^2, and in Figure 4–3c where the same (implied) social indifference curve S^2 is tangent to the Societal Production-Possibility Curve *P-P'*.[14]

Importantly, as suggested above, the social welfare function cannot reveal a true ordering of preferences *through economic analysis.* In other words, a societal value judgment must establish the "effective" state of distribution which makes a *specific* social welfare function applicable (tangent) to the utility frontier. The true ordering of social preferences becomes a *reality* only when this state of *ex ante distribution* is established, causing one social welfare function (social indifference curve) to become the "effective demand" of the society for public and private goods. It is the voting power of income and wealth distribution which determines such effective demand in the private sector and political voting power which determines the effective demand for public goods. The actual intersector resource allocation which follows from this "effective demand" for public and private goods establishes also the ultimate pattern of real income and consumption distribution, in a welfare or living standard sense, for the individuals of the society. This latter distribution concept may be referred to as *ex post distribution.*

Thus, in summary, *ex ante distribution* determines the relevant social welfare function (social indifference curve) which becomes tangent to the utility frontier with a resulting *actual allocation* of economic output between public and private goods and the ultimate *ex post distribution* of these goods among the consumers of the society. Hence, in a genuine sense, *actual allocation* and *ex post distribution* become essentially synonymous concepts.

A number of experts, such as Bergson, have analyzed the role of "value" judgments in the determination of the "prevailing" social welfare function or social indifference curve.[15] These ethical judgments may be those of an economist, legislature, or any individual person or group in the society. Yet, some "composite" societal value judgment is "effective," in a collective sense, at any one time. The distinction between *positive* and *welfare* economics is relevant to the present discussion. *Positive economics* concentrates upon the microeconomic

---

[14] The optimal allocation point *H* in Figure 4–3d is comparable to the optimal intersector allocation point established in Chapter 1, Figure 1–4. In Figure 4–3d, the utility frontier *fg* suggests the same resource constraint that is indicated by the production-possibility curve *P'* in Figure 1–4. In addition, the social welfare functions, S^1, S^2, and S^3, in Figure 4–3d, are analogous to the social indifference curves, S^1, S^2, S^3, and S^4, in Figure 1–4.

[15] A. Bergson, "A Reformulation of Certain Aspects of Welfare Economics," *Quarterly Journal of Economics,* February 1938, pp. 310–34.

and macroeconomic principles which operate toward the attainment of goals in the economy. It is *not* concerned with the "desirability" of the goals. In other words, it is not "normative" in scope. On the other hand, *welfare economics* is normative in the sense that it establishes *rules*—and judges their desirability—mostly from noneconomic value judgments. The Bergson social welfare function discussion represents an appreciation of the distinction between positive and welfare economics. That is, a "given" social welfare function must be specified through normative decisions in *welfare economics* before the meaningful attainment of allocation goals can be evaluated through the established principles of *positive economics*. In other words, once an *ex ante* state of distribution is assigned, positive economics can help point the way to the optimal welfare goal along the Pareto utility frontier.

The inability to apply the exclusion principle to a pure public good complicates the revelation of the true preferences which have been made effective by the *ex ante* state of distribution. This is to be contrasted with conditions as they would exist in a society of competitive markets (Walrasian general equilibrium) in which the price system would accurately reveal the demands for divisible private goods.[16] The fact that a pure public good is consumed "equally" by all individuals motivates a single individual to avoid voluntary payment for the good in a situation where a large number of individuals are consuming the good. Compulsion thus becomes an extremely logical, though not necessarily the only, means of financing a pure public good. This *basic* allocation problem involved with "indivisible" public goods, as developed in the Samuelson model, will now be treated in a more comprehensive fashion. In order to do this, the Samuelson result will be integrated with the voluntary-exchange model introduced earlier in this chapter (see Figure 4–2).

Thus, in Figure 4–4 curves MRS_a and MRS_b, summed "vertically," comprise the total demand for the Pure Public Good Z as indicated by curve ΣMRS. The supply or production constraint side of the analysis is shown through the marginal rate of transformation (marginal cost) curve marked $MRT(MC)$.[17] The MRS curves and the MRT curves in Figure 4–4 are drawn to reflect the slopes of the individual indifference curves in Figures 4–3a and 4–3b and the societal production-possibility curve in Figure 4–3c, respectively. An equilibrium is established where the ΣMRS curve intersects the MRT curve at point E. The "summation" of the marginal rates of substitution between the consumption of Public Good Z and Private Good W is *equal* at this point to the marginal rate

---

[16] See Chapter 2.

[17] The term "marginal rate of transformation" more closely fits the MRT curve than does the designation "marginal cost," though the latter is not invalid.

of transformation in the production of the two goods. This result is also consistent with tangency point a in Figure 1–4 of Chapter 1.

The conditions of equilibrium in the supply and demand of a collectively consumed pure public good thus differ radically from those of a *divisible* pure private good. This is an extremely important observation.

FIGURE 4–4
Optimal Allocation of a Pure Public Good: Combined *Voluntary-Exchange* and *Samuelson* Approaches

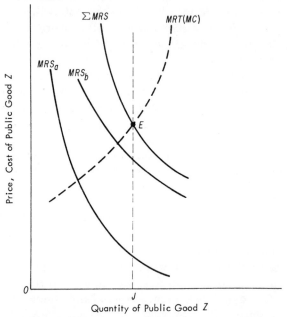

Source: Adapted from Paul A. Samuelson, "Diagrammatic Exposition of a Theory of Public Expenditure," *Review of Economics and Statistics*, November 1955, Chart 5, p. 354.

In the case of a divisible private good, a difference in marginal price between two individuals would present an unexploited "trading opportunity." In the case of the *indivisible* pure public good, however, no such trading opportunity is present. Individuals are unable to adjust their purchases among varying quantities even though they place different marginal evaluations on the good. The same quantity is consumed by all individuals.[18] Since the various individuals in the society cannot independently adjust the quantities which they consume of a pure public good, a "two-party exchange" is impossible. Yet, *all* in-

---

[18] For an excellent discussion of the difference between the allocation of a pure public good and a pure private good, see Buchanan, *Demand and Supply of Public Goods*.

dividuals in the society would have to be involved in the "contract" or "exchange" if market-type efficiency were to be attained. The trade of a private good, on the other hand, implicitly involves "unanimity." Otherwise, a third party could prevent an exchange by offering more attractive conditions to one of the two individuals involved in the trade. Such implicit unanimity is an inherent characteristic of "private goods trade."

Not only is such trade impossible for a pure public good, the complications multiply when the society is considered in terms of a "large group" or "many" individuals rather than only two individual members (as in the Samuelson model). Explicit agreements among all members of a large group to finance a jointly- and equally-consumed economic good are essentially impossible to attain, especially when the *costs of attaining such agreement* are considered. This involves the same conditions of "market failure" which were developed in Chapter 2 on the basis of zero marginal cost and collective consumption conditions.

Furthermore, in a small group society such as the two-person Samuelson model, there is the attraction for each individual to act in a "strategic manner," that is, to "bargain" in an effort to improve his terms of trade. This is true even for a pure public good, not just for a divisible private good. However, an individual in a large group society cannot expect to influence the behavior of other societal members through his own behavior. Thus, he is not similarly motivated to act in a "strategic" manner. In the *void* of bargaining, he will necessarily adjust his behavior to that of the collectivity without the hope that his actions will change that collective behavior. It is critically important that he will *not* be motivated to "voluntarily" *pay* for an economic good under such circumstances. He is content to be a *free rider* in the sense that he wishes to secure the benefits of a public good without contributing toward the financial support of its production costs. The "free rider" situation provides a logical argument for the introduction of "compulsion" in the form of "coercive agreements" in the political decision-making process, though once again the argument for governmental allocative action must be evaluated on a case-by-case basis which considers the comparative benefits and costs of such action.

It is one of the primary aims of the political decision-making process, in the allocation of economic goods, to remove the effects of the "free rider" problem and to allow the individual members of the large group society to select more "rationally" among alternative budget policies. The significance of the efficiency of political decision making in the allocation of economic goods is considered under the title of "welfare politics" or "public choice" in the following chapter. First, however, there will be a slight digression to consider the *compensation principle*. This concept relates to an adjustment possibility for the purpose of improving the "operational nature" of the Pareto-optimum social welfare norm.

THE COMPENSATION PRINCIPLE AS A SOCIAL WELFARE NORM

A decisive element in the determination of optimal intersector resource allocation and public goods allocation is the selection of a social norm toward which social welfare decisions can be directed. As observed above, the Pareto-optimum norm considers societal welfare to be improved if one person gains from an economic reorganization while other persons are not made worse off by the change. In an attempt to improve this norm, to reduce value judgments, and to widen the area of welfare application, J. R. Hicks, Nicholas Kaldor, and Tibor Scitovsky introduced the *compensation principle*.[19] This principle considers the welfare of society to be "increased" if the gainers from a resource reallocation evaluate their *gains* at a higher "monetary" figure than the losers evaluate their *losses*. The implication is that the former could reimburse the latter for their losses, still experience a net gain in utility, and thus increase societal welfare. The principle does not require *actual* compensation for the welfare improvement to occur, but only that the gainer be willing *potentially* to pay the compensation from his gains.

Scitovsky considers this version of the compensation principle to be inconsistent since a given resource reorganization may provide a higher gain for the gainers than for the losers, while a reversal of this reorganization may provide a higher gain for the previous losers than for the previous gainers.[20] In this instance, there is no criterion for saying which circumstance represents the preferred improvement. "Continuous" best positions, *not* a "single" or "discrete" best position, would exist. Scitovsky asserts that an improvement would have to pass the test of both the "initial" resource reallocation and its "reverse" reallocation.

Although this "double criterion" test is a welcome refinement to the compensation principle, the principle itself still faces rather serious theoretical and operational difficulties. For example, it becomes logically inconsistent in the sense that "monetary" values are *not* good indicators of "interpersonal utility" differences. Thus, Consumer *A* may suffer much more disutility from a $50 loss than Consumer *B* enjoys in

---

[19] J. R. Hicks, "The Foundations of Welfare Economics," *Economic Journal,* December 1939, pp. 696–712; Nicholas Kaldor, "A Note on Tariffs and the Terms of Trade," *Economica,* November 1940, pp. 377–80; and Tibor Scitovsky, "A Note on Welfare Propositions in Economics," *Review of Economic Studies,* November 1941, pp. 77–88.

[20] This phenomenon, as demonstrated by Scitovsky, could result when two "utility possibility curves" intersect. See Scitovsky, "Note on Welfare Propositions in Economics."

additional welfare from a gain which he values at $500. Relatedly, the compensation principle can be applied effectively only if there is knowledge as to how much compensation should be paid. The very nature of public goods (the usual presence of indivisibilities) makes such knowledge difficult to attain. In addition, there is the problem of the need for an ethical or value judgment by the society through the political process to determine the amounts and distribution of the compensation payments. Finally, if true preferences are revealed better through the political process, there is less need to use the compensation principle for attaining the Pareto-optimum goal. The chapter which follows will describe the evolving discipline of *welfare politics* or *public choice theory*—the goal of which is to improve political decisions through institutional means which improve the revelation of consumer preferences for public and quasi-public goods.

5

Political Institutions and Public Sector Decision Making

In this chapter the problems involved in the revelation of societal resource allocational preferences through the political process will be analyzed. Given the distributional value judgments which render these preferences "effective," the political process may function to "varying degrees of efficiency" in implementing the preferences in the form of actual allocation results. The free rider problem is an inherent part of such implementation efficiency. The more precisely that societal allocational preferences are revealed, the closer *actual* intersector resource allocation will be to *optimal* intersector resource allocation. The ultimate welfare achievement, of course, is the attainment of Pareto-optimal conditions. This important subject matter constitutes the area of "political economy" known alternately as *nonmarket decision-making* or *public choice theory*.

In essence, this subject matter involves a study of the "Economics of Political Decision-Making." The same consumers who individually demand "private-type goods" through the *market* are viewed here as demanding "public-type goods" through the *political process*. As seen in the previous chapters, partial market failure leads to an acceptance of governmental allocative intervention despite a market-oriented culture. Yet, the political process itself also is characterized by its own problems of economic inefficiency. Nonetheless, differences in the nature of certain public-type economic goods—such as the trait of collective consumption—require public sector allocational intervention if these goods are to be effectively supplied. However, interpretation of the demand for public-type goods creates problems of preference revelation unlike those found in the market sector of the economy.

An effort will be made herein to describe the "difficulties" encountered in revealing preferences without the presence of a market mechanism. That is, as observed in the preceding chapters, a pure public good cannot be allocated through a "two-person" market-type exchange. Moreover, the discussion will attempt to isolate some potential "institutional improvements" in the revelation of societal preferences for public-type goods. In other words, some of the possibilities which exist for the improvement of public sector economic decision-making for allocational purposes will be discussed. At this point, it should be reiterated that there are two important dimensions to the subject of public goods allocation: (1) the "value-judgment determined" distribution of political voting power or influence among individuals in the political decision-making process which, along with the distribution of market voting power in terms of income-wealth distribution, determines the "effective" social indifference curve (social welfare function). It is this "effective" social indifference curve which becomes tangent to the production-possibility curve (utility horizon)—thus providing optimal allocational conditions as demonstrated in Figures 1–4 and 4–3d, respectively, and (2) the political techniques used to reveal these true (effective) preferences within the public sector. A primary contributor in the latter regard was the late Swedish economist, Knut Wicksell, who built his economic analysis of democratic political decision-making on the *voluntary-exchange theory of public goods allocation* (described in the previous chapter). Wicksell's insights and contributions to this important and rapidly-evolving area of knowledge will now be discussed.

THE WICKSELL APPROACH TO REVEALING SOCIAL PREFERENCES—ABSOLUTE AND RELATIVE UNANIMITY

The political process is extremely important to the attainment of an efficient societal allocation of resources. Yet, if a society adopts a "democratic" political system using the "majority voting" rule, the institutional problems involved in revealing individual preferences for economic goods may be considerable. For example, preferences based on an "equal vote for all" concept, which is the benchmark of democratic individualism, are unlikely to be revealed and implemented effectively by a system of *simple majority voting* whereby a majority of 50 percent plus one vote may carry a decision. Thus, a minority of 50 percent minus one of the citizens may be obliged to help pay for a public-type economic good with their taxes though they do not desire the allocation

economic good with their taxes though they do not desire the allocation of the good. Wicksell was alert to the importance of this fact.[1]

It was demonstrated by Wicksell that *absolute unanimity* (100 percent approval) in the political process is analogous to the efficient *competitive solution* in the market. However, under "less than absolute unanimity" conditions, the efficient allocation of public goods "breaks down." In other words, the "two-party exchange," which is possible for divisible market goods without conventional externalities, is impossible for indivisible public goods consumed in a large group situation except under the condition of complete or absolute unanimity. The motivation for individuals in the large group to be *free riders*, and thus not "voluntarily" pay for the economic good, creates an inherent impasse in the financing of a pure public good if conditions of "less than complete" unanimity are present.

The objective of an "allocationally-efficient" political process is to reduce or eliminate this impasse so that the individual may feel that his own selection among alternatives will influence the consumption of others in the group, as is true in the two-person exchange of a pure private good. It is the elimination of this "free rider" motivation in large group decision-making that absolute or complete unanimity accomplishes. It is accomplished by the fact that the "effective size" of the group is reduced to a situation analogous to the "two-party exchange" condition for divisible private goods. In other words, the individual now may consider himself to be trading with "all others" as a unit. That is, by his single negative vote he can void a transaction or allocation policy and deny the public good to all other consumers in the society.[2] Of course, the problems of "strategy" or "gaming" are reintroduced when the free rider problem disappears as the large group situation is reduced to that of a two-party exchange. Nonetheless, it is important that motivation has been reestablished for the individual to achieve Pareto-optimal conditions through individual trade or exchange.

Since a single negative vote would block a budgetary policy under conditions of absolute unanimity, the inducement for "strategy" would tend to allow few, if any, budget policies to be approved under the rule. Thus, since absolute unanimity would lead to an essentially "inactive" budget system, Wicksell endorsed what he considered to be a "next best" concept of *relative unanimity* or, as it is alternately known, *qualified majority voting*. This rule suggests that an "approval percentage"

---

[1] See Knut Wicksell, "A New Principle of Just Taxation," in Richard A. Musgrave and Alan T. Peacock (eds.), *Classics in the Theory of Public Finance* (London: Macmillan & Co., 1958), pp. 72–118. Also, see the discussion of the Wicksellian position in James M. Buchanan, *Demand and Supply of Public Goods*, and Carl G. Uhr, *Economic Doctrines of Knut Wicksell* (Berkeley: University of California Press, 1960), pp. 164–90.

[2] See Buchanan, *Demand and Supply of Public Goods*, chap. 5.

for a budgetary policy should be as close to 100 percent (absolute unanimity) as possible without inducing "excessive" vetoing strategy. Generally, he recommended a five-sixths (5/6s) approval percentage for the relative unanimity criterion. Importantly, this means that an individual in a large group situation will know that his own negative vote, by itself, cannot block a budget proposal. Consequently, he will not be as strongly motivated to exploit others through a negative strategy as he would under an absolute unanimity rule. If a proposal promises some benefits for him, he may accept it even though under a benchmark of absolute unanimity he might be tempted to strategically block the same policy. Thus, under a five-sixths relative unanimity rule, it is more likely that a sufficient number of individuals in the society would follow "nonstrategic" behavior so as to allow an acceptable number of collective decisions to be made.

Once a relative unanimity rule has been established, the various percentage approvals for alternate budget policies may be compared and thus, in general terms, it can indicate relative approval preferences for alternative policies by the individuals of the society. A movement "toward" Pareto optimality, though not actually to the frontier of Pareto-optimal points (see Figure 4–3d), may thus be accomplished. In other words, some of the "potential" gains from trade can be realized. Moreover, the rule of relative unanimity, as opposed to the conventional simple majority rule, allows greater protection for the "minority" in the society on a particular fiscal decision. To the contrary, it could be argued against the Wicksellian relative unanimity approach, as compared to a simple majority rule, that it renders a budgetary decision so difficult to approve that it works against the general "well-being of the majority" and in favor of the minority.

Finally, it may be observed that Wicksell contended that "expenditure" and "tax" decisions should be made *simultaneously* by the legislature. This means, of course, a "symmetrical" tie-in between spending and revenue decisions. Hence, the marginal benefit from a public expenditure should be related to the marginal tax-cost of providing the public good—and then, the relative unanimity (qualified majority voting) rule should be applied to the "joint" decision. This is consistent with his preference for the voluntary-exchange approach to public goods allocations, as discussed in the previous chapter.

THE VOTING-EXTERNALITY AND DECISION-MAKING COSTS OF DEMOCRATIC VOTING

More recent analysis by James M. Buchanan and Gordon Tullock has added further insight concerning the economic issues involved in the process of revealing individual economic preferences through a democratic political system.[3] Figure 5–1 demonstrates some of the more significant of these issues. For example, the expected *political-interaction costs* (discounted to present-value) from collective democratic decision-making are measured on the vertical axis while the *percentage of the group required* for the approval of a collective fiscal decision are measured along the horizontal axis. The political-interaction costs are two-fold in nature: (1) the "voting-externality" cost component, and (2) the "decision-making" cost component.

FIGURE 5–1
Political-Interaction Costs

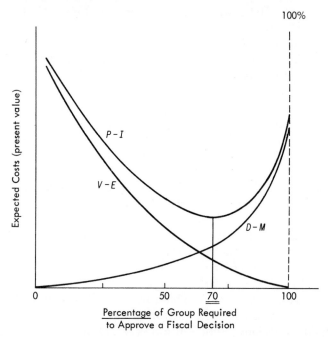

A *voting-externality cost*, in political-interaction terms, refers to the cost incurred by a voter who has voted against a fiscal choice which, nonetheless, has been approved by the required proportion of voters necessary to carry the decision for approval. Such an individual must abide by the collective decision even though his individual preferences did not "opt" for its approval. Assume a group of 100 voters. If the proportion of voters required to approve a collective action is only 1 percent, then one of the 100 voters can oblige the remaining 99 voters

---

[3] See James M. Buchanan and Gordon Tullock, *The Calculus of Consent* (Ann Arbor, Mich.:, University of Michigan Press, 1962).

to abide by his political decision. Quite obviously, the potential negative voting externalities extended to the remaining 99 voters who may oppose the decision are considerable. However, the potential voting externalities would continuously decline as the percentage required to approve a political decision increases. Ultimately, at an absolute (complete) unanimity rule of 100 percent approval, voting externality costs in the form of negative voting externalities would reach zero as no voter could be bound by the collective political decision of other voters. In other words, a single voter would retain the "right to veto." The nature of voting-externality costs are represented by *Curve V-E* in Figure 5–1.

A *decision-making cost*, in political-interaction terms, refers to the bargaining cost required to reach a group political consensus or agreement. Essentially, these are real resource costs in terms of both "direct" labor, material, and capital outlay as well as "opportunity cost" considerations inclusive of the value of time spent in bargaining. Decision-making costs may be expected to increase as the proportion of the voting group required to approve a decision becomes larger. That is, under conditions requiring higher percentage approval, more effort is normally required to gain agreement. The highest cost would be expected at the point of 100 percent approval (absolute or complete unanimity) since the potential for strategy would reach a peak at this point. This would be true because a single voter would be capable of negating a choice which conceivably every other voter would prefer. *Curve D-M* in Figure 5–1 represents the nature of decision-making costs. Assuming a group of 100 voters, a 1 percent approval rule would incur no bargaining costs while approval by all 100 voters would likely incur substantial decision-making costs.

Curve P-I in Figure 5–1 reflects the performance of the overall *political-interaction costs*. The curve is a summation of its two components, the voting-externality cost curve (*V-E*) and the decision-making cost curve (*D-M*). In this particular graph, given the character of the voting-externality and decision-making cost functions, the "most efficient" proportion of the group required for political approval is 70 percent.[4] That is, this proportion yields the lowest political-interaction cost per voter for a particular fiscal decision.

REVEALING SOCIAL PREFERENCES THROUGH MAJORITY VOTING—ARROW'S "IMPOSSIBILITY THEOREM"

Kenneth Arrow has provided an additional analysis of the problems involved in making societal decisions consistent with individual prefer-

---

[4] Note that the most efficient proportion is not determined by the "intersection" of the *V-E* and *D-M* curves.

ences in *group voting* within a democratic-political process.[5] Arrow
pays particular attention to the efficiency of the "majority voting" rule.
He argues that the following conditions must be met if collective decisions reached under majority voting conditions are to accurately reveal
the individual economic preferences which constitute the "effective"
social indifference curve (social welfare function):

1. Social choices must be "transitive" (consistent). That is, if Policy
X is preferred to Policy Y, and Policy Y is preferred to Policy Z, then
Policy Z cannot be preferred to Policy X in the social welfare function.
A *unique social ordering* must exist regardless of the manner in which
individuals in the society "order" their alternative choices.

2. The social welfare function must be "nonperverse" in the sense
that an alternative policy which might otherwise have been chosen by
the society must not be rejected because any individual has *changed
the relative ranking* of that alternative. For example, if Policies W, X,
Y, and Z are ranked in that order, and X is changed so that the resulting
ranking will be X, W, Y, and Z, such a change will *not* be "perverse"
because X is still ranked above Y and Z.

3. The rankings of the choices in the social welfare function between
two alternatives must not be dependent on the ranking by individuals
of other alternatives which are irrelevant to the choice between the
two alternatives. That is, the *elimination of any one alternative* must
not influence the ranking of the other alternatives in the social welfare
function. For example, if Policy X is eliminated from a Z, W, X, Y
ranking, the result should be a Z, W, Y ranking. In other words, there
should be no interdependence among alternative policies.

4. Voters must have *free choices* among all alternative policies.

5. *Social choices must not be dictatorial.* That is, they must *not* be
based solely on the preferences of one individual independently of the
choices of the other individuals.

Table 5–1 displays a situation whereby majority voting violates the
set of conditions necessary for consumer sovereignty to be maintained
in collective democratic decision making, especially through the violation of the "transitivity condition" (condition number one). Assume
three voters (A, B, and C) who are selecting between three budget
policies (X, Y, and Z). Since a majority of the voters (in this example,
two out of three) prefer Policies X to Y, Y to Z, and Z to X, the result

---

[5] Kenneth Arrow, *Social Choice and Individual Values* (New York: John Wiley & Sons,
Inc., 1951). Critical evaluations of the Arrow hypothesis include: Clifford Hildreth, "Alternative Conditions for Social Orderings," *Econometrica,* January 1953, pp. 81–94; Leo A.
Goodman and Harry Markowitz, "Social Welfare Functions Based on Individual Rankings," *American Journal of Sociology,* November 1952, pp. 257–62; and James S. Coleman, "The Possibility of a Social Welfare Function," *American Economic Review,*
December 1966, pp. 1105–22. The Coleman evaluation will be discussed later in this
chapter.

TABLE 5–1
Example of Majority Voting: Individual Preferences for
Alternative Budget Policies

Results: (1) Intransitive.*

	Policy Alternatives		
Voter	Preference 1	Preference 2	Preference 3
A	X	Y	Z
B	Y	Z	X
C	Z	X	Y

* Summary: Voters A and C prefer Policy X to Y; A and B prefer Policy
Y to Z; B and C prefer Policy Z to X; thus a majority (two of three individuals
in this case) prefer Policy X to Y, Y to Z, and Z to X. This result is *intransitive*
(inconsistent) and violates condition number 1.

is *intransitive* (inconsistent).[6] It is thus maintained by Arrow that
majority voting cannot assure social decisions which are consistent with
individual preferences when a choice must be made in a democratic
political process between three or more alternative policies.

Though Arrow's requirments for rational collective decision-making
through majority voting are rigorous, his analysis nonetheless indicates
some basic problems present in collective decision-making of the
democratic-individualistic variety. However, one condition seems unduly rigorous, that is, condition number 3 which says that the elimination of any one alternative policy shall not influence the ranking of the
other alternative policies in the social welfare function.[7] There can be
no interdependencies among alternative policies. Or, stated differently,
the relative intensities of preference among voters for different policies
is not a relevant consideration.

For example, one half of the community may prefer improved highways and streets to solve traffic congestion in an urban area while the
other half may prefer a government-subsidized mass transportation
system to meet the problem. Assume the cost to be equal for both traffic

---

[6] It is assumed in this example that Policies X, Y, and Z relate to "basically different"
budgetary items, not to "different degrees" of the same item. For example, the "intransitivity paradox" could be avoided in the following situation: Policy X = $50,000 expendi-
ture for a community fire station; Policy Y = $25,000 expenditure for a community fire
station, and Policy Z = *no* expenditure for a community fire station. In this case, a ZXY
ranking would be *unrealistic* and unlikely to occur since it would represent a movement
from a "no fire station" choice to one of "maximum expenditure" for a fire station—thus
skipping over the "intermediate choice." Without a ZXY ranking, of course, the intran-
sivity paradox would not occur.

[7] Later in the chapter the overly rigorous nature of this condition will be analyzed
in greater detail under the discussion of the "Coleman approach" to the social welfare
function.

congestion solutions. If those who prefer the highway solution rank traffic congestion as a "much lower priority" program among various program alternatives than those who prefer the mass transportation system, the particular traffic congestion solution selected, if money is to be spent for this purpose, should be the mass transportation system because of the "higher relative intensities of preference" of those who prefer it. Condition 3, however, stipulates essentially that a consideration of this preference intensity is "irrelevant."

The Arrow approach thus tends to understate the *intensity of desires* among alternative policy choices. It is difficult, of course, for a system of social choice which ignores these basic preference considerations to accurately interpret individual demands in the political process. In addition, the *order* in which votes are taken may influence the nature of the effective social welfare function. For example, this would happen if the timing of decisions between alternative policies allowed an interplay of "strategy" so that some voters could understate their true preferences for public-type economic goods until a time of choice which would allow them "net economic gains."

REVEALING SOCIAL PREFERENCES THROUGH "POINT VOTING"

The previous sections of this chapter have exposed some of the problems encountered in the effort to reveal individual economic preferences through majority voting techniques. One prospective solution was considered in the form of the *relative unanimity* concept of Knut Wicksell. Another approach encompasses the understanding of *political-interaction costs*. Still another alternative to simple majority voting in the derivation of the social welfare function is *point voting*.

The *point method* of voting, unlike simple majority voting, emphasizes the relative "intensity" of preferences among alternative policies. For example, 51 voters out of a group of 100 voters can bind a minority of 49 voters to a budget policy which is not preferred by the minority even though the welfare losses of the 49 voters may exceed the welfare gains of the majority of 51. The simple majority rule has merely counted the numbers of winners and losers. Importantly, the relative preference intensities of the voters for the budget policy has been ignored. Point voting, as described below, attempts to overcome this problem.

Assume in Table 5–2ab that Voters *A, B,* and *C* of the society are each given 50 points whereby they can specify their relative intensities of desire among three alternative budget policies—*X, Y, Z*—on any divisional basis which they prefer. Then, suppose that the following occurs: Voter *A* allots 40 points to Alternative *X,* and 5 points each to Alternatives *Y* and *Z:* Voter *B* gives 25 points to Alternative *Y,* 20 points to Alternative Z, and 5 points to Alternative X, and Voter C allots 20 points to Alternative X, 20 points to Alternative Y, and 10 points to Alternative Z. Policy Alternative X is thus selected and the margin of preference for it is obvious. The total points, as shown in Table 5–2a, are: Policy $X = 65$ points; Policy $Y = 50$ points, and Policy $Z = 35$ points. Though intransitivity is avoided under the point voting rule, a stalemate or tie could occur. Table 5–2b indicates this possibility. It may be observed in this table that the three voters—A, B, and C—now have preferences which create a situation in which the total score for each policy alternative is equal to 50 points.

TABLE 5–2
Examples of Point Voting (50 point maximum for each individual) for the Revelation of Social Preferences

a. *Results:* (1) Transitive; (2) No tie.

Voter	Points assigned to Policy Alternatives		
	X	Y	Z
A.	40	5	5
B.	5	25	20
C.	20	20	10
Total	65	50	35

b. *Results:* (1) Transitive; (2) Tie.

Voter	Points assigned to Policy Alternatives		
	X	Y	Z
A.	20	20	10
B.	10	10	30
C.	20	20	10
Total	50	50	50

Consumer sovereignty, in the market sense, appears to be approximated more closely in point voting than in simple majority voting. Relatedly, greater attention is paid to preference patterns through the consideration of relative preference intensities. Why, then, should not the political process be structured so as to significantly increase the use of this voting method? Well, in one sense, point voting already does prominently exist in American society. For example, some voters, through a variety of methods, will invariably exert greater influence on a budgetary decision than will others. Such influence may well reflect a greater desire on their part for the particular policy. Nonetheless, such varying degrees of influence on a governmental policy decision may also reflect the uneven ex ante distribution of political voting influence among the members of a society.

However, the formal structuring of a point voting system would incur numerous institutional and administrative problems of change. Moreover, the significant issue of *strategy* must be considered. Though point voting tends to reveal social preferences better than simple majority voting, the "increased knowledge" diffused throughout the society through the more accurate revealing of individual preferences would allow "strategy" to become more pronounced. Of course, the opportunity for strategy would also tend to reduce the "free rider" problem whereby "voluntary" payments for indivisible public goods are not forthcoming. On the other hand, the *costs* of reaching agreements in a large group may be massive when ample opportunity for strategy is present.

Thus, a paradox seems to exist: If strategy is neutral, then point voting seems preferable because it reflects the relative intensity of desires. On the other hand, if new opportunities for strategy are introduced, simply majority voting may still be the best voting technique available for revealing social preferences, even though it is far from ideal, due to the costs of negotiating large-group agreements on an individualistic basis, and especially without generalized political or fiscal rules (these will be analyzed later in the chapter). In any event, majority voting arrangements, as presently constituted, are an imperfect method of revealing the effective social welfare function in the political process.

THE COLEMAN APPROACH TO REVEALING SOCIAL PREFERENCES

The importance of *relative intensities of preferences* between various policy alternatives in the aggregation of individual preferences to achieve group decision-making in the public sector has been further emphasized by Coleman.[8] Essentially, Coleman questions the third condition for efficient majority voting provided by Arrow. That is, the Coleman approach demonstrates that the Arrow theorem is relevant only to those social choice mechanisms in which relative intensities of desire between policy alternatives cannot be expressed. In other words, the elimination of a policy alternative, even though it may be low in priority to the voter, would *not* alter the behavior of a rational individual concerning other alternatives. Coleman avoids this unrealistic assumption by using an approach in which the problems of "individualistic choice" and "social welfare" are viewed in terms of *utility maximization under risk*. Unlike the market sector in which a consumer can

---

[8] Coleman, "Possibility of Social Welfare Function."

purchase or reject an economic good, a voter in the political sector can only partially control a policy outcome. Thus, uncertainty and risk become relevant dimensions of the public-sector allocational problem.

When the outcome of a policy choice is uncertain, each individual voter attaches a "subjective probability" to each possible outcome. This amounts to a decision regarding *expected utility* under these conditions of imperfect knowledge and risk. He will consider (1) the ordering of his utilities from different policies, as he would do for rational behavior under conditions of "certainty," and (2) he will also consider the *relative sizes of utility (welfare) differences* between various possible outcomes, as rational behavior would require under conditions of "risk." Importantly, the "expected utility" consideration under risk is an *inherent* part of the collective decision-making process. It *is not* externally imposed.

Table 5–3 (a, b, c) may be used to discuss further this "expected utility under risk" approach. Table 5–3a represents an intransitive result for

TABLE 5–3
Collective Decision Making with "Vote Exchanges" under Conditions of "Expected Utility and Risk"

a. *Results:* (1) Intransitive.

	Policy Alternatives		
Voter	Preference 1	Preference 2	Preference 3
A	X	Y	Z
B	Y	Z	X
C	Z	X	Y

b. *Results:* (1) Intransitive.

	Policy Alternatives		
Voter	Preference 1	Preference 2	Preference 3
A	X'	Y'	Z'
B	Y'	Z'	X'
C	Z'	X'	Y'

c. *Results:** (1) Transitive; (2) No Tie.

	Utility "Expected" from Budget Policy					
Voter	X	Y	Z	X'	Y'	Z'
A	10	5	1	10	9	8
B	8	10	9	8	10	9
C	9	8	10	9	6	10

* After voting changes based on "expected utility" differences from alternative budget policies.
   Source: Part (c) of table adapted from James S. Coleman, "The Possibility of a Social Welfare Function," *American Economic Review*, December 1966, p. 1113.

Policy Alternatives X, Y, and Z similar to the basic Arrow model covered in Table 5–1. In Table 5–3b, three additional Policy Alternatives (X', Y', Z') are added for the three voters of the society (Voters A, B, and C), and intransitivity once again occurs. Table 5–3c provides the *relative intensities of preference* of the three voters for the six alternative budget policies in terms of the relative sizes of utility differences between possible outcomes. Assume that Voter A knows the various orderings of the other two voters among the six policy alternatives. Thus, he possesses "expected utilities" among a range of six possible alternatives. Now he has the power to induce an action from another voter in response to his own action. Indeed, gains can be made from trade even though outcomes are "probable" and not "certain."

Observe at this point that the utility differences for Voter A between Policy Alternatives X, X', Y', and Z' are small while the utility differences for the same voter between these alternatives and Policy Alternatives Y and Z are large (see Table 5–3c). The same phenomenon is evident from the "multipeaked" preference function presented in Figure 5–2. Hence, Voter A may well consider an *exchange of votes* with another voter, such as Voter C, so that Policy Alternatives X and Z' would win. Thus, both Voter A and Voter C would attain a top priority policy alternative as well as a high priority second policy. In fact, Voter B would likely not oppose the vote trade either since he would receive a substantial total of 17 units of "expected utility" from the two policies (X and Z') as contrasted to 18 units for Voter A and 19 units for Voter C.[9] In political terms, the vote exchange may well be termed *logrolling*. Significantly, the "intransitive" results of Tables 5–3a and 5–3b have been converted into a "transitive" situation in Table 5–3c by the application of analysis based upon "utility-maximization under risk."

An important conclusion from the above example is that when an individual is released (1) from the "restriction" of voting on only one issue, and also (2) from the "restriction" of a complete lack of information about the behavior of others, rational individual behavior suggests that every policy alternative which possesses some "subjective probability" of occurrence may affect maximizing behavior.[10] In fact, this is true even for policy alternatives of "low" priority. Obviously an individual acting in a rational economic manner would be willing to give up some resources in order to achieve an "expected" *net gain* in welfare or utility from giving them up. In the present context, this would amount to the giving up of votes on some "low priority" issues in order

---

[9] An effort is made in Table 5–3c *only* to demonstrate a particular vote exchange situation which is beneficial to both voters involved in the trade. No effort is made to isolate any other beneficial vote exchanges which may be implicit in the table.

[10] Even the Wicksellian *absolute unanimity approach* limits its direct consideration to a single-policy alternative.

FIGURE 5–2
Multipeaked Preference Functions of Voters A, B, and C (based on Table 5–3c)

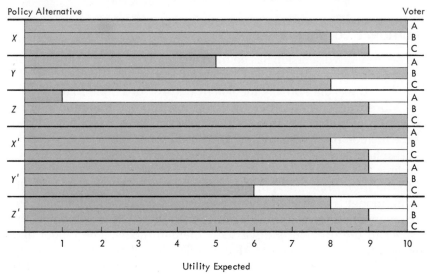

Policy Alternative   Voter

Utility Expected

to receive a utility gain from votes in support of other "higher priority" policy alternatives.

Significantly, *vote trading (logrolling)* by elected political representatives does occur through various techniques in the political structure of a nation such as the United States. Yet, in a distributional sense, voting influence among the individuals of a society is often quite uneven. An equal right to vote in an election does not constitute equal political influence in the ultimate "policy determination" sense. This unevenness of influence includes the "differential" effects exerted on policy formation by various pressure groups and lobbies. Hence, the "distribution of political voting power," as discussed at several earlier points in the book, takes on an especially important meaning in the present discussion.

It should be recognized that a precise and formal application of the "expected utility under risk" approach would face massive costs of "individual" negotiation as well as a potential free rider problem in a large number group. However, elected *legislatures* and other political institutions can act as "proxies" for the individual members of a political community in a manner that might well move the society closer to Pareto optimality than would be true under a simple majority voting rule on each issue with no consideration being given to relative preference intensities. In effect, logrolling provides the opportunity for a person or group to obtain what he or it "wants most" at the expense of what he or it "wants least." Relatedly, minorities can establish coalitions and thus better attain their more intense preferences.

ADDITIONAL VOTING MODELS

The previous discussion has pointed out both the de facto nonattainability of the "conceptually ideal" Wicksellian absolute unanimity model as well as the "conceptually inefficient nature" of simple majority voting. Moreover, certain other modified institutional techniques of revealing preferences in the political process have been considered. These include the "point voting" and "utility-maximization under risk" approaches. Now several additional democratic voting models will be considered.

In the *logrolling model* of Buchanan and Tullock, a simple majority voting model is examined under conditions whereby individuals may exchange their votes on one issue for another.[11] It is similar in this respect to the previously discussed Coleman model. The model then suggests that small groups of elected officials will be motivated to exchange their votes on particular issues or policy alternatives in a manner which will assure "majority support" for alternatives which are of special advantage to the groups or jurisdictions which they represent. Importantly, as in the Coleman analysis, the approach used by Buchanan and Tullock goes beyond the consideration of a single budgetary alternative.

In a general sense, an individual voter can array all possible budgetary alternatives according to the relative intensities of his preferences for them. Accordingly, his welfare position could be improved if he accepts a decision against his interests in an area where these preferences are low in exchange for a decision in accordance with his preferences in an area where his welfare or utility assessment is high. Thus, "bargains" or "vote exchanges" can be mutually beneficial. Basically, an individual should exchange until the "marginal cost" of voting for a policy alternative which he disapproves, but concerning which his disapproval is weak, equals the "expected marginal gains" of the vote or votes obtained in return support for issues in which he has higher preferences. The total bargaining or exchange mechanism should thus allow a *net gain* to the individual.

The rational individual voter would attempt to acquire the agreement of only a simple majority (50 percent plus one vote) of the voters, not all of the voters. He can initially ignore the remaining minority of the voters. However, the reverse also is true. That is, exchanges will most likely be made in which the individual voter does *not* participate,

---

[11] Buchanan and Tullock *Calculus of Consent.*

but for which he must bear some part of the costs of the action undertaken. In essence, these would constitute "voting externality costs" as discussed earlier in this chapter. The ultimate result from the exchange mechanism of "logrolling" or "vote trading" will be to yield the individual benefits from only slightly more than one half of the total exchanges that are made. Thus, a simple majority voting rule in group or collective decision making in the political process of a democracy will cause *external costs* as well as *internal gains* from the bargaining process. This situation would persist unless the simple majority voting rule were changed so as to allow the minority to receive compensation payments from the majority. Finally, it should be observed that even though the logrolling model of Buchanan and Tullock provides an improved analytical framework for understanding the "efficiency problems" which arise under majority voting conditions, it does not assure the attainment of a close approximation to Pareto optimality due to several factors including institutional complexities and informational problems.

Another approach to the revelation of individual preferences in the political process takes the form of the *competitive model* of Downs.[12] This model emphasizes the role of "political parties" in the decision-making process of the public sector. Specifically, it views a political party in terms of its "vote-maximization" motivation for the purpose of survival in office. The politicians have no direct interest in "welfare maximization," but only "vote maximization." Thus, party platforms are designed to conform with the consensus preference of large groups of voters. Assumedly, individuals will vote for the party which best represents their welfare or, in other words, the party which maximizes their net benefits (over tax costs) from public sector decisions. The greater the "consensus" of the population on major issues, the more effective the process becomes. However, where significant disagreement exists on major issues, two or more major political parties are likely to exist with the possibility that no single party is likely to exert a majority influence.

"Adequate information" is a basic requirement for the efficient operation of this system. Ideally, such information would include complete knowledge of voter preference patterns for both public and private goods and, in addition, complete knowledge of the effects of alternative budget policies. Neither condition is likely to be present to a substantial degree.[13] Moreover, considerable knowledge of voter preference patterns would allow additional "strategy" to ensue with significant com-

[12] Anthony Downs, *An Economic Theory of Democracy* (New York: Harper & Row Publishers, 1957).

[13] For a relevant discussion, see J. G. Head, "The Theory of Public Goods," Conference on Economic Policy, University of Queensland, Australia, August 1967, pp. 21–22.

plications in the costs of negotiating agreements in a large number group. Hence, the competitive model, though analytically useful in broadening the understanding of the political decision-making process, cannot be relied upon to provide conditions closely approximating Pareto optimality.

Next, mention will be made of the *spatial mobility* approach to decision-making efficiency in the political process. This approach was initially developed by Charles Tiebout.[14] Its focal point is the "market-type decision" which occurs when an individual "voluntarily" selects the particular political jurisdiction in which to establish his residence. As long as individuals can move freely among jurisdictions, they are afforded the opportunity of selecting the particular "budgetary mix" of expenditures and taxation which best meets their "fiscal preferences." Undoubtedly, some reflection of consumer sovereignty and its attendant allocational efficiency qualities are implicit in this approach. Nonetheless, a menu of "alternative fiscal mixes" is *not* a realistic option for many individuals due to inflexible employment options and numerous other causes. Hence, the *spatial mobility* approach—though conceptually valid—is limited in its overall scope. It cannot serve as a general efficiency framework for making individual economic decisions within a democratic political process.

THE POLITICAL CONSTITUTION AND FISCAL RULES[15]

Indeed, the *theory of public goods* must be complemented by a *theory of political institutions.* Institutional choice must have an economic "reference point," that is, it must possess the means for a comparison of economic benefits and costs over a range of alternative budget policies and over a period of time. Moreover, the basic theory of the demand and supply of public goods, and of the political decision-making process which responds to these demand and supply forces, must also consider the "means of financing" these goods. Thus, various "tax-sharing schemes" become highly relevant to the total analysis. Furthermore, the important fact should be recognized that considerable costs usually must be incurred in reaching collective decisions in the public sector.

In the typical large group situation, the costs of attaining "voluntary agreements" among individuals become prohibitive and decisions ordinarily will *not be made* unless some agreement can be reached among

---

[14] See Charles M. Tiebout, "A Pure Theory of Local Expenditures," *Journal of Political Economy*, October 1956. The "spatial mobility" approach will also be considered in the "intergovernmental fiscal relationships" analysis of Chapter 20.

[15] For an excellent discussion of this subject, see Buchanan, *Demand and Supply of Public Goods*, chaps. 7 and 8.

the individual members of the society on "decision-making procedures." These include: (1) the basic *political constitution* such as the adoption of a simple majority democratic voting system which makes the political process "operational," and (2) the establishment of specific *fiscal rules* within the framework of the political constitution. Regarding such fiscal rules, if a society can predict that fiscal decisions will be made on a yearly basis, and that these decisions will be similar in a number of respects, the individual members of the society may reach an agreement to impose upon themselves through their legislative assemblies various on-going fiscal rules. For example, the society may select a system of tax-sharing arrangements for distributing tax burdens which may remain in effect for a long period of time. Such a tax structure need not be changed every time that specific decisions concerning the allocation of public goods are made during a particular fiscal year. Decision-making costs are accordingly reduced if a "new tax structure" does not have to be set up for each successive fiscal year. Tax-sharing schemes and tax structures have usually been guided in real-world situations by the orthodox *ability-to-pay* and *benefit* principles of tax equity.[16]

In summary, the theoretical *demand and supply of public goods* concept must be integrated in the real world with *political conventions* and *fiscal institutions* which help to implement the society's preferences for public goods. In other words, the individual members of a society adopt procedures of "public choice" in the political process. That is, since the indivisible (collective consumption) nature of public goods denies the effective use of market principles in political decision-making, the individual members of a society, in order to reach "group decisions" and achieve the potential *gains from trade* which are available, must establish a general political constitution and specific fiscal rules, including financing schemes, in order to provide the public and quasi-public goods desired by the individual members of the society. Hence, society elects to accept compulsion in the form of "coercive governmental action" in order to circumvent the "free rider" or "nonaction" problem, to reduce negotiation costs, and thus to establish greater efficiency in public sector decision-making.

THE CURRENT STATE OF PUBLIC CHOICE THEORY

The important subject area of "nonmarket decision-making" or "public choice theory" is presently receiving considerable attention from scholars. Yet, the current state of knowledge in this area must be

---

[16] These "tax-equity" principles, first introduced in Chapter 4 in connection with the marginal utility and voluntary-exchange approaches to intersector resource allocation, are discussed in greater detail in Chapter 7.

considered to be only "partially developed" at this point of time. Nonetheless, an understanding of the nature of nonmarket decision-making is a necessary adjunct to a rational theory of "public sector economics." Wicksell's analysis provided an early important "break-through" for the integration of "welfare economics" and "public choice theory." Moreover, this provided the foundation for the subsequent development of the latter area of study. Other early contributions were made by a number of Italian economists working independently of Wicksell. Their names include de Viti de Marco and Pantaleoni.[17] Wicksell recognized that market-type decisions are duplicated in the political process only by absolute (complete) unanimity. This constituted an outstanding contribution, especially coming as it did during the 19th century when most focus in public finance was upon taxation considerations. Then, more recent twentieth century contributions to the development of public choice theory by Kenneth Arrow, James Coleman, James Buchanan, Gordon Tullock, Anthony Downs, and others have been significant.

The present stage of development in "public goods theory" allows a suitable understanding of the primary nature of public-type economic goods. Moreover, the present state of knowledge in "public choice theory" allows an understanding of the major problems of political decision making which impede the revelation of individual economic preferences through a democratic political process. Solutions to the latter problem, as noted above, are only in a partial stage of development. Nonetheless, one should not be too pessimistic regarding the future in this regard. Technology in the form of "social innovation" has played an outstanding role in the history of mankind. It is entirely conceivable that conceptual and institutional improvements in fiscal decision-making techniques to better reveal societal preferences can be provided through the rational research efforts of man in modern society. It would not be expected, of course, that complete attainment of "Pareto-optimum" conditions could be realized. Nonetheless, it does seem likely that improved "second-best" positions closer to Pareto optimality can be realized through innovation in the social decision-making process.

Finally, it may be observed that economists and political scientists, interested in improving upon the above problem, can further widen the scope of their analyses along *interdisciplinary* lines. Thus, Jerome Rothenberg argues that a better understanding of the social welfare function may be attained by focusing upon the interacting and interdisciplinary characteristics of group behavior in a society.[18] He points out

---

[17] See A. de Viti de Marco, *Il carattere teorico dell'economia finanziana* (Rome, 1888) and M. Pantaleoni, *Contributo alla teoria del riparto delle spese* pubbliche (1883).

[18] Jerome Rothenberg, *The Measurement of Social Welfare* (Englewood Cliffs, N.J.: Prentice-Hall, Inc., 1961), chap. 13.

that social psychologists, anthropologists, and sociologists, are developing a concept of social choice which stresses the high degree of culturally implemented "value consensus" which exists in any going society. This consensus integrates the several institutional networks in the society in order to avoid conflict. Thus, values are not imposed externally upon a system of social institutions, but instead "values and institutions are mutually engendering, mutually reinforcing, mutually sustaining."[19] It is thus suggested that welfare economics should be interrelated with intellectual advancements in cultural anthropology, learning theory, psychoanalysis, individual and group field theory, political theory (as here in the discussion of "public choice theory"), and sociological theory in order to better reveal individual economic preferences in the form of the social welfare function.

---

[19] Ibid., p. 315.

part two

Public Sector Revenues

6

Fiscal Rationality Criteria

THE NEED FOR FISCAL RATIONALITY CRITERIA

The purpose of this chapter is to develop a broad framework within which the principles of public sector economics may be applied in an efficient manner to the four functional areas of economic activity. That is, the allocational, distributional, stabilization, and economic growth performance of the economy should be promoted in a rational manner through the constitution of the public sector budget. In order to accomplish these objectives the traditional *fiscal (tax) neutrality concept* is selected as the "starting point" of the analysis. Then, this orthodox principle of fiscal neutrality is broadened along several lines. The ultimate result is a *comprehensive* set of *fiscal rationality criteria.*

Because of the organizational plan of the book, these criteria necessarily will be applied "retroactively" to the five chapters already covered. These chapters were basically concerned with the *allocation* branch of public sector economics. The analytical precepts developed in these earlier chapters may now be further viewed in terms of their fiscal rationality content. For the other functional areas of public sector economics—*distribution, stabilization,* and *economic growth,* as well as for the additional analytical developments which are of an "allocational" nature, the criteria will be applied as the relevant concepts are developed throughout the remainder of the book.

THE TRADITIONAL FISCAL NEUTRALITY CONCEPT

As suggested above, the analytical development of a comprehensive set of fiscal rationality criteria will be initiated by means of a discussion of the traditional approach to *fiscal neutrality*. Historically, the neutrality principle has been defined in terms of the imposition of taxes in such a manner that they do not change private sector, allocational behavior. Hence, the orthodox interpretation of "fiscal" neutrality, which in effect is a concept of "tax" neutrality, suggests that a tax should neither alter the satisfaction-motivated behavior of consumers nor the profit-motivated behavior of businesses in the private sector of the economy. If such allocational effects do occur, *nonneutrality* is said to exist. In this context, *neutrality* is deemed desirable while its opposite, *nonneutrality*, is considered undesirable.

Similarly, the literature of public finance has often referred to "nonneutrality" or "noneutral effects" as constituting an *excess burden* or *distortion* resulting from a tax. That is, the tax is said to interfere with market decision-making of a consumptive or productive nature and thus to reduce both efficient resource allocation and aggregate real income in the society. The *reduction in real income* may be considered, according to this line of thought, the measure of the *excess burden*. This narrow interpretation of neutrality and nonneutrality is based, of course, upon the assumption that the initial, pretax, allocation of resources in the market is optimal. If such is the case, any alteration of private sector behavior would necessarily introduce allocative inefficiency.

The traditional fiscal neutrality concept thus concentrates upon resource allocation in an optimally-functioning private sector. This emphasis, along with the attention paid by orthodox public finance to "equity in the distribution of tax burdens," has caused Anglo-American public finance for many years to be extremely "asymmetrical" or "narrow" in scope.[1] Moreover, the focus of the traditional approach has been on the *tax* side of the budget rather than upon the entire budget inclusive of governmental expenditures. These restrictive qualities strongly suggest the need to develop a comprehensive set of fiscal rationality criteria to help guide public sector budgetary decisions in a more rational manner.

COMPREHENSIVE FISCAL RATIONALITY CRITERIA

The restrictiveness and asymmetry of the orthodox fiscal neutrality approach is in sharp contrast both to the various functional areas of

---

[1] Theoretical principles relating to the distribution of tax burdens are discussed, in detail, in Chapter 7.

economic activity which are influenced by budgetary decisions as well as to the symmetrical nature of the budget itself. Moreover, the unlikelihood of an optimally-functioning market sector should be acknowledged. The concept of "neutrality," in order to serve adequately as a fiscal rationality benchmark, must be treated in a comprehensive, symmetrical, and realistic fashion. Thus, it will be desirable to broaden the traditional neutrality approach into a set of fiscal rationality criteria which will recognize the following points:

1. The fact that nonneutralities may be either beneficial or harmful in a system already functioning at a "suboptimal" equilibrium.
2. The fact that governmental budgetary decisions may exert nonneutral effects in all of the functional areas of economic activity—allocation, distribution, stabilization, and economic growth.
3. The fact that all governmental revenue-gathering and expenditure activities—not just taxation—may exert nonneutral effects.
4. The fact that many levels and units of government make budgetary decisions, "each" of which exerts *separate* nonneutral effects, but "all" of which together exert *aggregate* nonneutral effects.

These relevant points may then be synthesized into the following set of fiscal rationality criteria:

✗ 1. The public sector may exert *nonneutral effects* (*nonneutralities*) in any functional area of economic activity—allocation, distribution, stabilization, or economic growth. Moreover, these nonneutralities may *not* be "harmful" or "negative" if the previously-existing allocational, distributional, stabilization, or economic growth equilibrium is nonoptimal (suboptimal). Rather, they may instead be "beneficial" or "positive."

2. Since governmentally-exerted nonneutralities may be beneficial in nature, rational public sector economic policy can be formulated to better achieve the various allocational, distributional, stabilization, and economic growth goals of the society. Such rational economic policy will deliberately attempt to create "positive nonneutralities." Public sector "economic policy" may take a variety of forms, of which one form is "fiscal" ("budget") policy.

3. Fiscal policy may be initiated from "any facet" of a governmental budget ranging from expenditure policies to the various forms of governmental revenue-gathering activities.

4. *All* levels and units of government in the public sector may exert allocational, distributional, stabilization, and economic growth nonneutralities on the private sector. Moreover, governments may exert *intergovernmental economic effects* on each other.

Public Sector Nonneutralities, both "Positive" and "Negative," Exist in All Functional Areas of Economic Activity

The narrow (orthodox) fiscal neutrality concept, which emphasizes "allocational" effects, is not comprehensive enough to serve as a general fiscal rationality benchmark. Instead, it must be recognized that the public sector may exert nonneutralities on *any* functional area of economic activity. Moreover, these nonneutral effects may be received "independently" within a particular functional area or they may pass "interdependently" among several functional areas, with the latter being the more common result. Thus, a "comprehensive" fiscal rationality concept should include the ability of governmental economic activities to exert allocational, distributional, stabilization, and economic growth effects in a "mixed," two sector, economic system. The overall relevance of this phenomenon will be described in the present chapter. However, more elaborate applications of the ability of the public sector to influence *all* functional areas of economic activity will be provided in the various parts of the book which deal primarily with each functional area.

A further important dimension to a comprehensive fiscal rationality approach is the appreciation of the fact that a "nonneutrality" may be either beneficial or harmful in terms of a particular economic goal. For example, if an initial *allocational* equilibrium is nonoptimal, a government-exerted nonneutrality may be just as likely to improve allocational efficiency by increasing real income as it is to lessen allocational efficiency through a reduction in real income. Similarly, the public sector may exert nonneutralities which either improve or make worse income and wealth *distribution* objectives, the performance of *stabilization* aggregates such as employment and price levels, and the rate of *economic growth*. Thus, it is important to observe that in a society already operating at "suboptimal" points in terms of the four functional goals, a nonneutrality could either improve or make worse fiscal rationality by moving the society "closer to" or "further away" from optimal performance points. Moreover, it was shown in Chapter 2 that a pure market economy cannot be expected to achieve an optimal resource allocation position. Similar proofs concerning *market failure* will be developed later in the book for the distribution, stabilization, and economic growth goals of society. Thus, given these potential conditions of "nonoptimality" ("suboptimality"), a nonneutrality may provide either beneficial—or harmful—results. This is true for nonneutral effects pertaining to a "specific" goal as well as to those which are "intergoal" in nature. A nonneutrality which moves society closer to an economic goal, or goals, will be designated a *positive nonneutrality*. On the other hand, a nonneutrality which causes society to move further away from the economic goal, or goals, will be termed a *negative nonneutrality*.

Public Sector Economic Policy Should Be Designed to Exert Positive Nonneutralities in All Functional Areas of Economic Activity

Government in a "mixed," two-sector, economic system will *inevitably* exert nonneutral effects in all functional branches of economic activity whether it does so in a "consciously rational" manner or not. Thus, it is only logical to expect that the government sector should organize its economic activities along rational lines, using established economic principles, so as to promote greater allocational, distributional, stabilization, and economic growth efficiency in the economy. That is, it should structure its economic policies so as to exert *positive nonneutral effects* in terms of these goals. Admittedly, specific goals of income redistribution, the rate of economic growth, and the like, tend to be controversial. Nonetheless, society does seem to establish certain priorities and consensuses of action in relationship to these goals. Hence, the concept of "positive nonneutral effects" carries a legitimate policy inference.

The public sector may use various *economic policy* "tools" or "instruments" to create positive nonneutralities. Mainly, these instruments may be placed into three primary categories: (1) *fiscal (budget) policy*, (2) *monetary* (money and credit) *policy*, and (3) a *direct regulatory or incomes policy*. Only the first of these tools—fiscal policy—is directly relevant to the subject matter of this book though, indeed, it should be recognized that the various major forms of policy may interact with each other in influencing economic objectives. Finally, it should be observed that the term "fiscal policy" may be applied appropriately to governmental budgetary policy directed toward *any* of the four functional economic goals. Nonetheless, popular usage of the term has often confined its meaning to *macroeconomic* stabilization and economic growth goals. The discussion below will avoid this narrow interpretation as it explores the ability of governmental budgetary policy to exert positive nonneutral effects on all functions of the economy.

Allocational Effects. The nonneutral effects on *resource allocation* of public sector budgetary actions may take several forms. For example, a tax or expenditure may distort the utility-maximizing behavior of a *consumer*. Or, in similar fashion, a budgetary action may change the profit-maximizing behavior of a *producer*. These are examples of "disaggregate" allocational effects. However, allocation patterns may also be changed by a governmental budgetary action in the sense of "aggregate" behavior. Thus, a tax or spending change may well move the society either closer to, or further from, the point of optimal intersector resource allocation and, in so doing, may either improve or worsen societal welfare.[2]

The "disaggregate" allocational effects of a budgetary change will now be discussed in greater detail. A tax, for example, may cause both a "substitution effect" and an "income effect." Through a *substitution effect,* the relative prices between two or more economic goods or resources are altered with a subsequent direct change in allocational patterns. Through an *income effect,* the tax will change the level of real income or real outlay available to a consumer or business and thus alter the quantity of goods or resources which may be purchased. In turn, such a change in real income may or may not yield a significant "secondary" allocational effect. In any event, allocational effects may result either directly or indirectly from a change in governmental tax policy. Once these changes occur, a different pattern of resource allocation would exist as compared to that which existed in the "prebudgetary change" equilibrium.

A selected example of such "disaggregate" reallocation is provided in Figure 6–1a. In this graph, the original price ratio between two economic goods, X and Y, purchased by Consumer A, is indicated by the slope of the budget lines AB. The consumer is maximizing his welfare at point a on indifference curve I^2. In equilibrium, he purchases OX_1 units of Good X. Then, assume that the price of Good X is increased by the imposition of an excise tax on the good. Meanwhile, no comparable tax is imposed on Good Y. The budget line thus shifts from AB to AB^1 as the relative prices of the two goods have changed and Consumer A finds a new equilibrium consumption position at point b on indifference curve I^1. Here he purchases OX_3 units of Good X following the imposition of the excise tax. The total allocational change resulting from the imposition of the tax is indicated by the quantity purchased differences between points a and b. Thus, quantity OX_1, minus OX_3 equals the *total effect* of the tax.

The *total effect,* however, is of two forms: a *substitution effect* and an *income effect.* These two effects may be discerned by the following analysis: as the price of Good X rises due to the tax, Consumer A suffers a diminishment in real income. This is shown by the fact that he consumes along the lower indifference curve I^1 instead of along the higher indifference curve I^2 prior to the tax. Now, let it be assumed that Consumer A is given a sufficient amount of money income to compensate him for the loss in real income resulting from the tax. This would allow him to remain on the higher indifference curve I^2. This may be

---

[2] See Chapters 1 and 4.

FIGURE 6–1

Selected Examples of Public Sector Allocational Nonneutrality:

a. "Disaggregate" Effects Exerted on an Individual Consumer

b. "Aggregate" Effects Exerted on Intersector Resource Allocation

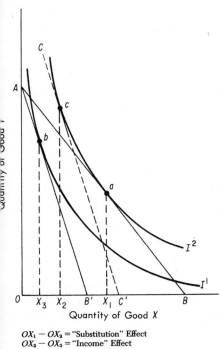

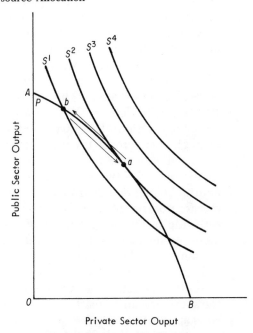

$OX_1 - OX_2 =$ "Substitution" Effect
$OX_2 - OX_3 =$ "Income" Effect

$a =$ Point of "Optimal" Intersector Allocation
$b =$ A Selected Point of "Suboptimal" Intersector Allocation

indicated graphically by placing a "fictitious" budget line tangent to the original (pretax) indifference curve I^2 with the "same slope" as the new price ratio curve AB^1. In Figure 6–1a, this is represented by the line CC^1 which is tangent to the original indifference curve I^2 at point c. The substitution effect from the tax is shown by the movement from the "original" equilibrium position a to the "fictitious" equilibrium position c, with both points "importantly" being on the original indifference curve I^2. Thus, quantity OX_1 minus OX_2 is equal to the *substitution effect*. It represents the change in the quantity demanded of Good X resulting from the change in its relative price, after compensating Consumer A for his reduction in real income. The *income effect*, in turn, is equal to quantity OX_2 minus quantity OX_3. It represents the change in the quantity demanded of Good X resulting from the change in real income alone. The *total effect*, of course, is equal to quantity OX_1 minus quantity OX_3. The imposition of an excise tax has thus caused an allocational nonneutrality which may be viewed from both "substitution effect" and "income effect" standpoints.

In Figure 6–1b, which is based on Figure 1–4 in Chapter 1, budgetary actions may cause the "aggregate" society to move either closer to or further away from the point of optimal intersector resource allocation at point *a*. Thus, if the society is at point *b*, which is a point of suboptimal intersector allocation, "rational" government tax or spending changes may move the society toward point *a*. Conversely, "irrational" budgetary policy may move the society away from point *a*.

Distributional Effects. The state of *real income* and *wealth distribution* in the private sector may also be influenced by a governmental budgetary action. The direct transfer of funds between individuals through a system of taxes and transfer payments, for example, may "redistribute" *real income* among the members of the society via a redistribution of purchasing power.[3] This would be viewed as a "nonneutral" effect of a distributional nature. However, tax-transfer activities are not the sole means of redistributing real income. The expenditure side of the budget through the process of allocating public and quasi-public goods to the members of the society can also significantly influence the distribution of real income in the society.

Figure 6–2, using a Lorenz curve approach, demonstrates how public sector budgetary behavior can influence both real income flows, in the short run, and wealth accumulation in the long run. In this particular example, the budget is used to render the distribution of real income more equal, though clearly fiscal behavior could redistribute real income in the direction of a greater degree of inequality.

Stabilization Effects. Public sector revenue-gathering and spending can also exert *stabilization nonneutralities.* That is, governmental tax and expenditure policy may influence the level of labor employment and real capital (plant and equipment) utilization. Moreover, it may affect the level of both product and input prices in the economy. In addition, the performance of the economy in the world of "international economics," as evidenced by the nation's "balance of international payments," may be influenced by the public sector budget. Changes in governmental tax rates and expenditures, or changes in the level of a government budget, will tend to provide a variety of "multiplier effects" capable of influencing these various aspects of "aggregate economic performance."[4] Generally, expenditure increases and tax rate reductions exert an "expansionary" multiplier effect on aggregate demand while expenditure reductions and tax rate increases are "contractionary" in their multiplier effects. Moreover, an increase in budget

---

[3] "Transfer payments" will be defined more explicitly later in this chapter.

[4] See Part Four of the book for a detailed discussion of the ability of government budgets to influence aggregate economic performance.

FIGURE 6–2

Selected Example of Public Sector *Distribution* Nonneutrality: A Change in the *Distribution* of Real Income*

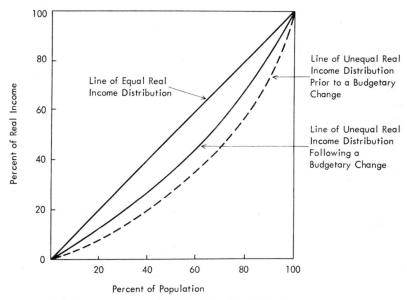

* See Table 21–1 for actual income distribution data for the United States.

size tends to be "expansionary" while a decrease tends to be "contractionary."[5]

Figure 6–3 may be used to demonstrate some of the stabilization effects resulting from public sector budgetary action. In this graph, Curve P is the production-possibility curve and Curves S^1–S^4 are the set of social indifference curves for the society. Point a reflects optimal intersector allocation, as discussed in Chapters 1 and 4, and in Figure 6–1b above. Importantly, the economy may be allocating between public and private goods at a point within the production-possibility curve P, such as Point b on social indifference curve S^1. Thus, rational governmental revenue-gathering and spending actions may move the aggregate performance level of the society toward full resource employment as represented by production along (at any point on) production-possibility curve P. Thus, a "positive" *nonneutral* effect of a "stabilization" nature would be the result of such action. Though not displayed graphically at this point, it should be clear to the reader that governmental budgetary actions, including the overall relationship between total revenues and expenditures, may exert a significant effect on *price levels* in the economy. The same may be said for *balance-of-payments* per-

[5] See the discussion of the "balanced budget multiplier" in Chapter 24.

FIGURE 6–3
Selected Example of Public Sector *Stabilization* Nonneutrality

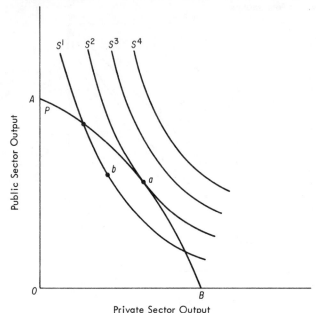

a = Point of Optimal Intersector Allocation and Full Resource (Labor and Capital) Employment.
    b = Point of Suboptimal Intersector Allocation and Underfull Resource Employment.

formance as it may be influenced by government taxes and spending policies.

Economic Growth Effects. Governmental budgetary policy may also affect the rate of *economic growth* in the society. This may be said to apply both to underdeveloped as well as to developed or mature economic systems. Specifically, the economic growth goal of an economy seeks to maintain, over a period of years, a "value judgment-determined" satisfactory rate of increase in real per capita output and income.

Figure 6–4 exhibits some aspects of the capability of public sector budgetary policy to exert *nonneutral* effects on the economic growth function. However, its point of reference is on the growth of "aggregate," not "per capita," output. In this graph, society production-possibility curve *P* reflects the aggregate production potential of the economy at a given time. Over a period of time, the resource base of the economy may be expanded so as to allow a greater production level along production-possibility curve P^1. A number of alternative revenue

FIGURE 6–4
Selected Example of Public Sector *Economic Growth*
Nonneutrality

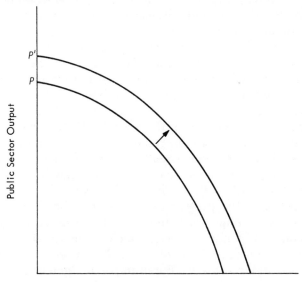

Private Sector Output

and expenditures techniques may be employed to achieve this positive nonneutral result. These will be discussed further in Part Four of the book. It is sifficient to conclude now, however, that the public sector may significantly influence the economic growth function through budgetary policy.

Intergoal Nonneutrality. It is essential to observe that governmental budgetary policy directed toward the attainment of a specific economic goal will often exert *nonneutral effects* on other public sector goals. These nonneutral effects may be termed *intergoal nonneutralities*. Fiscal policy directed toward a goal of income-wealth redistribution, for example, may either restrict or promote the achievement of the allocation, stabilization, and economic growth goals of the society. In the event of a restriction of a second goal, a *tradeoff* would be established between the two goals. In addition, conflicting "subgoals" may exist within a particular functional area or goal. Thus, full-employment stabilization policy may conflict with stabilization objectives of a price level or balance-of-payments nature. Furthermore, governmental budgetary policy may influence short-run performance and long-run economic growth through the particular *composition* of the revenue and expenditure flows. An investment credit tax subsidy for certain strategic growth industries, for example, may stimulate investment of the sort that will increase the rate of long-run economic growth as well as short-run aggregate demand in the economy. Also, federal expenditures in support of research may improve the efficiency of production functions in certain private industries and thus increase short-run aggregate output as well as promote economic growth.

Often, *intergoal nonneutralities* exist between the allocation and stabilization branches of economics. Two important examples follow: *First*, tax and expenditure policies directed toward full employment may harm the "economic incentives" of both businesses and consumers in the private sector. This occurred during the 1930s when deliberate federal fiscal policy programs of the Franklin D. Roosevelt New Deal administration were initiated to remove the depression conditions of the economy. Today, the widespread acceptance of federal fiscal policy directed toward stabilization and economic growth goals tends to reduce this disincentive effect. Thus, most incentive effects from federal fiscal policy at the present time appear to be of the "positive" variety which encourage consumption and investment. *Second*, governmental tax and spending policies which "directly" affect the allocative behavior of producers will often yield "indirect" or "secondary" aggregate performance results. For example, budgetary policies which distort or alter the choice between work effort and leisure, or those policies which directly influence resource combinations in the productive process, will tend to exert primary reallocation results which are followed by subsequent aggregate performance results in the form of a change in the *level of real income* in the society. If the level of real income has been diminished, it may be said that "inefficiencies" have been introduced into the private sector production process by the governmental budgetary actions.

The existence of *intergoal nonneutrality* makes it necessary for public sector policy makers to consider the interrelated allocational, distributional, stabilization, and economic growth effects which are likely to result from a given tax or expenditure action. "Social priorities" must be established and "social choices" must be made between various possible budgetary actions. These social choices must reflect the relative emphasis placed upon the various economic goals by the society. In other words, a comprehensive system of priorities is required for the application of rational fiscal behavior. In addition, the *relationship* between the selection of societal economic goals through "value judgments," on the one hand, and the "positive" budgetary policies enacted to help achieve these goals, on the other hand, must be recognized. In other words, it is necessary to discern between the role played by "value judgments" and that played by the "methodology" of public sector economics. Table 6–1 demonstrates some of the critical areas of

TABLE 6–1
Some Critical "Social Choice" Areas of Public Sector Economics

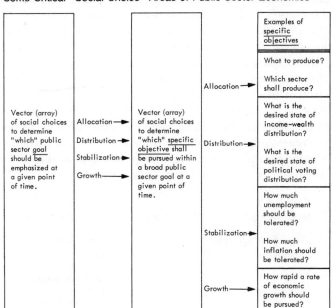

"social choice" which face public sector decision makers. These include both major goals, such as represented by the four functional areas of economics, and subgoals within the major goal areas.

Public Sector Fiscal Policy Should Be Symmetrically Approached since Any Type of Governmental Expenditure or Revenue-Gathering Activity May Exert Nonneutralities

A symmetrical concept of public sector budgeting must equally emphasize both governmental expenditures and revenues in order to assess the full economic effects of governmental budgetary activity. Table 6–2 lists the major types of public sector revenues and expenditures. These will be discussed below including the "primary purposes" for which spending and revenue decisions are made.

Governmental Expenditures. Public sector *expenditures* may be divided into two main categories known as "exhaustive" and "nonexhaustive" (transfer) expenditures. An *exhaustive* expenditure is one whose initial effect is "allocational" in nature since it directly absorbs resources into governmental production. Such resources, assuming full employment in the economy, would be absorbed from alternative allocational uses elsewhere in the economy.[6] On the other hand, a *nonexhaustive* government expenditure is one whose initial effect is upon the distribution of income" in the society. It does not directly absorb resources. A payment is received by an individual without an exchange of productive resources for that payment. It is merely a "transfer" of tax funds between the taxpayers of a society. In fact, nonexhaustive or transfer expenditures are sometimes referred to as *negative taxes*. In fact, this is the source of the term "negative income tax"—a concept discussed later in this book. Finally, it should be observed that even though a change in income distribution cannot "directly" change resource allocation, it is nonetheless capable of "indirectly" exerting such a change once the incremental purchasing power made available through the transfer payment is put into the spending stream.

TABLE 6–2
Major Categories of Public Sector Expenditures and Revenues

Expenditures	*Revenues*
Exhaustive	Tax
	1. General
	2. Earmarked
Nonexhaustive (Transfer)	Nontax
	1. User-Price
	2. Administrative
	3. Debt

Governmental Revenues.   Public sector revenues are of the "tax" and "nontax" varieties. Typically, *taxes* are the primary source of governmental revenues, though the proportion of tax revenues to total governmental revenues varies considerably between levels and units of government and between nations, including even those nations with comparable federal political systems. A *tax* may be defined as a "compulsory" contribution exacted from an individual for the purpose of meeting some governmentally-established goal or goals. Tax burdens are ultimately borne by individuals even though taxes may be formally paid by business entities which are owned by individuals. Most taxes go into the *general* treasury fund of a unit of government. The federal personal and corporation income taxes, for example, accrue to the general treasury fund of the federal government. Some taxes, however, are *earmarked* for a specific purpose and thus go into a "separate" budget or trust fund. The federal excise tax on gasoline, which enters the special Interstate Highway Trust Fund, is an example of this kind of tax. An earmarked tax is often tied to a particular type of private sector expenditure which correlates with the payment of the tax. The pay-

---

[6] The discussion of Figure 1–4 in Chapter 1 is closely related to the present discussion.

ment of a gasoline tax into a road construction and maintenance fund thus involves an approximate quid pro quo relationship between the nature of the tax and the ultimate use of the tax revenues.[7]

Most taxes serve more than one purpose or goal, though a single purpose typically is dominant. All taxes, of course, "by their very nature" provide revenues for the unit of government which imposes the tax. In most instances, this is the primary motive for the existence of the tax. In some instances, however, a tax may exist primarily, or at least very importantly, for regulatory purposes. Taxes may be regulatory in either a "microeconomic" or in a "macroeconomic" sense. In the former case, for example, they may influence the consumption of a particular good or the utilization of a particular productive resource. In this context, an excise tax on alcoholic beverages or tobacco products and a severance tax imposed on natural resource usage are typical.[8] A regulatory tax designed to "discourage" the consumption of a particular item, such as that on alcoholic beverages or tobacco products, is termed a "sumptuary" tax. An important additional regulatory purpose of taxation is represented by the example of the federal personal (individual) income tax which is adaptable to macroeconomic fiscal policy directed toward stabilization and economic growth goals.

Nontax revenues may take the following forms of
(1)   user prices (user charges),
(2)   administrative revenues, or
(3)   the governmental borrowing of funds (debt).

The collection of *user prices*, also known as "commercial revenues," involves the sale of economic goods or resources by government for a specific charge or price. The government may both produce and sell the good, such as state toll road facilities, or it may merely sell a privately-produced good as in the case of state liquor store monopolies. "User prices" differ from "earmarked taxes" in that the former represent the outright sale of an economic good or resource by a unit of government while the latter usually represent the application of a tax to the sale of an economic good or resource by the market sector of the economy.

In user pricing, the "exclusion principle" is applied in a manner comparable to its application in the acquisition of private sector output. Examples of governmental user charges include the payments made for postal service, highway and bridge tolls, tuition to public educa-

---

[7] Conceivably, an earmarked tax could be placed in a trust fund, the use of which is *not* correlated meaningfully with the nature of the tax. However, this is not the manner in which earmarked taxes have been traditionally used in the United States.

[8] The characteristics of different taxes, including excise and severance taxes, are discussed in detail later in this section of the book.

tional establishments, buying water from a municipal water utility, the purchase of liquor from a state-owned liquor store, and the purchase of a state government lottery ticket. The goods to which user prices are applied under the commercial principle of government enterprise are usually characterized by specific "private" benefits to the individual purchaser and, at times, also by significant "collective consumption" or "externalities," either of a benefit or cost variety. Moreover, they are ordinarily not "by-products" of a general administrative function of government. In most instances, those goods subject to user prices could be provided by either the public or private sectors of the economy, though not necessarily with equal economic efficiency.

On the other hand, those allocative actions which are basically concerned with the general administrative functions of government usually involve the use of *administrative revenues*. In a broad sense, the buyer has free choice concerning payment of the various types of administrative revenues to government. Hence, the exclusion principle generally applies to such fiscal behavior. Often, however, there is not a direct or close correlation between the payment of an administrative revenue and the receipt of a specific economic good by the purchaser. Indeed, government units collecting such revenues sometimes attempt to tie them to broad functional categories of expenditure. The relationship, however, is often loose. As a result, administrative revenues should not be confused with the much more precise *quid pro quo* relationships which ordinarily exist in the cases of both earmarked taxes and user prices. Administrative revenues include such revenue sources as licenses, permits, (some) fees, fines, forfeitures, escheats, and special assessments.

A final primary source of governmental revenue is the ability of the public sector to create *debt*. As shall be observed in Chapter 27, the public sector is unique in several important ways, as opposed to the private sector, in its ability to create and maintain debt. Government debt, of course, is created when the current nondebt revenues of a government unit are less than its current expenditures. That is, debt is created to fill the residual deficit through the borrowing of funds by the public sector.

Tax Base-Rate Relationships. Returning now to a more detailed discussion of taxation, it may be observed that taxes may be imposed on any of four primary "tax bases." These tax bases consist of *income, wealth, transactions,* and *people.* "Income" represents a flow of current earnings in such forms as wages, salaries, profits, rents, royalties, and interest payments. "Wealth" refers to a stock of assets, both real (such as land) and intangible (such as a bond), upon which a tax may be imposed. "Transactions" refer to the sale of goods and resources in the market. "People" may serve as the direct object of taxation if a tax is imposed on a person himself rather than on that person's income, wealth, or market purchase.

The most common usage of *income* as a tax base in the United States is found in the imposition of personal (individual) and corporation income taxes. *Wealth* taxes in prominent use include property, death, and gift taxes.[9] *Transactions* taxes in substantial use by the American public sector include the general retail sales tax imposed on a broad base of purchases as well as a variety of narrowbased excise taxes imposed on particular items of purchases. *Personal* taxes imposed on people as such, as characterized by a "lump-sum tax," are not common in the United States. Table 6–3 summarizes the primary tax bases and the particular

TABLE 6–3
Primary Tax Base Alternatives and Types of Taxes

Tax Base	Major Types of Taxes Applied to Base	
Income	1.	Personal (Individual) Income Tax
	2.	Corporation Income Tax
Wealth	1.	Property Tax
	2.	Death (Estate, Inheritance) Taxes
	3.	Gift Tax
	4.	Net Wealth Tax
Transactions	1.	General Retail Sales Tax
(Sales, Expenditures)	2.	Value-Added Tax
	3.	Turnover Tax
	4.	Excise Tax
	5.	Severance Tax
People	1.	Lump-Sum (Head, Capitation, Per Capita) Tax

taxes which are aligned to each tax base. These taxes will be described in detail in subsequent chapters.

As observed above, the *tax base* is that object to which the tax rate is applied. The *tax rate,* in turn, is the amount of tax applied per unit of tax base. Thus, the tax base multiplied by the tax rate equals the *tax yield* to the government. The yield to the government is the same as the *tax burden* to the taxpayer, except for certain differentials resulting from tax administration costs to the government and tax compliance costs to the taxpayer. The *technical* relationship between the size of the base and the rate of any particular tax would result in a tax being

---

[9] Some economists prefer to classify "death" and "gift" taxes under the *transactions* category since they involve the "transfer" of wealth. However, since a transfer of this variety is not a "market transaction" in a buying and selling sense, the author prefers to classify them in this book as *wealth* taxes.

termed *progressive* if the tax rate increases as the tax base grows larger. To the contrary, a tax rate which decreases as the size of the tax base increases is *regressive* in its technical structure while a tax with a constant rate structure as the tax base grows larger may be termed *proportional* (proportionate). It will be very important to distinguish between the terms "progressive," "regressive," and "proportional" used here in the technical sense of the statutory (legal) design of the tax, and their usage later in the book in the sense of equity in *the distribution of tax burdens*. Figure 6–5 graphically demonstrates these tax base-rate relationships in technical terms.

FIGURE 6–5
Various Tax Base-Rate Structures in "Technical"* Terms

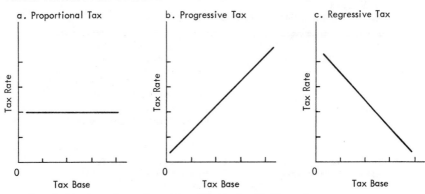

* *Not* in the "distributional equity" terms that will be introduced in Chapter 7.

The distinction between technically progressive (graduated), regressive, and proportional taxes may be viewed further in terms of *average* and *marginal* tax rates. The average tax rate is computed by dividing the *total* tax liability by the *total* tax base. The marginal tax rate is computed by dividing the *change* in total tax liability by the *change* in total tax base. If the tax structure is *proportional*, in technical terms, the marginal rate must be equal to the average rate as the tax base increases in size. If the tax structure is *progressive*, the marginal rate must be higher than the average rate as the tax base increases. If the tax structure is *regressive*, the marginal rate must be less than the average rate as the tax base increases. Table 6–4 demonstrates these relationships.

The Revenue Productivity of Taxes—the Concept of Income Elasticity.
As observed above, the primary purpose of taxation is to provide revenues to the public sector for the support of its economic activities. The revenue-raising capacity of a tax, or of an entire tax system, is thus basically important to the functioning of the public sector. Yet, different

types of taxes (See Table 6–3) may vary significantly in their revenue-raising capabilities. This is especially important when the dimension of *time* is added to the analysis. "Time" is linked to the "revenue productivity" of taxes primarily through the concept of the *income elasticity of a tax* (or *tax system*).[10] Symbolically, this concept may be designated Y_ϵ.

Thus, if the "revenue yield" (RY) from a tax is viewed as a function of "income" (Y), the rate of change overtime in RY, divided by the rate of change over time in Y, will yield the *income elasticity* of the tax for

TABLE 6–4
An Example of the Relationship between Marginal and Average Tax Rates and *Proportional, Progressive,* and *Regressive* Tax Structures*

			Tax Rate (Percent)	
(1) *Rate Structure*	(2) *Tax Liability*	(3) *Tax Base*	(4) *Average* (2) ÷ (3)	(5) *Marginal* Δ (2) ÷ Δ (3)
Proportional	$1,000	$ 50,000	2	
	2,000	100,000	2	2
Progressive	1,000	50,000	2	
	4,000	100,000	4	6
Regressive	1,000	50,000	2	
	1,500	100,000	1.5	1

* "Proportional," "Progressive," and "Regressive" in technical (statutory, legal) terms, *not* in the distributional equity terms that will be introduced in Chapter 7.

the period of time in question. Table 6–5 demonstrates the basic "income elasticity" formula. Moreover, under the concept of income elasticity, the changing revenue yield must be "statistically isolated" as a function of changing income via an empirical study. That is, the revenue yield effects of other causal variables such as a change in the "tax rate structure" or in the "tax base" must be treated as constant or unchanging.

The *income elasticity* concept is particularly important to the fiscal well-being of governments since changing income brings with it varying degrees of changing governmental expenditure responsibilities. The critical question, and one which receives detailed analysis in Chapters 19 and 20, is whether revenue yields will grow in a manner com-

---

[10] The *income elasticity* concept is sometimes referred to as the *marginal propensity to tax,* especially when applied to "macroeconomic fiscal policy." See Chapter 24 in this regard.

mensurate with these growing expenditure obligations.[11] Figure 6–6 demonstrates three categories of revenue response to income change:

1. If the change in revenue yield (RY) from a tax or tax system occurs at a greater rate than changes in income (Y), the income elasticity of the tax (or tax system) of a government is said to be *elastic* ($Ye > 1$). For example, a 1 percent change in income might induce a 1.1 percent change in revenue yield.

2. If the change in revenue yield (RY) occurs at the same rate as changes in income (Y), the income elasticity of the tax (or tax system) of a government is said to be *unitary* ($Ye = 1$). For example, a 1 percent change in income might induce an equivalent 1 percent change in revenue yield.

3. If the change in revenue yield (RY) occurs at a lesser rate than changes in income (Y), the income elasticity of the tax (or tax system) of a government is said to be *inelastic* ($Ye < 1$). For example, a 1 percent change in income might induce a 0.9 percent change in revenue yield.

TABLE 6–5
The Income Elasticity of a Tax or Tax System

$$Ye = \frac{\frac{\Delta RY}{RY_0}}{\frac{\Delta Y}{Y_0}}$$

$\Delta RY =$ Change in *revenue yield* between time *"0"* and time *"1"*
$RY_0 =$ *Revenue yield* at time *"0"*
$\Delta Y =$ Change in *income* between time *"0"* and time *"1"*
$Y_0 =$ *Income* at time *"0"*

A close relationship exists between the "technical" nature of a particular tax or tax system and its resulting income elasticity. Generally, a technically-*progressive* tax yields *elastic* results, a technically-*proportional* tax structure provides results near *unitary,* and a technically-*regressive* tax *inelastic* results. The reason for this phenomenon is obvious, that is, as the tax base increases, taxpayers move into higher tax rate brackets under a technically-*progressive* tax, thus yielding increasingly greater revenues to government. The opposite occurs under a technically-*regressive* tax with a *proportional* tax yielding intermediate results.

Under an *income* tax, the tax base "immediately" and "directly" increases as income increases since "income" itself is the independent variable in the income elasticity formula. The association is "less" immediate and direct with *wealth* taxes, such as property and death taxes,

---

[11] The changes in "income" over time may be viewed, if desired, within the framework of the "political jurisdiction" in question, that is, "national income" for the *federal* government, "state income" for *state* governments, and so on.

FIGURE 6–6
Various Categories of Income Elasticity of a Tax or Tax System

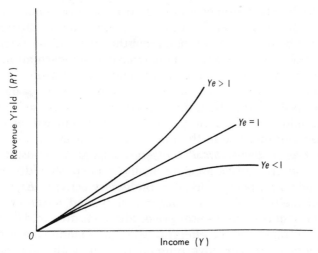

and with *transactions* taxes of the sales tax variety. Nonetheless, increasing short-run income flows do lead to a greater long-run accumulation of wealth or assets, but admittedly there is a time-lag present here which is absent with the income tax. Also, growing income induces greater expenditures or transactions, but with some delay as well as with a saving leakage from income. Moreover, some sales taxes are imposed on goods of an "income inelastic" nature whose purchases would be nearly as substantial out of lower income as higher income. Finally, a tax utilizing a *personal* base, such as the lump-sum tax, would tend to yield "no revenue response" to increasing income as it provides no linkage between the tax base and income. In other words, the income elasticity of a lump-sum tax would tend to be zero ($Ye = 0$).

Selecting Among Alternative Tax Sources. It is important in terms of the revenue productivity of a tax, as well as in reference to its overall economic effects, to consider the fact that several "alternative tax sources" are ordinarily available at any given time to a unit of government. Thus, the public sector possesses an option to use one or another tax source, or a combination of sources, to varying degrees. In this sense, it is necessary to define the *capacity* of a given tax. A rational government would first use the tax with the lowest marginal social costs.[12] When this tax reaches a certain level of revenue, however, further utilization of the tax may cause it to have marginal social costs "greater"

---

[12] Social costs, in this context, refer essentially to the opportunities foregone in private sector consumption due to the payment of taxes.

than those which would result from another tax. At this point, it would be said that the first tax has "reached its capacity."[13] Additional revenues should then be raised by a second tax until its marginal social costs become greater than those for a third tax, and so on, as alternative tax sources are used in an efficient manner at the "margin" in the provision of tax revenues to government. Policymakers can learn an important lesson from such analysis: "Thus, an income tax may seem to be much better than, say, an excise on sugar, but an increase in an income tax is not necessarily 'better' than the imposition of that excise."[14] In other words, the addition of a new tax to the tax system will at times be preferable to an increase in the rate of a present tax.[15]

The Need for a "Symmetrical" Budgetary Approach. Thus, it may be said that a comprehensive fiscal rationality concept should "symmetrically" include *all* aspects of fiscal or budgetary activity. *Expenditures*, whether of the exhaustive or transfer variety, and *revenues*, whether of the tax or nontax variety—user price, administrative, and debt—"all" exert nonneutral economic effects in the four functional areas of economic activity. Moreover, governmental revenue-gathering and spending activities interact importantly with each other. The following discussion, which focuses on the *distribution* function of economics, provides significant evidence of this fact. Taxes, which are the primary source of public sector revenues, impose "burdens" on those who ultimately pay them. They involve "compulsory" contributions to government with the "burdens" taking the form of the foregone private sector purchasing power. On the other hand, governmental *exhaustive* expenditures provide economic goods which yield "benefits" to those who consume them. Hence, the *real income* enjoyed by each resident of a political jurisdiction must necessarily reflect the pattern by which these burdens and benefits are distributed among the residents.

The term *incidence* is applied to mean the "ultimate" or "final" resting place of a tax burden or of an expenditure benefit, that is, the distribution of the final burdens and benefits among the residents of the political jurisdiction. Importantly, the locus of an "initial" tax burden, know as the point of *tax impact*, may be different from the point of "ultimate" *tax incidence*. This involves the complex concept of *tax shifting*, a topic which will be analyzed in detail in Chapter 8. In that

---

[13] See Amotz Morag, *On Taxes and Inflation* (New York: Random House, Inc. 1965) pp. 8–9.

[14] Ibid.

[15] It is sometimes argued that all taxes are ultimately paid out of "income." If this argument is accepted, then the concept of "taxable capacity" is meaningful only in terms of income. This point is related to the discussion of the *ability-to-pay principle* of tax burden equity, to be presented in the next chapter.

chapter, the symmetrical and general equilibrium nature of *budgetary incidence* can be fully more appreciated.

The Various Governments Comprising the Public Sector Will Exert Intergovernmental Nonneutralities on Each Other as well as on the Economy as a Whole

The existence of three levels and more than 78,000 units of government in the political structure of the American federation creates a situation of both diversified influence on the private sector and of substantial economic interdependence between the various levels and units of government within the public sector. Importantly, the four goals of an economic system will be influenced, for better or for worse, by the nature of this interdependence. That is, aggregate societal preferences for a goal, or goals, may be either "better achieved," or "thwarted," depending upon whether the various levels and units of government reinforce or neutralize each other's efforts to meet the preferences of the society.

These intergovernmental fiscal nonneutralities assume two dimensions.[16] First, intergovernmental budgetary relationships exist between levels of government in a federation. This may be referred to as *vertical intergovernmental fiscal relations.* The fiscal interaction between the federal and state or between the state and local levels of government in the United States exemplifies this dimension of the concept.[17] For example, a partial (80 percent) credit against federal estate tax liability for death taxes paid to the states, enacted by Congress in 1926, stimulated the state level of government to substantially use death taxation. Second, the interrelationship between different segments of government can take the form of fiscal interaction between different units of government at the same level. This may be termed *horizontal intergovernmental fiscal relations.* This can occur, of course, only at the state and local levels of government since only one unit of government exists at the federal level. Thus, the influence of the budgetary actions of one state on other states, or of the actions of one municipality on other municipalities, exemplify this dimension of intergovernmental fiscal behavior. Moreover, some intergovernmental fiscal relationships are characterized by both *vertical* and *horizontal* interaction.

Rational intergovernmental fiscal policy should take into account whether the budgetary action in question will promote or retard the

---

[16] Intergovernmental fiscal relationships in a federal system, with special reference to the United States are discussed, in detail, in Chapters 19 and 20.

[17] It should be noted, however, that the local level of government is not "sovereign," but instead receives its right to exist from the "sovereign" state level of government.

collective goals of the society. Indeed, a comprehensive fiscal rationality concept must consider the actions of the "aggregate public sector" in the context of *intergovernmental nonneutralities*.

A SUMMARY OF THE COMPREHENSIVE FISCAL RATIONALITY CRITERIA

Fiscal rationality criteria should be "symmetrical" and "comprehensive" in nature if they are to provide *efficiency* guidelines for all aspects of public sector economic activity. The fiscal rationality criteria developed above meet these requirements, unlike the orthodox fiscal (tax) neutrality benchmark which emphasizes tax distortion in the allocation branch. A desirable fiscal rationality approach should observe that a nonneutrality exerted by the budgetary action of government may be either positive or negative in its influence depending upon whether it moves the society closer to or further from an optimal goal. Moreover, it should consider all functional areas of economic activity—allocation, distribution, stabilization, and economic growth—and the goals set by society in terms of these functions. In addition, it should include all revenue gathering and expenditure activities of government. Also, the interaction between the budgetary policies of different levels and units of government is a necessary consideration in a comprehensive fiscal rationality approach especially in a decentralized federation like the United States.

Finally, the reader should recognize that the comprehensive fiscal rationality criteria do not in themselves prescribe explicit techniques to achieve economic goals. Instead, these techniques are developed in the analysis of each particular branch of public sector economics. For example, in the early chapters of the book important principles relating to optimal intersector resource allocation have been developed. In subsequent chapters, many additional analytical tools will be developed including the principles of tax burden distribution as well as the various "budgetary multipliers" which pertain to the economic stabilization and economic growth goals. Thus, it may be said that the *comprehensive fiscal rationality criteria* provide an overall framework within which the specific techniques directed toward particular functional goals may be applied.

7

Principles of Distributional Equity in Taxation

Several hundred years of attention have been devoted in public sector economics (public finance) to the importance of distributing tax burdens equitably among taxpayers. The impressive list of "interested economists" includes names such as Smith, Locke, Petty, Ricardo, Mill, Seligman, Wagner, Edgeworth, and Pigou. In fact, equity in taxation has been an obsession of public sector economics for many years. Unfortunately, this "asymmetrical" emphasis on the *tax* side of the fisc (budget) has led to an underemphasis on the ability of *governmental* expenditures to influence the distribution of real income as well as other functional areas of economic activity. Moreover, the determination of a given "tax burden distribution" rests largely outside the framework of economic analysis and, instead, depends largely upon noneconomic value judgments. This is true because economics itself is unable to provide a "substantive" benchmark for an *optimal* state of income and wealth distribution. However, it can provide a "methodological" benchmark for the attainment of any given *value judgment-selected* state of income and wealth distribution.

Hence, noneconomic value judgments, in the form of a collective consensus, must determine the substantive nature of market and political voting distribution, and thus of real income and wealth distribution, in the American economy. Accordingly, American society as well as other Western societies have adopted "operational systems" which, in essence, advocate specific tax equity principles as part of their fiscal institutions. These principles have helped to guide the design of Western tax structures. However, they do so largely in the sense of distributing tax burdens at the ultimate point of *tax incidence*, not in the initial sense of the point of *tax impact*.[1] An analysis of these various tax equity principles, including those norms most in use in the United States, constitutes the primary subject matter of this chapter.

THE PRINCIPLE OF ABSOLUTE EQUITY

A very strict interpretation of equity in the distribution of tax burdens would entail application of the principle of *absolute equality*. The statistical computation of individual tax burdens would be very simple in this case since the total spending of the government unit is merely divided by the number of taxpaying units, the resulting quotient being the tax liability of each taxpaying unit. Under this approach, each unit would pay an equal absolute amount of tax.

Suppose, for example, that spending by the federal government is defined, for purposes of this approach, as "that amount of expenditure which appears in the official budget for a particular fiscal year." Then, suppose that taxpaying units are defined in terms of "family" and "unmarried adult" spending units. If the expenditures in the total budget amount to $300 billion, and the number of spending (taxpaying) units is 100 million, the resulting quotient of $3,000 constitutes the tax liability per spending (taxpaying) unit. Importantly, this approach completely ignores the "differential abilities" of the respective units to pay taxes, as determined by such factors as income and wealth differences among the units. It is conceivable, for example, that the income of the spending unit may not even equal the amount of tax liability.

A specific application of the principle of "absolute equity" in taxation would occur in the hypothetical case of a tax system consisting totally of *lump-sum* (per capita, head) tax revenues.[2] In this event, though individual circumstances may vary as to income and wealth, taxpayers are identical in the sense that each individual is a single human being and each pays an equal amount of tax. American society, of course, has rejected in its operational establishment of a public sector tax structure this principle of absolute equity. Accordingly, a universal lump-sum tax has been rejected along with the absolute equity approach.

MODIFIED EQUITY PRINCIPLES

Since the absolute equity approach is viewed as "too extreme" by society and thus "undesirable," it is necessary to seek a *modified ap-*

---

[1] See the discussion of the distinction between *tax impact* and *tax incidence* in the previous chapter, and in the following chapter.

[2] This type of tax was discussed in the previous chapter and will be discussed further in Chapter 14.

proach to tax equity. Two specific modified equity principles have been developed theoretically and applied institutionally in the public sectors of Western nations: These are the *ability-to-pay* and the *benefit* principles.

The Ability-to-Pay Principle

While the *absolute equity* principle determines equity on a "monetary contribution" basis, the ability-to-pay principle determines equity on a "sacrifice" basis. It suggests that all taxpayers should bear an "equal sacrifice" in the payment of taxes. As was observed in Chapter 4 concerning the marginal utility theory of public goods allocation, which is based on the ability-to-pay approach, the payment of taxes to the public sector constitutes a "sacrifice" to the taxpayer in terms of the alternative uses forgone of the tax monies in the private sector. Thus, the subjective *sacrifice of utility (satisfaction, welfare)* in the payment of taxes comprises the basic tenet of the ability-to-pay principle of tax equity. This basic tenet may be described more fully in terms of the concepts of "horizontal" and "vertical" tax equity.

According to the concept of *horizontal equity* in taxation, "equals should be treated equally." According to the concept of *vertical equity* in taxation, "unequals should be treated unequally." Thus, horizontal equity suggests that individuals with the same amount of taxpaying ability should bear equal tax burdens. Vertical equity, on the other hand, suggests that persons of differential taxpaying circumstances or abilities should pay different amounts of tax. The definition of "taxpaying ability," of course, is highly significant to the application of these concepts. Yet, positive economics cannot provide an explicit definition of "taxpaying ability." Instead, noneconomic value judgments, collectively undertaken in a distributional sense by the society, must be relied upon to provide a benchmark for judging the ability to pay taxes. Anglo-American society has generally selected *income differences* between taxpayers as the primary indicator of ability to pay though, to a lesser extent, *wealth differentials* have also been used as a major benchmark.

The ability-to-pay approach may be viewed in terms of three sacrifice theories. These are the (1) equal absolute sacrifice theory, (2) equal proportional sacrifice theory, and (3) equal marginal sacrifice (minimum aggregate sacrifice) theory.[3] Each of these theories defines "sacrifice" in terms of "consumption disutility," that is, the pleasure foregone in alternative private sector uses due to the payment of taxes.

The *equal absolute sacrifice* approach would require that a tax imposed on a higher-income individual cause him an amount of disutility

---

[3] For an excellent discussion of these theories, see Richard A. Musgrave, *The Theory of Public Finance* (New York: McGraw-Hill, 1959), Chapter 5.

equal to that borne by a lower-income taxpayer. For example, the tax might be designed, within the "constraint" of the amount of revenue required by the government from the tax, to cause 10 units of disutility to all taxpayers.

The *equal proportional sacrifice* approach, on the other hand, suggests that a tax should cause each individual to give up the same percentage of his total utility (which "foregone utility" is synonymous to "disutility"). For example, if Taxpayer *A*'s higher income would allow him 200 units of consumptive utility while Taxpayer *B*'s lower income would allow him only 100 units of utility, the higher-income taxpayer should suffer 20 units of disutility (20/200) if Taxpayer *B* bears 10 units of disutility (10/100).

The *equal marginal sacrifice* (*minimum aggregate sacrifice*) approach suggests that each taxpayer bear an equal marginal decrease in the utility of his income from the payment of a tax. Thus, if the marginal tax dollar paid by Taxpayer *A* causes him 5 units of disutility while that paid by Taxpayer *B* renders him 15 units of disutility, Taxpayer *A* should pay more taxes and Taxpayer *B* should pay less taxes until their marginal disutilities are equal. This theory, unlike the equal absolute sacrifice and equal proportional sacrifice theories, is "aggregate" rather than "individual" in scope since it seeks to minimize the combined sacrifices from taxation of all taxpayers in the political jurisdiction. It would cause government revenues to be collected first from the highest income individuals and, then, from successively lower income groups as additional revenues are required. This would result ultimately in after-tax disposable income being equalized for all taxpayers if government revenue requirements were sufficiently large that all income brackets except the lowest were taxed.

The equal marginal sacrifice (minimum aggregate sacrifice) theory suggests a highly progressive rate structure. In fact, it would result in the elimination of all high incomes through taxation if revenue requirements were sufficiently large. In effect, it applies a marginal tax rate of 100 percent to the highest income group for that income differential which separates it from the next highest group, and so on through successively lower income brackets. As a theory, it constitutes the "other extreme" from the absolute equity theory discussed above.

Table 7–1 provides a comparison of the absolute equity and equal marginal sacrifice theoretical "extremes" as well as the "intermediate" theoretical approaches represented by the equal absolute sacrifice and equal proportional sacrifice theories. In addition, it includes the "benefit" principle alternative to the "ability-to-pay" approach to tax equity, which principle will be discussed later in the chapter.

Implications for Progressive Taxation. The three sacrifice approaches to the ability-to-pay principle, when the following assumptions are ac-

TABLE 7-1

Continuum of the Major Theoretical Approaches to "Equity" in the Distribution of Tax Burdens

	The Ability-to-Pay Approach (Equity in Terms of "Sacrifice")		
Absolute Equity* (Equality in Terms of "Equal Monetary Contribution")	Equal Absolute Sacrifice†	Equal Proportional Sacrifice‡	Equal Marginal Sacrifice (Minimum Aggregate Sacrifice)§

← ─── →

	Modified Equity Principles Based on the Concepts of Vertical and Horizontal Equity

	The Benefit Approach‖ (Based on "Market Principles")

Characteristics

* Absolute equity—Everyone pays an equal monetary amount of tax.
† Equal absolute sacrifice—Everyone bears an equal absolute amount of disutility from paying taxes.
‡ Equal proportional sacrifice—Everyone sacrifices the same proportion of his total utility in paying taxes.
§ Equal marginal sacrifice (minimum aggregate sacrifice)—Everyone suffers the same marginal disutility in paying taxes.
‖ Benefit—Applies market criteria to the public sector, but is essentially applicable only where the "exclusion principle" applies to economic goods.

cepted, may be used to suggest the desirability of a *progressive income tax* system of taxation. These assumptions are: (1) it is possible to compare "consumptive utilities" and "taxation disutilities" among taxpayers, (2) the utilities of individuals are equal within a particular income level, and (3) the marginal utility of income diminishes at "an increasing rate" as income increases. These are very strict assumptions. In fact, they run into a quantitative measurement roadblock since utility cannot be measured in cardinal (absolute) measurement terms. Thus, "progressive taxation," as implemented into practice, must rest on a collective consensus or value judgment justification rather than on an empirically provable economic fact.

The ability-to-pay concept, given the above assumptions, implies that the ability to make tax payments increases more than proportionately with increases in income because the marginal utility of income declines at an increasing rate as income becomes greater. Hence, it is argued that, in order to maintain equal sacrifices among taxpayers of differential incomes, the marginal rate of taxation must increase as the income base increases. For example, the last or marginal dollar of income to a man with a $50,000 annual income is said to provide lower marginal utility to him than the last dollar of income earned by the $5,000 per year income individual (other considerations such as family size being constant between the two individuals).

This analysis attempts to draw an analogy between additional income, which may be used for a variety of purposes including both consumption and saving, and the additional consumption of a particular economic good such as food. Admittedly, the successive consumption of additional units of food within a reasonably-defined time period is likely, after a certain point in consumption, to provide "diminishing" marginal amounts of pleasure. However, when an individual's entire income is viewed, the analogy is weakened since the person may switch his consumption patterns to other economic goods with higher marginal amounts of pleasure, or he may derive considerable pleasure from saving the incremental income, or from investing it, or from the prestige which many societies place upon high income, large accumulations of wealth, and prestigious consumption. These represent several of many alternative uses of incremental higher income which may provide high marginal amounts of utility to the high-income taxpayer.

Nonetheless, since lower income individuals tend to allocate most or all of their incomes for the purchase of *necessity* goods, while higher income individuals spend a greater proportion of their incomes for *nonessential* or *luxury* goods, a reasonable "judgment" argument, though *not* an "empirically-provable" one, may be made for the acceptance of the "interpersonal comparisons of utility" concept and its application in the form of the "diminishing marginal utility of income." Despite the inability to achieve cardinal (absolute) measurement of utility, it may be argued that the *interpersonal comparisons of utility* and the *diminishing marginal utility of income* concepts should not be totally rejected. In reality, there must be such a thing as utility or pleasure from the receipt and use of income. Interdisciplinary observations in psychology and sociology indicate that the individuals of a given society tend to possess certain similarities of behavior. These behavioral similarities may well include diminishing "income utility" as income increases. Moreover, ordinal measurement, in a behavioral sense, may substitute in part for the failure of cardinal measurement.

In any event, Western societies have generally made collective value judgments in support of the ability-to-pay principle for application in operational terms.[4] *Income* is considered as the primary "indicator" of taxpaying ability and *progressive* (graduated) tax systems are generally advocated as the type which best serve the goal of "equity in the distribution of tax burdens."

The Benefit Principle

This tax equity principle is the primary alternative to the ability-to-pay theory. The benefit approach has the advantage of directly relating

---

[4] This does not suggest, of course, the complete absence of opposition to the application of the ability-to-pay principle in these societies.

the revenue and expenditure sides of the budget to each other.[5] It involves basically an approximation of market behavior in the allocative procedures of the public sector. That is, an individual voluntarily exchanges purchasing power in the form of taxes for the acquisition of government economic goods—a quid pro quo arrangement whereby the individual consumers pay directly for the economic goods of the public sector from which they derive satisfaction or profit.

"Equity" is suggested in this approach by neither the "monetary" nor a "sacrifice" benchmark, but instead by the dual facts that: (1) the exchange of purchasing power for the economic good is "voluntary," as it would be in the market sector, and (2) the "payments" are made in accordance with the "benefits" that are received. The benefits, in turn, may be priced either according to the governmental *cost* of providing the service or according to the *value* of the service to the purchaser, or by a combination of these considerations.

The institutional application of the benefit approach is greatly restricted, however, by the inherent nature of collective consumption. That is, public goods are characterized by the fact that the exclusion principle cannot be effectively applied to all, if any, of the benefits of the economic goods in question. Unless *compulsion* exists to require the consumers to pay, they will benefit by behavior as "free riders" to avoid payment. They will not pay "voluntarily." Thus, many public sector economic goods, not being subject to a market-type pricing mechanism, cannot be provided under the benefit approach. The benefit theory is thus not comprehensive enough in its "application" to serve as a general benchmark of equity in the distribution of tax burdens, though it does possess merit where it can be utilized due to its application of market principles to the public sector. It is generally applicable, of course, in those cases in which government applies the *user-price* or *earmarked tax* devices.

PROGRESSIVE, PROPORTIONAL, AND REGRESSIVE TAXES IN DISTRIBUTIONAL EQUITY TERMS

It has been observed above that the collective consensus of Western society has approved the underlying vertical and horizontal equity concepts and the progressive tax systems which implement these concepts. This does not mean, of course, that all existing taxes in the Western world are progressive in the ability-to-pay sense. Nonetheless, the predominant benchmark in academic and policy circles has historically

---

[5] This is essentially the same approach as used for the discussion of "optimal intersector resource allocation" under the designation of the *voluntary-exchange approach* in Chapter 4.

been one which uses *income differences* as the preferred indicator of the ability-to-pay taxes and *progressive taxation* as an equity reference point.

The societal consensus which allows the use of income as the indicator of taxpaying ability causes "equity" semantics to differ from "technical" semantics concerning the relationship of tax base and tax rate concepts. The latter meaning was developed in the previous chapter. Thus, it is necessary now to carefully develop the meaning of progressive, proportional, and regressive taxation in terms of *equity in the distribution of tax burdens.*

In a "technical" sense, it was noted that the *base* of a tax is that object to which the tax rate is applied. This object may be income, wealth, transactions, or people. Although these technical definitions of progressive, proportional, and regressive taxes are necessary for the purpose of understanding the detailed discussion of the different types of taxes throughout Part Two of this book, "distributional equity" considerations nonetheless require a somewhat different definition of these terms. Moreover, it should be recognized that the latter definitional approach serves today as the more popular usage in both academic and nonacademic circles. The significant *equity* interpretation of the terms derives, of course, from the overall acceptance by society of (1) the ability-to-pay principle of tax equity, and (2) interpersonal comparisons of utility along with the diminishing marginal utility of income concept. The acceptance of these concepts by society has led to *income* being selected as the best indicator of taxpaying ability and, thus, to its general use as the "tax base" for reference to progressivity, proportionality, or regressivity in distributional equity terms.

Thus, in a "distributional equity" sense, a tax (or tax system) is said to be *progressive* if the tax paid as a percentage of income increases as income increases. This is true regardless of the type of tax in question, that is, whether it be revenues derived from any form of income, wealth, transactions, or personal tax which increase as a proportion of income. However, if the tax paid as a percentage of income remains unchanged as income increases, the tax is termed *proportional.* Or, if the tax paid as a percentage of income diminishes as income increases, the tax is said to be *regressive.* Figure 7–1 (a, b, c) demonstrates these distributional equity relationships in graphical form.

Only a tax such as a progressive personal income tax is "progressive" in both distributional equity and technical terms. This occurs because "income," which is the indicator of taxpaying ability as the *equity benchmark,* is also the *technical base* of the tax unlike, for example, a general retail sales tax whose technical base is stated in terms of the value of transactions or a property tax whose technical base is stated in terms of wealth. Taxes such as the latter are usually "proportional"

in their "technical" structure, but *regressive* in the sense of tax paid as
a percentage of income.

The following example will demonstrate the regressive nature, in
equity terms, of the general retail sales tax which is used as a revenue
source by 46 states (in 1974) and by a substantial number of local governments: Suppose that Consumer A earns an income of $50,000 annu-
ally, from which he spends $25,000 or 50 percent for consumption of
goods, the remainder being saved. Thus, the *average propensity to
consume* of Consumer A is 50 percent. On the other hand, suppose that
Consumer B earns an annual income of $5,000, from which he spends
$4,800 or 96 percent for consumption goods. The *average propensity
to consume* of Consumer B is 96 percent. Moreover, assume equal

FIGURE 7–1
Various Tax Base-Rate Relationships in "Distributional Equity" Terms

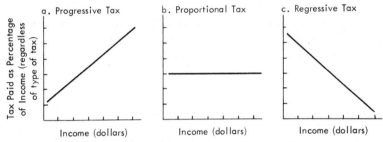

family size for both consumers and the existence of a broad-based retail
sales tax of 4 percent on the consumption purchases of each consumer.

In this instance, Consumer B pays $192 in sales taxes from his $5,000
annual income and Consumer A pays $1,000 in sales taxes from his
$50,000 annual income. Significantly, the sales tax paid by the lower
income taxpayer, Consumer B, constitutes 3.84 percent of his income
while the higher income taxpayer, Consumer A, pays only 2 percent
of his income in the form of a general sales tax. Thus, even though the
actual (technical) tax rate is 4 percent for each taxpayer, the effective
tax rate in distributional equity terms decreases as income increases—
from a rate of 3.84 percent at $5,000 of income to 2 percent at $50,000.
The sales tax thus tends to be regressive, in distributional equity terms,
due to the fact that the average propensities to consume of lower
income taxpayers tend to be higher than those of the higher income
groups.[6] Figure 7–1c would typify the regressive nature of the sales tax,

---

[6] The distributional regressivity of general retail sales taxes, as well as of certain other
taxes, can be reduced by certain fiscal techniques. These techniques will be discussed in
the subsequent chapters on particular types of taxes, wherever appropriate, and in Chapter 21.

in a *distributional equity* sense, as opposed to its *technical* proportionality.

EQUITY AND EFFICIENCY IN TAX ENFORCEMENT

Tax Equity in the Enforcement Sense

The term *tax equity* is, perhaps, as important a consideration in the "enforcement" sense as in the conceptual "distribution of burden" sense. Tax equity must mean more than a theoretically rational tax system. It must consider also the equitable enforcement of the tax structure upon all taxable subjects, seeing to it that no one illegally transfers his tax burden to other taxpayers. Tax equity, in this connotation, requires the consistent and unbiased imposition of taxes upon all those prescribed by the law as taxpayers. Though a good enforcement system cannot improve the rationality of an irrational tax structure, a poor system of enforcement can undo the advantages of a rational tax structure. The importance of equitable enforcement cannot be doubted.

Tax Evasion, Tax Avoidance, and Tax Delinquency

It is necessary to distinguish three terms in relationship to tax enforcement, namely, tax evasion, tax avoidance, and tax delinquency. *Tax evasion* involves a fraudulent or deceitful effort by a taxpayer to escape his legal tax obligations. This is a direct violation of both the "spirit" or "intent" and the "letter" of tax law. On the other hand, *tax avoidance* may involve a violation of the spirit of tax law, but it does not violate the letter of the law. Tax avoidance occurs when a taxpayer manipulates his economic behavior in such a manner as to maximize his posttax economic position, that is, to minimize his tax obligations. This may be accomplished in the short run by cleverly taking advantage of loopholes in the tax laws, primarily through the "expert" advise of tax lawyers and tax accountants, and in the long run by influencing tax legislation through the support of pressure groups and the lobbies which represent the special interests of the taxpayer. Tax avoidance is lawful, while tax evasion is unlawful. *Tax delinquency* refers to the failure to pay the tax obligation on the date when it is due. Ordinarily, tax delinquency is associated with the "inability" to pay a tax because of inadequate funds. However, the term does cover the possibility of nonpayment even though adequate funds are available. In any event, tax delinquency usually is only a "temporary" escape from tax payment since the government unit which is owed the tax can place liens on property and future earnings as well as use other devices to eventually secure the tax money.

Techniques of Tax Enforcement

Various techniques of tax enforcement are used within the United States public sector.[7] One of the most commonly employed devices in the United States is that of *voluntary taxpayer compliance*. This technique is especially important for the collection of income taxes. The federal personal income tax and many state personal income taxes also use the *withholding* technique of tax administration whereby tax funds are collected at the income source of the taxpayer for wage and salary income. This device was used first by the federal government during World War II when there was an extremely critical need for immediate federal funds to finance the war and when inflationary pressures were severe.[8] Importantly, the *private sector* provides a considerable monetary contribution to tax enforcement in the United States. The combination of voluntary taxpayer compliance and withholding means that both consumer and business units bear a significant part of "explicit" enforcement costs. The economic value of this contribution is even greater if one includes the "implicit" costs incurred by individual taxpayers who compute their obligations on their own labor time.

Auditing, whether computerized or clerical, is basic to any tax enforcement program. The federal government in recent years has expanded its use of computers to assist tax administrators in their enforcement efforts. Moreover, taxpayer account numbers are required by law as part of the federal income tax enforcement program. Tax auditing by government requires adequate information. *Information* of tax evasion may be gathered in a variety of ways. Among the most important techniques in use, especially by the federal government, are: (1) the routine check of tax returns by a tax enforcement agency; (2) the check of large or unusual business transactions; (3) the appraisal of relevant newspaper reports, court proceedings, and legal filings; (4) the routine check of the business activities of gangsters and racketeers (here the revenue motive of taxation is supplemented by the "regulatory" motive); (5) the exchange of information with other agencies within the same unit of government and also between units and levels of government; (6) information obtained from business, as required by law, to report various information items such as wages, dividends, and interest paid to taxpayers; and (7) the use of tax informers.

---

[7] Enforcement techniques will also be discussed in subsequent chapters when the particular types of taxes are analyzed.

[8] Secretary of the Treasury Henry Morgenthau and Beardsley Ruml pioneered the withholding technique during World War II.

Tax Enforcement Agencies

The primary tax enforcement agency of the federal government is the Internal Revenue Service (IRS), formally called the Bureau of Internal Revenue, which was established as part of the Treasury Department during the Civil War. The IRS is responsible for the collection of *internal* (domestic) tax revenues. The other tax collection agency of the federal government, the Bureau of Customs, enforces taxes of an *external* nature such as tariffs placed on the importation of economic goods. It also operates under the Treasury Department. At the state level of government, tax commissions serve as the tax collection agencies for the various state taxes such as general retail sales taxes, specific sales (excise) taxes, and state income taxes. The various units of local government use somewhat diverse tax collection techniques, though the collection of property taxes through county assessor offices is a common practice throughout the nation.

It is generally conceded that economies of scale exist in centralized tax collecting. Thus, the central government is said to be able to collect revenue dollars at lower cost per unit of revenue than state and local government. Though empirical studies in this regard are somewhat scarce, the "economies of scale in centralized tax collection" argument is probably a valid one. In this connection, it may be observed that tax collection operations in the United States are considerably decentralized. On the other hand, nations of similar federal structures such as Canada allow for techniques such as the "piggybacking" of income taxes. This means that the federal government offers to collect provincial income taxes through part of the federal government tax administration mechanism. Most Canadian provinces have accepted this federal government offer. The beginning of such a system for the United States is made possible by the much publicized federal revenue sharing legislation of 1972.[9] Moreover, certain exchanges of tax information take place between units and levels of government in the United States.

Finally, a rational tax requires that its direct monetary costs of enforcement not be an exceedingly high percentage of the revenues collected from the tax. This is particularly true when reasonable tax source alternatives are available to the unit of government in question. In the present context, the term "enforcement costs" should be construed to include both the direct administrative costs of the public sector and the voluntary compliance costs of the private sector.

"Secondary Effects" from Tax Enforcement

Various *secondary effects* such as "negative" allocational nonneutralities in the form of "disincentives" of consumption and investment

---

[9] See Public Law 92–512, 92nd Congress, H.R. 14370, October 20, 1972, Title II: "Federal Collection of State Individual Income Taxes."

may result from irritating and irrational tax enforcement efforts. This is undesirable. On the other hand, tax evasion—the target of enforcement efforts—is also undesirable. Thus, tax enforcement efforts, though justified, should be efficient and rational so as to avoid unnecessary disincentives. Yet, due to the fear of creating excessive disincentives from "overenforcement," the degree of tax enforcement effort is normally not extended to the point where the "marginal cost of enforcement" is equal to the "marginal tax dollar" derived from such enforcement.

Another secondary result of tax enforcement activities is that some potential evasion "never occurs" because taxpayers know that an adequate tax enforcement system is in operation and, consequently, they tend to diminish their evasion efforts. Although the additional revenues collected *directly* as a result of the detection of tax evasion can be estimated, the additional revenues which *indirectly* accrue because potential tax evasion is discouraged cannot be determined. Yet, this latter amount may constitute a considerable revenue value.

8

Principles of Tax Shifting and Incidence

THE SYMMETRICAL AND GENERAL EQUILIBRIUM NATURE OF BUDGETARY INCIDENCE

The *distributional* branch of the economy may be significantly influenced by the public sector activities of both "taxing" and "spending." Yet, academic public finance in the Anglo-American part of the Western world has historically approached the distribution issue in an "asymmetrical" fashion. It has focused on the tax or revenue side of the budget to attain distributional objectives while neglecting until recently detailed analysis of the influence of governmental expenditures on distribution. This is not to suggest, of course, that actual governmental spending failed to exert redistributional effects during the period. Nonetheless, the conceptual approach to public sector distribution policy placed its major emphasis on "equity" in the distribution of tax burdens. Relatedly, the political consensus in Western nations has generally indicated a preference for the ability-to-pay approach to equity in the distribution of tax burdens along with the concepts of horizontal and vertical tax equity.[1] The result has been an overall "value judgment-imposed" mandate, wherever feasible, for progressive tax structures which, in turn, reflects an acceptance (at least implicit) of the diminishing marginal utility of income concept with interpersonal comparisons of utility.

Importantly, the tax equity goals established through this political

---

[1] See Chapter 7.

144

consensus must encompass the important concept of "tax shifting." That is, the "legal" point of *tax impact* may be situated at a different taxpaying locus than the ultimate or final resting place of a tax after various market adjustments have occurred. This ultimate point of tax burden is commonly known as the point of *tax incidence.* If it differs from the point of impact, *tax shifting* has taken place. A tax equity principle such as the "ability-to-pay principle," of course, is more fundamentally concerned with the ultimate or final burden rather than the initial burden of a tax.

Moreover, the tax or revenue side of the budget should not be treated in isolation. Instead, the incidence of public sector *expenditures,* in a "benefit" sense, should be considered in a *symmetrical* manner alongside the incidence of *taxes,* in a "burden" sense. In other words, the distribution of *real income* among the people of the society, in the actual consumption or resource usage context, may be influenced by either the tax or expenditure side of the public sector fisc. Thus, the incidence of *taxes,* which create a real "burden" through private sector consumption forgone, and of *expenditures,* which provide real "benefits" through either expanded purchasing power from the receipt of transfer payments or direct resource consumption in the form of public and quasi-public goods, are both equally relevant to the determination of the state of real income distribution among the members of a society.

Unfortunately, the efforts which have been made to empirically measure the redistributional results of total budget changes have been somewhat disappointing. However, this is not surprising due to the extremely complex nature of the interacting variables which are functionally involved in the determination of *budgetary incidence.*

In fact, the ultimate incidence of a tax or expenditure change can be conceptually determined only in a *long-run, general equilibrium* sense.[2] That is, the distribution of real income, as influenced by a budgetary change, must reflect all long-run price and output adjustments,

---

[2] The initial "breakthrough" article demonstrating the merits of a general equilibrium approach to tax incidence was written by Arnold C. Harberger, "The Incidence of the Corporation Income Tax," *Journal of Political Economy* (June, 1962), pp. 215–40.

For an excellent recent article concerning the general equilibrium nature of taxation, see Charles E. McLure, Jr., "Tax Incidence, Macroeconomic Policy, and Absolute Prices," *Quarterly Journal of Economics,* May 1970, pp. 254–67. Specifically, McLure argues that "tax incidence," which is defined in terms of changes in "relative" *product* and *factor* (resource) *prices* as determined by a change in the structure of taxation, does not in itself determine a change in the absolute price of a product or resource. In addition, it is also necessary to know how the aggregate economic policies which accompany the tax change influence the "general level" of product or factor prices. Thus, it is argued that changes in both general price levels and relative prices determine the "posttax-change" price of a product or resource. Also, another excellent article on the subject is: Peter M. Mieszkowski, "On the Theory of Tax Incidence," *Journal of Political Economy,* June 1967, pp. 250–62.

in both product and factor markets, that are relevant to the fiscal change. Normally, this would incorporate many markets and many price-output changes. In fact, it would conceptually involve the entire economic system. Relatedly, effects exerted on such relevant considerations as capital/labor ratios in firm production functions and on work/leisure choices will also help to determine the ultimate incidence of a tax or expenditure change.

In addition, aggregate output effects will also bear upon the incidence of a tax or expenditure change due to the ability of such changes to influence the important macroeconomic variables of consumption, saving, and investment, with resulting changes in such variables as production, employment, national income, and price levels. To complicate still further, the incidence of a budgetary policy may also be affected by policies which are not directly intended to be of a distributional nature. In other words, an allocational or economic growth policy might well bear significant distributional implications, even though it is not primarily looked upon as a distributional policy. Thus, *intergoal nonneutrality* also deserves consideration in any comprehensive analysis of the tax and expenditure incidence of the public sector budget.

As suggested above, empirical efforts to isolate tax or expenditure incidence, in the real income sense, face severe obstacles. For example, many of the benefits derived from public and quasi-public goods are indivisible in nature. That is, these goods are characterized by indivisibilities which cannot be quantified to the individual consumer. The benefits are jointly consumed. Moreover, such benefits do not relate ordinarily to any particular revenue measure (earmarked taxes excepted). In addition, though a "comparative statics" type of analysis which compares two distinct equilibriums can be somewhat helpful, it is difficult to isolate the "strict" tax or expenditure incidence from the influence of other parameters (variables) which may have changed between two points of time. On the other hand, the more desirable long-run general equilibrum analysis involves an extreme complexity of multiple interacting variables and thus faces formidable practical problems of empirical testing and measurement. Moreover, such considerations as *interstate* or *interregional* tax incidence, which is concerned with the "exporting" of tax burdens from one political jurisdiction or region to another, or *dynamic* tax incidence which is concerned with the economic growth aspects of the subject including changes in the overall supply of factor inputs, carry significant implications for incidence analysis though they also involve the complex interaction of many variables.

Tax incidence studies, in general, may follow either a *differential incidence* or a *balanced budget incidence* methodology. Under the "differential incidence" methodology, the level of government expenditures remains unchanged while one tax is substituted for another tax of equal revenue yield to the government to finance these expenditures. Hence, the redistributional effects of alternative taxes can be compared. On the other hand, under the "balanced budget incidence" methodology, the effect of the overall tax-expenditure process on the level of private sector income is considered as the level of government expenditures, matched by additional taxes, is increased.

THE MONETARY OR ABSOLUTE INCIDENCE OF A TAX

Unquestionably, the comprehensive and symmetrical nature of budgetary incidence, as described above, is a fact that must be appreciated. Nonetheless, disaggregated and asymmetrical studies of either tax or expenditure incidence alone, as well as the application of *partial equilibrium* rather than general equilibrium analysis, may still be useful. Most budget incidence studies until recent years have been of the "partial equilibrium" variety for "taxes" in that they have emphasized incidence in the sense of the "monetary" burden of a tax or "absolute price changes." They have not directly considered "real resource effects" nor "relative price changes." That is, they have attempted to define and measure tax "shifting" and "incidence" in terms of a higher *absolute* selling price for an economic good, or in terms of a lower *absolute* purchase price for a productive resource, but they have not emphasized changes in *relative* product and resource prices in the context of the interrelationship of many variables in a general equilibrium system. Yet, even though the relevance of the *general equilibrium* approach to tax shifting and incidence is fully appreciated, this section of the chapter will focus upon some of the orthodox criteria of *tax incidence* and the related concept of *tax shifting* as they are approached in a *partial equilibrium* context. The most significant of these criteria will be described separately as if each were the only determinant of ultimate tax incidence, though clearly together they exert a composite effect. This procedure will be followed in order to isolate the probable direction of the effects which the criterion in question would exert. Meanwhile, some incidence effects will be considered separately in other chapters of Part Two of this book under the application of the *fiscal rationality criteria* to particular types of taxes.

In order to understand the nature of "tax shifting" in the monetary or absolute sense, further discussion of the terms "tax impact" and "tax incidence" is desirable. *Tax impact* may be designated as the point which receives the *initial burden* of a tax in a legal or statutory sense. Since individuals are the fundamental claimants of all factor incomes, this point of impact must be upon an individual or individuals.[3] One way of looking upon tax impact is to ask the question: "Who pays the

---

[3] Businesses, including corporate businesses, are correctly viewed as earning income for their individual owners. Thus, only these owners may receive the impact (initial monetary burden) of a tax.

tax to the government?" This is *not* meant to suggest the technical or administrative handover of tax funds, but instead, the person who bears the initial financial burden of paying the tax. For example, the employer by means of payroll deductions may actually turn over personal income tax funds to the government. Yet, the worker from whose income the tax is withheld certainly bears the immediate impact. As observed earlier, *tax incidence*, as distinguished from tax impact, is the point where the *ultimate* (final) burden of the tax rests.

Tax shifting can be demonstrated by a comparison of the impact and incidence points of a tax. If the point of incidence is identical with the initial point of impact, the burden rests ultimately where it initially fell and tax shifting, that is, transference of the tax burden among individuals, *does not* occur. On the other hand, if part or all of the burden of the tax rests at a point or points other than the point of impact, tax shifting, at least to some extent, *does* occur. Tax shifting may be partial; it may be complete; in some instances, due to the taxpayer taking advantage of "unrealized gains," it may be greater than 100 percent.[4] Thus, a range exists from zero, or no tax shifting, at the one extreme, to greater than 100 percent tax shifting, given sufficient unrealized gains, at the other extreme.

Tax shifting takes place through the market mechanism of supply and demand. Taxes induce *allocational* adjustments in productive and consumptive behavior which, in turn, yield *redistributional* results in both a real tax burden and real income distribution sense. These allocational adjustments, in essence, are substitution effects. While every tax exerts an "income effect," every tax *except one*—a lump sum tax—also yields some form(s) of "substitution effect." Allocationally speaking, tax shifting will occur through a change in the *absolute price* of an economic good or productive resource, in the partial equilibrium sense, or through a change in *relative* product and factor prices, in the general equilibrium sense.

In terms of partial equilibrium analysis, two possibilities are important. If the absolute price of an economic good is *increased* as the result of a new or higher tax, and this allows part or all of the tax burden to be transferred to someone else, it may be said that the burden has been "shifted forward." Or, if the result of the tax is to decrease the absolute price of a factor (resource) of production, and this allows transference of part or all of the tax burden, it may be said that the burden has been "shifted backward." Thus, *forward tax shifting* under partial equilibrium conditions ordinarily results from a rise in the absolute price of an economic good in a product market and *backward tax shifting* ordinarily results from a reduction in the absolute price of a productive

---

[4] The definition of "unrealized gains" and their relationship to tax shifting and incidence will be discussed later in the chapter.

resource in a factor market. In the first instance, the burden of the tax may be said to have been "shifted forward" to the consumer while in the latter case the burden may be described as having been "shifted backward" to the owner of the factor of production through the price changes.

A related technique by which a tax may be shifted is that of *tax capitalization*. Again, the shifting takes place through a change in price, but in the tax capitalization case the price is the capitalized value of the expected future earnings of the asset subject to the tax. This technique is particularly important in the case of a property tax involving commercial property. The following example will illustrate the possibility of transferring a property tax burden through tax capitalization.

Suppose that the average annual net income of a motel investment is $10,000. Suppose also that 10 percent is the normal rate of return needed in the community to attract capital into the motel business. In this instance, since $10,000 is 10 percent of $100,000, the capitalized value of the motel may be estimated at $100,000 (excluding depreciation considerations). Now, suppose that property taxes imposed on the motel are increased by $1,000 per year. This tax increment lowers the aftertax income of the motel to $9,000 from $10,000. Since $9,000 is 10 percent of $90,000, the capitalized value of the motel in terms of its earning potential is decreased by $10,000 to $90,000 as the property tax rates are increased.

If the owner of the motel decides to sell the asset, and is able to sell it at the "pretax increment" capitalized value of $100,000, he has shifted the burden of the tax increment by selling the property. If the owner sells the property at the "posttax increment" value of $90,000, he absorbs the incremental property tax. If the owner sells at any price over $90,000, but less than $100,000, part of the tax burden is transferred through the process of tax capitalization. Tax shifting, in this example, is assisted by imperfect market knowledge by the purchaser of the property after its capital value has declined. Moreover, long-run considerations may allow an adjustment which would increase the room prices charged by motels as some reduction of motel capacity takes place in the community because of reduced posttax earnings. The tax capitalization example demonstrates a peculiar market method whereby, under favorable conditions, tax shifting can occur.

Tax shifting is sometimes disguised by an *implicit* rather than an outward (external) price change. This would occur, for example, when the quality or size of an economic good or productive resource is reduced while price is held constant in order to shift a tax. Thus, a special excise tax levied on candy bars may be shifted forward to consumers by reducing the quality or size of the candy bar while its price remains stable. Implicitly, and effectively, the price is raised when a reduced quality or size is attained at the same per unit price. Thus, in an indirect and disguised manner, the burden of the tax may be transferred (at least partially) through a market adjustment involving a quality or size change rather than a direct price change.

Attention will now be directed toward several criteria or determinants which influence the ability to *shift* the monetary or absolute burden of a tax under partial equilibrium conditions. These incidence criteria are the market structure and unrealized gains, industry cost conditions, price elasticity, type of tax, and political jurisdiction criteria. There is no intention, however, to imply that only five determinants exist. Instead, a multiple of interacting variables, both these and others, will influence the final result. The criteria analyzed in this chapter are among the most important determinants of tax shifting and incidence. They are not discussed in any intended order of relative importance. All five are considered to be significant.

The Market Structure and Unrealized Gains Criterion

The extent to which the monetary burden of a tax is shifted, either forward or backward, may be importantly affected by the nature of the *market structure* within which the seller or buyer functions. In order to explain the effects of different market structures, let us look at the possibilities of tax shifting in both the short and long run, and under pure competition, monopolistic competition, pure monopoly, and oligopoly conditions. In these cases, it will be initially assumed that the sellers are maximizing profits.

Pure (Perfect) Competition. The purely competitive (perfectly competitive) market is characterized by many sellers and buyers of homogeneous (nondifferentiated) goods. In Figure 8–1a, the initial "pretax" equilibrium position for the purely competitive firm is indicated at point *a* and for the purely competitive industry in Figure 8–1b at point a^1. The firm is producing an output of 25 units and selling at a price of $10, as determined by the intersection of its marginal cost curve, *MC*, with marginal revenue (*MR*) and price (*AR*), as set by the industry. Then, assume that an excise tax of $5 per unit is imposed on the good.

The individual firm can initiate no effort on its own to shift the tax forward via a higher selling price since it has no control over price. It completely lacks monopoly power due to the homogeneity of its product and the fact that it is one of many sellers. Thus, any forward shifting which may occur can take place *only* through "industry forces." In the *immediate* or *market* period, this will not occur. In the *short run,* industry forces may allow "partial shifting" of the tax, though the overall possibility of shifting is reduced by the inability of the individual firm to influence price. Any shifting which does occur through industry

FIGURE 8-1

Pure Competition: Long-Run Tax Shifting under Constant Cost Conditions

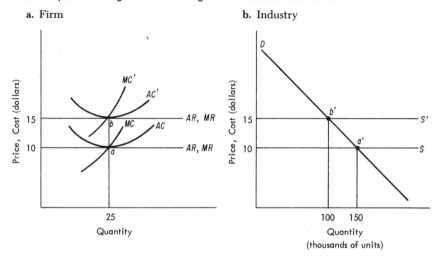

a. Firm

b. Industry

forces in the short-run would not involve the exit of firms from the industry. However, in the *long-run,* under "constant cost" supply conditions, the tax will be "fully shifted" forward to the consumer due to the action of industry forces in the form of an exodus of some firms from the industry.[5] That is, over the *long-run,* some firms will leave the industry because the industry determined short-run price increase was not equal to the amount of the new excise tax burden. When this occurs, the industry supply schedule will shift upward until market price has risen sufficiently so that the representative firm again can earn a normal profit. This is demonstrated for the industry in Figure 8–1b at point b^1 where the industry supply schedule S has shifted upward by the amount of the tax to become the "posttax" supply schedule S^1. Industry price increases from $10 to $15 and the firm can now sell all of its output at the higher price. The burden of the tax has thus been fully shifted forward though, significantly, this has not occurred through monopoly power by the individual firm, but instead through the operation of long-run competitive industry forces. For the purpose of the example, such forward shifting assumes constant factor (resource) prices and hence the impossibility of backward shifting. The final equilibrium price ($15) is higher than the initial price ($10) by the amount of the tax ($5).

Monopolistic Competition. This type of market structure, which is characterized by a substantial number of sellers and buyers of differen-

---

[5] Only partial shifting could occur in pure competition under long-run "increasing cost" conditions of supply.

tiated goods, provides tax shifting results somewhat similar, but not identical, to those found in purely competitive markets. Similar to pure competition, the firm is one of many sellers which detracts from its ability to influence price. However, product differentiation may allow the firm, at times, to exert a modest amount of shifting influence which could not occur under the "homogeneous product" conditions of the purely competitive market. In the long-run, the exit of some firms from the industry because of the higher costs resulting from the tax will tend to shift the excise tax, at least partly, to consumers as the industry moves toward, if not to, a normal profit position.

Pure Monopoly. As depicted in Figure 8–2, the pure monopoly firm which is identical with the industry since no competitors exist, is in "pretax" equilibrium producing output OQ, charging price OP, and earning monopoly profits $PABC$. Assume first that an *excise tax* is imposed on the economic good produced by the monopoly. As a result, the marginal cost curve MC and the average cost curve AC shift upward and become MC^1 and AC^1, respectively. Thus, a new "posttax" equilibrium is set at output OQ^1 and price OP^1 which yields monopoly profits equal to the rectangle P^1DEF. In this example, the profit rectan-

FIGURE 8–2
Pure Monopoly: Tax Shifting Considerations

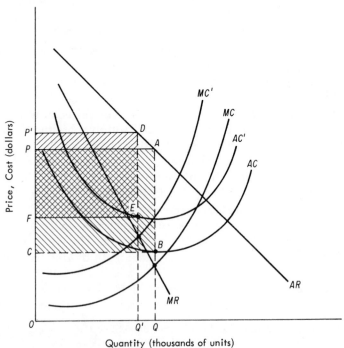

Quantity (thousands of units)

gle is smaller than the profit rectangle *PABC* which existed before the excise tax was imposed. Hence, the pure monopoly firm in this case *does not fully shift* the "excise" tax. In fact, the extent which it can shift any part of the tax will be determined by numerous factors (some of which are discussed below) such as cost conditions and the price elasticities of demand and supply. Importantly, however, the pure monopoly firm could initiate a price change on its own due to the absence of competitors, and it could do so in either the short-run or the long-run time period.[6]

In the above example, the monetary burden borne by the monopolist is equal to the difference between the "pretax" and "posttax" profit rectangles. The ultimate change in absolute price is a measure of the amount of the tax that is "shifted forward" while the difference between the original and the ultimate average cost curves, if any, would illustrate the absolute amount of the tax which has been "shifted backward" in the form of lower prices paid for productive resources—as made possible by "monopsony power" in factor markets. However, it is assumed for simplicity in Figure 8–2, as it was above in Figure 8–1 for pure competition, that no change in average cost occurs (except for the tax) and, therefore, that only forward tax shifting takes place.

Next, assume that a 50 percent *corporation (business) income tax* is imposed on the net income of a pure monopoly firm. In this instance, the tax is levied upon a "surplus" or "residual," that is, upon the "profits" of the firm as such. Thus, in Figure 8–2, if the pure monopoly firm is maximizing profits, the corporation income tax would be imposed on rectangle *PABC*. The corporation income tax, unlike the excise tax imposed on the good produced by the monopoly firm, does not result in an increase in the marginal and average cost curves of the firm. Thus, it does not pay for the firm to increase price to help cover the increased costs and thus shift part of the tax. In the case of the corporation income tax, the firm's "posttax" profits are simply reduced by the amount of the tax. Importantly, the most profitable "posttax" price-output point remains unchanged from the "pretax" profit-maximizing price-output point. Assume, for example, a 50 percent tax on corporate profits. Thus, 50 percent (after paying the corporation income tax) of the largest profit

---

[6] The comparative shiftability of an excise tax by a *pure competition* firm as opposed to a *pure monopoly* firm, in different time periods, may be summarized as follows:

Time Period	Pure Competition	Pure Monopoly
Short-Run	Little, if any, shifting, and through "industry forces only."	Shifting, to varying degrees, possible through "firm monopoly power."
Long-Run	Full shifting, and through "industry forces only." (constant cost conditions)	Shifting, to varying degrees, possible through "firm monopoly power."

rectangle available ($PABC$) leaves the firm with more net aftertax income than 50 percent of any smaller nonprofit-maximizing profit rectangle (such as P^1DEF). No increase in price, such as in the response to the excise tax, can change this fact. However, the nonshiftability of a corporation net income tax is based upon the strict assumption that the firm is operating in its "pretax" status at the profit-maximation point where marginal cost equals marginal revenue ($MC = MR$). If this premise is accepted, then it is only logical to conclude that the tax cannot be shifted.

The Unrealized Gains Phenomenon. An often overlooked, though highly significant, point relevant to tax shifting is suggested in the above discussion. That is, a firm may *not* be operating at the $MC = MR$ position and, thus, "unrealized gains" may be present in its production circumstances.[7] An *unrealized gain* may be defined as the amount of incremental profits (or of reduced losses) which could be obtained if the firm were operating at its "best profit point" ($MC = MR$) rather than at a "suboptimal price-output position" apart from this point. Among the various types of market structures, the only "impossible" occurrence of unrealized gains is for the firm operating under long-run, purely (perfectly) competitive conditions. In this situation, since the firm is earning only "normal economic profits," it must produce at the $MC = MR$ point in order to survive in the industry in the long run. However, any imperfectly competitive firm (monopolistic competition, oligopoly, pure monopoly) may operate in both the short-run and long-run apart from the $MC = MR$ point due to the possible presence of monopoly profits. Thus, an imperfectly competitive firm which is not operating at the profit-maximization point will be in a possible position to shift a corporation (business) income tax if there exists a "buffer area" of unrealized gains within which price-output rearrangements can be made. Figure 8–3, which is described below, demonstrates this phenomenon. First, however, the highly significant question must be asked: Why would a firm choose not to maximize profits at the $MC = MR$ point?

Such considerations as imperfect market and production knowledge, the fear of antitrust action, the fear of an unfavorable public image, the fear of attracting new entrants into the industry, the fear of stimulating union wage demands, and public utility regulation may prevent a firm from achieving, or even attempting to achieve, an optimal profit position—especially in the short run. Instead, the firm may follow such rules or benchmarks as: the maximization of gross receipts (sales); achievement of a target rate of return on investment; maintenance of stable

---

[7] In this chapter, *unrealized gains* will be spoken of in terms of business profits, though the principle involved applies equally to all productive resources and their earnings such as an individual's compensation for labor input.

FIGURE 8–3

Unrealized Gains as a Condition of Shifting a Business Income Tax by
a Firm in Imperfect Competition

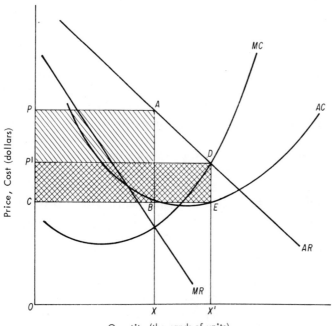

Quantity (thousands of units)

Explanation:
  Rectangle *PABC* = Maximum Profits where *MC* = *MR* at output *X*.
  Rectangle *P¹DEC* = Profits at output *X¹* which is a position of suboptimal profits.
  The "Excess" of *PABC* over *P¹DEC* = *Unrealized Gains*, thus allowing the "possibility"
  of shifting the burden of a profits tax as price is increased toward *P* and output is decreased
  toward the profit-maximization output *X*.

prices on goods produced by the firm; the application of a percentage
markup price over average (unit) cost; or the improvement of the firm's
relative sales position within the market as a whole. When such rules
or benchmarks are followed, the firm usually does *not* attain an optimal
price-output position. Consequently, in this "gray area" of *unrealized
gains,* a margin is created from which tax shifting becomes increasingly
possible (assuming that the other criteria permit the tax shifting). In
other words, the possibility of shifting the monetary or absolute burden
of a business profits tax is enhanced by the existence of unrealized gains.

Reference will now be made to Figure 8–3 to demonstrate the above
phenomenon. Observe that rectangle *PABC* at the "profit-maximization" point, *MC* = *MR*, exceeds rectangle *P¹DEC* at the "nonprofit-max-
imization" point shown on the graph. In this situation, imperfect knowledge, fear of antitrust action, and/or one of the other reasons
mentioned above causes the firm to allow the unrealized gains "excess"

of *PABC* over P^1DEC to exist by charging a lower than profit-maximizing price (P^1) and producing a larger than profit-maximizing output (X^1). The firm, in terms of the profit-maximization goal, would like to restrict output and utilize its monopoly power to increase price from P^1 to P at profit-maximizing output X. Then, given the imposition of a new profits (income) tax, or a rate increase in a present profits tax, the firm may choose to push aside antitrust or other considerations which impede tax shifting and change price upward toward the profit-maximization position. In so doing, part, or all, or possibly more than 100 percent of the tax burden may be shifted.[8] Significantly, the shifting, if it occurs, is not accomplished through "equilibrating" market forces, as in the purely competitive case, but instead is accomplished through individual firm policy decisions as assisted by "market power" in an imperfectly competitive industry.

Public utility firms appear to be in a unique institutional position to shift tax burdens through unrealized gains. These privately-owned, publicly-regulated, firms are ordinarily allowed to earn a particular rate of return on invested capital but, because of the nature of their market and production conditions, they are not allowed to charge profit-maximizing prices nor to produce profit-maximizing outputs. Thus, *unrealized gains*, operating through the institutional arrangement of "public utility regulation," are built into the price-output policies of public utility firms. When additional profits (income) tax burdens are imposed, the "posttax" earnings on investment of these companies tend to decline and a case is created for the firms to request higher prices (rates) from the regulatory commissions. Often, such requests are granted. The quantity demanded of the economic good, moreover, does not ordinarily decline greatly as price increases due to the typical inelastic demand for public utility goods. Farris contends that public utility firms tend to pass along increased taxes through regulatory approval, but at the same time are reluctant and are not pressed strongly by the regulatory commissions to lower prices on the occasion of tax reductions.[9]

Oligopoly. Significant interdependence between a few dominant sellers, and thus "uncertainty," characterizes oligopoly market structure. In the case of a new *excise* tax or an increase in the rate of a present excise tax, however, the degree of uncertainty is reduced since each firm recognizes that every other firm also has its costs increased by the amount of the tax. Thus, unless industry demand is elastic, or unless considerable differentiation exists between the products of the

---

[8] Greater than 100 percent tax shifting would require extreme deviation by a firm from its pretax profit-maximization position and would likely also require both extensive forward and backward tax shifting opportunities.

[9] Martin T. Farris, "Tax Reductions and Utility Rates," *Public Utilities Fortnightly,* August 27, 1964, pp. 30–36.

oligopoly firms, it is likely that *each* firm will add the tax to its selling price in an effort to shift the tax. Unlike pure competition, the individual firm will be able to initiate such a price change on its own. Moreover, the existence of unrealized gains in an oligopolistic industry may allow at least partial shifting of a *corporation (business) profits* tax, given the presence of favorable demand and supply elasticity conditions and other determinants. This would be especially possible if the few oligopoly firms voluntarily act in unison on prices in product and/or factor markets. Given "unrealized gains," the actual degree of shifting of the corporation (business) income tax, just as with an excise tax, will depend upon the "weighted influence" of numerous tax shifting determinants. Thus, unrealized gains become a "necessary," but *not* a "sufficient," condition for the shifting of a corporation income tax in imperfect markets.

The Cost Conditions of the Industry Criterion

A second criterion of tax shifting, in the partial equilibrium sense of "monetary" or "absolute" burden, derives from the *cost conditions* present in the industry in which the attempt to shift the tax takes place. In this regard, an industry may be classified as (1) a *constant cost industry* if the average cost of production remains unchanged as output expands, (2) an *increasing cost industry* if average cost rises with expanding output, and (3) a *decreasing cost industry* if average cost declines as output expands. Industry cost conditions are a "long-run" phenomenon involving the concept of scale economies and diseconomies. Also, it should be qualified that long-run decreasing cost conditions are not conceptually consistent with purely (perfectly) competitive markets.

Figure 8–4a represents an industry operating under *constant* average costs of production. Assume the imposition of an excise tax on the product sold by this industry. The marginal cost schedules of the firms in the industry will increase by the amount of the tax. The initial "pretax" equilibrium is determined at point a by the intersection of the supply curve S and the demand curve D, establishing price P. After the long-run market adjustment, the "posttax" equilibrium is reached at point b resulting in price P^1. Importantly, the absolute price of the economic good has increased by the amount of the tax. In this case, full forward shifting of the tax has taken place.

Figure 8–4b represents an industry operating under *increasing* average costs of production. The initial "pretax" equilibrium is once again at point a and the "posttax" equilibrium is at point b. After the long-run market adjustment, the absolute price of the economic good, P^2, has increased by less than the amount of the tax. Thus, full forward shifting

FIGURE 8–4
Cost Conditions of the Industry and Tax Shifting (industry graphs)

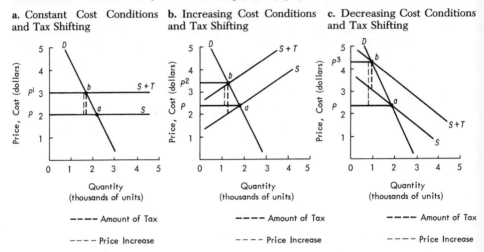

a. Constant Cost Conditions and Tax Shifting   **b. Increasing Cost Conditions and Tax Shifting**   **c. Decreasing Cost Conditions and Tax Shifting**

has *not* occurred. On the other hand, under *decreasing* industry cost conditions, the absolute price of the economic good, P^3, increases by more than the amount of the tax. This may be observed by comparing points *a* and *b* in Figure 8–4c. In this instance, more than 100 percent shifting has taken place. Thus, decreasing cost conditions are the most conducive and increasing cost conditions the least conducive to tax shifting.

The Price Elasticity Criterion

Price Elasticity of Demand. A third significant partial equilibrium determinant of tax shifting and incidence concerns the price elasticity of demand of the economic good or the price elasticity of supply of the productive resource in question. The elasticity concept relates the sensitivity of the response of a quantity (demanded or supplied) change to a change in price. Such variables as product or factor substitutability, and the price of the good or resource in relation to the buyer's total income or outlay, help determine the elasticity value for a good or resource. By affecting the quantity demanded or supplied at various prices, and thus total revenue or gross income (price times quantity demanded) and total cost (average cost times quantity supplied), demand and supply elasticity help to determine the "net income" level of a firm at the posttax equilibrium. The relationship of the posttax net income level to the pretax net income level will help to indicate the extent to which shifting may have occurred.

Generally, the more sensitive (elastic) the quantity demanded is to a change in price, the more difficult it is to shift the monetary burden of a tax forward through a higher selling price. Conversely, the more inelastic or insensitive the quantity reaction to a price change, the greater the possibility of forward shifting the tax. Suppose that an excise tax is levied upon a particular economic good. In Figures 8–5a, 8–5b, and 8–5c, let the S curve represent the supply and curve D represent the demand for the good. Constant cost conditions of supply are assumed. In Figure 8–5a, demand is *relatively elastic* throughout the relevant portion of the demand curve while in Figure 8–5b demand is *relatively inelastic* throughout the relevant portion. In Figure 8–5c, the demand for the good is *perfectly* (completely) *inelastic* throughout the entire curve. When the excise tax is imposed, the price of the good is initially increased by the amount of the tax as the average and marginal cost schedules of the firms in the industry are increased by this amount. Whether the tax is successfully shifted or not will be influenced by the nature of the demand elasticity for the product. The supply curve S will shift upward and become the new supply curve $S + T$ in each graph as the tax is added on to the original selling price of the product. Thus, the new selling price is P^1 in each graph as opposed to the pretax selling price P.

The greatest quantity reduction to the higher price occurs in the *relatively elastic* demand case (Figure 8–5a). In this instance, tax shifting is difficult because the total revenue or gross income (price X quantity) of a firm would decline. In Figure 8–5b, where the demand is *relatively inelastic*, as the price increases from P to P^1 (by the amount of the tax) the quantity decrease from X to X^1 is less than proportionate to the price increase. As a result, total revenue (gross income) to the firm does *not* decline and tax shifting is more likely to take place. The most likely occurrence of tax shifting is found in Figure 8–5c, where

FIGURE 8–5
Price Elasticity of Demand and Tax Shifting

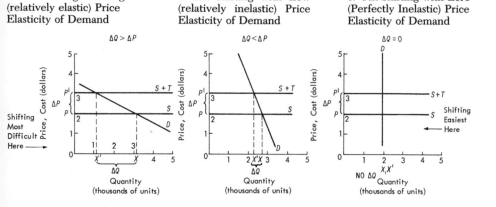

a. Tax Shifting with High (relatively elastic) Price Elasticity of Demand

b. Tax Shifting with Low (relatively inelastic) Price Elasticity of Demand

c. Tax Shifting with Zero (Perfectly Inelastic) Price Elasticity of Demand

the demand is *perfectly inelastic,* since there is no quantity reaction as the price increases from P to P^1. The initial quantity X and the posttax quantity X^1 are the same.

The student should continue to bear in mind, of course, that other criteria are at work in any single tax shifting situation. However, considering the price elasticity of demand criterion alone, it is an accurate generalization to say that the greater the price elasticity of demand, the lesser the opportunity for transferring a tax burden forward. Conversely, the greater the price inelasticity of demand, the more likely forward tax shifting is to occur.

Price Elasticity of Supply. While "forward shifting" is ordinarily concerned with obtaining a higher selling price for an economic good, "backward shifting" ordinarily relates to an effort to pay a lower buying price for a productive resource. The following generalizations may be made concerning backward tax shifting as it would be influenced by price elasticity of supply: (1) the more elastic the resource supply, the less the amount of the tax that can be shifted back to the factor of production since the quantity supplied of the resource decreases sharply as the offer price for the resource declines, and (2) the more inelastic the resource supply, the greater the amount of the tax that can be shifted backward to the factor of production since the lower offer price induces little supply reduction. A comparison of Figures 8–6a and 8–6b demonstrates this result. In the limiting cases, a perfectly elastic resource supply could completely prevent the backward shifting of the

FIGURE 8–6
Price Elasticity of Supply and Tax Shifting

a. Tax Shifting with High (relatively elastic) Price Elasticity of Supply   **b.** Tax shifting with Low (relatively inelastic) Price Elasticity of Supply

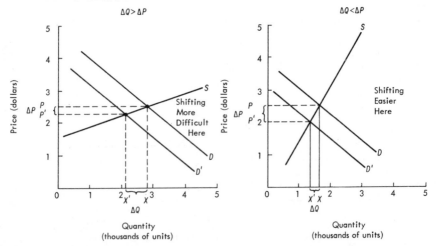

Quantity
(thousands of units)

tax to the resource owner while a perfectly inelastic supply could allow the total burden to be borne by the resource owner. However, the presence of other tax shifting determinants might prevent these results.

The Type of Tax Criterion

The nature of the tax, as determined by such characteristics as whether it is (1) direct or indirect, and (2) broad-based or narrow-based, will also help to determine its shiftability and incidence. Generally, the more *direct* the tax the more difficult shifting becomes, and the more *indirect* the tax the greater the possibility of transferring its burden from the point of impact to another point of incidence. This is explained by the fact that a direct tax usually is applied to a tax base closely identifiable with an individual such as his income and wealth. The most direct tax possible would be a lump-sum (per capita) tax on the individual himself. Direct tax bases, in most instances, are further removed from subsequent market transactions after the taxes are imposed than are the bases of indirect taxes. Thus, *direct taxes,* such as the personal income tax, are not especially conducive to the further market transactions which are necessary for the shifting of a tax. On the other hand, *indirect taxes,* such as the general retail sales and excise taxes, are more closely associated with further market transactions. Hence, they are more conducive to tax shifting, generally speaking, than are direct taxes.

In terms of the "extent" of the tax base, the more *broad-based* a tax, the easier it is to shift the tax.[10] Oppositely, the more *narrow-based* the tax, the more difficult tax shifting becomes. When the tax base is narrow, demand tends to be *elastic* since distortions in consumer decisions are more likely to occur through the operation of a "substitution effect." Hence, as price is changed in the effort to shift the tax, the change in quantity demanded tends to be more than proportionate to the change in price due to the availability of "untaxed" or "lower-taxed" goods. This phenomenon relates closely to the "price elasticity" criterion discussed above. Thus, when such movement to substitutes is possible, it will be very difficult to raise the product price in order to shift the tax. That is, the demand schedule of the taxed good tends to be *elastic* due to the availability of the untaxed or lower-taxed substitutes. The opposite is true, of course, when the tax is broad-based, in which case, demand tends to be less elastic and shifting becomes easier.

A tax on movie theatre tickets in a community where other forms

---

[10] The reference to broad-based and narrow-based taxes under this criterion is concerned with the "nature of the tax," not with the "geographical size" of the political jurisdiction imposing the tax. The latter is treated below as a separate tax shifting determinant.

of recreation are not taxed, for example, would likely cause consumption patterns to change somewhat away from movie theater consumption to substitute forms of recreation such as bowling, baseball games, or miniature golf if movie prices were increased in an effort to shift the tax. On the other hand, if the sales tax in question were broadbased and applied equally to all substitute recreational items in the community, the consumer would have no price incentive to move between the alternative forms of recreation and the sellers of recreation would be in a better position to raise prices in order to shift the tax.[11]

The Political Jurisdiction Criterion

The *geographical nature of the political unit* which levies a tax also helps to determine its shiftability. In this context, a political unit may be a local, state, national, or even international government. Generally, the *narrower* the geographical limits of a political unit, the more difficult it is for sellers to shift the tax. For example, a sizable new (or increased) general retail sales tax in a city may lead to consumption readjustments in the form of increased purchases outside the city (in other cities or counties). The retail merchants in the city would probably absorb at least part of the tax since they would tend not to raise prices if similar taxes were not applied in nearby cities and counties. Efficient communications and transportation increase the possibility of buying outside a limited geographical (political) area.

Taxes levied at the state level, since they involve a wider geographical area of political jurisdiction than those imposed at local levels of government, improve the possibility of forward tax shifting by sellers in the form of higher prices. There are reduced opportunities for buyers to purchase in "no-tax" or "lower-tax" areas. Furthermore, states normally attempt to reduce tax escape by imposing *use taxes* whereby the residents of a state may be made subject to a tax applied in lieu of the state sales tax which they have failed to pay because they have purchased items elsewhere.

Since taxes levied at the national level comprehend a wider geographical area than do those of individual state governments, the chance of tax shifting is enhanced under this criterion by national taxes. The opportunities for purchases to move to no-tax or lower tax political jurisdictions are very limited for national taxes. In fact, this can be accomplished only by purchasing outside of the national political jurisdiction, that is, by purchasing within the political boundaries of another nation. A tax which was imposed and administered *uniformly* through-

---

[11] If a tax is *direct* instead of *indirect*, then it will be difficult to shift the tax burden even though the tax may be broadbased. For example, a progressive personal income tax, even if applied to *all types* of income, would not be particularly conducive to tax shifting because the direct nature of the tax would tend to exclude it from a further market transaction.

out the world—a true international tax—would provide the strongest potential for shifting according to the political jurisdiction criterion. In this case, no political jurisdiction would remain in which taxes might be lower or nonexistent.

In summary, the narrower the geographical limit of political jurisdiction imposing a tax, the more difficult it is to shift a tax because there are more alternative geographical areas available where a good or resource might be purchased. Hence, the seller will be hesitant to raise the price by the amount of the tax. The following example is relevant:

A five cent tax per package of cigarettes imposed by a city government may lead to increased consumption purchases outside the city in other cities or counties. Thus, tax shifting by the seller is difficult.

A five cent tax per package of cigarettes imposed by a state government may lead to increased consumption purchases outside the state in other states. However, the geographical availability of such purchases is reduced as compared to the city government example above. Hence, tax shifting by sellers becomes increasingly possible.

A five cent tax per package of cigarettes imposed by a national government may lead to increased comsumption purchases outside the nation in other nations. However, this is difficult to accomplish and is not an avoidance technique available to most smokers. Thus, tax shifting by sellers is considerably enhanced and is the most likely among the three examples so cited.

A five cent tax per package of cigarettes imposed by an international agreement among all nations would leave no geographical (political) area to which consumption could transfer in order to escape the tax. In this instance, tax shifting is the most likely of the four political jurisdiction situations presented here.

Summary

Thus, it has been observed that many forces influence the ability to "shift" the monetary or absolute burden of a tax from its initial point of *impact* to a different taxpaying locus or point of final *incidence*. Some of the most important of these determinants relate to market structure conditions and the presence or not of unrealized gains, long-run industry cost conditions, the price elasticities of demand and supply, the nature of the tax, and the geographical extent of the political jurisdiction imposing the tax. Moreover, it has been indicated that the monetary or absolute burden of a tax involves only a "narrow" concept of incidence. Though difficult in terms of measurement, the ideal conceptual approach to *incidence* is one which considers:

1. Both the revenue and expenditure sides of the budget
2. Both short- and long-run analysis

TABLE 8–1

Taxes Paid as a Percentage of Adjusted Total Income,* by Adjusted Money Income Intervals, 1968

	Total Taxes	Federal Taxes				State and Local Taxes		
		Total	Income Tax	Corp. Profits Tax	Social Security Tax	Total	Property Tax	Sales Tax
Under $2,000................	25.6	11.5	0.6	3.1	3.9	14.0	8.3	3.4
$2,000 to $4,000...........	24.7	13.4	2.5	3.1	4.6	11.2	5.3	3.5
$4,000 to $6,000...........	27.9	17.1	4.7	3.2	6.1	10.9	4.3	3.7
$6,000 to $8,000...........	30.1	19.4	6.5	3.2	6.8	10.7	3.8	3.6
$8,000 to $10,000..........	29.9	19.6	7.6	2.9	6.4	10.3	3.7	3.4
$10,000 to $15,000.........	30.9	20.6	9.1	3.0	6.0	10.3	3.8	3.1
$15,000 to $25,000.........	31.1	21.4	10.3	4.1	4.8	9.7	3.8	2.5
$25,000+..................	38.5	30.9	16.0	10.8	2.0	7.6	2.5	1.6

* Adjusted Total Income is defined as the total household claims on the nation's product after the receipt of transfer payments and the payment of taxes to finance the transfer payments.
Source: Roger A. Herriot and Herman P. Miller, "Changes in the Distribution of Taxes Among Income Groups: 1962 to 1968," American Statistical Association—1971 Proceedings of the Business and Economic Statistics Section, Table 3, p. 108.

3. Intergoal effects
4. General equilibrium conditions with a focus on relative product
and resource price changes as determined by a budgetary change.

INCIDENCE OF THE TOTAL TAX STRUCTURE

In this final section of the chapter, brief attention will be paid to the "incidence" of the *total public sector tax structure* inclusive of all levels and units of American government. In other words, after making estimates and assumptions concerning tax shifting, the question may be asked: "how are the overall tax burdens of the American public sector distributed among different income classes?" Table 8–1 summarizes the findings of one such study which shows federal and state-local taxes paid as a percentage of "adjusted total income" in 1968. This constitutes the "effective rates of tax" or, in other words, the "incidence" of the taxes by income class.

It may be observed from Table 8–1 that the aggregate public sector tax structure is generally *progressive,* in distributional equity terms, though the degree of progression is somewhat moderate. Moreover, the table demonstrates the *progressivity* of the overall "federal" tax structure, which derives revenues mainly from the personal and corporation income taxes with their graduated (progressive) rate structures, and the overall *regressive* nature of the "state-local" tax structure which depends heavily on sales and property taxation.

Table 8–2, which presents the estimated burdens of *certain major*

TABLE 8–2
The Estimated Burden of Major Federal, State and Local Taxes for a Hypothetical Family of Four, for Various Family Income Groups, 1972*

Type of Tax	Estimated Tax as a Percent of Family Income by Income Group					
	$5,000	$7,500	$10,000	$20,000	$25,000	$50,000
Federal Personal Income Tax.............	3.0	6.2	8.4	13.4	15.1	23.2
Social Security Tax (OASDHI)............	5.2	5.2	4.7	2.3	1.9	0.9
Major State and Local Taxes...............	6.9	6.3	6.4	6.5	6.5	6.9
Property	4.6	3.6	3.5	3.1	2.9	2.5
Personal Income	0.5	1.1	1.5	2.3	2.7	3.7
General Sales	1.8	1.6	1.4	1.1	0.9	0.7
Total.................	15.1	17.7	19.5	22.2	23.5	31.0

* Assumes all income from wages and salaries earned by one spouse.
Source: Advisory Commission on Intergovernmental Relations, *Federal-State-Local Finances: Significant Features of Fiscal Federalism* (Washington: U.S. Government Printing Office, 1974), Table 38, p. 53.

federal and state-local taxes for a family of four in 1972, demonstrates the progressivity of *both* the federal and state-local personal income taxes. In addition, it shows the regressivity of the federal social security tax as well as the regressive nature of state-local property and general sales taxes.

9

Income Taxation: The Personal Income Tax

ALTERNATIVE CONCEPTS OF INCOME

The definition of *income* for the purpose of establishing an income tax base involves both theoretical and institutional complexities. Economists disagree somewhat concerning the theoretical ideal of "what should be taxed." Moreover, accounting concepts of income, stressing the "internal control" of a business, differ from those used in economics. Government policymakers (legislators and tax administrators), meanwhile, "institutionalize" the concept by using a hybrid definition of income which is consistent with neither the economic nor the accounting concepts. Yet, if income is to be accepted as the primary indicator of the ability to pay taxes, and if the income tax is to be used prominently within the U.S. public sector, the definition of income selected for tax base purposes should meet the test of "fiscal rationality."[1]

The majority of economists accept the *economic accretion* concept of taxable income.[2] This concept defines *taxable income* for a specified time period as an "accretion to wealth" equal to the sum of (1) the monetary value of an individual's consumption, *plus* (2) any increase in the individual's *net worth (personal wealth)* during the period. Thus both "current consumption" and "net worth gains" constitute *taxable income* under this concept. A "decrease" in net worth, of course, would

---

[1] See Chapter 6.

[2] See Henry C. Simons, *Personal Income Taxation* (Chicago: University of Chicago Press, 1938), for a basic representation of this concept.

cause a reduction in the "taxable income" base. Moreover, the consumption and net worth gains constitute "taxable income" regardless of their financial origin. Thus, "factor earnings" such as wages, interest, rents, or profits may make possible the consumption or net worth increase as also may transfer payments, inheritance, gifts, and gambling winnings. Table 9–1 provides some examples of the *economic accretion* concept of "taxable income."

In practice, the concept of "taxable income" used institutionally within the American public sector does not follow closely, though it does resemble in part, the "economic accretion" benchmark. In the United States, for example, "taxable income" is generally looked upon as a current flow of "monetary receipts" received by a "family spending

TABLE 9–1

Some Examples of the *Economic Accretion* Concept of "Taxable Income"

Taxpayer (1)	Consumption (2)	Change in Net Worth (3)	Taxable Income (column 2 plus or minus column 3) (4)
A............	$20,000	$+5,000	$25,000
B............	20,000	0	20,000
C............	20,000	−5,000	15,000

unit" for its provision of resources to the productive process. It includes only part of the value of gains in the value of capital assets or net worth increases. This deviation is primarily due to administrative expediency since the cost of collecting accurate information on all net worth changes, both realized and unrealized, would be considerable. A second-best approximation to the theoretical ideal, however, may still be considered to be a worthy policy objective.

THE FEDERAL PERSONAL INCOME TAX

Historical Development

The first federal personal (individual) income tax was enacted by Congress in 1861 during the Presidential administration of Abraham Lincoln. Before the beginning of the Civil War in 1861, the federal government had relied heavily upon revenues derived from tariffs and from the sale of public lands. Under the stress of wartime spending, however, increased reliance was placed upon excise, inheritance, and *income* taxes. Though the federal government had never previously enacted a personal income tax, several states had experimented with them and some still had them in force at the beginning of the Civil War.[3]

Congress deliberated in 1861 between the adoption of a direct tax on real property and a personal income tax, but adopted the latter because it seemed less likely that an income tax would require apportionment among the states according to population.[4] It was feared, moreover, that a real property tax would place undue tax burdens upon the agricultural areas along the frontier, primarily in the Midwest and West. Before the collection machinery for the 1861 income tax law had been arranged, Congress enacted the income tax law of July 1, 1862 which superseded the earlier legislation. The first federal income tax revenues were actually collected under the 1862 legislation. The basic characteristics of the 1862 law prevailed, with some modification in rates, until repeal of the tax in 1872.

The Civil War income tax provided adequate revenues despite many enforcement problems. During the period 1863–73, a total of $376 million was collected.[5] Subsequently, the tax was challenged in the courts and found to be constitutional despite its close identification with the economic characteristics of a direct tax. The Supreme Court of the United States thus held in *Springer* v. *United States* (1880) that direct taxes, within the meaning of the Constitution, referred only to capitation taxes and to taxes on real estate, and that the federal personal income tax was "within the category of an excise or duty."[6]

The next adoption of a personal income tax by the federal government was motivated by reform movements rather than by an emergency need for revenues. President Grover Cleveland had been elected in 1892 on a platform which promised to reduce the importance of tariffs in the federal revenue system and to fill the gap by reintroducing the income tax. As a result, a second federal personal income tax became law in 1894, though it was so altered by the Senate from its proposed form that President Cleveland allowed it to become law without signing the bill.[7] Basically, however, the 1894 personal income tax resembled its Civil War predecessor.

Soon after its enactment, a test case was introduced in the courts challenging the constitutionality of the new law. The case pivoted upon

---

[3] However, these state personal income taxes possessed little revenue significance.

[4] The Constitution requires in Article I, Section 9, that direct taxes must be apportioned among the several states according to the census.

[5] Joint Economic Committee, Congress of the United States, *The Federal Tax System: Facts and Problems* (Washington, D.C.: U.S. Government Printing Office, 1964), p. 14.

[6] *Springer* v. *United States,* 102 U.S. 586 (1880).

[7] E. R. A. Seligman, *The Income Tax* (2d ed.; New York: The Macmillan Co., 1914), pp. 499–505.

the interpretation of direct tax as intended by the founding fathers of the Constitution. Are *only* land and capitation taxes direct, or should the income tax also be considered a direct tax? The Supreme Court, in the case of *Pollock* v. *Farmers' Loan and Trust Co.* (1894), reversed the earlier opinion handed down in the *Springer* decision and declared the tax to be unconstitutional on the grounds that it taxed income earned from real estate, from personal property, and from state and local government bonds.[8] Hence, the 1894 income tax died an early death and only $77,000 in revenue was collected from it.[9]

The social reformers, however, refused to accept defeat. A more powerful reform campaign concerned itself with the need for an amendment to the Constitution which would clearly exempt the personal income tax from the requirement that direct taxes be apportioned among the states according to population.[10] In 1913, the Sixteenth Amendment to the Constitution was ratified. This amendment makes abundantly clear the right of Congress to impose personal and corporation income taxes without apportionment among the states according to population. The Sixteenth Amendment states:

> The Congress shall have power to lay and collect taxes on incomes, from whatever source derived, without apportionment among the several States, and without regard to any census or enumeration.

The path having been opened by the ratification of the Sixteenth Amendment, Congress enacted income taxes applying to both individuals and corporations as part of the Tariff Act of 1913.

Subsequently, the federal income taxes gained considerable revenue importance during America's involvement in World War I (1917–18). For example, the maximum rate of the personal income tax, which had been 7 percent from the enactment of the 1913 bill until 1915, was increased to 77 percent by 1918. By 1917, income tax revenues (both personal and corporate) had surpassed customs revenues, and by 1920 approximately two thirds of total federal revenues were derived from the two income taxes.

---

[8] *Pollock* v. *Farmers' Loan and Trust Co.*, 157 U.S. 429 (1894); rehearing: 158 U.S. 601 (1895).

[9] *The Federal Tax System*, p. 14.

[10] Obviously, a personal income tax would be unworkable, on traditional "distributional equity" grounds involving the ability-to-pay principle, if it had to be apportioned among the states according to population. For example, two states may have identical populations, but one state may be twice as wealthy in productive resources and produce twice the amount of income as the other state. Yet, each state would be required to pay the same "absolute amount" of income tax under the constitutional requirement that direct taxes be apportioned—even though one state has "much greater taxpaying ability" than the other.

Personal income tax rates were reduced during the 1920s causing absolute income tax revenues to decline. Then, during the depression of the 1930s federal income tax collections (both personal and corporate) declined still further. This is exemplified by the drop in income tax revenues from a level of $2.4 billion in 1930 to less than $750 million in 1933. Income tax receipts then rose again to $2.1 billion by 1940, though this was still less than their total in 1930. Income tax collections, moreover, represented only 40 percent of the total federal tax revenues collected in 1940 while they had amounted to approximately 67 percent of federal tax revenues 10 years earlier.

The decline in the absolute and relative importance of federal income taxation during the depression decade of the 1930s was reversed by America's involvement in World War II (1941–45). The advent of World War II turned the federal personal income tax into a tax "on the masses" and established the overriding importance of the federal personal and corporation income taxes to the federal revenue structure. In terms of enforcement, the mass personal income tax was made feasible by the adoption of "withholding" at the source of wage and salary income. In addition to providing an enormous increase in the revenues needed to finance the war, the income taxes also helped to combat inflationary pressures. By 1945, the personal income tax had reached an all-time high in rates with a marginal rate range between 23 and

TABLE 9–2
Federal Personal Income Tax Marginal Rate Ranges* and Personal Exemptions, Selected Years, 1861–1974

| | Rate (in Percent) | | Personal Exemption (Single |
Year	Minimum	Maximum	Individual)
1861.................	3	3	$ 800
1862.................	3	5	600
1865.................	5	10	600
1894.................	2	2	4,000
1913.................	1	7	3,000
1918.................	6	77	1,000
1929.................	3⁄8	24	1,500
1939.................	4	79	1,000
1945.................	23	94	500
1954.................	20	91	600
1964 to Present.......	14	70†	750‡

* Only the maximum and minimum rates are shown. The taxable incomes at which the rates apply are not shown in the table.
† Dropped to 50 percent on "earned" (salary and self-employment) income as a result of the Tax Reform Act of 1969.
‡ The personal exemption of $600 in 1964 was increased to $750 by the Tax Reform Act of 1969.

94 percent. In 1945, some 50 million taxpayers filed personal income tax returns, a substantial increase over the 6 million who filed returns during 1937.

Personal income tax rates were reduced in 1945 and again in 1948. The Korean War emergency during the early 1950s, however, motivated Congress to increase rates. After the Korean War ended, the personal income tax rates were lowered in 1954 to their pre-Korean War levels. The Revenue Act of 1964 established the present federal personal income tax rate structure while the Tax Reform Act of 1969 made certain significant changes in the overall composition of the tax. The present composition of the tax will be described below. Meanwhile, Table 9–2 summarizes the historical pattern of federal personal income tax rates, as discussed above, from the Civil War until today.

Federal Personal Income Tax Base and Rate Structure

The procedure required to establish *tax liability* under the federal personal income tax is a "complex" one due to the existence of numerous exclusions, deductions, personal exemptions, tax credits, and the like. These "adjustments" represent the source of considerable deviation between gross income, in a conceptual sense, and ultimate taxable income. In the sequence of their administrative application, the adjustments are:

1. Exclusions from gross income.
2. Deductions from gross income.
3. Deductions from adjusted gross income.
4. Personal exemptions.
5. The application of the rate schedule to the *taxable income* base.
6. Tax credits.
7. The application of the "minimum income tax" rule.

These will be discussed in a general "procedural" context now with the more important provisions being discussed in depth later in Chapters 9 and 10.

A wide variety of personal receipts may be treated as *exclusions from gross income.*[11] Moreover, "income in kind," though not excluded ex-

---

[11] Exclusions from gross income include:
1. Social security benefits.
2. Unemployment compensation.
3. Relief payments.
4. Payments under the Railroad Retirement Act.
5. Veterans' pensions, except retirement pay based on age or length of service.
6. Life insurance payments made upon reason of death.
7. Death benefits, up to a certain maximum, paid to the beneficiary of an employee by an employer upon the death of the employee.
8. Workmen's compensation, damages for illness or injury, accident and health insurance payments. (cont.)

plicitly from gross income, has not in practice been included in the gross income concept under the *Internal Revenue Code*. This includes such goods and services as food produced and consumed on farms and the rental value of owner-occupied nonfarm dwellings. In 1970, the estimated "net" value of such income in kind and imputed income was $45 billion. Yet, some of the other exclusions bear even greater monetary significance. For example, federal transfer payments—including (social security benefits,)(veterans' benefits) and (military pensions—) amounted to nearly $80 billion.

Once exclusions from gross income have been considered, the next step in computing tax liability under the federal personal income tax is to apply various *deductions from gross income.*[12] It should be pointed out that most deductions from gross income constitute ordinary and necessary "business and trade expenses." These deductions would apply, for the most part, to professional people and those operating businesses under the (proprietorship) and (partnership legal forms. The income concept which remains at this point of tax accounting—after exclusions and deductions from gross income adjustments have been made—is that of "adjusted gross income."

The third step in determining federal personal income tax liability is to apply various *deductions from adjusted gross income.*[13] These

9 Contributions by employers to qualified employee pension, annuity, accident, or health plans.

10. Gifts and inheritances.

11. Interest paid on state and local government securities.

12. Fellowship and scholarship grants (subject to limitations).

13. Dividends received from domestic corporations, up to $100 annually per taxpayer.

14. Income earned abroad, up to $20,000, for a taxpayer living abroad for 17 out of 18 months, and $25,000 for a bona fide resident abroad for three or more years.

[12] Deductions from gross income include:

1. All ordinary and necessary expenses paid or incurred during the taxable year in carrying on any trade or business, except in the performance of services as an employee. Allowable deductions include wages and salaries, depletion, depreciation, interest, and taxes.

2. Certain employee expenses incurred in behalf of an employer, including those as an outside salesman and for travel while away from home.

3. One half of net long-term capital losses up to a $1,000 maximum on a joint return.

4. Expenses which may be attributed to the production of rent and royalty income.

5. Certain deductions of self-employed individuals for pension, annuity, profit-sharing, and bond purchase plans.

6. The expenses of moving because of a change in job locations by new or continuing employees (subject to various limitations).

[13] Deductions from adjusted gross income include:

1. Various taxes such as *state and local* personal property, real property, income, general sales, and gasoline taxes.

2. Interest on indebtedness (subject to various limitations).

3. Contributions to certain nonprofit institutions, such as religious, educational, scientific, and charitable organizations (subject to various limitations).

4. Various expenses associated with the occupation of the taxpayer, such as union dues, membership fees in professional associations, subscriptions to professional journals,

deductions, such as a portion of medical expenses and charitable contributions, are essentially of a (nonbusiness or personal nature.) They must be itemized on the taxpayer's return unless he prefers to use the standard deduction.

The fourth step in computing federal personal income tax liability is to deduct *(personal exemptions.)* Under legislation enacted in 1969, the taxpayer now receives an exemption of $750 for himself and additional exemptions of $750 for his spouse and for each dependent. Also, additional $750 exemptions are allowed for a taxpayer who is age 65 or over, for his spouse if 65 years of age or over, for a blind taxpayer, and for a blind spouse. In 1970, the personal exemptions on tax returns bearing ultimate tax liability amounted to $107 billion, with the amount being significantly greater if nontaxable returns are included.

The first four steps establish the *taxable income base* of the federal personal income tax. It is to this base that the *rate schedule* is applied (step 5). The rate structure of the federal personal income tax is progressive in both "technical" and "distributional equity" terms. Table 9–3 shows the marginal and average statutory rates of tax now in effect for the federal personal income tax. In all, there are 25 different taxable income brackets at which the rates are applied. Obviously, the average rates represent a lower "range" of rates (14 to 55.5 percent) than do the marginal rates (14 to 70 percent) because they encompass the effects of the lower marginal rates on all previous lower income marginal brackets as well as the higher marginal rate of the highest income bracket attained by the taxpayer. For example, on $2,000 of taxable income the *marginal* rate of 14 percent would apply on $1,000 of the total amount and the marginal rate of 15 percent on the remaining $1,000. The *average* rate is thus 14.5 percent on the total $2,000 because one half of the total amount was taxed at a 14 percent instead of at a 15 percent rate.

A special adjustment is made for taxpayers with sharply fluctuating income over a period of years. The adjustment made in this situation, known as *(income averaging,)* will be described more fully in a subsequent section of the chapter. Furthermore, legislation during 1969 provided a new *maximum tax on earned income.* This statutory provision places a maximum marginal rate limit of 50 percent on salaries or self-employment income. However, such preferential treatment will be

---

uniforms, other types of special work apparel, and educational expenses incurred to maintain or improve skills required in the taxpayer's employment, trade, or business, or to meet the requirements of the taxpayer's employer.

5. Medical expenses incurred on behalf of the taxpayer, his wife, and dependents, if not reimbursed by insurance (subject to various limitations).

6. An amount equal to the excess over $100 of each loss due to fire, theft, or other casualty to the extent that the loss is not compensated by insurance.

7. Alimony and separate maintenance payments to the extent that these amounts are includable in the recepient's gross income.

TABLE 9–3
Federal Personal Income Tax Rate Structure,* Marginal and Average Rates of Tax, for Married Persons Filing Joint Returns

Taxable Income Bracket	Tax Rate (Percent)	
	Marginal	Average†
$ 0– 1,000	14	14.0
1,000– 2,000	15	14.5
2,000– 3,000	16	15.0
3,000– 4,000	17	15.5
4,000– 8,000	19	17.2
8,000– 12,000	22	18.8
12,000– 16,000	25	20.4
16,000– 20,000	28	21.9
20,000– 24,000	32	23.6
24,000– 28,000	36	25.4
28,000– 32,000	39	27.1
32,000– 36,000	42	28.7
36,000– 40,000	45	30.3
40,000– 44,000	48	32.0
44,000– 52,000	50	34.7
52,000– 64,000	53	38.2
64,000– 76,000	55	40.8
76,000– 88,000	58	43.2
88,000–100,000	60	45.2
100,000–120,000	62	48.0
120,000–140,000	64	50.3
140,000–160,000	66	52.2
160,000–180,000	68	54.0
180,000–200,000	69	55.5
over 200,000.	70	55.5–

* The introduction of a "maximum rate" on *earned income* by the Tax Reform Act of 1969 reduces the likelihood of many taxpayers being in the high marginal brackets even beyond the escape from high brackets allowed by the various special preferences that have historically benefited higher income taxpayers.

† Based on maximum figure in each taxable income bracket rather than on minimum figure or mean figure of the bracket.

reduced by other income received by the taxpayer if that income is accorded special tax treatment under other provisions to the extent that such other income exceeds $30,000 per year.[14] This option is not available to those taxpayers who use the income averaging provision.

Tax credits also may influence federal personal income tax liability (step six).[15] A tax credit reduces the tax liability computed in the proce-

---

[14] Specifically, if the value of tax preference income in the current year, or the "average" tax preference income during the current year and four previous years, whichever is higher, exceeds $30,000, the preferential "earned income" feature is reduced.

[15] Tax credits include:

1. A credit for foreign income taxes paid (subject to various limitations). This is applicable *only* if a deduction is not applied for this amount.

2. A credit for partially tax-exempt interest on certain federal government securities, subject to a maximum limit.

3. A retirement income credit for persons 65 or over, and for those under 65 who are retired under a public retirement system (subject to various limitations).

dures of step five by the amount of the credit itself. Such credits may be of two types. First, a credit such as that for foreign income taxes paid reduces, in a "complete" sense, the true tax liability of the taxpayer to the federal government. On the other hand, a credit for tax withheld at the source of income, though reducing the tax amount owed to the federal government at the time of submission of the individual's tax return, does not represent a genuine reduction in the true tax liability of the taxpayer.

A *final* step (step seven) in establishing "ultimate" tax liability under the federal personal income tax involves application of the recently enacted (1969) *minimum income tax* rule. This provision is intended to reduce the capability of high-income taxpayers to completely escape the federal personal income tax. The amount of "tax-sheltered" income is summed and $30,000 is subtracted from that income. Then, the regular income tax liability of the taxpayer is subtracted from the remainder and a 10 percent *minimum tax* is assessed on this amount. The most important of the various *special provisions* of the federal personal income tax law alluded to in the above "procedural" discussion will now be discussed in depth in the section which follows.

Special Characteristics of the Federal Personal Income Tax[16]

The Exclusion of State and Local Government Bond Interest. Interest income received from state and local government securities is one of the major "exclusions" from gross income. Moreover, this exclusion has been in existence, despite reaching a vote in Congress on a number of occasions, since the establishment of the present federal personal income tax in 1913.[17] The significance of the exclusion has been increasing in recent years. This is due to the rapid post-World War II growth of state and local government debt.[18] The twofold effects of this growing significance for the exclusion are (1) the growing revenue loss to the federal government and (2) the increasing impact of the violation

---

[16] Certain features of federal income tax law which are applicable to *business income* are common both to the federal personal income tax, now being discussed in Chapters 9 and 10, and to the federal corporation income tax, discussed in Chapter 11. Several of these provisions, such as those pertaining to depreciation and depletion, are discussed in the latter chapter, but are equally relevant to the personal income tax chapters (Chapters 9 and 10) if the business income is that of a proprietorship or partnership instead of a corporation.

[17] The most recent challenge to the exclusion from gross income of state and local government bond interest was in the enactment of the Tax Reform Act of 1969. However, an avalanche of lobbying efforts on behalf of state and local governments succeeded in continuing the exclusion.

[18] See Chapter 27.

of the "ability-to-pay" principle of equity in the distribution of tax burdens. As an example of the latter, it may be observed that an average interest yield on "tax-exempt" state and local government bonds of 6.35 percent would represent nearly a 13 percent yield on a taxable security if the taxpayer is in the 50 percent marginal rate bracket.

Additional disadvantages of the exclusion of state and local government bond interest from the federal personal income tax base include the distortion of resource allocation both within the private sector as well as between the public and private sectors of the economy. If the exclusion is used to encourage the establishment of industrial development projects to attract private firms through tax-exempt facilities, an allocative distortion within the private sector occurs. In the event that a state or local government issues tax-exempt bonds to finance "commercial" type undertakings in the public utility or housing areas, intersector allocation distortion tends to occur.

One argument in behalf of the tax-exempt status of such interest stresses the need to preserve state and local government fiscal autonomy in a federal system. Thus, even if the exclusion were replaced by a partial or complete intergovernmental transfer or subsidy to state and local governments from the federal government, there would remain the fear that central government control over state and local governments would increase. In retrospect, it is clear that a policy "trade-off" regarding the tax-exempt security issue exists between the violation of the ability-to-pay principle of tax equity, since the loophole is primarily used by individuals with high incomes, and the political problem of a "proper" division of fiscal powers between the two sovereign levels of government (federal and state-local) in the American federation.

The Preferential Treatment of Capital Gains. Net *long-term* capital gains realized on the sale or exchange of capital assets held for more than six months receive "preferential tax treatment."[19] On the other hand, net *short-term* capital gains realized on the sale or exchange of capital assets held for less than six months are "fully taxable" as ordinary property income. One-half of the net *long-term* capital gains of individuals, to the extent that they exceed net short-term capital losses, may be excluded from the tax base thus causing such gains to be taxed at one half of the ordinary income tax rates on property income. Moreover, the tax rate is limited to 25 percent on the first $50,000 of gain

---

[19] *Capital assets* are defined by the *Internal Revenue Code* to include all property held by the taxpayer except certain specified categories such as: (1) stock in trade; (2) property held primarily for sale to customers in the ordinary course of the taxpayer's trade or business; (3) property used in trade or business which is subject to an allowance for depreciation; (4). real property used in trade or business; (5) a copyright, literary, artistic, or musical composition which is the product of the personal efforts of the taxpayer; (6) accounts or notes receivable acquired in the ordinary course of trade or business; and (7) certain government obligations which are sold at a discount.

with the maximum limit of 35 percent applying to amounts exceeding $50,000.[20] This 35 percent maximum marginal long-term capital gains tax rate is equal to one half of the maximum marginal rate of 70 percent on ordinary property income.

A controversy exists over the "rationality" of treating capital gains in a preferential manner from the treatment of ordinary income. Indeed, a complete adoption of the economic accretion definition of income described earlier in the chapter would require the full taxation of "all" capital gains as they "accrue" annually. Moreover, if income is to serve as the primary indicator of taxpaying ability in reference to the ability-to-pay principle of distributional tax equity, capital cains income should be taxed on an equivalent basis with other sources of income, including labor income. In fact, at times capital gains represent an "unearned" increment of income in the sense that such occurrences as an increase in the site value of land, a discovery of oil, or a rise in bond prices due to changes in the market rate of interest may be gains for which the asset holder is not directly responsible by his own initiative or actions. Hence, it is argued the such gains should be taxed on an equal basis with ordinary wage and salary income—if not taxed more heavily. Furthermore, the preferential treatment of capital gains income provides an extraordinary tax avoidance loophole which is especially attractive to higher income taxpayers. The overall magnitude of lost revenues to the federal government from this loophole, not to mention its violation of the ability-to-pay principle, is estimated to exceed $6 billion annually. Finally, it is contended that the preferred treatment of capital gains income under federal income taxation provides a negative nonneutral effect on capital markets by encouraging the "retention" or "plow back" of profits within corporations.

On the other hand, those who favor preferential treatment for capital gains, even to the point of imposing no tax at all on such gains, use a variety of arguments. Among these are the argument that an investor may feel "locked in" if his asset or investment has increased significantly in value. Thus, he may hestitate to sell the asset because of the existence of a capital gains tax, with a resulting distortion of business and investment decision making. On the other hand, if capital values decline, many taxpayers may be induced to sell in order to deduct the capital losses. Thus, distortion occurs in investment decisions concerning the retention of capital. Furthermore, it is argued that if the capital gain is taxed in the particular year in which the gain accrues, though is not realized, an undue burden may be placed on the taxpayer since

---

[20] However, since capital gains are classified as a "tax preference item" under the "minimum income tax" provision, the *effective* maximum rate becomes 36.5 percent when this provision is taken into account.

an immediate "income flow" is not available for payment of the tax. In addition, it is contended that the preferential tax treatment under the federal personal income tax of capital gains income stimulates the accumulation of capital by individuals who subsequently make much of it available in the capital markets where new or growing firms may acquire it. Finally, it may be argued that capital gains serve as rewards through preferential tax treatment for those individuals who undertake the risk of investment to promote a changing and growing economy. Since capital losses are not fully deductible, this argument receives additional reenforcement.

Personal Deductions and Exemptions.   Various *personal deductions* from adjusted gross income are allowed in the computation of a taxpayer's liability under the federal personal income tax. With certain specific limitations, these personal deductions include medical and dental expenses, taxes paid to state and local governments, contributions to religious, charitable, educational, and other organizations, and interest expenses. A taxpayer may either present *itemized* deductions or select a *standard deduction*. Under the standard deduction, a taxpayer can either deduct 15 percent of adjusted gross income up to a maximum of $2,000, or a flat amount of $1,300. The latter option, which is known as the *low-income allowance,* is more advantageous for taxpayers with adjusted gross incomes up to $8,667 since it puts a minimum or floor under the standard deduction. For example, the flat deduction of $1,300 is equal to 15 percent of $8,667.

Personal exemptions, which comprise the fourth step in the computation of federal personal income tax liability as described above, allow the taxpayer to deduct an exemption for himself and additional exemptions for his spouse and for each dependent. Also, additional exemptions are allowed for a taxpayer who is age 65 or over, for his spouse at 65 years of age or over, or a blind taxpayer, and for a blind spouse. The amount allowed for each personal exemption is $750.

Family Status and Taxable Income.   As observed above, personal exemptions allow a special preference to family size because of the allowance of separate exemptions for each dependent child as well as for both husband and spouse. In addition, the federal personal income tax accords significant preferential treatment to the *family taxpaying unit* through the technique of "income splitting." This device provides an important rate modification for married couples filing a joint tax return since they may compute their joint tax liability by applying the statutory tax rates to one half of their combined taxable income and then multiplying this result by two. With a progressive tax rate structure, married couples thus enjoy tax savings from this technique as long as either spouse has a taxable income in excess of the maximum taxable income in the first of the 25 rate brackets.

Under this arrangement, discrimination is practiced against single taxpayers as well as widows, widowers, and divorced people. Even when such an individual can be classified as the "head of a household," only partial tax relief is obtained as compared to a married couple filing a joint return. However, the Tax Reform Act of 1969 provided for a partial reduction of this preferential treatment. Under this legislation, effective in 1971, a new rate schedule for single people was initiated. The new rate schedule allows the tax of a single person to exceed no more than 120 percent of the amount owed by a married couple with the same income. Previously, the differential could run as high as 141 percent. Furthermore, a new rate schedule to provide relief for widows, widowers, and divorced people who qualify for "head of household" status went into effect in 1971 to provide reduced tax differentials as compared to the married couple filing a joint return

The preferential treatment of *family status* may be supported in an "equity" context in the sense that the ability to pay taxes is an "inverse" function of family size since families with children have greater requirements for space, food, health services, and educational services, among other expenses. On the other hand, it may be argued that deductions for family size encourage large families and thus contribute to a long-run population problem.

Income Averaging. Fluctuating income over a period of years, as opposed to more stable earnings, may penalize the taxpayer under a progressive rate structure in the absence of an "averaging" device. For example, a married couple filing a joint return who earn $8,000 of taxable income during *each* of the next five years would incur a cumulative total tax liability for the five-year period of $6,900 on the $40,000 of income.[21] However, if the same couple earned $40,000 of taxable income during the five-year period—with *all* of the earnings being made in a single year—they would pay a much larger tax of $12,140 in the absence of an averaging device. Hence, the need for an averaging device is apparent.

Prior to the Revenue Act of 1964, only slight consideration was provided for fluctuating incomes. Some occupations were covered by averaging devices or other special rules while others were not covered. The 1964 legislation replaced the scattered provisions with a general averaging device. Subsequent important legislation in this regard replaced the law which required for "averaging eligibility" that taxable income be more that 133⅓ percent of the average taxable income of the prior four years by lowering the percentage to 120. Moreover, the averaging technique may be used for previously ineligible income such as long-term capital gains and income from gambling However, those

---

[21] These computations assume current tax rates.

using income averaging must forego certain other tax privileges including the maximum rate limitation on earned income.

Maximum Rate on Earned Income. Until the legislation of 1969, the only specific "personal" allowances to taxpayers were deductions for certain business expenses, for certain personal expenses, and for personal exemptions. Earlier, the federal personal income tax between 1924–31 and 1934–43 had allowed an additional "earned income" adjustment. This practice is still commonly followed in a number of other Western nations. The "earned income" concept gives preferential consideration to earnings from *labor effort* as opposed to income derived from the ownership of the property factors of production. In the Tax Reform Act of 1969, a modest reintroduction of this concept occurred.

Thus, a maximum tax rate of 50 percent is imposed on the "earned income" of an individual. This applies essentially to wage, salary, and self-employment income. For example, adjustments are made under this provision so that if a single taxpayer has $100,000 of salary income and $20,000 of dividend income, the former will not be taxed at a marginal rate above 50 percent while the dividend income would be taxed at the top bracket marginal rate of 70 percent. However, the benefit from this earned income provision is reduced to the extent that the taxpayer has other income which derives from the various "preferential sources" contained in the "minimum income tax" plan, which is further described below. Specifically, the amount designated as "earned income" will be reduced by any income from such "preferential sources" which totals more than $30,000 per year.

Minimum Income Tax. Some of the important tax avoidance loopholes which allow high-income taxpayers to escape most, and at times all, income tax liability were "limited" by a new rule contained in the Tax Reform Act of 1969. Thus, a "minimum" tax of 10 percent is levied on "tax preference income" after the deduction from such income of the taxpayer's regular federal income tax liability, and $30,000 ($15,000 each) for a married couple filing a joint tax return.

For example, if the taxpayer receives $200,000 of income from preferential sources and pays $50,000 of regular personal income tax, he would first subtract this $50,000 from his preferential income. The residual is $150,000. Then the taxpayer would subtract the $30,000 allowance (for a married couple filing a joint return) from the $150,000 leaving $120,000. The 10 percent minimum tax would thus be applied to the $120,000 and the tax liability under the minimum income tax concept would be $12,000. Hence, the total tax would be $62,000 ($50,000 of regular personal income tax plus $12,000 under the minimum income tax rule).

"Preferential sources," under the minimum income tax concept, include: accelerated depreciation gains on personal property which is subject to a net lease; accelerated depreciation gains on real property; amortization of certified pollution control facilities; amortization of railroad rolling stock; tax benefits from stock option; the excess of percentage over cost depletion; and one half of net long-term capital gains (over net short-term capital losses). On the other hand, the minimum income tax rule does not include interest earnings from tax-exempt state and local government securities. Hence, this major tax avoidance loophole, used primarily by high-income taxpayers, remains fully in force.

Erosion of the Federal Personal Income Tax Base

A divergence exists between the conceptual definition of "taxable income," in the *economic accretion* sense, and the effective base of the federal personal income tax. U.S. Treasury Department data reveal that there were 367 individuals in 1966 who earned $100,000 or more income who paid no federal personal income tax. The reported income of these individuals totaled $140 million. In 1967, the number of such "tax-free" individuals increased to 399 with combined reported income of $185 million. Once more, these data reflect only "reported" incomes. They do not reflect, for example, "exclusions from gross incomes" such as interest earned on tax-exempt state and local government bonds. In addition, there were 18 individuals in 1966 and 23 individuals in 1967 who had incomes in excess of $1,000,000 and who paid no federal personal income tax. During 1967 the total "reported" income of these individuals amounted to $95 million. Furthermore, there were 394 individuals with annual incomes in excess of $100,000 who paid no federal personal income tax in 1970, 276 such individuals in 1971, and 402 individuals in this category during 1972.

Indeed, a complexity of tax avoidance loopholes exist, many of which are effectively available only to upper income taxpayers, which contribute to considerable erosion of the federal personal income tax base. The overall impact of this is reflected in Tables 9–4, 9–5, and 9–6. In Table 9–4, for example, it may be observed that the "statutory" or "nominal" *average tax rate* of the federal personal income tax during 1966 varies sharply from the "effective" or "actual" *average tax rate* as adjusted gross income reaches the higher income brackets. Thus, the "statutory" tax rate on adjusted gross income below $5,000 is 15.3 percent while the "effective" tax rate is 15 percent—a very small differential representing very little tax base erosion at the low income levels. On the other hand, on adjusted gross income in excess of $1,000,000 the "statutory" *average tax rate* of 55.5 percent greatly exceeds the "effective" *tax rate* of 32.7 percent—a large differential representing considerable tax base erosion. Moreover, these differences at the higher income

TABLE 9–4
"Statutory" and "Effective" *Average Tax Rates,* in Percent, by Adjusted Gross
Income Bracket, 1966

Adjusted Gross Income Bracket	"Statutory" or "Nominal" Average Tax Rate	"Effective" or "Actual" Average Tax Rate
$5,000 and under	15.3	15.0
$5,000 to $10,000	16.4	16.2
$10,000 to $20,000	18.1	17.8
$20,000 to $50,000	24.0	22.8
$50,000 to $100,000	35.8	32.6
$100,000 to $200,000	45.6	37.8
$200,000 to $500,000	52.3	37.9
$500,000 to $1,000,000	55.3	35.8
$1,000,000 and over	55.5	32.7

Source: U.S. Treasury Department

brackets are actually understated since substantial sources of income such as interest from state and local government bonds are excluded from the table. Despite this erosion of its base, the effective tax rate range of the federal personal income tax remains "progressive" (15–32.7 percent), but much less so than its statutory rate structure (15.3–55.5 percent) would suggest.

The concept of *personal income,* as defined and measured by the Department of Commerce, varies significantly in monetary magnitude from the *taxable income base* of individuals, as measured by the Treasury Department. Nonetheless, the "personal income" figure of the Department of Commerce is an excellent starting point for establishing a "potential" income tax base which is "comprehensive" in nature. Table 9–5 disaggregates these two concepts for the calendar year 1970 in order to reconcile the differences between them. As a result, further evidence is provided regarding the erosion of the federal personal income tax base. For example, *exclusions* inclusive of transfer payments, imputed income, and the like, are 22 percent of the total personal income figure, but are not included in the total taxable income of individuals. However, certain conceptual adjustments involving the legal and economic definitions of income, totalling $48 billion, reduce this figure by 6 percent, to 16 percent. Thus, *adjusted exclusions* constitute $134 billion, or 16 percent, of personal income.

Another $62 billion, or 8 percent of personal income, escapes tax liability by being either filed on *nontaxable returns* or by *not being reported.* This includes items which may be classified as either "avoided" or "evaded." *Personal deductions,* both itemized and stan-

TABLE 9–5
The Relationship of Personal Income to Taxable Income under the Federal Personal Income Tax, Calendar Year, 1970

Income Concept		Amount (billions of dollars)	Significant Percentage Ratios
Personal income		$ 806	
Deduct: Portion of personal income not included in adjusted gross income.		−182	
Transfer payments*	80		
Other labor income†	32		
Imputed income and income in kind‡	45		
Other types of personal income	$\dfrac{25}{182}$		$\left\{\dfrac{\text{Exclusions}}{\text{Personal income}}\right.$ → $\dfrac{182}{806} = 22\%$
Add: Portion of adjusted gross income not included in personal income.		+48	
Employee and self-employed persons contributions for social insurance	28		
Net gains from sale of capital and other assets	10		
Other types of income	$\dfrac{10}{48}$		$\left\{\dfrac{\text{Exclusions (adjusted)}}{\text{Personal income}}\right.$ → $\dfrac{134}{806} = 16\%$‖
Equals: Adjusted gross income of taxable and nontaxable individuals.		672	$\left\{\dfrac{\text{Adjusted gross income}}{\text{Personal income}}\right.$ → $\dfrac{672}{806} = 83\%$
Deduct: Nontaxable and nonreported adjusted gross income§		−62	$\left\{\dfrac{\text{Nontaxable and nonreported income}}{\text{Personal income}}\right.$ → $\dfrac{62}{806} = 8\%$
Equals: Adjusted gross income of taxable individuals		610	
Deduct: Deductions of taxable individuals.		−102	
Standard deductions.	18		
Itemized deductions	$\dfrac{84}{102}$		$\left\{\dfrac{\text{Personal deductions}}{\text{Personal income}}\right.$ → $\dfrac{102}{806} = 13\%$
Equals: Net income of taxable individuals		508	
Deduct: Personal exemptions of taxable individuals		−107	$\left\{\dfrac{\text{Personal exemptions}}{\text{Personal income}}\right.$ → $\dfrac{107}{806} = 13\%$
Equals: Taxable income of individuals		401	$\left\{\dfrac{\text{Taxable personal income}}{\text{Personal income}}\right.$ → $\dfrac{401}{806} = 50\%$

* Excludes fees and pay of military reservists.　† Excludes military retirement pay.

‡ Net total of imputed items in disposable personal income such as estimated value of food and fuel consumed on farms.

§ Includes income on nontaxable returns, income disclosed by audit, estimated income of tax evaders, and the like.

‖ The *adjusted exclusions* figure is 16 percent after certain "conceptual adjustments" amounting to $48 billion are taken into consideration.

Source: Data from U.S. Department of Commerce; U.S. Treasury Department.

dard, amounted to $102 billion in 1970. This represented nearly 13 percent of personal income. Furthermore, *personal exemptions* totaled $107 billion or 13 percent of personal income. Other than exclusions, personal exemptions during 1970 thus constituted the largest single category of erosion between personal income and taxable income.

Hence, this series of "escape provisions" lowered a "potential" comprehensive *personal income tax base* of $806 billion to an *actual taxable income base* of $401 billion during 1970. Importantly, the latter figure represents only about 50 percent of personal income. Once again, the significant erosion of the federal personal income tax is apparent. Moreover, though not shown in the table, it is interesting to note that during 1970, federal personal income tax revenues constituted only 11 percent of personal income, 13 percent of adjusted gross income, and 22 percent of taxable income.

Finally, Table 9–6 and Figure 9–1 provide additional evidence of the erosion of the federal personal income tax base. Particularly, they demonstrate the distribution of the various federal personal income tax preference loopholes by *income class*.[22] The "Adjusted Gross Income" (AGI) classes used in both the table and the graph are "expanded" from the statutory definition of AGI provided by the Internal Revenue Code to meaningfully include the estimated value of numerous exclusions and other tax preference income not statutorily included in AGI.

In Table 9–6, it may be observed that the bulk of tax benefits from capital gains,[23] and also from tax exempt interest, dividend exclusions, and excess depletion are received at the "higher income" levels. Meanwhile, the bulk of tax benefits resulting from transfer payments, including social security payments, and from personal exemptions for age and blindness are received at the "lower income" levels. On the other hand, the "middle income" classes receive the greatest benefits from homeowners' preferences such as the exclusion of the services (imputed rent) of owner-occupied homes and the deductibility of mortgage interest and property tax payments. Also, the middle income levels receive the greatest preferential treatment resulting from the nontaxation of interest on life insurance savings. Figure 9–1, in turn, demonstrates the rapid tapering off of the increase in "effective" federal personal income tax rates at the higher income levels. Moreover, it shows the expanding

---

[22] Table 9–6 and Figure 9–1 are based on a recent study by Joseph A. Pechman and Benjamin A. Okner which was published in *The Economics of Federal Subsidy Programs,* A Conpendium of Papers submitted to the Joint Economic Committee, Part 1, General Study Papers, 92d Congress, 2d sess. (1972), pp. 13–40.

[23] *Capital gains* are defined in the Pechman-Okner study to include the "tax advantage" effects of excluding both one half of realized capital gains and also excluding gains transferred by gift or bequest from the personal income tax base.

TABLE 9–6
Percentage Distribution of Features Increasing the Tax Base under a Comprehensive Income Tax, by Income Classes, 1972 Income Levels
[Income classes in thousands]

(Expanded Adjusted Gross Income Class)*	All Features	Capital Gains‡	Features Affecting the Tax Base†							
			Tax Exempt Interest, Dividend Exclusion, Excess Depletion, and Other Preference Income	Life Insurance Interest	Homeowners' Preferences§	Transfer Payments	Other Itemized Deductions	Percentage Standard Deduction	Additional Exemptions for Age and Blindness
Under $3	100.0	0.8	0.5	1.1	4.4	24.0	0.5		68.9
$3 to $5	100.0	.9	.4	1.3	4.2	57.1	.5		35.7
$5 to $10	100.0	3.1	.9	4.0	10.3	62.3	3.0	1.3	15.2
$10 to $15	100.0	5.0	1.3	7.3	18.3	37.8	3.6	21.6	5.1
$15 to $20	100.0	7.2	1.9	8.5	24.0	27.3	5.1	23.5	2.6
$20 to $25	100.0	10.2	2.4	7.5	25.4	25.7	7.5	18.4	3.0
$25 to $50	100.0	21.6	3.9	5.5	23.6	21.3	10.3	11.4	2.3
$50 to $100	100.0	53.0	7.1	1.0	15.9	3.0	15.4	2.9	1.8
$100 to $500	100.0	68.4	14.5	.3	5.9	(#)	9.7	.4	.7
$500 to $1,000	100.0	80.4	11.9	.1	2.0		5.4	.1	.1
$1,000 and over	100.0	88.8	6.6	.1	.8		3.6	(#)	(#)
All classes	100.0	15.7	3.0	5.5	17.3	33.2	5.9	12.6	6.9

* Expanded adjusted gross income is adjusted gross income as defined in the Internal Revenue Code modified to include the following additional income items: one half of realized capital gains; constructive realization of gain on gifts and bequests; tax exempt state and local government bond interest; excess of percentage over cost depreciation and accelerated over straight-line depreciation; dividend exclusion; interest on life insurance policies; homeowners preferences; transfer payments, and personal exemptions and deductions.

† Beginning with the Revenue Act of 1971 as it applies to 1972 income and going to a comprehensive tax base.

‡ Includes effects of excluding ½ realized capital gains and taxation of gains transferred by gift or bequest.

§ Includes effects of eliminating itemized deductions for mortgage interest and real estate taxes.

Less than 0.05.

Note: Details may not add to totals because of rounding.

Source: Joseph A. Pechman and Benjamin A. Okner, "Individual Income Tax Erosion by Income Classes" (Washington: *The Economics of Federal Subsidy Programs*, Joint Economic Committee, Compendium of Papers, Part 1, *General Study Papers*, 92d Cong. 2d sess., 1972), p. 25.

FIGURE 9–1

Influence of Various Provisions on Effective Rates of Federal Personal Income Tax, 1971 Act*

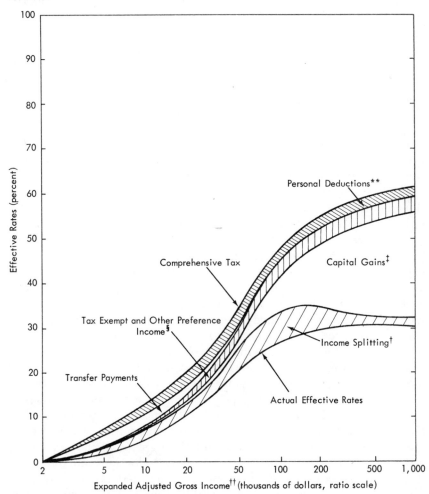

Expanded Adjusted Gross Income[††] (thousands of dollars, ratio scale)

* Rates, exemptions, and other provisions of the Revenue Act of 1971 scheduled to apply to calendar year 1972 incomes.

† Includes effect of removing maximum tax.

‡ Includes effect of full taxation and constructive realization of capital gains.

§ Includes effect of taxing of interest on state-local bonds and life insurance policies; taxing net imputed rent (including effect of disallowing personal deductions for mortgage interest and real estate taxes); disallowing excess of percentage over cost depletion; disallowing excess of accelerated over straight-line depreciation; and removing dividend exclusion.

** Includes effect of removing additional exemptions for age and blindness and retirement income credit.

†† Expanded adjusted gross income is adjusted gross income as defined in the Internal Revenue Code modified to include the income items listed in Table 9–6.

Source: Joseph A. Pechman and Benjamin A. Okner, "Individual Income Tax Erosion by Income Classes" (Washington: *The Economics of Federal Subsidy Programs,* Joint Economic Committee, Compendium of Papers, Part 1, *General Study Papers,* 92d Cong. 2d sess., 1972), p. 28.

importance of the preferential treatment of "capital gains"[24] as income increases at the higher levels.

Indeed, the above discussion indicates that the effective progressivity of the federal personal income tax deviates considerably from the fundamental theoretical concepts of horizontal and vertical tax equity as espoused by the ability-to-pay principle. Yet, as Table 9–4 and Figure 9–1 demonstrate, there still remains some "effective" progressivity after tax avoidance loopholes are taken into account. However, this is much less than the nominal progressivity that would be suggested by the marginal tax rate brackets which range between 14 percent and 70 percent. Obviously, the various items which differentiate a comprehensive definition of personal income from taxable income erode the tax base to a considerable extent. Whether they do so from a rationality standpoint, of course, is another question. The determination of rationality in this regard is an extremely elusive proposition primarily because the definition of taxable income impinges upon the "sacred" value judgment of determining distributional equity.

It is contended by opponents of the various tax avoidance loopholes that elimination or significant modification of these loopholes would greatly increase the revenue potential of the federal personal income tax and/or allow a substantial reduction in the range of tax rates applied to the tax base. Pechman has suggested a tax simplification plan whereby the federal personal income tax rate range of 14 to 70 percent could be reduced to a range of 7 to 35 percent.[25] The proposed plan would involve the taxation of income from *all* sources which, of course, would mean the elimination of special treatment for certain types of income such as captial gains, state and local bond interest, and dividends. In so doing, it would approximate the broader concept of income represented by the *economic accretion* approach. Meanwhile, deductions would be limited under the plan to such strategic items as large medical expenses, casualty losses, and charitable contributions above 2 percent of income. Other less important deductions, including the then-existing standard 10 percent optional deduction, would be removed. However, the personal exemption concept would be retained under the proposal. Relatedly, a Canadian Royal Commission (in 1967) and the Executive Branch of the Canadian federal government have suggested the adoption of a comprehensive income tax system for Canada.[26] Some aspects of these recommendations have been implemented in Canada.

---

[24] See the definition of "capital gains" in footnote 23 for its meaning in this statement.

[25] What's Wrong with Our Tax System?," a discussion by Frank Fernbach, Joseph Pechman, and Martin Gainsburgh, *Challenge,* July-August 1966. p. 17. See also the alternative tax rate reduction alternative for the federal personal income tax as presented in Pechman and Okner, *Economics of Federal Subsidy Programs,* pp. 29–33.

[26] See the relevant discussion in Chapter 22.

Proponents of an eroded federal personal income tax base contend that the difference between personal and taxable income is accounted for by items which either cannot be included in taxable income on the basis of practical administration and compliance, or which conflict with other basic objectives of public policy. Undoubtedly, certain validity is contained in these arguments. However, it does not seem likely that the degree of erosion which now exists can be considered *rational* in a society which basically has espoused the concepts of horizontal and vertical tax equity and the use of "income" as the indicator of taxpaying ability under the guidance of these benchmarks.

STATE AND LOCAL PERSONAL INCOME TAXES

History of State and Local Personal Income Taxes

At the beginning of the twentieth century, some *states* still carried statutes providing for personal income taxes which had been enacted during the nineteenth century. These flat rate (proportional) taxes, which were administered by local property tax officials, were quite ineffective as revenue producers and can scarcely be considered the legitimate forerunners of the present state personal income taxes. The "new era" of personal income taxation at the state and local levels was initiated in 1911 when Wisconsin adopted a well-planned state personal income tax which was centrally administered by a state tax commission. The Wisconsin tax, moreover, provided progressive rates and personal exemptions.

The success of the Wisconsin tax led to the early adoption of similar personal income taxes by several other states. By 1920, 9 states (plus the Territory of Hawaii) imposed such taxes. During the 1920s, 5 additional states adopted personal income taxes. The depression of the 1930s provided strong impetus for additional state adoptions of the tax and 16 states imposed personal income taxes between 1931 and 1937. Only one state, Alaska (then a territory), adopted a personal income tax between 1937 and 1961—a period equal to nearly one quarter of a century. However, a resurgence of state personal income tax adoptions occurred during the decade of the 1960s and the early 1970s. For the most part, the use of personal income taxes by local governments is a post-World War II phenomenon. However, the city of Philadelphia initiated the trend toward local government personal income taxation in 1939.

Present Status of State Personal Income Taxes

Personal income taxes are imposed by 44 states and the District of Columbia. This total includes the New Hampshire tax which applies only to dividend and interest income and to commuters, the Tennessee tax which applies only to dividends and interest, the Connecticut tax which applies only to capital gains, and the New Jersey tax which, in effect, applies only to New York residents who derive income from New Jersey sources. Table 9–7 lists the states currently using personal income taxes including the years in which they were adopted.

Despite the growing use of the personal income tax by state and local governments, especially the former, the tax remains primarily a source of federal government revenue. For example, 88 percent of the $98.1 billion of personal income taxes collected by the American public sector during 1972 were federal government revenues. Meanwhile, only 10 percent of the total represented state personal income tax collections and local government personal income tax revenues constituted merely 2 percent of the total. However, the personal income tax presently constitutes the second major revenue source of state governments. Only sales taxation is a more important revenue producer. Moreover, as compared to five years earlier (1967), it is interesting to note that the federal share of total personal income tax revenues declined from 91 percent to 88 percent while the state proportion increased from 7 to 10 percent of the total.

Several reasons may be offered for the growth in the relative importance of personal income taxes to lower levels of government (state and local government) during recent times. Among these are the fact that aggregate personal income has grown greatly during recent decades, thus greatly expanding the potential income tax base. Closely related to the growth of aggregate personal income is the significant upward shift of a large segment of the population on the income scale. Since most of the state personal income taxes possess "progressive rate structures," this leads to an *income elastic* revenue elasticity for the tax. Finally, some revenue increases were derived from the improved state personal income tax enforcement which has resulted from the additional use of "withholding at the source," and the growing "exchange of tax records" with the federal government.

Those state personal income taxes which do apply progressive (graduated) tax rate structures generally provide for only a moderate degree of progression. For example, they typically impose a much lower range of marginal rates than does the federal personal income tax. Moreover, some of the state personal income taxes apply a proportional rate—thus avoiding progression altogether. For the average state using a personal income tax, the "effective" median rate at a taxable income level (adjusted gross income) of $25,000 was more than six times greater than the "effective" rate at the $5,000 taxable income level (in 1970), though at higher income levels the taxes tend to become regressive where the deductibility of the federal personal income tax from the state personal

TABLE 9–7

States Using Personal Income Taxes and the Years of Their Adoption

Period of Time	Number of States Adopting Tax	State	Year Adopted
1901–10 1		Hawaii	1901
1911–20 9		Wisconsin	1911
		Mississippi	1912
		Oklahoma	1915
		Massachusetts	1916
		Virginia	1916
		Delaware	1917
		Missouri	1917
		New York	1919
		North Dakota	1919
1921–30 6		North Carolina	1921
		South Carolina	1922
		New Hampshire*	1923
		Arkansas	1929
		Georgia	1929
		Oregon	1930
1931–40 16		Idaho	1931
		Tennessee†	1931
		Utah	1931
		Vermont	1931
		Alabama	1933
		Arizona	1933
		Kansas	1933
		Minnesota	1933
		Montana	1933
		New Mexico	1933
		Iowa	1934
		Louisiana	1934
		California	1935
		Kentucky	1936
		Colorado	1937
		Maryland	1937
Since 1940 12		Alaska	1949
		New Jersey‡	1961
		West Virginia	1961
		Indiana	1963
		Michigan	1968
		Nebraska	1968
		Illinois	1969
		Connecticut§	1969
		Maine	1969
		Rhode Island	1969
		Pennsylvania	1971
		Ohio	1971
Total 44			

* Applies to dividend and interest income only except that it serves also as a commuters' income tax.
† Applies to income from stocks and bonds only, namely, dividend and interest income.
‡ In effect, applies only to New York residents who derive income from New Jersey sources.
§ Applies to capital gains income.
Source: Advisory Commission on Intergovernmental Relations.

TABLE 9-8
State Personal Income Tax Rates and Related Data (as of September 1, 1972)

State	Lowest bracket		Highest bracket		Maximum personal exemption and credit for dependents[a]			Optional tax table or standard deduction	Federal income tax deductible[b]	Withholding of salaries and wages
	Rate (percent)	To net income of	Rate (percent)	Income above	Married or head of family	Single	Each dependent[c]			
Alabama	1.5	$1,000	5	$5,000	$3,000	$1,500	$300	Yes	Yes	Yes
Alaska	(d)	(d)	(d)	(d)	1,400	700	700	Yes	No	Yes
Arizona[e]	2	1,000	8	6,000	2,000	1,000	600	Yes	Yes	Yes
Arkansas	1[g]	2,999	7	25,000	35[f]	17.50[f]	6[f]	Yes	No	Yes
California[e]	1[g]	2,000	11[k]	15,500	50[f]	25[f]	8[f]	Yes	No	Yes
Colorado[i]	3	2,000	8	10,000	1,500	750	750	Yes	Yes	—
Connecticut[j]	6	all[j]	—	—	2,000[j]	1,000[j]	—	—	—	Yes
Delaware	1.5	1,000	18	100,000	1,200	600	600	Yes	Yes[k]	Yes
Georgia	1	1,000	6	10,000	3,000	1,500	700	Yes	No	Yes
Hawaii	2.25[l]	500	11[l]	30,000	1,400	700	700	Yes	No	Yes
Idaho[e]	2[m]	1,000	7.5[m]	5,000	1,400	700	700	Yes	No	Yes
Illinois	2.5	all	—	—	2,000	1,000	1,000	No	No	Yes
Indiana	2	all	—	—	2,000[n]	1,000	1,000	No	No	Yes
Iowa	.75	1,000	7	9,000	30[f]	15[f]	10[f]	Yes	Yes	Yes
Kansas	2	2,000	6.5	7,000	1,200	600	600	Yes	Yes[k]	Yes
Kentucky	2	3,000	6	8,000	40[f]	20[f]	20[f]	Yes	Yes[k]	Yes
Louisiana[e]	2	10,000	6	50,000	5,000[o]	2,500[o]	400[o]	Yes	Yes	Yes
Maine	1	2,000	6	50,000	2,000	1,000	1,000	Yes	No	Yes
Maryland	2	1,000	5	3,000	1,600[f]	800	800	Yes	No	Yes
Massachusetts	5[p]	all	—	—	4,600[p]	2,000[p]	600[p]	No	No	Yes
Michigan	3.9	all	—	—	—	—	—	No	No	Yes
Minnesota	1.6	500	15	20,000	42[f]	21[f]	21[f]	Yes	Yes	Yes
Mississippi	3	5,000	4	5,000	6,000	4,000	400	Yes	No	Yes
Missouri[r]	1.5	1,000	6	9,000[q]	2,400	1,200	400	Yes	Yes	Yes
Montana[r]	1	1,000	11	35,000	1,200	600	600	Yes	Yes	Yes
Nebraska	(d)	(d)	(d)	(d)	—	—	—	Yes	No	No[h]
New Hampshire[j,s]	4.25	all[j]	—	—	—	—	—	No	No	Yes[h]
New Jersey[s,t]	2	1,000	15	25,000	1,200[f]	600[f]	650[f]	Yes	No	Yes
New Mexico[e]	2[u]	500	9	100,000	1,300[f]	650[f]	700	Yes	No	Yes
New York[t]	3[v]	1,000	15[u]	25,000	1,400	700	650	Yes	No	Yes[h]
North Carolina	3	2,000	7	10,000	1,300	650	600	Yes	No	Yes
North Dakota	1[v]	3,000	11[v]	15,000	2,000	1,000	600	Yes	Yes	Yes
Ohio	.5	1,000	3.5	40,000	1,200	600	500	Yes	No	Yes
Oklahoma	.5	1,500	6	11,500	1,000	500	500	Yes	Yes	Yes
Oregon	4	all	10	5,000	1,500	750	750	Yes	Yes	Yes
Pennsylvania	2.3	(d) all	(d)	(d)	—	—	—	No	No	Yes
Rhode Island	2	all[j]	7	10,000	1,400	700	700	Yes	No	Yes
South Carolina	2	2,000	7	—	1,600	800	800	Yes	Yes[k]	Yes
Tennessee[r]	6	—	—	—	1,400	700	—	No	No	No
Utah[r]	(d)	(d)	(d)	10,000	1,200	600	600	Yes	Yes	Yes
Vermont[r]	2	1,000	6.5	5,000	—	—	—	Yes	No	Yes
Virginia	2.1	3,000	5.75	12,000	2,000	1,000	300	Yes	No	Yes
West Virginia	3.1	2,000	9.6	200,000	1,200[f]	600	600	Yes	No	Yes
Wisconsin	2[u]	2,000	11.4	14,000	30[f]	15[f]	15	Yes	No	Yes
District of Columbia	2[u]	1,000	10[u]	25,000	2,000	1,000	500	Yes	No	Yes

a Does not include exemptions or credits granted for age or blindness, to offset sales or property taxes paid, or for any other special purpose.

b In general, each state which permits the deduction of Federal income taxes limits such deductions to taxes paid on that part of income subject to its own income tax.

c In some states "head of families" are taxed at slightly different rates. A taxpayer with head of family status is generally disallowed deductions for dependents.

d Applies to Federal income tax liability attributable to sources of income within the state. Rate of 16% in Alaska; 15% in Nebraska; 15% in Rhode Island; and 25% in Vermont.

e Community property state in which, in general, one-half of the community income is taxable to each spouse.

f Amount deducted in lieu of exemption, except in New Jersey where credits of $25 for married couple or head of household and $12.50 for single taxpayer are in effect.

g For residents and nonresidents except heads of household, for whom rate is 1% of taxable income not over $3,000, and 11% of taxable income over $16,500. A 2.5% tax is imposed on taxable items of tax preference.

h Withholding on nonresidents only.

i A surtax of 2% on income in excess of $5,000 received as dividends and interest. A credit equal to ½% of net taxable income is allowed on the first $9,000 of net taxable income.

j Tax limited to interest and dividends or capital gains income. The Connecticut tax applies only to dividends and capital gains income; exemption modified by size of Federal adjusted gross income. Those of New Hampshire and Tennessee apply to income in the form of interest and dividends only.

k Deductions limited in Delaware, Kansas, and Kentucky. In South Carolina, deduction limited to $500.

l An alternative tax is permitted on capital gains. A taxpayer may deduct 50% of capital gains and pay an additional tax of 4% of such gains.

m An additional $10 is paid by every taxpayer or taxpaying unit except persons who are blind or recipients of public assistance.

n For joint returns, each spouse may subtract the lesser of $1,000 or the adjusted gross income of each, but not less than $500 apiece.

o Personal exemptions are deductible from the 2% bracket only.

p On income from professions, employment, trade or business. Rate is 9% on interest, dividends, and capital gains from sales of intangibles. Exemptions listed apply to earned income.

q The entire taxable amount of each net income shall be computed at only the one rate wherein the income falls.

r A surcharge on personal income tax of 40% is levied in Montana, and of 15% in Vermont.

s In New Hampshire a 4% tax on commuter's income is imposed. In New Jersey the tax applies to commuters only. Rates shown apply to New York commuters. A tax of 2.3% of Federal income is imposed on Pennsylvania commuters.

t In New Jersey and New York a 6% tax on those subject to the Federal minimum tax on "tax preference items". A 2.5% surcharge is imposed on regular income taxes and on the tax on "tax preference items".

u Income of unincorporated businesses is taxed at 5½% in New York and 7% in D.C.

v An additional 1% tax is imposed on net income derived from a business, trade, or profession other than as an employee. Effective after January 1, 1972, a temporary second additional 1% tax is imposed.

Source: *Facts and Figures on Government Finance—1973* (New York: Tax Foundation, Inc., 1973), pp. 192–93.

income tax base is allowed.[27] Thus, in addition to the rate structures, the pattern of deductions, exemptions, and credits may help influence the "effective" progressivity of state personal income taxes.

A majority of state personal income tax bases resemble the federal personal income tax. The Advisory Commission on Intergovernmental Relations classifies 17 state personal income tax bases as "moderately" conforming to the federal base, 6 others as "substantially" conforming, and 4 others as providing "virtually complete" conformance.[28] Similar to the federal tax, most state taxes allow personal exemptions. The exemptions are ordinarily allowed as a deduction from income, but some states provide the exemptions as a tax credit. Moreover, a number of states in recent years have added credits against state personal income tax liability to minimize or offset the regressivity of general sales and property taxes against lower income taxpayers.[29] In fact, the use of the credit device in this manner usually amounts to the existence of a state "negative income tax" since the taxpayer actually receives a payment from the government when the amount of the tax credit is greater than the income tax liability.

There is a modest trend toward the adoption of the federal personal income tax base for state personal income taxes. This is advantageous from the standpoint of assisting voluntary taxpayer compliance in paying the tax. Moreover, it would be conducive to federal government collection of state personal income taxes as is allowed by the federal "Revenue Sharing Legislation" of 1972. Even those states which do not define "adjusted gross income" in the same or a similar manner as the federal tax often provide other specific provisions which are similar, if not identical, to the federal tax. These provisions include those for capital gains and losses, depreciation, depletion, deductions for charitable contributions, deductions for medical expenses, and deductions for interest paid. Four states—Alaska, Nebraska, Rhode Island, and Vermont—compute the state personal income tax liability of the taxpayer as a percentage of his or her federal personal income tax liability.

The federal personal income tax allows the payment of state personal income taxes as a deduction in computing federal personal income tax liability. However, less than one half of the states allow the federal personal income tax to be deducted against the state personal income tax. As suggested above, the deduction of the federal tax tends to reduce the effective rate progressivity of the state tax. Of course, such influence may be offset by an appropriate structure of rates and exemptions at

---

[27] The effective median rates cited here are for a married couple with two dependents.

[28] *State-Local Finances: Significant Features and Suggested Legislation* (Washington, D.C.: Government Printing Office, 1972), p. 213.

[29] These tax credits are described in detail in Chapter 21.

the state level. Table 9–8 summarizes some of the major features of the state personal income taxes. It is apparent that considerable diversity still exists among the various state taxes.

A significant problem in the administration of a personal income tax by a lower level of government involves the inherent conflict between taxation of income on the basis of the residence or domicile of the taxpayer versus taxation on the basis of site or place where the income is earned. No completely satisfactory solution to this problem has been found and, in fact, the problem tends to get worse as the mobility of individuals becomes greater. This problem is found in large metropolitan areas where the majority of income may be earned in a central city, but the majority of middle to higher income taxpayers may live in the suburbs which, at times, are even located in another state.

States using the personal income tax rely upon it to varying degrees for revenues. In 1970, for example, one state (Oregon) relied upon the tax for nearly 50 percent of its total tax revenues. At the other extreme, Connecticut's "limited" personal income tax on only dividend and capital gains income yields less than one percent of that state's tax revenues. Overall, state personal income taxes provide a continually expanding long-run revenue source in a growing economy due to their "income elasticity" being considerably in excess of unity ($Ye > 1$). See Table 9–9 in this regard.

TABLE 9–9
Income Elasticity of State and Local Personal Income Taxes: Summary of Empirical Studies

Study	Year Published	Area Covered	Elasticity Coefficient
Harris	1966	Arkansas	2.40
ACIR*	1971	Kentucky	1.94
ACIR	1971	New York	1.80
Harris	1966	United States	1.80
Groves and Kahn	1952	United States	1.75
Netzer	1961	United States	1.70
ACIR	1971	Hawaii	1.47
Arizona Planning Division	1971	Arizona	1.30
Harris	1966	New Mexico	1.30

* Advisory Commission on Intergovernmental Relations
Studies cited above: Advisory Commission on Intergovernmental Relations, "State-Local Revenue Systems and Educational Finance," unpublished report to the President's Commission on School Finance, November 12, 1971; Arizona, Department of Economic Planning and Development, Planning Division, *Arizona Intergovernmental Structure: A Financial View to 1980*, Phoenix, 1971; Groves, Harold M., and Kahn, C. Harry, "The Stability of State and Local Tax Yields," *American Economic Review* (March 1952), pp. 87–102; Harris, Robert, *Income and Sales Taxes: The 1970 Outlook for States and Localities*, Chicago: Council of State Governments, 1966; Netzer, Dick, "Financial Needs and Resources Over the Next Decade," in *Public Finances: Needs, Sources, and Utilization*, Princeton: Princeton University Press, 1961.
Source: Advisory Commission on Intergovernmental Relations, *State-Local Finances: Significant Features and Suggested Legislation* (Washington, D.C., U.S. Government Printing Office, 1972), p. 301.

Present Status of Local Personal Income Taxes

Personal income taxes are used by local governments in 9 states and the District of Columbia (as of January 1, 1972). The states which permit the tax are Alabama, Delaware, Kentucky, Maryland, Michigan, Missouri, New York, Ohio, and Pennsylvania. The local government personal income tax is used most extensively in Ohio and Pennsylvania. In Ohio, 18 major cities with populations over 50,000 and 306 cities and villages under 50,000 population impose a personal income tax. In Pennsylvania, 16 major cities or townships and more than 3,000 other units of local government use the tax. A number of the largest cities in the nation employ personal income taxation. These include the cities of Akron, Baltimore, Birmingham, Cincinnati, Cleveland, Columbus, Dayton, Detroit, Kansas City, Louisville, New York, Philadelphia, Pittsburgh, St. Louis, Toledo, Washington, D.C., and Wilmington, Delaware. In all nine states which allow a "local" personal income tax to be imposed, the "state" government also levies such a tax. This results in the payment of three personal income taxes to three different levels of government, namely, a federal, state, and local personal income tax.[30] Table 9–10 summarizes the usage of personal income taxation at the local government level (as of September 1, 1972).

Many of the local government income taxes are imposed at low, flat (proportional) rates. However, important exceptions include the "progressive" resident personal income taxes used in New York City and Washington, D.C. The taxes are usually levied on the gross wage and salary earnings of individuals and the net profits of professions and unincorporated business. Thus, income from wages and salaries is generally taxed on a gross basis, without exemptions or deductions, and with the full amount of the tax withheld by the employer. Dividend, interest, rent, and capital gains income received by individuals are normally exempt from the tax. While some states share their personal income tax collections directly with local government, the increased usage of local personal income taxes per se represents a distinct trend. While in 1955 only 370 local units of government used the tax, the number imposing it by 1970 had grown to more than 3,500 localities.

---

[30] Such "vertical tax overlapping" involving the imposition of the same tax by three different levels of government is not undesirable per se. This point will be discussed in detail in Chapter 19 which is concerned with "intergovernmental fiscal issues."

TABLE 9–10
Local Personal Income Tax Rates, by State[a] (as of September 1, 1972)

State and locality	Rate (percent)	State and locality	Rate (percent)
Alabama		Ohio—continued	
Birmingham	1.0	Euclid	1.0
Gadsden	2.0	Hamilton	1.5
3 cities under 50,000	1.0	Kettering	1.0
Delaware		Lakewood	1.0
Wilmington	.25 or 1.5[b]	Lima	1.0
Kentucky		Lorain	1.0
Covington	2.5	Parma	1.0
Lexington	1.5	Springfield	1.5
Louisville	1.75	Toledo	1.5
22 cities under 50,000	.5–2.0	Warren	1.0
2 counties	.5–1.75	Youngstown	1.5
Maryland	(% of state tax)	306 cities and villages	
Baltimore	50.0	under 50,000	.25–1.5
23 counties	20.0–50.0	Pennsylvania[d]	
Michigan		Abington Township	1.0
Detroit	2.0	Allentown	1.0
Flint	1.0	Altoona	1.0
Grand Rapids	1.0	Bethlehem	1.0
Lansing	1.0	Chester	1.0
Pontiac	1.0	Erie	1.0
Saginaw	1.0	Harrisburg	1.0
9 cities under 50,000	1.0	Johnstown	1.0
Missouri		Lancaster	1.0
Kansas City	1.0	Penn Hills Township	1.0
St. Louis	1.0	Philadelphia	3.3125
New York		Pittsburgh	1.0
New York City	.7–3.5[c]	Reading	1.0
Ohio		Scranton	2.0
Akron	1.5	Wilkes Barre	.5
Canton	1.5	York	1.0
Cincinnati	1.7	Approx. 3,000 other local	
Cleveland	1.0	jurisdictions	.25–1.0
Cleveland Heights	1.0	District of Columbia	
Columbus	1.5	Washington	2.0–10.0[c]
Dayton	1.0		

[a] Rates shown separately for cities with 1960 population of 50,000 or more. Where rates differ for resident and nonresident income, only rates on residents are given. In Ohio and Pennsylvania cities, rates are the same; the nonresident rate is markedly lower in New York City and is half the resident rate in most Michigan cities.

[b] The tax is not graduated. If taxable income is below $4,000, there is no tax; if between $4,000 and $6,000, the tax is 0.25%; if over $6,000, tax is 1.5% of total taxable income.

[c] New York City and Washington, D. C. resident income tax rates are progressive. New York rates range from 0.7% on taxable income of less than $1,000 to $673 plus 3.5% of excess over $30,000. Washington rates range from 2% on taxable income less than $1,000 to $1,770 plus 10% of excess over $25,000.

[d] Except for Philadelphia, Pittsburgh, and Scranton, the total rate payable by any taxpayer is limited to 1%. When other local government units such as school districts levy income taxes, the tax is usually divided equally between jurisdictions.

Source: *Facts and Figures on Government Finance—1973* (New York: Tax Foundation, Inc., 1973), p. 250.

10

Income Taxation: The Personal Income Tax (Continued)

FISCAL RATIONALITY CRITERIA APPLIED TO THE PERSONAL INCOME TAX

The personal income tax will now be evaluated in terms of the "fiscal rationality criteria" developed in Chapter 6. These criteria, it may be recalled, relate importantly to the economic concept of *neutrality*. In the present context, the personal income tax will be examined in terms of its influence on resource allocation decisions, distributional considerations, and aggregate economic performance with an emphasis on the influence of the *federal* personal income tax. Of course, the exertion of such influence involves a *nonneutral effect*. As observed in Chapter 6, nonneutralities may be either positive (beneficial) or negative (harmful) in terms of a given societal goal. The subject of the economic effects deriving from personal income taxation is a comprehensive one. Consequently, the discussion which follows will present only a "selected menu" of topics concerning the neutrality (nonneutrality) of personal income taxes. Moreover, some of the discussion is equally applicable to both the federal personal and federal corporation income taxes which contain a number of identical or similar provisions.

Is a Personal Income Tax or an Excise Tax More Neutral?

For many years economists believed that a personal income tax was more neutral toward private sector behavior than were excise taxes.[1]

---

[1] This approach is represented in M. F. W. Joseph, "The Excess Burden of Indirect Taxation." *Review of Economic Studies,* June 1939, pp. 226–31, and in several other sources.

This viewpoint is demonstrated in Figure 10–1. Point *A* represents the initial equilibrium for the representative consumer. Given (1) the preferences of the consumer for Goods *X* and *Y* as represented by indifference curves I^1-I^3, (2) the prices of Goods *X* and *Y*, and (3) the consumer's income as indicated by budget line *WX*, Point *A* reflects the equality of the marginal rate of substitution between the two goods in consumption as well as the "effective demand" of the consumer to acquire the goods.

FIGURE 10–1
Personal Income Tax versus Excise Tax Neutrality—the Traditional Argument

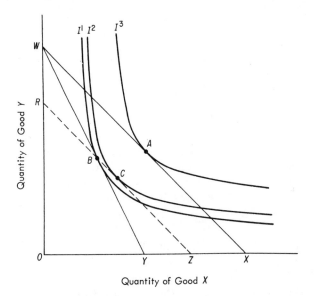

Source: Adapted from M. F. W. Joseph, "The Excess Burden of Indirect Taxation," *Review of Economic Studies,* June, 1939, Figure II, p. 227.

Then, assume that an excise tax is placed on Good *X* with no change occurring in the income of the consumer nor in the prices of the two goods except for the tax. The result is a new equilibrium at point *B* which is the point of tangency between the new "post-excise-tax" budget line *WY* and consumer indifference Curve I^1. Significantly, point *B* is on a lower indifference curve, I^1, than indifference curve I^3, which represents the attainable "pre-tax" level of consumption. Yet the same amount of revenue could be provided to government by a personal income tax, as shown by budget line *RZ*, which passes through point *B* and provides an equilibrium at point *C.* Since an income tax, unlike an excise tax on one of the two goods, does not change the relative prices between the goods, that is, since it does not cause a "direct" substitution effect, budget line *RZ* and the original budget line *WX* possess the same slope. This absence of a relative price change means that point *C* is on a higher consumer indifference curve, I^2, than is provided at point *B* on indifference curve I^1 when the excise tax is used. Hence, the personal income tax is alleged to be more neutral, and thus superior, to the excise tax because it results in less distortion in the form of welfare sacrificed. That is, the loss in welfare between indifference curve I^3 and I^2, under the personal income tax, is less than the welfare loss between indifference curves I^3 and I^1, under the excise tax. Hence, the excise tax is said to yield an "excess burden."

This orthodox analysis was challenged subsequently by other economists and, as a result, the issue has been further clarified.[2] Friedman attacked the traditional approach on the grounds that it uses a *partial equilibrium* methodology which ignores technical production possibilities and, relatedly, disregards the alternative uses to which tax revenues may be put.[3] He agrees that the orthodox conclusions would hold for an "isolated individual," but demonstrates that such partial equilibrium analysis cannot provide a "general" conclusion for the entire community. Such generalization is deemed incorrect because it supposes that an excise tax reduces the range of alternatives to an individual in a way which is calculable by simply taking the differences in alternatives available between budget lines *WX* and *WY* in Figure 10–1 and multiplying them by the number of individuals. Yet, this supposition is invalid, according to Friedman, because the imposition of an excise tax does not in itself change technical production possibilities. The resources available to the society remain unchanged. The tax, indeed, may reduce the flow of productive resources to Goods *X* and *Y,* but in so doing may increase the production of a third economic good such as *Z.*

Hence, the traditional analysis is said to falter because it is "partial equilibrium" in nature and ignores the technical production possibilities for other goods. Relatedly, it is asserted that the traditional approach is inadequate because it does not consider the fact that the excise tax receipts may be used either to subsidize the production of

---

[2] See Milton Friedman, "The Welfare Effects of an Income Tax and an Excise Tax," *Journal of Political Economy,* February 1952, pp. 25–33 and his *Price Theory* (Chicago: Aldine, 1966), pp. 56–67; I. M. D. Little, "Direct vs. Indirect Taxes," *Economic Journal,* September 1951, pp. 577–84; and Richard A. Musgrave, *The Theory of Public Finance* (New York: McGraw-Hill Book Co., 1959), pp. 140–48.

[3] *Friedman,* "Welfare Effects of an Income Tax and an Excise Tax," pp. 27–29.

Good X or Good Y, they may be used for general consumer subsidies, or even impounded and held idle. Undoubtedly, this critical analysis of the traditional approach adds further dimensions of understanding to the complex issue of personal income versus excise tax neutrality.

The alternative approach, briefly described above, is presented in more detail in the discussion of Figure 10–2 (a, b). In Figure 10–2a,

FIGURE 10–2
Personal Income Tax versus Excise Tax Neutrality—Friedman Argument

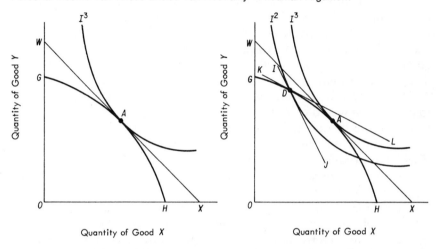

Source: Milton Friedman, "The Welfare Effects of an Income Tax and an Excise Tax," *Journal of Political Economy*, February 1952, (© 1952 by the University of Chicago) Figure 3, p. 30, and Figure 4, p. 31.

"production possibilities" are introduced into the analysis and a "general equilibrium" approach results.[4] Competitive market conditions exist. Let GH represent the transformation function (production-possibility curve) for the *production* of Goods X and Y and let I^3 represent the relevant indifference curve for the representative individual of the society[5] in the *consumption* of Goods X and Y. Furthermore, assume that WX is *both* the "budget line" for the representative consumer in the *purchase* of the goods and the "constant receipts" line for the producer in the *sale* of the goods. Thus, point A represents the competitive equilibrium with each individual consuming at point A. At this point, the marginal rate of substitution in consumption (the slope of the

---

[4] It is assumed that the society is composed of many identical individuals, that is, identical in preferences and in the resources owned by each. In such a society, each individual would have the same income and consume the same bundle of goods and hence the position of the entire society can be represented by that of any single individual. This is implicit in the analysis of Figure 10–2 (a, b).

[5] See Footnote 4.

consumption indifference curve I^3) is equal to the marginal rate of substitution in purchase on the market (the price ratio in purchase as shown by the slope of the budget line WX) which, in turn, is equal to the marginal rate of transformation in production (the slope of the transformation function GH) and the marginal rate of substitution in sale on the market (the price ratio in sale as shown by the slope of the constant receipts line WX).

If the desired amount of revenue is raised through a "personal income tax" (assume a "proportional" personal income tax), the neutrality effect will depend upon how the revenue is used. Thus, if the revenue is used to grant a "per capita subsidy," there would be no change in the equilibrium position in Figure 10–2a since neither a personal income tax nor a subsidy would change the relative prices of Goods X and Y, the transformation curve GH, nor the consumer indifference curve I^3. However, if the revenue is used to produce Good Z, a new transformation curve would be required since resources are being drawn away from the production of Good X and/or Y. Importantly, the change in the transformation curve would depend *only* on the quantity of Good Z which is produced and *not* on the "type of tax" which is used to raise the revenue. That is, if the amount of Good Z is assumed to be *given* or *fixed*, the new transformation curve will be the same whether a "personal income tax" or an "excise tax" is imposed. Thus, while pursuing the difference between income and excise tax effects, curve GH may be considered the transformation curve after resources have been subtracted to produce Good Z. Thus, Figure 10–2a can be said to represent the situation both "before" and "after" the imposition of a proportional personal income tax in order to compare that tax with an excise tax.

Accordingly, in Figure 10–2b the equilibrium point under a personal income tax is indicated at point A on transformation curve GH. Also, the equilibrium position after an excise tax is levied on one of the goods would be on transformation curve GH—but *not* at point A. Hence, the question must be asked: What is the equilibrium point of allocation after an excise tax is imposed on one of the goods (say Good X)? A highly relevant consideration in this regard is that the excise tax causes a divergence between the "price paid by the consumer" and the "price received by the producer." Hence, the "budget line" price ratio in the purchase of the good by the consumer is no longer equal to the "constant receipts line" price ratio in the sale of the good by the producer. That is, the rate at which individuals substitute the goods in purchase is "different" from the rate at which producers substitute the goods in sale. Yet, "optimal equilibrium" requires that the consumption indifference curve be tangent to the "budget line" and that both of these be equal to the transformation curve which is tangent to the "constant receipts line." This is not attained under the excise tax because the terms on which the consumer can substitute one good for another "in purchase," while keeping total spending constant, must be calculated from prices *inclusive of the tax* while, on the other hand, the terms on which the producer can substitute one good for another "in sale," while keeping total receipts constant, must be calculated from prices *exclusive of the tax*. This phenomenon relates closely to the possibility that the producer may shift (transfer) part or all of the excise tax burden through a higher selling price.

In Figure 10–2b, point *D* represents the "suboptimal" equilibrium point for both consumers and producers under the excise tax with the conditions described in the preceding paragraph. Line *IJ* is the "budget line" as it appears to the consumer while line *KL* is the "constant receipts line'" as it appears to the producer. At point *D*, the "budget line" *IJ* is tangent to the "consumer indifference curve" I^2 while the "constant receipts line" *KL* is tangent to the "transformation curve" *GH*. Yet, it is important to observe that the "budget line" price ratio of the consumer (*IJ*) is *not* tangent to this "constant receipts line" price ratio of the producer (*KL*) at point *D*. This causes consumption at a socially "less desirable" point on a lower indifference curve (I^2) under the excise tax than would be the case (I^3) under an income tax.

However, now drop the assumption of "competitive" conditions and assume that "monopolistic" market conditions place the representative consumer at point *D* even without government taxation. These monopolistic conditions are now providing the same distortive allocational effects as the previously existing excise tax on Good *X*. If an excise tax identical to this previously existing excise tax on Good *X* is placed on Good *Y*, these monopoly effects are offset and, once again, Point *A* becomes the equilibrium. Thus, "optimal" conditions prevail as no divergence exists between the "budget line" price ratio in purchase by the consumer and the "constant receipts line" price ratio in sale by the producer at point *A*. In other words, an excise tax on Good *Y* which is *identical* to the monopoly effects on Good *X*, or to an identical excise tax on Good *X*, *neutralizes the previous relative price changes between Goods X and Y* as caused by the monopoly effects or by the excise tax effects on Good *X* alone. However, if only the monopoly or excise tax effects on Good *X* are retained, without an excise tax being applied to Good *Y*, the imposition of an income tax—in addition to these monopoly or excise effects on Good *X*—would cause a divergence between the price ratios of the "budget line" and the "constant receipts line." Thus, once again, a "suboptimal" equilibrium would be re-established at point *D*, but this time by the use of income rather than excise taxation.

Thus, in terms of a *neutrality* comparison between the comparative economic effects of personal income versus excise taxation, the following observations are relevant:

1. An income tax is preferable to an excise tax on one of two economic goods.
2. Identical excise taxes on two economic goods are preferable to an income tax superimposed on an excise tax on one of the goods.
3. Either an income tax or identical excise taxes on two goods will yield equally preferable results.

The obvious conclusion is that it is impossible to state categorically whether a "personal income tax" or an "excise tax" is superior in terms of fiscal rationality. The most that can be generally inferred is that the broader the tax base and the more equal its incidence, the less likely it is to distort the relevant marginal rates of substitution described above. However, such considerations as the rate of substitution between work effort and leisure and between consumption and savings are outside the "direct" scope of the above analysis. Several of these additional tax rationality phenomena and their relevance to the personal income tax will now be considered.

Labor Nonneutrality and the Personal Income Tax

Effect of Personal Income Tax on Work Effort. A personal income tax can distort the "tradeoff" between *work effort* and *leisure* and thus create "nonneutral effects."[6] Such nonneutrality, however, may be either "positive" or "negative" in its allocative effects depending upon whether the previous work-leisure allocation is optimal. The work-leisure distortion tends to be rather insignificant, in general terms, because of two "offsetting" effects which would result from personal income taxation. On the one hand, income taxation impairs work incentives by reducing the net monetary reward from work effort, thus causing leisure to be "substituted" for work effort at the margin. On the other hand, income taxation lowers the disposable income of the taxpayer and places pressure upon him to earn more in order to maintain a desired living standard. The latter *income effect,* which stimulates work effort, thus tends to neutralize the former *substitution effect,* which tends to retard work effort. Yet, no a priori statement can be made concerning the predominance of one or the other effect. Instead,

---

[6] See Musgrave, *Theory of Public Finance,* pp. 232–49. Also, for pertinent discussions of the topic, see Richard Goode, "The Income Tax and the Supply of Labor," *Journal of Political Economy,* October 1949, pp. 428–37; and George F. Break, "Income Taxes and Incentives to Work: An Empirical Study," *American Economic Review,* September 1957, pp. 529–49.

each individual case will be separately influenced depending upon such factors as (1) the degree of control by an individual over "time worked," (2) the desire to work for power, prestige, or other "noneconomic motives," and (3) the overall level of "income," and thus of "living standard," for the individual.

The degree of nonneutrality tends to increase as personal income tax rates become more "progressive," as opposed to "proportional," since it is the *marginal tax rate* which influences the work-leisure choice and, of course, the marginal rate exceeds the average rate under a progressive tax. Figure 10–3 displays this as well as other relevant relationships. It may be observed that income is measured on the vertical axis and the tradeoff between work and leisure, in terms of the time available for each, is measured on the horizontal axis. It is assumed that the same amount of governmental revenue is collected under any type of tax which may be imposed. Line *AZ* represents the income of the taxpayer

FIGURE 10–3
Work Effort-Leisure *Tradeoffs* under Different Personal Income Tax Arrangements

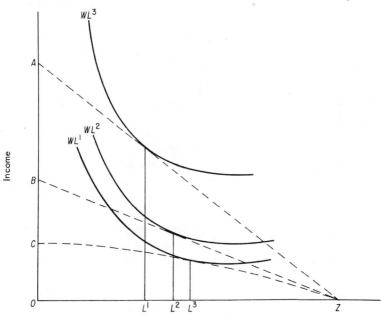

Time Available for Work or Leisure

AZ = Pre-tax disposable income—
      L^1Z work, OL^1 leisure tradeoff
BZ = Disposable income under proportional personal income tax—
      L^2Z work, OL^2 leisure tradeoff
CZ = Disposable income under progressive personal income tax (less than 100 percent marginal rate)—
      L^3Z work, OL^3 leisure tradeoff
OZ = Disposable income under personal income tax with 100 percent marginal rate.
      No work, OZ leisure tradeoff

prior to the payment of an income tax. Line *BZ*, on the other hand, represents the disposable income of an individual after the application of a *proportional* income tax. Moreover, line *CZ* represents the disposable income of the taxpayer after a *progressive* tax has been applied. However, in the latter case, the progressive tax is one for which the marginal tax rate is less than 100 percent. Finally, the extreme or polar case of income taxation is represented by line *OZ*, along the horizontal axis, which demonstrates the disposable income of the taxpayer following the imposition of a personal income tax with a marginal rate of 100 percent. Lines WL^3, WL^2, and WL^1 represent indifference curves for the taxpayer regarding his work-leisure tradeoff and a desire to earn income.

In the pretax case, the individual is providing L^1Z work effort and retains OL^1 time for leisure. When the proportional personal income tax is applied, the demand for work effort by the taxpayer reduces to quantity L^2Z while his demand for leisure increases to OL^2. Furthermore, when a progressive personal income tax is applied, with a marginal rate of less than 100 percent, the desire to work is reduced to L^3Z while the preference for leisure increases to OL^3. In the extreme case of a 100 percent marginal personal income tax rate, the individual offers no work effort since the entire amount of earnings is taxed, and the substitution effect yields a demand for leisure equal to OZ. Thus, it may be concluded that there is a general tendency for the desire for leisure to increase, and the subsequent preference for work effort and income to decline, as the rate of a personal income tax increases in progressivity. In other words, the substitution effect between leisure and work tends to become more significant as the personal income tax rate structure becomes more progressive.

Effect of Personal Income Tax on Labor Mobility. It has been asserted that the federal personal income tax retards *labor mobility* between jobs or professions since it encourages "deferred compensation programs.[7] This is said to be especially true when the pension rights under the program are *not* "vested." Thus, if an employee were to lose most or all of his pension accumulation through a change of jobs, it would appear likely that he would be motivated *not* to change. In particular, it would seem that older workers would be so affected.

As plausible as these assertions appear to be, they have not been substantiated in several empirical studies. In one such study, the proposition that "the American labor force is being immobilized by the at-

---

[7] Many firms develop deferred compensation programs for their executives in order to spread their incomes over retirement years and thus to increase their long-term aftertax earnings. Deferred compensation, in addition, may take the form of various fringe benefits negotiated by labor unions with management for the benefit of nonmanagement employees.

tractions of seniority and negotiated fringe benefits" is examined.[8] The secular trend of the "quit rate" in manufacturing industries is charted in this study and, after adjustment for business cycle variation data, the weight of evidence comes out against the hypothesis. Though a long-term decline in the quit rate is detected, it does not appear to be due to seniority and to deferred compensation programs. This is evident when the data are disaggregated and related to years of service. When this is done, no decline is demonstrated where it would need to take place to support the hypothesis, namely, among workers who have been with a firm for a considerable number of years. Instead, the quit rate for older workers remains relatively constant while the decline in the overall quit rate is caused by a substantial decline in the rate for younger workers. This is attributed, in turn, to the forces of unionization and prosperity.

Another study concentrates on the effect of nonvested pensions on labor mobility in the higher education industry.[9] Here, as in the previous study, an attempt is made to empirically test the hypothesis that "the effect of nonvested pensions is to reduce the mobility of labor." Faculty separation rates are compared for both vested and nonvested pension programs. It is concluded that the mobility of labor in the higher education industry is as large from institutions with nonvested pension programs as with vested programs. Consequently, the hypothesis is rejected. The effects of the federal personal income tax on labor mobility through the encouragement of deferred compensation programs thus may not be as restrictive as originally suspected.

Effect of Personal Income Tax on the Choice of a Profession. The personal income tax appears to exert only a modest influence on the choice of a profession. To the extent that such effects occur, however, the patterns of production, money wages, and prices will tend to be influenced and thus affect both the allocation of resources and income-wealth distribution. A relevant study provides a survey of randomly selected graduating seniors at a major American university to ascertain whether the progressive federal personal income tax influenced their selection of an occupation.[10] Not one student mentioned on his own accord that taxation had influenced his decision.

There are, nevertheless, several ways by which a personal income tax could influence the selection of a profession. Progressive personal income taxes, for example, may be expected to discourage the kinds

[8] Arthur M. Ross, "Do We Have a New Industrial Feudalism?" *American Economic Review,* December 1958, pp. 903–20.

[9] Melvin Lurie, "The Effect of Non-Vested Pensions on Mobility: A Study of the Higher Education Industry," *Industrial and Labor Relations Review,* January 1965, pp. 225–37.

[10] Herbert G. Grubel and David R. Edwards, "Personal Income Taxation and the Choice of Professions," *Quarterly Journal of Economics,* February 1964, pp. 158–63.

of work which entail the largest amount of nondeductible costs. Also, a progressive personal income tax may encourage nonmarket work effort as opposed to market work effort since labor which escapes an explicit monetary transaction is difficult to assess and thus difficult to tax. Self-employed professions are favored in this regard. In addition, self-employment offers greater opportunity for tax evasion due to the fact that earnings are not subject to withholding as are wages and salaries. On balance, however, these effects on occupational choice tend to be insignificant.

Saving-Investment Nonneutrality and the Personal Income Tax

Effect of Personal Income Tax on Saving. The ability of the personal income tax to influence saving is demonstrated in the following example.[11] Assume the existence of a single economic good. Thus, the only possible allocation distortion is between the present and future consumption of this good. In the "optimal" pretax equilibrium, the consumer's "marginal rate of substitution" between *present* and *future* consumption equals the producer's "marginal rate of transformation" between *present* and *future* goods. However, the application of a proportional personal income tax will distort the equality of these two rates since it reduces the rate at which future consumption may be substituted for present consumption. Thus, the personal income tax reduces the *net* rate of interest on consumption if interest income is taxable. At the same time, no effect is exerted on the mix of productive resources used by the firm. In other words, the *net* rate of interest upon which the marginal rate of substitution by the consumer depends is reduced while the *gross* rate of interest which affects the firm's transformation (production) decision is not changed. The condition of optimal allocation is distorted because the two rates are now "unequal." Moreover, the "nonneutrality" or "distortion" would be accentuated if the personal income tax were "progressive" because the degree of inequality between the marginal rates of substitution and transformation depends upon the marginal tax rate.

A relevant study emphasizes the possible effect of changes in the degree of personal income tax progression on the saving behavior of individuals.[12] The results of this empirical analysis indicate that increases in the degree of income tax rate progression tend to reduce individual savings in both an absolute sense as well as in terms of the saving/income ratio.

Attention should be paid also to the various effects on personal saving

---

[11] Musgrave, *Theory of Public Finance*, pp. 152–53.

[12] Paul E. Smith, "Individual Income Tax Rate Progression and the Savings Function," *Quarterly Journal of Economics*, May 1964, pp. 299–306.

which may result from the encouragement of deferred compensation programs by the personal income tax. When personal saving is "institutionalized," saving may be increased beyond the amount desired by an individual. This is especially true in the case of group retirement plans where the individual has little choice in the matter. In addition to this possible allocation nonneutrality, another allocation distortion occurs to the extent that pension trusts make funds available which must necessarily go into low-risk, relatively high-priced issues, thus driving their prices up and reducing the funds available to speculative, high-risk firms.

Regarding intergoal nonneutrality, pension funds may serve as an automatic stabilization device to the extent that fund contributions, and thus saving, expand during periods of prosperity and decline during periods of recession.[13] However, pension funds may at times also become destabilizers through their influence on stock and bond markets due to the long-term inflexible nature of such investments. The above analysis thus suggests that saving may be significantly affected by a personal income tax, especially one which is progressive.

Effect of Personal Income Tax on Risk-Taking and Investment.   The structure of a personal income tax may influence the investor's decision whether or not to invest and the magnitude of his investment. For example, if an investor must pay a 25 percent capital gains tax on his net gains, and a tax offset for capital losses is *not* allowed, the expected net gains (yield) after taxes will be less than if a tax offset were allowed. In effect, the degree of risk is increased when tax offsets for capital losses are not allowed. Moreover, if the investor has a liquidity preference, it is likely that a large investor has an advantage over a small investor in risk-taking since he will tend to have more income against which to offset a loss. Hence, a possible policy objective with both allocation efficiency and distributive equity in mind would be the creation of equally favorable loss offsets for *all* types of investors and income classes.

Finally, the personal income tax, in conjunction with the lower rate tax on capital gains, may be said to result in a bias favoring the retention of earnings by corporations rather than paying profits out in the form of cash dividends. This is true because stockholders in high tax brackets tend to prefer compensation in the form of the price realization of their securities, which are taxed as capital gains (when realized), rather than in the form of cash dividends, which are taxed at higher rates as ordinary personal income.[14] This not only results in an allocation nonneu-

---

[13] The "stabilization" effects of taxation can be more fully understood after the student has read Part Four of this book.

[14] Some tightening of provisions in this regard were contained in the Tax Reform Act of 1969.

trality, in the sense that investments financed from retained earnings may be undertaken which otherwise would not have been warranted, but it also encourages the market concentration of larger enterprises and the resulting increase in market structure imperfection.

Undoubtedly, a personal income tax will tend to affect investment incentives, risk-taking, and the supply of capital. The *specific* effects, however, will depend upon the existence (or not) of such "fiscal techniques" as the preferential treatment of capital gains, loss offsets, and investment credits.

Distributional Equity, Stabilization, and Economic Growth Effects from a Personal Income Tax

Most of the nonneutral effects discussed above pertain to the "allocation" branch of economics. In the broader sense, however, the personal income tax also exerts important nonneutralities in the "distribution," "stabilization," and "economic growth" branches. Concerning *distributional equity,* it was observed in the previous chapter that significant "erosion" of the federal personal income tax base occurs. As a result, the "effective" progressivity of the tax is much less than the nominal or statutory rates of the tax would suggest. Nonetheless, the federal personal income tax remains *de facto* "progressive" and its *net* effect is that of redistribution of income from higher to lower income individuals. Ultimately, however, the overall distributional effects of the tax should also reflect the pattern of distribution of the benefits financed by the income tax revenues. This subject is considered in Chapter 21. It may be observed at this time, however, that the societal goal of distributional equity in accordance with the *ability-to-pay* principle is served to a degree by the progressive federal personal income tax.

A theoretically rational tax remains rational only if it is efficiently implemented in practice. Thus, tax rationality in the "enforcement sense" is also a critical distributional consideration for a totally efficient and equitable tax. The federal personal income tax appears to pass the enforcement efficiency test though further improvements, indeed, are possible. In addition to the largely measurable "direct" revenue results of income tax enforcement efforts, an untold additional amount of personal income taxes are collected due to the "indirect" persuasion which an effective tax enforcement system provides. In any event, the aggregate revenues collected, both directly and indirectly, from the federal personal income tax greatly exceed the monetary enforcement costs incurred by the federal government. Furthermore, the tax avoids the creation of severe disincentives to consumption, saving, and investment behavior in the market.

The enforcement structure of the federal personal income tax may now be described in brief fashion. Essentially, it is one of "voluntary taxpayer compliance." The taxpayer assesses his own liabilities and reports them to the federal government on the appropriate tax return. The federal government, in turn, provides an administrative structure which assists the taxpayer in his efforts of voluntary compliance. It coordinates the overall program, collects the taxes, and audits part of the returns for accuracy. The administrative unit of the federal government exercising this authority is the Internal Revenue Service (IRS), a division of the Treasury Department.

The IRS assists the taxpayer in his self-assessment and voluntary compliance efforts through the following programs: (1) direct personal taxpayer assistance by district and local offices in answering questions and filing returns, (2) publication of tax guides covering specific tax situations, (3) dissemination of information to taxpayers by a broad public information program through various communications media, and (4) the preparation and distribution of regulations, rulings, tax forms, and instructions. The actual collection and enforcement of the federal personal income tax by the Internal Revenue Service involves such varied specific techniques as: (1) withholding from wage and salary income, (2) payments of estimated tax (3) information returns at the source of income (4) auditing, (5) rewards to informers, and (6) the assessment of penalties. Of course, it should be recognized that a significant portion of overall federal personal income tax enforcement costs are incurred by the taxpayers themselves either through their own time inputs or by hiring the services of an accountant or lawyer to assess their tax liabilities.

While the final tax return for a calendar year need not be filed before the following April 15, "provisional payments" are normally required during the course of the year. Primarily, this involves the *withholding* of wage and salary income at the source of the income, on a graduated (progressive) basis depending upon the level of income, and quarterly payments of *estimated tax* by certain taxpayers who are required to do so because of excessive income "not subject to withholding." Later, when the final return is submitted, the taxpayer credits the amounts withheld from wages and estimated tax payments against his final tax liability. If additional tax is due, it must be paid when the final return is submitted. If the provisional payments exceed the final liability, the excess may be, at the discretion of the taxpayer, either refunded, or applied as a credit against the following year's income tax liability.

The Internal Revenue Service is assisted in its enforcement efforts by information returns from employers regarding wages and salaries paid and taxes withheld. Copies of such returns go to both the Internal Revenue Service and to the employee. Moreover, information returns are also provided to both the taxpayer and the federal government regarding the payments of dividends and interest during the year. Such information is extremely important in the effort to provide effective tax enforcement. Moreover, such information can be used with increasing effectiveness as the *auditing* efforts of the IRS become increasingly computerized.

A less-known, though long-established, technique of personal income tax enforcement by the federal government is a payment of rewards to *tax informers*. This device was used with the first federal personal income tax during the Civil War and is still in use today. During the 1969 fiscal year, rewards totaling nearly $300,000 were paid by the Internal Revenue Service to 426 tax informers, mostly for income tax enforcement. Overall, it appears that the federal personal income tax is effectively administered by the Internal Revenue Service in conjunction with the voluntary compliance efforts of taxpayers. In other words, distributional equity in the enforcement sense is not violated by the tax.

Finally, it may be observed that the federal personal income tax also performs important *stabilization* and *economic growth* functions. Since these topics are discussed in detail in Part Four of the book, only a brief discussion will be provided in this chapter. Positive stabilization non-neutralities include the "automatic" anticyclical effects of the tax. Federal personal income tax revenues increase at a faster rate than national income as national income increases and diminish at a more rapid rate than national income as national income declines. Thus, increasing proportions of private sector purchasing power are taken from aggregate demand as potentially-inflationary prosperity approaches while increasing proportions are left in the private sector when national income declines in a recession or depression.

Mainly, it is the progressive rate structure of the federal personal income tax which gives it the *income elastic* $(Ye > 1)$ revenue characteristics responsible for its automatic anticyclical performance. In addition, this feature provides an excellent long-run revenue source in a growing economy with an expanding national income. A study by Blackburn gives a possibly conservative income-elasticity estimate of 1.4 for the federal personal income tax[15]—a figure below that of most estimates for the less progressive state and local government personal income taxes.[16] That is, there is a 1.4 percent increase in federal personal income tax revenues for every 1 percent increase in income per taxpayer. Another study by Snowbarger and Kirk also estimates the income elasticity of the federal personal income tax to be 1.4.[17]

---

[15] John O. Blackburn, "Implicit Tax Rate Reductions with Growth, Progressive Taxes, Constant Progressivity, and a Fixed Public Share," *American Economic Review*, March 1967, pp. 162–69.

[16] See Table 9–9.

[17] Marvin Snowbarger and John Kirk, "A Cross-Sectional Model of Built-in Flexibility, 1954–1969," *National Tax Journal*, June 1973 pp. 241–49.

In addition to its "automatic" anticyclical characteristics, "discretionary" changes in the structure of the tax can be used to provide further anticyclical effects. Moreover, the application of various personal income tax features, such as accelerated depreciation, can be used to promote economic growth in the society. Accelerated depreciation is also an important feature of the "federal corporation income tax" which will be the topic of the following chapter.

11

Income Taxation: The Corporation Income Tax

FEDERAL CORPORATION INCOME TAX

Federal tax law provides for the partially differential tax treatment of business and trade profits depending upon the legal form of organization under which the business functions. Businesses which are legally organized as *corporations* are thus taxed as separate entities and have a particular scale of tax rates applied to them.[1] This specific base-rate structure constitutes the *federal corporation income tax*. On the other hand, businesses organized as *proprietorships* or *partnerships* are not taxed under the federal corporation income tax and all taxable profits are reported on the individual returns of the owners.[2]

Historical Development

A federal corporation "excise tax" was levied on the net income of corporations in 1909. However, this was in essence an "income tax" since "net income" was used as the *indicator* of the tax base. Finally, following the Sixteenth Amendment, legislation in 1913 recognized the tax as an income tax by passing a new corporation income tax law which

---

[1] Nonetheless, numerous features of federal income tax law apply commonly to *business income* whether it be earned under a proprietorship, partnership, or corporate legal form. Among the provisions which are similar or identical in this regard are those pertaining to depletion, depreciation, and capital gains.

[2] Under certain limited conditions, "noncorporate" businesses may elect to be subject to the corporation income tax instead of to the personal income tax.

eliminated the hypocrisy of calling it an excise. The 1913 legislation imposed a 1 percent proportional rate on taxable corporate income. Subsequently, the rate was increased to a 12 percent level in 1918 (World War I) and varied between proportional rates of 10 percent and 13.5 percent during the 1920s. Progressive rates were first introduced in 1936 with a range between 8 and 15 percent along with a supplemental surtax ranging from 7 to 27 percent on "undistributed profits." The undistributed profits surtax was repealed two years later (in 1938).

Federal corporation income tax rates ranged from 25 to 40 percent throughout most of World War II (1941–45). These were supplemented by an excess profits tax between 1943–45, which brought the combined maximum tax rate on corporate income to 80 percent. Rates ranged from 21 to 38 percent during the early postwar years (1946–49). In 1950, the system of progressive rates for corporations with taxable incomes under $25,000 was replaced by both a single normal tax rate, which was applicable to the full amount of taxable income, and a surtax which was applicable to taxable income in excess of a specific $25,000 surtax exemption.[3] The Korean War caused both the normal and surtax rates to be increased and an excess profits tax again to be levied. Hence, the combined corporation income tax rate reached a ceiling of 70 percent during the Korean War. The excess profits tax was allowed to expire at the end of the war.

Between 1952 and 1963, the normal tax rate was 30 percent and the surtax rate was 22 percent, for a combined rate of 52 percent on taxable corporation income in excess of $25,000. The present rate structure, described later in the chapter, resulted from the Revenue Act of 1964 which reduced the combined maximum rate to 48 percent.

The Federal Corporation Income Tax Base and Rate Structure

Taxable corporation income is computed by deducting from gross income the expenses which are incurred in creating that income. Such expenses must be "ordinary and necessary" to the operation of a trade or business. Among the deductible expenses are wages and salaries, remuneration of executives, rents, royalties, material costs, bad debts, casualty losses, taxes, advertising expenses, interest payments, and the depreciation cost of fixed capital for the year in question. Dividends paid to stockholders are *not* deductible as expenses, except in certain cases involving the preferred stock dividends of public utility companies. Thus, in effect, the tax base of the federal corporation income tax consists of the return to equity capital.

---

[3] In effect, however, the combined "normal" and "surtax" rates constitute a progressive rate structure with "one bracket change."

In addition to these deductible expenses, certain other expenses are deductible, though subject to rather stringent qualifications. Among these are contributions to charity, contributions to profit-sharing plans and pension funds, and entertainment expenses. The federal corporation income tax base is influenced, moreover, by several special provisions which are applicable to certain types of corporations and to certain types of income and expenditures. In most instances, the special provisions for certain types of income and expenditures apply under the federal income tax structure to both corporate and noncorporate businesses.

Some corporations receive preferential treatment under the federal corporation income tax on the basis of qualification as "nonprofit" institutions. These include such organizations as those organized for charitable, religious, scientific, literary, and educational purposes. No part of the net profits of these corporations may be applied, however, to the benefit of any individual, nor can the organization substantially engage in propaganda or participate in political activity. Additional preferential treatment is provided for labor and agricultural organizations, business leagues and chambers of commerce, credit unions, recreational clubs, fraternal organizations and, under certain circumstances, small mutual life insurance companies and farmers' producer cooperatives.

Moreover, insurance companies have historically received preferred treatment under the federal corporation income tax structure, though recent years have witnessed a significant reduction in these advantages. The first of these important modifications occurred under the Life Insurance Company Income Tax Act of 1959. Prior to this act, life insurance companies were taxed on only a portion of their net investment income. The 1959 legislation, however, provided for taxing one half of underwriting income when earned and the other half when distributed, and also provided for the taxation of investment income under a new formula which measures the taxable margin of investment earnings on an individual company basis. Furthermore, capital gains of these companies are now taxed.

Other corporate organizations receiving preferred treatment under the tax include commercial banks, mutual savings banks, savings and loan associations, cooperatives, and regulated investment companies. However, legislation enacted in 1969 placed further restrictions on the deduction of "bad debt reserves" by such companies.

At the present time, the rate structure of the federal corporation income tax consists of a normal tax on the full amount of taxable income and a surtax on the amount of taxable income above a $25,000 surtax exemption. The normal rate on the first $25,000 of taxable corporate income is 22 percent and the surtax rate is 26 percent. Hence, the rate structure of the federal corporation income tax, combining both the normal and surtax rates, ranges between 22 and 48 percent with only *one* "step" ("bracket") change.

Long-term capital gains realized by corporations on property not considered part of normal operations are taxed at the rate of 30 percent.[4] Unlike the federal personal income tax, the federal corporation income tax does not allow a lower rate on the first $50,000 of long-term capital gains. However, similar to the personal income tax, these gains arise from the sale or exchange of capital assets held for "more than six months." Capital gains tax treatment is afforded certain types of income, not otherwise defined as gains, arising from the sale of "specialized" capital assets. These certain types of income include profits from the sale of depreciable and real property, profits from the sale of certain draft, breeding, or dairy livestock, coal and iron ore royalties, income from timber-cutting operations, and profits from the sale of unharvested crops on land sold or exchanged. Net losses realized from these sources of income may be deducted (subject to limitations) against other sources of taxable income.

The "effective" rate structure of the federal corporation income tax may also be affected by tax credits. One such credit of considerable significance was enacted in the Revenue Act of 1962, namely, the *investment credit* against income tax liability for expenditures on depreciable machinery and equipment used in a trade or business within the United States. This credit was repealed, however, by the Tax Reform Act of 1969 for "anti-inflation" reasons, but was later reenacted during 1971 for "anti-recession" reasons. The basic credit is equal to 7 percent of qualified investment.

Differential treatment is also available to small corporations which may elect *not* to pay a corporation income tax if all stockholders consent to the taxation of the income of the corporation at the stockholder level under the personal income tax. The qualifications for such tax treatment are rigorous, however, and many small corporations are excluded from the option.[5]

The Internal Revenue code provides special provisions to inhibit the use of the federal corporation income tax by high-bracket taxpayers to avoid the higher marginal rates of the federal personal income tax. A

---

[4] However, corporations with less than $25,000 of taxable income pay only a 22 percent rate on capital gains.

[5] To qualify for this choice, a corporation must be a domestic corporation with no more than 10 shareholders, each of whom must be an individual or an estate, and no one of whom may be a nonresident alien. In addition, the corporation must have only one class of stock and it may not be a member of an affiliated group of companies eligible to file a consolidated tax return. Furthermore, the corporation must not receive more than 80 percent of its gross receipts from sources outside the United States nor may it receive more than 20 percent of its gross receipts from rents, royalties, dividends, interest, annuities, and gains from the sale or exchange of stocks and securities.

corporation which accumulates earnings in excess of the "reasonably anticipated" needs of the business, for example, may legally be required to pay a penalty tax on the excess in addition to the regular corporation income tax. The burden of proof regarding "improper accumulations" generally falls upon the Internal Revenue Service (IRS). Another special provision provides a tax at the rate of 70 percent on the undistributed income of companies defined by the law as "personal holding companies."[6]

Some Special Characteristics of the Federal Corporation Income Tax

Treatment of Depreciation. Business expenditures for capital assets such as plant and equipment cannot be fully deducted, under ordinary circumstances, in the year in which they are acquired. Instead, the deduction must be apportioned over the estimated "useful life" of the asset. The income of each year's operation is charged with a proportion of the cost of the capital asset. Allowances for depreciation may be taken only for that property used in trade or business, or otherwise held for the production of income. The depreciation allowance cannot exceed the original cost of the capital asset. Though the firm may use *any* estimated useful life for tax purposes which is consistent with retirement practices, depreciation guidelines, known as "guideline lives," are provided by the Treasury Department. These "guideline lives," in effect, are "tax lives" which theoretically would correspond to the actual "useful lives" of the assets. However, the tendency has been to allow "tax life" depreciation deductions to occur at rates faster than the actual using up of the capital assets.

There have been three primary methods of computing depreciation in use since The Revenue Act of 1954. Thus, a taxpayer may select from among the "straight-line," "double-declining balance," and "sum-of-the-years'-digits" method of depreciation. Moreover, he may use "any other consistent method" which, during the first two thirds of the life of the asset, does not result in depreciation charges greater than those which would be obtained under the "double-declining balance" method.

Under the *straight-line* method of depreciation, the acquisition cost of an asset is written off (depreciated, deducted) in equal annual installments during the useful life of the asset. Thus, a $20,000 capital asset

---

[6] In general, a corporation is considered to be a personal holding company if it is controlled by not more than five individuals, and if its personal holding company income (such as dividends, interest, royalties reduced for depletion deductions, and rents reduced by depreciation, taxes, and interest) constitutes up to 60 percent or more of its gross income reduced by the amount of deductions for depreciation, depletion, interest, and taxes.

with a useful life of 20 years would be deducted at a depreciation rate of 5 percent, or $1,000 per year.

The *double-declining balance* method of depreciation is one by which a fixed percentage of the unrecovered cost (undepreciated balance) is deducted annually starting at a rate double that of straight-line depreciation, and then continuing that rate on the remaining balances. Thus, referring to the same capital asset as in the above example, a depreciation rate of 10 percent of $20,000, or $2,000 would be applied in the first year with the rate being 10 percent of the unrecovered cost of $18,000, or $1,800 in the second year and so on.

The *sum-of-the-years'-digits* method of depreciation produces a depreciation pattern somewhat similar to that of the double-declining balance method, but without leaving an undepreciated balance considerably in excess of salvage value at the end of the useful life of the asset. Again, using the same example, this method would sum the useful years of life of the asset $(20 + 19 + 18 + 17 . . . + 1 = 210)$ and then calculate depreciation allowances in each year, beginning with the highest-number year, as that year is a proportion of the sum of the years $(20/210, 19/210, 18/210 . . . 1/210)$. This fraction is then multiplied by the cost of the asset ($20,000). Thus, $20/210$ $(2/21)$ times $20,000 or (approximately) $1,905, is deducted during the first year with $19/210$ times $20,000, or (approximately) $1,810 in the second year, and so on.

The latter two of these depreciation methods—the double-declining balance method and the sum-of-the-years'-digits method—allow the writing off of a capital asset in greater proportions in the earlier than in the later years of the life of the asset. This is known as *accelerated depreciation.* In 1962, following an extensive study of depreciation rules, methods, and existing practices, the Treasury Department issued an administrative ruling which substantially reduced suggested "tax lives," thus allowing for still greater "accelerated depreciation." The practice of accelerated depreciation increases the amount of money capital available (in the shorter term) for "reinvestment" by a business since it allows a cost writeoff for a capital asset "more rapid" than the actual physical "using up" or "obsolescence" of the asset. That is, the net taxable income of the corporation is reduced and its capital expenditure potential increased in the short run by the use of "accelerated depreciation."

In 1971, depreciation procedures received significantly greater liberalization with the introduction of the asset depreciation range (ADR) system. This system allows a taxpayer to select a "tax life" ("guideline life") for an asset up to 20 percent shorter than the liberal guideline lives already in existence. The ADR technique applies to "tangible personal property" such as machinery, but *not* to "real property" such as buildings.

Taxation of Income from Natural Resources. Various special provisions for the taxation of income derived from natural resources are provided by the Internal Revenue Code. *Depletion allowances* may be applied to capital sums invested in the development of natural resource properties. For mineral properties, depletion allowances are computed by either a "cost depletion" or a "percentage depletion" method.

Under the *cost method,* which must be used for timber resources, the "adjusted basis" (see definition below) of the property is divided by the total number of units estimated to remain in the deposit or property (for example, barrels of oil, tons of ore, and board feet of lumber), and the result is multiplied by the number of units sold during the year. When the "adjusted basis" of the property is lowered to zero, the cost depletion allowance ceases. For example: If the adjusted basis (original cost plus any additional capital costs less the total of all depletion allowed) is $100,000, and the number of recoverable units is 100,000, and 5,000 units were sold during a final year, the total depletion allowance would be ($100,000/100,000 $\times$ 5,000) = $5,000.

Under the *percentage depletion method,* "depletion" is computed as a specific percentage of the annual gross income from the property. It cannot, however, exceed 50 percent of the net taxable income from the property. The percentage depletion rates for various minerals are as follows:

1. 22 percent for oil and gas, sulfur, and uranium and, if mined in the United States, for asbestos, bauxite, cobalt, lead, manganese, mercury, nickel, platinum, thorium, tin, titanium, tungsten, zinc, molybdenum, and 23 other minerals.
2. 15 percent for gold (domestic), silver, oil shale, copper, and iron ore.
3. 14 percent for certain clays, asphalt, vermiculite, and certain other metals.
4. 10 percent for asbestos, coal, lignite, salt, and certain other minerals.
5. 5 percent for brick and tile clay, gravel, sand, clam and oyster shells, peat, pumice, sand, scoria, shale, rough stone, and certain brine well products.
6. 14 percent for "all other minerals" except soil, sod, dirt, turf, water, or mosses or minerals from sea water, the air, or similar inexhaustible resources.[7]

---

[7] Certain exceptions apply to group 6 above. For example, some of these minerals may be listed in (1) above if they are produced in the United States. All of these minerals, moreover, are subject to a "use test," that is, they are restricted to a 5 percent rate, whether produced domestically or not, when they are used for purposes comparable to common sand, gravel, or rough stone.

The Internal Revenue Code provides special treatment, other than depletion allowances, for certain capital expenditures incurred in bringing mineral properties into production. A taxpayer is allowed, for example, to write off as "incurred" the costs of *exploring* for mineral deposits (except oil and gas wells which are treated preferentially under separate provisions), or to set these costs up as deferred expenses to be deducted ratably as the deposit is exhausted. These expenses include expenditures to determine the existence, location, extent, and quality of mineral resources. Deductions for exploration expenditures are limited to $100,000 per year per taxpayer and to a total of $400,000 per taxpayer over an unspecified number of years. Another special provision permits a taxpayer either to write off as "incurred" the costs of *developing* a mineral deposit (except oil and gas wells which again are treated separately), or to set these up as deferred expenses to be deducted ratably as the mineral deposit is exhausted. Expenditures for development include the costs of mine shafts, tunnels, and strip mine activities. No dollar limitation is placed upon deductions for development costs.

The statutes also grant a special provision to oil and gas operators by providing an option of either "capitalizing," or by charging as "current expenses," so-called *intangible* drilling and development costs of oil and gas wells. These deductible expenses include costs of fuel and power, labor, materials, tool rental, repairs of drilling equipment, and the like. No dollar limit is placed upon these deductions.

Among the other special provisions for taxpayers in the extractive industries is the one which pertains to the recipients of grants from the United States for the encouragement of exploration, development, and mining of minerals or metals which are strategic for national defense. Such grants may be excluded from taxable income. Moreover, special treatment is provided to income arising from certain types of timber-cutting and iron and coal mine operations. A taxpayer owning timber, or the contract right to cut timber for a six-month period prior to the beginning of the taxable year, may elect to treat the proceeds received from cutting the timber as a long-term capital gain. Also, a taxpayer owning timber, coal, or iron ore for a period of six months before its disposal, and who retains an economic interest following such a disposal, may treat the royalties received as a long-term capital gain. In all, "depletion" and other special "tax privileges" for exhaustive industries contribute significantly to the *erosion* of the federal corporation as well as the federal personal income tax bases.

Taxation of Income from Foreign Sources. A critical problem of equity arises when the same income is subject to tax by more than one nation.[8]

---

[8] This subject is discussed in greater detail in Chapter 22 entitled "The Public Sector in Other Nations."

In the absence of special provisions, American individuals and corporations could be fully taxed on foreign income by both the federal government and by the government of the foreign nation in which the income is earned. However, the Internal Revenue Code, in conjunction with more than 30 tax treaties or conventions between the United States and foreign nations, does provide special tax treatment for income earned from foreign sources. The Code directly determines, for the taxpayer's return filed with the Internal Revenue Service, what income is to be taxed, when it is to be taxed, and what credits or deductions are to be given for foreign taxes paid. Tax treaties or conventions influence the manner in which the foreign nations tax residents of the United States as well as the manner in which the United States taxes foreign residents who derive income from economic activity in the United States.

The Multiple (Double) Taxation of Dividend Income. Corporate dividends are taxed by the federal personal income tax as taxable income to shareholders and again by the federal corporation income tax as part of corporate profits.[9] Technically, this is a form of "intra-unit" multiple (double) taxation, that is, the same tax base is taxed more than once by the same unit of government. Opponents of the imposition of dual income taxes upon dividend income, among other things, contend that the burden of multiple taxation is particularly heavy on low-income taxpayers who receive dividends.

Meanwhile, proponents of the multiple taxation of dividend income contend that the effective extent of multiple taxation is exaggerated. They argue that a substantial portion of the tax is shifted both backward to wage earners in the form of lower wages and forward to consumers in the form of higher prices.[10] To the extent that the tax is not shifted, moreover, it is claimed that stockholders do not generally base their decisions with respect to stock purchases on "pretax" corporate earnings per share, but instead upon the "aftertax" earnings available for distribution. It is thus argued that stockholders take full account of the existence of the corporation income tax in determining the price which they will pay for corporate stock. Hence, the burden would be limited to those who purchase stock before an increase in corporation income tax rates occurs.

Probably, the primary reason for the retention of the federal corporation income tax, despite its "multiple taxation" characteristics, is the fact that it is such an important revenue producer for the federal government. In fiscal 1973, the tax produced $36 billion in federal tax

---

[9] A modest "exclusion" is allowed under the federal personal income tax for the first $100 of dividends received from qualifying domestic corporations.

[10] See the relevant discussion of the incidence of the corporation income tax later in this chapter.

revenues, an amount surpassed only by the federal personal income tax and by the combined federal payroll (employment) taxes.

STATE AND LOCAL CORPORATION INCOME TAXES

Historical Development

States began to charge fees for incorporation and to levy capital stock taxes during the nineteenth century.[11] The modern period of state corporation income taxation, however, was not initiated until the enactment of the Wisconsin personal and corporation income taxes in 1911, though the Territory of Hawaii had enacted a corporation income tax in 1901. Between 1911 and 1920, 7 additional states passed corporation income tax laws. During the 1920s, 8 states passed such legislation while 15 additional states added the corporation income tax during the 1930s. After 1947, 13 more states and Alaska (as a territory) adopted the tax, bringing the present total to 45 states plus the District of Columbia.

While the corporation income tax accounts for about 20 percent of federal government tax revenues (1971), state corporation income tax revenues represent only about 7 percent of total state tax revenues. A number of cities also impose corporation income taxes, though concentration of the cities occurs within a small number of states. These taxes are usually "supplementary" taxes to the low-rate personal income taxes and the taxes on the net profits of unincorporated business levied by the cities. In terms of revenue productivity, state and local corporation income taxes in the nation as a whole are estimated to be slightly "income elastic." A study by Harris estimates the income elasticity coefficient to be 1.16 ($Ye = 1.16$) while another study by Netzer estimates an income elasticity value of 1.10 ($Ye = 1.10$).[12]

State–Local Corporation Income Tax Base and Rate Structures

Table 11–1 summarizes the state corporation income tax structures. It may be observed that the majority of state corporation income taxes

---

[11] See the Advisory Commission on Intergovernmental Relations, *Tax Overlapping in the United States—1964* (Washington, D.C.: U.S. Government Printing Office, 1964), and the Advisory Commission on Intergovernmental Relations, *State and Local Finances—Significant Features 1967–1970* (Washington, D.C.: U.S. Government Printing Office, November 1969), for material related to this section.

[12] Robert Harris, *Income and Sales Taxes: The 1970 Outlook for States and Localities* (Chicago: Council of State Governments, 1966); Dick Netzer, "Financial Needs and Resources over the Next Decade: State and Local Governments," in *Public Finances: Needs, Sources, and Utilization* (Princeton: Princeton University Press, 1961), pp. 23–65.

TABLE 11–1

Summary of State Corporation Income Tax Rates[a] (as of September 1, 1972)

State	Flat rate or lowest bracket		Highest bracket		Minimum tax	Federal income tax deductible[b]
	Rate	To net income of	Rate	Net income over		
Alabama	5.0%	All	—	—	—	Yes
Alaska	18% of Federal income tax		—	—	—	No
Arizona	2.0	$11,000	8.0	$6,000	—	Yes
Arkansas	1.0	3,000	6.0	25,000	—	No
California[c]	7.6	All	—	—	$200	No
Colorado	5.0	All	—	—	—	No
Connecticut	8.0[d]	All	—	—	45	No
Delaware	6.0[e]	All	—	—	—	No
Florida	5.0	All[f]	—	—	—	No
Georgia	6.0	All	—	—	—	No
Hawaii	5.85	25,000	6.435	25,000	—	No
Idaho	6.5[g]	All	—	—	—	No
Illinois	4.0	All	—	—	—	No
Indiana	2.0[h]	All	—	—	—	No
Iowa	6.0	25,000	10.0	100,000	—	Yes[i]
Kansas	4.5[j]	All	—	—	—	Yes[i]
Kentucky	4.0	25,000	5.8	25,000	—	No
Louisiana	4.0	All	—	—	—	No
Maine	4.0	All	—	—	—	No
Maryland	7.0[k]	All	—	—	—	No
Massachusetts	7.5[l]	(l)	(l)	(l)	100	No
Michigan[m]	7.8	All	—	—	—	No
Minnesota	12.0	All	—	—	10	No
Mississippi	3.0	5,000	4.0	5,000	—	No
Missouri	5.0	All	—	—	—	Yes
Montana	6.25[n]	All	—	—	50[o]	No
Nebraska	3.0[p]	All	—	—	—	No
New Hampshire	7.0	All	—	—	—	No
New Jersey[q]	5.5	All	—	—	—	No
New Mexico	5.0	All	—	—	—	No
New York	9.0[d]	All	—	—	125	No
North Carolina	6.0	All	—	—	—	No
North Dakota	3.0[r]	3,000	6.0	15,000	—	Yes
Ohio	4.0	25,000	8.0	25,000	50	No
Oklahoma	4.0	All	—	—	—	No
Oregon	6.0	All	—	—	10	No
Pennsylvania	11.0	All	—	—	—	No
Rhode Island	8.0[d]	All	—	—	—	No
South Carolina	6.0	All	—	—	—	No
Tennessee	6.0	All	—	—	—	No
Utah	6.0	All	—	—	25	Yes
Vermont	6.0	All	—	—	25	No
Virginia	6.0	All	—	—	—	No
West Virginia	6.0	All	—	—	—	No
Wisconsin	2.3	1,000	7.9	6,000	—	Yes[i]
District of Columbia[s]	7.0	All	—	—	25	No

[a] A special tax on financial institutions is levied in all states, and is based either on net income or generally on the value of shares of capital stock.

[b] In general, each state which permits the deduction of Federal income taxes, limits such deduction to taxes paid on that part of income subject to its own income tax.

[c] Financial corporations other than banks are allowed a limited offset for personal property taxes and license fees.

[d] Alternative methods of computation are used if tax yield is greater.

[e] A surcharge equal to 20% of the tax due is imposed on taxable income earned during the period August 1, 1971, through June 30, 1973.

[f] An exemption of $5,000 of net income allowed each corporation.

[g] Each corporation filing return pays additional $10.

[h] Based on adjusted gross income from sources within Indiana.

[i] Deductions limited. For Kansas the deduction is suspended for tax years beginning after 1971 and before 1973.

[j] A 2¼% surtax is imposed on taxable income in excess of $25,000.

[k] Domestic corporations deduct franchise taxes in excess of $40.

[l] Corporations pay an excise tax equal to the greater of the following: (1) $7 per $1,000 of value of Massachusetts tangible property not taxed locally or net worth allocated to Massachusetts, plus 7½% of net income; or (2) $100, whichever is greater. Interstate corporations not subject to the corporation income tax pay a tax of 4% of net income. In addition, a surtax of 14% is imposed.

[m] In addition, cities are authorized to levy a 1% tax (2% in Detroit) on corporations.

[n] For taxable years ending on or after February 28, 1971, and before February 28, 1973, the rate is 6.75%.

[o] $10 for small business corporations.

[p] The tax rate is increased to 3.75%, for taxable years beginning January 1, 1973.

[q] All corporations pay additional tax on net worth.

[r] An additional 1% tax is imposed for the privilege of doing business in the state, and a temporary second additional 1% tax is imposed.

[s] For tax years beginning after December 31, 1973, the rate is 8%.

Source: *Facts and Figures on Government Finance—1973* (New York: Tax Foundation, Inc., 1973), p. 196.

are applied with flat (proportional) rates. The rate structures of the state taxes are low as compared to the federal corporation income tax. The rates range from a minimum rate of 1 percent in one state to a maximum rate of 10 percent in another. One state, Alaska, uses the "tax supplement" approach whereby it assesses the tax at 18 percent of the federal corporation income tax liability of the business. Corporation income taxes used by *local* governments tend also to be low, proportionally rated taxes. The local corporation income taxes overlap state corporation income taxes in a number of cities including New York City, Baltimore, Detroit, Kansas City, and St. Louis.

Increasingly, state corporation income taxes are being made more similar to the federal corporation tax base. In fact, well over one third of the states which now levy corporation income taxes have substantially adopted the federal corporation income tax base, with certain modest deviations. Finally, one irritating problem deriving from multistate use of the tax should be noted, that is, the fact that some 125,000 companies do business in more than one state. This raises the delicate question of "allocating" the taxable income base among the various states.

INCIDENCE OF THE CORPORATION INCOME TAX

The chapter will now turn its attention to a discussion of the incidence of the corporation income tax. Such a discussion will be useful prior to the overall evaluation of the tax in the final "fiscal rationality" section of the chapter. Moreover, the discussion seems justified in light of the renewal of interest during the 1960s in this subject which has led to a number of significant empirical studies.[13] Moreover, some of these studies have tended to consider corporation income tax incidence in a "general equilibrium" sense rather than in the more narrow framework of "partial equilibrium" analysis. Although the studies as such have not been conclusive, the broadening of the empirical analysis which they represent warrants the attention of anyone interested in the current state of knowledge regarding tax (and total budgetary) incidence.

Some earlier efforts during the 1950s provided analyses of the relationship between, on the one hand, *corporate income tax rates* and, on the other hand, *corporate rates of return* and *factor shares* (the proportion of the income originating in the corporate sector which is received by capital in the form of profits). These include studies by Lerner and

---

[13] An excellent appraisal of these studies, as well as of the current state of incidence theory in general, may be found in Peter Mieszkowski, "Tax Incidence Theory: The Effects of Taxes on the Distribution of Income," *Journal of Economic Literature*, December 1969, pp. 1103–24.

Hendrikson in 1956 and by Adelman in 1957.[14] The Lerner-Hendrikson study attempted to determine the relationship between federal corporation income tax rates and the *rates of return* to capital in various American industries for the period 1927–1952. The authors consider that a decline in the posttax rate of return following a tax increase would suggest the absence of complete short-run shifting of the tax. On the other hand, a constant or rising posttax rate of return would indicate substantial shifting of the tax. The Lerner-Hendrikson study concludes from its evidence that complete short-run shifting of the federal corporation income tax did *not* take place during the period.

The Adelman study focused upon *factor shares* in that it compared the proportion of "pretax" corporate profits to total income originating in the corporate sector of the economy for the periods 1922–1929 and 1946–1955. The proportion of "pretax" corporate profits was approximately 23 percent during both the prosperous, *low-tax*, period between 1922–1929 and also during the prosperous, *high-tax*, period between 1946–1955. Adelman thus concludes that substantial shifting of the federal corporation income tax had *not* occurred since the ratio of "pretax" corporate profits to total income originating in the corporate sector remained constant. On the other hand, a higher "pretax" proportion in the later high-tax period would be required, if the higher tax is to be offset through shifting.

Both studies, though worthwhile, are generally conceded to have failed to account for the significant *nontax forces* which affect corporate rates of return or factor shares, respectively. That is, they fail to separate the "nontax variables" from the "federal corporation income tax" as forces which determine corporation profit-making behavior.

An important study, one which broadened the scope of corporate income tax incidence analysis into the *general equilibrium* context, was provided by Harberger in 1962.[15] The Harberger study, which emphasizes long-run capital flows from the corporate to the noncorporate sector of the economy, is concerned initially with the incidence of the tax under *competitive* conditions. Given these conditions, he observes:

> It is hard to avoid the conclusion that plausible alternative assumptions about the relevant elasticities all yield results in which capital bears very close to 100% of the tax burden. The most plausible assumptions imply that capital bears more than the full burden of the tax.[16]

---

[14] E. M. Lerner and E. S. Hendrikson, "Federal Taxes on Corporate Income and the Rate of Return on Investment in Manufacturing, 1927–1952," *National Tax Journal,* September 1956, pp. 193–202; M. A. Adelman, "The Corporate Income Tax in the Long Run," *Journal of Political Economy,* April 1957, pp. 151–57.

[15] Arnold Harberger, "The Incidence of the Corporation Income Tax," *Journal of Political Economy,* June 1962, pp. 215–40.

[16] Ibid., p. 234.

Moreover, in an appendix to the article, the author concludes that when *monopoly* elements in the corporate sector are recognized, the results are not substantially modified from those which occur in competitive markets. Relatedly, Mieszkowski remarks:

> It is easy to show, by extending the Harberger approach, that if concentrated industries make investments on the basis of a target rate of return criterion, the sharp decrease in the use of capital in these industries can drive down the rate of return in the competitive sectors of the economy to an extent that the return on all capital falls by considerably more than the yield of the corporate profits tax.[17]

An important implication which may be derived from the Harberger general equilibrium study is that even if *short-run* forward shifting by large segments of the corporate sector does occur, the overall burden of the tax in the *long run* still might fall on "capital in general."

The *econometric* technique was comprehensively applied to the subject of corporation income tax incidence in the much discussed study by Krzyzaniak and Musgrave in 1963.[18] This study focused upon the influence of the federal corporation income tax on the *rate of return* using multiple regression techniques and a profit-behavior model for the years 1935–1959 (the war and early postwar years, 1943–1947, are excluded). An attempt is made to determine the extent of *short-run shifting* by comparing the actual behavior revealed by existing data with the bahavior that would be indicated by the profit-behavior model when the tax determinant is excluded. If successfully implemented, the model would thus isolate the functional relationship between the federal corporation income tax and profit-behavior as it influences the rate of return; the other (exogenous) determinants would be separated from this main functional relationship. A correlation between *high* "pretax" corporate profits (rates of return) and *high* corporate tax rates would thus indicate forward shifting of the tax.

On this basis, they conclude that the federal corporation income tax is shifted by more than 100 percent in the short-run. That is, for every $1 increment in corporate tax liabilities per unit of capital, pretax corporate profits would increase by $1.34. The authors acknowledge that such a ratio represents some "overstatement" of the extent of shifting due to the lack of initial correction for factors such as inflation and governmental expenditure effects in the standard "all manufacturing case" which they develop. When these forces are considered, however,

---

[17] Mieszkowski, "Tax Incidence Theory," pp. 1120.

[18] M. Krzyzaniak and R. A. Musgrave, *The Shifting of the Corporation Income Tax* (Baltimore: The Johns Hopkins Press, 1963).

it is still concluded that a high degree of short-run shifting exists.[19] Needless to say, the "policy implications" of substantial short-run shifting of the federal corporation income tax would be significant.[20]

A number of studies have challenged the conclusions reached in the Krzyzaniak-Musgrave analysis. Among these studies are those by Goode, Slitor, Gordon, and the one by Cragg, Harberger, and Mieszkowski.[21] The basic criticism contained in these reactions to the Krzyzaniak-Musgrave model is that the model fails to adequately reflect *aggregate* or *cyclical changes* in the national economy during the period under study (1935–59). Yet, this was a period characterized by both depression and prosperity as well as by wartime mobilization, though the years 1943 through 1947 are excluded from the Krzyzaniak-Musgrave study. Thus, the correlation between high corporate tax rates and high pretax corporate profits (rates of return) may well be caused by *nontax cyclical variables* and it does not necessarily suggest the shifting of the federal corporation income tax. The critics believe that little a priori justification can be established for the nontax variables used in the Krzyzaniak-Musgrave model.

Some of the forces which tend to make corporate earnings high at a time when corporate income tax rates are high include high capacity utilization of capital in particular, and of productive resources in general, which relate to the high effective demand typically found during periods of peacetime prosperity and during mobilization and war years. The Cragg-Harberger-Mieszkowski study, in order to adjust for the alleged inadequacies of the Krzyzaniak-Musgrave model, introduces a "cyclical variable" in the form of the *employment rate* and a "dummy variable" to represent *wartime mobilization* for the years 1941, 1942, 1950, 1951, and 1952—all war-related years covered in the Krzyzaniak-Musgrave study. The results of these adjustments cause Cragg, *et al.* to conclude that capital bears approximately 100 percent of the tax. The studies by Goode and Slitor, in an effort to fill the nontax (cyclical) variable void represented by aggregate economic conditions, add the

---

[19] Moreover, studies by Roskamp [K. W. Roskamp, "The Shifting of Taxes on Business Income: The Case of West German Corporations," *National Tax Journal*, September 1965, pp. 247–57] and Spencer [B. G. Spencer, "The Shifting of the Corporation Income Tax in Canada," *Canadian Journal of Economics*, February 1969, pp. 21–34], using the Krzyzaniak-Musgrave model, indicate 100 percent shifting of the corporation income tax in West Germany and Canada, respectively.

[20] See Gordon, cited in footnote 21 below, for a list of some of these important policy implications.

[21] R. Goode, "Rates of Return, Income Shares, and Corporate Tax Incidence," in M. Krzyzaniak (ed.), *Effects of Corporation Income Tax* (Detroit: Wayne State University Press, 1966); R. E. Slitor, "Corporate Tax Incidence: Economic Adjustments to Differentials under a Two-Tier Tax Structure" in Krzyzaniak, *Effects of Corporation Income Tax;* R. J. Gordon, "The Incidence of the Corporation Income Tax in U.S. Manufacturing 1925–62," *American Economic Review*, September 1967, pp. 731–58, and J. G. Cragg, A. C. Harberger, and P. Mieszkowski, "Empirical Evidence on the Incidence of the Corporation Income Tax," *Journal of Political Economy*, December 1967, pp. 811–21.

ratio of "actual to potential GNP" to the Krzyzaniak-Musgrave model. None of these studies yields results consistent with the short-run shifting conclusion reached in the Krzyzaniak-Musgrave study. However, a subsequent study by Dusansky—using a rate-of-return approach and a cyclical variable proxy—estimated 100 percent forward shifting of the tax in the short run.[22]

Other nontax variables which should be considered concerning the Krzyzaniak-Musgrave study, and which are also relevant to any study of corporation income tax incidence, include those effects exerted by increases in *capital productivity,* and changes in the *capital-output ratio* in firm production functions. For example, the higher "pretax" rates of return which allow "posttax" rates of return to remain constant, after higher tax rates are in effect, may be due to an increase in the productivity of capital rather than due to tax shifting. Or, under the factor shares approach, a higher "pretax" share of corporate profits out of total income originating in the corporate sector, after higher corporate income tax rates are in effect, may be due to an increase in the capital/output ratio in the corporate sector.

In terms of methodology, it should be noted that the study by Gordon integrates the "rate of return" and "factor share" approaches and thus, in addition to its point of disagreement with the Krzyzaniak-Musgrave conclusions, provides a methodological sophistication to the study of corporation income tax incidence by combining the two approaches. Moreover, the Gordon model is based on a "markup pricing" technique which relates to a realistic "real world" situation in terms of the existence of unrealized gains. Also, mention should be made of the "production function" approach used by Hall, which relates changes in the "productivity of capital" to corporate rates of return, and also the study by Kilpatrick which attempts to establish a positive relationship between "industry concentration," in a market structure sense, and the forward shifting of the corporation income tax.[23]

In summary, it may be said that recent times have witnessed an active interest in the incidence of the corporation income tax even though the various studies have left "unresolved" the actual direction of that incidence.[24] Relatedly, this also reflects a revival in tax (and budgetary) incidence theory in general. Significantly, some of the re-

[22] R. Dusansky, "The Short-run Shifting of the Corporation Income Tax in the United States," *Oxford Economic Papers,* November 1972, pp. 357–71.

[23] C. A. Hall, "Direct Shifting of the Corporation Income Tax in Manufacturing," *American Economic Review,* May 1964, pp. 258–71; R. W. Kilpatrick, "The Short-run Forward Shifting of the Corporation Income Tax," *Yale Economic Essays,* Fall 1965, pp. 355–420.

[24] For a later version of the corporation income tax incidence controversy, see M. Krzyzaniak and R. A. Musgrave, "Corporation Tax Shifting: A Response," *Journal of Political Economy,* July–August 1970, pp. 768–73, and J. G. Cragg, A. C. Harberger, and P. Mieszkowski, "Corporation Tax Shifting: Rejoinder," pp. 774-77.

cent corporation income tax incidence studies move toward a general equilibrium approach. This, in itself, represents a fuller appreciation for the need to broaden the concept of tax incidence, to the extent feasible, from the *partial equilibrium* concept into the more comprehensive *general equilibrium* approach, as discussed in Chapter 8. Moreover, the application of the econometric technique of analysis offers hope for more conclusive future studies of corporation income tax incidence.

FISCAL RATIONALITY CRITERIA APPLIED TO THE CORPORATION INCOME TAX

The economic effects of the corporation income tax, with particular emphasis on the federal government version, will now be further analyzed in terms of the fiscal rationality criteria developed in Chapter 6. The economic effects of the tax will be approached below from the dual standpoints of both *aggregative* and *disaggregative* analysis. The *former* approach will consider the influence of the corporation income tax upon "overall" investment incentives and capital availability in the national economy, as well as stabilization effects. The *latter* will consider the impact upon such allocative decisions as internal versus external financing and equity versus debt financing. Moreover, the reader should once again be reminded that duplicative provisions in the federal personal and corporation income taxes render some of the following analysis applicable to either tax.

The Corporation Income Tax and Aggregate Nonneutral Effects

Effect of the Corporation Income Tax on Investment Incentives. It is often asserted that the corporation income tax has a negative or retarding effect on *aggregate* investment expenditures in the economy. Indeed, an unshifted corporation income tax does reduce net "aftertax" profits on new investments, which would tend to reduce investment incentives. Moreover, such profit reduction would occur whether the investments would have been for the expansion of present capacity or for the replacement of existing facilities. Yet, there exist certain important forces which tend to reduce or neutralize the retardation effect of the corporation income tax on business investment.[25] The corporation income tax, for example, is *not* the only tax which corporations must pay. Since other taxes also require consideration when investment decisions are made, the relative impact of the corporation income tax on decisions is subsequently lessened. Furthermore, the assumption

---

[25] Gerhard Colm, "The Corporation and the Corporate Income Tax," *American Economic Review,* May 1954, pp. 486–503.

that the corporation income tax is not shifted is an uncertain one, especially if one assumes "nonshiftability" in the sense that not even "partial shifting" of the tax occurs.[26]

Still other forces may help to neutralize the retarding effect on aggregate investment resulting from the corporation income tax.[27] These forces include: (1) the inelasticity, in many instances, of investment demand; (2) the fact that many businesses use the rate of return "before taxes" as an earnings goal; (3) the fact that many businesses look to the "loss potential" as well as to the "rate of return" from an investment; (4) the fact that businesses, particularly modern corporations, may have other goals in addition to the earnings goal, and (5) the fact that the volume of investment is determined, in many instances, by "bottleneck factors" such as management size and the availability of internal funds. For example, for a company to expand beyond a point, a subsidiary staffed with its own management hierarchy may have to be established. In other words, it may not be possible to expand output along a linear homogeneous input/output curve.

No definite conclusions can be reached regarding the retardation of aggregate investment incentives by the corporation income tax. The variables mentioned above, and many others, will help to determine the result in any one case. Moreover, these parameters may be expected to change over time. Thus, only generalizations and not specific conclusions can be rendered. Among the most relevant generalizations are: (1) the observation that a shiftable corporation income tax is less likely to reduce aggregate investment incentives than is one which cannot be shifted; (2) the fact that investment incentives are less likely to be harmed by a corporation income tax during a cyclical upswing than during a cyclical downturn since, when the demands for their products are relatively high, stronger motivation exists for businesses to modernize equipment and to expand output and inventories, and (3) the fact that high personal and corporation income tax rates, combined with a low rate on capital gains, encourages the retention and subsequent reinvestment of earnings by corporations.

Accelerated Depreciation under the Corporation Income Tax. In recent decades, *accelerated depreciation* allowances have been used as a fiscal device, in part to offset the general investment retardation effects of the corporation income tax discussed above, and in part to encourage business investment in a direct manner.[28] However, this is *not* to sug-

---

[26] See the discussion earlier in this chapter of the incidence of the corporation income tax.

[27] John Lintner, "Effect of Corporate Taxation on Real Investment," *American Economic Review*, May 1954, pp. 520–34.

[28] See the discussion in Chapter 25 regarding the nature of accelerated depreciation as well as the use of this device as a fiscal policy tool.

gest that presently-existing accelerated depreciation procedures are designed only to promote investment. Instead, they are designed also to provide a realistic measure of "taxable income" since capital assets tend to use up value faster in the early years of their useful lives than in the later years. Yet, by the extent to which accelerated depreciation influences investment decisions, it may still exert significant economic effects.

As discussed earlier in the chapter, "accelerated depreciation" refers to a tax write-off for the wearing out of a capital asset over a period of time "shorter" than the actual physical wearing out or obsolescence of the asset. To the extent that "normal depreciation" allowances delay and sometimes prevent the full recovery of capital from the earnings of a new asset, "accelerated depreciation" will be effective in reducing the discouragement of investment.[29] The rapid recovery of capital made possible by accelerated depreciation offers an interest (time discount) gain to investors and permits growing firms to finance more of their capital requirements from retained earnings. Moreover, it serves to make investment projects more lucrative because risk and uncertainty are reduced.

The introduction of accelerated depreciation tends to stimulate investment more by lowering a tax burden rather than by creating new incentives.[30] Hence, the potential significance of accelerated depreciation depends upon the severity of the burden presented by the income tax under normal depreciation methods. The "attitude" of the investor is an important variable. Accelerated depreciation will significantly influence those investors who apply a fairly heavy, though not excessive, discount for interest and risk and who adopt a payoff period considerably shorter than the normal useful life of the asset, but still long enough to permit recovery of a substantial fraction of the investment outlay during the payoff period by means of the accelerated depreciation.[31]

The stabilization effects of accelerated depreciation may not be as satisfactory as the allocation and economic growth effects discussed above. It is argued, for example, that accelerated depreciation is very likely to intensify economic fluctuations, that is, widen the range of the cycle in terms of both output fluctuation and cycle duration.[32] These results will tend to follow because the accelerated allowance will encourage investment when profits are high and tax extraction is consid-

---

[29] Richard Goode, "Accelerated Depreciation Allowances as a Stimulus to Investment," *Quarterly Journal of Economics*, May 1955, pp. 191–220.

[30] *Ibid.*

[31] *Ibid.*

[32] Evsey D. Domar, "The Case for Accelerated Depreciation," *Quarterly Journal of Economics*, November 1953, pp. 493–519.

erable while, in the absence of profits during a cyclical downturn, it will become ineffective or, even worse, it may make it worthwhile to postpone investment until profits reappear and advantage can be taken of larger allowances. Furthermore, the heavy amortization of investment during prosperity leaves little depreciation to charge during a depression. Taxable profits will thus be understated in the first instance (prosperity), and overstated in the second instance (depression), with parallel undesirable movements in the magnitude of tax liabilities.

Accelerated depreciation may also be criticized in the sense of its "single tax" characteristic. Thus, it is argued that to be effective it must be introduced only once and tax rates must not be raised in the future.[33] If legislative behavior causes investors to expect that permissible rates of depreciation will increase in the future, for example, investors effectively receive an "announcement" that the capital values of assets acquired at the present time will decline in the future. Such knowledge would tend to discourage investment by distorting its "time dimension."

The above analysis suggests that accelerated depreciation provides "mixed" economic results yielding both *positive* and *negative* nonneutralities. On balance, however, accelerated depreciation appears advantageous in terms of its allocation and economic growth effects, though somewhat negative in terms of stabilization. Thus, a "stabilization distortion" cost may be paid in terms of intergoal nonneutrality in order to achieve positive results in the allocation and economic growth areas.

Accelerated depreciation, of course, is only one of a number of alternative economic policies which may be used to induce investment. Tax rate reduction, tax credits, and interest rate reduction are among the other alternatives. The comparative influence of accelerated depreciation, the investment tax credit, and an interest rate reduction upon the present value of a prospective investment may be briefly considered.[34] Each of these devices tends to increase the "present value" of an investment, but they involve substantially different "secondary" effects from one another.

The *accelerated depreciation* method appears to incur a substantial "revenue disadvantage" as a secondary effect since the achievement of a given increase in present value requires a large reduction in government revenues—a reduction much greater, for example, than under the investment credit which benefits the taxpayer *only* when profits exist. In addition, the accelerated depreciation method has the charac-

---

[33] J. A. Stockfisch, "Investment Incentive, Taxation, and Accelerated Depreciation," *Southern Economic Journal,* July 1957, pp. 28–40.

[34] See E. Cary Brown, "Tax Incentives for Investment," *American Economic Review,* May 1962, pp. 335–44.

teristic that, after large transitional revenue losses have been sustained, a particular firm will receive no extra reduction in income tax unless its current investment exceeds normal depreciation.[35] On the other hand, the *investment credit* draws no similar distinction between firms which are growing and those which are stable. Even if outlays were to fall below some kind of past average, a tax credit would nevertheless be given on these outlays. The accelerated depreciation technique has the advantage of being more "selective" than the *lower interest rate* alternative since the benefits are restricted to those who acquire new depreciable assets.

Effect of the Corporation Income Tax on Consumption. The influence of income taxation on consumption differs, among other things, depending upon whether the tax is a "personal" or a "corporation" income tax.[36] In the case of an "unshifted" corporation income tax, a change in the tax rate or base may be reflected in either a change in *retained earnings* or a *change in dividends.* To the extent that "retained earnings" are affected, personal income and personal consumption expenditures tend to be unchanged. Hence, the *substitution* of a corporation income tax for a personal income tax would increase consumption since personal tax liabilities would decline, thus increasing disposable income, while "dividends" would be maintained. On the other hand, the reverse, the *substitution* of a personal income tax for a corporation income tax, would decrease consumption. The distinction between a tax on personal income and a tax on business income is less profound if the business tax is on the "profits of unincorporated firms" since there is a close relationship in unincorporated businesses between personal income and business income.

The Corporation Income Tax as an Automatic Stabilizer. Although federal corporation income tax receipts vary sharply in a countercyclical direction during cyclical movements in the economy, the tax is generally conceded to perform rather modestly as an *automatic stabilizer.*[37] This is true, in part, because its effects on "aggregate demand" in the form of consumption and investment spending tend to be "indirect" rather than "direct." For example, when profits decline during a recession, many corporations tend to maintain dividend payments due to established policy. Hence, the "disposable income" of consumers is maintained at a relatively stable level. Yet, this is accomplished only through the "indirect" nature of corporate dividend policy, which causes dividends to be maintained at the expense of diminished corpo-

---

[35] *Ibid.*

[36] See Richard A. Musgrave, *The Theory of Public Finance* (New York: McGraw-Hill Book Co., 1959), pp. 173–74 and chap. 12.

[37] The full implications of "automatic stabilization devices" are analyzed in chapters 24 and 26.

rate saving, rather than through a "direct" reduction in personal income tax liabilities. Moreover, corporate investment decisions tend to be influenced more by the present and prospective demand for the products of a company, and by the related rates of return, than by a change in corporation income tax liability.

The Corporation Income Tax and Disaggregate Nonneutral Effects

The Corporation Income Tax and Distributional Equity. Next, the *disaggregate* nonneutral effects of the corporation income tax will be considered. The "first" disaggregative consideration focuses upon the ability-to-pay principle of equity in the *distribution* of tax burdens and to the related concept of "horizontal tax equity."[38] This concept stipulates that "equals should be treated equally" in the payment of taxes. It is implied, of course, that only individuals, *not* legal corporate business entities, can bear tax burdens. Since businesses are owned by individuals, business income taxes should be collected from the owners if horizontal distributional equity is to be achieved. "Retained earnings," however, pose a problem and, if the corporation income tax were to be eliminated, a way would have to be found to tax such earnings as if they were distributed. To do so, however, does not pose an insurmountable problem.

Moreover, some of the features discussed in connection with the federal personal income tax also bear a "tax equity" connotation for the federal corporation income tax. For example, many individuals as corporation shareholders—especially those in the higher income brackets—ultimately realize the tax advantages offered under the federal corporation income tax for capital gains, accelerated depreciation, and depletion allowances. This is true even though the formal format of the tax lists net "corporate income," not "personal income," as the base of the tax. Moreover, the special tax preferences cited earlier in this chapter, such as those provisions which favor banks, savings and loan associations, and insurance companies, tend to erode the base of the federal corporation income tax and, in addition, to "differentiate" tax burdens among individuals depending upon the source and type of income received. There is a strong likelihood that many features which erode the federal corporation income tax base create "negative nonneutral effects," in light of the "ability-to-pay" principle of equity in the distribution of tax burdens.

---

[38] The distribution of corporation income tax burdens is also closely related to the *incidence* of the tax—a subject which is devoted considerable attention earlier in the chapter.

Effect of the Corporation Income Tax on Investment Decisions. The
following example will focus upon the ability of a corporation income
tax to exert investment nonneutralities on the decision by a firm to
purchase *real capital assets.* In particular, the influence of alternative
"depreciation methods" and "tax rate schedules" will be emphasized.
The example, which is summarized in Table 11–2, is based on the
following assumptions for the firm in question:

1. The firm possesses a short-run profit-maximazation objective.
2. It wishes to increase rapidly in size so as to gain a larger share
   of the market.
3. It wishes to utilize all possible internal sources to finance its
   capital acquisitions.
4. The relevant capital asset has a cost of $24,000 and a useful life
   of five years.
5. The income generated by the use of the asset is $10,000 annually.
6. All funds remaining after the payment of taxes are invested.

The alternative *depreciation methods* are straight-line, double-declining balance, sum-of-the-years' digits, or "no" depreciation at all. The
alternative tax rate schedules are proportional, progressive, and regressive.

First, if a "proportional" tax rate of 28.8 percent is applied, the firm
will have $8,502 remaining for investment after the corporation in-
come tax is paid if the *straight-line* method of depreciation is used.
However, the more rapid the depreciation write-off during the first
year, the more the firm will have left over to invest after paying the
first year's taxes.[39] Thus, according to the Table, $9,885 would be left
over for investment under the *double-declining balance* method of
depreciation and $9,424 under the *sum-of-the-years' digits* method. At
the other extreme, only $7,120 would remain out of the $10,000 income
for investment if *no depreciation* is allowed and a "proportional" tax
rate is applied.

Next, it may be observed in Table 11–2 that both the "progressive"
and "regressive" tax rate schedules diminish the first-year investment
funds under the *straight-line* method of depreciation as compared to
the results of the "proportional" tax. On the other hand, under *double-
declining balance* depreciation, the "progressive" tax rate schedule
increases the amount of posttax investment funds, as compared to the
"proportional" tax, but the "regressive" rate schedule leaves fewer
investment aftertax funds than the "proportional" tax. Similarly, under
sum-of-the-years' digits depreciation, "progressive" taxation leaves

---

[39] Yet, it should be noted that the larger depreciation and smaller tax *now* result in
smaller depreciation and a larger tax in the *future,* in the absence of other offsets.

TABLE 11-2

Investment Nonneutralities as Influenced by the "Method of Depreciation" and the "Rate Structure" of a Corporation Income Tax*

Income, Asset, and Tax Parameters	Item	Depreciation Method Used			
		Straight line	Double-declining balance	Sum-of-the-year's digits	No depreciation
A. 1. Annual pretax and predepreciation income from asset = $10,000	Depreciation	4,800	9,600	8,000	0
2. Life of asset = 5 years	Taxable income	5,200	400	2,000	10,000
3. Cost of asset = $24,000	Income tax	1,498	115	576	2,880
4. Proportional tax rate = 28.8%	Remaining funds	8,502	9,885	9,424	7,120
B. 1. Annual pretax and predepreciation income from asset = $10,000	Depreciation	4,800	9,600	8,000	0
2. Life of asset = 5 years	Taxable income	5,200	400	2,000	10,000
3. Cost of asset = $24,000	Income tax	1,630	80	450	3,950
4. Progressive rate schedule:† 0–$1500 .... 20% 1500– 3000 .... 30% 3000– 6000 .... 40% 6000 up 50%	Remaining funds	8,370	9,920	9,550	6,050
C. 1. Annual pretax and predepreciation income from asset = $10,000	Depreciation	4,800	9,600	8,000	0
2. Life of asset = 5 years	Taxable income	5,200	400	2,000	10,000
3. Cost of asset = $24,000	Income tax	2,010	200	950	3,050
4. Regressive rate schedule:† 0–$1500 .... 50% 1,500– 3000 .... 40% 3,000– 6,000 .... 30% 6,000 up 20%	Remaining funds	7,990	9,800	9,050	6,950

* Nonneutral effects (nonneutralities) are based on the first year of use of a capital asset by a firm.

† The tax rates represented here are "marginal," not "average," rates. For example, under the *progressive* tax rate schedule and a $5,200 taxable income, the first $1,500 of taxable income is taxed at a rate of 20 percent, the next $1,500 at 30 percent, and the remaining $2,200 at 40 percent—yielding an income tax of $1,630.

more investment funds than the "proportional" tax, but "regressive" taxation leaves fewer funds than the "proportional" tax. *Without depreciation,* the most investment funds are left under the "proportional" tax schedule and the least under the "progressive" tax schedule. In *all* of the examples, regardless of the tax rate structure, the aftertax first year investment funds are largest under the double-declining balance, second largest under the sum-of-the-years' digits, third largest under straightline depreciation methods and, of course, least when no depreciation is allowed. Thus, it has been observed that the method of depreciation and the rate structure of a corporation income tax may each be expected to exert nonneutral effects on the decision of a firm to purchase real capital equipment.

The Corporation Income Tax and Inefficiency in Corporate Management. Another efficiency effect of the federal corporation income tax, definable in terms of both allocative and technical efficiency, is the influence of the tax upon inefficiency or waste in corporate management. There are certain facts which suggest that a corporation income tax with high marginal rates invites extravagance in business management.[40] This waste may occur in the form of "excessive compensation to executives" which can be charged as a business expense to the corporation. Moreover, liberal spending by businesses for advertising, for participation in goodwill campaigns, and for investment in the beautification of factories may be partially explained by the high marginal rates of the federal corporation income tax.

The Corporation Income Tax and Industrial Location. An additional allocative effect of the corporation income tax may be found on the state and local level in the sense of a geographical redistribution of industrial location. Industries tend to move, for example, from areas which have high state and/or local corporation income taxes to areas which either do not have corporation income taxes, or which impose them at "low" tax rate or "narrow" tax base levels. Admittedly, many other factors such as comparative labor costs and comparative property taxes also influence industrial location, but comparative differences in the corporation income tax between states and localities still must be included as a pertinent consideration.

The Corporation Income Tax and the Preferential Treatment of Certain Types of Business and Sources of Income. As suggested earlier in the chapter, one of the most critical areas of allocational distortion resulting from the federal corporation income tax exists in the preferential treatment given to certain types of businesses and to certain sources of income. An earlier, though still meaningful, study in this regard concentrates upon exemption from the federal corporation income tax as a

---

[40] Colm, "Corporation and the Corporate Income Tax," pp. 497–98.

factor which gives certain kinds of businesses competitive advantage over other business units subject to the tax.[41] Two types of tax-exempt business are analyzed, namely, the cooperative and the government-owned utility.

It is concluded that the exemption of the net income of cooperatives encourages the economically unwarranted growth of these institutions. For example, 1949 data indicate that an exempt cooperative in the retail grocery field could charge its customers 1.2 percent less than a competing business corporation, and make the same profits for its stockholders, because of exemption from the federal corporation income tax. Furthermore, it was observed that prices in the farm implements field could be 8.6 percent less, in the oil business 3.3 percent less, and in the electric utility 6.3 percent less than for comparable businesses *not* exempt from the federal corporation income tax as it was then structured. In addition, cooperatives, by escaping the corporation income tax, could reinvest the tax savings for growth. Moreover, since patronage dividends were treated as refunds on sales and were taxed neither to the corporation nor to the recipient, a strong incentive was created to pay patronage dividends instead of regualr stock dividends. While the disparity in tax rates has now been narrowed, the essence of the argument remains intact.

In the case of government-owned utility operations, a local government owning its own utility escapes the federal corporation income tax. In 1948, for example, this resulted in the fact that consumers using private power from a company subject to the federal corporation income tax were paying 7 percent more than if they had been buying from a municipal power company.[42] Also, many municipal utilities purchase power from federal hydroelectric sources which themselves enjoy a special tax position, including the sale of tax-exempt bonds for capital.

Thus, exemptions from the federal corporation income tax appear to have exerted significant nonneutralities by encouraging the growth of farm cooperatives and government-owned utilities. The differential rates of taxation applied to various types of corporations, however, are equally important in their nonneutrality influence. Commercial banks, for example, have traditionally been taxed at a higher rate than either savings and loan or life insurance companies, though some reduction of this differential has taken place in recent years. Moreover, a professional investment survey stated in 1965 that its studies indicate that the maximum federal income tax rate for savings and loan companies is

---

[41] See Harry G. Guthman, "Competition from Tax-Exempt Business," *Journal of Finance,* June 1951, pp. 161–77.

[42] *Ibid.,* p. 174.

likely to be 19.2 percent, far below the 48 percent levy on the profits of industrial corporations.[43] This income tax differential results not only in a "direct" stimulant to these lower-taxed financial institutions, but it can also "indirectly" affect the allocation of resources throughout the entire economy because of the substantial importance of financial intermediaries within the economy. The degree of taxation, in addition, is a critical element in determining the specific portfolio policies of financial institutions. Commercial banks, for example, maintain a large volume of tax-exempt securities because of the high tax rates which they must pay on their taxable income. On the other hand, savings and loan associations and life insurance companies hold fewer tax-exempt securities because they pay lower federal corporation income tax rates.

Loss Carryovers under the Corporation Income Tax. Another allocational effect from the corporation income tax involves the "carryover of losses" in computing tax liability. The loss carryover device may encourage mergers and industrial concentration in the economy. Hence, although loss carryover may ameliorate the disincentive impact of the corporation income tax on investment, it could, on the other hand, encourage a firm with substantial profits to reduce its tax liability by merging with a company which has substantial losses. By this device, the profitable firm acquires a loss offset against its substantial profits and, in addition, may be adding diversification to its holdings. The result is an increased tendency, through mergers, toward the monopolization of markets. Thus, allocative nonneutrality exists, though it may be (at least partially) rational or beneficial. A benefit would result, for example, if the losing firm were made technically more efficient by the management of the profitable firm, or if the losing firm eventually exits the market because of insufficient market demand for its product(s).

Effect of the Corporation Income Tax on the Choice Between External and Internal Financing. Another area of possible "distortion" from corporation income taxation involves the decision between "internal" and "external" financing. Federal income taxation can influence this choice in three ways, namely, by: (1) influencing the level of profits, (2) influencing the decision by business management to retain or to distribute these profits, and (3) affecting the terms on which external or outside capital can be acquired.[44]

An "unshifted" corporation income tax will directly reduce corporate profits, and will thus tend *either* to restrict expenditures on business investment *or* to stimulate an increased reliance on external financing.[45] For many small corporations, the expected rate of return on

---

[43] *The Value Line Investment Survey*, Vol. XX, 26, Arnold Bernhard and Co., April 16, 1965.

[44] J. Keith Butters, "Federal Income Taxation and External vs. Internal Financing," *Journal of Finance*, September 1949, pp. 197–205.

[45] *Ibid.*, p. 200.

an investment financed by external capital needs to be higher than that for an investment using internal capital because of the importance of self-employed factors of production. Thus, higher income taxes which reduce the internal sources of funds will tend to curtail the investment expenditures of these small firms rather than stimulate external financing. Large firms, however, which can raise external capital more easily than small firms, will tend to react to the reduction in internal funds by diversion to external sources of capital rather than the curtailment of investment.

In addition, a corporation income tax will tend to impair the terms on which equity capital can be obtained since it subtracts from the earnings potential of a company. Hence, whether the equity or debt form of external financing is selected may also be influenced by the corporation income tax. This nonneutral effect on equity financing will tend to be more severe for rapidly growing companies than for mature firms. Furthermore, the federal corporation income tax encourages a corporation to increase its debt/equity ratio by allowing the deduction of bond interest in computing tax liability. Although the "lower-rate" capital gains tax tends to reduce the distortion against equity financing, the "less-than-complete" offset for capital losses reduces the ability of the capital gains tax to be a full offsetting force.[46]

The Federal Corporation Income Tax and Enforcement Efficiency. The federal corporation income tax adequately meets the criterion of "enforcement efficiency." The tax provides a large volume of tax revenue at a relatively low governmental collection cost. Moreover, business compliance costs are small relative to the overall magnitude of federal corporation income tax collections. Similar to the federal personal income tax, the system of enforcement of the federal corporation income tax is essentially one of "voluntary compliance." The importance of this enforcement technique is accentuated for the corporation income tax by the fact that the number of returns filed is only a small fraction of the number of personal income tax returns submitted to the Internal Revenue Service. Yet, voluntary compliance works effectively even in personal income tax collection. Moreover, a small percentage of the corporate returns filed provide most of the taxable corporation income. It should be observed, however, that corporation income tax returns tend to be more complex than personal income tax returns which reduces somewhat this corporate tax enforcement advantage. The Revenue Act of 1964 provided for the payment of the corporation income tax on a basis similar to the "estimated tax" technique used for the personal income tax.

---

[46] Paul L. Howell, "The Effects of Federal Income Taxation on the Form of External Financing by Business," *Journal of Finance*, September 1949, pp. 208–22.

12

Wealth Taxation: The Property Tax

HISTORY OF THE PROPERTY TAX

Use of the property tax dates from the colonial period in the United States and from at least as far back as the feudal period in Europe. Historically, the property tax has been used in one form or another by all levels of government in this nation, but primary usage of the tax has been reserved to state and local units of government. Yet, Congress did impose a federal property tax on real estate on several occasions during the 1800s. This tax, which was apportioned among the states according to population as required for a "direct" tax by the Constitution, was typically ineffective. During the twentieth century, state governments have sharply reduced their reliance on property taxation and have turned to other tax sources such as general sales, income, and excise taxes. Thus, the states derive only 2 percent of their total tax revenues from property taxes at the present time as compared to more than 50 percent at the beginning of the century. Meanwhile, local governments continue to rely heavily upon property taxation as is indicated by the fact that 85 percent of their total tax revenues presently come from this source.

The nature of the property tax, as used in the United States, has changed considerably during its more than 200 years of usage.[1] Initially, it was largely a *classified (differentiated, selective)* tax imposed on

---

[1] Jesse Burkhead, *State and Local Taxes for Public Education* (Syracuse, N.Y.: Syracuse University Press, 1963), p. 20.

"specified" classes of wealth. Then, over a period of some 100 years the tax gradually evolved toward the status of a *general* property tax applying "broadly" to most or all classes of real and personal property. Since the Civil War, this trend has been reversed with a gradual narrowing of the tax base so that classified property taxes have tended once again to replace the general tax. The states have exempted some classes of property by constitutional amendment or statute. Moreover, personal property, both tangible and intangible, has been increasingly excluded from the tax base—if not by specific exemption, then by the implicit action of assessors who have difficulty discovering this type of property. In addition, differential tax rates have been applied to various types of property in some states.

PRESENT STATUS OF THE PROPERTY TAX IN THE UNITED STATES

The Property Tax Base

As one would expect, there is considerable variation among the property tax bases of the many units of state and local government imposing this type of tax. In other words, there is not *one* nationwide system of property taxation. Instead, there are *many* different systems encompassing 50 states and the District of Columbia. Moreover, there exist differential procedures for imposing the tax within each state due to the fact that much of the administration of the tax is performed at the local level of government by a large number of counties, cities, and special districts. Nonetheless, there is a meaningful "similarity" among the various property taxes in the sense that the property tax, as employed within the U.S. public sector, tends to be a "classified" (differentiated, selective) property tax rather than a "general" property tax.

A *general* property tax, in the pure or complete sense, would be one imposed on "all" classes or types of property in an identical manner regardless of the "nature of the property" or the circumstances of its "ownership" or "use." On the other hand, a *classified* property tax may be defined as one which treats property differently depending upon the "nature of the property" or the circumstances of its "ownership" or "use."[2]

Regarding the "nature of property," a general property tax may be "classified" into two major categories: *realty* and *personalty*. Realty is

---

[2] In reality, it is the *degree of differentiation* which distinguishes a classified from a general property tax since neither a "completely comprehensive" nor a "completely differentiated" property tax actually exists. Unfortunately, there is no general agreement as to the "particular" degree of differentiation which may serve as the demarcation line between a classified and general property tax.

known as "real property" and personalty as "personal property." Realty, which consists of land and structures or permanent-type improvements on the land, may be subcategorized into "land" and "improvements" segments. On the other hand, personalty may be further classified into "tangible" and "intangible" categories. Table 12–1 displays these classifications and subclassifications including examples of each type of property.

TABLE 12–1
Property Classifications for Tax Purposes

Realty (Real Property)	*Personalty* (Personal Property)
A. Land	A. Tangible
1. Farm	1. Farm machinery
2. Residential	2. Furniture
3. Commercial	3. Merchandise (business inventories)
4. Forest	4. Motor vehicles
B. Improvements	B. Intangible
1. Farm buildings	1. Stocks
2. Homes or residences	2. Bonds
3. Business buildings	3. Mortgages
4. Fences, sidewalks, etc.	4. Bank deposits

A *general* property tax may be converted into a *classified* property tax through a variety of "differentiating" techniques. These include:

1. Differentiation achieved by the partial or complete exemption of a certain class or classes of property. For example, intangible personal property, such as stocks and bonds, may be exempt from the base of the tax.
2. Differentiation based upon the circumstances surrounding the ownership of the property. For example, property owned by veterans, widows, or religious institutions may be partially or totally excluded from the base of the tax.
3. Differentiation achieved by the application of differential ratios of "assessed value" to "market value" ("sales value") depending upon the use of the property. For example, business property may be assessed at 40 percent of its market value while residential property may be assessed at 20 percent of its market value.
4. Differentiation in the form of applying different tax rates to different properties depending upon their class or use. For example, a rate of $2 per $100 of assessed valuation may be imposed on realty and a rate of $1 per $100 of assessed valuation on personalty.

The first three techniques "classify" or "differentiate" the property tax by affecting the *base* of the tax while the fourth technique directly affects the *rate* structure of the tax. Nonetheless, all four techniques tend to convert a "general" into a "classified" property tax. Moreover, each of the four techniques is used in at least one state while many states employ a combination of two or more of them.

Typically, the property tax base is predicated upon the ownership of property, regardless of any liens which may exist against it, and is measured in terms of estimated monetary value. In some instances, however, the property tax is levied upon leaseholds. In four states (Delaware, Hawaii, New York, and Pennsylvania), the tax is a *real estate tax* on land and improvements and ignores personal property. In the remaining 46 states and the District of Columbia, the property tax base also includes varying combinations of personal property such as household goods, livestock, business inventories, machinery, money, and stocks and bonds. Even in these states, however, the primary part of the tax base consists of real estate, especially improved realty. Considering the nation as a whole, 78 percent of the $492 billion assessed value of property subject to local property taxes (1966) consisted of real property. The remainder consisted of personal property (13 percent) and state-assessed property, owned mainly by railroads and public utilities (9 percent).

Most states either exempt tangible personal property such as household goods entirely or allow partial exemptions of some fixed amount. In addition, most states exempt intangible personal property such as money, stocks and bonds, and accounts receivable from the property tax though a few apply the tax to selected intangibles on a very low-rate basis. The great difficulty involved in discovering personal property, particularly intangible personal property, is the primary reason for the tendency to exempt it.

Certain specific exemptions based on "ownership" or "use" of property supplement those general exemptions which are based primarily on the "class" or "type" of property. For example, the property tax is classified in many states through partial exemptions for homesteads, veterans, and aged people. Such partial exemptions on real property amounted to $14.9 billion in 1966. In addition, billions of dollars worth of educational, religious, and governmental real estate are exempted— for the most part "totally"—from the property tax base.

Another means of taxing property in a differential manner is to vary the ratios of assessed values to market values for the different uses of property. Bureau of the Census data for 1966 suggests considerable variation of property classes since the national average ratio of assessment for *all locally assessed real estate* was approximately 33 percent of market (sales) value while the average for *nonfarm residential property* was 36 percent and that on acreage and farm property was 19 percent.[3]

The Property Tax Rate Structure

The property tax is shared by two "levels" of American government—state and local. The latter includes county, municipal, school district, road district, and other special district governments. Hence, the owner of property typically pays *several different property taxes* levied upon the same tax base. Moreover, for each of these separate property taxes the unit of government imposing the tax may "classify" the tax by applying differential rates to the property depending upon its "type" or "use." Thus, although the classified property tax is primarily structured by the techniques of *exemption* and *differential assessment ratios* which affect the "tax base," differential treatment may also be accomplished by applying *variable rates* to different properties.

In some instances, the property tax rate is *limited* "explicitly" by constitution or statute, or "implicitly" by popular tax consciousness which attaches great importance to holding down the rate. Under such circumstances, pressure for additional revenue is likely to find an outlet in increased assessment levels. In all cases, the presence of other revenue sources such as federal or state grants to local government, or the use of nonproperty taxes such as general sales and income taxes by local government, will help to offset the amount of revenue that must be raised for local government through the property tax. With all nonproperty revenue factors taken into account, the decision then turns upon the expenditures required for desired services as weighed against the requirements that such expenditures place upon the property tax rate. As one expert comments, "this judgment reflects the socio-economic variables—income, attitudes toward government, elements of strategy, bargaining, and conflict—that characterize public sector decisions."[4]

At this point, a distinction should be made between "nominal" or "mill" and "effective" property tax rates. The *nominal (mill)* rate is the annual tax liability assigned to the property expressed as a percentage of the "taxable assessed value" of the property (the value of the property for tax purposes). On the other hand, the *effective* rate is the annual tax liability assigned to the property expressed as a percentage of the estimated market value of the property. Table 12–2 provides an exam-

---

[3] U.S. Department of Commerce, Bureau of the Census, *Taxable Property Values, 1966, 1967 Census of Governments* (Washington, D.C.: U.S. Government Printing Office), Table 9.

[4] Burkhead, *State and Local Taxes*, p. 23.

TABLE 12–2
Example of Distinction between "Nominal" and "Effective" Property Tax
Rates

a. "Market Value" of Property   = $100,000
b. "Gross Assessed Value" of Property   =   30,000
   Assessment Ratio $(b \div a) = 30$ percent
c. Exemptions (such as homestead or homeownership
   and veterans exemptions)   =   5,000
d. "Taxable Assessed Value" of Property $(b - c)$ =   25,000
e. Annual Property Tax Liability   =   1,500
   Nominal Tax Rate $(e \div d) = 6$ percent
   Effective Tax Rate $(e \div a) = 1.5$ percent

ple of this distinction and, in addition, demonstrates other relevant
concepts.

Because of substantial interstate variation in *assessment ratios* (taxable assessed value of property expressed as a percentage of market
value), "nominal" rates cannot be compared between states in a meaningful fashion. However, valid interstate property tax comparisons can
be made by relating the property tax liability in a state to the market
value of the taxed property in the state. This constitutes, of course, the
"effective" property tax rate concept defined above. Table 12–3 provides estimates of such effective property tax rates on middle income
homes in the 50 states. It may be observed that the effective rates vary
widely from a low of 0.4 percent in Louisiana to a high of 3.0 percent
in New Jersey. The overall average effective property tax rate on middle income homes for the nation is 1.8 percent.

Another study, which estimates effective property tax rates for single-family houses in 122 major American cities for 1966, is summarized
in Table 12–4. In this table, it may be noted that the heaviest concentration of effective rates falls between 1.5 and 1.99 percent. Only two cities
have rates above 4 percent and only nine have rates below 1 percent.
Finally, Table 12–5 reveals the *inverse* relationship which exists between the level of "nominal" property tax rates and "assessment ratios"
in the 122 cities. Relatively high nominal rates tend to combine with
relatively low-assessment ratios, and vice versa. This again suggests that
direct comparisons of nominal rates between governments, especially
on an interstate basis, is meaningless and reinforces the contention that
the "effective" rate concept is superior for purposes of analysis.

Property Tax Administration

Assessment. Administration of the property tax consists of the
threefold tasks of *assessment, rate setting,* and *collection.* The first of
these three functions, assessment, involves the discovery and evalua-

TABLE 12–3

Effective* Property Tax Rates on Middle Income Homes for the 50 States, 1969

Alabama	0.7%	Nebraska	2.9%
Alaska	1.8	Nevada	1.5
Arizona	1.9	New Hampshire	2.8
Arkansas	1.1	New Jersey	3.0
California	2.2	New Mexico	1.5
Colorado	2.3	New York	2.6
Connecticut	2.3	North Carolina	1.4
Delaware	1.2	North Dakota	1.9
Florida	1.3	Ohio	1.5
Georgia	1.3	Oklahoma	1.4
Hawaii	1.0	Oregon	2.2
Idaho	1.4	Pennsylvania	2.0
Illinois	2.0	Rhode Island	2.1
Indiana	1.7	South Carolina	0.7
Iowa	2.3	South Dakota	2.7
Kansas	2.2	Tennessee	1.3
Kentucky	1.2	Texas	1.7
Louisiana	0.4	Utah	1.5
Maine	2.3	Vermont	2.5
Maryland	2.1	Virginia	1.2
Massachusetts	2.9	Washington	1.4
Michigan	1.8	West Virginia	0.7
Minnesota	1.7	Wisconsin	2.5
Mississippi	0.9	Wyoming	1.4
Missouri	1.7	UNITED STATES	1.8
Montana	2.0		

* *Effective* property tax rates are computed by dividing the annual property tax liability by the market (sales) value of the taxed property.

Source: Advisory Commission on Intergovernmental Relations, *State-Local Finances: Significant Features and Suggested Legislation* (Washington, D.C.: U.S. Government Printing Office, 1972), p. 234.

TABLE 12–4

Median Effective* Property Tax Rates for Single-Family Houses in 122 Major American Cities, by Region, 1966

Median Effective Tax Rate	Number of Cities				
	Total	North-east	North Central	South	West
Total	122	25	34	39	24
4.0 percent or more	2	2	—	—	—
3.5 to 3.99 percent	2	2	—	—	—
3.0 to 3.49 percent	9	6	2	1	—
2.5 to 2.99 percent	13	8	5	—	—
2.0 to 2.49 percent	27	3	8	7	9
1.5 to 1.99 percent	39	2	16	11	10
1.0 to 1.49 percent	21	2	3	12	4
Less than 1.0 percent	9	—	—	8	1

* *Effective* property tax rates are computed by dividing the annual property tax liability by the market (sales) value of the taxed property.

Source: U.S. Department of Commerce, Bureau of the Census, *Taxable Property Values—1967 Census of Governments* (Washington, D.C.: U.S. Government Printing Office, 1968), p. 15.

TABLE 12–5
Median Assessment Ratios and Average Nominal* Property Tax
Rates for Single-Family Houses in 122 Major American Cities in
1966

Median Assessment Ratio	Number of Cities	Average Nominal Tax Rates (percent)
Less than 15 percent	7	18.80
15 to 19.9 percent.................	20	9.33
20 to 24.9 percent.................	17	8.85
25 to 29.9 percent.................	16	7.86
30 to 34.9 percent.................	12	6.23
35 to 39.9 percent.................	11	5.37
40 to 49.9 percent.................	17	5.24
50 to 59.9 percent.................	8	5.23
60 percent or more...............	14	3.64

*Nominal property tax rates are computed by dividing the annual property tax liability by the taxable assessed value of the property.
   Source: U.S. Department of Commerce, Bureau of the Census, *Taxable Property Values—1967 Census of Governments* (Washington, D.C.: U.S. Government Printing Office, 1968), p. 15.

tion of the property subject to tax. Discovery of realty such as land and buildings is relatively easy. The discovery of personal property, however, is much more difficult. In most states, the taxable value of railroad and public utility property is determined by the central tax agency of the state. Usually, this agency will arrive at a unit value on the entire operating property of the railroad or public utility company and then distribute the total valuation on some "equitable" basis among the taxing jurisdictions within which the properties of the company are located. The state agency in some states, in addition, appraises other types of specialized business property such as mines and business inventories.

Meanwhile, local assessors determine the vast majority of the assessed taxable value of property. Typically, local assessors are selected either by election or from appointment by popularly elected government officials. Considerable interstate variation exists in local assessment organization ranging from 28 states in which the country is the primary assessing jurisdiction to 12 states in which hundreds of cities, villages, and townships use assessors to discover and evaluate the property subject to tax. In only one state, Hawaii, is property tax administration completely centralized at the state level. All of the remaining states, however, influence the administration of the tax by determining how the assessment and collection machinery is organized, including the division of responsibility between state and local government officials. Some states with efficient state tax agencies provide considerable direct assistance and guidance to local officials. In many other instances, however, the assessment of property remains subject to the arbitrary judgment of the assessor. In some areas the assessors are part-time workers and are poorly trained for the complexities of their assignment

Ordinarily, as observed above, property is assessed at a value less than its current market or sales value. This policy, of course, cannot be defended on logical grounds. Lower assessment levels simply mean that tax rates must be higher in order to provide the same revenue yield. Clearly, the tax liability to the taxpayer would be unchanged, for example, if property tax rates were lowered by one half while the assessed value of the property was doubled in amount. At times, the administrators of some local units of government such as counties deliberately evaluate property within their jurisdictions at lower ratios of market value than the ratios used by other counties in order to lower their shares of state property tax collections. This is referred to as "competitive underassessment" and it can be controlled only by an effective state tax agency which will *equalize the assessment ratios* used by the local units of government within the state.

Also, part and parcel with efficient enforcement procedure is the need for an adequate system of "local review" to equalize assessments of particular parcels of property, within a given classification, in accordance with the applicable property tax law. Many of the abuses attributed to the property tax arise because of inadequate assessment procedures and an important aspect of this failure falls within the area of inadequate equalization procedures between different parcels of property of the same class or use. The state laws are clear—assessments must be uniform within the same class or use of property. The Fourteenth Amendment to the Constitution stipulates, moreover, that fair treatment must be provided in the apportionment of the tax burden. Yet, review and equalization procedures are ineffective in many states. Presently, the states are putting more emphasis on the improvement of assessment procedure than on the need for improved review and equalization. The state efforts for improved supervision of assessment, improved training for assessors, and statewide revaluations, indeed, are desirable programs. Efforts for improved review and equalization procedures, however, also need to be expanded.

Rate Setting. The ultimate tax liability of the property owner is determined by the legislative body (bodies) of the jurisdiction (jurisdictions) in which the property is located. A tax rate (or rates) must be applied as a multiple to the property tax base. Each unit of government determines the amount of its expenditures. Its administrative officers then determine the amount of revenues available from nonproperty taxes and other sources. The amount which remains to be financed by the property tax is divided by the total assessed valuation in order to arrive at the tentative rate, which is expressed usually either as a number of mills or as so many dollars of tax per $100 or per $1,000 of assessed valuation. If the amount to be financed is $4 million, for example, and the assessed valuation is $400 million, the tax rate is equal to 1 percent or $1 per $100 of assessed valuation.

Collection. Once the tax rate is set, the assessment roll which contains the assessed valuation of each parcel of taxable property in the jurisdiction is provided to the tax collector. The collection officials then multiply the assessed valuation of the particular parcel of property by the tax rate in order to determine the tax liability which attaches to each parcel of property. In 20 states, property tax collection is exclusively a function of the county, and the county collector bills the taxes for all other jurisdictions within the county such as municipalities, school districts, and special assessment districts. Eight other states provide for centralized county collection but allow cities to collect their own property taxes, with the option of contracting with the county for tax collecting services.

The property tax is usually collected in the year following the one in which the assessments are made. Until fairly recently, the entire annual tax was ordinarily paid in a single sum on or before a specified day. There is a current trend, however, toward the use of installment-type payments on a semiannual, quarterly, or monthly basis, the last of these being closely associated with monthly mortgage payments on residences.

Delinquent property taxes require the imposition of penalties. Normally, a monetary penalty is imposed immediately after the tax payment becomes delinquent. In addition, interest charges at the legal rate are imposed upon unpaid taxes for as long as they remain unpaid. In most states, if the tax is unpaid for a specified period, the government may foreclose on the tax lien and assume the property in essentially the same manner that a private mortgage holder can foreclose if the debtor fails to meet his payment obligations. The government later may sell the tax lien. If not redeemed, the purchaser can procure a deed, normally referred to as a tax deed or treasurer's deed, after a specified period of time.

Table 12–6 depicts the various steps of property tax administration.

The Single Tax on Land

David Ricardo espoused the doctrine that a tax on the non-reproducible properties of the soil is a tax on *economic rent* and, thus, cannot be shifted forward by a higher selling price.[5] This would be the case

---

[5] See Chapter 8 for a complete discussion of the concept of "tax shifting."

TABLE 12–6
Example of the Determination of Local Government Property Tax
Revenue from Realty

> 1975 Assessment roll
>   +   New taxable construction
>   −   Demolition of taxable property
>   =   "Physical roll"
>   ±   Revaluations induced by:
>   Market Forces
>   Public Policy
>   =   1976 Assessment roll
>
> 1976 Expenditure requirements
>   −   Nonproperty tax revenue plus federal and state aid
>   =   Property tax requirements for revenue
>   ÷   1976 Assessment roll
>   =   1976 tax rate (frequently subject to legal limitations)
>   +   Special district assessments
>   =   Tax rate for specific properties
>
> 1976 Assessment roll × 1976 tax rate = 1976 tax levy
>   (potential property tax yield)
>   −   Delinquencies
>   =   1976 Property tax collections (actual property tax yield)

Source: Adapted from Jesse Burkhead, *State and Local Taxes for Public Education*, (The Economics and Politics of Public Education Series, Vol. 7 [Syracuse, N.Y.: Syracuse University Press, 1963]), Figure 1, p. 21.

because land, on the one hand, is "constant in supply" while, on the other hand, a "contraction of supply" would be required to forward shift a tax in the form of a higher selling price. Henry George, in his famous book *Progress and Poverty* (written in 1879), applied the Ricardian analysis to urban land. Hence, a productive resource *fixed in supply*, such as urban land which earns an "economic rent" or "site value," may be taxed with no resulting nonneutralities (distortions of economic activity). However, since the supply of "improved realty" is *not fixed*, it is argued that reproducible improvements should not be taxed due to the nonneutralities which would result from such taxation. It is reasoned that economic rent (site value) is a logical tax base because it provides a "socially created" income rather than one derived from direct labor effort. The tax was called a *single tax* because allegedly it alone could have provided all of the tax revenue required for the entire nation at the time when it was proposed.

"Economic rent" should not be confused with the "net income" from land. Idle land, for example, creates no net income, but it still may have a market value (site value, economic rent). In addition, land in use may be poorly managed and yield no net income; yet such land may have a market value. Orthodox followers of the single-tax theory would apply a rate of 100 percent to economic rent on an annual basis.

A practical disadvantage of the single tax involves the difficulty experienced in distinguishing the "land rent" from the "business rent." In other words, how much of the earnings is derived from the site or location value and how much from the reproducible assets and from the business entrepreneurial factor? In order to be equitable, moreover, the tax must be applied when land is first acquired. Otherwise, unearned wealth becomes diffused through the purchase and sale of property and also through inheritance. The price of land becomes a fixed parameter in the businessman's or investor's profit-motive decisions and, as a result, a single tax cannot effectively be applied unless it is imposed before land changes ownership.

A concerted effort was made to introduce the single-tax notion into the public sector of the United States during the latter years of the nineteenth century. This effort, however, found only limited success. Nonetheless, its basic concept "lives on" in the minds of those who today advocate "differentially higher" property taxes on land as compared to other property.

FISCAL RATIONALITY CRITERIA APPLIED TO THE PROPERTY TAX

As with the previous analyses of various types of taxes, fiscal rationality criteria will be used as benchmarks for an analysis of the fiscal efficiency of the property tax. Final judgment concerning the fiscal effects of property taxation, however, should reflect a "comprehensive" approach. For example, an individual should not appraise the influence of the property tax upon his economic behavior solely by the "rate" of tax. Other critical variables such as the ratio of assessed value to market value, the exemption of certain classes of property from the tax base, and the distribution of economic goods to taxpayer which are financed by property tax revenues are all relevant.

The Property Tax and Intergovernmental Nonneutrality

Many instances of intergovernmental nonneutral effects resulting from property taxation could be cited. The Advisory Commission on Intergovernmental Relations, for example, observes that several "negative" nonneutralities result from the use of constitutional or statutory property tax *rate limitations*.[6] The Commission suggests that while property tax restrictions initially may have had some influence in limiting tax rates, local governments have managed to increase their prop-

---

[6] See the Advisory Commission on Intergovernmental Relations, *State Constitutional and Statutory Restrictions on Local Taxing Powers* (Washington, D.C.: U.S. Government Printing Office, 1962).

erty tax revenues in the long run by other means. Meanwhile, the negative distortions placed on the structural and fiscal operations of local governments have been substantial. Property tax rate limitations, for example, have stimulated the creation of special assessment districts for the primary purpose of gaining additional taxing authority. This has caused a distortion by needlessly adding to the proliferation of local governments—some without rational economic and political justification. In addition, financial distortions have been introduced in the sense that rate limitations have made necessary the use of short-term financing in order to meet operating deficits. Such debt ultimately has to be funded. The rate limitations, furthermore, have encouraged long-term borrowing for activities which may have been financed more efficiently from current revenues.

Another study focuses upon the long-run effects of the property tax limitation movement of the 1930s.[7] It suggests that the following allocational and distributional effects occurred: (1) the decline in the relative importance of the property tax as a state and local government revenue source, (2) a shift of some of the weight of taxation away from real estate with a consequent increase in the prices of real estate, (3) transference of some of the tax burden from urban to rural areas because the tax rate limitation often did not apply to rural property, (4) the imposition of heavier tax burden on low- and middle-income taxpayers and the reduction of tax burdens on high-income individuals and corporations, and (5) the encouragement of state government assumption of responsibilities formerly considered within the domain of local government.

Influence of the Property Tax on Residential and Industrial Location

The property tax can influence allocational efficiency through its effects on "residential" and "industrial" location. Individuals in metropolitan areas may *select their residence* on the basis of property tax differentials. Moreover, this is sometimes decided in an irrational fashion. For example, an individual may select a residential location on the basis of tax liability disparities rather than upon differences in the quantity and quality of governmental services within the various political jurisdictions. The property tax, moreover, is increasingly becoming a tax upon improvements to real estate. As such, it tends to discourage investment in heavily taxed real estate improvements and to encourage the speculative purchase of lower-taxed, unimproved land. Such distorted behavior may exert significant effects in rapidly growing commu-

---

[7] James W. Martin, "Relationship between the Property Taxes and the Economy," *Proceedings of the National Tax Association, 1952*, pp. 47–55.

nities where it can result in the existence of large tracts of unimproved land within the metropolitan community. This phenomenon, which is more commonly known as "urban sprawl," makes necessary the existence of additional miles of streets, gas, electric, and telephone lines, extensive areas of police and fire protection, and increased commuting costs and travel time. This is an outstanding case of a negative allocative nonneutrality resulting from the structure of the property tax.

The use of property tax differentials by state and local government to *attract industry* is becoming increasingly prominent. Two approaches are used in this regard: *One* approach, which is quite direct, is simply to exempt the property of the invited industrial firm from state and/or local property taxes. The exemption may be either partial or complete. Normally, the exemption is for a specified period of time. The *second* approach involves the sale of industrial development bonds by a state or local unit of government. These bonds provide funds for the acquisition of land and the construction of plant facilities which, in turn, are usually exempt from state and local property taxes since they are governmentally owned and only leased to the private firms. Under either approach, however, nonneutral effects (distortions) are introduced into the selection of business-operating sites and patterns of allocative behavior are thus influenced by the subsidies. Nonetheless, these allocational nonneutralities may be either "positive" or "negative" depending upon whether they attract resources to a location of "greater" or "lesser" production efficiency than would have prevailed in the absence of the property tax inducement. The allocational distortions are further intensified by the fact that interest earned on the state and local bonds is exempt from the federal personal and corporation income taxes and, frequently, from state income taxes as well. Hence, the financing is accomplished at a lower cost than the firm could have acquired by itself. Moreover, if the company buys a part of the new bond issue, it receives tax-free income from what amounts to an "investment in itself."

General versus Classified Property Taxes and Nonneutral Effects

A *general* property tax applied to "all" assets held by an individual or institution will reduce the expected income from each asset and thereby reduce the overall capitalized values of the assets. A general property tax, moreover, tends to discriminate against income from nonhuman sources, such as capital equipment, as opposed to income derived from human sources through the labor factor of production. The latter, of course, is not included in the property tax base.

A *classified* (selective) property tax, on the other hand, will produce differential results depending upon the pattern of selectivity. The present *de facto* exemption of intangible personal property, for example, tends to encourage some individuals to hold their wealth in this form rather than to invest it in that property which is includable in the property tax base. In addition, the homestead exemption, combined with federal income tax deductions for interest payments, has encouraged owner-occupied housing, though admittedly the exemption of certain other types of property from the tax tends to increase the overall tax burden on buildings. Homeowners, moreover, often benefit from more favorable assessment practices than those afforded to many other types of property. The effective tax rates on owner-occupied residential property thus are usually below the average for all property. On the other hand, it has been observed that relatively unfavorable treatment is often afforded to enterprises such as public utilities, commercial enterprises, department and food stores, service shops, residential rental housing, and residential rental offices which must be part and parcel of the city in order to exist.[8] Another noteworthy differentiation under the property tax is the typical exemption granted to the property of nonprofit religious, educational, and charitable organizations. This exemption tends to encourage the holding of property by such institutions relative to property held by profit-oriented institutions.

The Property Tax and Urban Economic Problems[9]

An interesting current property tax issue concerns the effects exerted on property taxation by the annexation of suburban areas by central cities. One study of this phenomenon concludes:[10]

1. Suburban residental areas which are undergoing rather intense development are likely to experience a sharp increase in school property taxes. If areas such as these were to annex to the central city, there is a strong possibility that their school tax would stablize or decline;

2. Suburban districts which are annexed to the central city are virtually certain to experience a sharp increase in their basic (general) property tax. However, properties remaining outside the city report, in the short run, very moderate general property tax increases. These are primarily due to inflation rather than to any change in governmental services;

---

[8] George W. Mitchell, "Property Taxation in Relation to Investment in Urban Areas," *Journal of Finance*, June 1951, pp. 200–08.

[9] This topic is also discussed in Chapters 19 and 20 in relationship to "intergovernmental fiscal issues."

[10] R. B. Andrews and Jerome J. Dasso, "The Influence of Annexation on Property Tax Burdens," *National Tax Journal*, March 1961, pp. 88–98.

3. Properties which remain outside the central city for a prolonged period, and which are part of an area undergoing intense suburbanization, will have general property tax bills in the long run which are comparable to those òf the city, and school property taxes which are even higher;

4. A short-run pattern of tax bill change emerges whereby suburban properties experience a general property tax increase when they are annexed while their school property tax tends to decline. On the other hand, properties which do not annex will, in the short run, experience a stable or mildly increasing basic property tax accompanied by a sharply increasing school tax if they are located in an area experiencing intense development;

5. Primarily as a result of the influence of the school tax, total property taxes in two of the three areas studied by the authors were higher for unannexed properties on the average. In the third area, the differential, though favoring the unannexed area, was quite narrow; and

6. If suburban areas are annexed as they develop, the adjoining township property taxes will stay at a much lower level for comparable properties. Conversely, there is a tendency toward comparatively heavier property tax burdens, as the price which must be paid for continuing independence from the city, for suburban areas which are heavily developed and which rely on property taxes as their main financial source. It thus may be observed that a significant interplay exists between the political procedure of suburban annexation and property tax patterns regarding the distribution of tax burdens among political jurisdictions and the allocation of governmental services.

The question as to the relationship between the economic activities which occur within a city and the fiscal status of its government is a significant one. One study, which examines this issue for the metropolitan area surrounding the central cities of San Francisco and Oakland, concludes:[11] (1) the municipal property tax rate is higher for "business cities" (central cities) which have a high rate of jobs for their residents within their boundaries than for "dormitory cities" (suburban cities). This higher rate is a function of their much higher public expenditures per capita, their lower real property values, and the insufficient fiscal advantage which they receive from nonproperty-type revenues; (2) the public expenditures of "business cities" are both higher and more inelastic relative to wealth than those of "dormitory cities." Therefore, the lower the per capita wealth of business cities, the greater their per capita tax burdens; (3) the per capita value of taxable property of business cities is lower than that of "dormitory cities," and (4) doubt is cast

---

[11] Julius Margolis, "Municipal Fiscal Structure in a Metropolitan Region," *Journal of Political Economy*, June 1957, pp. 225–36.

upon the rationality of a program which encourages industrial and commercial land use in the suburbs.

These findings suggest that, accompanying the business use of suburban land, there will be a change in the nature of residential uses and an expansion of public services so that tax costs per dollar of property value will increase. The overall findings of the study are consistent with the hypothesis of "suburban exploitation of central cities," but a more intensive evaluation of this hypothesis is desirable—especially in the sense of an examination of the "governmental services" provided by the respective local governments.

The Property Tax and Distributional Nonneutrality

According to *traditional* analysis, the goal of "equitable tax burden distribution" is poorly served by the property tax.[12] This is said to be true whether one uses the "ability-to-pay" or the "benefit" benchmark for judging distributional equity. In terms of the *ability-to-pay* principle, the tax is said to be "regressive" in that it tends to take a higher proportion of the income of lower-income taxpayers than it does of higher-income taxpayers.[13] Table 12–7 demonstrates the distribution of property tax burdens by income class on the basis of three alternative assumptions: (1) Column A assumes that the tax on buildings is borne exclusively by capital; (2) Column C, on the other hand, assumes that the tax is shifted forward entirely to renters and consumers; and (3) Column B assumes an intermediate position of partial absorption of the tax by capital and partial forward shifting to renters and consumers. Column C, which represents the traditional viewpoint, shows the tax to be regressive throughout the entire range of incomes. However, if the tax is assumed to be borne entirely by capital (column A), the burden distribution is U-shaped with the tax being regressive on incomes up to $15,000. Importantly, regardless of which assumption is made, the tax still remains regressive for a majority of American families since 70 percent of the families earn annual incomes of $15,000 or less.

Following the traditional viewpoint, the reasons for regressivity include (1) the fact that housing expenditures—a major source of the property tax base—tend to be a greater proportion of income for lower-income taxpayers than for those of higher-income, and (2) the adminis-

---

[12] For a comprehensive study of alternative propositions of property tax incidence, both traditional and nontraditional, see Peter Mieszkowski, "The Property Tax: An Excise Tax or a Profits Tax?," *Journal of Public Economics* (1972), pp. 73–96.

[13] A recent paper by Henry J. Aaron, "Views on Property Taxation," presented at the 1973 Annual Meetings of the American Economic Association, concludes that the tax tends to be "progressive" in its distributional effects.

TABLE 12–7

Incidence of the Property Tax Under Alternative Assumptions, 1972

Income Class	Property Tax Burden as Percent of Income Assuming that the Tax on Improvements is Born by		
	Capital Only* A	Intermediate Cases B	Renters and Consumers Only† C
$ 0– 2,999	7.2	10.1	13.0
3,000– 4,999	5.4	6.7	8.0
5,000– 9,999	3.6	4.8	5.9
10,000– 14,999	2.6	3.8	4.9
15,000– 19,999	2.9	3.8	4.7
20,000– 24,999	3.7	4.1	4.4
25,000– 49,999	5.7	5.1	4.4
50,000– 99,999	14.1	8.9	3.7
100,000–499,999	22.4	13.0	3.5
500,000–999,999	24.5	13.8	3.0
1,000,000 and over	18.2	10.2	2.1
All Incomes	**5.0**	**5.0**	**5.0**

Note: Property taxes include all levies by state and local governments on automobiles; livestock; commercial, industrial, and residential property; etc. *Income is equal to the sum of federal adjusted gross income, transfer payments, state and local government bond interest and long-term capital gains excluded from federal income taxation.* The tax on land is distributed on the basis of income from capital under all sets of assumptions. (The exclusion of imputed income from owner-occupied homes from the definition of income somewhat overstates the estimated progressivity of the tax in columns A and B. Imputations in the national income accounts for interest, net rent, and proprietors' income associated with owner-occupied homes amount to some 18 percent of total proprietors' income, rents, dividends and interest.)

* Property taxes other than levies on nonfarm motor vehicles and agricultural property are distributed on the basis of total property income; the tax on cars is distributed using the value of cars owned by the family; and agricultural taxes are distributed on the basis of gross farm value.

† It is assumed that the tax on owner-occupied homes falls on the owner-occupier and that the tax on apartments rests on tenants in proportion to rents paid. The tax on commercial and industrial improvements is allocated on the basis of general consumption, and the tax on farm improvements is allocated among farmers and consumers in general.

Source: Advisory Commission on Intergovernmental Relations, *Financing Schools and Property Tax Relief* (Washington, D.C., January 1973), Table 13, p. 34. This table is derived by the Advisory Commission on Intergovernmental Relations from the following additional source: Charles L. Schultze. Edward R. Fried, Alice M. Rivlin, and Nancy H. Teeters, *Setting National Priorities. The 1973 Budget* (Washington: Brookings Institution, 1972). Columns A and C are from p. 445. Other column from ACIR staff computations based on p. 445 and p. 447.

trative tendency to assess higher-value residences at a lower percentage of market value than lower-value residences. Moreover, an analogy can be made to the "diminishing marginal utility of income" argument for progressive taxation[14] if one assumes a comparable "diminishing marginal utility of wealth" as wealth increases. In this case, the "proportional" tax rates which characterize the American property tax would be implicitly regressive in their affects because a "progressive" tax rate would instead be required if sacrifices among individuals in the payment of taxes are to be equalized.

To make even worse the performance of the property tax in ability-to-pay terms, one may observe that "income" does not always reflect the immediate "monetary ability" to pay property taxes. Property such

---

[14] See Chapter 7.

as vacant lots, for example, may have "present value" in a tax assessment sense and still not yield income until some future date. Moreover, owner-occupied residential dwellings do not provide a "direct" relationship to taxpaying ability. Instead, the ability to pay taxes must derive ultimately from either current income or from the long-term accumulation of an adequate amount of wealth which can be converted to cash when needed. The value of an owner-occupied dwelling quite obviously does not relate necessarily to either course of ultimate taxpaying capability. Relatedly, elderly people on fixed incomes may have their properties "appreciate" in value, and thus have them assessed at higher levels, but not realize corresponding increments in their monetary ability to pay property taxes. Moreover, two businesses may have properties assessed at identical values, but one business may be profitable while the other is operating at a loss. Once again, the assessed value of property fails to serve as an accurate indicator of the monetary capacity to pay taxes.

Property taxation also fails to meet the test of the *benefit* principle of tax equity. The "payment" of property taxes, in many instances, does not follow a quid pro quo relationship with the "benefits received" from the consumption of public-type goods financed by the taxes. A childless couple, for example, will pay school property taxes on an identical basis with a couple who has several children to be educated. Moreover, fire and police protection usually do not correlate closely with the assessed value of property and the taxes paid on that property. A modern, fireproof apartment building of high assessed value, for example, may require less actual fire protection effort than an old firetrap apartment. Nonetheless, its owner will pay much higher property taxes based upon the assessed value of the respective properties than will the owner of the lower-valued apartment building. Indeed, distributional equity in the bearing of tax burdens tends to be approached irrationally by the property tax whether viewed in terms of the ability-to-pay or the benefits-received benchmark.

A number of states have enacted legislation in recent years in the form of *tax credits* to alleviate some of the regressivity of the property tax against elderly low-income taxpayers.[15] These constitute a "credit against the state personal income tax liability" of the taxpayer for property taxes paid by the taxpayer. Such credits may actually result in a "negative income tax" if the credit leads to a cash payment from the state government to the taxpayer when the amount of the credit exceeds the state personal income tax liability of the taxpayer. Traditionally, state efforts to reduce property tax regressivity have also included

---

[15] These credits will be discussed in detail in Chapter 21 which is concerned with the problem of poverty in the United States.

the *exemption* from the property tax base of low-value, owner-occupied dwellings (homestead exemptions) and of homes owned by widows.

Further deterioration of distributional equity results from the many problems associated with the "administration" of the property tax. This is particularly true in jurisdictions where, as observed above, higher-valued property is assessed at a lower percentage of market value than is lower-valued property. Relatedly, "inflation" combined with "poor administration" may introduce severe inequities into the distribution of property tax burdens since tax officials often fail to adjust the effective property tax rate in a manner consistent with changing property values. For example, an assessor may increase the tax roll by adding new construction while, at the same time, failing to adjust the valuation of old property for inflation. Hence, the ratio of assessed value to market value may vary greatly between property of different ages. In addition to creating residential inequities, this can also lead to serious competitive distortions between businesses.

The Property Tax in Reference to the Revenue Productivity and Stabilization Criteria

The overall allocational and distributional nonneutralities associated with property taxation, many of which tend to be "negative" in nature, must be weighed against the substantial revenue importance of the tax before a conclusive evaluation of it can be rendered. Next to income and sales (including excise) taxes, no other tax supplies as much revenue to the American public sector. Although the relative importance of the property tax for the state level of government has declined during this century, its absolute magnitude has increased for both state and local governments. Moreover, its relative importance to local government has been largely maintained. In addition, the value of the property tax as a source of revenue continues despite the difficulties present in the administration of the tax. It is reasonably flexible in terms of being adjustable to the revenue needs of local government in any given year. Moreover, its enforceability is largely assured by the practice of applying liens on property for which the property tax is delinquent.

The property tax possesses a lower *income elasticity* (*Ye*) coefficient than does the personal income tax. The results of 12 empirical studies of the income elasticity of property taxes are summarized in Table 12–8. It may be observed that 8 of the 12 studies estimate that the tax is "income-inelastic" (*Ye* < 1) while only 3 suggest that it is "income elastic" (*Ye* > 1). The remaining study concludes that the tax is "unitary elastic" (*Ye* = 1).

Since property tax revenues do not respond to changes in the aggregate performance level of the economy, as measured by national money

TABLE 12–8
Income Elasticity of State and Local Property Taxes: Summary of Empirical Studies

Study	Year Published	Area Covered	Elasticity Coefficient
ACIR*................ 1971		New York City, N.Y.	1.41
Mushkin.............. 1965		United States	1.30
ACIR*................ 1971		Baltimore City, Md.	1.25
Netzer 1961		United States	1.0
Bridges.............. 1964		United States	0.98
ACIR*................ 1971		Honolulu Co., Hawaii	0.89
ACIR*................ 1971		Multnomah Co., Oreg.	0.84
McLoone 1961		United States	0.80
Rafuse............... 1965		United States	0.80
ACIR*................ 1971		Jefferson Co., Ky.	0.50
ACIR*................ 1971		Newark, N.J.	0.38
ACIR*................ 1971		Albany City, N.Y.	0.34

* Advisory Commission on Intergovernmental Relations studies cited above: "State-Local Revenue Systems and Educational Finance." Unpublished report to the President's Commission on School Finance, November 12, 1971.

Other Studies: Bridges, Benjamin, Jr., "The Elasticity of the Property Tax Base: Some Cross Section Estimates," *Land Economics,* 40:449–51 (November 1964); McLoone, Eugene P., "Effects of Tax Elasticities on the Financial Support of Education," Unpublished Ph.D. dissertation, College of Education, University of Illinois, 1961; Mushkin, Selma, *Property Taxes: The 1970 Outlook,* Chicago, Council of State Governments, 1965; Netzer, Dick, "Financial Needs and Resources Over the Next Decade," in *Public Finances: Needs, Sources, and Utilization,* Princeton, Princeton University Press, 1961; Rafuse, Robert W., "Cyclical Behavior of State-Local Finances," in Richard A. Musgrave (ed.), *Essays in Fiscal Federalism,* Washington: Brookings Institution, 1965.

Source: Advisory Commission on Intergovernmental Relations, *State-Local Finances: Significant Features and Suggested Legislation* (Washington, D.C., U.S. Government Printing Office, 1972), p. 301.

income, to the same degree of sensitivity that income tax revenues respond, there is a "revenue advantage" in the sense that property tax revenues, except in a time of a major depression like the 1930s, remain relatively stable during downward phases of the business cycle. On the other hand, there is a "revenue disadvantage" in that the relative ine-lasticity of the tax with respect to national income often causes it to lag behind the rapid growth of local government expenditures which, in turn, are responding to an elastic demand for local government eco-nomic goods in a growing economy. This leads to the often-heard state-ments that the property tax is being "overworked."

The property tax does *not* serve well in a compensatory manner for economic stabilization and growth purposes. For example, the income inelasticity of the tax causes it to perform inadequately as an "auto-matic" stabilization device while it does not perform adequately as a "discretionary" stabilizer due to the fact that it is not centrally adminis-tered, but instead is under the direction of a multitude of state and local governments.[16]

[16] The full meaning of "automatic" and "discretionary" stabilization devices is pre-sented in Part Four of this book. Meanwhile, it may be said that a budget policy which, when once established, continues to function by its very nature to counteract the business cycle is an "automatic" stabilizer while one which is instituted on an *ad hoc* basis to meet a presently-recognized cyclical problem is a "discretionary" stabilizer.

Nonetheless, it has been suggested that the property tax could be converted into a stabilization tool during periods of recession by allowing those who are unemployed to pay their current property taxes to state and local governments via "personal notes."[17] The notes could then be sold at discount to the federal government. When prosperity returns and the unemployed are back on the job, the federal government could ask employers to withhold part of the pay of the employees so as to make the property owner pay back the tax debt on an installment basis. It is argued that the results would be the same as would derive from changes in the property tax rate and base, that is, the redistribution of the tax burden from recession to prosperity. Moreover, this would be accomplished without the attendant problems of rate and base changes. However, the machinery necessary to administer such a program might prove to be complex and expensive. The plan has not been adopted.

Improvement in Property Tax Administration

Many states are presently undertaking efforts to improve the mechanics of the property tax. These efforts are important from a number of aspects, especially the need to maintain the revenue importance of the tax, and the need to make it more equitable in an enforcement sense. Furthermore, organizations such as the National Association of Tax Administrators, the International Association of Assessing Officers, and the federally sponsored Advisory Commission on Intergovernmental Relations, and other groups, are supporting these state government efforts.

Meanwhile, the "politico-geographic" jurisdiction for "property assessment" has been moving gradually toward centralization at the county level of government with the subsequent elimination of overlapping jurisdictions. In addition many states now conduct "assessment-ratio studies" which use sampling techniques to reveal variations in assessment between political jurisdictions and among property classes within a particular jurisdiction. These studies indicate the lack of assessment uniformity between areas and provide a useful tool for the correction of such inequities and for the installation of a meaningful equalization procedure. It is likely that more states will employ assessment-ratio studies as the studies become more sophisticated and when sufficient competent personnel are available to apply them. Indeed, states are responsible for providing adequate revenue sources to local government since it is the states which create the very existence of local

---

[17] Pao L. Cheng and Alfred L. Edwards, "Compensatory Property Taxation, an Alternative," *National Tax Journal*, September 1959, pp. 270–75.

government as an offshoot from their own sovereignty. Thus, it appears that the states must increasingly provide leadership for improving the administration of this important source of revenue to local governments.

In order to achieve the goal of more efficient property tax administration, the Advisory Commission on Intergovernmental Relations suggests that the states:[18]

1. Eliminate features from property tax laws which are impossible to administer and which, as a result, encourage administrators to condone evasion and encourage taxpayers to ignore the law.
2. Remove details about property tax administration from state constitutions.
3. Take a critical look at exemptions which eat away at the property tax base and repeal those which would not be valid as a continuing part of state budget appropriations.
4. Reimburse local governments for revenues lost when the state does prescribe the exemption of property from the property tax base.
5. Consolidate small primary assessment districts into districts large enough to support an efficient assessment operation.
6. Provide a strong state supervisory and coordination agency for the property tax headed by a career administrator of recognized professional ability.
7. Transfer to the state agency the responsibility for assessing property which customarily lies within more than one assessment district, or which requires appraisal specialists not available to most local districts.
8. Require local assessors to be appointed to office on the basis of professional qualifications.
9. Conduct continuing studies on the quality of local assessment practices and regularly publish the findings.
10. Simplify assessment review and appeal procedures for the protection of taxpayers.

Adoption of these recommendations would improve the revenue productivity of the property tax and, in addition, would render it a more equitable tax instrument by removing many of the administrative inequities encountered in its enforcement. The conceptual inequities of the tax, of course, would remain along with numerous negative allocational nonneutralities. Yet, it may be predicted with considerable confidence that "death and taxes—especially some form of property or wealth tax—will always be with us." The revenue importance of this form of taxation will assure its continued use.

---

[18] Advisory Commission on Intergovernmental Relations, *The Role of the States in Strengthening the Property Tax*, June 1963, Vol. 1.

AN ALTERNATIVE TO THE "PROPERTY TAX"—THE "NET WEALTH TAX"

A number of nations employ a net tax on personal wealth though such a tax is not used in the United States.[19] A *net (personal) wealth tax*, which may also be termed a *net worth tax*, is levied upon the aggregate wealth (assets, properties) of an "individual owner" rather than upon the "specific item of wealth" itself.[20] In this sense, it contrasts sharply with the property tax which does not concern itself with the overall wealth status of the owner of the property. Moreover, it contrasts with the property tax in the important sense that it is a "net" rather than a "gross" tax. That is, the net wealth tax allows the deduction of liabilities (claims) against the property from the base of the tax while the property tax does not allow such deductions. In the case of corporate stocks and bonds, the net wealth tax is imposed upon these assets as they are held by individuals, but not directly upon the business itself. The tax is a comprehensive levy on virtually all real and personal property.

The net wealth tax would appear to serve the goal of distributional equity more consistently than does the property tax. This would be true because the overall wealth position of the owner of the property is the basis for the tax. This adds a dimension to "taxpaying ability" which is ignored by the traditional property tax as used in the United States. Moreover, the net wealth tax achieves greater distributional equity than the property tax through its allowance of the deduction of claims against the property from the base of the tax. Thus, if two individuals each possess "gross" wealth of $25,000, but one of the individuals has claims of $10,000 against his wealth (making his "net" wealth $15,000) while the other has no claims against his wealth (making his "net" wealth $25,000), the latter individual clearly possesses greater taxpaying capabilities than the former. Although the overall fiscal rationality effects of net wealth taxation are beyond the scope of the present discussion, the tax in concept does seem worthy of further investigation for possible usage in the American public sector.

---

[19] These nations include "developed nations" such as Germany, Japan, the Netherlands, Sweden, and Switzerland as well as "developing nations" such as Ceylon, India, and Pakistan.

[20] For an excellent discussion of *net worth taxes* and their place in the public sector revenue structure, see Lester C. Thurow, *The Impact of Taxes on the American Economy* (New York: Praeger, 1971), and his "Net Worth Taxes," *National Tax Journal*, September 1972, pp. 417–423.

13

,

Wealth Taxation: Death and Gift Taxes

DEATH AND GIFT TAXES

The Federal Estate and Gift Taxes

Death taxes consist of two main types—estate taxes and inheritance taxes. An *estate* tax uses the entire property which is transferred at death as its tax base. On the other hand, an *inheritance* tax uses a tax base consisting of only that portion of the property which is received by a particular beneficiary. While the base of a death tax clearly is "wealth," more specifically the tax is imposed on the "transfer of wealth" by reason of death. In this regard, it resembles an excise tax on the transfer of property. The federal government has imposed death taxes on an intermittent basis since 1798.[1] However, the present federal estate tax dates from 1916. The first federal gift tax was levied for the two years, 1924 and 1925. In 1932, the present federal gift tax was introduced.

A sizable segment of Congress viewed the federal estate tax of 1916 as a temporary measure. Competition between states for wealthy residents during the early 1920s, however, provided important support for its continuance. Some states had begun to advertise in national publications regarding immunity from death taxation in their jurisdictions.

---

[1] For an excellent discussion of federal estate and gift tax history, see The Advisory Commission on Intergovernmental Relations, *Tax Overlapping in the United States—1964* (Washington, D.C.: U.S. Government Printing Office, 1964), chap. 10.

Several states, moreover, had amended their constitutions to guarantee freedom from death taxes to those who established residence within their political boundaries. The Revenue Act of 1926 took an important step for continuance of the federal estate tax within the federal revenue structure by permitting an *80 percent credit* offset of federal estate tax liability for death taxes paid to the states. This helped to reduce interstate competition for wealthy residents since each state could collect death taxes up to 80 percent of the federal tax liability without increasing the overall death tax burden. For example, if federal estate taxes on an estate are $100,000 while no state death tax is imposed on the estate, the overall death tax burden would be $100,000 even though the state receives no death tax revenues. However, the state could have collected $80,000 in death tax revenues (80 percent of the $100,000 federal estate tax liability) without increasing the overall (federal plus state) death tax burden since the 80 percent credit would reduce the federal estate tax liability to $20,000 ($100,000 − 80,000). Thus, any state not levying a death tax up to the limit of the credit would be sacrificing revenues to the federal treasury which it otherwise could possess.[2]

Substantial revisions were made in 1932 in the federal estate tax structure along with the adoption of the federal gift tax. Gift tax rates were set at 75 percent of the estate tax rates, a ratio still in effect. The estate tax exemption was reduced from $100,000 to $50,000 and the maximum rate was increased from 20 to 45 percent. Subsequent legislation during the 1930s further reduced the exemption and further increased the rates. Another rate revision in 1941 established the schedule which is now in effect. In 1942, the exemption level was increased to its present $60,000 level. Though actual rates have remained unchanged since 1941, effective rates of the federal estate and gift taxes were lowered in 1948 through the introduction of marital deductions for the two taxes.

The federal tax credit for death taxes paid to the states achieved its primary goal of reducing interstate competition for wealthy residents. However, it has not been completely successful in achieving satisfactory federal-state death and gift tax coordination nor has it made death and gift taxation a major revenue producer for state governments. In fact, its capacity to achieve these results has been dwindling over the years with the nature of federal tax legislation subsequent to the legislation of 1926 being a contributing factor. During this period, federal estate tax rates have been increased and exemptions have been reduced. In

---

[2] The "tax credit" technique used here by the federal government to help coordinate state death tax activity resembles the approach used in the Social Security Act of 1935 to encourage states to adopt payroll taxes for unemployment compensation programs. See Chapter 15 in this regard.

addition, the federal gift tax which was imposed in 1932 at rates equal to 75 percent of the federal estate tax rates, and with a separate exemption, has contributed to the decline in the importance of state death and gift taxes by further usurping revenue sources. Obviously, the distribution of property through gifts during a person's lifetime, as encouraged by the lower-rate federal gift tax, reduces the size of the estate subject to taxation at death. State death tax revenues are thus reduced. In 1935, the states received about 75 percent of total death and gift tax revenues. In 1971, they collected only 23 percent of the total. Moreover, these taxes contributed only 2.1 percent of total state tax revenues.

The Federal Estate Tax Base and Rate Structure. The base of the federal estate tax consists of the gross estate transferred after adjustments are made for certain exemptions and deductions. The gross estate includes the total amount of property which, according to estate tax law, is deemed to have been transferred at death. The value of property may be determined for tax purposes either as of the date of death or as of one year after death. The executor may exercise this option.

Specific provisions govern the extent to which certain property interests of the decedent, such as those in trusts, joint tenancies, community properties transferred during the lifetime of the decedent, and insurance proceeds are included in the tax base. The tax base is also influenced, of course, by the $60,000 specific exemption which is large enough to eliminate most estates from liability under the tax. Furthermore, deductions from the base are allowed for such items as charitable bequests, administrative expenses, funeral expenses, and unpaid mortgages or other debt claims upon the estate properties. In addition, a martial deduction is allowed for property which passes to the decedent's wife or husband.

The rate structure of the federal estate tax is progressive (graduated) with marginal rates ranging from 3 to 77 percent through 25 different tax rate brackets. Table 13–1 displays this rate structure. An estate tax return must be filed for any gross estate in excess of the specific $60,000 exemption. Generally, the return and tax payment are due within 15 months of the date of death. However, if the estate primarily consists of an interest in a "closely held business" such as a sole proprietorship, certain small partnerships, and certain small corporations, the tax may be paid in installments over a 10-year period.

Various tax credits are allowed against the federal estate tax liability, one of which is the previously mentioned credit for the payment of state death taxes. This credit may go up to *80 percent of the 1926 federal estate tax,* or $8,400, with the maximum allowable credit being expressed as a percentage of the taxable estate in excess of $40,000. The law provides a graduated rate table for computing the credit. Credits

TABLE 13–1
Marginal Tax Rates of the Federal Estate and Gift Taxes

Taxable Net Estate or Gift	Marginal Tax Rates (Percent) Estate	Gift
$ 0 to $ 5,000............. 3		2.25
5,000 to 10,000............. 7		5.25
10,000 to 20,000............ 11		8.25
20,000 to 30,000............ 14		10.50
30,000 to 40,000............ 18		13.50
40,000 to 50,000............ 22		16.50
50,000 to 60,000............ 25		18.75
60,000 to 100,000............ 28		21.00
100,000 to 250,000............ 30		22.50
250,000 to 500,000............ 32		24.00
500,000 to 750,000............ 35		26.25
750,000 to 1,000,000............ 37		27.75
1,000,000 to 1,250,000............ 39		29.25
1,250,000 to 1,500,000............ 42		31.50
1,500,000 to 2,000,000............ 45		33.75
2,000,000 to 2,500,000............ 49		36.75
2,500,000 to 3,000,000............ 53		39.75
3,000,000 to 3,500,000............ 56		42.00
3,500,000 to 4,000,000............ 59		44.25
4,000,000 to 5,000,000............ 63		47.25
5,000,000 to 6,000,000............ 67		50.25
6,000,000 to 7,000,000............ 70		52.50
7,000,000 to 8,000,000............ 73		54.75
8,000,000 to 10,000,000............ 76		57.00
10,000,000 and over................. 77		57.75

against the estate tax also are allowed for gift taxes paid by the decedent on transfers made during his lifetime, but included in the gross estate, and for the payment of death taxes on the property to foreign governments.

The Federal Gift Tax Base and Rate Structure.   The federal gift tax is levied upon a base comprised of the value of property transferred as gifts (see Table 13–1). The tax is the liability of the *donor*, that is, the person who makes the gift. It is not imposed on the *donee* or recipient of the gift. In computing the gift tax base in any one year, the first $3,000 of gifts to each recipient may be excluded. If a husband and wife agree to each contribute one half of a gift, each may claim a $3,000 annual exclusion, bringing the total exclusion for a married couple to $6,000 per recipient. Moreover, in addition to this annual exclusion, a specific exemption of $30,000 of total lifetime gifts to all donees is provided by the law. This exemption may be taken, at the discretion of the taxpayer, either in a single year or over a period of years until it is used up. If a married couple treats gifts as each contributing one half of the gifts, this specific exemption is doubled to $60,000. Table 13–2 provides an example of federal gift tax exemptions.

In computing the gift tax base, certain important deductions are allowed. These include gifts made to charitable, civic, religious, and public organizations. In these instances, the gifts may be deducted in full. Moreover, one half of the value of gifts made between a husband and wife after April 2, 1948 may be deducted from the net aggregate gifts subject to the gift tax. This marital deduction is similar to that used for estate tax purposes.

TABLE 13–2
Example of Federal Gift Tax Exemptions

Year	Size of Gift	Annual Exemption	Increments to $30,000 Lifetime Exemption
Assume that donor A gives the following gifts over a four-year period to donee B:			
Year 1	$ 4,000	$ 3,000	$ 1,000
Year 2	21,000	3,000	18,000
Year 3	10,000	3,000	7,000
Year 4	7,000	3,000	4,000
4-year total	$42,000*	$12,000	$30,000

* This $42,000 total of gifts could have been given to 14 "different donees" at $3,000 per gift, in any one year or throughout the four-year period without incurring any federal gift tax liability, and without using up any of the $30,000 lifetime exemption.

The federal gift tax, like the federal estate tax, resembles an excise tax on the transfer of wealth. The rate structure is progressive and, as noted above, the tax is levied at marginal rates equal to 75 percent of those under the federal estate tax. The tax is cumulative in the sense that it applies each year to the aggregate sum of all taxable gifts made since enactment of the present tax in 1932.

State Death and Gift Taxes

The first state death tax—an inheritance tax—was imposed by Pennsylvania in 1825. Subsequently, several other states enacted death taxes. Most of these fell into disuse following the Civil War, but a revival in their importance was initiated by New York in 1885 with its adoption of a 5 percent tax on the transfer of property to collateral heirs. In 1903, Wisconsin adopted an inheritance tax which set a pattern followed by many other states on such matters as progressive rates and central administration. Presently, all states except Nevada impose death taxes.

Most state death taxes are of the "inheritance" variety and are "progressive" in rate structure. Usually, this progressivity in marginal rates is based on the twofold consideration of (1) the size of the individual shares of the estate, and (2) the basis of the relationship between the decedent and the heir with the rate being lowest for the closest relative. The taxes may be placed into several classifications as summarized in Table 13–3. Six states use only a *pickup* tax which, as it were, "picks up" the full amount of the federal tax credit in that it imposes a tax liability equal to the maximum credit allowed against the federal tax. Two states use only an *estate* tax and two others use only an *inheritance* tax. Most states (30) impose a combination of inheritance and pickup taxes with the latter assuring that the full federal credit will

TABLE 13–3
Types of State Death Taxes (1973)

Description of Tax		State
"Pickup" tax only	(6)	Alabama, Alaska, Arkansas, Florida, Georgia, New Mexico.
Estate tax only	(2)	Mississippi, North Dakota.
Estate tax and "pickup" tax	(7)	Arizona, New York,† Ohio, Oklahoma,† South Carolina,† Utah, Vermont.†
Inheritance tax only	(2)	South Dakota, West Virginia.
Inheritance tax and "pickup" tax	(30)	California,† Colorado,† Connecticut, Delaware,† Hawaii, Idaho, Illinois, Indiana, Iowa, Kansas, Kentucky, Louisiana,† Maine, Maryland, Massachusetts, Michigan, Minnesota,† Missouri, Montana, Nebraska, New Hampshire, New Jersey, New Mexico, North Carolina,† Pennsylvania, Tennessee,† Texas, Virginia,† Washington,† Wisconsin,† Wyoming.
Inheritance, estate, and "pickup" taxes	(2)	Oregon,† Rhode Island.†
No tax	(1)	Nevada.

† Also has gift tax (16 states).
Source: Advisory Commission on Intergovernmental Relations, *Federal-State-Local Finances: Significant Features of Fiscal Federalism* (Washington, D.C.: U.S. Government Printing Office, 1974), p. 296.

be utilized. Seven other states levy a combination of estate and pickup taxes while 2 states—Rhode Island and Oregon—apply all three types of taxes (inheritance, estate, and pickup).

The considerable variation between state death tax structures includes differences in deductions, exemptions, and rates. Rates and exemptions even vary sharply among those states which impose the same type of death tax. Among the states with estate taxes, for example, exemptions range from $2,000 to $100,000. Inheritance tax exemptions among the states, moreover, range from no exemption to complete exemption for certain types of heirs. Though state death tax rates generally are progressive, one state uses an estate tax with a *proportional* rate and another utilizes a proportionally-rated inheritance tax.

Gift taxes are imposed by 16 states. These are generally integrated with the state death taxes. Consequently, considerable interstate variation exists in rates and exemptions. The Wisconsin gift tax is imposed each year without regard to the gifts of previous years while other states follow a cumulative system.

FISCAL RATIONALITY CRITERIA APPLIED TO DEATH AND GIFT TAXES

The analysis which follows will primarily concentrate on the economic effects of the *federal* estate and gift taxes, though many implications also exist for state death and gift taxes. The important efficiency effects of death and gift taxation are essentially of an allocational and distributional nature. The influence of death and gift taxation on the economic stabilization and growth goals tend to be modest, but the latter goal could be significantly influenced in a society where death taxes bear heavily upon the acquisition and accumulation of real capital.

Allocational Effects of Death and Gift Taxes

Business Mergers and Property Management. The effect of estate taxation on the business merger movement will first be considered. Two aspects of the estate tax exert an influence on business practice in closely held (family-type) corporations.[3] These are the uncertainty regarding the amount of the tax, and the fear of insufficient liquidity to pay the tax. The major areas of *uncertainty*, in turn, reside in the difficulty in evaluating closely held securities, the application of the attribution rules which determine inheritance rights, and the variety of court decisions which may exist on the same point of law. The *illi-*

---

[3] See Harold M. Somers, "Estate Taxes and Business Mergers: The Effects of Estate Taxes on Business Structure and Practices in the United States," *Journal of Finance*, May 1958, pp. 201–10.

quidity (liquidation) problem, on the other hand, results from the fact that stock shares in closely held corporations may be difficult to sell upon the death of one of the owners. Moreover, even if a buyer is available, there is danger of bringing an individual into the business who may disrupt the operations of the firm to the detriment of the surviving owners or heirs.

Several property management approaches may be undertaken to reduce the severity of the uncertainty and illiquidity problems. For example, the owner in the case of merger may receive either cash or the listed securities of the larger corporation. Neither he nor his estate pays a capital gains tax if he receives securities. The brunt of the estate tax is lessened in such instances. Motivation thus exists for the merger of small business units with large corporations. As a result, an allocational distortion occurs and market (industry) structures tend to become more imperfect.

The illiquidity problem may also be viewed in terms of its effects on the "composition of assets" held in an estate.[4] The need to liquidate part of the estate to raise money to pay the tax tends to discourage the acquisition or retention of assets with a "thin market." A general bias is thus created by heavy death taxes toward the holding of highly marketable securities as opposed to real estate, works of art, libraries, and the securities of small corporations.

Finally, it should be recognized that allocational effects in the form of pressure for sale or merger, or which induce changes in the composition of assets, will tend to be alleviated somewhat by the one-year installment payment privilege adopted in 1958, which is applicable to estates consisting largely of a closely held business. Moreover, the law permits the tax-free redemption of stock in closely held companies for the payment of estate tax liabilities. Furthermore, an individual has an opportunity to utilize the exemptions available under the federal gift tax law during his lifetime for the tax-free transfer of part of his property in a closely held business to members of his family.

The Work—Leisure Choice. Another area of possible allocative nonneutrality is the impact of the estate tax on the choice between work and leisure. A death tax may affect a person's decision to stay on the job, or to retire, in a manner similar to that of the income tax.[5] On the one hand, the price of leisure in terms of the aftertax net estate is reduced by the amount of the marginal rate of tax upon the estate. The individual may thus desire to purchase more leisure by working less since leisure is now a comparatively cheaper commodity than before. As a result, the *substitution effect* is adverse to work effort.

---

[4] Earl R. Rolph and George F. Break, *Public Finance* (New York: The Ronald Press Co., 1961), pp. 261–64.

[5] *Ibid.*, pp. 264–65.

On the other hand, the *income effect* may be either adverse or advantageous to work effort. The individual is motivated to work more in order to leave the same amount of wealth to his survivors. He may work less, however, since the amount of wealth he could bequeath with the same work effort is decreased by the amount of the tax. Thus, since the income effect could either expand or contract work effort at a time when the substitution effect would retard it, a determinate answer is not forthcoming.

However, it is unlikely that the work habits of people are significantly affected by estate taxes because the contemplation of death taxes will likely affect only the older segment of the population. A substantial fraction of this group will not have a choice concerning the date of retirement. Furthermore, some of those who do have a choice are people who enjoy their work and do not wish to retire. Hence, the possibility of estate taxes affecting the work-leisure choice in a significant manner can be dismissed as being unlikely.

The Consumption—Saving Decision. Another possible allocational effect of estate taxes is their influence upon the choice between consumption and saving.[6] Again, as with the work-leisure choice, the substitution effect and the income effect are relevant. By reducing the cost of a dollar of consumption in terms of its estate consequences, the tax will have a *substitution effect* favorable to consumption and unfavorable to saving. Since the *income effect* may go in either direction, however, as with the work-leisure choice, the answer is again indeterminate.

It would appear, however, that the overall influence of the estate tax on the consumption-saving decision is insignificant since by the time people have reached the age when estate considerations bear heavily on their thinking, they have reached an age when radical departures from previous modes of living are unlikely to occur. In addition, it is generally agreed that death taxes have less of an effect on the incentive to save and invest than income taxes. This is because income taxes reduce the return for effort and risk taking from "current income" while death taxes are "postponed" to a later date and are paid by the estate and its beneficiaries rather than by the person who earns the income.

The above discussion indicates the ability of estate and gift taxation, particularly the former, to influence resource *allocation.* The most significant areas of influence include the effects of such taxation on the encouragement of business mergers and on the composition of the assets held in an estate. To a lesser extent, the estate and gift taxes may at times influence the choice between work and leisure as well as that between consumption expenditures and saving.

---

[6] *Ibid.,* pp. 265–66.

Distributional Effects of Death and Gift Taxes

Progressive death taxes have long been advocated in Western society. During the nineteenth century the famous British economist, John Stuart Mill, argued that a severe limit should exist on the amount of wealth that any individual might receive through inheritance. He thus called for "progressive death taxes."[7]

Assuming a societal consensus for "greater equality" in the distribution of wealth, the performance of death and gift taxation in the United States is "mixed" in relationship to this goal. Of course, since the rate structures of the federal estate and gift taxes and of most state death and gift taxes are "progressive," some redistribution of income and wealth toward greater equality can be expected to occur. The $60,000 federal estate tax exemption and the federal gift tax exemptions, moreover, help to intensify this redistribution effect by exempting wealth transfers of modest value.

Indeed, the estates of only a relatively small proportion of the adults who die each year are subject to federal estate tax liability. Less than 46,000 estate tax returns were filed in 1961, for example, though some 1.5 million adult deaths occurred that year.[8] Moreover, 30 percent of the estate tax returns filed during the year carried no tax liability. The redistribution effect of the estate tax is also exemplified by the fact that taxable returns listing gross estates valued at $150,000 or less accounted for 51 percent of all returns filed in 1961, but contributed only 4 percent of the total estate tax yield. On the other hand, taxable returns with gross estates valued at $1 million or more accounted for 50 percent of the total tax yield though constituting only 3 percent of the returns filed. In addition, tax liabilities as a percentage of "gross estates," that is, prior to the application of credits, exemptions, and the like to the potential tax base—which constitutes the *effective federal estate tax rate structure*—ranged from an average of less than 2 percent on returns with gross estates between $60,000 and $70,000 to an average of 21 percent on returns listing gross estates at $20 million or higher. The redistributional effects of the gift tax appear to be similar. During 1961, for example, over 78,000 gift tax returns were filed with a total gift value of $2.3 billion. More than one half of the value of the gifts ($1.2 billion), however, was reported on less than 25 percent of the returns (less than 18,000 returns).

The federal estate and gift taxes also contribute to greater distribu-

---

[7] John Stuart Mill, *Principles of Political Economy* (New York: Longmans, Green, 1909), Book Two.

[8] Admittedly, the returns filed during 1961 pertained mostly to deaths which had occurred prior to 1961. The adult death totals between 1961 and earlier years, however, cannot be expected to vary significantly. Hence, the comparison of the 46,000 returns to 1.5 million adult deaths seems valid for discussion purposes.

tional equity by helping to close an implicit tax avoidance loophole. Specifically, the estate tax can include certain items in its tax base which escape the federal personal income tax base. The interest on state and local government securities, for example, is exempt from the federal personal income tax base but the value of the securities which earn this interest is includable in the federal estate tax base. In addition, the existence of the gift tax serves to control tax avoidance by those who would escape both the income and estate taxes by giving property away. It may be argued, however, that the differential rates which exist between the federal estate and gift taxes create some inequity in themselves because they penalize those individuals who cannot easily transfer property during a lifetime as compared to those who can easily transfer it. The latter group, of course, will pay a 25 percent lower rate under the gift tax than under the estate tax. However, the overall influence of the federal estate and gift taxes as a deterrent of tax avoidance is a favorable one.

Despite certain significant "positive" distributional nonneutralities, death and gift taxes also yield "negative" distributional effects. For example, the impact of death taxes will depend largely on the amount of legal skill and effort applied to the "planning" of an estate. Many individuals—due to a variety of reasons including early death—do not have an opportunity to minimize death taxes through planning. Moreover, the direct relationship between "stock prices" and the "size of an estate tax base" creates an additional problem of inequity.[9] This results from the fact that a large percentage of the gross assets of individuals in many taxable estates consists of corporate stock. Varying stock prices over time thus lead to varying estate tax bases and tax liabilities. That is, two persons with identical estates in real terms (number of shares of the same stocks) would bear different tax liabilities, with constant tax rates, if the values at which the assets are appraised for tax purposes vary due to fluctuating stock prices and different times of death.

Horizontal and vertical tax equity may be further violated in federal estate taxation through the "specific techniques" employed in the transfer of property. These include the use of trusts, gifts to charitable foundations, and the special tax treatment of property transfers between husband and wife. In fact, trusts have become a major deterrant to the "effective" (as opposed to the "nominal" or "statutory") rate progressivity of the federal estate tax. A trust, of course, is a legal arrangement whereby funds are administered for an individual or organization. Federal estate tax law permits trusts to pay income to one

---

[9] C. Lowell Harriss, "Stock Prices, Death Tax Revenues, and Tax Equity," *Journal of Finance*, September 1950, pp. 257–69.

or more successive generations of heirs while giving the property ultimately to a still-later generation. For example, a wealthy individual
may establish a trust at the time of his death naming his wife and
children as successive "life tenants" entitled to receive income from
the trust, and naming his grandchildren as the ultimate owners of the
property (known as "remaindermen"). When the trust is terminated,
the property in the trust becomes legally that of the remaindermen.
Importantly, even though the man who established the trust had to pay
an estate tax on the amount of the trust, the transfer of the property
by successive life tenents (like by his wife to his children and by his
children to his grandchildren) is not subject to the estate tax. In fact,
an estate (or gift) tax is not paid again unless the remainderman himself
transfers the property. Such "generation-skipping" in estate taxation
constitutes a major tax avoidance loophole within the structure of the
federal estate tax. Moreover, it is a loophole utilized primarily by
wealthy individuals capable of transferring large segments of property
at the time of death. Indeed, the existence of death and gift taxes have
failed in an overall sense to achieve one of their primary initial social
objectives, namely, the prevention or constraint of the "continuing
accumulation" through successive generations of very large family concentrations of wealth.

The Revenue Productivity of Death and Gift Taxes

The *revenue importance* of death and gift taxes to the American
public sector is modest. Federal and state governments, for example,
collected approximately $4.8 billion in death and gift tax revenues
during the 1971 fiscal year. This amounted to some $3.7 billion for the
federal government, or only 2.7 percent of total federal tax revenues,
and to $1.1 billion for the *states* which constituted only 2.1 percent of
total state tax revenues. The estate and gift taxes were most important
(relatively) to the federal tax structure during the 1930s. They contributed 6.5 percent of total federal tax receipts in 1939, for example,
as compared to only 2.7 percent at the present time. The federal and
state death taxes are relatively easy to enforce. On the other hand, the
gift tax is more difficult to collect, particularly in the case of the "state"
gift taxes. The *income elasticity* of death and gift taxes is "modestly
progressive" with an estimated coefficient of 1.1 for state death and gift
tax collections as related to GNP and 1.2 for such taxes as related to
personal income.[10]

---

[10] Selma J. Mushkin and Gabrielle C. Lupo, "Project 70: Projecting the State-Local
Sector," *Review of Economics and Statistics*, May 1967, p. 243.

14

Sales Taxation: Broadbased and Narrowbased Sales Taxes

Nature of the Sales Tax Base

Sales taxes, which are taxes imposed on "economic transactions" involving a "buyer" and "seller" relationship, may be levied at the various stages of economic activity. Among the alternative points of placement are the manufacturing, wholesale, and retail levels of transaction. These comprise the various stages of production and distribution (in the marketing sense) of an economic good. A sales tax may be placed at any "one" or "combination" of these transaction points. In the former case, the tax is referred to as a *single-stage* sales tax and, in the latter case, it is known as a *multistage* or *multiple* sales tax. A "single-stage" sales tax imposed upon an economic good at the time when it is sold by its producer may be referred to as a *manufacturer's* sales tax. One imposed upon a commodity when it is sold by a wholesaler to a retailer, in turn, may be called a *wholesale* sales tax while one levied on the final sale of the commodity to its ultimate purchaser is known as a *retail* sales tax. "Multistage" sales taxes, which are applied vertically at two or more stages of economic activity, normally take the form of either a *turnover* or a *value-added tax* (VAT).

In addition to being differentiated by means of the various levels of economic activity at which they may be placed, sales taxes also bear the fundamental characteristic of possessing tax bases which are either *narrow* or *broad* in scope. In this regard, a sales tax applied to one, or to a few, economic goods is considered *narrowbased* while sales tax levied on a wide range of goods is called a *broadbased* sales tax. Moreover, a sales tax base may be further classified in terms of whether it measures the monetary value or the physical number of units purchased. If the tax base is defined in terms of the monetary value of the purchased item or items, like the broadbased state general retail sales taxes, the tax is *ad valorem* in nature. If the tax base is defined in terms of the number of units of the commodity purchased, like gallons of gasoline under the federal and state gasoline taxes, the tax is termed a *specific* tax.

Narrowbased Sales Taxes

A *narrowbased* sales tax often is referred to as an *excise* or *selective* sales *excise* tax. Such a tax may be imposed either "externally" or "internally." An *external* excise is applied to the movement of an economic good across an international boundary. External excise taxes are commonly known as customs duties or tariffs. Such taxes may be imposed either by the nation exporting or by the nation importing the economic good. Thus, an external excise may be either an "export duty" or an "import duty." Though external excise taxes are taxes in every meaningful sense of the word, they will not be discussed at length in this book since the emphasis herein is intended to be upon internal or domestic public finance.

An *internal* excise tax may be applied to any one or any small number of items involving business transactions within the political boundaries of a sovereign nation. Many different commodities are, or have been, subject to excise taxes in the United States. These include the excise taxes on tobacco products, alcoholic beverages, motor fuels, jewelry, cosmetics, luggage, and transportation. Internal excises may be imposed for a variety of reasons other than the primary reason (in most cases) of providing revenue. For example, some excises are applied on "luxury" goods with an "income redistribution" motive in mind. Other excises, known as "sumptuary taxes," are intended to discourage the consumption of certain so-called "undesirable" commodities such as liquor and tobacco products.

Another use of internal excise taxes involves the benefit principle of taxation. Here an attempt is made to tie the payment of the excise to the consumption of a particular quasi-public good. The federal gasoline tax, for example, goes into a special trust fund whereby the tax funds are earmarked for the provision of an interstate highway system. It should thus be noted that the revenues from an excise tax may go either into a *general treasury fund* for "nonearmarked" purposes, or they may enter a *particular trust fund* where they are "earmarked" for a specific purpose. A final use of excise taxes involves their occasional application in order to control or ration the consumption of certain commodities in times of extreme scarcity or general inflation. Such application of the excise tax technique is most often found under wartime conditions of scarcity and inflationary pressure in the economy.

Broadbased Sales Taxes

Sales taxes which are applied to a wide variety of economic goods may be referred to as *broadbased* sales taxes. The tax base of a broadbased sales tax generally is *ad valorem* in nature because of the difficulty in applying a *specific* tax to a large number of economic goods. Broadbased sales taxes may be imposed either at one or at more than one level of economic activity. Hence, they may be either "single-stage" or "multistage" in nature.

Primary types of "single-stage" broadbased sales taxes include the *general retail sales* tax and the *spendings* tax. The "typical" state or local government general sales tax in the United States is imposed at the *retail* level and applies a flat rate to a broad base of purchases (with certain exemptions). A spendings or expenditure tax, which is not utilized in the United States, would be imposed upon the total money value of a taxpayer's consumption expenditures during a certain period of time, plus any increase in his net worth during that period, under the assumption that such expenditures indicate the taxpayer's "ability-to-pay" taxes.[1] The tax would tend to resemble the typical personal income tax in terms of progressive rates, exemptions, and deductions. The spendings tax has been used in India and Ceylon without significant success.

Primary types of "multistage" broadbased sales taxes are the *value-added* tax and the *turnover* tax. Minor variations of the turnover tax, in turn, include the *gross income* and the *transactions* taxes. The *turnover* tax is imposed on the *gross* monetary value of all business transactions, both productive and distributive, through which a tangible economic good passes. This tax differs from a *gross income* tax in the sense that the latter tax also includes "intangible services" as well as tangible economic goods. The *transactions* tax, in turn, is differentiated from both the turnover and the gross income taxes in that it extends beyond those exchange transactions for tangible economic goods and intangible

---

[1] See the relevant discussion of "income concepts" and "taxpaying ability" at the beginning of Chapter 9. Also, for a detailed advocation of this tax concept, see Nicholas Kaldor, *An Expenditure Tax* (London: Allen and Unwin, 1955).

services and includes also such transactions as the depositing of money in banks.

The *value-added* tax, though also applied at multiple stages of business activity, differs from the other three multistage broadbased sales taxes in that it defines the tax base at each level only in the *net* sense of the "value added" at that particular stage of production or distribution.[2] The "value added" is ascertained "conceptually" by subtracting the purchase cost of a taxable good from its selling price. That is, each firm would pay a tax on the increase in value of an economic good for which its productive or distributive activities are responsible. "In practice," however, administrative considerations induce those nations using value-added taxation to levy the tax on the basis of the "sales value" of the good at a particular stage of economic activity, not directly on the "value added" at that stage, with the firm then receiving a tax credit for the value-added tax which it has paid on its purchased inputs. Of course, the overall results are essentially the same as they would be if the tax were levied directly on the value added at that stage of production. However, the credit approach possesses an administrative advantage in that it entails separate itemization of the tax on all invoices which, in turn, reduces the opportunities for evasion of the tax.

The value-added tax is used prominently in Europe and has been the subject of serious discussion recently for possible use by the federal government in the United States. In fact, it is often proposed as a replacement for the federal corporation income tax in the United States though its adoption in other nations usually has been as a substitute for some other form of sales tax. This important proposal will be treated in greater detail in a later section of the present chapter.

Meanwhile, Table 14–1 demonstrates the conceptual differences between the two most prominent types of "multistage" broadbased sales taxes—the *turnover* and *value-added* taxes—and the "single-stage" *general retail sales* tax. Ordinarily, either multistage tax would be administered more efficiently by a "national" unit of government, but coordinative arrangements may be worked out between national and "subnational" governments if the tax is imposed by both levels of government. At a given tax rate, the turnover tax would yield more tax revenues than a value-added tax since its "cumulative base" would be larger, that is, it would be imposed on the "gross" value ($18 in the example) instead of upon the "net" value ($6 in the example) of the multiple transactions. Alternatively, it can yield the same volume of revenues at an appropriately lower tax rate.

---

[2] For an excellent appraisal of the value-added tax, see Charles E. McLure, Jr., "The Tax on Value Added: Pros and Cons," in *Value Added Tax: Two Views* (Washington, D.C.: American Enterprise Institute for Public Policy Research, 1972), pp. 1–68.

Moreover, a turnover tax is more likely to encourage the "vertical integration" of firms in production and distribution, with resulting market structure distortion, than is a value-added or general retail sales tax. In Table 14–1, for example, assume (as is usually the case) that internal transactions or transfers within a single business firm are exempt from the tax. In this case, the tax base under the turnover tax for a firm with full vertical integration would be $6—the gross monetary value of the final good. Yet, if the productive and distributive process involves a number of separate business firms (the absence of vertical integration), the cumulative base of the turnover tax would be $18. However, the tax base is $6 under a value-added tax whether vertical integration exists or not. Clearly, a motivation exists to seek vertical integration in the case of the turnover tax. Finally, if full vertical integration does exist

TABLE 14–1*

Comparison of "Turnover," "Value-Added," and "General Retail Sales" Tax Bases

Stage (Level) of Transaction	Selling Price (Value)	Value Added	General Retail Sales Tax
Bauxite ore prior to mining...................	$ 0	$	
Mining of ore	1 ——→ 1		
Processing of ore	2 ——→ 1		
Manufacture of pan for cooking.................	4 ——→ 2		
Wholesale distribution of pan	5 ——→ 1		
Retail (final) sale of pan to consumer...........	6 ——→ 1		6
TAX BASE............	$18	$6	$6

"Cumulative" base of *turnover* tax   = $18.
"Cumulative" base of *value-added* tax   = $ 6.
"Single-stage" base of *general retail sales* tax = $ 6.
* This table assumes the existence of firms which are *not* "vertically integrated" in production and distribution.

for a turnover tax, it and the value-added tax become similar in effect to the general retail sales tax with a de facto single-stage application of the tax on the common tax base of $6. (see Table 14–1).

Finally, the "revenue productivity" of a sales tax, either narrowbased or broadbased, imposed by a state or local unit of government may be threatened by the possibility of purchasing taxable economic goods in another political jurisdiction. In order to discourage such tax avoidance efforts, all states levying broadbased retail sales taxes also impose a *use* tax which applies a special sales tax to economic goods purchased outside the state by its residents, but subsequently brought into the state. The use tax is somewhat difficult to enforce because of the problems involved in discovering out-of-state purchases.

SELECTIVE SALES (EXCISE) TAXATION IN THE UNITED STATES

Historical Development of Selective Sales Taxes

Federal Excise Taxes. The *federal* government has collected both internal and external excises since the early days of the Republic. Meanwhile, state and local governments are forbidden by the Constitution to levy external excise taxes (tariffs, customs duties), though during the latter part of the twentieth century these levels of government have actively engaged in the imposition of interal excise taxes.

External excise taxes served as the primary source of federal revenue between 1790 and the beginning of World War I. Internal excise taxes, nonetheless, were imposed during the period extending from 1791–1802 and again during the emergency surrounding the War of 1812. Then, during the Civil War, internal excises once again became a prominent part of the federal revenue structure. At this time the taxes were imposed upon a long list of economic goods including tobacco products and alcoholic beverages (distilled spirits). After the Civil War, most of the excise taxes were repealed though the ones on tobacco and alcoholic beverages were retained. As the century progressed, these internal excises increased in importance.

Following the earlier wartime pattern, the Spanish-American War brought about the introduction of miscellaneous new excise taxes, most of which were repealed by 1902. Later, important use was made of a wide variety of excise taxes during World War I. During the prosperous 1920s, most existing excises either were repealed or reduced sharply and by the end of the decade the only important federal excise tax remaining was that levied on tobacco products. The alcoholic beverage excise remained in effect, but declined greatly in importance due to the existence of prohibition. The repeal of prohibition during the early 1930s, however, revived the importance of this tax. Meanwhile, a federal excise tax on gasoline, following the mass production of the automobile, was enacted into law during 1932 and has remained in continuous use since that time.

Most of the manufacturer's excise taxes still in use today had been revived during the early 1930s as a depression tax device in lieu of adopting a manufacturer's general sales tax. As a result, federal excise tax revenues increased substantially throughout the remainder of the 1930s. Federal excise tax rates were increased during World War II and both retailer's and transportation excise taxes were introduced. Extensive excise tax reductions were enacted by Congress in 1954 and again in 1965 with isolated reductions occurring in several other years. The legislation in 1965, in particular, was substantial and involved the outright repeal of many excise taxes as well as reductions in the rates of others.

State and Local Excise Taxes. The use of excise taxes at the *state and local levels of government* has largely been a twentieth-century phenomenon. The gasoline tax was initiated by 5 states, led by Oregon, in 1919. This excise spread rapidly and by the end of the decade of the 1920s all of the "then 48" states were using the tax. Meanwhile, 29 states adopted excises on alcoholic beverages during the decade of the 1930s and 4 additional states have adopted them since that time, bringing the present total to 33 states. The remaining 17 states use a government liquor monopoly means of selling distilled spirits. All 50 states levy an excise tax on beer. The first state excise tax on cigarettes was adopted by Iowa in 1921. There were 7 additional enactments during the 1920s, 19 during the 1930's, and 23 since that time.[3] Thus, all 50 states now impose cigarette excise taxes.

Most state amusement taxes are also relatively recent in origin. Though a wide assortment of amusement taxes were in existence during the 1920s (and earlier) the taxes did not assume significant revenue importance until the 1930s. The first state admissions tax was enacted by Connecticut in 1921. Meanwhile, state public utility taxes on intrastate public utility gross receipts, gross earnings, or units of service sold, date from the latter part of the nineteenth century. Most states presently obtain revenue from such taxes imposed on telephone, telegraph, transportation, and other public utility companies. Local levels of government in the United States, to varying degrees, impose excise taxes on gasoline, alcoholic beverages, tobacco products, amusements, and public utility companies. The time origin of these local excise taxes is primarily a twentieth-century phenomenon and, for the most part, followed the adoption of such taxes by state governments.

Present Status of Selective Sales Taxes

Federal Excise Taxes. Significant legislation passed by Congress during 1965 substantially reduced the federal excise tax burden on American taxpayers. Many federal excise taxes were either repealed or sub-

---

[3] North Carolina, in 1969, became the 50th state to impose a cigarette excise tax.

stantially reduced by the legislation. Prior to this action, federal excise taxes had been applied to a wide variety of economic goods.[4] Depending upon the particular excise tax in question, these federal excises were applied at proportional rates on either an *ad valorem* or a *specific* basis. The following summarizes the major changes enacted by the federal excise tax legislation of 1965 as well as the subsequent modification of some of these changes:

1. Repeal of the 10 percent excise taxes on furs, jewelry, luggage, handbags, cosmetics, room air conditioners, business machines, cigarette lighters, cameras and film, musical instruments, pens, radio and television sets, phonographs and records, and sporting goods (except fishing equipment).

2. Repeal of the 5 percent manufacturer's excise taxes on household appliances, refrigerators, freezers, and movie projectors.

3. Repeal of miscellaneous excise taxes on playing cards, pipe tobacco, pinball machines, pool tables, bowling alleys, and safe-deposit boxes.

4. Repeal of the excise taxes on club dues, admissions, cabaret bills, telegraph service, private phone lines, auto parts and accessories, electric light bulbs, wire and equipment service, and documentary stamps.

5. Reduction of the excise tax on new (domestic) automobiles from 10 percent to 7 percent, effective June, 1965, and to 6 percent by January, 1966, and also reduction of the excise tax on local and long-distance telephone service from 10 percent to 3 percent, effective January, 1966. For reasons of aggregate economic policy, these reductions were short-lived. However, in 1971 the excise tax on new automobiles was fully deleted.

---

[4] *Alcoholic beverages,* including distilled spirits, still wines, sparkling wines, liqueurs, and cordials.

Tobacco products, including cigarettes, cigars, chewing and smoking tobacco, and snuff.

Stamp taxes, documentary, etc., including those on bond issues, bond transfers, stock issues, stock transfers, deeds, conveyances of realty, foreign insurance policies, and playing cards.

Manufacturer's excise taxes, including air conditioners; automobiles; business machines; cameras, lenses, and film; cigarette lighters; electric, gas and oil appliances of a household variety; electric light bulbs and tubes; firearms, shells, and cartridges; fountain pens, mechanical pencils, and ballpoint pens; gasoline and lubricating oil; matches; musical instruments, phonographs and records, radio and television sets, and components; pistols and revolvers; refrigerators, refrigerating apparatus, and quick-freeze units of a household variety; and sporting goods and equipment.

Retailer's excise taxes, including those on furs and fur articles; jewelry; luggage and handbags; and toilet preparations.

Miscellaneous excise taxes, including those on admissions; bowling alleys, billiard and pool tables; cabaret and roof garden bills; club dues and initiation fees; coin-operated amusement or gaming devices; diesel fuel for highway vehicles and special motor fuels; leases of safe-deposit boxes; telephone, telegraph, radio, and cable facilities; transportation of persons by air; truck use tax on vehicles in excess of 26,000 pounds; and wagering.

TABLE 14–2
Federal Excise Tax Rates on Selected Items

Item Taxed	Tax Rate	
	In Dollars	*In Percent*
Liquor Taxes		
Distilled spirits (per proof or wine gallon)	$10.50	
Still wines (per wine gallon 14% alcohol or less)....	.17	
Fermented malt liquors (per 31 gallon barrel)......	9.00	
Champagne and sparkling wines (per wine gallon) .	3.40	
Tobacco Taxes		
Cigars, large (per thousand)*	2.50 to 20.00	
Cigarettes (per thousand weighing not more than 3 pounds)†.................................	4.00	
Manufacturers' Excise Taxes		
Lubricating oil (per gallon).....................	.06‡	
Gasoline (per gallon)...........................	.04§	
Tires used on highways and other tires (per pound, respectively)...........................	.10‖, .05	
Inner tubes (per pound)#.......................	.10	
Tread rubber (per pound)**.....................	.05	
Trucks and buses (sale price)††		10
Truck parts and accessories‡‡		8
Firearms, shells, and cartridges (sales price)........		11
Pistols and revolvers (sales price)		10
Airway User Taxes		
Annual registration............................	25.00	
Poundage fees (aircraft over 2500 pounds) Propeller-driven (per pound)	.02	
Turbine-powered............................	.35	
Highway Motor Vehicle Use Tax		
(for each 1,000 pounds of gross weight over 26,000 pounds)...............................	3.00	
Miscellaneous Excise Taxes		
Local and toll telephone service and teletype-writer service (amount charged, respectively)....		10, 10§§
Air transportation persons (domestic flights, amount paid)		8
(International flights)	3.00	
Airfreight (domestic waybills)...................		5
Wagers (amount wagered, except parimutuel)......		10
Retailers' Excise Taxes		
Diesel fuel (per gallon)‖‖	.04	
Gasoline and jet fuel used in noncommercial aviation (per gallon, respectively)..................	.03, .07	

* Rates graduated with retail prices of cigars. Small cigars (less than 3 pounds per thousand) are taxed at $.75 per thousand.
† Cigarettes weighing more than 3 pounds per thousand are taxed at $8.40 per thousand.
‡ Refund of tax for oil not used in highway vehicles, beginning January 1, 1966.
§ Scheduled to drop to $.015 per gallon on October 1, 1977.
‖ Scheduled to drop to $.05 per pound on October 1, 1977.
Scheduled to drop to $.09 per pound on October 1, 1977.
** Scheduled to disappear on October 1, 1977.
†† Scheduled to drop to 5% on October 1, 1977.
‡‡ Scheduled to drop to 5% on October 1, 1977.
§§ Scheduled to drop in steps to 1% by 1981.
‖‖ Scheduled to drop to $.015 on October 1, 1977.

At the present time, items upon which federal excise taxes are imposed include alcoholic beverages, tobacco products, lubricating oil, gasoline, diesel fuel, tires, trucks and buses, guns, telephone service, air transportation, and returns from bets or wagers. Among these, the alcohol, gasoline, and tobacco excises are the biggest revenue producers (in that order) for the federal government. Table 14–2 summarizes the major federal excise tax base and rate structures now in effect.

State and Local Excise Taxes. *Motor Fuel Taxes.* The federal government, all 50 states, the District of Columbia, and some units of local government impose *motor fuel taxes* with "gasoline" serving as the primary base of the tax.[5] Motor fuel taxes collected by the public sector in 1971 totaled $10.6 billion of which $6.7 billion was collected by state governments, $3.8 billion by the federal government, and the relatively small remaining amount by local units of government. State gasoline tax rates range from 5 cents per gallon in two states to 10 cents per gallon in one state. Eighteen states impose a rate of 7 cents per gallon. See Table 14–3 for specific details.

Diesel fuel and liquefied petroleum are taxed by the District of Columbia and by all states except Vermont. Vermont, however, levies additional highway registration fees on motor vehicles using fuels other than gasoline. The tax rate on diesel fuel is the same as the gasoline tax in all except 11 states. In these 11 states, except Michigan and Oklahoma, diesel fuel is taxed at a higher rate. Various exemptions exist for the state motor fuel taxes. For example, interstate sales, export sales, and sales to government units ordinarily are exempt. In addition, tax refunds are generally allowed on motor fuels purchased for nonhighway use such as those in agriculture, manufacturing, construction, and marine activities. Local government motor fuel taxes are used in 6 states. These tend to be levied at lower rates than the federal or state motor-fuel taxes. In a few instances, counties and municipalities levy taxes on motor fuels other than gasoline.

Tobacco Taxes. The primary source of tobacco tax revenue is the excise tax imposed on cigarettes. The federal government, all 50 states, the District of Columbia and local units of government in several states impose cigarette excises. Slightly more than one half of all tobacco tax revenues accrue to state governments with most of the remainder going to the federal government. State cigarette tax rates vary between 2 cents and 21 cents "per standard package" of 20 cigarettes (See table 14–4). Hawaii and New Hampshire impose an ad valorem tax on cigarettes. Local cigarette tax rates range from 1 to 10 cents "per standard package" of cigarettes. As an alternative to specifically authorized local

---

[5] The gasoline excise is discussed in the context of an "earmarked" tax in Chapter 15.

TABLE 14-3
State Gasoline Tax Rates, 1973* (per gallon)

Under 7¢	7¢	7½¢	8¢	8½¢	9¢	10¢
Hawaii (5¢)†	Alabama*	Georgia	Alaska	Arkansas*	Kentucky	Connecticut
Nevada (6¢)	Arizona	Illinois	Delaware†	Idaho	Maine	
Oklahoma (6.58¢)*	California	Massachusetts	Florida	Nebraska	Maryland	
Texas (5¢)*	Colorado		Indiana	West Virginia	Michigan*	
	Iowa*		Louisiana		Mississippi*	
	Kansas*		New Jersey		New Hampshire	
	Minnesota		New York*		North Carolina	
	Missouri		Pennsylvania		Vermont*	
	Montana*		Rhode Island		Virginia	
	New Mexico		South Carolina§		Washington	
	North Dakota		Dist. of Columbia			
	Ohio					
	Oregon					
	South Dakota					
	Tennessee*					
	Utah					
	Wisconsin					
	Wyoming					
Number 4	18	3	11	4	10	1

* In most states diesel fuel is taxed at the same rate as gasoline. The states which tax diesel fuel at a different rate are: Alabama, 8¢; Arkansas, 9.5¢; Iowa, 8¢; Kansas, 8¢; Michigan, 7¢; Mississippi, 10¢; Montana, 9¢; New York, 10¢; Oklahoma, 6.5¢; Tennessee, 8¢; Texas, 6.5¢. In all but a few states liquified petroleum is taxed at the same rate as gasoline. Vermont does not tax diesel fuel or liquified petroleum.

† Excludes the following county rates, determined by the county in which the fuel is used: Honolulu, 3½¢; Hawaii, 3¢; Maui, 5¢; and Kauai, 4¢.

‡ Increased from 8¢ to 9¢ effective from August 1, 1973 until June 30, 1974.

§ The tax on gasoline sold, consigned, used, shipped, or distributed is 8¢ per gallon. The tax on gasoline imported or stored in South Carolina is 7.67¢ per gallon.

Source: Advisory Commission on Intergovernmental Relations, *Federal-State-Local Finances: Significant Features of Fiscal Federalism* (Washington, D.C., U.S. Government Printing Office, 1974), p. 310.

TABLE 14–4
State Cigarette Tax Rates, 1973 (cents per standard pack of 20)

7¢ or less	8¢	9¢	10¢	11¢	12¢	13¢	14¢ or more
Dist. of Col. (6¢)	Alaska	Missouri	Arizona	Kansas	Alabama	Iowa	Arkansas (17¾¢)
Indiana (6¢)	Hawaii*	Oregon	California	Louisiana	Georgia	Nebraska	Connecticut (21¢)
Kentucky (3¢)	Utah	Idaho (9 1/10¢)	Colorado	Michigan	Illinois	Oklahoma	Delaware (14¢)
Maryland (6¢)	Wyoming		Nevada	Mississippi	Montana	Rhode Island	Florida (17¢)
North Carolina (2¢)				New Hampshire†	New Mexico	Tennessee	Maine (14¢)
South Carolina (6¢)				North Dakota	South Dakota		Massachusetts (16¢)
Virginia (2½¢)					Vermont		Minnesota (18¢)
					West Virginia		New Jersey (19¢)
							New York (15¢)
							Ohio (15¢)
							Pennsylvania (18¢)
							Texas (18½¢)
							Washington (16¢)
							Wisconsin (16¢)
Number 7	4	3	4	6	8	5	14

* Hawaii with a rate of 40% of wholesale price is estimated at 8¢.
† New Hampshire with a rate of 42% of retail price is estimated at 11¢.
Source: Advisory Commission on Intergovernmental Relations, *Federal-State-Local Finances: Significant Features of Fiscal Federalism* (Washington, D.C.: U.S. Government Printing Office, 1974), p. 301.

cigarette excises, a number of states share their state cigarette excises directly with cities and counties. A total of 23 states impose an excise tax on cigars. In addition, excise taxes are placed on smoking tobacco by 21 states, on chewing tobacco by 20 states, and on snuff by 17 states. Moreover, a number of states tax cigarettes under a general retail sales tax as well as under the selective excise tax on cigarettes.

Alcoholic Beverage Taxes. Excise taxes on distilled spirits are imposed by the federal government, 33 states, and by some units of local government. In addition to these specific excise taxes, the "group" of alcoholic beverage taxes includes occupational license taxes imposed on the privilege of engaging in the alcoholic beverage business. Many states which have special excise taxes on alcoholic beverages also impose general retail sales and use taxes on their purchase. All 50 states impose an excise tax on beer. Hawaii levies an *ad valorem* instead of a *specific* excise tax on distilled spirits. Moreover, approximately three fourths of the states levy an excise on "wines." Sixteen states exercise monopoly power over the distribution of distilled spirits by operating state-owned liquor stores while one other state, North Carolina, utilizes county- and municipally-operated liquor stores, supervised by the state, for this purpose. Alcoholic beverages are subject to local government excise taxes in only a few states, but the application of local general retail sales taxes to the purchase of alcoholic beverages is more common.

Miscellaneous Excises. Lower levels of government also impose excise taxes on such things as telephone service, the "transfer" of real estate, and entertainment. In 1972, the general retail sales tax included charges for telephone services (with a few exemptions) in its tax base in 29 states. Moreover, telephone companies are subject to gross receipts taxes as well as to corporation income taxes in many states. The gross receipts taxes frequently apply also to other public utility companies. In addition, local governments in a number of states impose "nonproperty" taxes on local telephone service. Most of these taxes are also gross receipts taxes. In a few states, however, local units of government impose special excises on local telephone service.

Excise taxes levied on the "transfer" of real estate and capital stock and on the issuance of corporate bonds and other evidences of indebtedness (such as mortgages) are known as *documentary* taxes. Thirty-four states and the District of Columbia impose a documentary tax on real estate transfers. Interestingly, most of the states first enacted the tax during the decade of the 1960s. Moreover, in some states local governments also use this tax. Ordinarily, the tax is ad valorem in nature and requires that stamps be affixed to the pertinent documents. Though only a few states, including New York, directly impose "stock transfer" taxes, almost all stock market transactions are subject to a state documentary tax since 90 percent of stock market transactions occur in that state. During 1966, a proposed 50 percent increase in this tax on the transfer of stock created rumors of relocating the New York Stock Exchange.

General admissions to entertainment events are subject to taxation by state-local governments through a variety of techniques. These include (1) special admissions or amusement taxes, which may be levied on either the "admission charge" or upon the "admission receipts" of amusement operators, (2) inclusion of admission charges in the base of the general retail sales tax, (3) inclusion of admission receipts in the base of a business gross receipts tax, or (4) a combination of taxation under both the business gross receipts tax and the general retail sales tax. In addition, the majority of states apply a special admissions tax on boxing or wrestling exhibitions, or both, while a few states apply such a tax to some or all forms of horse and dog racing. In many instances, these special admissions excise taxes are levied on top of the general admissions excise tax of the state. Parimutuel betting on thoroughbred and harness horse racing and on dog racing is also subject to excise taxation in a large number of states. Only a few states levy specific excise taxes on cabaret charges, club dues, and initiation fees, though in some cases the state general retail sales tax is applied to these items. In addition, some states allow local governments to impose admissions taxes. However, this device is extensively used in only a few states.

GENERAL RETAIL SALES TAXATION IN THE UNITED STATES

Historical Development of General Sales Taxes

The federal government has never employed a broadbased *general retail sales tax* though Congress has considered the matter on a number of occasions. However, most states use such a tax at the present time. This use by the states of broadbased general sales taxes is a twentieth-century phenomenon. More specifically, the retail sales tax movement grew out of the Great Depression of the 1930s. Though some states had imposed taxes on gross business receipts during the 1920s, the first permanent general retail sales tax was enacted by Mississippi in 1932. The next few years witnessed an avalanche of adoptions of similar taxes. At the close of the depression, approximately one half of the states were using the tax, though several states which had adopted it earlier in the 1930s had discontinued its use by that time. A revival of state general sales tax adoptions occurred following World War II and again during

TABLE 14–5
Years of Adoptions of State General Retail Sales Taxes

Period	Number	State	Year Adopted	Period	Number	State	Year Adopted
1931–40.... 24		Mississippi	1932	1941–50 ... 5		Connecticut	1947
		Arizona	1933			Maryland	1947
		California	1933			Rhode Island	1947
		Illinois	1933			Tennessee	1947
		Indiana	1933			Florida	1949
		Iowa	1933	Since			
		Michigan	1933	1950 16		Georgia	1951
		New Mexico	1933			Maine	1951
		North Carolina	1933			South Carolina	1951
		Oklahoma	1933			Pennsylvania	1953
		South Dakota	1933			Nevada	1955
		Utah	1933			Kentucky	1960
		Washington	1933			Texas	1961
		West Virginia	1933			Wisconsin	1961
		Missouri	1934			Idaho	1965
		Ohio	1934			New York	1965
		Arkansas	1935			Massachusetts	1966
		Colorado	1935			New Jersey	1966
		Hawaii	1935			Virginia	1966
		North Dakota	1935			Nebraska	1967
		Wyoming	1935			Minnesota	1967
		Alabama	1936			Vermont	1969
		Kansas	1937	Total			
		Louisiana	1938	(1931–69).. 45			

Source: Advisory Commission on Intergovernmental Relations.

the 1960s. Presently, 45 of the 50 states impose the tax. Table 14–5 summarizes the time pattern of state adoptions of the tax since 1932.

Meanwhile, the use of general sales taxes by local units of government derives primarily from their desire to relieve the pressure on the property tax. Only two major cities, New York City and New Orleans, used the tax prior to World War II. New York City had adopted retail sales taxation in 1934 and New Orleans in 1938. Following World War II, a local general sales tax movement was initiated in California and spread to a number of other states. At the present time, local governments in 25 states impose general retail sales taxes and, during 1969 alone, 5 additional states passed "enabling legislation" to permit local governments to impose the tax. The overall role of broadbased general retail sales taxes in the local government revenue picture, however, remains relatively insignificant as is indicated by the fact that in 1971 only 3 percent of total local government revenues (excluding intergovernmental transfers) came from such taxes. Nonetheless, they are of considerable revenue importance to certain individual units of local government.

TABLE 14-6
State General Retail Sales Tax Rates, 1973 (percent)

2	2.5	3	3.5	4	4+	5	Over 5
Nevada*	Nebraska	Arizona	Tennessee	Alabama	California (4-¾)	Kentucky	Pennsylvania (6%)
Oklahoma		Arkansas		Florida	Washington (4-½)	Maine	Connecticut (6.5%)
		Colorado		Hawaii		Mississippi	
		Georgia		Illinois		New Jersey	
		Idaho		Indiana		Rhode Island	
		Iowa		Maryland		District of Columbia	
		Kansas		Michigan			
		Louisiana		Minnesota			
		Massachusetts		New Mexico			
		Missouri		New York			
		North Carolina		North Dakota			
		Vermont		Ohio			
		Virginia		South Carolina			
		West Virginia		South Dakota			
		Wyoming		Texas			
				Utah			
				Wisconsin			
Number 2	1	15	1	17	2	6	2

* Excludes the one percent mandatory county tax.

Source: Advisory Commission on Intergovernmental Relations, *Federal-State-Local Finances: Significant Features of Fiscal Federalism* (Washington: U.S. Government Printing Office, 1974), p. 239.

Present Status of State and Local General Sales Taxes

During the 1971 fiscal year, state and local governments collected $17.8 billion in general sales tax revenues, $15.5 billion of which accrued to the states. The general sales tax accounts for 30 percent of *all* state government tax collections despite the fact that 5 states do not use the tax. The rates of state general retail sales taxes are applied ordinarily to the sales of "tangible personal property" and "specific services" at the *retail level* of business activity. State general sales tax rates are proportional in their statutory structure and range from 2 percent in 2 states to 6.5 percent in one state. The most common rate in 1973 was 4 percent in 17 states followed by the 3 percent rate used in 15 states. Despite the proportional technical structure of general sales (and most excise) taxes, they are "regressive" in terms of an income base and related distributional equity considerations.[6] Table 14–6 provides a summary of *state* general retail sales tax rates.

General retail sales taxes, as observed above, are imposed by *local* governments in 25 states. Several of the largest cities in the nation including New York City, Chicago, Los Angeles, Washington, D.C., San Francisco, and New Orleans use the tax. The taxes are locally administered in some states and are administered through cooperation between the state and local, or between county and municipal governments in others. All of the states in which *local* general retail sales taxes are used, except Alaska, also impose *state* general retail sales taxes. Under this condition of dual general sales taxation, the local government rate tends to be quite low. A number of states share part of their general sales tax revenues with local governments.

FISCAL RATIONALITY CRITERIA APPLIED TO SALES TAXES

Allocational Effects

First, the allocational effects of "excise taxes" in an economy where "imperfect market structure" dominates will be analyzed.[7] *Four* basic patterns of excise tax effects, each of which is based upon the assumption of a "fixed supply of labor," can be isolated. Further assumptions for the present analysis include: (1) an initial condition of *full employment,* (2) a given or constant level of *governmental expenditures,* and (3) a *tax structure* consisting solely of a 10 percent proportional income

---

[6] See Chapter 7.

[7] See George F. Break, "Excise Tax Burdens and Benefits," *American Economic Review,* September 1954, pp. 577–94.

tax. What would happen if the proportional income tax were removed and replaced by a set of partial ad valorem excise taxes levied at rates sufficient to maintain governmental revenues.

One possible result would be to increase the prices of "taxed" goods and to lower the prices of "untaxed" commodities. Thus, a substitution effect is virtually certain to occur.[8] Nevertheless, the excise does *not* necessarily lead to an "inferior" allocation of resources after the substitution effect occurs. The imposition of the set of partial excise taxes, indeed, does move the system from one full-employment resource allocation point to a different full-employment point. Yet, the posttax resource allocation position may be either "superior" or "inferior" to the pretax position. Thus, unless the pretax allocation of resources is optimal—and this seems unlikely in a world of imperfect markets—the excise may create either a "positive" nonneutral effect in terms of an "excess benefit" or a "negative" nonneutral effect in the sense of an "excess burden," depending upon the circumstances of each individual case.

The conclusion changes if one drops the assumption of full employment.[9] Prices in the "taxed" industries will increase while there need be no decrease in prices in the "untaxed" industries. Consumers and resource owners, in general, are worse off since the overall level of prices has increased while disposable income has remained relatively constant (the effect of the income tax reduction is offset by the decline in employment and the payment of excise taxes). An "excess burden" is thus imposed upon consumers through *inflation* and upon resource owners through *involuntary unemployment.*

A third case assumes that the government combines the excise tax with a government-induced expansion of the money supply.[10] In this instance, both consumption prices and consumer incomes are higher and no excess burden exists. The final case considers what happens if the increase in monetary demand comes from the private sector.[11] In this case, the result of the excise again will be in the form of both higher prices and higher incomes and an excess burden does not occur.

Hence, the primary conclusion concerning the allocational effects of excise taxes is that such taxes meet the orthodox definition of "excess burden," resulting from a "substitution effect," *only* under certain circumstances.[12] Moreover, when the orthodox position is upheld, it is typically for reasons other than those traditionally given. For example,

---

[8] See the analytical description of "substitution" and "income" effects in Chapter 6.

[9] *Ibid.*

[10] *Ibid.*, p. 585.

[11] *Ibid.*, p. 588.

[12] See the discussion of the *fiscal neutrality* concept, both in the narrow (orthodox) and comprehensive context, in Chapter 6.

the "excess burden" argument, in the narrow or orthodox sense, is based traditionally upon the assumption that the reduction in the output of the "taxed" good is *not* compensated by an increase in the output of other commodities.[13] In the orthodox sense, consumers are thus said to have had their real income (welfare) reduced. Such an approach, however, clearly implies that the reduced resources "disappear" from the economic scene. To answer the question whether a particular tax change exerts an "overall" *negative allocational nonneutrality,* in the form of an *excess burden,* it is necessary to consider the gains in the output of "nontaxed" items occasioned by the reallocation of productive resources.[14] When the problem is viewed in this fashion, it is evident that excise taxes may either improve or worsen allocation efficiency and thus living standards or welfare. In other words, if the initial equilibrium is *not* one of optimal resource allocation, the nonneutral effects of the excise tax may be "positive," that is, these effects may improve instead of worsen resource allocation.

Next, the analysis will turn to indirect taxes, such as sales taxes, as they may exert possible nonneutral effects on "fiscal choice through *time.*" One relevant study emphasises the problem of "individual choice" in a *long-run* setting characterized by "intertemporal adjustments."[15] In this setting, various types of taxes are viewed as "institutions" and not merely as "analytical devices" without the realistic dimensions of space and time.

In a *one-period* or *short-run* analysis, as opposed to long-run analysis, the following order of tax instruments would generally be preferred in a range from "least" to "most" distortion or nonneutrality: (1) a lump-sum or per capita tax levied on a person "as a person," (2) a proportional personal income tax, (3) a progressive personal income tax, (4) a general expenditure or spendings tax on the total consumption of an individual, and (5) a selective excise tax on the consumption of an economic good. In other words, the lump-sum tax results in the least market distortion through a substitution effect and the selective excise tax in the greatest market distortion.

However, *long-run* analysis provides a "different ordering" of tax instruments, in terms of "nonneutrality," when the following assumptions are made:[16] (1) the individual knows his future income; (2) his current decision-making process reflects consideration of expected fluc-

---

[13] Earl R. Rolph and George F. Break, "The Welfare Aspects of Excise Taxes," *Journal of Political Economy,* February 1949, pp. 46–54.

[14] See the related discussion in the first part of Chapter 10 concerning the neutrality of income versus excise taxation.

[15] See James M. Buchanan and Francesco Forte, "Fiscal Choice through Time: A Case for Indirect Taxation?" *National Tax Journal,* June 1964, pp. 144–57.

[16] *Ibid.*

tuations in wants and needs over time; (3) the individual saves only for the purposes of retiring debt or of accumulating funds for future consumption; and (4) the capital market is "imperfect" in the specific sense that differential interest rates exist between loans to consumers and loans for the business acquisition of productive capital—the latter rates being lower because offsetting productive assets are provided.

Thus, if the capital market is imperfect, an individual will tend to choose the tax which minimizes his need to go into the capital (loan) market for funds. As a result, if "income" is *less stable* than "needs" over time, the individual will prefer the "progressive tax on income earned in each period" to either the lump-sum tax, the proportional personal income tax, the general spendings tax, or the excise tax because the intertemporal flexibility of income will allow the *tax liability to be concentrated* in periods when the marginal utility of overall consumption spending is "low."[17]

The analysis leads to a different conclusion, however, if "needs" are *less stable* than "income" over time. In this instance, an "excise tax imposed on a luxury good" would likely involve less overall distortion than even a progressive personal income tax because it would allow postponable *luxury good purchases to be concentrated* in time periods when the marginal utility of overall consumption spending is "low."

The comparative welfare effects of indirect and direct taxes may also be viewed in terms of (1) the choice between work and leisure and (2) the choice between savings and consumption. Regarding the effect on the *"work-leisure" choice,* it should be recognized that no a priori case can be established in favor of "direct" taxation (such as income taxes), since both types of taxes affect this choice. Regarding the *saving-consumption choice,* there is a tendency for income taxation to reduce the rate of saving more than does a consumption tax of equal revenue yield.[18] However, the nature of the federal corporation income tax causes the "welfare costs" deriving from the influence of that tax on the rate of saving to be less than that exerted by the differential tax treatment of various types of capital income. It is estimated, for example, that the misallocation of capital caused by the special provision for percentage depletion allowances, and related provisions, amounts to a total ranging from $0.5 billion to $1.0 billion per year.[19] Finally, it is estimated that the influence of "direct" taxation on the saving-consumption choice may reduce the economic growth of the nation by as

---

[17] Ibid., p. 150.

[18] See Arnold C. Harberger, "Taxation, Resource Allocation, and Welfare," in *The Role of Direct and Indirect Taxes in the Federal Revenue System,* A Conference Report of the National Bureau of Economic Research and Brookings Institution (Princeton, N.J.: Princeton University Press, 1964), pp. 25–81.

[19] Ibid., p. 62.

much as two tenths of 1 percent due to the retardation of capital formation. Thus, a change from "direct" to "indirect" taxation could conceivably increase the rate of economic growth by this amount.[20]

Distributional Effects

Next, focus will be placed upon sales taxation in reference to the
principles of equity in the *distribution of tax burdens.*[21] The general
retail sales taxes and most selective sales (excise) taxes used in the
American economy utilize "technically-proportional" tax rate structures. However, these statutorily proportional rates tend to yield a
regressive tax burden distribution in light of the *ability-to-pay principle*
of equity in the distribution of tax burdens with *income* as the accepted
indicator of taxpaying ability. Since marginal and average propensities
to consume tend to be lower at higher-income levels, the purchase of
items subject to the sales taxes (except excises on luxury goods) is ordinarily a smaller proportion of income for higher-income taxpayers.
Moreover, the regressivity is accentuated when services are exempt
from the tax base of a general retail sales tax since these tend to be
consumed in greater proportions by higher-income taxpayers. The regressivity of a "general retail sales tax" is exemplified graphically in
Figure 14-1, but similar effects may be assigned also to other broadbased sales taxes such as the "value-added tax" and to numerous narrowbased excise taxes.[22]

Thus, since the *general retail* sales tax is the largest single source of
state tax revenues, and since all states use *selective* sales taxes, the
potential influence of sales taxation on income and wealth distribution
is very significant. Of course, the "effective progressivity" of the federal
tax structure may be viewed as a somewhat neutralizing offset to the
regressive distributional effects of state and local general sales and excise taxes. Moreover, it should be noted that to the extent that selective
sales (excises) taxes are imposed on luxury goods, the burden of such
tax payments tends to fall more heavily on higher income taxpayers,
thus reducing the regressive effects. Yet, it also must be acknowledged
that excise taxes imposed on luxury goods provide a small part of total

---

[20] Ibid., pp. 62–70.

[21] See the relevant discussion in Chapter 7.

[22] A recent study of the regressivity (progressivity) of federal excise taxes shows a
"regressivity index" of – 2.8 for all federal excises prior to the comprehensive federal
excise tax revisions of 1965 and a – 2.9 regressivity for excises repealed during that year.
(Note: A "negative" value indicates regressivity; a "positive" value indicates progressivity, and "zero" indicates proportionality. Moreover, "larger" negative or positive value
reflects greater regressivity or progressivity, respectively.) A wide range of results was
demonstrated for particular excises. For example, the individual items varied from an
extremely regressive – 37.1 for the excise on smoking tobacco to a progressive + 14.2 for
the excise on furs (now repealed). For the detailed study, see Thomas W. Calmus, "The
Burden of Federal Excise Taxes by Income Class," *Quarterly Review of Economics and
Business,* Spring 1970, pp. 17–23.

sales tax revenues. Finally, it should be recognized that the *exemption of food and medicine* (basic consumption necessities) from the general sales tax base in certain states, and also the occasional use of *income tax credits,* reduce the effective regressivity of the tax.

Since the "income tax credit" means of alleviation sales tax regressivity constitutes a form of "negative income taxation," it will be discussed in Chapter 21 which deals specifically with the problem of poverty. However, further discussion of the "exemption" technique will now be undertaken. Table 14–7 summarizes *food and medical exemptions* from the general retail sales tax bases of various states. It may be observed that 29 states exempt medicine from their general sales tax bases while 19 of these and the District of Columbia also exempt food along with medicine. Thus, 58 percent of the states (29 out of 50) employ some version of "food-medical exemption" as a means of reducing the regressivity of general sales taxation. Interestingly, however, the exemption of clothing from the general retail sales tax base, as contrasted to the exemption of food and medicine, tends to make the tax "more" instead of "less" regressive.[23]

In some instances, excise taxes are earmarked to special trust funds for specific uses related to the nature of the tax itself. To the extent that this occurs, the *benefit principle* of tax burden distribution may be

FIGURE 14–1
The Regressive Nature of General Retail Sales Taxes

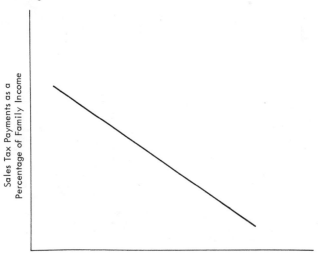

Sales Tax Payments as a Percentage of Family Income

Family Income (dollars)

---

[23] Two studies which demonstrate the fact that "clothing exemptions" increase sales tax regressivity are: Jeffrey M. Schaefer, "Sales Tax Regressivity Under Alternative Tax Bases and Income Concepts," *National Tax Journal,* December 1969, pp. 516–27, and David G. Davies, "Clothing Exemptions and Sales Tax Regressivity: Note," *American Economic Review,* March 1971, pp. 187–89.

TABLE 14-7
Exemption of Food and Medicine in State General Retail Sales Taxes, 1973

State	Tax rate (percent)	Food†	Medicine‡
Alabama	4	—	x§
Arizona	3	—	x
California	4¾	x	x
Colorado*	3	—	x
Connecticut	6.5	x	x
Dist. of Columbia*	5	x‖	x
Florida	4	x	x
Idaho	3	—	x
Indiana	4	x	x
Kentucky	5	x	x
Louisiana	3	x#	x#
Maine	5	x	x
Maryland	4	x	x
Massachusetts	3	x	x
Michigan	4	—	x**
Minnesota	4	x	x
Nebraska*	2.5	—	x
Nevada	2	—	x
New Jersey	5	x	x
New York	4	x	x
North Carolina	3	—	x
North Dakota	4	x††	x
Ohio	4	x	x
Pennsylvania	6	x	x
Rhode Island	5	x	x
Texas	4	x	x
Vermont	3	x	x
Virginia	3	—	x
West Virginia	3	—	x
Wisconsin	4	x	x

Note: In South Carolina effective March 31, 1970 persons aged 65 or older may apply to the Tax Commission for reimbursement of sales tax paid for prescription medicine.

* Also allows personal income tax credit or cash rebate for sales tax paid on food.

† Food exemptions usually apply to "food for human consumption off the premises where sold." Restaurant meals are taxable in all States, although meals costing less than a specified amount are exempt in some States.

‡ The exemption is usually applicable to medicine sold on prescription or compounded by druggists, and often to medical and dental aids or devices such as artificial limbs, eye glasses, and dentures. Some States exempt patent medicines and household remedies.

§ Limited to medicines prescribed by a physician for persons aged 65 or older.

‖ Rate on food is 2 percent.

The rate on food and prescription medicine is 2 percent.

** The exemption is applicable only to 50 percent of the amount charged for recorded drug prescriptions. Full exemption applies to artificial limbs and eyes.

†† Limited to specified items.

Source: Advisory Commission on Intergovernmental Relations, *Federal-State-Local Finances: Significant Features of Fiscal Federalism* (Washington, D.C.: U.S. Government Printing Office, 1974), p. 251.

applied to help justify the tax.[24] A primary example of such an ear-marked excise tax is the federal excise tax imposed on motor fuel (gasoline, diesel fuel) which goes into a special federal trust fund for the support of the interstate highway program.

Ultimately, equity in the distribution of tax burdens must encompass the ability to effectively "enforce" and "collect" the tax in question. The general and selective sales taxes used in the United States tend to meet this criterion in an adequate fashion. Moreover, the administrative costs of sales tax enforcement is generally modest, though some differences in enforcement costs exist depending upon the type of sales tax used and the political jurisdiction imposing the tax. Collection costs incurred by the states for the general retail sales tax average about 1.5 percent of the total revenues collected. The total cost of enforcement, however, is increased further by "taxpayer compliance" costs which often entail additional labor and equipment inputs. To compensate for these business-incurred collection expenses, a number of states allow "discounts" to retailers on the total amount of general sales tax revenues paid to the government. These discounts tend to range from 1 percent to 5 percent of total tax receipts. Moreover, vendors often collect more than the tax liability based on their total sales through use of the "bracket system" of tax assessment whereby small sales bring in more than the established rate. In a number of states using general sales taxes, the vendors are allowed to retain these excess receipts which are known as "breakage." Most states not providing discounts to vendors allow the vendor to keep the breakage.

Approximately one half of the states using general retail sales taxes administer the tax through an agency headed by a single director appointed by the governor of the state. In a few states, elected state comptrollers administer the tax. A number of other states use appointive or elected boards (tax commissions). Normally, general retail sales taxes are collected by the state agency directly from the vendors of the taxable commodities, who collect the tax from the purchasers when the commodities are sold. All states require vendors to register with the state tax collection office. Approximately one half of the states require monthly returns and the remainder generally require returns on a quarterly basis.

Federal, state, and local selective sales taxes (excises) are collected with varying degrees of efficiency. The Alcohol and Tobacco Tax Unit of the Internal Revenue Service is responsible for collecting the important federal "sumptuary" excises on alcoholic beverages and tobacco products. Federal taxes on tobacco are collected directly from the manufacturer while state tobacco taxes are collected from wholesale distributors of tobacco products. Obviously, the federal enforcement

---

[24] See Chapter 7.

approach is more easily accomplished because there are relatively few manufacturers of tobacco products as compared to the number of wholesale distributors of tobacco products within a state. The federal government does not require that stamps be attached to the tobacco product packages, but most states do attach stamps as evidence of payment of the tax. No discount for collection efforts is allowed to manufacturers for the federal tobacco excise, but most states do allow discounts to distributors. These discounts generally range between 1 percent and 10 percent of sales.

It may be concluded that the *enforcement efficiency* of sales taxes, both general and selective, meets the test of adequacy. A satisfactory ratio exists between collection costs and the total revenues collected. Nonetheless, some variation does exist in the cost-revenue ratio depending upon the "type of sales tax" employed and the "particular political jurisdiction" imposing the tax. Finally, it may be noted that enforcement of general and selective sales taxes in the United States successfully avoids widespread evasion efforts.

Stabilization-Growth, Revenue Productivity, and Intergoal Performance

As compared to the personal income tax, sales taxes perform rather poorly as "automatic" fiscal stabilizers. This is the result of a lower degree of revenue response to income changes. That is, the income elasticity (Ye) of general and selective sales taxes tends to be significantly lower than that for the personal income tax. However, the use of "discretionary" sales tax policy, particularly of the selective or excise variety, may still yield some macroeconomic effects of a "positive" nature. For example, the imposition of *wartime excise taxes* during periods of war-induced inflation and consumer goods scarcity tends to discourage the effective demand for these goods. In addition, the use of an *interest-equalization tax*[25] to discourage the outflow of domestic capital to foreign nations represents a technique employed for the purpose of improving the nation's balance of international payments. Since 1963, the federal government has imposed such an excise tax on foreign common stock, bonds, and loans acquired by Americans (Canada excepted).

The more insensitive income-elasticity performance of "sales taxes," as compared to "income taxes," also restricts the long-run *revenue productivity* of these taxes. This can have significant fiscal implications for jurisdictions relying upon sales taxation since long-run demands for public-type economic goods may grow at a more rapid rate than sales tax revenues.[26] Table 14–8 summarizes the results of various "income

---

[25] See Chapter 24.

[26] See Chapter 19 for an elaboration of this point.

TABLE 14–8

Income Elasticity of State and Local General Retail Sales Taxes: Summary of Empirical Studies

Study	Year Published	Area Covered	Elasticity Coefficient
Davies..................	1962	Arkansas	1.27
Rafuse..................	1965	United States	1.27
ACIR*..................	1971	Maryland	1.08
Peck....................	1969	Indiana	1.04
Netzer..................	1961	United States	1.0
Harris..................	1966	United States	1.0
Davies..................	1962	United States	1.0
Friedlaender- Swanson-Due.........	1973	United States	< 1.0†
ACIR..................	1971	Kentucky	0.92
Arizona Planning Division..............	1971	Arizona	0.87
Davies..................	1962	Tennessee	0.80

* Advisory Commission on Intergovernmental Relations.
† An average general sales tax "income elasticity" for *all states* is not presented in this study. However, the "income elasticities" of general sales taxes presented for the *individual states* are generally "inelastic" with only one state displaying an "elastic" coefficient.
Studies Cited Above: Advisory Commission on Intergovernmental Relations, "State-Local Revenue Systems and Educational Finance," Unpublished report to the President's Commission on School Finance, November 12, 1971: Arizona Department of Economic Planning and Development, Planning Division, *Arizona Intergovernmental Structure: A Financial View to 1980*, Phoenix: 1971; Davies, David G., "The Sensitivity of Consumption Taxes to Fluctuations in Income," *National Tax Journal*, September 1962, pp. 281–90; Friedlaender, Ann F.; Swanson, Gerald J.; and Due, John F., "Estimating Sales Tax Revenue Changes in Response to Changes in Personal Income and Sales Tax Rates," *National Tax Journal*, March 1973, pp. 103–110; Harris, Robert, *Income and Sales Taxes: The 1970 Outlook for States and Localities*, Chicago: Council of State Governments, 1966; Netzer, Dick, "Financial Needs and Resources Over the Next Decade," in *Public Finances: Needs, Sources, and Utilization*, Princeton: Princeton University Press, 1961; Peck, John E., "Financing State Expenditures in a Prospering Economy," *Indiana Business Review*, July 1969, pp. 7–15; Rafuse, Robert W., "Cyclical Behavior of State-Local Finances," in Richard A. Musgrave (ed.), *Essays in Fiscal Federalism*, Washington, Brookings Institution, 1965.
Source: (Except for Friedlaender-Swanson-Due Study) Advisory Commission on Intergovernmental Relations, *State-Local Finances: Significant Features and Suggested Legislation* (Washington, D.C., U.S. Government Printing Office, 1972), p. 301.

elasticity studies" of the *general sales tax*. Although the results vary, the mean (average) result would fall in the vicinity of *unitary* income elasticity, that is, $Ye = 1$. While no table is presented here for the income elasticity of *selective sales (excise)* taxes, all of 18 separate studies which have been undertaken suggest an *inelastic* income coefficient ($Ye < 1$) for the "motor fuel" and "tobacco" excises.[27]

Next, the "interrelated" effects of a general retail sales tax on the goals of allocation and stabilization will be considered.[28] One possibility

---

[27] See Advisory Commission on Intergovernmental Relations, *State-Local Finances: Significant Features and Suggested Legislation* (Washington, D.C., U.S. Government Printing Office, 1972), p. 301.

[28] See the discussion by George F. Break, *Federal Excise Tax Structure*, Panel Discussion before the Committee on Ways and Means, House of Representatives, 88th Cong., 2d sess. (Washington, D.C.: U.S. Government Printing Office, June 15–16, 1964), Part Two, pp. 33–35.

is that resources would be transferred from the production of consumer goods into the production of capital goods. An immediate burden would thus be placed on consumers, but one that would be lessened gradually as the additional capital goods created by the reallocation of resources were brought into the production of consumer goods. Another effect of a general sales tax would involve the nature of the reaction of the consumers to the higher prices. For example, if producers increase prices to cover the taxes, consumers will either have to increase their money expenditures, and thereby accept the tax burden themselves, or they will have to reduce their purchases, in which case producers may be forced to either accept unemployment or reduced money income. The probable result would be mixed, that is, there would be some lowering of employment and wage levels and some shifts within the economy away from luxury goods. The general sales tax burden will tend to be shared between consumers and producers, though the proportion of sharing will depend upon numerous other variables. Thus, sales taxes (like other taxes) may pose an issue of "intergoal nonneutrality." Such intergoal nonneutrality, of course, can be either "positive" or "negative" if the pretax equilibrium is suboptimal. However, if it is optimal, the distortion can only be negative.

A further example of intergoal nonneutrality follows: Suppose that a nation places top priority on economic growth and relies heavily upon sales taxes to restrict present consumption and thus make additional resources available for the accumulation of real capital. If aggregate demand is inadequate due to diminished consumption, however, the result may be additional unemployed resources instead of increased investment in real capital. The tax, in addition, may alter the distribution of income in the society. Furthermore, the sales taxes, especially those of the "excise" variety, may distort resource allocation decisions through a substitution effect. Even a sales tax policy which successfully increases investment, and thus the economic growth and performance level of the economy, may provide distorting side effects on income distribution and resource allocation with subsequent indirect effects on aggregate performance. In conclusion, it should be recognized that a sales tax policy, just as any budgetary action, should reflect the "intergoal" effects of such a policy in terms of the "priorities" of the society.

THE PROPOSED SUBSTITUTION OF A FEDERAL VALUE-ADDED TAX FOR THE FEDERAL CORPORATION INCOME TAX

Background

Recent years have witnessed a growing discussion of the proposal that the federal government enter the field of broadbased sales taxation via the introduction of a multistage *value-added tax* (VAT).[29] Primarily, a federal VAT has been suggested as a replacement, complete or partial, for the federal *corporation income tax* (CIT), though other recommendations have included its utilization in relationship to the reduction of state and local government property tax burdens. The present discussion will concentrate upon the economic effects of the substitution of a value-added tax for the corporation income tax at the federal level of government.

Many European governments have adopted value-added taxes during recent years. However, these essentially have served as "replacements" for the less effective turnover tax which was already in use in these countries as well as for promoting the Common Market (European Economic Community) goal of economic unity for its member nations. Neither of these purposes is directly relevant to the present economic circumstances of the American public sector.

Different Types of Value-Added Tax

Value-added taxes may be of either the *income* (VAT$_i$) or *consumption* (VAT$_c$) varieties, the difference resulting from the manner in which

TABLE 14–9
An Example of the "Income" and "Consumption"
Varieties of Value-Added Tax for Firm *A**

Tax Base of *Income-type* VAT (VAT$_i$)
$$VAT_i = S - I - D$$
$$\$50,000 = 100,000 - 40,000 - 10,000$$

Tax Base of *Consumption-type* VAT (VAT$_c$)
$$VAT_c = S - I - C$$
$$\$40,000 = 100,000 - 40,000 - 20,000$$

*Key: Sales (*S*) = $100,000.
  Cost of Intermediate Goods (*I*) = $40,000.
  Depreciation Costs (*D*) = $10,000.
  Capital Costs or new investment (*C*) = $20,000.

"capital goods" are treated in computing the tax base. Under an "income-type" VAT, the tax base for a firm consists of sales (*S*) minus both the cost of purchasing intermediate goods (*I*) and depreciation costs (*D*).[30] Under a "consumption-type" VAT, the tax base for a firm consists of sales (*S*) minus both the cost of purchasing intermediate goods (*I*) as well as the costs of purchasing capital goods (*C*). Thus, a consumption-

---

[29] For two excellent discussions of the economic effects of federal "value-added taxation," see McLure, "Tax on Value Added," and Musgrave, Richard A., "Problems of the Value-Added Tax," *National Tax Journal*, September 1972), pp. 425–30.

[30] For example, an automobile acquired by a dealer for sale at the retail level constitutes an "intermediate good" for that dealer.

variety VAT would deduct capital costs (new investment) immediately while a VAT of the income-variety would allow the capital offset to be applied only as the capital assets "depreciate." European nations have generally opted for use of the consumption-type VAT since, among other reasons, it is administratively more simple. The comparative administrative simplicity of VAT_c results largely from the fact that it does not require detailed depreciation schedules. Table 14–9 depicts the major characteristics of each variety of value-added tax. Since the "consumption-variety" of value-added tax is the more likely candidate for American usage, the continuing discussion below will focus upon this version of the tax.

The Economic Effects of an "Unshifted" Corporation Income Tax versus a Value-Added Tax

The economic effects resulting from the substitution of a "consumption variety" value-added tax for the federal corporation income tax may be evaluated in terms of the allocational, distributional, stabilization, and economic goals of society. In comparing the economic effects of the two taxes in reference to these goals, it becomes necessary to distinguish between a corporation income tax whose tax burden has been shifted forward to consumers via higher selling prices and one whose burden is absorbed entirely by the owners of the corporation.[31] Of course, much greater certitude exists concerning the "distributional impact" of the federal corporation income tax, that is, its *initial* payment by the shareholders of the corporation, as opposed to the less certain issue of whether the burden has been transferred from this initial impact point to other taxpayers. In fact, as is observed in Chapter 11, numerous empirical studies have yielded inconclusive results concerning the latter point.

First, it will be assumed that the "distributional impact" of the federal corporation income tax is coincident with the ultimate "distributional incidence" of the tax. That is, it is assumed that the owners of the corporation are unable to transfer the burden of the tax to other individuals or, in other words, the tax remains *unshifted*. In this instance, a federal VAT would generally be considered superior to a federal CIT, on *allocational* grounds, since its broadbased nature would tend to minimize "nonneutral effects" as contrasted to the performance

---

[31] Chapter 8 develops the subject of "tax shifting" in greater detail. Also, it should be noted in the continuing discussion of the present chapter that tax shifting may be "partial"—thus yielding results which are *intermediate* between the extremes of "complete" shifting and "no" shifting of the corporation income tax burden.

of the much more distortive CIT.[32] A VAT of the consumption variety would impose an idential tax rate on all economic goods, thus not interferring with the relative price relationships between different economic goods. On the other hand, the corporation income tax exerts numerous nonneutral effects including the preferential treatment of equity versus debt financing, corporate versus noncorporate business structure [with subsequent discrimination between products], and capital versus noncapital resources. Nonetheless, the VAT would introduce a new nonneutrality of its own, namely, a preferential treatment of "retained corporate profits" since these profits would be subject to federal income taxation *only* if distributed. If distributed, they would become subject to the federal personal income tax. This nonneutrality, on the other hand, could be mitigated by either an integration of the personal and corporation income taxes or by the more rigorous taxing of capital gains under the personal income tax.

Unlike the above "allocational" analysis which favors value-added taxation, an unshifted CIT may be seen to distinctly out-perform the VAT when the *distributional equity* benchmark of "ability to pay" is brought into consideration. The distributional impact of a federal (consumption-type) VAT would be similar to that of the general retail sales tax. That is, it would be "regressive" against lower-income taxpayers since the tax is a broadbased consumption tax which requires greater tax payments as a proportion of income from lower-income taxpayers, with their higher consumption propensities, than it does from higher-income taxpayers. The progressively-rated federal corporation income tax, on the other hand, would largely avoid these negative distributional effects.

The comparative *aggregate economic effects* of a value-added tax and an "unshifted" corporation income tax are less definitive than are the "allocational" and "distributional" effects. Yet, it would appear, in general, that the CIT would perform better as an *automatic fiscal stabilizer* than the VAT due to its relatively greater income elasticity (Ye). On the other hand, the VAT should be less restrictive on those saving and investment decisions necessary to the *economic growth process* than the CIT. The two taxes appear about equal in their *discretionary stabilization policy* performances. Either tax could be made the focus of tax base and tax rate changes directed toward employment and price level goals. Furthermore, their respective influences on *international balance of payments* performance would appear to be about the same,

---

[32] However, it still must be remembered (see Chapter 6) that "neutrality" is necessarily preferable to "nonneutrality" only under the strict assumption that the existing pretax equilibrium is "allocationally optimal." Otherwise, a nonneutral effect may be either "positive" or "negative" in its effects on allocational efficiency.

though negligible, in each case. For example, an unshifted federal corporation income would *not* tend to increase the prices of those consumption goods subject to export. However, a federal VAT, which *would* increase such prices domestically, could be rebated from exports via a *border tax adjustment* (BTA). Thus, export prices should remain the same in either case.

The Economic Effects of a "Shifted" Corporation Income Tax versus a Value-Added Tax

Next, it will be assumed for purposes of analysis that the corporation income tax is *fully shifted* forward to consumers in the form of higher selling prices. In this event, certain comparative economic effects between the two taxes differ from those described above under the assumption that the corporation income tax is "unshifted." For example, the full shifting of the corporation income tax lessens the degree of *allocational nonneutrality*. However, one important segment of nonneutrality would still remain, namely, the bias against the products of corporate versus noncorporate businesses since the former would bear relatively higher prices as the "shifted" corporation tax finds its way into product prices. However, *distributional nonneutrality* would change to an even greater degree than would allocation under a shifted corporation income tax since full shifting of the tax would increase the prices of consumer goods in a matter similar to that which would occur under the broadbased value-added tax. The VAT, of course, is regressive in "ability-to-pay principle" terms and so would be a fully shifted corporation income tax.

The comparative *aggregate economic effects* would remain essentially unchanged for *stabilization* policy, both automatic and discretionary, regardless of the shifting or not of the CIT. The comparative *economic growth* advantage, on the other hand, would likely remain with the VAT, but to a much lesser extent since a "shifted" corporation income tax burden would certainly not bear the same negative saving and investment influence on business decision-making as would an "unshifted" corporate income tax. Finally, while an unshifted CIT, and a VAT with a "border tax adjustment" deleting the tax from exports, would yield an equally impassive effect on the balance of international payments, the results would vary sharply if one assumes that the corporation income tax is shifted. In this case, the VAT becomes the superior instrument since the higher "domestic" prices which it causes can be taken off a good at the border, when "exported," via a border tax adjustment, while a similar adjustment is not compatible with the CIT.

Intergoal Conflict

The above discussion appraises the comparative economic effects of the federal corporation income tax and a value-added tax under the polar assumptions of either the *nonshifting* or the *full shifting* of the corporation income tax. However, the results may be "intermediate" since *partial shifting* of the CIT is not only possible, but likely, thus adding additional complexity to the analysis. Moreover, still further complications enter the analysis when the *conflict between economic goals* is considered. For example, an effort to reduce the *regressivity* of the VAT through the exemption of items such as food and medicine, among other things, from the base of the tax would interfere with the *allocational neutrality* of the tax by changing the relative prices of various economic goods. McLure points out that the tax base for a federal value-added tax applied at uniform rates to all economic goods in 1970, with no exemptions, would have been $615.8 billion.[33] Yet, various exemptions for such consumptive items as food, medicine, medical expenses, housing, electricity, and the like would reduce this tax base by more than one half—thus largely removing the "allocational neutrality" merits of the tax.[34] However, a more *comprehensive* alteration of the federal fiscal structure could employ the interrelated "negative income tax" and "income tax credit" technique,[35] instead of "exemptions," to reduce the regressivity of the VAT and thus preserve many of the "allocational neutrality" advantages of the tax. Whether such alternatives would be more likely to be incorporated into the federal fiscal structure than exemptions is open to question.

In conclusion, it should be observed that the proposal to substitute a federal value-added tax for part, or all, of the presently-existing federal corporation income tax has many important ramifications. Clearly, an introduction of the VAT by the federal government in the United States would not be comparable to the recent adoptions of the tax in Europe. There it has largely been a matter of the national governments substituting one *national* broadbased sales tax, the value-added tax, for another broadbased sales tax, the turnover tax. By contrast, its adoption by the federal government in the United States would involve the imposition of a *national* broadbased sales tax of the "value-added" variety on top of the already-existing broadbased "general retail sales taxes" of *subnational* state and local governments. The distributional equity implications of such "expanded regressivity" are significant. Yet, attempts to mitigate this regressivity through exemptions would reduce

---

[33] McLure, "Tax on Value Added," p. 26.

[34] Ibid., pp. 26–32.

[35] See Chapter 21.

the primary advantage of the VAT—its allocational neutrality. In retrospect, it is suggested that the proposed replacement of the federal value-added tax must be tested within the framework of the overall economic goals of American society. Moreover, additional research and analysis is desirable before such an important societal judgment is rendered.

A VARIETY OF OTHER TAXES

Severance Taxes

More than half the states (28) impose severance taxes. A *severance* tax, which is a form of sales tax, my be defined as a special gross receipts or gross production tax imposed upon removal from land or water of natural resources including oil, gas, other minerals, coal, timber, and fish. Severance taxes imposed on timber-cutting operations are usually ad valorem "gross receipts" taxes based on the stumpage value of the cut timber, such as 12 percent of the monetary value of the timber. Also, some of the state severance taxes on other natural resources are gross receipts taxes. Most state severance taxes, however, are "gross production" taxes which impose *specific* rates such as 1 cent per ton of coal, or 5 cents per barrel of oil, multiplied by the gross number of resource units extracted from the land or water.

In a sense, severance taxes are a "rationing" device which ideally would help establish an optimal societal "rate of use" of the resource in question. Yet, as contrasted to rationing the "short-run" use of a capital resource to avoid congestion and overuse, they instead are a "long-run" rationing device to discourage reckless exploitation of land and water resources. They have been levied, at times, in lieu of property taxes which have a built-in tendency to encourage natural resource usage.[36] Although severance taxes as replacements for property taxes could involve a short-run revenue loss, they may well also cause a long-run revenue gain by helping to conserve natural resources for economically rational long-term usage. Moreover, it should be noted that severance taxes offer a high potential for *exportability* to the residents of other political jurisdictions in a decentralized public sector since they occur at an early stage of the productive process.[37]

Under certain conditions, severance taxes, if unevenly applied

---

[36] For example, the "actual cutting" of timber would lower the assessed value of land under a *property tax*, thus reducing property tax liability, while there would, in fact, not even be a *severance tax* liability if the timber is not cut. Hence, the owner of the property would be more likely to "cut" the timber in order to reduce a property tax liability, but to leave it "uncut" to avoid a severance tax liability.

[37] See Chapter 19.

among several states and among several types of substitutable resources, could yield undesirable allocation and distribution nonneutralities. For example, a severance tax levied on copper ore, but not upon bauxite which is the source of aluminum and a competitor of copper for many residential and industrial uses, would cause an allocational distortion as some users would substitute aluminum for copper because of the tax-induced price differentials. Moreover, the owners of copper mines would bear an aftertax income distribution bias as compared to the owners of bauxite property.

The "overall" revenue importance of severance taxes to the states is modest. In fiscal 1972, for example, the total collection of severance taxes by the states amounted to $758 million, or 1.3 percent of total state tax revenues. However, in some states severance taxes are an important source of tax revenue. These included Texas, Louisiana, Oklahoma, and New Mexico, which together collected $666 million of the $758 million total severance tax revenues collected by all 28 states using the tax in 1972.

Capital Stock Taxes

Some states impose *capital stock* taxes—a business tax uniquely applicable to only the corporate form of ownership. Essentially, the tax serves as a franchise or privilege tax for the right to do business as a corporation and, in this regard, is somewhat like an excise tax on the acquisition of this privilege except, of course, the privilege is acquired from government and not from the private sector. It was originally intended, however, in many instances, to serve as a property tax on intangible personal property in the form of corporation stocks. The tax may be imposed on a base consisting of either (1) the par value of "authorized" capital stock, (2) the market value or the par value of capital stock" actually issued," (3) the "number of shares," either authorized or issued, of no par stock, or (4) the "real" physical capital used by the corporation in the state. At times, capital stock is taxed under a "franchise," "privilege," "license," or "occupational" tax or fee.

The capital stock tax tends to violate the principles of distributive equity. The par value of capital stock, for example, does little to indicate the genuine "taxpaying ability" of a corporation and its stockholders. Par value of stock may be vastly different from market value. Bonds, moreover, may be an important part of the financial structure of a corporation. Yet, they are not ordinarily considered when the capital stock tax base is computed. In addition, capital stock taxes do not fit a precise quid pro quo relationship as required by the benefit principle of equity. The tax may be reasonably adequate, however, if it is levied at low rates and considered as an excise tax on the privilege of doing business as a corporation. The revenue productivity of capital stock taxes is quite modest.

The Lump-Sum Tax

The *lump-sum* (head, capitation) tax represents a separate form of taxation, that is, it is a tax on neither income, wealth, nor transactions. Instead, it is a tax imposed upon *a person as a person,* not upon his income, his property, nor his purchases. However, since it is a rare tax in actual usage, with insignificant revenue importance, it will not receive "separate chapter treatment" in this book as do the other basic forms of taxation.

Usage of the lump-sum tax dates back to ancient Greece and Rome and to medieval England. It was transplanted to the American colonies during the seventeenth century. The tax involves the payment of a "set" or "fixed" amount of money to the government. In other words, each taxpayer pays the same amount of tax. At times, it has been related to the privilege of voting within the political jurisdiction levying the tax. This variation of the lump-sum tax is known as a *poll* tax. The Twenty-Fourth Amendment to the Constitution outlawed use of the poll tax as a prerequisite to voting in federal elections. During 1966, the U.S. Supreme Court declared the state poll taxes of Virginia, Mississippi, Alabama, and Texas unconstitutional as a prerequisite to voting in any election—federal, state, or local. This action discourages the use of state poll taxes which were used by nine states during 1965. Poll taxes also have been used by some local governments in the United States. The poll tax, when used, is ordinarily limited to adults, but various exemptions from the tax apply for such disabilities as deafness, blindness, and insanity. Poll tax rates tend to be very low—generally ranging from $2 to $5 per person annually.

A pure *lump-sum* tax avoids allocational nonneutralities since it exerts "no substitution effect." This is because it is not involved with any "economic activity." That is, it does not relate to the earning of *income,* nor to the accumulation of *wealth,* nor to any economic *transaction.* Instead, it is imposed only on a *person,* not on that person's "economic activity." It is the *only* tax which exerts just an "income effect," which *all taxes* exert by nature since the very payment of taxes "reduces disposable income."

However, the lump-sum tax seriously violates the ability-to-pay principle of equity in the distribution of tax burdens. The tax, which is imposed as a flat fee per person, is *extremely regressive* if income differences are used as the indicator of the "ability to pay" taxes. An individual with a $1 million annual income, for example, would pay the same absolute amount of tax as the individual with a $1,000 annual income. It is, in fact, an example of the extreme "absolute equity" type of tax distribution criterion.[38] Moreover, there is no significant quid pro quo relationship of a cost-benefit nature to justify the tax under the benefit principle of tax equity.

---

[38] See Chapter 7.

15

The Financing of Quasi-Public Goods: Earmarked Taxes, User Prices, and Administrative Revenues

ALTERNATIVE TECHNIQUES FOR THE FINANCING OF QUASI-PUBLIC GOODS

It was observed in Part One of this book that few, if any, economic goods are "polar" in the sense of being pure private or pure public goods. Instead, the vast majority of goods are "mixed" between traits of the "market" and "public" sectors. This does not suggest, of course, that a given economic good may not be primarily "private" or "public" in nature. Thus, an economic good characterized largely by such a trait as the nonjoint (divisible) consumption of benefits under the application of the exclusion principle may be termed a *quasi-private* good. On the other hand, a good which is consumed largely under conditions of "large group" joint consumption may be termed a *quasi-public* good. Or the phenomenon of decreasing production costs at the relevant output scales of an important economic good may add "publicness" to its nature. Yet the application of the exclusion principle may, to some degree, be feasible with these goods. Though an a priori case for significant public sector allocational influence cannot be made for *all* quasi-public goods which possess such characteristics, it nonetheless can be said that the case for governmental allocational influence is strengthened by the presence of these conditions.[1]

The exclusion principle, of course, can be applied more readily to the benefits of some quasi-public goods than to those of others. More-

---

[1] See Part One.

over, government may, for "revenue" or "sumptuary" reasons, intervene in the allocation of economic goods totally subject to the exclusion principle. This chapter will consider essentially the influence of the public sector on the allocation of those quasi-public goods which are reasonably conducive either to the application of, or to some proxy for the application of, the exclusion principle. The primary techniques for financing such goods, unless they are financed from general tax revenues or from debt creation, are *earmarked taxes* and *user pricing* and, to a lesser extent, *administrative revenues.*

An *earmarked tax* may be imposed on the production and/or sale of an economic good. Under this "proxy-type" arrangement for the exclusion principle, the tax revenues are placed in a "separate" budget account which is set apart from the general revenue fund of the governmental unit imposing the earmarked tax. Such a special budget account is generally known as a *trust fund.* The tax is normally tied to a particular type of productive or consumptive expenditure which, according to the benefit principle of taxation, correlates in some meaningful quid pro quo fashion with the payment of the tax. The federal gasoline tax, for example, goes into a special trust fund to help finance the interstate highway system. Broadbased taxes such as a personal income tax or a general retail sales tax, by comparison, are not conducive to "earmarking" since they do not relate closely to any particular governmental function or expenditure. On the other hand, narrowbased taxes such as a selective sales (excise) tax may sometimes be associated with a particular functional type of economic activity. In general, an earmarked tax may be described as an excise tax whose revenues go into a separate trust fund for specific expenditure purposes which are related meaningfully to the nature of the tax. Moreover, it is possible to control the supply of a quasi-public "bad" through an earmarked tax. Thus, a special excise tax on "leaded gasoline" could be "earmarked" for a special fund to finance the alleviation of air pollution.

The *user price (user charge, commercial)* technique for the financing of quasi-public goods (resources) involves the sale of the good (resource) by the public sector in a manner analogous to the market. That is, the good (or resource) is priced and, thus, is not available to the user unless he voluntarily pays for it. Yet, the question may be asked: Why should the public sector become involved significantly in the allocation of these goods in a market-oriented society if the market can allocate the good through the price mechanism? The answer may be that such goods are characterized by elements of joint consumption or by the presence of important externalities which escape the pricing mechanism and thus lead to an undersupply of the good. The "publicness" of these conditions, of course, is greatly accentuated if the relevant interaction group is large. The benefits of university education, which are jointly but not equally consumed by all members of the society, exemplify such a good. Moreover, user prices may help to reflect the desired level of demand for the goods including long-run capacity requirements. In any event, the allocation of a quasi-public good under the user pricing technique by government is indicative of a collective consensus that it is in the "public interest" for the public sector to directly allocate the good. Broadly speaking, this public interest could even include the "revenue productivity" of the good as a source of governmental funds or its use as a "regulatory" device to discourage the consumption of certain economic products. For example, the consumption of a quasi-public bad such as river pollution may be reduced by the application of a "user charge" for the right to dump effluents into the water. Hence, the user price technique—just as an earmarked tax—may be designed either to increase the supply of an economic good or to reduce the supply of an economic bad.[2]

Those economic goods which are by-products of the general administrative functions of government are frequently financed through *administrative revenues.* In a broad sense, the buyer often has a free choice concerning payment of the various types of administrative revenues to government. Hence, the exclusion principle generally applies. However, there is usually not a direct or close correlation between the payment of an administrative revenue and the receipt of a specific economic good by the purchaser. Admittedly, governmental units collecting such revenues sometimes attempt to tie the revenues to a functional category of expenditure. This relationship, however, is often obscure. As a result, administrative revenues should not be confused with the more precise quid pro quo relationships which ordinarily exist in the case of both earmarked taxes and user prices. Examples of administrative revenues include licenses, permits, (some) fees, fines, forfeitures, escheats and special assessments.

The governmental unit allocating an economic good must determine whether general taxes, debt financing, earmarked taxes, user prices or administrative revenues, or some combination of these financing techniques, will pay for the good. Since broadbased taxes such as the personal income, general sales, and property taxes are most appropriate in financing those *public goods* for which considerable difficulty arises in applying the exclusion principle, they will not be considered as relevant alternatives in the present discussion. Debt, moreover, will also be excluded from this discussion since it is discussed in Chapter 27. Thus, *earmarked taxes, user prices,* and *administrative revenues*—all of which are capable, at least to some extent, of utilizing or approximating

---

[2] See Chapter 3.

the exclusion principle when used as financing techniques—will be emphasized in the remainder of this chapter.

EARMARKED TAXES AND TRUST FUNDS

Federal Social Security Programs

The federal social security programs comprise the primary usage of the trust fund allocation technique in the American public sector. The Social Security Act, enacted by Congress during the depression year 1935, became effective in 1937. The initial legislation provided for old-age and survivors insurance, certain welfare payments, and unemployment compensation benefits. Later, provisions for disability benefits were added in 1956 and for medical care for the aged and needy in 1966. These programs are financed by earmarked federal *payroll* (*employment*) taxes of an excise variety. The same technique is used to support a separate social security program for railroad employees. The various federal social security programs under the Social Security Act are described below.

The Old-Age, Survivors, Disability, and Health Insurance Program (OASDHI). The earmarked payroll taxes collected under this program feed three separate trust funds, namely, the old-age and survivors insurance, the disability insurance, and the health insurance trust funds. During fiscal 1972, these three trust funds received $52.2 billion of the $73.2 billion in receipts collected for all federal trust funds. Amounts equivalent to collections of OASDHI taxes are appropriated to these trust accounts and, subsequently, are invested in securities of the federal government. Both employers and employees pay the taxes, which are levied upon a tax base consisting of wage or salary earnings up to a certain maximum. In addition, self-employed persons have been eligible since 1951 to pay taxes under a different formula to obtain coverage by the program. The original legislation had exempted from coverage various categories of employment such as agricultural labor, domestic service in private homes, casual labor, services performed for religious, charitable, scientific, literary, and educational organizations, and services performed for the United States, a state, or its political subdivisions. Many of these exemptions, however, have since been eliminated. Some exceptions are federal civilian employees, who have their own substitute program, self-employed persons whose annual income from self-employment is less than a certain amount, and domestic and farm workers when they earn less than a specified amount from a single employer.

Old-age and survivors insurance in some ways resembles a private insurance system, but it differs in several important respects including the fact that its "premiums" are really "taxes," that is, they are *compulsory* and not voluntary. The compulsory premiums (payroll taxes) are calculated on a very rough actuarial basis and reserves are accumulated to strengthen the trust fund and to assure payments when the claims of policyholders are due. A private insurance company being run on strict actuarially computed principles, however, would have to charge thousands of dollars annually for such benefits and privileges. Hence, the comparison between social and private insurance on an actuarial basis is somewhat loose. However, the program is in close accord with certain other private insurance principles. For example, only "insured" or "covered" workers (whose pay has been taxed) are eligible to receive benefits. The benefits, moreover, belong to the workers by right. No embarrassing proof of poverty or need is required. Furthermore, the programs are operated as separate financial operations with earmarked taxes (analogous here to premiums) going into special trust funds to help provide the benefits. It must be acknowledged, nonetheless, that the scale of benefit payments is not strictly proportional to the size of the tax payments. Relatedly, present beneficiaries as a group are receiving benefits much larger than their payroll tax contributions would entitle them since an effort is made to keep the benefits consistent with rising "prices" and "wages" in the economy over a period of time. In fact, benefits now rise automatically whenever the annual rate of inflation exceeds a specified percentage in the Consumer Price Index.

Benefits are payable to individuals who have worked a sufficient number of quarters to be covered by the program and to their dependents and survivors. Monthly old-age insurance benefits are payable to a retired worker covered by the program, beginning at age 62. Benefits are also payable to the wife of a retired worker if she is either 62 or has a child in her care who is entitled to child's benefits. Child's benefits are payable to a retired worker's unmarried children under the age of 18 or, regardless of age, to any of his children who become permanently and totally disabled before the age of 18. Benefits, moreover, are payable to a dependent husband who has reached the age of 62.

The old-age insurance benefit is based on the monthly average earnings of the insured worker, the benefit for each amount of average monthly earnings being stated in the law. The average monthly earnings are calculated by adding the worker's total earnings in "covered" employment over the number of years specified in the law (generally, the years between 1951 and the age of 65, or 62 for women) and dividing by the total number of months in those years. However, the five years in which earnings are lowest and periods of disability are excluded from the average monthly earnings calculation. Benefits for dependents and survivors are based on a percentage of the benefit payable to the insured worker.

Full survivor benefits are payable to the widow of an insured worker if she has reached the age of 62 (reduced benefits are payable at age 60), or has a child in her care who is entitled to benefits. In addition, survivor benefits are payable to unmarried children of such a worker under 18, unless the unmarried child is a student in a college or trade school, in which case benefits are payable until age 22 is reached. Moreover, unmarried children of such a worker, if over 18, may receive benefits if he or she becomes disabled before age 18. Benefits are payable also to a dependent parent aged 62 or more, and to a dependent widower aged 62 or more. In addition, a lump-sum benefit equal to three times the worker's monthly benefit amount, but not to exceed a specified amount, is payable on the death of an insured worker.

As of January 1, 1973, the average monthly retirement benefit for a worker was $180 with the range varying between a minimum possible benefit of $84 per month to a maximum possibility of $250. For a worker with spouse retiring at age 65, the average benefit per month was $271 with a range of possible monthly benefits between $126 and $375. In terms of survivors insurance, the average monthly payment to a widow with two children was $308.

Disability insurance benefits are payable to a worker under age 65 who is unable to engage in any substantial gainful work because of a disability that can be expected to last for a long and indefinite period of time, or that can be expected to result in death. The dependents of a disabled worker may receive benefits under the same conditions that the dependents of retired workers receive them. Disability payments are made until an individual recovers and can return to work, or until age 65 when retirement benefits would begin.

In 1965, Congress amended the Social Security Act to provide for a *health insurance trust fund.* This encompasses the medicare and medicaid programs. "Medicare" provides for the aged, regardless of income, a hospital insurance plan as well as an optional supplementary insurance plan, at low rates, covering doctors' fees. The monthly premium in the voluntary insurance plan is matched by the federal government. Most of the nation's aged have subscribed to this voluntary insurance plan. Certification by a physician is required before benefits will be paid. Hospitals and doctors are free to select their own collection agencies. The program, moreover, remains individualistic in the sense that the doctor may charge more than the fee which the "reasonable customary charge" schedule provided by the government lists for the service. The doctor's fee is negotiated between the doctor and his patient, as previously was the case. In addition, the patient may go to any doctor he chooses.

"Medicaid" is set up within the framework of the federal-state public assistance programs.[3] It offers federal revenues to the states amounting to a portion of the cost of providing an approved program for medical assistance to specified needy persons. Moreover, no maximum spending limitation is imposed on a state's outlay for such a program. In order to qualify for the federal aid, a state is required to establish a new medical assistance program to replace and liberalize the coverage under previous public assistance programs.

The employer and the employee pay identical *payroll tax* rates to finance the various old-age, survivors, disability, and health insurance benefits.[4] As of 1974, the employer and the employee each pay a proportional (flat) rate of 5.85 percent on a tax base consisting of the first $13,200 of taxed wages and salaries. Thus, the combined employer-employee tax rate is 11.7 percent. Moreover, present law allows for the tax base to be automatically adjusted as price levels change. The tax rate for self-employed persons covered by the programs is somewhat greater than either the employer or employee tax above, but less than the combination of the two. There is, of course, no matching contribution from an employer in the case of self-employed persons. Payroll tax rate increases are scheduled well into the future. Table 15–1 presents a summary of the OASDHI tax rates dating from the first rates in 1937 to those scheduled up to 1997. In general, it reflects the sharp increases in tax rates and the expansion of the maximum taxable base during recent years. Moreover, the social security payroll tax for support of the OASDHI programs performs poorly in relationship to the principles of equity in the distribution of tax burdens—a point which will be discussed further at a later point in this chapter.

Federal-State Public Assistance Programs. In addition to the OASDHI program, the Social Security Act provides for grants-in-aid from the federal government to the states to support the needy aged, blind, widowed and orphaned, and the physically and mentally handicapped who are unable to contribute to their own support.[5] This assistance is "direct relief." It is based upon *need.* These programs are administered by the states, but the federal government contributes to the expenses incurred in the programs as long as certain minimum standards set by the Social Security Administration are met. At the present time, more than 50 percent of the funds used for these joint federal-state programs are provided by the federal government. States with low per capita

---

[3] Federal-State assistance programs are described below.

[4] Although, technically speaking, OASDHI consists of three separate payroll taxes, since these taxes are collected simultaneously under one combined rate, they will be referred to in the present discussion as a singular tax.

[5] As noted above, medicaid is also set up within the framework of the federal-state public assistance programs.

TABLE 15-1
Federal Old-Age, Survivors, Disability, and Health Insurance Tax Rates, 1937–1997*

	(1)	(2)	(3)	(4)	(5)
			Combined OASDHI Tax Rate (percent)		
Year	Maximum Taxable Base	Employer or Employee Alone	Combined Employer- Employee	Self- Employed Person	Maximum Combined Employer- Employee Payment (Col. 1 X Col. 3)
1937–49	$ 3,000	1.0	2.0	†	$ 60
1950...................	3,000	1.5	3.0	†	90
1951–53	3,600	1.5	3.0	2.25	108
1954...................	3,600	2.0	4.0	3.0	144
1955–56	4,200	2.0	4.0	3.0	168
1957–58	4,200	2.25	4.5	3.375	189
1959...................	4,800	2.5	5.0	3.75	240
1960–61	4,800	3.0	6.0	4.5	288
1962...................	4,800	3.125	6.25	4.7	300
1963–65	4,800	3.625	7.25	5.4	348
1966...................	6,600	4.2	8.4	6.15	554
1967...................	6,600	4.4	8.8	6.4	580
1968...................	7,800	4.4	8.8	6.4	686
1969–70	7,800	4.8	9.6	6.9	748
1971...................	7,800	5.2	10.4	7.5	811
1972...................	9,000	5.2	10.4	7.5	936
1973...................	10,800	5.85	11.7	8.0	1,263
1974...................	13,200	5.85	11.7	7.9	1,544
1975–77	‡	5.85	11.7	7.9	—
1978–80	‡	6.05	12.1	8.1	—
1981–85	‡	6.30	12.6	8.35	—
1986–97	‡	6.45	12.9	8.5	—

* Disability insurance included for 1956 and thereafter; health insurance included for 1966 and thereafter.
† Not covered until January 1, 1951.
‡ Maximum taxable base will vary depending upon automatic cost-of-living adjustments.
Source: Department of Health, Education, and Welfare.

income receive relatively larger proportions of federal assistance than do high per capita income states. The public assistance component of the federal social security system has declined in relative importance as the OASDHI coverage has been extended.

The public assistance component of the Social Security Act includes federal grants to state health and welfare agencies for the support of services rendered to mothers and children. These services include maternal and child health services, services for crippled children, and child welfare services. Such programs are state administered and require state funds to match the federal grants. In 1970, Congress considered, but did not adopt, an entirely different approach to the various public assistance programs described in this section. The new approach would have entailed the "guaranteed annual income" concept as implemented through a version of the *negative income tax.*[6]

In addition to the federal social security programs, various other social welfare services are provided by state and local governments independently of federal support. These include the state-sponsored workmen's compensation programs, used in all states, which provide medical services and cash benefits to a worker injured in connection with his job. More than three fourths of all nonagricultural employees are covered by such laws. The essence of most of the state workmen's compensation laws is that the employer is responsible for injuries resulting from any accident "arising out of or in the course of employment," and thus for insuring workers in the event that such injuries occur. The quality (coverage) of the programs, however, varies greatly between the states. Many of the programs are inadequate in terms of their coverage, the length of the benefit period, and the amount of benefits. It would appear that an indirect gain derived from the existence of such legislation is the encouragement of plant safety.

Unemployment Compensation Program.   The Social Security Act of 1935 also established an unemployment compensation program. This program, just as the public assistance programs, involves a combination of federal and state fiscal action. The initial legislation motivated state governments to cooperate in the program by placing a federal excise tax on employers, and by stipulating that if a state unemployment insurance law and administration meets certain requirements, the federal government will pay 100 percent of the administrative expenses and will permit employers to *credit* state excise taxes against the major portion (90 percent) of the federal taxes. Thus, for every dollar of federal tax, the existence of a state unemployment excise would reduce the dollar of federal tax liability for the employer to 10 cents via the *tax credit* technique. Within a short time, all states passed unemployment compensation laws providing for state excise taxes on payrolls. Though all states participate in the program, considerable differentiation exists among the programs of the 50 states. States may determine such basic features of their programs as coverage, benefits, the rate of the state tax, eligibility, and disqualification provisions.

The Social Security Act of 1935 imposed a federal excise tax of 1 percent on the payrolls of employers of eight or more workers in covered employment for the financing of the unemployment insurance program. Beginning in 1939, the tax was applied only to the first $3,000 of each covered employee's annual earnings. The federal tax rate was raised to 3 percent in 1938 and remained at that level until 1961. In 1961, the tax was increased to 3.1 percent and in 1970 to 3.2 percent.

---

[6] The negative income tax is discussed in greater detail in Chapter 21 as a "poverty alleviation" device.

Moreover, the 1970 legislation increased the tax base to $4,200 of wages, effective in 1972. The additional tax rate, which is earmarked for the federal share of the tax, is to assist in meeting the increasing administrative costs of the program and to provide additional money for the "loan fund." The latter supports advances made to states whose unemployment reserves become depleted. Credits for state taxes paid by employers continue to be computed on the basis of a 3 percent federal tax. Thus, 90 percent of the 3 percent federal rate—a rate of 2.7 percent—may be credited against state taxes paid by employers. Though no federal tax is levied on employees, three states impose unemployment compensation payroll taxes on employees. The employer must have four or more employees on at least one day in each of 20 weeks in the calendar year in order to be liable for the federal tax. All states use *experience-rating systems* to determine the degree of "unemployment risk" of particular employers. Some "low risk" employers thus pay taxes of less than 2.7 percent of their federally covered payrolls to the states, though they still retain the full 2.7 percent credit against the federal tax.

Taxes collected by the states are deposited in a separate unemployment trust fund. The individual states have their own accounts in the fund against which they draw as required for the payment of unemployment benefits. The weekly system of benefit payments is geared to pay about 50 percent of gross wages up to a fixed maximum. This results in benefits which are usually higher than 50 percent of take-home pay, especially in the case of beneficiaries without dependents. Most wage earners are covered by the unemployment insurance program. In fact, some 60 million Americans are covered under some form of government-sponsored unemployment compensation program—with 89 percent of these being covered under the state-sponsored programs described above. In addition to the long-established unemployment compensation programs, emergency legislation was passed by Congress in 1958, and again in 1961, to finance temporary unemployment compensation payments to individuals who had exhausted their benefit rights under regular state programs.

In all, it should be observed that federal payroll (employment) taxes, inclusive of both the OASDHI and unemployment taxes, comprise approximately 25 percent of all federal government revenues. Indeed, their magnitude suggests potential significant influence on the allocational, distributional, and aggregate economic performance of the economy.

Interstate Highway and Other Trust Funds

Though the federal government has been continually assisting the states in highway development since 1916, a marked policy change occurred with the passage of the interstate highway legislation of 1956. This legislation not only provided for the long-term development of a 42,500 mile interstate highway system, but also changed the philosophy of federal highway financing. Previously, federal assistance to the states had been derived from general tax funds. Federal gasoline tax revenues went to the general treasury just as was true of any other nonearmarked tax. The legislation of 1956, however, changed this basic philosophy and *earmarked* various highway user tax revenues, including those of the federal gasoline tax, for a special Highway Trust Fund which would be used to finance highway construction. Specific excise taxes on gasoline, tires, trucks, and other economic goods closely connected to highway use thus became the revenue sources for the separate federal highway trust account. The trust fund provides 90 percent of the costs of interstate highway construction, the remaining 10 percent being contributed by the states. Legislation enacted by Congress during 1973 "opened" a limited portion of the highway trust fund revenues for use in the development of urban mass transit systems.

In all, the federal government has more than 100 special trust or deposit funds. Some of the more important ones, which will not be discussed specifically in this book, are the Railroad Retirement Trust Fund, the Federal Employees' Retirement Funds, the National Service Life Insurance and Government Life Insurance Fund, and the Federal Deposit Insurance Trust Fund. In addition, state and local governments use the trust fund technique to finance some quasi-public goods. The participation of state governments in the unemployment compensation program under federal social security, as discussed above, is representative of their participation in this technique. Moreover, state and local governments participate in various other earmarked financing programs such as those for workmen's compensation and retirement. The magnitude of those state-local government earmarked revenues of an insurance nature, including unemployment compensation, approached $12 billion in Fiscal 1971. The state highway user tax trust accounts would add significantly to this total.

Economic Analysis of Earmarked Taxes and Trust Funds

Allocational Effects. Economists disagree concerning the economic efficiency results of earmarked taxes. Margolis and Heller, in separate papers, suggest that earmarking tends to reduce the willingness of taxpayers to approve expenditures on specific public services.[7] On the other hand, Rolph and Break, Burkhead, and the Tax Foundation sug-

---

[7] Julius Margolis, "Metropolitan Finance Problems: Territories, Functions, and Growth," in *Public Finances: Needs, Sources, and Utilization* (New York: National Bureau of Economic Research, 1961), pp. 261–66; Walter Heller, "CED's Stabilizing Budget Policy after Ten Years," *American Economic Review*, September, 1957, pp. 634–51.

gest earmarking as a device to generate taxpayer support for expansion of certain governmental services.[8]

Buchanan, in a study on the economics of earmarked taxes, reaches two conclusions.[9]

1. Earmarking may increase allocational efficiency by insuring more rational individual choice since, with earmarking, the individual can appraise more closely the relevant costs and benefits of a particular project. The individual is thus able to adjust the amount consumed of each quasi-public good in order to attain his most preferred consumption position. This is not true in general fund financing which is similar to a "joint-product sale" in the sense that to get one commodity the consumer must also purchase another. The individual consumer of quasi-public goods, in the latter case, is subject to an allocational distortion since his independence of choice is reduced.

2. General fund financing will tend to attract a greater supply of publically-supplied economic goods with "elastic" demands than will earmarked financing. A bachelor, for example, is likely to vote against funds which are earmarked *only for education* (thus an "elastic" demand for education by the bachelor), but is more likely to vote for a *bundle of additional goods* to be financed from a general fund which happens to include education. Thus, when "general fund financing" is used, society receives a greater proportion of those economic goods with highly elastic demands since they are tied in with the acquisition of other goods, and it receives a smaller proportion of those goods which possess less elastic demands.

Moreover, it is sometimes argued that the federal social security program should be financed from "general" instead of "earmarked" taxes since a negative allocational nonneutrality can result from an excise tax on wages alone, but not on capital. It is claimed, for example, that payroll taxes, by increasing the cost of hiring new employees, encourage the substitution of capital for labor since capital is not subject to the payroll tax. Therefore, it is argued that labor will be forced into "noncovered" employment while capital is drawn to employment "covered" under social security. It is thus concluded that an important allocational nonneutrality takes place.

Distributional Effects.   The performance of the earmarked federal payroll taxes are largely inadequate in terms of the established principles of "distributional equity" and, especially, in relationship to the *ability-to-pay principle.* The proportionally-rated OASDHI tax, for example, is distinctively *regressive* when "income" is used as the indicator

---

[8] Earl Rolph and George Break, *Public Finance* (New York: The Ronald Press Co., 1961), p. 62; Jesse Burkhead, *Government Budgeting* (New York: John Wiley & Sons, Inc., 1956), p. 469; Tax Foundation, *Earmarked State Taxes* (New York, 1955).

[9] James M. Buchanan, "The Economics of Earmarked Taxes," *Journal of Political Economy,* October 1963, pp. 457–69.

of "taxpaying ability" in conjunction with the ability-to-pay principle. The OASDHI payroll tax applies only to the first \$13,200 of annual wages and salaries. Thus, a worker who earns that amount (the taxable wage ceiling) would, at the rate of 5.85 percent, pay a tax of \$772.20, the same absolute amount that would be paid by an executive with a salary of \$100,000. Yet, the "effective" tax rate, in ability-to-pay terms, would be 5.85 percent of wages for the lower-income wage earner, but less than 1 percent of the salary of the executive. If, as many experts believe, part or all of the "employer's" matching tax of 5.85 percent is shifted "backward" to the wage earner, the regressivity is further accentuated. Moreover, it should be pointed out that the OASDHI payroll tax, which exempts income (wages) *above* a maximum level (\$13,200) from the tax base, works in an exactly opposite pattern to the federal personal income tax which exempts income *below* a certain level from the base of the tax. The "regressive" effects of the former arrangement and the contrasting "progressive" effects of the latter arrangement are obvious. Furthermore, since the tax exempts nonwage (land and capital) income from the base of the tax, still greater regressivity results. This is because nonwage income tends to be concentrated among the higher-income classes. In addition, the tax discriminates against "multiworker" and in favor of "single worker" families since the former pays additional taxes for benefits which are partially redundant. Table 15–2 provides empirical evidence of the regressivity of the

TABLE 15–2
Distributional Effects of the Federal OASDHI Payroll Tax, 1969

Earnings Class (thousands of dollars)	Number of Earners (millions)	*(billions of dollars)*			Tax Rate* (percent)
		Total Earnings	Taxable Earnings	Tax	
\$15.0 and over........	3.72	\$ 92.62	\$ 33.40	\$ 2.933	3.17
12.0–15.0............	3.28	43.60	27.20	2.482	5.69
9.0–12.0............	8.82	90.35	70.79	6.565	7.27
7.8–9.0............	6.48	54.26	51.01	4.778	8.81
6.6–7.8............	6.90	49.53	49.53	4.661	9.41
4.8–6.6............	12.29	69.52	69.52	6.542	9.41
4.2–4.8............	4.77	21.41	21.41	2.015	9.41
3.6–4.2............	5.04	19.60	19.60	1.844	9.41
3.0–3.6............	5.06	16.64	16.64	1.566	9.41
Under 3.0	36.44	45.11	45.11	4.245	9.41
Total................	92.80	\$502.64	\$404.21	\$37.631	7.49

* Ratio of *tax* to *total earnings*.
Social Security Administration data.
Source: John A. Brittain, *The Payroll Tax for Social Security* (© 1972 by the Brookings Institution, Washington, D.C.), Table 4–3, p. 104.

OASDHI tax as contributed to by the "exemption above the ceiling" provision.

Efforts to alleviate the regressivity of the federal OASDHI payroll tax may take a number of different directions. For example, a *low-income exemption* could be affixed to the "employee portion" of the tax. Moreover, additional upward movements in the *taxable wage ceiling* (see Table 15–1 for recent changes upward) would reduce the regressivity of the tax, or the ceiling could be removed entirely thus allowing the imposition of significantly lower employer and employee tax rates. A more basic reform would involve a movement towards the *general tax financing* of social security benefits from the progressive federal personal income tax. This would make the financing of social security more equitable in ability-to-pay terms. The latter course of action would reflect the long-term trend away from the initial "private insurance" intent for the social security program and would recognize, instead, that its benefits primarily represent a "redistributional" program toward lower-income groups rather than a precise quid pro quo exchange of costs and benefits.[10] This important point will receive further attention in Chapter 21 which deals with the distributional problem of poverty.

Stabilization Effects. The unemployment compensation trust fund operates as an automatic fiscal stabilizer for the national economy.[11] That is, benefit payments tend to exceed payroll tax collections during recession while tax payments tend to exceed benefit payments at times of full employment. An expansionary multiplier effect is thus initiated by the unemployment compensation program during recession and a restrictive or negative multiplier is provided at times of inflationary pressure. This result occurs even without "on the spot" discretionary changes in tax rates or benefits. The magnitude of the stabilization effects resulting from the unemployment compensation program can be increased, of course, if deliberate rate or benefit changes are enacted.

THE COMMERCIAL PRINCIPLE AND USER PRICES

The Extent of Commercial Activity by American Government

Commercial revenues derive from the production and/or distribution and sale of economic goods and resources by one unit of govern-

---

[10] The schedule of benefits is designed to favor workers whose lifetime earnings are below average. However, part of this redistribution reflects a transfer from the "youthful poor" to the "elderly poor" due to the overall structure of both OASDHI taxes and benefits.

[11] This point will be discussed more thoroughly in Part Four of the book.

ment to private purchasers or to other units of government. The government enterprises providing the goods and resources apply *user prices (user charges)* to their sale. All levels of government in the United States participate in this type of activity.

At the *federal* level, the examples of commercial activity include the Postal Service, Panama Canal, Alaska Railroad, various power and reclamation projects such as the Tennessee Valley Authority and the Rural Electrification Administration, national forests and parks, various loan and insurance funds such as the Commodity Credit Corporation and the Federal Housing Administration, and the sale of surplus military goods. In 1973, outstanding direct domestic loans by federal agencies exceeded $51 billion while outstanding guaranteed and insured domestic loans totaled an additional $189 billion. During the same year, the gross expenditures of federal enterprises amounted to some $32 billion as compared to applicable receipts of $26 billion generated from these activities.

An outstanding application of the commercial principle at the *state* level is found in the operation of state universities and colleges. Tuition is the user price charged for the purchase of educational services, though typically the tuition amount only partially covers the costs of providing the education. This is especially true for "in-state" as compared to "out-of-state" students since the tuition charged to the nonresidents usually is higher than the amount charged to the residents of a state.

Another example of state commercial activity is found in the operation of toll roads. This type of public enterprise activity underwent a temporary slowdown period around 1960, after having experienced a period of rapid growth following World War II. Recently, however, interest in toll road activity has revived. Thus, some highway services in the United States are financed by "user prices" though the greater part of such services are financed by the "earmarked tax" technique. In addition, some states operate bridges and tunnels and charge prices for their use. Examples include the Golden Gate and San Francisco Bay bridges in California and the Lincoln Tunnel operated by the Port of New York Authority, the latter actually an "interstate" government compact between New York and New Jersey as approved by Congress through its jurisdiction over "interstate commerce." The Port of New York Authority, which holds nearly $2 billion in assets, was founded in 1921. Another state government usage of the commercial principle is found in the monopoly operation of liquor stores in 17 states, with one of these states following a policy of state government supervision of local government liquor monopolies. During fiscal 1971, these states collected over $1.8 billion in gross revenues from the sale of liquor and associated products in state liquor stores. Moreover, "miscellaneous state charges," some of which are user prices and not administrative revenues, amounted to nearly $10 billion during the year.

During recent years a number of American states have engaged themselves in the "sale of risk" through the establishment of *public lotteries*.[12] In effect, this constitutes a *user price* being charged by government for the voluntary purchase of a lottery ticket by an individual who hopes to win a monetary sum in excess of the ticket price. Public lotteries are used in many nations of the world to provide government revenues. In the United States, New Hampshire initiated a public lottery in 1963, followed by New York in 1967, New Jersey in 1970, and by Connecticut, Illinois, Maryland, Massachusetts, Michigan, Pennsylvania, and South Dakota since that time. Lottery revenues are "earmarked" for educational purposes in several of the states. In addition to public lotteries, *private gambling* provides revenue to many American states through such devices as the "legalized betting on horse races" accompanied by the imposition of special "parimutuel excise taxes" on the gains of successful gamblers. In particular, Nevada benefits revenue-wise from the varied legalized gambling operations which take place in that state.

Significant operation of public enterprises exists also at the *local* level of government. The two most pronounced fields of local government commercial activity are found in the provision of water and in the generation and/or distribution of electricity. Other important local government enterprises include the operation of transit and gas supply systems. During fiscal 1971, local governments derived $7.3 billion in gross revenues from utility operations and an additional $15 billion from miscellaneous licenses and other charges, some of which are classifiable as user prices. In some instances, local governments operate toll bridges and tunnels.

It is evident from the above discussion that commercial charges in the form of *user prices* are an important revenue source to the public sector. Moreover, *nontax revenues in general* are expanding in both absolute and relative importance at all levels of government. Hence, the critical question once again arises: what economic justification exists for governmental production and/or sale of those economic goods and resources whose benefits are at least partially subject to the *exclusion principle* in a society orientated toward private sector economic activity? This important question shall be considered in detail on the following pages.

---

[12] For a discussion of state government lotteries, see: Frederick D. Stocker, "State Sponsored Gambling as a Source of Public Revenue," *National Tax Journal*, September 1972, pp. 437–41.

Fiscal Rationality and Government Commercial Activity

The Choice Between Private and Public Provision (Allocation) of Quasi-Public Goods.[13]   A unit of government may undertake commercial activities for a variety of reasons. The most obvious reason would appear to be the need to obtain *revenue* for the support of governmental functions. In a society collectively preferring the market allocation of quasi-public (quasi-private) goods, however, this motivation cannot be considered the dominant reason for the engagement of the American public sector in commercial activities. Instead, the prevailing reasons for governmental participation in such activity focus upon the overall characteristics of quasi-public goods which, in certain cases, confer substantial degrees of "publicness" upon particular economic goods. Within this context, "publicness' is conferred upon a particular economic good by such circumstances as the presence of decreasing production costs at relevant output scales, elements of joint consumption, or important externalities. Such conditions warrant the consideration of "possible" public sector influence upon the supply of that good—if the goal of fiscal rationality is to be attained. Table 15-3, which relates nontax revenues such as user prices derived from certain governmental enterprise activities to total public sector expenditure on these activities, demonstrates clearly that "revenues" are *not* the primary purpose for governmental allocational involvement. Of those functions listed, only liquor store operations show a "profit" and this function is accompanied by a "regulatory" motive.

Figure 15-1 provides a framework for analysis of the relevant question of government versus market allocation of quasi-public goods. Since "imperfect" market structure, particularly that of an oligopolistic variety, characterizes American industry, the graph depicts "monopolistic" elements. Furthermore, since many instances of governmental allocational influence on the supply of quasi-public goods exist within decreasing cost industries, the graph also depicts economies of scale in production.[14] The price-output combination at point a is set under conditions of *profit-maximization pricing* $(MC = MR)$, that at point b under circumstances of *average cost pricing* $(AC = AR)$, and that at point c under conditions of *marginal cost pricing* $(MC = AR)$.

The major alternatives available for allocation of quasi-public goods

---

[13] The discussion which follows in this chapter will concentrate upon the provision (allocation) by government of final *economic goods,* not upon the provision of resources which may be employed to produce these goods. In addition, *provision (allocation)* will be defined to mean either the actual "production" of the goods, or its subsequest sale at a "later stage" of economic activity, such as the sale by state government liquor stores of privately-produced alcoholic beverages.

[14] See Francis M. Bator, *The Question of Government Spending* (New York: Harper & Row Publishers, 1960). Bator estimates that approximately 97 percent of federal administrative budget expenditures are for economic goods with significant decreasing cost-public good characteristics.

TABLE 15–3
Selected Nontax Revenues as Percentages of Direct Expenditures on
Associated Functions, All Levels of Government, Fiscal 1966

Function	Revenue as Percent of Expenditure on Function 1966
Postal Service...............................	80.3
Education	10.6
Institutions of higher education..............	30.5
Hospitals	24.6
Sewerage and other sanitation...............	30.7
Local parks and recreation..................	14.7
Natural resources...........................	32.6
Housing and urban renewal..................	40.7
Nonhighway transportation..................	24.9
Utilities....................................	83.9
Liquor stores...............................	125.0

Source: U.S. Department of Commerce.

are: (1) unregulated (except for antitrust) private sector provision of the
good, (2) private provision of the good under direct governmental (public utility) regulation, (3) private sector production of the good with
governmental subsidy, (4) a combination of (2) and (3), or (5) public
sector production of the good.

If economies of scale exist over a wide range of output scales, the

FIGURE 15–1
Various Price-Output Alternatives for a Firm Operating under Decreasing
Production Costs in an Imperfect Market

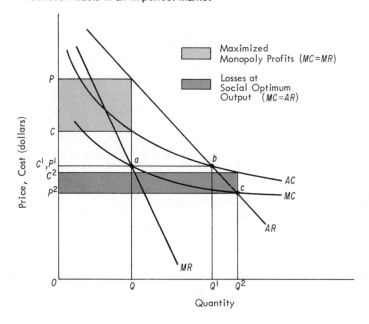

unregulated private industry likely will consist of either one pure monopoly firm or of a few oligopoly firms which dominate the industry. The pure monopoly firm, or the oligopoly firms if perfect or near perfect collusion exists, prefer to produce at the profit-maximizing price and output determined by the intersection of marginal cost and marginal revenue at point *a* in Figure 15–1.[15] Thus, Output *OQ*, Price *OP*, and Cost *OC* reflect the relevant magnitudes at the profit-maximizing position. No direct governmental regulation exists to compel lower prices and greater output. Distributional distortion will result from the "exploitative" monopoly price and allocational distortion will result because output is restricted below the optimal social welfare allocation point where marginal cost equals average revenue (price).[16] The condition of exploitative monopoly price will tend to be accentuated if the economic good is characterized by a highly inelastic price elasticity of demand. If the economic good does *not* possess important externalities or other traits of "publicness," the best practical *allocation* approach (though not theoretically optimal) will likely be that of unregulated private production. This is especially true for a society whose preferences favor market allocation and where most markets are imperfect so that output is *not* typically carried to the social optimum allocation point where marginal cost is equal to average revenue (price).

A second alternative for allocating the quasi-public good in question is the application of the public utility concept. This approach, while continuing to allow private production of the good, provides for *direct regulation* of the private producer or producers of the good regarding such basic matters as price, quantity, and quality of output. In Figure 15–1, the firm subject to public utility regulation ordinarily would be allowed to produce at a price-output combination in the vicinity of point *b*. At this output (OQ^1), average revenue equates average cost, giving Price OP^1 and Cost OC^1. This is known as *average cost* or *full cost pricing*. The firm, in this instance, is earning a normal return on investment since alternative uses of the self-employed factors are compensated in a manner consistent with their opportunity cost values

---

[15] The firm may choose not to maximize profits for fear of attracting new entrants to the industry, an antitrust crackdown, or suffering a public image deterioration, or it may be unable to maximize them because of inadequate production and market knowledge. It seems reasonable to assume, however, that the firm will ordinarily come as close to point *a* as possible in its price-output combination.

[16] It is not argued that the public sector should compel output at or near the $MC = AR$ point for all economic goods produced in a world of imperfect markets. Relatedly, for a comprehensive model which precludes overall application of the marginal cost pricing technique ($MC = AR$) to all industries (as in a socialist economy in which all industry has been "nationalized"), and which substitutes an alternative rule, see William J. Baumol and David F. Bradford, "Optimal Departures from Marginal Cost Pricing," *American Economic Review*, June 1970, pp. 265–83.

elsewhere. A public utility firm frequently is allowed to operate at a price-output combination slightly to the left of point b, thus earning modest monopoly profits.

By comparison with the unregulated case, it may be observed that public utility regulation provides a greater output at a lower price, $OQ^1 - OP^1$, as compared to the unregulated price-output, $OQ - OP$. Thus, if the good possesses substantial traits of publicness, direct governmental regulation likely will increase welfare by increasing output from OQ to OQ^1—the latter output being closer to the social optimal output OQ^2. At any output to the left of OQ^2, the price which consumers are willing to pay for the good exceeds the marginal cost of supplying the good, thus distorting the ability of the market to meet consumer preferences. In addition to its beneficial allocational effects, public utility regulation may also reduce those distributional nonneutralities which lead to greater income inequality because it does not allow the full exploitative monopoly price to be charged. This result would be consistent with American society's overall value judgments concerning distributional goals.

A third major alternative for the allocation of quasi-public goods is for the private sector to produce the good at the social optimum output OQ^2, and the nonmonopoly price OP^2, with government subsidizing the loss (the vertical excess of OC^2 over OP^2 for each unit produced). This would represent a variety of *marginal cost pricing* in which there is "private sector" production and "public sector" subsidization. Fourth, government might compel a public utility to produce quantities of the good somewhere between OQ^1 and OQ^2 and then subsidize the loss to the private firm. If the fifth alternative—government production of the good—is selected, production by the public sector ordinarily must be justified by some strong traits of publicness in the good itself and/or by the ability of the public sector to supply the good at lower costs than the private sector. In this case, another variety of *marginal cost pricing* would exist if output is carried to OQ^2 where $MC = AR$.

A private firm, of course, could not earn a profit producing optimal Social Output OQ^2 and charging Price OP^2 because average cost exceeds price (average revenue) at that output. This *always* would be the case when decreasing production costs are being realized at the output where marginal cost equals price because marginal cost must be below average cost when average cost is declining.[17] Government production of the good, or the subsidization of private production, is thus required if the good is to be allocated in optimal quantities.

At times, a quasi-public good which possesses certain undesirable

---

[17] See the relevant discussion in Chapter 2.

characteristics may be supplied by government if, by the government so doing, price can be kept high and the quantity exchanged reduced. Private allocation at the $MC = AR$ point thus is purposefully avoided because of a higher priority social interest of a regulatory nature. In addition, a uniquely scarce good or resource with social importance may be allocated by government with a high price so as to ration use of the good. Of course, such rationing could also be performed by direct governmental mandate without charging a user price. In any event, if strong traits of publicness are present in a quasi-public good, governmental production or governmental regulation and/or subsidization of private production of the good may be the most efficient means of allocation.

The Choice Between General Tax and User Price Financing of Quasi-Public Goods. If "government" production and/or distribution of a quasi-public good is considered desirable, a variety of financing techniques are available to the unit of government providing the good. Emphasis in the next few pages will center upon the choice between the *general taxation* and *user pricing* techniques as alternative revenue means of paying for quasi-public goods. Other possible financing techniques such as earmarked excise taxes, administrative revenues, and debt financing are discussed elsewhere.

Pure public goods, which are not subject to the exclusion principle, cannot be allocated by the commercial principle. Quasi-public goods, on the other hand, can often be priced since their benefits are often partially subject to the exclusion principle. Yet, quasi-public goods can also be allocated and financed through general taxation. The choice between general taxation and user prices as financial allocative techniques is thus relevant for quasi-public goods, but irrelevant for pure public goods.

The case for general taxation as the means of financing quasi-public goods rests upon several related points. First, general tax financing seems preferable to user pricing in those instances where the short-run marginal cost of an additional unit of output is very low or zero and the price elasticity of demand of the good is highly inelastic. The low or zero short-run marginal cost means that additional units of the good do not withdraw resources in any substantial way from alternative uses. For example, the marginal cost of additional usage of a park or playground up to capacity is negligible as is that of tuning in another television set to receive a program which is being transmitted anyway. Moreover, if the demand for an economic good is highly inelastic, there would be little purpose in charging a price for "rationing" the use of the good within its short-run capacity since the quantity demanded of the good would be largely insensitive to price changes.

Another argument in behalf of the general tax financing of quasi-public goods emphasizes the fact that pricing quasi-public goods with important joint consumption characteristics may cause a seriously short supply of these goods. Thus, if the total cost of a university education were financed through tuition charges, with no general fund financing, there would likely be an undersupply of this important economic good due to the free-rider problem. This result would be assured further by the economies of scale which seemingly exist in the provision of higher education. As a result, even though the user price may initially be set equal to marginal cost, providing a socially optimal output, the decreasing cost nature of the industry would not allow this price to cover unit costs of production. If costs are to be covered fully, and if general fund financing is not to be used, a higher tuition price would have to be charged. The higher price, of course, would tend to reduce the quantity demanded of and the output of educational services below the social optimum.

A further argument in favor of the general tax financing of quasi-public goods concerns the cost of administering a user price system. If collection costs for user prices are substantial, general taxation would appear to be the preferred method of financing from this standpoint. Severe inconvenience to users from the collection system, moreover, may be looked upon as an important reduction in the utility derived from the consumption of quasi-public goods financed by user prices. If tolls were collected for the use of all streets, roads, and highways, for example, the inconvenience would cause considerable consumptive disutility to their users, not to mention added resource costs including the opportunity costs of wasted time.

The pursuit of certain distributional objectives provides another argument in defense of the general fund financing of quasi-public goods. The community may decide, for example, to make its real (ex post) income and wealth distribution more equal by means of either *direct* transfer payments or through the *indirect* method of concentrating first on the reallocation of resources. Transfer payments, however, are incompatible with the user pricing technique since they do not participate in resource-absorbing activities. There is no opportunity to apply the exclusion principle. *Direct* redistribution through transfer payments thus would have to depend upon some other form of general financing (either tax or debt). Moreover, the *indirect* redistribution of income and wealth, as achieved by the reallocation of resources toward the provision of additional amounts of certain desirable quasi-public goods, would tend to require at least partial dependence upon general financing techniques. For example, if these goods are priced above the purchasing power means of lower-income individuals, such people will be unable to acquire the goods in adequate quantities unless they are financed, at least in part, from other sources such as general tax revenues. Medical services or school lunches thus may not be available in adequate quantities to certain low-income people if they are available *only* on a direct pricing basis. The argument again suggests a preference for the general tax financing of quasi-public goods as opposed to the user price alternative.

For the most part, the arguments in support of user pricing rest on the converse of the above points. The free provision of goods without the involvement of a pricing mechanism, for example, loses sight of any long-term investment criterion or guide. User prices, on the other hand, provide at least a partial benchmark for long-run changes in capacity. Moreover, use of the commercial principle provides short-run prices which help to prevent overuse of short-run capacity. In addition, general fund financing may induce an oversupply of those quasi-public goods which are characterized by highly elastic price elasticities of demand.[18]

Another argument for use of the commercial principle is found in those quasi-public goods whose economic effects are mostly subject to the exclusion principle. This is true of electricity consumption, for example, as compared to education. Thus, in the *absence* of significant "positive" externalities, the argument for general tax financing loses strength and user pricing may be preferable. On the other hand, the *presence* of substantial "negative" externalities may call for user prices at high levels to discourage consumption of the good—to the extent that the exclusion principle can be applied to the good.

In addition, when the costs of collecting user prices are lower than the expenses of general tax administration for the same revenue yield (other things equal), the former means of financing is to be preferred. Certain distributional goals, moreover, may be better met through user pricing than through tax financing. Since the consumption of electricity primarily benefits the purchaser, for example, the application of user prices conforms to the overall distributional philosophy accepted in American culture and demonstrated through the obvious community preference for market-type allocation and pricing. Moreover, the benefit principle of tax equity is "approximated."

User Pricing of Quasi-Public Goods by Government: Pricing Alternatives. As noted earlier in the chapter, the commercial principle may be implemented by the public sector through either *profit-maximizing pricing,* *average cost pricing,* or *marginal cost pricing.* It was also observed that negative allocational and distributional nonneutralities tend to be reduced as output is expanded toward the marginal cost = average rev-

---

[18] See the relevant discussion of the similiarity between "general fund financing" and "joint product sale," as developed in James M. Buchanan, "Economics of Earmarked Taxes," and described earlier in the chapter.

enue equality (the social welfare optimal allocation point). However, the reader should, once again, be reminded that "isolated" examples of *marginal cost pricing* in a society where imperfect markets prevail do not necessarily constitute an optimal allocation solution, though in many cases they likely would constitute an improvement in allocation. The strongest case for marginal cost pricing would likely center around an important economic good possessing significant joint consumption characteristics over a large group and/or the presence of decreasing production costs at the relevant output scales. Yet, an administrative problem of effectively applying the exclusion principle may well arise. Moreover, the implicit danger remains that pursuit of the marginal cost pricing rule for public-type goods, at a time when it is not being followed generally within the economy as a whole, will irrationally expand the supply of public versus private goods. The point of "actual" intersector resource allocation would thus be distorted and would move further away from the society's "optimal" point of division between public and private goods.[19]

However, since the basis for governmental allocation of quasi-public good rests primarily upon the degree of "publicness" which the goods possess, and upon the institutional failure of the market as an "equally efficient" allocative technique in providing these goods—especially under large group conditions, an expanded supply of socially desirable goods may still be deemed rational despite the above intersector allocation objection. Thus, use of the marginal cost pricing technique in the allocation of quasi-public goods may be considered, at times, as an acceptable "second-best solution" in a world inextricably associated with imperfect market structures, joint consumption, and externalities.

Use by government of the *profit-maximizing price* as determined by the intersection of marginal cost and marginal revenue ($MC = MR$), in allocating a quasi-public good, would best serve only the "revenue goal" unless the isolated case exists where the society is trying to reduce the consumption of an "undesirable" economic good. *Average cost pricing,* a third alternative, is generally preferable to profit-maximizing pricing since it helps to reduce negative allocational and distributional distortions. However, *marginal cost pricing* appears to be the most desirable of the three "less than optimal" alternatives for governmental pricing of important quasi-public goods. Marginal cost pricing, nonetheless, faces several problems as mentioned above. Yet, the impediments to efficient marginal cost pricing may be reduced by certain modified (hybrid) financing techniques.

One important economic problem which occurs when marginal cost pricing is used in a society characterized by substantial market imper-

---

[19] See Chapters 1 and 4.

fections is that the government enterprise operating under decreasing production costs will incur a loss at the social welfare optimal allocation point where $MC = AR$. Figure 15–2, which essentially reproduces the Point c conditions of Figure 15–1, displays this result. Thus, in allocating quantity OQ^2 of the good while charging price OP^2, the government in allocating the economic good is suffering a loss to the extent of the rectangle $wxyz$. The loss per unit of output is OC^2 minus OP^2. Since the user price does *not* cover the cost of producing output OQ^2, the difference could be met through tax revenues.

FIGURE 15–2
Losses with Governmental User-Pricing Technique at Social
Optimum Output under Decreasing Production Costs

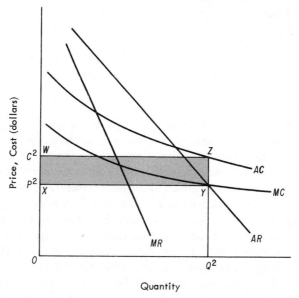

Under certain conditions, *mixed financing* utilizing both user prices and general tax revenues would constitute the most rational alternative for financing quasi-public goods. Under other circumstances, it may provide negative allocational and distributional nonneutralities. The use of mixed financing may be rational if the good possesses both substantial joint consumption effects, which benefit the society as a whole and which remain outside the exclusion principle, and also important private benefits. Tax funds would thus finance the community or social benefits while user prices would finance the individual or private benefits. Moreover, the use of general fund financing to cover the loss rectangle in Figure 15–2 is rational if it is collectively determined by the community that fiscal means of this sort should be used to redistribute real income by increasing the allocation of the quasi-public good in question. The combined use of general fund financing and user pricing (tuition charges) to finance public university education in the United States seems to meet both of the above rationality points since the benefits of education are both social and private in nature and, in addition, improving the education of the poor is an effective means of improving their long-term real income position.

On the other hand, the absence of sufficient joint consumption benefits to justify tax (or debt) subsidization of the loss rectangle, or the absence of a sufficient community-approved redistribution objective, would make the mixed financing technique irrational. This could be true because private users would derive most or all of the benefits from the consumption of the good and few, if any, social benefits would exist. Yet, general tax funds collected from the society as a whole would subsidize part of the cost of the private consumption. The results would be both a redistribution of income in favor of the private consumers of the quasi-public good as well as an allocational distortion.

Another related problem present in the decreasing cost case is the fact that "subsidized output" at the optimal social allocation point distorts long-run investment planning. There is no "profit test" to indicate the proper long-run allocation of resources toward the production of the good. In other words, price is not rationing resources among alternative uses in an adequate manner because the price does not cover full costs. A partial solution to this problem is offered by the *multipart* or *peak-load* pricing approach. This approach is a "hybrid" between marginal cost pricing and average cost pricing. All costs are covered by price. Yet, the price schedule is divided into at least two parts: one part for the "opportunity to acquire" the commodity and the other for the "actual quantities demanded." A "flat price" may thus be charged for the standby opportunity to use a quasi-public good and an "incremental price" can be charged for each specific usage to cover short-run marginal costs as well as to suggest long-run investment needs. Such multipart pricing techniques are uniquely applicable to industries which produce "nonstorable" commodities, such as electricity and transit services, and whose product demands are "uneven" over the relevant period of time. It is here, in particular, that multipart pricing takes on the name "peak-load pricing."

Peak-load pricing suggests that prices charged at periods of maximum or peak use of capacity should be higher than those charged at off-peak hours. The reasoning behind this approach is that "higher prices" will more effectively ration short-run use of the capacity at peak-load periods of demand and, at the same time, will help to determine future capacity requirements as well as to help cover the costs

of these requirements. Both short-run rationing and long-run investment criteria are thus served by this technique. Though such an approach involves differential prices, this does not necessarily mean that
price discrimination exists since the differential prices may be proportional to differences in marginal costs. If so, true price discrimination,
which consists of charging different purchasers different prices for the
same economic good when such price differentials are not justified by
cost differences, is not present.

The following example, related to Figures 15–3a and 15–3b, demonstrates the peak-load pricing approach. Consider the case of a govern-

FIGURE 15–3

Peak-Load Pricing of a Government-Supplied Quasi-Public Good

a. Off-Peak   b. Peak-Load

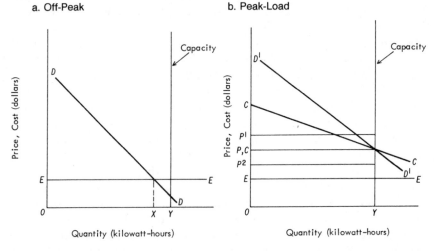

Quantity (kilowatt–hours)   Quantity (kilowatt–hours)

ment-owned electric utility. Assume that the peak demand is "firm,"
that is, it will not change as the multiprices under consideration are
introduced. The marginal cost in off-peak periods of electricity consumption is merely the cost of the energy itself. On the other hand, the
marginal cost in peak periods is the sum of the energy cost and the cost
of capacity. Suppose that the demand is divided into two equal parts.
Thus, one half of the day represents peak demand for electricity and
the other half of the day represents off-peak demand.

The long-run solution to the problem is demonstrated in Figures
15–3a and 15–3b. There is no need to increase capacity to meet the
energy cost in the off-peak period. The marginal energy cost is represented by curve *EE* and the off-peak demand is represented by demand
curve *DD* in Figure 15–3a. At the intersection of the marginal energy

cost and the off-peak demand curves, the quantity purchased of off–peak electricity is determined. This quantity is equal to OX on the horizontal axis, but it is "less" than the capacity quantity OY.

In Figure 15–3b, the long-run "capacity cost" is added to the "energy cost" for the peak demand situation. Capacity, of course, must be greater to meet the peak demand as opposed to the off-peak demand for electricity. Hence, line CC represents the long-term marginal cost for electricity inclusive of both energy and capacity requirements. It is a downward sloping curve in order to characterize a decreasing cost industry such as is frequently associated with quasi-public goods. Line EE, once again, represents marginal energy costs. Line $D^1 D^1$ represents the peak demand for electricity. It should be observed that line $D^1 D^1$ in Figure 15–3b is higher than line DD in Figure 15–3a because of the greater "on-peak" than "off-peak" demand for electricity. At the intersection of the peak demand curve $D^1 D^1$ and the long-run marginal cost curve CC, the quantity purchased of peak demand electricity is determined. This quantity is equal to OY on the horizontal axis.

The determination of long-run equilibrium conditions would have been attained through the following adjustments: If the price at peak demand is equal to the sum of the marginal energy cost and the marginal capacity cost and the entire available capacity is allocated (quantity OY), optimal capacity exists and there is no reason to change capacity ($P = C$ at quantity OY). If the price exceeds the sum of the marginal energy cost and the marginal capacity cost, as under high demand conditions, the results comprise a long-term investment signal that capacity should be expanded ($P^1 > C$ at quantity OY). The price in excess of long-run marginal costs, moreover, will help to pay for the expansion of capacity. On the other hand, if the price is less than the sum of the marginal energy and capacity costs, as under low demand conditions, the loss per unit of electricity signals the need for retrenchment in capacity during the long-run time period ($P^2 < C$ at quantity OY).

Hence, multipart or peak-load pricing, under certain conditions, may improve rationality in the use of the commercial principle by government. Yet, it offers only a second-best solution. It must be stressed, once again, that the social welfare optimum of marginal cost pricing serves perfectly as a pricing technique only if all industries are pricing in this manner (as in a general equilibrium world of perfect competition). This is an unrealistic assumption, however, for the American economy. Nevertheless, marginal cost pricing and, under certain conditions, its multipart pricing modification, may still be the best available means for application of the commercial principle by government in the allocation of quasi-public goods.

ADMINISTRATIVE REVENUES

Administrative revenues are collected by a unit of government from individuals as part of the performance of general governmental functions. These general governmental functions are primarily regulatory in nature. For example, government must protect persons and property. It must also provide a certain basic framework within which private economic activity will take place, In the performance of these and other general functions, government frequently charges a fee, levies a fine, receives an escheat, or otherwise collects revenue from individuals. The correlation between the payment of an administrative revenue by an individual, and the subsequent service or right acquired by the individual, is usually broad and imprecise. Only in a general sense, therefore, may it be said that a quid pro quo relationship exists in the case of administrative revenues.

Fees, licenses, and *permits* are very similar in nature. They all provide administrative revenues to government as part of a regulatory function and all involve the granting of permission by government to the individual to behave in a particular way. A fishing license, for example, allows a person to fish in public waters within the political jurisdiction of the grantor. A business license allows an individual or firm to participate in a particular trade. Admittedly, permission to behave in a particular manner can be regulated without requiring a monetary payment to government by the individual receiving the privilege. The revenue motive used by government for requiring payment, however, may still be deemed worthwhile. Collection costs usually are low while the revenue productivity of the administrative charge can be high. Since the charges are frequently uniform to all taxpayers, they do not perform well in reference to the "ability-to-pay" principle of tax equity. Moreover, since the quid pro quo relationships generally are less than precise, the charges also fail to satisfactorily meet the "benefit" principle.

Fines and *forfeitures* clearly involve the performance of a regulatory function by government. Fines are monetary charges levied by a governmental unit as a penalty for a violation of law. Forfeitures, similarly, are penalties. They involve the sacrifice of bail or bond for failure to appear in court, or to complete contracts as prescribed. Except for isolated local government examples (such as "traffic trap" cities), the relative revenue importance of fines and forfeitures to the American public sector is slight.

According to the American legal system, the state level of government possesses the legal right to be the ultimate claimant of property left by deceased persons who have no legal heirs. This legal right of the state to absorb such property is known as an *escheat.* Escheats thus constitute another source of administrative revenues. As with fines and forfeitures, the overall revenue importance of escheats to the public sector is slight.

Special assessments, though usually classified as administrative revenues, are very similar to "user prices." Moreover, they contain some traits of both "general" and "earmarked" taxes in the sense that they resemble what might be termed an "earmarked property tax." It is not inconsistent, however, to classify them as "administrative revenues" since they often are closely related to the overall governmental regulatory function of administering community development programs. A special assessment charge for the installation of sewers, street lights, or paved streets as part of the development plan of a community may thus be viewed as a by-product of the general administrative function of government. Special assessment districts, at times, are set up which are not coterminous with already existing levels of government. In this sense, such an assessment district may be said to constitute a separate unit of local government.

Special assessments normally are characterized by the allocation of costs and benefits resulting from the improvement of land. The basis for assessment is usually not in terms of value, but instead is in terms of area or frontage. This tends to negatively distort the ability-to-pay principle of tax equity. Considerable procedural variation exists among the various levels and units of government which utilize the special assessment technique for allocating quasi-public goods.

part three

The Public Sector Budget: Trends, Techniques, and Issues

16

The Aggregate Public Sector Budget: Growth Trends and Analysis

Although the "symmetrical" character of the budgetary process is emphasized in Part Three as well as throughout the book as a whole, the present chapter will approach public sector growth trends and changes in a somewhat "asymmetrical" fashion. Although the tax or revenue side of the budget will still be used to help demonstrate governmental fiscal trends in the United States, the primary emphasis herein will be upon changes in public sector *expenditure* patterns which serve as ideal "indicators" of governmental fiscal trends since they show the functional reasons for which governmental economic activity occurs. Meanwhile, the tax, or revenue, side of the budget has received primary emphasis in Part Two while the residual of certain tax-expenditure arrangements, government debt, is considered in Part Four. Finally, the last section of this chapter will consider several theoretical attempts to explain "public sector growth."

EXPENDITURE PATTERNS

Prior to 1900

Federal expenditures display a secular growth trend throughout American history. The growth, however, has been cyclical rather than continuous. Moreover, even after adjustment for both intertemporal price level differences and for population growth, federal expenditures in real per capita terms still display an interrupted pattern of growth.

Real per capita federal expenditures, for example, were either station-ary or declined between 1794–1811, 1817–46, 1866–84, and 1899–1916.[1]

The huge magnitude of federal expenditures at the present time may be compared to the very small federal expenditure base at the begin-ning of the sovereign history of the United States. During the first full year of its existence, 1789–90, the federal government spent less than $1 million. Federal expenditures did not reach $10 million until 1800, more than a decade after national sovereignty had begun. Federal spending first reached the $20–$30 million range during the War of 1812, but it took many additional years before they "shot past" the $40 million dollar mark to $57 million in 1847, a figure more than double the spending in the previous year, 1846. The first year in which federal expenditures exceeded the billion-dollar mark was the last year of the Civil War, 1865, when they totaled nearly $1.3 billion. Following the war, they dropped sharply and stayed under $1 billion until the nation's entry into World War I in 1917. The ratio of federal expenditures to gross national product was generally lower during the nineteenth cen-tury than it is today. In fact, it was as low as .5 percent during extended periods of America's early history while today it stands at a ratio above 20 percent.

The fiscal activities of *state* governments, after a relatively slow be-ginning, increased significantly during the second quarter of the nine-teenth century.[2] At this time, the states assumed the responsibility for many internal improvements of a social capital nature from the federal government as well as considerable responsibilities in the fields of charity and corrections from local government.[3] In addition, the states initiated aid to schools, with most of the funds coming from the sale of public lands. Some states furnished financial assistance to private col-leges and several states in the South and West established state universi-ties prior to the Civil War. Still others, particularly New York, founded free teachers colleges. State expenditures, which were correlated closely with the business cycle during this period, increased sharply during prosperities and declined during depressions.

During the latter half of the nineteenth century, conservative politico-economic philosophies were influential in restraining state gov-ernment participation in the provision of internal improvements and

---

[1] M. Slade Kendrick, *A Century and a Half of Federal Expenditures,* Occasional Paper 48 (New York: National Bureau of Economic Research, 1955).

[2] For an excellent coverage of the expenditure activities of state and local govern-ments prior to 1900, see Paul Studenski and Herman E. Krooss, *Financial History of the United States* (New York: McGraw-Hill Book Co., 1963), chaps. 12 and 17.

[3] A classic example of state internal investment in social capital is the Erie Canal Project sponsored by New York State between 1817–1825. This project initiated exten-sive state investments in internal improvements.

in furnishing credit to private enterprise. Nevertheless, the states indirectly provided for such functional expenditure activities by making it legally possible for local units of government to undertake them. The states, in addition, gave local government the powers to organize basic educational activities.

During the 1860s and 1870s, most state expenditures were dominated by the Civil War and its consequences. Compensation was paid to volunteers during the war and to veterans and their survivors after the war. Considerable state revenues were allocated during the 1870s to the repayment of debts accumulated during the Civil War era. Subsequently, a significant increase in state expenditures occurred between 1880 and 1900 as the states extended their regulatory, educational, and social service functions.

Local government fiscal activity prior to 1900 followed a pattern similar to that of state governments during the early part of the period. Like the state governments, local governments were beginning by the second quarter of the nineteenth century to meet the increased demand of the population for internal social capital improvements and for various social services—objectives which both levels of government had met quite modestly prior to 1825.

These activities intensified as the incipient American industrial revolution and heavy population immigration led to a rapid growth of American cities during the second quarter of the century. Thus, municipal governments increasingly provided such social capital items as water systems, sewer systems, all-weather streets, and such social services as fire protection, police protection, and free public education.[4]

During the latter part of the century, local government further increased its internal improvement and assistance to private enterprise activities. The continuing growth of sheer numbers in urban area population justified this action. In the 40 years between 1860 and 1900, urban population increased from 20 percent to 40 percent of the growing total population. The expansion in local government expenditures occurred mostly during prosperities, with subsequent slowing down of expenditure growth, or even retrenchment, during business cycle downturns.

Twentieth-Century Expenditure Trends

Public sector expenditures have increased significantly as a percentage of gross national product (GNP) during the twentieth century. Of

---

[4] Some municipalities, with at least implicit state government approval, provided for the organization of *independent school districts* to administer the public education needs of the community. Significantly, such school districts possess the important symmetrical budgetary functions of both tax collecting and spending.

course, this is a direct indication that the point of "actual" resource allocation in the American economy is increasing in the direction of greater relative resource allocation by the public sector.[5]

Table 16–1 shows that public sector expenditures have more than quadrupled as a percentage of gross national product during the century. A more than threefold increase may be detected between 1929, the end of the prosperous 1920s, and 1971. Moreover, during the height of World War II (1944) the expenditures of American governments were nearly one half of GNP while in 1971 they stood at slightly less than one third.

TABLE 16–1

Total Public Sector Expenditures as a Percentage of GNP, Selected Calendar Years, 1902–71*

Year	Percent	Year	Percent
1902	8.0	1950	21.3
1913	8.5	1955	24.5
1929	10.0	1960	27.0
1940	18.5	1965	27.3
1944	49.0	1968	31.3
1947	18.3	1971	32.2

* Expenditures are from the U.S. Department of Commerce's National Income and Product Accounts. These are presented on an accrual basis and include government trust fund transactions, but exclude those capital transactions not representing current production.

Source: U.S. Department of Commerce; author's estimates for data prior to 1929, with reference given to national product data from Simon Kuznets, *National Product Since 1869* (New York: National Bureau of Economic Research, 1946).

Total public sector expenditures, in current prices, have increased from $1.6 billion in 1902 to over $369 billion in 1971. (See Table 16–2). The federal government accounted for $226 billion, or 61 percent of the total, in 1971 while state and local governments accounted for nearly 21 percent and 18 percent, respectively. Significantly, federal government expenditures have increased from approximately one third to nearly two thirds of total public sector spending during the twentieth century. At the same time, state government expenditures have nearly doubled in importance, but local government spending has decreased sharply from more than one half to less than one fifth of the total. Hence, the "combined" state-local component of the public sector, under the influence of the significantly diminished importance of local government, has declined from roughly two thirds to one third of total government spending during the century. Nonetheless, the relative proportions of the federal and state-local components have remained essentially unchanged during the past 25 years.

A disaggregation of these aggregate expenditures into four com-

---

[5] See Chapters 1 and 4 for the discussion of "optimal" and "actual" intersector resource allocation.

TABLE 16–2

Federal, State, and Local Government Expenditures,* by Level of Government, Selected Fiscal Years, 1902–71

a. Absolute Dollar Terms (millions of current dollars)

| Year | Total | Government Level | | |
		Federal	State	Local
1902.........	$ 1,660	$ 572	$ 179	$ 909
1913.........	3,215	970	372	1,873
1927.........	11,220	3,533	1,882	5,805
1932.........	12,437	4,266	2,562	5,609
1936.........	16,758	9,165	3,144	4,449
1940.........	20,417	10,061	4,545	5,811
1944.........	109,947	100,520	4,062	5,365
1950.........	70,334	44,800	12,774	12,761
1955.........	110,717	73,441	17,400	19,875
1960.........	151,288	97,284	25,035	28,970
1965.........	205,550	130,050	35,726	39,765
1968.........	282,645	184,464	50,046	48,135
1971.........	369,423	226,157	75,882	67,384

b. Percentage Distribution

| Year | Total | Government Level | | | Combined State-Local |
		Federal	State	Local	
1902.........	100.0	34.4	10.8	54.8	65.6
1913.........	100.0	30.2	11.6	58.3	69.9
1927.........	100.0	31.5	16.8	51.7	68.5
1932.........	100.0	34.3	20.6	45.1	65.7
1936.........	100.0	54.7	18.8	26.5	45.3
1940.........	100.0	49.3	22.2	28.5	50.7
1944.........	100.0	91.4	3.7	4.9	8.6
1950.........	100.0	63.7	18.2	18.1	36.3
1955.........	100.0	66.3	15.7	18.0	33.7
1960.........	100.0	64.3	16.5	19.2	35.7
1965.........	100.0	63.3	17.4	19.3	36.7
1968.........	100.0	65.3	17.7	17.0	34.7
1971.........	100.0	61.2	20.6	18.2	38.8

* Expenditures are treated in terms of the financing rather than the final spending level of government; i.e., by treating amounts represented by intergovernmental transactions as expenditures of the originating rather than the recipient government.

Source: Tax Foundation, Inc.

ponents—direct, intergovernmental, utility and liquor store operations, and trust fund-financed expenditures—reveals a number of significant trends: (1) intergovernmental expenditures of the federal government have increased from a negligible amount in 1913 to approximately 12 percent of total federal expenditures in 1971; (2) trust fund expenditures have grown to a position of substantial importance (in 1913, these expenditures were insignificant at all levels of government, but now they are extensively used by the federal government and used prominently, though to a lesser extent, by state governments), and (3) expenditures for the operation of utilities and liquor stores by state and local governments have increased manyfold since 1913.

If total public sector spending is disaggregated into the functions undertaken by the different levels of government, the following observations may be made for present-day expenditures: The federal government provides the highest percentage of such functional expenditures as national defense, health, natural resources, air transportation, interest on debt, and insurance trust fund activities. State governments, meanwhile, lead the way with the highest percentage expended on highways and public welfare while local governments, in turn, spend the most for such functions as education, utility operations, and hospitals. Importantly, the substantial growth in both defense-related activities and in transfer payments, the latter inclusive of trust fund operations of a social insurance nature, are provided primarily by the federal component of the public sector.

A functional distribution of *federal* expenditures for the fiscal year 1971 demonstrates the considerable influence of national defense (national security) on the federal budget. Over 35 percent of federal budget expenditures, including trust fund spending, went for "direct"

TABLE 16–3
Federal Expenditures* by Function, Fiscal Year 1971 (unified federal budget)†

	Absolute Terms ($ millions)	Percent of Total
Total expenditures	$211,424	100.0‡
National defense	77,661	35.4
International affairs and finance	3,095	1.4
Space research and technology	3,381	1.5
Agriculture and rural development	5,096	2.3
Natural resources	2,716	1.2
Commerce and transportation	11,310	5.1
Community development and housing	3,357	1.5
Education and manpower	8,654	3.9
Health	14,463	6.6
Income security	55,712	25.4
Veterans benefits and services	9,776	4.4
Interest	19,609	8.9
General government	3,970	1.8
Undistributed intragovernmental transactions	−7,376	

* Includes net lending.
† The nature of the *unified federal budget* will be described in detail in the following chapter.
‡ Total may not equal 100 percent due to rounding. Percentages are based on $218,800 billion expenditure total prior to subtraction of $7,376 billion for "undistributed intergovernmental transactions".
Source: Office of Management and Budget data.

TABLE 16–4
Federal "War-Related" Expenditures* as a Percentage of Total Federal Expenditures, Fiscal Year 1971 (unified federal budget)

1.	National defense	35.4%
2.	International affairs and finance...............	1.4
3.	Veterans benefits and services.................	4.4
4.	Interest on federal debt.......................	8.9
	Total war-related expenditures (lines 1, 2, 3, 4) as a percentage of total federal expenditures...............................	50.1%

* Includes net lending.
Source: Office of Management and Budget data.

defense, as demonstrated in Table 16–3. In addition, more than 50 percent of federal budget expenditures during the year may be classified as *defense spending* if the concept is broadened to encompass such "indirect" defense items as: (1) international affairs and finance (including foreign aid), (2) veterans benefits and services, and (3) interest on the federal debt, much of which was accumulated during periods of war or high-defense spending. (See Table 16–4). Moreover, defense spending, so defined, amounted to 10.5 percent of GNP during 1971.

The possibility of a significant reduction during future years of the absolute and relative importance of *defense spending* to the federal budget opens up a meaningful discussion of the alternative usage of the potentially-displaced funds. The importance of assessing expenditure *priorities* in public sector decision-making, of course, cannot be questioned in terms of allocative efficiency. This was apparent in Chapter 1 in noting the changing emphasis of the current social balance discussion and it will be further evident in Chapter 18 which is concerned with benefit-cost analysis and budgetary efficiency. Hence, the consensus of the public must somehow, though "imperfectly" due to the imperfections inherent in the political decision-making process, be prepared to select among such alternative "domestic" uses of displaced defense funds as the problems of poverty, cities, environmental pollution, and crime control, as well as such "international" problems as the support of the economic development of underdeveloped nations and the combating of world poverty and hunger. Importantly, it is evident that a federal government budget (fiscal 1971) of well over $200 billion, which shows over 35 percent of all expenditures to be for "direct" and more than 50 percent for "direct" plus "indirect" national defense purposes, is "massive" in its *opportunity cost potential* for application to other important areas of functional expenditure need. Then, of course, the long-term "fiscal dividend" potential of the "income-elastic" federal revenue structure can further supplement displaced military revenues for meeting additional high-priority needs.

TABLE 16–5
Total *State* Direct Expenditures* for Own Functions, and Percentage† Distribution by Function, Selected Fiscal Years, 1902–71

Year	Total Direct Expenditures (millions of current dollars)	Percentage Distribution by Function								
		Education	Highways	Public Welfare‡	Health & Hospitals	Natural Resources	Financial Administration	Other§	Insurance Trust	Liquor Stores
1902	$ 136	—	8.8	5.4	17.8	4.7	12.8	32.0	—	—
1913	297	18.5	35.4	2.8	11.7	6.5	6.6	17.1	4.9	—
1927	1,451	15.0	41.6	3.6	10.6	5.9	5.6	15.9	3.1	—
1932	2,028	13.7	30.8	17.3	9.0	3.8	5.3	12.5	3.2	5.9
1936	2,445	12.2	22.3	14.8	8.4	4.1	4.2	12.4	16.9	6.3
1940	3,555	10.6	16.3	17.4	10.0	4.9	4.9	12.2	6.8	12.8
1944	3,319	14.7	19.1	12.2	8.4	4.4	3.4	17.2	12.9	8.7
1948	7,897	13.7	23.7	13.1	10.5	5.0	3.3	10.8	13.1	6.7
1952	10,790	13.8	28.8	10.6	9.7	4.4	3.2	10.5	13.1	5.6
1956	15,148	14.1	27.4	10.1	8.6	3.8	3.0	12.2	15.6	4.1
1960	22,152	15.3	26.8	9.8	8.4	4.0	3.0	11.3	15.6	3.2
1963	27,698	17.9	23.7	10.8	8.5	4.5	3.0	12.1	10.7	3.0
1967	39,704	23.6	23.7	10.8	8.5	4.5	3.0	12.1	15.6	3.0
1971	66,200	23.9	18.6	15.9	8.2	3.8	2.9	12.1	12.6	2.1

* Direct expenditures include all resource-absorbing and transfer expenditures regardless of the source of the expended funds.
† Totals may not equal 100 percent due to rounding.
‡ Primarily categorical public assistance.
§ Primarily police, correction, interest, and social insurance administration.
Source: U.S. Department of Commerce, Bureau of the Census.

Changes in the functional distribution of direct *state* government expenditures during the twentieth century may be observed in Table 16–5. Several significant trends or patterns are evident from the data. These trends or patterns (summarized below) occurred within an environment of rapid growth in the absolute magnitude of state spending during the century. State direct expenditures in 1902, for example, amounted to only $136 million and they totaled only $297 million in 1913. However, at the present time direct spending by state governments exceeds $66 billion. The following patterns of direct state expenditure may be summarized from the data for the 58-year period, 1913–1971, except for point (8) which represents a somewhat shorter period:

1. State expenditures for education increased from less than one fifth to nearly one fourth of the total.
2. State expenditures for highways more than doubled in relative importance.
3. Public welfare expenditures by states nearly tripled in relative importance.
4. State spending on health and hospitals were reduced to approximately one half of its earlier relative importance.
5. Natural resource expenditures by the states were reduced by about one fourth in relative importance.
6. Financial administration (general control) expenditures were reduced in 1971 to less than one fourth of their 1913 importance.
7. "Other" expenditures, mostly for police, correction, bond interest, and social insurance administration, decreased from about one third to about one eighth of total direct spending by the states.
8. Insurance trust and liquor store activities, both nonexistent in 1913, became operational during the period, with the former constituting about one eighth of total direct spending in 1971.

Expenditures for education and highways presently constitute 42.5 percent of the total direct spending of state governments.

Total direct spending by *local* governments has also increased enormously during the twentieth century. Table 16–6, for example, reveals an increase in direct spending from $959 million in 1902 to nearly $105 billion during 1971. The following patterns of direct local government expenditures may be summarized from the data for the period 1902–1971 though points (9) and (10) represent a somewhat shorter period:

1. Local expenditures for education increased from approximately 25 percent to more than 40 percent of total local government spending.

TABLE 16-6

Total *Local* Direct Expenditures* for Own Functions, and Percentage† Distribution by Function, Selected Calendar Years, 1902–71

Year	Total Direct Expenditures (millions of current dollars)	Percent Distribution of Total Direct Expenditures										
		General Expenditure							Utility	Liquor Stores	Insurance Trust
		Education‡	Highways	Public Welfare	Health & Hospitals	Police & Fire	Financial Administration	Other§			
1902	$ 959	24.8	17.8	2.8	2.9	9.4	12.3	21.6	8.4	—	—
1913	1,960	26.6	20.1	1.8	2.8	8.4	8.8	21.6	9.5	—	0.4
1927	6,359	31.7	20.4	1.8	2.9	7.3	5.0	22.6	7.7	—	0.6
1932	6,375	31.9	14.1	5.8	3.8	8.0	5.6	21.8	8.1	—	0.9
1936	6,056	31.0	11.1	6.7	4.1	8.2	6.1	22.3	9.1	0.1	1.3
1940	7,685	29.4	10.2	8.2	4.0	7.4	5.3	20.1	14.2	0.1	1.1
1944	7,180	32.1	9.2	7.7	4.5	8.7	6.1	18.0	11.4	0.5	1.8
1948	13,363	32.2	11.4	8.5	4.2	7.4	4.6	17.7	12.1	0.6	1.3
1952	20,073	34.0	10.4	6.9	5.2	7.1	4.1	19.2	11.2	0.5	1.4
1956	28,004	39.6	9.2	5.5	4.6	6.8	3.9	17.5	11.1	0.4	1.4
1963	47,002	40.4	7.9	5.8	4.9	6.6	3.4	19.2	10.0	0.3	1.4
1967	66,274	43.1	6.8	5.9	5.0	6.2	3.2	19.0	9.1	0.2	1.5
1971	104,566	41.7	5.5	7.4	5.6	6.4	3.2	20.3	8.3	0.2	1.4

* Direct expenditures include all resource-absorbing and transfer expenditures regardless of the source of the expended funds.
† Totals may not equal 100 percent due to rounding.
‡ Primarily elementary and secondary schools.
§ Includes natural resources, sanitation, recreation, interest on general debt, housing and urban renewal, nonhighway transportation, correction, local libraries, general public buildings, and other general government.

Source: U.S. Department of Commerce, Bureau of the Census.

2. The relative importance of highway expenditures by local government decreased in 1971 to less than one third of their importance in 1902.
3. Public welfare expenditures nearly tripled in relative importance during the period.
4. The relative importance of health and hospital spending by local government nearly doubled during the period.
5. Police and fire expenditure declined by about one third in relative importance.
6. In 1971, financial administration (general control) expenditures were only about one fourth of their relative position in 1902.
7. "Other" expenditures—including those for natural resources, sanitation, debt interest, correction, and the like—declined slightly in relative importance during the period.
8. Utility spending decreased slightly in relative importance.
9. Between 1936 and 1971, liquor store expenditures by local government doubled in relative importance.
10. Insurance trust fund activities were nearly four times more important in 1971 than in 1913.

Expenditures for education presently constitute the single largest functional item of local government expenditure (41.7 percent of total direct expenditures).

The considerable absolute growth in public sector spending is shared by all levels of government and is sizable even when converted to a

TABLE 16–7
Federal, State, and Local Expenditures* per Capita, Selected Fiscal Years, 1902–72 (current dollars)

Year	Total	Federal	State	Local
1902................	$ 21	$ 7	$ 2	$ 12
1913................	33	10	4	19
1927................	95	30	16	49
1936................	132	72	25	35
1940................	156	77	35	44
1944................	821	751	30	40
1950................	467	297	85	85
1955................	676	449	106	121
1960................	846	544	140	162
1964................	1,033	662	176	195
1968................	1,420	927	251	242
1972................	1,979	1,195	420	364

* Total expenditures include spending for liquor stores, utilities, and insurance trust funds. Grants-in-aid are counted as expenditures of the level of government which first disburses the funds.
Source: U.S. Department of Commerce; Tax Foundation, Inc.

per capita basis.[6] While total public sector spending (in current dollars) was only $21 per capita in 1902, it reached $1,979 per capita in 1972. The federal component was the largest single contributor of per capita government spending in 1972 though local government had been in the first position in 1902. The state level of government ranked third among the three levels in per capita spending in 1902, but is second at the present time. It should be observed in this discussion of public sector expenditure growth, however, that a rapidly growing national income and product during the twentieth century has been able to adequately support the burden of the rapidly growing per capita governmental expenditures.

REVENUE PATTERNS

Prior to 1900

Federal revenues exceeded expenditures during 74 of the first 110 years of federal budgetary history. The minute nature of early federal budgetary behavior is exemplified by the fact that the federal government's budget displayed a surplus during its first fiscal year despite revenues of only $4.4 million. In fact, federal revenues did not reach $10 million until the year 1800. Moreover, it was not until during the Civil War in 1863 that federal receipts first surpassed $100 million. Furthermore, federal nondebt receipts stayed under $1 billion until America's entry into World War I in 1917.

Table 16–8 displays characteristics of the federal revenue structure between 1790–1916 as arranged by time-period groupings. Expectedly, a high percentage of total federal revenue consisted of "tax revenue" during each time period. Nevertheless, "nontax revenues" such as land sales provided substantial receipts, in relative terms, during several of the time periods. Significantly, the primary source of tax revenue as late as the latter part of the nineteenth century consisted of external taxes (tariffs or customs) rather than internal (domestic) taxes.

State revenue sources required expansion when the considerable growth in state expenditures took place during the nineteenth century.[7] Investment revenues (such as dividends on bank stock), land sales, and lotteries were insufficient to meet the growing state revenue requirements. State revenue needs were thus met during the first half of the nineteenth century by bank taxes, particularly on capital stock, and by the general property tax. The bank taxes were used regularly following the War of 1812, and property taxes were used steadily for

---

[6] See Table 16–7.

[7] See Studenski and Krooss, *Financial History of the United States,* chaps. 12 and 17, for an excellent discussion of state and local government revenue patterns prior to 1900.

TABLE 16–8

Characteristics of the Federal Revenue Structure, by Time-Period Groupings, 1790–1916 (millions of dollars)

						Nontax Revenues		
		Average Annual Tax Revenues						
Number of Years	*Time Period*	*Customs*	*Income & Profits*	*Other*	*Total*	*Land Sales*	*Other*	*Total Revenues*
22	1790–1811	9.3	*	0.4†	9.7	0.3	0.1	10.1
4	1812–15	9.5	‡	2.9§	12.4	1.1	0.4	13.9
21	1816–36	22.8	‡	0.8§	23.6	4.1	0.2	27.9
25	1837–61	35.8	—	—	35.8	3.5	1.4	40.7
4	1862–65	121.0	22‖	71.0	213.0	1.0	9.0	223.0
25	1866–90	200.0	12‖	136.0	348.0	6.0	4.0	358.0
26	1891–1916	235.0	15#	245.0	495.0	7.0	15.0	517.0

* Tax on bank dividends, 1796–1802—no separate data.
† Levied 1791–1802 only.
‡ Tax on bank dividends yielded about $0.1 million annually, 1815–1818.
§ Levied 1814–1817 only.
‖ Levied 1863–1872 only.
\# Beginning 1910 on corporate profits.
Source: Selected from table compiled by Paul B. Trescott and appearing in "Some Historical Aspects of Federal Fiscal Policy, 1790–1956," *Federal Expenditure Policy for Economic Growth and Stability,* Joint Economic Committee, 85th Cong., 1st sess. (Washington, D.C.: U.S. Government Printing Office, November 5, 1957), p. 68.

the first time during the 1840s. State governments, however, were forced at times during the century to borrow to meet their functional expenditure requirements, especially those of a social capital (internal improvement) nature. State government debts totaled $175 million during the late 1830s at which time no federal government debt existed. Another state government "borrowing spree" took place during the 1850s.

Continued pressure for state government revenues during the latter half of the nineteenth century caused the states to seek additional tax sources. Thus, taxes on insurance companies, franchise taxes on railroads and public utilities, general corporation franchise taxes, inheritance taxes, and liquor license taxes became important supplementary sources of state revenue. State debts, meanwhile, reached a post–Civil War high of $450 million during the 1870s, but then declined throughout the remainder of the century.

Local government relied heavily upon the property tax to support its expanding functional expenditures during the nineteenth century. The increased utilization of the property tax, however, was still inadequate and many large capital outlays by local government had to be financed through debt creation. Municipal debt, for example, was approximately equal to state debt, and exceeded the federal debt by a ratio of three to one, in 1860. The depression of 1873 caused severe problems for municipal finance, which led to more restrained and more competent financial behavior by city government during the remainder of the century. The property tax continued to be the single most important revenue source for municipalities and for other forms of local government. Property tax rates eventually were further increased and assessed valuation rose sharply, particularly for "real" as opposed to "personal" property, as the century progressed.

Twentieth-Century Revenue Trends

During the 42–year period between 1929 and 1971, public sector tax collections in the United States increased from approximately 10 per-

TABLE 16–9
Public Sector Tax Revenues, Total and by Levels of Government, as Percentages of Net National Product, Selected Calendar Years, 1929–71

	Tax Revenues* as a Percentage of Net National Product†		
Year	*Total Public Sector*	*Federal*	*State- Local*
1929	10.8	3.9	6.9
1930	11.8	3.6	8.2
1935	16.2	6.0	10.2
1940	18.3	9.3	9.0
1944	25.1	20.4	4.7
1948	23.7	17.7	5.9
1952	27.3	20.8	6.5
1956	27.6	20.1	7.5
1960	29.6	20.9	8.7
1964	29.2	19.8	9.3
1968	32.2	22.0	10.2
1971	32.3	20.7	11.6

* Tax revenues as they appear in the National Income and Product Accounts. Business taxes are treated on an accrual basis. Contributions for social insurance are included and tax revenues are net of refunds.
† Net national product, which consists of gross national product minus capital consumption allowances, is used since it is assumed that the tax burden does not fall on national product allocated to replace consumed capital.
Source: U.S. Department of Commerce.

cent to more than 30 percent of net national product. (See Table 16–9). This represents a growth in "direct" allocational influence by the public sector during the period to the extent that governmental "exhaustive" (as opposed to "transfer") expenditures are involved. The relative growth in public sector tax receipts is shared by both the federal and state-local categories of government. The primary growth, however, is that of the federal government which at the present time collects approximately two thirds of total public sector taxes. Between 1929 and

1971, federal tax receipts as a percentage of net national product increased by more than five times while combined state-local tax collections less than doubled during the period.

Table 16–10 demonstrates the present pattern of "tax revenue sources" for the three levels of government in the American public sector (employment or payroll taxes excluded). It may be observed that personal and corporation income taxes bear the brunt of federal tax revenue requirements constituting 82 percent of total federal tax revenues during fiscal 1971. Meanwhile, 57 percent of the state government total was derived from sales and gross receipts taxes. On the other hand, property taxes were the major tax revenue source for local governments contributing 84 percent of the total.

When the three levels of government are "aggregated" into the total public sector, Table 16–10 reveals that the federal government receives 88 percent of all income tax revenues, the state governments receive over one half of the sales and gross receipts tax revenues, and local governments receive 97 percent of the revenues derived from the property tax. Interestingly, income taxes for the federal government and general sales taxes for the state governments were nonexistent as revenue sources at the beginning of this century. However, property taxation was the primary revenue source for the local level of government both at the beginning of the twentieth century and at the present time.

Within the *federal* revenue structure, the personal and corporation income taxes have contributed more revenues than any other tax source since soon after the adoption of the Sixteenth Amendment in 1913.[8] Moreover, payroll taxes under the Social Security Act have gained considerable prominence since the mid-1930s. A number of changes have occurred also in the relative importance of certain *state* tax sources during the twentieth century. For example, 30 percent of state tax revenues came from the general sales tax category (including gross receipts taxes) during 1971. As noted above, the general sales tax was nonexistent in 1900. Furthermore, personal and corporation income taxes, which contributed more than 26 percent of state tax revenue in 1971, contributed virtually no revenue in 1902. In addition, the motor fuels tax, which provided nearly 13 percent of state tax revenue in 1971, was nonexistent in 1902. To a lesser extent, similar trends may be observed for the tobacco tax, motor vehicle and operator's license fees, and the severance taxes collected by state governments.

On the other hand, the relative importance of certain other state taxes declined during the century. This is particularly true of the property tax which decreased from 52.6 to a 2.2 percent ratio of total state

---

[8] See Chapter 9.

TABLE 16–10

Public Sector Tax Revenues, Percentage Distribution by Type of Tax* and Level of Government, Fiscal Year 1971

Item	By Type of Tax†				By Level of Government‡			
	All	Federal	State	Local	All	Federal	State	Local
Total	100.0	100.0	100.0	100.0	100.0	59.1	22.2	18.7
Property	16.3	—	2.2	84.6	100.0	—	3.0	97.0
Sales and Gross Receipts	22.7	14.1	57.4	8.4	100.0	36.9	56.2	7.0
Custom Duties	1.0	1.9	—	—	100.0	100.0	—	—
General Sales and Gross receipts	7.7	—	30.0	5.4	100.0	—	86.9	13.1
Selective Sales and Gross receipts	13.8	12.2	27.4	3.0	100.0	55.8	40.5	3.8
Motor Fuel	4.6	2.8	12.9	0.1	100.0	37.0	62.6	0.4
Alcoholic Beverages	2.7	3.5	3.0	0.1	100.0	75.0	24.0	1.0
Tobacco Products	2.1	1.6	4.9	0.3	100.0	45.2	51.9	2.9
Public Utilities	1.7	1.5	2.0	1.7	100.0	54.5	26.3	19.1
Other	2.9	2.8	4.6	0.8	100.0	58.4	36.4	5.2
Income Taxes	55.3	82.3	26.3	4.0	100.0	88.0	10.6	1.3
Personal	42.3	62.9	19.7	4.0	100.0	87.9	10.3	1.8
Corporation	13.0	19.5	6.6	—	100.0	88.7	11.3	—
Motor Vehicle Licenses	1.4	—	5.7	0.4	100.0	—	94.1	5.9
Death and Gift	2.1	2.7	2.2	—	100.0	77.2	22.8	—
All Other	2.3	0.8	6.2	2.6	100.0	20.3	59.2	20.5

* Excluding payroll taxes.
† Read table "vertically."
‡ Read table "horizontally."
Source: U.S. Department of Commerce, Bureau of the Census.

tax revenue between 1902 and 1971—an intentional result of state government efforts to improve the "revenue picture" of local governments. Also experiencing downward relative trends, but to a lesser extent, during the period were sales and license taxes on the sale of alcoholic beverages, death, and gift taxes. Intergovernmental "shared" revenues, which were less than 5 percent of all state revenues in 1902, were 24 percent during 1971. This trend will be evaluated later in Part Three under the discussion of fiscal federalism.

The general pattern of *local* government tax sources also demonstrates significant changes during the twentieth century. The property tax, however, remained stable in relative importance contributing 88 percent of total tax revenues at the beginning of the century and 84.6 percent in 1971. Several local government tax sources increased their relative importance between 1902 and 1971, namely, sales, income, and insurance trust fund (payroll) taxes. Importantly, there has been a considerable increase in local government revenues derived from intergovernmental sources. Between 1902 and 1971, the proportion of total local government revenues received from state governments increased from 5.7 percent to 30.8 percent of total revenues and that received from the federal government grew from 0.4 percent to 3.4 percent of total local government revenues.

Functional Analysis of Twentieth-Century Expenditure and Revenue Trends

The functional reasons for the relative expansion of the public sector within aggregate economic activity in the United States may be classified into two broad categories: (1) the more *intensive* application of governmental economic activity within areas of allocation previously provided by the public sector, and (2) the lateral or *extensive* movement of government into new areas of economic activity. The latter movement may involve, for example, the allocation either of economic goods previously allocated by the private sector or of newly developed goods resulting from technological innovation and previously allocated by neither sector.

The primary causes of the relative growth of the public sector in the United States may be found within the first category which refers to the more intensive performance of established governmental functions. War or defense, education, and highways are long-established public sector activities in the American economy. For example, "direct" military spending by the federal government grew from $191 *million* in 1900 to $77.6 *billion* in 1971. The significance of defense spending to public sector growth, of course, is indicated even more sharply if "indirect" defense spending is included in the defense total.[9]

---

[9] See Table 16–4.

The influence of war upon public sector spending may be dramatized further by the following facts.[10] The federal government spent more money financing the Civil War between 1861 and 1865 than it had spent from its beginning in 1789, under George Washington's first administration, until Abraham Lincoln's first administration. The federal government, moreover, spent in its next major war, World War I, whose primary influence covered the years 1917–20, more than it had spent for all other purposes, including all previous wars, from the first administration of George Washington until Woodrow Wilson's second administration. The spending during World War I included loans to other Allied nations, most of which were never repaid.

Yet, the story has not ended! The federal government undertook more expenditures to conduct World War II between 1941 and 1945 than it had spent throughout its entire history for all purposes combined, other wars included, between the first administration of George Washington and the third administration of Franklin D. Roosevelt. This cumulative spending total includes those measures employed to alleviate the depression of the 1930s, a fact which exposes the prevalent mythology that New Deal domestic economic policy primarily caused the relative growth of the federal component of the public sector as well as that of the entire public sector as a proportion of aggregate economic activity during the twentieth century.[11] Furthermore, the data for 1971, which show that over 35 percent of federal budget expenditures are for "direct" defense purposes and that more than 50 percent are for defense in a "broadly defined" sense, suggest that no fundamental diminishment in the importance of the defense function has yet occurred.

While war and defense were causing the federal government to perform more intensively its time-honored function of national protection, state and local governments were expanding their expenditures to meet the growing demands of an urban-industrial population for education, highways, police and fire protection, public health, and other services. Ever-improving technology, and related cultural adjustments connected with an urban-oriented society, help to explain the growing demands for these governmental economic products. As demonstrated previously, state governments have assumed the primary responsibility for highway services and local governments for educational services.

---

[10] See Troy J. Cauley, *Public Finance and the General Welfare* (Columbus, Ohio: Charles E. Merrill Books, Inc., 1960), pp. 39–41.

[11] Admittedly, the above comparisons are presented in terms of current dollars and thus do not adjust for secular inflationary trends. Inflation, however, does very little in an overall sense to counteract the impressive influence of war and defense expenditures upon relative federal government and public sector growth trends in the United States.

It has been observed that the lateral expansion of government into new areas of allocation has been a less significant cause of absolute and relative public sector growth than has the more intensive performance of established functions. Three areas of lateral expansion, however, deserve comment, namely, social security measures, macroeconomic anticyclical and growth policies, and microeconomic regulatory policies. During the twentieth century, government in the United States has accepted a mandate from the people to increase the allocation of social welfare services. These services include old-age plans for retirement, survivors insurance, unemployment compensation, medical care for the aged, and industrial accident benefits. Though the historical evolution of public sector allocation of these services was initiated in other Western nations (such as Germany and England), the public sector in the United States has moved to a present position where these have become prominent areas of economic influence. Importantly, the provision of such services by the public sector may be essentially viewed as a new function of government in the United States as compared to long-established functions such as the provision of defense and roads.

Government also has moved during the twentieth century into the deliberate influencing of aggregate economic activity in terms of production, employment, income, price level, balance of payments, and economic growth goals.[12] This may be considered alternately as anticyclical policy or as "regulation" in a macroeconomic sense. The development of Keynesian economics has led to widespread acceptance in the Western world of aggregate *fiscal policy*. The United States was among the last of the major Western industrial nations to accept the deliberate fiscal policy technique.[13] The federal tax reductions of 1964 and 1965, however, are good evidence of the culmination of an evolutionary pro-fiscal policy movement which had been historically initiated in the United States in the form of the New Deal "public works" measures of the 1930s and supported in principle by the Employment Act of 1946. Aggregate fiscal policy of both the tax and expenditure variety undoubtedly represents an important movement by American government into a new functional area of responsibility.[14]

---

[12] See Part Four of this book for a detailed analysis of this subject.

[13] For a thorough analysis of the evolution of aggregate fiscal policy in the United States, see Herbert Stein, *The Fiscal Revolution in America* (Chicago: University of Chicago Press, 1969).

[14] There is, of course, a strategic interrelationship between the fiscal policy goals of stabilization and economic growth and such functionally important areas of expenditure as the long-established defense function. During the last 30 years, for example, part of the contribution to stabilization and growth made by the federal government has been achieved through increases in aggregate demand caused by war and defense expenditures.

The public sector in the United States also has moved laterally during the last 100 years into new areas of microeconomic regulation. This expansion takes the form of such allocative techniques as general anti-trust laws and public utility regulation. This is not to suggest, however, that American government ever completely avoided microeconomic regulatory influence. Nonetheless, the preindustrial American economy of the pre–Civil War era did not require allocative regulation to the extent that it is required today. That is, big business and big labor today require governmental guidance and restraint in a manner unknown to agricultural societies. Growing population and urbanization, moreover, both of which are related to America's industrial revolution, create additional demands for governmental allocative influence. Regulation of the microeconomic variety may thus be considered a lateral expansion of government into a new area of economic activity.

In summary, the public sector in the United States has grown both in *relative* and *absolute* terms during this century. The primary explanations of this growth are found in the category of more intensive performance of traditional governmental functions. The lateral movement of government into new areas such as social welfare, macroeconomic regulation, and microeconomic regulation, however, has also been significant. Nevertheless, these have been far overshadowed by the impact on the public sector of the long-established governmental functions of defense, highways, and education—especially defense.

THEORETICAL ANALYSIS OF PUBLIC SECTOR GROWTH

The experience of the Western world during the last half of the nineteenth century and in the twentieth century has been one of growth in the public sectors of most industrial nations. This growth has been evident not only in an *absolute* sense—which would be expected in an environment of expanding population, output, and complexity in economic activity—but also on a *relative* basis. Thus, while the resources allocated by both the public and private sectors have increased in absolute terms, a higher proportion of total resources are now being allocated through the influence of government. Some of the theoretical efforts to explain this phenomenon, as well as to explain the "patterns" of this change, are discussed in this section of the chapter.

Wagner's Hypothesis of Increasing Governmental Activity

Statement of the Hypothesis. Adolph Wagner, the famous German political economist (1835–1917), believed that a functional "cause-and-effect" relationship exists between the growth of an economy and the relative growth of its public sector. According to Wagner, relative growth of the government sector is an inherent characteristic of industrializing economies. He referred not only to Britain, which essentially had completed its industrial revolution before Wagner's time, but to nations such as the United States, France, and Germany (in the West) and Japan (in the East) whose industrial revolutions were contemporary to Wagner's life. Hence, the *Wagner Hypothesis of Increasing Governmental Activity* holds that as per capita income and output increase in industrializing nations, the public sectors of these nations necessarily grow as a proportion of total economic activity.[15] This may be shown as

$$\frac{RPCOPG^1}{RPCI^1} < \frac{RPCOPG^2}{RPCI^2}$$

with *RPCOPG* representing the "real per capita output of public goods," *RPCI* representing "real per capita income," and with "1" indicating an earlier and "2" a later point of time.

Wagner believed that social progress was the basic cause of the relative growth of government in industrializing economies. The "chain-reaction" circumstances described by Wagner are that social progress leads to a growth in government functions which, in turn, leads to the absolute and relative growth of governmental economic activity. The hypothesis is clearly secular (long-term) in nature.

In his attempt to validate the hypothesis, Wagner distinguished certain types of governmental activities or functions. One function is that of providing the law and order essential for the "environmental conditions" within which a market functions.[16] Second, Wagner described governmental participation in the material production of economic goods, including the provision of certain "social products" like communications, education, and monetary-banking arrangements in the face of "market failure."

It is argued that need for the *first* type of public sector activity, *law and order*, increases along with economic growth and its increasing per capita output because the inevitable accompanying growth in centralized administration results in an impersonalization and automation of many social and economic institutions. Economic growth and centralization of administration thus increase labor specialization and cause greater complexities and interdependencies in economic and social life. Efficient performance of the economy, given the existence of these

---

[15] Adolph Wagner, *Finanzwissenschaft* (3rd ed.; Leipzig: 1890). For a comprehensive analysis of the Wagner hypothesis, see Richard M. Bird, *The Growth of Government Spending in Canada* (Toronto: Canadian Tax Foundation, 1970), chap. 4.

[16] See Chapter 2.

interdependencies and the desirability of maintaining qualitative governmental services, suggests the need for additional public sector economic influence.

Wagner believed, *secondly*, that *government corporations* must produce certain economic goods requiring large fixed investment because private corporations cannot undertake such investment on a profitable basis. The similarity of this viewpoint to those of Smith, Mill, and others is obvious. These industries often are characterized by natural monopoly conditions of production which involve heavy fixed costs, or by joint consumption conditions, or by significant consumption externalities (*not* Wagner's terminology) which give the goods an "income elastic demand" during a period of industrialization. Such goods take on important characteristics of publicness and thus incur a social (collective) interest in their allocation.

Graphical Presentation of the Wagner Hypothesis. The Wagner hypothesis of increasing governmental activity is demonstrated in Figure 16–1. In this graph, the real per capita output of public goods

FIGURE 16–1
Wagner Hypothesis: The Relative Expansion of Public Sector Economic Activity over Time

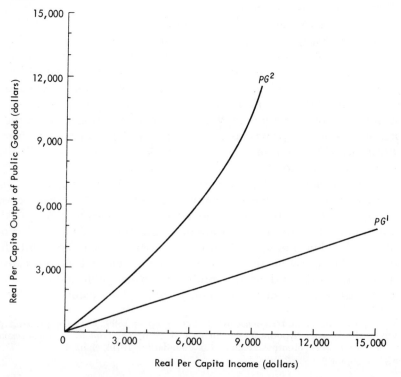

(RPCOPG) is measured on the vertical axis and real per capita income (RPCI) on the horizontal axis. Time is an important third dimension implicit to the graph because the growth both in the real per capita output of public goods and in real per capita income is realistically assumed to take place on a historical basis over an extended period of time. Line PG^1 represents a circumstance in which the public sector maintains a constant proportion of the total economic production of the society over time. In other words, as real per capita income increases due to the economic development of the society, the real per capita output of public goods remains at the same proportion of total economic activity. Thus,

$$\frac{RPCOPG^1}{RPCI^1} = \frac{RPCOPG^2}{RPCI^2}$$

The constant proportions line may now be used as a reference point to the graphical presentation of the Wagner hypothesis as depicted by Line PG^2. Along Line PG^2, the proportion of resources devoted to the output of public goods is expanding over time. That is,

$$\frac{RPCOPG^1}{RPCI^1} < \frac{RPCOPG^2}{RPCI^2}$$

Alternate graphical presentations of the *Wagner hypothesis* are presented in Figures 16–2 and 16–3 (a, b). These graphs are based upon Figures 1–1 and 1–4, respectively, in Chapter 1 which relate to the issue of "intersector resource allocation." In Figure 16–2, which corresponds to Figure 1–1, it is demonstrated that over time a society could move from point *a,* where the public sector allocates only 10 percent of the resouces of the society, to point *b* where it allocates one third of the resources. Of course, this would be characteristic of Wagner's hypothesis in an industrializing nation.

Figures 16–3a and 16–3b demonstrate the same phenomenon using an indifference graph approach. The corresponding analysis in Chapter 1 is presented in Figure 1–4. It may be observed in Figure 16–3a that the public sector allocates only 10 percent of the output in the nation with a $400 billion gross national product. However, as the resources of the society expand over time in the process of economic development, the societal production-possibility (transformation) curve (P) moves further to the right in Figure 16–3b, as compared to Figure 16–3a, and the total output of the nation expands from $400 billion to $900 billion. Importantly, economic development has caused societal preferences between "public" and "private" goods to change and the public sector is now providing one third instead of 10 percent of economic output. Once again, the graphical presentation is consistent with the Wagner hypothesis.

FIGURE 16–2

Wagner Hypothesis as Demonstrated by Graph Based on Figure 1–1

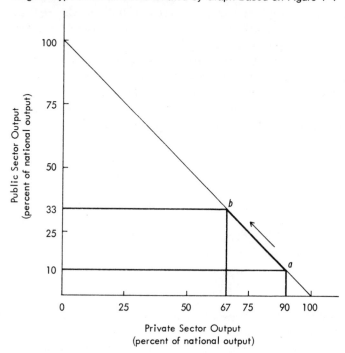

The Wagner Hypothesis: Preindustrial, and Postindustrial Maturity Stages of a Society's Economic Development. Since Wagner's analysis was directed toward industrializing nations, a discussion of the hypothesis should delimit the "industrialization era" in a nation's history from a possible earlier "preindustrial stage" and also from a possible later period of "postindustrial maturity" when living standards are affluent not only on an *average* basis but on a *distributional* basis as well.[17] Figure 16–4, which is based on the terminology of Figure 16–1, provides in line PG^2 an example of how the proportion of the real per capita output of public goods to real per capita income may change depending upon the particular stage of development in a nation's economy. It may be conjectured that the proportion $\dfrac{RPCOPG}{RPCI}$ will tend to decline in the "preindustrialization" and "postindustrialization" stages of a society's economic evolution. Thus,

---

[17] For a discussion of the "preindustrial" and "postindustrial" maturity stages of a society's economic development, see Walt Whitman Rostow, *Economic Growth* (New York: Cambridge University Press, 1960).

FIGURE 16–3

Wagner Hypothesis as Demonstrated by Graphs Based on Figure 1–4

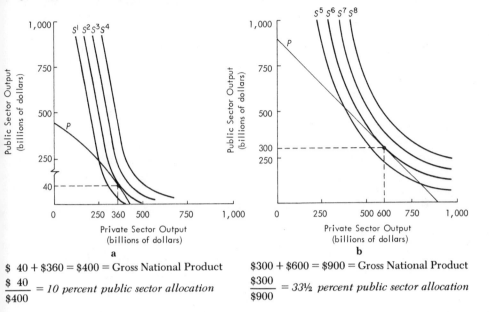

$40 + $360 = $400 = Gross National Product

$$\frac{\$\ 40}{\$400} = 10 \ percent \ public \ sector \ allocation$$

$300 + $600 = $900 = Gross National Product

$$\frac{\$300}{\$900} = 33\tfrac{1}{3} \ percent \ public \ sector \ allocation$$

$$\frac{RPCOPG^1}{RPCI^1} > \frac{RPCOPG^2}{RPCI^2}$$

would represent either of these stages. The reasons why this may occur are described below.

Most subsistence wants and goods have traditionally been provided by the private sector through market-type arrangements since food, clothing, and shelter are divisible goods to which the exclusion principle can be applied. Consequently, the gradual economic expansion of a preindustrial society would likely cause the real per capita output of private goods to become a greater proportion of real per capita income which would mean that the real per capita output of public goods would become a declining proportion of real per capita income.[18]

As real per capita income continues to increase, however, the relative allocative importance of each sector may be expected to change. For example, investment in social capital items such as communica-

[18] The following data for 1965 lend some evidence to this tendency: underdeveloped nations such as Bolivia, China (Taiwan), Colombia, Ghana, Jamaica, the Korean Republic, the Philippines, and Peru collect tax revenues at a ratio of less than 15 percent of gross national product while developed nations such as Austria, Belgium, Canada, Denmark, Finland, France, West Germany, Italy, the Netherlands, New Zealand, Norway, Sweden, the United Kingdom, and the United States have tax/GNP ratios of 25 percent or higher. Also, see the related discussion in Chapter 22.

tions, transportation, and education must take place as part of the economic development process. Since these goods tend to posses heavy fixed costs of production and collective consumption characteristics, they are often provided by the government sector of the economy rather than by the market. Thus, let us say that as real per capita income rises above $3,000 in Figure 16–4, the economy enters an industrialization stage and the real per capita output of public goods now becomes a greater proportion of real per capita income over an extended period of time. This stage, which represents the Wagner hypothesis, is largely explained by the fact that important social capital items provided by the public sector have now become part of aggregate demand. Ultimately, these social overhead items will be provided in sufficient quantities and the society will attain postindustrial maturity at a real per capita income level of (say) $10,500.

All spending units now possess an adequate standard of living in the

FIGURE 16–4

Relative Changes in Public Sector Economic Activity during Preindustrialization, Industrialization, and Postindustrialization Periods of Economic Development

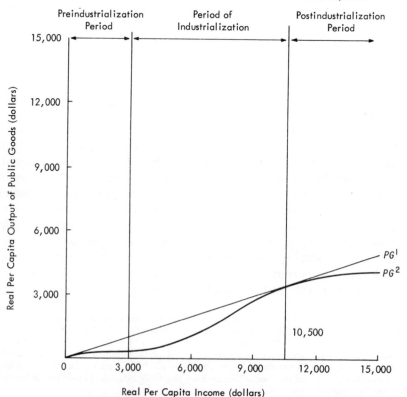

Real Per Capita Income (dollars)

postindustrial society. It seems plausible to suggest that, at this stage of economic development, government may already be providing adequate quantities of those economic goods with decreasing production cost and collective consumption characteristics so that society will turn increasingly to additional private sector output. Moreover, society may be resisting "too large" a public sector, in relative terms, due to a cultural preference for market activity with its greater individual freedom and with its absence of "compulsory taxation." Hence, the real per capita output of private goods may well become, once again, a larger proportion of real per capita income during the postindustrial maturity stage. Oppositely, the relative importance of the public sector may be expected to decline.

Critique of the Wagner Hypothesis. Though Wagner's hypothesis contains certain attributes, it also contains several defects. Primarily, it should be observed that the hypothesis deals with "interdisciplinary" phenomena though it is not essentially interdisciplinary in its analytical framework. Political science, economics, and sociology are among the several disciplines which must be involved in any theory of public sector expenditure. Such theories must consider the cultural characteristics of a society. It thus seems unlikely that the causal conditions described by Wagner, which essentially are of an economic nature, constitute *all* of the primary determinants of a relatively expanding public sector during industrialization and economic growth. Although the Wagner hypothesis possesses the attribute of accumulating and partially explaining important historical facts, its lack of a comprehensive analytical framework causes it to fall short in these explanations. Yet, it does provide a convenient framework for discussion and for further research.

It is observed by Peacock and Wiseman that the Wagner argument contains three serious defects:[19] (1) the fact that it is based upon an organic self-determining theory of the state, which is not the prevailing theory of state in most Western nations; (2) its omission of the influence of *war* on governmental spending; and (3) the fact that Wagner stresses a long-term trend of public economic activity which tends to overlook the significant "time pattern" or "process" of public expenditure growth.

The Displacement, Inspection, and Concentration Effects

Peacock and Wiseman, in their work published during the early 1960s, stress the "time pattern" of public spending trends.[20] Their

---

[19] Alan T. Peacock and Jack Wiseman, *The Growth of Public Expenditure in the United Kingdom* (Princeton, N.J.: Princeton University Press, 1961), p. xxiii.

[20] Ibid.

general approach is inclusive of three separate, though related, concepts. These are the *displacement, inspection,* and *concentration* effects. Using empirical data for the British economy after 1890, they observe that the relative growth of the British public sector has occurred on a "steplike" rather than on a "continuous growth" basis. Government fiscal activities, in other words, have risen "step by step" to successive new plateaus during the period studied. Most of the absolute and relative increases (steps upward) in taxing and spending by British government have taken place during periods of "major social disturbance" such as war and depression. These disturbances create a *displacement effect* by which the previous (lower) tax and expenditure levels are replaced by new and higher budgetary levels. After the social disturbance has ended, however, the new levels of "tax tolerance" which have emerged make the society willing to support a higher level of public expenditure since the society realizes that it is capable of carrying a heavier tax burden than it previously had thought possible. Thus, when the major social disturbance ends, no strong motivation exists for a return to the lower predisturbance level of taxation. The greater governmental revenues are used, instead, to support a permanently higher level of public sector allocation. Over the secular period 1890–1960, this displacement procedure occurred several times in Great Britian.

Figure 16–5 demonstrates the displacement effect. Time (in years)

FIGURE 16–5
The "Displacement Effect"

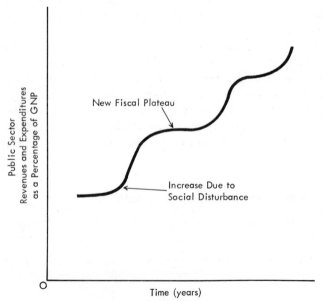

is measured along the horizontal axis while public sector revenues (mostly taxes) and public expenditures as a percentage of gross national product are measured along the vertical axis. It is suggested that as social disturbances cause a relative expansion of the public sector, the displacement effect which occurs helps to explain the "time pattern" by which the governmental growth took place. This displacement effect does not require that the new higher plateau of expenditure continue the same expenditure pattern that was created by the social disturbance. Although some of the increased expenditures, such as veterans benefits and debt interest, are direct results of a social disturbance, other expenditure items frequently involve the expansion of government into new areas of economic activity. Some of these new areas may have been provided formerly by the private sector while others may be the result of technological advancement which allows new goods to exist which have no previous allocational history. Moreover, war or other social disturbances frequently force people and their governments to seek solutions to important problems which previously had been neglected. This is referred to as an *inspection effect*.

In addition to the displacement and inspection effects, Peacock and Wiseman also describe a *concentration effect*.[21] This concept refers to the apparent tendency for central (national) government economic activity to become an increasing proportion of total public sector economic activity when a society is experiencing economic growth. This means, of course, that lower (subnational) levels of government necessarily will decline in relative importance within the public sector. Empirical data for the British economy are consistent with this hypothesis during the twentieth century. Data for the United States are less definitive in this regard and since World War II the federal government of the United States has been an essentially constant proportion of total public sector economic activity.[22]

In summary, Peacock and Wiseman conclude that in Great Britain: (1) the relative growth of the public sector tends to occur on a steplike basis ("displacement effect"), (2) an "inspection" process occurs whereby existing problems are more clearly defined with potential solutions more carefully studied during a major disturbance, and (3) a "concentration" process exists whereby central government becomes a larger proportion of the aggregate public sector: The Peacock and Wiseman approach to governmental spending trends is much more modest in what it purports to explain than is the Wagner hypothesis. It does not claim to be an immutable economic principle or law; it merely attempts to point out some characteristics of the growth pat-

---

[21] Ibid.

[22] See Table 16–2

tern, not to isolate *all* of the important causal variables involved in public sector growth. Both the Wagner and the Peacock-Wiseman arguments, however, contribute to the understanding of the process of public sector growth in industrial nations. Yet, neither should be placed in the high status of an economic law.

The Peacock-Wiseman approach would appear to apply less neatly to the pattern of public sector growth in the United States than it does to that of Great Britain. Nevertheless, the growth of governmental economic activity in the United States has been rather closely related to major social disturbances such as war (World Wars I and II) and depression (the 1930s). In this sense, some approximation of the steplike process of the "displacement effect" may be noted. Moreover, the twentieth century as a whole has experienced a significant relative expansion in the importance of the federal government component of the public sector while a significant relative decline in the local government component has occurred.[23] This would seemingly resemble the "concentration effect" segment of the Peacock-Wiseman hypothesis. The relationship of public sector economic activity to aggregate economic activity experienced a relative decline, however, after World Wars I and II which is inconsistent with the Peacock-Wiseman prediction that the new "disturbance-created" tolerance level of taxation would find additional expenditure outlets in other areas of economic activity in order to maintain the new tax collection level. Moreover, it should be recognized in any comparison of American public sector behavior with the functioning of the displacement and concentration effects in Great Britain that "national defense" has played a unique role in the United States. Thus, perhaps defense as such, and not the "tolerance level" of taxation and scale effects, should receive priority consideration in any cause-and-effect analysis of the phenomenon in the United States. In conclusion, it would seem that the Peacock and Wiseman hypothesis is only partially useful for application to the growth of the public sector in the United States.

The Critical-Limit Hypothesis

Another public sector hypothesis concerned with the tolerance level of taxation is the *critical-limit hypothesis*. This analysis was developed by the British economist, Colin Clark, immediately following World War II.[24] The critical-limit hypothesis concludes from the empirical data of several Western nations for the period between World War I and World War II that inflation necessarily occurs when the govern-

---

[23] See Table 16–2

[24] Colin Clark, "Public Finance and Changes in the Value of Money," *Economic Journal*, December 1945, pp. 371–89.

ment sector, as measured in terms of taxes and other receipts, exceeds 25 percent of aggregate economic activity. This is alleged to be true even under circumstances when the budget remains in balance.

The critical-limit hypothesis is based upon institutional factors. Clark suggests that: (1) when taxes collected by government reach the critical 25 percent ratio, community behavior patterns change and people become less productive since incentives are harmed by the fact that increasing proportions of additional income must be paid in taxes under a progressive tax system, and (2) people become less resistant to various inflationary means of financing government expenditures. The loss of incentive thus tends to reduce "aggregate supply" while the increased purchasing power resulting from inflationary financing techniques tends to expand effective "aggregate demand." Inflation tends to result from this new, "aggregate supply—aggregate demand equilibrium," under conditions of high resource employment.

The critical-limit hypothesis resembles the displacement effect in the sense that it concentrates upon institutional factors such as the tolerance level of taxation. Except for this similarity, however, the two hypotheses and their conclusions are quite distinct. The critical-limit hypothesis has received very limited support from academic circles, but has been more popularly received in the business community. Empirical evidence, however, demonstrates that a number of nations have violated the 25 percent limit during recent decades *without* significant inflationary results. Moreover, it is clear that inflation is a phenomenon characterized by multiple determinants. Part Four of this book will consider these multideterminants of inflation in reference to public sector stabilization policy.

17

The Aggregate Public Sector Budget: Fiscal Institutions and Budget Concepts

CONSTITUTIONAL DIVISION OF FISCAL POWERS

The federal *Constitution* is the basic legal document which allocates the "fiscal powers" of taxing and spending between the federal and state levels of government in the United States. The political structure of the public sector in the United States is that of a *federation* with a division of "sovereign" governmental power between the central government and the states.[1] This may be contrasted to a *unitary* system of government, such as that in Great Britain, where only the central government is sovereign. In both nations, the political structure is that of a representative democracy. Moreover, in each nation local governments are "nonsovereign." They are created through state government sovereignty in the United States and by the central government in Great Britain.

Two powers inherent in sovereign government give the public sector the "authority" to institute tax laws. These are the *revenue* and *police* powers of government. The former implies the basic right of government to collect revenues for the support of public sector functions. The latter gives authority to sovereign government to control persons and property for the purpose of promoting the general welfare. Most taxes exist for both revenue and welfare purposes, though one

---

[1] A sovereign government is one which possesses "independent" or "autonomous" authority. That is, it exists "by its own right" and not as a creation of some other unit of government.

motive or the other will usually be dominant.[2] For example, the American public sector uses excise taxes on tobacco and alcoholic beverage products for "sumptuary" or "control" purposes. Yet, these excises also provide significant revenues to the public sector. Moreover, the federal personal income tax, which exists primarily for revenue-raising purposes, still performs important "regulatory" functions. These functions include macroeconomic control in the sense of anticyclical or stabilization performance as well as microeconomic control in such matters as the detection and conviction of noted gangsters and racketeers.

The Constitution, by denying certain rights and powers to the federal and state governments, "reserves" them to the American people. Furthermore, it defines certain "enumerated" powers for the federal government. In turn, these are supplemented by other "implied" powers which have their basic origin in court interpretation. State governments also have certain powers "reserved" to them by the Constitution. In this regard, the Tenth Amendment to the Constitution states that "the powers not delegated to the United States by the Constitution, nor prohibited by it to the States, are reserved to the States respectively, or to the people."

The boundary between federal and state authority is difficult to define in a precise manner. While a unitary system of government can rely primarily upon unwritten traditions for its political-economic direction, a federal system requires a written constitution and subsequent judicial interpretation of the laws which are legislated under the constitution. The trend in the United States during much of the twentieth century has been toward a more liberal interpretation of the Constitution in behalf of greater central government authority in setting the political-economic direction of the society. Moreover, a perennial conflict exists between the federal government's obligation "to promote the general welfare" and its constitutional inability "to compel coordination and uniformity" among the tax and expenditure policies of the various states.

An extremely important fiscal clause in the Constitution is that which gives Congress "Power to lay and collect Taxes, Duties, Imposts and Excises, to pay the Debts and provide for the common Defence and general Welfare."[3] This represents a very extensive grant of power from the Constitution to the federal government. The Constitutional Convention had been called in 1787 primarily for the purpose of solving the post-Revolutionary War financial crisis of the new nation. Prior to the adoption of the Constitution, the Continental Congress, which directed the new nation, possessed no taxing authority. Instead, only the

---

[2] See the relevant discussion in Chapter 6.

[3] *U.S. Constitution,* Art. I, Sec. 8.

states had the authority to impose taxes. As a result, a major financial crisis occurred. The extensive fiscal clause quoted above was the product of this crisis which received intense discussion at the Continental Congress. The interpretation of "general welfare" in this clause, as suggested above, has become more liberal in terms of central governmental authority over the years. In part, this has followed from a more liberal interpretation of the concept of "interstate commerce."

Fiscal Limitations on the Federal Government

The Constitution places several significant limitations on the fiscal activities of the federal government. *First,* the federal government is prohibited from taxing the export of goods to other nations. However, it is not prohibited from levying taxes (duties) on goods imported from other countries. The export clause was placed in the Constitution primarily at the insistence of the southern states which wanted their farm staples to remain competitive in world markets, that is, not made higher in price by export duties.

A *second* limitation placed on federal fiscal authority by the Constitution is the provision that "all Duties, Imposts and Excises shall be uniform throughout the United States."[4] This clause refers to geographical uniformity. For example, legal residence in one state rather than in another cannot be the basis for differential federal personal income tax rates. Or, the federal gasoline excise cannot be 10 cents per gallon in New York and 4 cents per gallon in California. Furthermore, the federal government could not impose a gasoline tax in one state without imposing it in all other states. However, it can legally tax an object which is "relevant" to only one or part of the states in the sense that it is found in some states and not in others. Hence, the recently-repealed manufacturer's excise on new automobiles could be imposed legally even though manufacturing of cars takes place in only a few states.

A *third* important federal government fiscal limitation in the Constitution is the clause which holds that "no Capitation, or other direct, Tax shall be laid, unless in Proportion to the Census."[5] This limitation has been more important historically than it is at the present time due to the ratification of the Sixteenth Amendment to the Constitution in 1913. The Constitution does not define clearly what is meant by a "direct" tax, though probably the founding fathers had property taxes and poll (lump-sum) taxes in mind. However, the clause was used historically to question the constitutionality of a federal personal income tax. This led supporters of the income tax to seek a constitutional

---

[4] *U.S. Constitution,* Art. I, Sec. 8.

[5] *U.S. Constitution,* Art. I, Sec. 9.

amendment. An income tax, of course, would be unacceptable if it had to be apportioned among the various states according to population.

For example, two states may each possess a population of 20 million people. However, one state may have a taxable income of $30 billion and the other (poorer) state may have a taxable income of only $15 billion. If the income tax is considered to be a "direct" tax, the taxpayers of each state would be required to contribute the same absolute amount of tax revenues to the federal government, in accordance with their equal populations, even though one state possesses much greater tax-paying ability than the other. Obviously, the tax would be unsatisfactory in distributional equity terms if "income" is accepted as an indicator of the ability to pay taxes. The tax, in effect, would be "regressive" against the residents of the lower-income state. Consequently, the Sixteenth Amendment to the Constitution, adopted in 1913, excludes the income tax from the direct tax apportionment limitation. It states:

> The Congress shall have power to lay and collect taxes on incomes, from whatever source derived, without apportionment among the several States, and without regard to any census or enumeration.

The constitutionality of federal income taxation is made abundantly clear by this amendment.

A *fourth* important public finance provision in the Constitution is found in the Fifth Amendment to the Constitution. This amendment states that "no person shall be . . . deprived of life, liberty, or property, without due process of law." The implication is that taxes and other fiscal actions cannot be so arbitrary or discriminatory so as to result in the "confiscation" of property or the denial of fundamental personal rights. Actually, the federal courts have not employed this clause to any great extent as a limitation on federal fiscal powers, but they have stated that the use of poll taxes by lower-level governments as a "condition" for voting in federal elections is unconstitutional.[6]

Fiscal Limitations on State Governments

There are several significant limitations imposed by the Constitution on the fiscal authority of state governments and, indirectly, on the local governments which they create: (1) State governments, like the federal government, are prohibited from taxing exports. (2) Moreover, they similarly are constrained by a "due process" provision similar to that described above for the federal government. This is found in the form of the Fourteenth Amendment to the Constitution. As applied to taxation, this provision prohibits the imposition of taxes by state and local

---

[6] See Chapter 14.

governments beyond their legal areas of jurisdiction as well as the prohibition of unduly arbitrary or confiscatory taxation. (3) In addition, the state governments are prohibited from levying import duties without the consent of Congress. (4) Furthermore, state governments are directly prohibited from the levying of tonnage taxes, based on the size or capacity of inland water carriers, without the permission of Congress. (5) Since states are "explicitly" forbidden to levy export, import, and tonnage taxes, it is implied, and also verified by judicial interpretation, that they cannot "tax interstate and foreign commerce." The Constitution directly relegates this authority to the federal government when it gives Congress the right "to regulate Commerce with foreign Nations, and *among the several* States, and with the Indian Tribes,"[7] (6) Finally, an indirect limitation on state fiscal authority results from the fact that the Constitution gives the federal government exclusive authority to make treaties with other nations. When such treaties relate to fiscal matters, state governments are bound to set their tax and expenditure actions in accordance with the terms of the treaties.

The Taxation of Governmental "Instrumentalities"

An important area of indirect legal limitation on both federal and state governments involves the taxation of *instrumentalities*. This is not stated explicitly in the Constitution, but instead has been developed through judicial interpretation. According to this limitation (which is replete with exceptions to the rule), state governments cannot tax federal instrumentalities and the federal government cannot tax state instrumentalities. Of course, such a concept could exist only in a federation where sovereign state or provincial governments exist alongside a sovereign central government. Governmental "instrumentalities" are difficult to define. One public finance scholar notes that "in its broadest scope" the term would include "all corporations (that get their charters from governments), all land (underlying title lies with state governments), banks, copyrights and patents, voting, college football games, sale to or by the government, government property, government bonds, and government enterprises."[8] In any case, governmental property, sales, and legal instruments would normally be classified as "instrumentalities" of government. Because of this limitation the federal government did not apply the federal personal income tax to most salaries paid by state and local governments until the Supreme Court reversed this position in 1938.

---

[7] U.S. *Constitution*, Art. I, Sec. 8.

[8] Harold M. Groves, *Financing Government* (New York: Holt, Rinehart & Winston, Inc., 1964), p. 434.

Fiscal Limitations Imposed by State Government Constitutions

State government constitutions also impose fiscal limitations, though considerable variation exists among the states as to the nature and extent of these limitations. The most common limitation found in state constitutions is that which stipulates that taxes must be uniform and/or equal. For example, property tax rates and assessments should be uniform for the same class of property in the same jurisdiction. Among the wide variety of other special fiscal provisions are the following:

1. Rate limitations on taxes, especially on property taxes, though sometimes on income and selective excise taxes.
2. Earmarked taxes, such as highway user taxes (typified by the state gasoline taxes which all 50 states use).
3. Property and income tax exemptions.
4. Origination of revenue bills in the lower house of the state legislature.
5. Specification that taxes must be for public purposes.
6. Prohibition of particular types of taxes such as income and poll taxes.

Thus, it has been observed that the federal Constitution and the various state constitutions place numerous limitations on the fiscal behavior of the public sector in the United States. None of the constitutions (federal or state), however, places any significant limitation upon the type of public purpose for which taxes may be imposed. As noted earlier, taxes may be imposed for revenue purposes, for regulatory or nonrevenue purposes, or (as is usually the case) for a combination of both objectives.

THE DEVELOPMENT OF FORMAL PUBLIC SECTOR BUDGETING IN THE UNITED STATES

Formal public sector budgets at the "executive" level of government were developed in the United States at a later date than in most other advanced nations of the world. Under this budgetary arrangement, the executive branch of government follows an established, legally approved, procedure in planning its expenditures and receipts. Moreover, the pattern of governmental budgetary development in the United States differs from that of most other industrial nations of the West in that it was initiated first at the local government level (later utilized by state governments) and then finally by the federal government.

There appear to be two major causes for the lag in the adoption of formal federal government budgeting procedures in the United States.

First, until the beginning of the present century, federal revenues exceeded expenditures in most fiscal years. These revenues were derived mostly from tariffs and from selective excises on tobacco and liquor. There was little popular effort to increase "efficiency" and "responsibility" in the federal government through budgetary control. Relatedly, the fact that the federal component of the public sector was a relatively less important component than combined state-local government created an environment in which no significant pressure was exerted for the adoption of a formal executive budget by the federal government.

A *second* basic explanation for the tardy acquisition of a federal executive budget rests in the historical desire for a "separation of powers" between the executive, legislative, and judicial branches of government. Considerable change had to occur in the conceptual and practical relationships between the executive and legislative branches before a federal executive budget was feasible. There was fear in the minds of the founding fathers at the Constitutional Convention regarding "excessive power" by the executive branch. Consequently, Congress was given the authority "to budget" as well as "to legislate," though it was not especially well qualified to perform the former function. The only important control by the President over the composition of the budget came through the right to veto, and this was to be restricted in practice by institutional behavior in the form of "riders" on appropriation bills, "pork-barreling," and "log-rolling."[9] The primary budgetary function of the executive was to execute the budget enacted by Congress, not to help formulate the budget.

Important changes had occurred by the third decade of the twentieth century which led to the adoption of formal budgeting procedures by the federal government. The relative importance of the federal component of the public sector had gradually increased following the Civil War as the federal government became involved increasingly in policies to regulate business and growing wealth concentration. Moreover, there had been a considerable increase in federal expenditures during World War I. These factors, along with the growing confusion surrounding the financial operation of a major nation without formal executive budgeting procedures, combined to accelerate the transition to formal federal budgeting. Moreover, the conceptual and practical interrelationships between the executive and legislative branches had changed enough to make formal executive budgeting feasible.

---

[9] A "rider" is an extraneous provision attached to a general appropriation bill with the belief that the Executive will not veto the entire bill because of the extraneous provision; "pork-barreling" refers to legislation favorable to a certain local district, and "logrolling" refers to the exchange of support among legislators for such pork-barrel legislation.

The transition to federal executive budgeting was assisted in an important way by the movement toward municipal budgeting in the United States. The municipal budget movement preceded the federal budget movement by at least one decade. The fact that the municipal budget transition came first is explained in part by the historic American fear of strong central government. This philosophy provided an "environment of reluctance" to improve the efficiency of federal fiscal activities. In the meantime, a strange marriage was occurring between two opposing groups which was to result in the strong movement toward municipal budgeting, as well as toward formal public sector budgeting in general, during the early twentieth century. One group was composed of "social reformers" who wanted to strengthen the ability of the public sector to meet social welfare objectives. The other group was composed of "businessmen" who were seeking retrenchment in government spending and who desired increased government efficiency in order to reduce their tax burdens. These two contrasting groups combined to guide the municipal budget movement to a successful conclusion.

State governments followed the municipalities, and slightly preceded the federal government, in moving to formal executive budgeting. Like the federal government, the states had not been forced to adopt efficient budgeting practices due, in part, to the long-run tendency for receipts to exceed, or at least to match, expenditures. Also, the stability of the property tax for revenue yield was partially responsible for the formal budget delay among state governments since it often provided adequate revenues even with a somewhat inefficient administration of the tax. Moreover, the tardy introduction of formal executive budgeting by the public sector in the United States—at all levels—may be attributed, in part, to the wealth of America's productive resources. That is, the momentum of economic development stemming from the application of increasing quantities of labor and capital to America's natural resource base tended to "more than offset" inefficient governmental budgetary practices.

Formal executive budgeting by the federal government grew out of the report of the Taft Commission, formally titled the *Commission on Economy and Efficiency,* which reported in 1912. This report became the direct stimulus for the "nine-year transition" to the establishment of a federal executive budget in 1921. In that year, the Budget and Accounting Act provided the following institutional changes in the federal government budgetary process:

1. The creation of the Bureau of the Budget (BOB) to assist the President in the preparation and execution of the budget. Thus, for the first time in American history, it became the obligation of the President to prepare a formal federal budget. The Bureau of the Budget was

subsumed in 1970 into the more comprehensive Office of Management and Budget (OMB).

2. The creation of the office of Director of the Budget, the Director being appointed by and responsible to the President and serving as the chief officer of the Bureau of the Budget (now the Director of the Office of Management and Budget).

3. The establishment of the Office of Comptroller General. This office is responsible to Congress in the authorization and auditing of federal government expenditures. The Comptroller General, as chief official of the General Accounting Office, is appointed for a 15-year term of office. It also performs a quasi-judicial function in the interpretation of the intent of many statutes.

4. The act established that there should be only two fiscal committees in each house of Congress, one on revenues and the other on expenditures. This replaced the multiplicity of committees previously existing. The *revenue* committees are the House Committee on Ways and Means and the Senate Finance Committee and the *expenditure* committees are the House and Senate Appropriation Committees, respectively. This reduced the extreme decentralization of fiscal decision-making which had previously existed in Congress. However, the revenue and expenditure sides of the budget are still "asymetrically" considered by different committees in each House of Congress despite the fact that the budget, in the ultimate sense, is a single "symmetrical" document.

In 1949, the *Commission on Organization of the Executive Branch of the Government,* known as the Hoover Commission, made many significant recommendations for further improvement in the federal fiscal process. The Commission recommended, for example, that "the whole budgetary concept of the Federal Government should be refashioned by the adoption of a budget based upon functions, activities, and projects."[10] This was the forerunner of the eventual movement to performance and program budgeting, benefit-cost analysis, and related governmental budgetary procedures.[11] A number of other recommendations made by the report, though not yet implemented, may yet find their way into improved budgetary procedures. Meanwhile, in 1972 Congress set up an ad hoc "joint committee" of the Senate and House to study ways that Congress might improve its budgetary procedures. The report of this special Committee, which was submitted during 1973, is receiving considerable attention from Congress. If adopted, an

---

[10] Commission on the Organization of the Executive Branch of the Government, *Budgeting and Accounting* (February 1949), p. 8.

[11] Planning-Programming Budgeting Systems (PPBS) and Benefit-Cost Analysis are discussed in Chapter 18.

important step will have been taken toward a "symmetrical" Congressional approach to fiscal decision-making.

FEDERAL BUDGETARY PROCEDURE

As observed above, the present federal budgetary process was basically designed by the Budget and Accounting Act of 1921. This budgetary procedure may be divided into four phases: (1) executive preparation and submission, (2) legislative review and enactment (3) executive implementation, and (4) auditing by the General Accounting Office. These four steps in federal budgeting will now be discussed in the sequence with which they are practiced.

Executive Preparation and Submission of the Budget

The proposed budget is formulated in the executive branch of the federal government. Preliminary planning begins some 16 months before a budget goes into effect. Federal agencies thus prepare estimates of their desired expenditures for the fiscal year which will begin 16 months later. For example, fiscal year 1976 begins on July 1, 1975, and ends on June 30, 1976.[12] Expenditure estimates by federal agencies would thus be prepared beginning in (approximately) March 1974 for the 1976 fiscal year. In May (approximately) 1974 these estimates would be submitted to the Office of Management and Budget (OMB) for preliminary review. By this time, the executive branch will have formulated its overall fiscal philosophy for the budget year in question. This will ordinarily be done by the President in consultation with the Director of the Office of Management and Budget, the Secretary of the Treasury, and the three members of the President's Council of Economic Advisors. These individuals will be assisted by revenue estimates and other analyses from the Treasury Department and by economic forecasts and other analyses from the Council of Economic Advisors.

It is the Treasury Department which assumes the primary responsibility for the vast amount of work involved in the preparation of the "tax recommendations" contained within a proposed budget. Within the Treasury Department, two staffs concentrate upon this task. These are the Office of Tax Analysis, composed primarily of economists and statisticians, and the Office of the Tax Legislative Counsel which is comprised primarily of attorneys with expertise in tax matters. The Office of Tax Analysis provides revenue estimates based on tax changes, overall revenue projections based on current taxes, and a general anal-

---

[12] The *fiscal year* of the federal government takes the name of the calendar year in which the fiscal period "terminates." Thus, the 1976 fiscal year begins on July 1, 1975.

ysis of tax issues and their effects on the economy. The Office of the Tax Legislative Counsel, on the other hand, provides legal and accounting analyses of tax issues and, in addition, drafts tax legislation and decides upon tax rulings and regulations.

Once the Office of Management and Budget receives the expenditure estimates from federal agencies, it reviews the budget requests and returns them to the agencies accompanied by both a statement of the administration's overall fiscal philosophy for the fiscal year in question, and suggested budgetary policies for the agencies. Following the sequence of the above example, in the summer of 1974 the agencies begin to recast their expenditure requests in accordance with the administration's philosophy and specific requests. The "revised estimates" are then resubmitted to OMB, which reviews and discusses them in detail with the respective agencies. The agencies may then be asked to defend or change their expenditure requests. The President possesses authority, operating through OMB, to reduce expenditure requests. Finally, by late fall of 1974, the Office of Management and Budget, following the desires of the President, assembles the various estimates into a "unified" budget document inclusive of both estimated revenues as well as proposed expenditures. The President then submits the proposed budget for fiscal 1976 to Congress in his budget message during the third week of January, 1975.

Legislative Review and Enactment of the Budget

Unlike a "parlimentary" system of government in which the legislature usually adopts the executive budget, especially its tax recommendations, substantially in the form in which it is presented, the executive budget in the American system is likely to be considerably altered by Congress. In fact, Congress has always guarded its budgetary authority, especially its "taxing power," jealously. After being submitted to Congress by the President, the budget is first referred to the Appropriations Committee of the House. This would occur in late January, 1975. Then, various subcommittees of the House Appropriations Committee conduct hearings at which the government agencies are asked to explain and defend their budget requests. The separate appropriations bills are subsequently returned to the House Appropriations Committee which submits them to the floor of the House for ultimate debate and passage. The Senate Appropriations Committee follows a procedure similar to that in the House.

When an appropriations bill is passed by both Houses of Congress, after differences have been ironed out, it goes to the President for signature. The Chief Executive does *not* have the authority of selective (item) veto. He must accept the bill totally, or not at all. This encourages, of course, the attachment of "riders" and the practices of "pork-barreling" and "logrolling." On the other hand, the selective (item) veto is used by many states. However, Congress traditionally fears that the selective veto represents a dangerous extension of Presidential power.[13] The need for a selective Presidential veto would be greatly intensified if Congress used an *omnibus* (all-inclusive, single) appropriations bill, as it attempted during the 1951 fiscal year. In our example, appropriations bills should be passed by July 1, 1975, for fiscal year 1976. Sometimes, the deadline is barely made; frequently, it is missed.

Tax bills as well as appropriations bills, according to constitutional provisions, must originate in the House of Representatives. The research work provided by two "joint committees" in Congress assists in the decision-making process regarding the enactment of a budget. These committees are the Joint Committee on Internal Revenue Taxation and the Joint Economic Committee. In fact, Congress has only one other permanent "joint committee," that is, the Joint Committee on Atomic Energy. Meanwhile, considerable lobbying pressures are exerted to influence the final legislation by Congress. Of course, such pressure had been initiated earlier on the executive branch to influence the budget submitted by the President to Congress. A large number of such pressure groups exists. They represent many segments of American society inclusive of business, labor, and state-local governments. Moreover, they include "internal lobbying" within the federal government by the respective agencies of the government, such as the Departments of Defense and of Health, Education, and Welfare.

Revenue bills eventually work their way from the House Committee on Ways and Means to the floor of the House and, when passed, to the Senate Committee on Finance. Subsequently, Senate revenue bills are considered in the Senate Committee on Finance, go to the Senate floor, and eventually are voted upon. When voted upon, the revenue bills reflect the compromise results of the Conference Committee composed of members of both the House and Senate. The membership of this committee is appointed by the Speaker of the House and the President of the Senate. Normally, this consists of three selected from the majority and two from the minority in each House of Congress. The Conference Committee is capable of exerting substantial influence upon the final bill enacted by Congress. Moreover, considerable authority and discretion rests with the Chairman of the Conference Committee. When reported out of the Conference Committee, and submitted to the Congress for enactment, the appropriations and tax bills then go to the President for signature. The President, of course, has the power of veto.

---

[13] For a discussion favoring the selective veto, see *Hearings before the House Expenditures Committee,* July 8 and 18, 1950, on H.R. 8054, 81st Cong. 2d sess. (Washington, D.C.: U.S. Government Printing Office, 1950).

As observed earlier, there is no formal consideration by Congress of the budget "as a whole." Tax bills and appropriation bills are considered separately by different committees in both the House and in the Senate. Furthermore, the bills are passed as separate statutes by Congress and are signed into law as separate statutes by the President. This decentralization of procedure differs vastly from budgetary procedure in many other mature Western nations. In particular, there is a sharp contrast to the consideration and enactment of a budget under the parlimentary system of government such as that in Canada and England. It is particularly difficult under the American system to relate program benefits and costs to each other and to generally apply efficiency criteria. It is also difficult to formulate fiscal policy for stabilization and economic growth objectives.

Executive Implementation of the Budget

The President has the obligation to implement (execute) the budget.[14] The Office of Management and Budget authorizes the various agencies to spend the appropriated funds on a quarterly basis. This is to prevent an agency from spending too much of its yearly appropriation early in the fiscal year. Once the budget authorizations are received, the agencies may purchase economic goods and productive resources, as needed, to perform their various functions. The Treasury Department releases funds in accordance with vouchers that have been prepared by the spending agencies. The funds are to be spent within the legislative intent of the appropriations bills, but a reasonable amount of discretion is left to the agencies.

Auditing of the Budget by the General Accounting Office

Congress has created the General Accounting Office (GAO), headed by the Comptroller General, to assure that appropriated funds are spent in accordance with provisions of the appropriations bill and to discourage fraud. This office reports directly to Congress. Several thousand accountants are employed by the GAO to help it perform its huge task. It is a quasi-judicial agency in the sense that it must interpret the intent which Congress had at the time the legislation was enacted.

The broad powers of the GAO include: (1) the authority to decide most questions involving payments made by government agencies; (2)

---

[14] The "extent" of this obligation is not clear. For example, in 1973 President Nixon followed a procedure of impounding (not spending) funds appropriated by Congress for certain governmental programs. The constitutionality of these actions is currently under court review with early indications being that impoundment is unconstitutional.

the auditing and settling of all public accounts; (3) settling, adjudicating, and adjusting all claims for and against the government; (4) describing systems and procedures for administrative appropriation and fund accounting, and (5) the investigation of all matters relating to receipts and disbursements of public funds, including the right to examine certain books, documents, papers, and records of government contractors and subcontractors. In addition, the Office of Comptroller General assists Congress by making specific studies and analyses of expenditure administration by the various governmental agencies.

The Concepts of "Contained Specialization" and "Incremental Decision-Making."[15] Despite its cumbersome nature and the presence of conflict, the federal government "somehow" makes and implements fiscal decisions. Disputes over policy are reduced to an operational reality. Two institutional devices which help to render the federal budgetary system operational may be termed "contained specialization" and "incremental decision making." *Contained specialization,* which summarizes a number of separate institutions and behavioral patterns, encompasses "the assignment of specialists within the legislative and executive branches to formulate taxing and spending decisions, the capacity of these specialists to reach decisions on controversial issues with a minimum of partisan bickering among themselves, and the tendency of other members in the legislative and executive branches to accept the specialists' recommendations."[16] Though conflict over policy remains, operational policies are established despite these conflicts. A sizable portion of the conflict is "contained" within institutions whose members possess the dual capacity to represent the various perspectives of a controversy while, at the same time, being able to accept a compromise position.

Incremental decision-making, on the other hand, institutionalizes decision-making by reducing and simplifying the range of decisions which need to be made. "The incrementalist does not attempt to write a tax or spending policy *de novo,* but accepts as given those policies already in force. He limits consideration to the *increment of change* that is proposed in taxes or expenditures."[17] This limited focus permits the decision maker to concentrate upon the relevant issues involved in the decision. Moreover, he accepts previous decisions as largely "fixed parameters" and thus he can avoid involvement in "lingering policy disputes" and can concentrate, instead, on the decision at hand. Indeed, it is through such *fiscal rules* as "contained specialization" and

---

[15] For an excellent discussion of these concepts as well as the overall institutional nature of public sector decision making in the United States, see Ira Sharkansky, *The Politics of Taxing and Spending* (Indianapolis: The Bobbs-Merrill Co., Inc., 1969).

[16] Ibid., p. 34.

[17] Ibid.

"incremental decision making" that the complex federal budgetary procedure becomes operational.[18]

TYPES OF GOVERNMENT BUDGETS

Public sector budgets exist for two substantially different purposes. One purpose of a government budget centers around the function of "accounting." An orderly arrangement for the control of expenditures and for their relationship to receipts is necessary in every management operation. Government is no exception. This purpose of public sector budgeting, however, is not connected directly to the four branches or goals of public sector economics. It is merely a "bookkeeping" function. On the other hand, the purpose of governmental budgeting relevant to public sector economics centers upon the economic problem of "resource scarcity" and the "related issues" that derive from it. In this context, the budget is viewed as an economic means whereby the *allocational, distributional, stabilization,* and *economic growth* performance of the society can be influenced through governmental revenue-gathering and expenditure behavior. The discussion that follows will emphasize the latter interpretation of the budget as it applies, primarily, to federal government budgeting.

The Unified Federal Budget

Until recently the federal government did not use a "single" official type of budget, but instead used three different budget concepts. The new *unified federal budget,* adopted in 1968, resulted from the recommendations of a special Presidential Commission on Budget Concepts which had been established in 1967. The new budget utilizes the best characteristics of the three previously employed federal government budgets—the administrative budget, the consolidated-cash budget, and the national-income-accounts budget. The national-income-accounts budget, however, still remains in separate use due to its value in isolating federal fiscal activity as a component of the Commerce Department's "National Income and Product Accounts."

The *unified federal budget* comprises an overall financial plan encompassing a set of comprehensive and integrated accounts. These accounts or subdivisions of the budget are: (1) budget authority; (2) budget receipts, expenditures, and net lending; (3) budget financing, and (4) outstanding federal securities and loans. Table 17–1 summarizes the major subdivisions of the unified federal budget.

The *first* section of the new budget provides a statement of the new appropriations requested by the President and relates these to appro-

---

[18] See the related discussion of "fiscal rules" in Chapter 5.

TABLE 17–1
The Unified Federal Budget

  I. *Budget Authority*
     (1) New proposals for action by Congress
     (2) Continuing appropriations approved at earlier sessions of Congress.
                  = *Total Appropriations*

 II. *Budget Receipts, Expenditures, and Net Lending*
     (1) *Expenditure Account*
         a) Revenues (general tax receipts, earmarked tax receipts, fees, receipts derived from sovereign authority)
         b) Expenditures (all nonloan expenditures and trust fund payments)
                  = *Expenditure Account Deficit or Surplus*

     (2) *Loan Account*
         a) Gross Loan Disbursements
         b) Gross Loan Repayments (including actual sales of loans)
                  = *Net Lending*

     (3) *Total Budget*
         a) Revenues [same as II (1) (a) above]
         b) Outlays (Expenditures and Net Lending) [same as II (1) (b) + II (2) above]
                  = *Budget Deficit or Surplus*

III. *Budget Financing*
     (1)
         a) Borrowing from the Public
                     } to finance a budget deficit
         b) Reduction of Cash Balances
     (2)
         a) Holding additional cash balances idle
                     } to dispose of a budget surplus
         b) Net repayment of borrowing
                  = *Total Budget Financing*

IV. *Outstanding Federal Securities and Loans, End of Year*
     (1) Federal Securities
         a) Gross Amount Outstanding
         b) Held by the Public
     (2) Federal Credit Programs
         a) Direct Loans Outstanding
         b) Guaranteed and Insured Loans Outstanding

priations that will become available during the fiscal year due to previous congressional legislative action. The summation of the newly proposed and previously approved appropriations amounts to "total appropriations" for budgetary action during the fiscal year in question.

The *second* section of the budget, and no doubt the most essential section, presents the receipts, expenditures, and net lending activities of the federal government. The *total* budget performance is derived from the disaggregation of federal budgetary activities into two accounts, namely, the "expenditure" and "loan" accounts. The *expenditure account* measures all tax receipts, whether general or earmarked, fees, and receipts derived through the sovereign authority of the federal government. In addition, it includes all nonloan expenditures and payments from federal trust funds.[19] The difference between total receipts and total expenditures in the expenditure account may be termed the "expenditure account *deficit* or *surplus.*"

The other major account—the *loan account*—separates the "lending activities" of the federal government from "ordinary" governmental expenditures. The separation is useful since it allows the "expenditure account deficit or surplus" to indicate whether these ordinary operations are acting to stimulate or restrict the performance of the national economy. Indeed, federal government lending programs should be considered separately from ordinary outlays since they may be expected to provide a different impact on the economy than normal expenditures and revenue collections. This tends to be true because lending activities involve an exchange of financial assets rather than direct income payments. That is, a loan received from the federal government by the private sector creates, at the same time, an obligation to repay the loan. Hence, though purchasing power in the private sector is increased, the reactions of firms and individuals to purchasing power changes incurred in this manner would tend to be different than if resources had been sold by the private sector to the public sector (exhaustive expenditures), or welfare-type payments had been received by the private sector (transfer expenditures). The loan account acquires a "net" figure by offsetting gross loan disbursements against gross loan repayments (including actual sales of loans).

Also, the *second* section of the unified budget culminates into a *total deficit or surplus* by means of relating total revenues to combined total expenditures and net lending. This constitutes the most basic part of the federal budgetary figures. If total revenues and total expenditures plus net lending are equal, the budget is said to be *balanced.* If total revenues are greater, the budget is said to be a *surplus* budget while an excess of expenditures plus net lending over revenues constitutes a *deficit* budget.

The *third* section of the budget describes the means of "financing" a deficit budget or "disposing" of a surplus budget. For example, it would indicate the amount of a deficit to be financed by such means as borrowing from the private sector, or through the reduction of cash balances. Moreover, it would indicate surplus disposal alternatives such as holding additional cash balances idle or the net retirement of debt.

---

[19] "Earmarked" taxes and payments from special trust funds were excluded from the previously emphasized administrative budget of the federal government. This constituted one of the major drawbacks of federal government budgetary procedure prior to 1968.

Finally, the *fourth* section of the new budget describes the composition and magnitude of outstanding federal securities and loans. Federal securities, in this regard, may be disaggregated in terms of the (1) gross amount of securities outstanding, and (2) that amount held by the public. In addition, federal credit programs may be enumerated in terms of (1) direct loans outstanding, and (2) outstanding guaranteed and insured loans.

The Federal Tax Expenditures Budget

A recently-introduced approach to federal budgeting estimates the value of tax revenues, by functional area of budgetary activity, which the government does *not* collect as a result of "special provisions" under federal income tax law. Thus, the estimated "tax loss value" of the numerous special exclusions, deductions, credits, differential rates, and the like are presented in terms of functional expenditure categories. Such an approach is significant since "taxes not collected" have the same *impact* on an eventual budget deficit or surplus as do the "direct expenditures" of the federal government. Table 17–2 provides an esti-

TABLE 17–2
Estimated Federal Budget Outlays and Tax Expenditures, Classified by Function, Fiscal Year 1975 (billions of dollars)

	Budget Outlays	Tax Expenditures	Total	Tax Expenditures as Percentage of Total
National defense	$ 87.7	$ 0.7	$ 88.4	0.8
International affairs and finance	4.1	.9	5.0	18.0
Space research and technology	3.3	0	3.3	0
Agriculture and rural development	2.7	1.1	3.8	28.9
Natural resources and environment	3.1	3.6	6.7	53.7
Commerce and transportation	13.4	24.4	37.8	64.6
Community development and housing	5.7	13.2	18.9	69.8
Education and manpower	11.5	1.0	12.5	8.0
Health	26.3	6.9	33.2	20.8
Income security	100.1	11.7	111.8	10.5
Veterans benefits and services	13.6	.5	14.1	3.6
Interest	29.1	0	29.1	0
General government	6.8	.1	6.9	1.4
Aid to foundations and charities	0	3.7	3.7	100.0
General revenue sharing aid to state and local governments	6.2	10.4	16.6	62.6
Allowances	1.6	0	1.6	0
Undistributed intergovernmental transactions	−10.7	0	−10.7	0
Total	304.4	78.2	382.7	20.4

Source: Tax Analysts and Advocates and Ben Okner, Senior Fellow, Brookings Institution, as presented in *The 1974 Joint Economic Report* (Washington, D.C.: U.S. Government Printing Office, 1974), Table 5, p. 47.

mate of the value of such "tax expenditures" for the federal government as well as their relative importance to the "total federal budget" for fiscal year 1975.

The Full-Employment Budget

The *full-employment budget* is a device utilized to shed light on the effects of federal budgetary activities on aggregate economic performance.[20] The *full-employment budget* "projects" either the national-income-accounts budget, or the unified budget, to what it would "look like" under conditions of *full resource employment* at a time when unemployment exists in the economy. Relatedly, "actual GNP" may be

TABLE 17–3
Federal Budget* Surplus and Deficit, Actual and Under Full-Employment Assumptions, 1969–74 Calendar Years

Calendar Year	Actual Budget Surplus or Deficit (−) (billions)	Budget Surplus or Deficit (−) at 4 Percent Unemployment Rate (billions)
1969	$ 8.1	$ 8.8
1970	−11.9	4.0
1971	−22.1	−2.1
1972	−15.9	−7.7
1973	0.6	5.8
1974	−4.6	6.0

* On *National-Income-Accounts* basis.
Source: *Economic Report of the President, 1974.*

compared to "potential GNP." Federal tax rates and expenditure patterns are viewed as "fixed" for this purpose.

The genesis of the full-employment budget concept derives from the work of the Committee for Economic Development which, in 1947, recommended that tax rates and expenditures be set so that a "slight" (not overly restrictive) surplus would exist at full employment. This budget concept has played a role in significant policy decisions. For example, it provided a framework for the "historic" federal personal and corporation income tax reductions of March 1964.[21] During the

---

[20] The significance of the *full-employment budget* concept will be better appreciated by the reader following the analysis contained in Part Four of this book.

[21] The income tax reductions of 1964 are termed "historic" by many people who assert that the tax cuts represent, for the first time, a "rational concensus" in favor of reducing taxes to promote employment and economic growth objectives.

early 1960s, the full-employment budget indicated that, under then existing federal fiscal patterns, a considerable "surplus" would exist at full employment. Hence, it was concluded that the persistent short-run unemployment, and also the lagging rates of long-run economic growth which had been plaguing the economy for several years following the termination of the Korean War, were to be explained by an "overly restrictive" federal budget. The concept thus served as an important reference point for the substantial income tax reduction bill enacted by Congress during 1964 which reduced the restrictiveness of the federal budget. Table 17–3 presents "full-employment budget" data for several recent calendar years.

The Capital Budget

A *capital budget* separates total government expenditure into "current" and "capital" items. This type of budget was suggested for the federal government by the Budget and Accounting Act of 1921. However, the federal government does not formally employ the concept. The "current" part of a capital budget would reflect *recurring* expenditures such as the salaries of government workers and office supplies. The "capital" component of the budget would reflect *nonrecurring* expenditure on capital assests of a durable nature. According to the capital budget concept, the budget is "balanced" if current tax collections (or other receipts except those from borrowing) equal current expenditures, including depreciation allowances for existing durable goods. It is thus implied that long-term capital items should be financed through borrowing (debt creation) activities.

The capital budget concept for central (national) governments was popular in Scandinavia, especially Sweden, during the 1930s and is now used in other nations, such as the Netherlands, England, Canada, India, Republic of South Africa, and Ecuador. Moreover, a number of American states employ the technique. In addition, it is used by many American municipalities which obviously cannot expect to always pay for acquisitions of new durable capital out of current receipts given the restricted nature of their taxing authority.

The capital budget may be defended on the grounds that it shows that government spending often results in the acquisition of durable, productive capital and, thus, is "not money poured down a rathole" as too many people mistakenly believe. Relatedly, the capital budget possesses the advantage of pointing up the often overlooked fact that the failure of current receipts to cover all expenditures, both current and capital, is not indicative per se of "fiscal irresponsibility."[22] On the other

---

[22] Fortunately, this version of "fiscal responsibility," and of its counterpart, "fiscal irresponsibility," is much less common than it was a generation ago.

hand, the capital budget could provide a "disservice" to society if it led to "excessive" investment in durable capital goods at the expense of current services, as well as at the expense of worthy investment in human resources by causing reduced expenditures for health, education, and safety. These items would not necessarily be treated as capital items under the capital budget concept. Indeed, the whole issue of classifying expenditures as "current" or "capital" is a complex one. Furthermore, though the failure of current receipts to cover all current expenditures is not indicative per se of fiscal irresponsibility, a complete divorcement from the orthodox idea of budget balance nonetheless could lead to irrational fiscal action.[23] A relevant recent study recommends against the adoption of capital budgeting for the federal government.[24]

Other Budget Concepts and Sources of Fiscal Information

An important newly emphasized area of governmental budgeting takes the form of the *planning-programming budgeting system* (PPBS) approach. However, since this is the primary subject of Chapter 18, it will not be discussed in detail at this point. Suffice it to say here that PPBS seeks to increase the *efficiency* of public sector decision-making. It relates closely to the established idea of "operations research" which is used so prominently in business decision making in the private sector of the economy. In general, these techniques involve the application of scientific methodology to decision making.

The notion of an *emergency budget* was first introduced by President Franklin D. Roosevelt during the 1930s. Under this concept, all depression-relieving expenditures were classified as part of an "emergency" component of the budget. It was, in turn, not expected that current tax receipts should cover such expenditures. The intent was to suggest that the government was being operated in a "fiscally responsible" manner since the ordinary, "nonemergency," functions of government were being financed on a "pay-as-you-go" basis through current tax collections. It was thus suggested that the budget was "balanced" in the ordinary sense and "unbalanced" with a deficit only because of the depression emergency. This budget concept did not "catch on" with the American public and was subsequently eliminated.

Regarding sources of fiscal information, a number of competent sources exist for the American public sector. For example, the *Federal Reserve System* provides "net" data on such federal government fiscal items as individual and corporate income taxes, excise taxes, customs

---

[23] This subject will be discussed in further detail in Chapter 26 entitled "Fiscal Policy Norms."

[24] Maynard S. Comiez, *A Capital Budget Statement for the U.S. Government* (Washington, D.C.: Brookings Institution, 1966).

receipts, estate tax receipts, gift tax receipts, fines, payments to the Treasury Department on federal reserve notes outstanding, as well as social insurance program data. Moreover, the Federal Reserve System data shows "net" purchases of goods and services by the federal government in a manner similar to that of the national income accounts.

The *Bureau of the Census* of the U.S. Department of Commerce also provides valuable fiscal information. Such information encompasses all levels of government—federal, state, and local—in the United States. Concerning the federal government, the Census data include all federal budget receipts and expenditures except those for unemployment compensation and for the District of Columbia. Intragovernmental fiscal transactions are treated similarly to their presentation in the national income accounts except for the inclusion of interest payments on Treasury securities to trust funds in both the receipts and expenditure accounts. Government loans are excluded from the Census data. Most data are presented on a "cash" rather than on an "accrual" basis. Another feature of the Census data is that government corporations are treated on a gross basis for both receipts and expenditures. Much of the important Commerce Department information is provided in the form of the *Census of Governments.*

Other sources of federal fiscal information include the various *Congressional Hearings* on tax and appropriation matters. In addition, the studies and reports of those special research groups created by the Employment Act of 1946, namely, the *Council of Economic Advisers* at the executive level and the *Joint Economic Committee* at the congressional level are extremely valuable for policy-making purposes. Moreover, the various Treasury Department statistics and publications add to the stock of economic information available concerning the impact of the federal government on the allocation, distribution, stabilization, and economic growth goals of the society. The publications include the *Treasury Bulletin* and the *Annual Report of the Secretary of the Treasury.* In addition, the Office of Management and Budget, a part of the Executive Office of the President, provides direct and valuable fiscal information. Finally, a wealth of fiscal information, primarily applicable to state and local governments, is provided by organizations such as the *Advisory Commission on Intergovernmental Relations* (a federal government-sponsored body), the *Council of State Governments, Commerce Clearing House, National Tax Association-Tax Institute of America,* and the *Tax Foundation.*

State and Local Government Budgets

There are "three major types" of *budget systems* in use by state and local governments in the United States. These may be termed the executive, committee or board, and legislative budget systems. The *executive* budget approach is similar to that employed by the federal government in that the chief executive of the state—the governor— must prepare and formally present a proposed budget to the state legislature. The governor is assisted in this regard by a budgetary agency or staff. Most states use the executive budget technique and it is used also by many large municipal governments. It is especially conducive to use by those municipalities which have a city manager format of local government administration

The *committee* or *board* budget approach is used by several states and many municipalities. This budget system fits in well with governmental organizations characterized by administrative decentralization. If employed by a state government, the "committee" typically consists of the governor and the administrative heads of the major departments of state government with, in some instances, representatives from the state legislature being included. Finally, there exists the *legislative* budget which is utilized primarily by smaller units of local government. This technique finds a legislative agency performing both the preparation and enactment functions. It is used mostly when the executive and legislative branches of government cannot be clearly distinguished, such as when a municipality is administered by a city council.

In general, the budgetary process tends to be somewhat less complex at the state-local level of government than at the federal level. Moreover, benefits derived from public sector expenditures tend to be somewhat easier to measure. However, there do exist greater constraints on revenues at the state-local level due to such factors as constitutional limitations on borrowing and the overall scarcity of good revenue sources. The latter point will be developed more thoroughly in the chapter which follows.

18

Benefit-Cost Analysis and Budgetary Efficiency

THE BENEFIT-COST CONCEPT

There can be no doubt about the *economic importance* of a public sector which spends over \$350 billion in a given year. The allocational, distributional, stabilization, and economic growth implications of the aggregate public sector budget in the United States are enormous. Thus, it is little wonder that questions are frequently raised concerning the *efficiency* of decision-making procedures in the government sector of the economy. Indeed, the mere size of the budgetary operation of government in the American public sector warrants such an interest. Moreover, the considerable decentralization of government in the American federation adds further complexities to the governmental decision-making process.

A pronounced effort to improve the public sector budgetary process has taken the form of *Benefit-Cost Analysis.*[1] This approach attempts primarily to compare the relative economic merits of alternative governmental capital projects. All of the relevant benefits and costs of a particular project or investment are determined and, to the extent possible, these benefits and costs are quantified and valued in monetary terms. In turn, projects may be compared with each other on the basis of their relative economic merits. Thus, benefit-cost analysis consists of

---

[1] For a comprehensive analysis of benefit-cost analysis, see A. R. Prest and R. Turvey, "Cost-Benefit Analysis: A Survey," *Economic Journal,* December 1965, pp. 155–207.

an effort to estimate and compare various gains (benefits) and costs which would result from alternative investment projects.

The integral components of the benefit-cost technique consist of the following:[2]

1. The *programs* (goals, objectives, or targets) need to be defined. In other words, what achievements need to be made in order to yield the benefits?
2. The *alternative investment projects* for obtaining these objectives need to be arrayed. These "projects" may be termed "systems" if they contain a substantial set of interrelated components.
3. The *costs,* that is, the benefits that must be "foregone" when one project is selected, must be estimated. This involves the basic economic doctrine of "opportunity cost."
4. Mathematical *models* may be constructed in order to assist in the estimation of benefits and costs and the subsequent choice between alternative projects or systems.
5. A *criterion of preferredness* or *social discount rate* must be established to help select the "best" investment alternative.

The selection among alternative investment projects may be guided by reference to the *benefit-cost ratio (B/C)* which relates the "present value" of the *total benefits (B)* which flow from a particular investment project to the "present value" of the *total costs (C)* of that project. Discounting the "future" benefit and cost streams from the long-run project to their "present" values is required because benefits derived in some future year will tend to be worth less than benefits derived at the present time, and the same is true for costs since opportunity costs represent the present value of foregone consumption. Thus, a *discount* or *interest* factor must be applied in order to estimate the "present" value of "future" benefits and costs.[3] Importantly, the selection of a particular rate of discount (interest) will influence the relative ranking of alternative investment projects depending upon the duration of each project. A higher discount rate, for example, will tend to favor shorter-term investment projects, and vice versa.

In the absence of budget constraint, any capital project with a *B/C*

---

[2] See the discussion in Roland N. McKean, *Public Spending* (New York: McGraw-Hill, 1968), pp. 136–38.

[3] The present value *(PV)* of an amount *(A)* due in a certain number of years *(n)*, discounted at a particular rate of interest *(i)*, is found by the following formula:

$$PV = \frac{A}{(1+i)^n}$$

or,

$$PV = \frac{A_1}{1+i} + \frac{A_2}{(1+i)^2} + \frac{A_3}{(1+i)^3} \cdots \cdots \frac{A_n}{(1+i)^n}$$

ratio of unity ($B/C = 1.0$), or greater than unity ($B/C > 1.0$), should be undertaken. However, if budget constraint is present, those investments with the higher B/C ratios should be carried out first—down to a B/C "cut-off point" which reflects the extent of the constraint. Thus, without budget constraint, if Project A yields a B/C ratio of 5.0; Project B one of 3.0; Project C one of 2.0, and Project D one of 0.5, Projects A, B, and C would be undertaken, but Project D would not be undertaken since the present value of the costs of Project D exceed its benefits. Yet, if the presence of budget constraint should impose a B/C ratio "cut-off point" of 2.5, only Projects A and B would be carried out and Project C would not be undertaken even though its B/C ratio of 2.0 is greater than unity.

The next major step in benefit-cost analysis is to select a *social discount rate*, or as it is also termed—a *preferredness criterion*, which may be applied to the alternative investment projects so that the projects can be compared in terms of their benefit-cost ratios. Certainly, an effective social discount rate must recognize that governmental investment decisions tend to be "long run" in nature. Thus, a "time-preference" element must be contained in any acceptable preferredness criterion. This is necessary, as observed above, because the present value of a dollar of benefits or costs would be worth more than the future value in 5, 10, or 20 years. Of course, this is a reflection of the "interest phenomenon" which is relevant to *all* investment decisions whether they be private or public in nature. Thus, an interest or discount factor must be applied in order to estimate the present value of future benefits and costs. Ideally, when applied in benefit-cost models, this interest factor, by aiding in the selection among various investment projects, would allow a comparison of the "social rates of return" between alternative public sector programs or goals. Moreover, it would also allow an efficient division of scarce resources between the private and public sectors of the economy. In other words, it would help yield optimal intersector resource allocation as discussed in Chapters 1 and 4.

One school of thought argues that the best approximation to an ideal social discount rate is the *net yield (return) on private investment* projects, that is, the "marginal productivity of capital in private investment." Technically, this would be a "weighted average" of the opportunity cost rate in private investment for *all* sectors of the economy from which the government investment would withdraw resources.[4] However, imperfections in capital markets do not allow a clear discernment of the "marginal productivity of private capital investment." In

---

[4] See William J. Baumol, "On the Discount Rate for Public Projects," in *The Analysis and Evaluation of Public Expenditures: The PPB System*, Vol. 1, Joint Economic Committee, 91st Congress, 1st sess. (Washington, D.C.: U.S. Government Printing Office, 1969), pp. 497–98.

practice, as will be observed later in the chapter, the discount rates utilized in the benefit-cost efforts of the federal government frequently have not approximated this version of the social discount rate. Instead, they have at times moved far away from it by using the "convenient" government borrowing rate, that is, the *average interest rate paid by the U.S. Treasury on government securities.* Of course, this represents an almost "riskless" type of investment, much unlike typical private investment. Thus, too low a discount rate tends to lead to the justification of too many governmental as opposed to private investment projects and, consequently, tends to distort intersector resource allocation. Although it is certain that the government borrowing rate is "too low," various adjustments may be used to "blend" this rate and the "imperfect" marginal productivity of private capital investment rule so as to provide a more rational social discount rate.

Admittedly, subjective judgments must be part of the decision-making procedure in the benefit-cost approach to governmental budgeting. Nonetheless, a "systematic" approach to benefit and cost comparisons, as provided by benefit-cost analysis, and the consideration of time-preference and the marginal productivity of private capital investment, should all help to provide a more rational manner of approaching governmental budgetary decisions than would be provided by an uncoordinated, haphazard, and intuitive approach. The results should allow public sector budget decisions to be made in a more rational manner than allowed by conventional budgeting procedures. Spending would be appraised in terms of *programs* or *objectives* instead of merely by spending agencies. The *total benefits* of expenditures for alternative investments would be considered alongside the *total costs* of the inputs. Long-run considerations of a *time-preference nature* would be included. Finally, the economic doctrine of *opportunity cost* would help serve as an efficiency reference point for budget decisions. The remaining two sections of the chapter will (1) describe the history and current status of benefit-cost analysis in the American public sector, and (2) evaluate its performance in terms of the "ideal" concepts described above.

HISTORY AND PRESENT STATUS OF BENEFIT-COST ANALYSIS IN THE AMERICAN PUBLIC SECTOR

The Federal Level of Government

The genesis of benefit-cost analysis at the federal level of government began in the early 1900s when Congress required the Army Corps of Engineers to take into account the benefits to commerce as well as the costs of river and harbor projects. Subsequently, more pronounced attention was paid to federal water development projects in benefit-cost terms during the 1930s. Then, a new burst of interest in this approach occurred in the post–World War II period after economists and military officers began pursuing their own separate courses in defense planning. More specifically, in the late 1940s specialists were at work at the Rand Corporation to determine the best strategic bomber for development and next generation use by the Air Force. However, each specialist emphasized his own area of technical competence and there was no agreement on what should be "minimized" in order to achieve the given strategic objective. Eventually, the economists prevailed and it was agreed that *dollars*, which could represent a "common denominator" for resource inputs, should be "minimized." In this manner, *cost effectiveness analysis*, which later became the basis of McNamara-Hitch "program packaging," was first integrated into the defense decision-making process.[5] However, "cost-effectiveness analysis," unlike pure "benefit-cost analysis," does not require an economic evaluation of output. Instead, it deals with a specific physical output and the different ways of producing that output. In any event, additional economists were brought into the military choice program and the concepts of variable proportions and opportunity cost, as applied to military problems, were further developed.

The application of these *economic concepts* to military decision-making was of particular importance. Previously, in the case of developing a strategic bombing capacity, those concerned with bombs had treated bombers as a *free good*.[6] Now a more sophisticated method was employed. If the "targets destroyed" are considered the output (in "low-level-optimization" terms since national security itself cannot be measured as an output), the two main inputs were "fissionable materials" and "delivery vehicles." Once the problem had been framed in these terms, it was a simple matter to establish the rate of substitution between one marginal bomber and a marginal kilogram of fissionable material. In addition, once the cost of acquiring and keeping a bomber was known, the use value of fissionable material was obviously the delivery cost which it saved. In the 1950s, the marginal use value of fissionable materials appeared to be several times larger than the Atomic Energy Commission's marginal cost of production. This suggested that the Oak Ridge gaseous diffussion plant should be operated more intensively. Such analysis was also applied to the substitution values between two uses—strategic versus tactical bomber systems. An estimate was made of the marginal values in dollars of x kilograms of fissionable materials as a substitute for strategic bombers and as a substi-

---

[5] The McNamara-Hitch approach will be explained further below.

[6] A *free good*, though capable of providing utility (satisfaction), is not influenced by the problem of resource scarcity. Obviously, such goods are rare, if not "nonexistent," in modern industrial societies where even "unpolluted air" is scarce.

tute for tactical bombers. The conclusion was reached that the nuclear stockpile needed to be reallocated, in part, with some new weapons being reserved for tactical air missions in NATO (North Atlantic Treaty Organization).[7]

Meanwhile, the subject of economic efficiency in defense economics was discussed brilliantly by Charles J. Hitch and Roland N. McKean in a book published in 1960.[8] This followed the significant application of benefit-cost analysis in several water resource studies during the late 1950s.[9] The Hitch-McKean "defense" study suggests that the essence of economic choice in military planning involves a comparison of all the relevant alternatives from the point of view of the objectives which each can accomplish and the cost which each involves, including opportunity costs, and the subsequent selection of the "best" alternative through the application of an appropriate preferredness criterion. In 1961, the Department of Defense "officially" adopted costing methods and analytical techniques similar to those which had evolved in the Rand Project. This was no coincidence since Charles Hitch had by then become Comptroller of the Department of Defense under Secretary of Defense, Robert McNamara, who was also familiar with the benefit-cost approach. Subsequently, the techniques became known as "program packaging." Thus, a full-fledged benefit-cost effort was underway at the federal government level as part of a new comprehensive budgetary efficiency system known as the *planning-programming budgeting system* (PPBS).

The PPBS approach is intended to reduce the inefficiency inherent in conventional budgeting procedures. "Conventional budgeting," for example, tends to emphasize the budget requests of government *agencies* which spend the public funds rather than the *programs* or *goals* for which the funds are expended. Moreover, many programs are *interagency* in nature which adds further confusion to the orthodox efforts to provide rationality in the public sector budget. In addition, the traditional stress has been on costs, in the sense of productive *inputs,* rather than upon the *output* of economic goods and the *benefits* which they provide. Furthermore, the conventional federal budgetary approach is generally of short duration—one year (except for items such as trust fund expenditures). Yet, many programs include expenditures and benefits which cover a long time period. Thus, fiscal rationality obviously

---

[7] There was difficulty in costing alternative and hypothetical delivery systems in the above analysis. The Air Force did not maintain cost data in such a form that a bomber wing could be costed. Thus, only approximations could be made.

[8] Charles J. Hitch and Roland N. McKean, *The Economics of Defense in the Nuclear Age* (Cambridge, Mass.: Harvard University Press, 1960).

[9] For example, see J. V. Krutilla and Otto Eckstein, *Multiple Purpose River Development* (Baltimore: The Johns Hopkins Press, 1958), and Otto Eckstein, *Water Resource Development* (Cambridge, Mass.: Harvard University Press, 1958).

must require that the costs of a long-term program not be evaluated solely in terms of its "down payment" cost in the initial budget year. Finally, conventional budgeting has an inherent tendency to *perpetuate programs*, with their associated agencies, departments, officials, and assorted "vested interests," even though the programs may yield benefits less than could be provided by alternative usage of the public sector funds. In other words, "program reviews" tend to be much too infrequent under orthodox budgeting procedures.

The *planning-programming budgeting system* approach was intended to avoid these obstacles to efficiency in conventional governmental budgeting. Basically, the "planning" aspect of the system carried the connotation of long-term evaluation as opposed to the short-run consideration of costs and benefits in only one or two fiscal years. The "programming" aspect of PPBS, on the other hand, carried the connotation of structuring the budget in terms of goals (programs). These programs or goals are frequently "intermediate" or "suboptimal" in nature. That is, an ultimate or final goal may need to be sacrificed, in "definitional terms," as a primary objective and substituted for by a lesser component of that objective due to the severe problems which arise in the measurement of economic goods characterized by joint consumption and externalities. Thus, a national security goal may be stated necessarily in terms of such components as "bomber strike capacity" instead of "national defense."

The PPBS approach, as assisted in its implementation by benefit-cost analysis, was extended to other agencies of the federal government through an executive order by President Johnson in 1965, but was terminated in 1971 during the Nixon administration. Between 1965 and 1971, more than 25 agencies, including all of the primary federal departments, made efforts to utilize these techniques. Through this process, the major *policy issues* in each agency were identified annually by the Bureau of the Budget (now subsumed into the Office of Management and Budget).[10] Then an *issue letter* was sent to the head of the agency requesting an analysis of the issue. Those analyses expected to be completed in a short period of time were submitted to the Bureau of the Budget in the form of *program memoranda*. On the other hand, those analyses which entail research covering a several month period were submitted later in the form of *special analytic studies*. These program memoranda and special analytic studies were expected (1) to help policy formulation within the agency, and (2) to serve as an instrument of budgetary control. Furthermore, the PPBS approach at the federal government level produced a document called *Program and*

---

[10] See the discussion in *Economic Analysis and the Efficiency of Government*, Joint Economic Committee, 91st Cong., 2d sess. (Washington, D.C.: U.S. Government Printing Office, 1970), p. 8.

Financial Plans. This document presented five-year projections of program budgets, as prepared by the agencies. These included the budgetary implications of previously-made commitments and, where possible, the projected program outputs for the period. Although PPBS was terminated in 1971 on a "government-wide" basis, benefit-cost analysis efforts continue in a number of federal government agencies.

The State and Local Levels of Government

A number of states use benefit-cost analysis in one form or another. The first to adopt a comprehensive PPBS program with benefit-cost analysis was Wisconsin under legislation enacted in 1964.[11] Subsequent measures in Wisconsin resulted in the refinement of the approach which is used (1) to define needs or goals along with budget or cost constraints; (2) to determine the primary needs or goals; and (3) to estimate the costs of attaining these goals and to fit them within the cost constraints. The Wisconsin approach classifies the needs or goals within broad functional areas or programs—commerce, education, environmental resources, human relations and resources, and general operational functions. Hopefully, this will allow decision makers to more efficiently consider alternative uses of state government revenues both between and within major categories of expenditure.

The Wisconsin structure may be exemplified as follows:[12]

1. The specific goal under the human relations and resources category may be to "assist the handicapped."
2. The most pressing subgoal may be that of "providing education and related training to crippled children."
3. The alternative means of doing this may be through:
    a. Orthopedic hospitals.
    b. Financial aids to individuals.
    c. Aids to orthopedic schools.
    d. Transportation aids.
4. Some or all of these four techniques may be utilized, within the given budget constraints, to attain the goal.

However, despite rather extensive efforts such as those by the state of Wisconsin, it must be admitted that the use of benefit-cost analysis is in an early stage of development at the state level of government.

Just as with the introduction of executive budgeting early in the

---

[11] See John W. Reynolds and Walter G. Hollander, "Program Budgeting in Wisconsin," *State Government,* Autumn 1964.

[12] Paul L. Brown, *An Operational Model for a Planning-Programming-Budgeting System* (State of Wisconsin, Department of Administration, January 1968), pp. 15–17.

twentieth century, local governments were among the pioneer inves-
tigators of program budgeting as a forerunner to present budgetary
efficiency developments in the American public sector. Yet, at the present time, benefit-cost analysis is still quite limited at the local government level with the exception of certain large municipalities and counties. Some of the early local government efforts involved the
programming of tax collections with the help of data processing equipment. The use of this equipment was often extended to payroll disper-
sion and, subsequently, to general dispersions of funds. In effect, however, the information supplied to decision-making bodies usually
amounted to little more than an indication of present and future "expenditure constraints."

However, several larger cities and counties now use a more comprehensive and sophisticated approach. New York City, for example, has
a "Division of Program Planning" within its Bureau of the Budget for
the purpose of analyzing the budget by function and objective. Guidelines are established for each agency for the purpose of (1) relating
capital proposals to program objectives, (2) for the identification of
alternative policies, and (3) for focusing attention on cost and effectiveness issues. Nonetheless, the use of benefit-cost analysis is in an early
stage of development, generally speaking, for the local government
sector just as it is for the state level of government. Moreover, though
the federal government has carried this approach to a more comprehensive level than any other component of the American public sector,
especially prior to 1971, even here its application is not very sophisticated.

In addition, since the majority of the states do not have a comprehensive benefit-cost effort, and since that of the federal government has
been suspended on a "government-wide" basis, an "integrated" intergovernmental system to improve vertical and horizontal intergovernmental fiscal relations has not been developed. However, the "initial"
path for improved intergovernmental fiscal coordination may be paved
by the "data exchanges" which exist between a number of states and
the Internal Revenue Service for income tax enforcement. These data
exchanges typically operate with relatively sophisticated data processing equipment. Moreover, another step toward improved fiscal coordination was provided in the 1972 legislation which made possible the
"federal government" collection of "state government" personal income taxes.

The final section of the chapter below will appraise the "theoretical"
and "practical" advantages and disadvantages of benefit-cost analysis
with particular emphasis on the effectiveness of its recent widespread,
though now diminished, use by the federal government as part of the
PPBS approach.

EVALUATION OF BENEFIT-COST ANALYSIS

Advantages

The budget efficiency phenomena discussed in this chapter essentially carry an *allocative* trademark. In a preliminary sense, the benefit-cost technique is offered as an effort to improve the "technical" efficiency of conventional public sector budgeting. More importantly, to the extent that technical efficiency is enhanced, the primary "allocative" efficiency objective is also served. Governmental decision-making bodies become better informed, as does the general public, on the "relevant considerations" for both goal selections and the allocational policies used to attain these goals. More specifically, alternative goals can be arrayed, intergoal comparisons can be made, alternative allocational techniques can be surveyed, and societal preferences can generally be revealed in a more accurate manner. Moreover, the use of such irrational decision-making techniques as "creeping incrementalism," that is, the increase of (say) 5 percent annually for each departmental budget, may be reduced. In the terminology of Part One of this book, an improvement in allocative efficiency means a movement toward (if not actually to) the point of optimal *inter*sector resource allocation.[13] Moreover, *intra*sector allocational efficiency may be enhanced. The ultimate objective is to employ society's resources so as to create the largest possible amount of welfare for the individuals of the society.

Although benefit-cost analysis is primarily allocational in its emphasis, it would be a mistake to conclude that it bears no distributional nor stabilization-growth implications. The following example should indicate the *distributional* implications of an application of benefit-cost analysis: Assume that the preferredness criterion (social discount rate) indicates, in an allocational sense, that an irrigation and flood control project should be developed in Montana. Farmer *X* in Montana, along with other farmers in the area, would incur monetary benefits from the project in the form of "increased income." Yet, assume also that the project is financed from general federal tax revenues contributed largely by people who do not directly benefit in a monetary sense from the project. Clearly, a redistributional effect, in terms of greater monetary income, accrues to the Montana farmer even though this was made possible largely by the tax payments of others who did not directly benefit. It might be said, for example, that a clerical worker in New York City is helping to pay for the irrigation project which benefits Farmer *X* directly, but which scarcely benefits the clerical worker at all. Indeed, the *incidence* both of the financial burden "costs" and of

---

[13] See Figure 1–4 and its explanation.

the "benefits" of governmental expenditures for a particular program does bear importantly on the question of distribution. Thus, only in an "initial" sense, may benefit-cost analysis be described as "distributionally neutral." Distributional effects are virtually certain to "ultimately" result from the allocational actions dictated through an initial benefit-cost decision. Thus, it is important for policymakers using this approach to be cognizant of the concept of *intergoal nonneutrality*.[14] In fact, the information provided by benefit-cost analysis should not only make it possible for policy makers to avoid "negative" distributional and stabilization-growth nonneutralities, it should also allow them to pursue "positive" objectives in these important functional areas of public sector economic activity.

Certainly, the information provided by benefit-cost analysis regarding current income distribution should assist in the achievement of positive distributional goals. Thus, if policy makers have an adequate estimate of "monetary" income distribution among the spending units of the society, and assuming that it is not the distribution desired by a societal consensus, it may be changed through budgetary action. In fact, even though historical emphasis has been focused on the effects of tax measures on "monetary" income distribution, the "real" income effects, in consumption terms, of expenditure decisions are equally important.[15] Yet, such symmetry has frequently been neglected in public sector budgetary calculations. Benefit-cost analysis, however, should allow an increase in focus upon the distributional effects of public sector spending decisions, thus encouraging a symmetrical approach.

Benefit-cost analysis is capable also of promoting the aggregate economic goals of *stabilization* and *economic growth*. For example, if a higher level of national output yields greater aggregate welfare to the people of a society than does a lower level of output, a movement toward the societal production-possibility curve from within the curve, or an outward shift of the curve itself, must be considered desirable.[16] A budget policy which leads to a movement from inside the production-possibility frontier to a point on the frontier would thus increase societal welfare by allowing the full employment of available societal resources. Or, an expansion of the resource base itself through economic growth would likewise increase societal welfare.

A movement toward the production-possibility frontier at a time when resources are not being fully employed, or an outward movement of the frontier itself over a period of time, may be assisted by PPBS and

---

[14] See Chapter 6.

[15] See also the relevant discussion in Chapter 8 entitled "Principles of Tax Shifting and Incidence."

[16] See Figure 1–4 in Chapter 1.

benefit-cost analysis. For example, the improved revelation of allocative preferences as the result of greater efficiency in the budgeting process could reduce involuntary unemployment. Moreover, governmental policies directed toward the prevention of illness and the rehabilitation of the handicapped can increase the number of labor hours applied in the productive process. The Department of Health, Education, and Welfare (HEW) has specifically utilized benefit-cost analysis in an effort to maximize the attainment of such benefits within the given constraints of the budget.

Unquestionably, a federal government expenditure total in excess of $250 billion annually carries considerable potential influence on stabilization and economic growth goals. Yet, the nature of conventional budgeting procedures often places considerable "budget inflexibility" into various programs, Table 18–1, for example, demonstrates the sizable "uncontrollable" portions of the federal government budget.[17] In fiscal 1972, for example, $158.5 billion of federal spending could be classified as "relatively uncontrollable." This amounted to well over one half of the federal expenditures for that year. This certainly presents an important obstacle to "discretionary" stabilization policy directed toward the full-employment and price stability goals as well as toward other functional goals.[18] To the extent that benefit-cost analysis can reduce this inflexibility, stabilization performance should be improved. This would be achieved by giving public sector decision makers greater control and insight over the controllable portion of the budget.

Finally, an eventual comprehensive application of benefit-cost analysis to the entire public sector would be expected to partially alleviate the pressing *intergovernmental fiscal problems* of the American federation. If the American people continue to assume that the maintenance of an "effective" federal system of government is desirable, then such problems as *equalization* (horizontal fiscal imbalance between different states and localities) and *noncorrespondence* (vertical fiscal imbalance between levels of government) cannot be ignored.[19] Various instruments such as unconditional revenue sharing have been implemented to help solve these problems. For example, unconditional revenue-sharing deals with concepts such as "revenue effort" and "need." Bene-

---

[17] Pioneering work on the concept and measurement of "uncontrollable federal expenditures" was done by Murray L. Weidenbaum. See his "Budget 'Uncontrollability' as an Obstacle to Improving the Allocation of Government Resources," in *The Analysis and Evaluation of Public Expenditures: The PPB System*, Vol. 1, Joint Economic Committee, 91st Cong., 1st sess. (Washington, D.C.: U.S. Government Printing Office, 1969), pp. 357–68.

[18] See the discussion of discretionary fiscal policy in Part Four.

[19] See Chapter 19 for a more extensive description of these intergovernmental fiscal problems.

TABLE 18–1

Relatively Uncontrollable Federal Budget Outlays, 1969 to 1974 Fiscal Years (in billions)

	1969	1970	1971	1972	1973*	1974*
Relatively uncontrollable under present law	$118.6	$130.2	$145.7	$158.5	$181.9	$201.8
Open-ended programs and fixed costs, total	76.5	88.7	105.5	119.3	141.3	152.6
Social insurance trust funds total	39.8	45.2	54.9	61.7	71.7	80.4
Social security	26.8	30.3	35.9	40.2	49.4	55.5
Medicare	6.6	7.1	7.9	8.8	9.6	12.6
Unemployment	2.3	3.6	6.1	6.9	6.1	5.5
Retirement and other	4.1	4.2	5.0	5.8	6.7	6.8
Interest	15.8	18.3	19.6	20.6	22.8	24.7
Veterans benefits—pensions, compensation, education and insurance	5.7	6.6	7.6	8.3	9.1	9.1
Medicaid program	2.3	2.7	3.4	4.6	4.3	5.2
Other public assistance grants	4.0	4.7	6.3	8.5	8.4	7.4
General revenue sharing	—	—	—	—	6.8	6.0
Military retired pay	2.4	2.8	3.4	3.9	4.4	4.7
Farm price supports (Commodity Credit Corporation)	4.1	3.8	2.8	4.0	3.4	2.7
Supplemental security income	—	—	—	—	.1	2.2
Food stamp program	—	.6	1.6	1.9	2.2	2.2
Housing payments	—	—	—	1.1	1.7	2.0
Postal Service	.5	1.5	2.2	1.8	1.7	1.4
Legislative and judiciary	.4	.5	.5	.7	.7	.8
Other	1.5	2.1	3.3	2.4	3.9	3.7
Outlays from prior year contracts and obligations	41.9	41.5	40.3	39.2	39.9	45.5
National defense	25.5	24.9	22.1	20.2	19.2	21.9
Civilian programs	16.4	16.6	18.2	19.0	20.7	23.6
Allowances for pay raises	—	—	—	—	.7	3.7
Department of Defense	—	—	—	—	.7	2.7
Civilian agencies	—	—	—	—	†	1.0

* Estimated.
† Less than $50 million.
Source: *Budget of the United States Government*, various fiscal years, and Tax Foundation, Inc., *Spending Control Issues and the U.S. Budget* (New York: Tax Foundation, Inc., 1973), Table 9.

fit-cost analysis could provide a better understanding of the critical interrelationships which exist between these variables. Moreover, it could assist in the operation and appraisal of an unconditional revenue sharing program. In addition, a flexible and continuous inflow of data could be employed to assist the intergovernmental fiscal decision making relevant to an unconditional revenue-sharing program.

Disadvantages

Opponents of a comprehensive benefit-cost approach, especially one which is completely absorbed within the PPBS methodology, sometimes assert that it amounts to "government by computer," that is, without human flexibility and administered by technicians rather than by the elected representatives of the people. Another objection contends that planning may be carried out in such detail that the costs of the planning are likely to exceed the benefits of many programs. Moreover, it is pointed out that in the Soviet Union, where planning is an integral component of the operation of the entire economy, costly "planning errors" have occurred. Also, it is argued that a comprehensive planning approach in the American public sector would tend, in the long run, to move the governmental structure in the United States away from federalism and toward a unitary system of government.

It is also contended that the new budget efficiency approach is faced with enormous problems of information collection and analysis. Great gaps in theoretical and applied knowledge are said to show up when the critical time arises for selecting and applying a *social discount rate* (*preferredness criterion*) to indicate the "social profitability" of various governmental programs. Input as well as output data require reasonable quantification—and the task is not easy. Joint consumption benefits and externalities, for example, escape the price mechanism and their economic value is difficult to measure. Moreover, when output quantification is at least partly attainable, there exists a danger that governmental programs subject to such quantification may be selected over equally desirable, or more desirable, programs which are less subject to quantification, and thus less sensitive to the basic operational techniques of benefit-cost analysis. Furthermore, some opponents of the new approach fear that administrators and political officials will be tempted to manipulate benefit-cost studies in a biased manner so as to attain support for their "favorite" projects.

As suggested in the preceding paragraph, it is difficult to obtain an adequate *social discount rate* (*preferredness criterion*) to indicate the relative "social profitabilities" of various programs. The problem has both conceptual and quantification dimensions. Ideally, the estimates of benefits and costs for use with the preferredness criterion would be based on observable *market-type prices* for public and quasi-public goods, which prices would accurately reflect the "social benefits" of the final goods and the "social costs" of the resources used in their production. In other words, "opportunity costs" would be used as a reference point. Yet, the very nature of public and quasi-public goods, inclusive of such traits as joint consumption benefits and externalities, reduces the feasibility of using market-type prices for public-type goods as an overall benchmark. Moreover, long-term investment considerations require that "time-preference" play a primary role in the selection between alternative governmental investment projects. Market prices, once again, fail to meet this requirement. To an extent, *shadow prices* —either imputed from consumer behavior and supply phenomena or acquired from similar goods sold in the private sector—may be utilized, but they cannot be relied upon to guide the preferredness criterion in an unambiguous manner.[20] Somers has argued recently that there is no conceptual foundation for a single appropriate social discount rate applicable by a unit of government to select between alternative investment projects.[21] Instead, it is said that a separate discount rate based on time preference exists for each project and, moreover, that the private rate of time preference is inapplicable to pure public goods. In the latter case, such institutional devices as public opinion polls and the study of public choice theory or welfare politics[22] become increasingly relevant.

Indeed, the problem of selecting an adequate preferredness criterion, and supplementing it with quantifiable data, is a significant one. There is a danger that the public sector will set a social discount rate lower than would be set by the market sector. This may well occur because governments generally do not need to worry about credit ratings, nonliquidity, and risk in the manner that private enterprise must consider these factors. Clearly, the lower the social discount rate applied, the greater will be the number of governmental investment projects adopted. This is evident from Figure 18–1 which measures the social discount rate on the vertical axis and the magnitude of governmental investment expenditures along the horizontal axis. The relationship between these two variables is inverse, as is indicated by the downward slope of the government investment curve *G*. That is, the lower the social discount rate, the greater the volume of governmental investment expenditures undertaken, and vice versa. Thus, to the extent that the social rate of return for governmental investment is set at a lower rate than that for the market sector, a nonneutral *intersector* allocational effect will occur which favors public sector resource allocation.

---

[20] See the discussion of *shadow prices* by Roland N. McKean, "The Use of Shadow Prices," in Samuel B. Chase, Jr., (ed.), *Problems in Public Expenditure Analysis* (Washington, D.C.: Brookings Institution, 1968), pp. 33–77.

[21] Harold M. Somers, "On the Demise of the Social Discount Rate," *Journal of Finance*, May 1971, pp. 565–78. Also, see the related discussion by Bernard P. Herber in the same journal on pages 581–83.

[22] See Chapter 5.

FIGURE 18–1

Governmental Investment Expenditures at Various Social Discount Rates

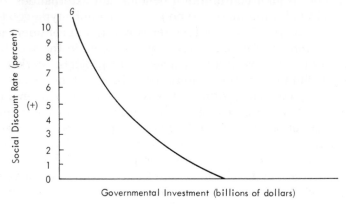

Moreover, by the extent to which different agencies of a unit of government use different social discount rates as part of their preferredness criterion, a similar negative *intragovernmental* distortion will take place.

Unfortunately, there is evidence that both of these criticisms may be applied to the comprehensive usage of the approach by the federal government as part of its PPBS efforts between 1965 and 1971. Some agencies, for example, used a discount rate equal to the rate paid by the U.S. Treasury Department to borrow money. In 1968, this would have amounted to about 3.2 percent if based upon the average rate payable on outstanding federal securities with maturity of 15 years or longer. Such a rate, of course, tends to be below a private sector rate where firms must account for such factors as nonliquidity and risk. Moreover, the social discount rates used by the various agencies of the federal government have ranged between 3 and 12 percent.[23] By comparison, it has been estimated that between 1961 and 1965 the rate of return in the private sector ranged from 4.1 percent for railroads to 15.4 percent for manufacturing firms.[24] However, if the value of corporate and personal income taxes forgone as a result of borrowing by the government to finance programs is added on to Treasury borrowing costs, the social rate of return for governmental projects would fall

---

[23] *Hearings before the Subcommittee on Economy in Government,* Joint Economic Committee, 90th Cong., 2d sess., (Washington, D.C.: U.S. Government Printing Office, 1968), p. 34.

[24] See Jacob A. Stockfisch, "The Interest Rate Applicable to Government Investment Projects," in *Hearings before the Subcommittee on Economy in Government,* Joint Economic Committee, 90th Cong., 1st sess. (Washington, D.C.: U.S. Government Printing Office, 1967), p. 137.

between 7 and 8 percent (in 1968). This would be more realistic, in terms of the opportunity costs of resources extracted from the private sector for use in public sector investment projects, than the 3.2 percent figure cited above. Moreover, the critical relationship of "time preference" to the conceptual and applied definition of a social discount rate, as mentioned earlier in the chapter, cannot be ignored.

As observed in the above appraisal of the advantages of benefit-cost analysis, the primary focus of the new budgetary approach is allocational in nature. Yet, it was observed also that distributional and stabilization-growth implications are inevitably present in any policy which may be selected. One danger of the new approach, indeed, is that such other effects may be totally ignored. It has been recommended that *equity* (distribution) be included as a "subset" of the *efficiency* (allocation) goal in benefit-cost analysis.[25] Thus, when equity effects are favorable, they could be included in the "benefits" of the program; when they are unfavorable, they could be included among the "costs." Admittedly, placing a value on equity or distributional effects poses a major problem. Nonetheless, society does make collective judgments concerning these goals. Thus, it seems appropriate that:

> Until means are developed for valuing distributional effects, their importance to policy makers makes it clear that economists who undertake or advise about benefit-cost analyses should at least spell out and discuss the forms of redistributive effects of a program, even if the end product of the research fails to place a value (positive or negative) on those effects.[26]

If such precaution is undertaken, the inherent danger of an overemphasis on the allocational implications of benefit-cost analysis can be reduced.

Musgrave warns that benefit-cost analysis, even if combined with traditional tax analysis, does not provide a comprehensive theory of public finance.[27] That is, even though opportunity cost considerations are included, and the revenue (tax) structure enters the picture, *no basic link* between the revenue and expenditure sides of the budget is provided by benefit-cost analysis. Hence, the economic goods provided by the public sector cannot be valued in a determinant manner. This is not to suggest, of course, that preferences cannot be better revealed with benefit-cost analysis in effect than in its absence. However, it does suggest that its basic limitations should be recognized in

---

[25] See Burton A. Weisbrod, "Income Redistribution Effects and Benefit Cost Analysis," in Samuel B. Chase, Jr. (ed.), *Problems in Public Expenditure Analysis* (© 1968 by the Brookings Institution, Washington, D.C.), pp. 177–222.

[26] Ibid., p. 180.

[27] Richard A. Musgrave, "Cost-Benefit Analysis and the Theory of Public Finance," *Journal of Economic Literature*, September 1969, p. 805.

the sense it does *not* provide a unique and comprehensive theory of public sector economics.

Final Evaluation of Benefit-Cost Analysis

Generally speaking, the new budgetary-efficiency approach which utilizes benefit-cost analysis for capital investment decisions gives evidence of being a worthy addition for the improvement of rationality in the public sector budgetary process. This is not to deny, however, that significant obstacles still need to be overcome. Moreover, caution needs to be taken so that the basic allocational nature of benefit-cost analysis does not cause policy makers to preclude relevant distributional and stabilization-growth implications. Instead, positive *distributional* (equity) and *stabilization-growth* objectives should be promoted through the additional data and information which are available.

Some of the explicit arguments against the approach, as enumerated in the "Disadvantages" section above, can be refuted on rather convincing terms. For example, the "government by computer" criticism could easily be altered to stress "government with the help of computers." Democratic decision-making in the public sector should be "assisted," not "replaced," by computers. Moreover, benefit-cost analysis, if properly utilized, is more likely to "strengthen federalism" through the alleviation of equalization (horizontal fiscal imbalance) and noncorrespondence (vertical fiscal imbalance) problems than to result in a "unitary" political system. Relatedly, the availability of more information and data for policy makers, both executive and legislative, and for the general public, should strengthen the democratic process. The growing interest in "public choice theory" should be complementary to this improvement. Furthermore, there is no excuse for "too low" a social discount rate, nor for considering only "quantifiable" projects, since both problems can be largely overcome by a properly designed and implemented approach.

The improvement in the technical efficiency of decision making should allow a better revelation of societal preferences for "particular" public and quasi-public goods. Moreover, this advantage should be extended also to include the "intersector allocation decision" between the public and private sectors, though admittedly the selection of a rational social discount rate is especially important at this point.

Furthermore, even though benefit-cost decisions are more feasible at lower than higher levels of decision-making in an agency or department—due largely to the easier quantification of goals, benefits, and costs at the lower stages—the approach still provides an overall "array of primary budgetary alternatives" to which "priorities can be applied" over a period of time. In all, it would appear that benefit-cost analysis improves the efficiency of public sector decision-making. Where adopted, spending is appraised in terms of goals. Long-run, intermediate, and short-run budgetary decisions are tied together through the consideration of time preference. Costs are arrayed alongside the benefits of public expenditures. Also, the economic calculus of the opportunity cost doctrine is applied to the economic operation of the public sector. Yet, despite all of these merits, the approach should be undertaken only within a framework which includes an awareness of its limitations. However, it would be difficult to imagine that such an approach would fail to yield results in which the overall advantages outweigh the disadvantages.

19

Intergovernmental Fiscal Problems in the American Federation

THE AGGREGATE PUBLIC SECTOR BUDGET CONCEPT

Chapter 17 considered the *institutional* nature of the federal system in the United States. The present chapter will describe the basic *intergovernmental fiscal problems* which tend to arise within the aggregate public sector of a federal nation with particular reference to the American federation. Chapter 20 will then analyze the *major fiscal techniques* or *instruments* which may be directed toward the alleviation of these problems. Also, it will focus on the controversial *division of fiscal powers* between the two sovereign levels of government in a federation—an area of decision-making in which noneconomic value judgments play a significant role. Overall, these chapters will be concerned with the subject of *fiscal federalism.*

The intergovernmental fiscal issues which arise in a federation stem primarily from the dual existence of two sovereign levels of government. Yet, a *federation* is generally conceded to be economically more efficient than a *balkan* arrangement in which the states or provinces would each operate as a separate nation. On the other hand, it might be argued that a *unitary* structure of government—with only a sovereign central government—would avoid the intergovernmental fiscal problems which derive from the dual sovereignty of two levels of government. For example, such a unitary system is employed in Great Britain. However, it would appear that an "operational" unitary democracy would be difficult, if not impossible, to attain in the United

States due to the great magnitude of the geographical area to be governed.[1] Centralized sovereign government, indeed, might impair the American cultural preference for individualistic involvement and representation in the political decision-making process. Thus, it will be assumed that the American people prefer a federal democracy over a unitary democracy because the latter, in practice, might deviate seriously from democratic goals in a nation covering a broad geographical area.

The *aggregate public sector* of the United States is composed of more than 78,000 separate units of government each capable of performing the basic fiscal functions of revenue-gathering (mainly taxation) and spending.[2] The overall allocational, distributional, stabilization, and economic growth performance of the American public sector, of course, will reflect the fiscal decisions of each of these separate governmental units. Though no single unit of government determines the entire aggregate effects, some units obviously exert greater influence than do others. The overall fiscal effects of federal budgetary behavior, for example, are of much greater significance than the budgetary actions of a local school district.

The federalistic basis of public sector structure in the United States complicates the aggregate operations of government in this nation as compared to nations with unitary political structures. Tax and expenditure policies often lack coordination in reference to national economic goals. A tax reduction at the federal level for stabilization-growth purposes, for example, may be partially or totally neutralized by tax increases at the state-local level.[3] The multiplicity of state and local units of government, moreover, tends to cause many conflicting policies within the same level of government (state or local) regarding the four public finance goals.

The nature of *intergovernmental fiscal relations* thus constitutes an extremely relevant consideration for the achievement of fiscal rationality within a decentralized political structure. The *aggregate public sector budget* concept, indeed, is an important one. Intergovernmental

---

[1] The same may be said to explain the use of the federal system in certain other democratic nations with large land areas such as Australia, Canada, and India.

[2] In 1972, the Bureau of the Census, U.S. Department of Commerce, reported the existence of 78,268 units in the United States, inclusive of the federal government, the District of Columbia, 50 state governments, and 78,216 local governments.

[3] The federal personal and corporation income tax reductions of March, 1964 were not followed immediately by state-local tax increases of any significant nature. The reasons for this relative status quo apparently were (1) the federal tax reduction came too late in the legislative year to influence the actions of most state legislatures, and (2) 1964 was an election year, at which time tax increases are politically unpopular. The latter point is supported by the fact that state-local tax increases were considerable during 1965, a nonelection year. Hence, the initial inaction of state-local government was only temporary.

fiscal relations assume two major dimensions: (1) intergovernmental budgetary influence between levels of government, which is referred to as *vertical* intergovernmental fiscal relations, and (2) intergovernmental budgetary influence between different government units at the same level, which is termed *horizontal* intergovernmental fiscal relations. The latter type of interrelationship is possible, of course, only at the state and local levels of government where more than one unit of government exists.

INTERGOVERNMENTAL FISCAL PROBLEMS

Vertical Fiscal Imbalance—The Problem of Noncorrespondence

As observed above, *federalism*—whereby two or more sovereign units of government coexist within the same political environment—provides the primary basis for the intergovernmental fiscal problems of the U.S. public sector. For example, it must be decided *which level of government* will perform the specific functions which community preferences require. In addition, the revenue sources necessary to finance these expenditure functions must be allocated in some manner among the various levels of government. This does not mean, of course, that each governmental level should possess exclusive rights to a particular type of revenue, but it does mean that overall consideration should be given to the *combined* effects of the revenue-gathering activities of *all* components of the public sector under the aggregate public sector budget concept.

A considerable divergence may exist between the sources of revenue and functional expenditure obligations among the governments of a federation. Thus, some governments may find it easier than others to meet their expenditure responsibilities from their own revenue sources. When this situation exists in the form of an imbalance of revenues and expenditures "vertically" between levels of government, it is referred to as the problem of *noncorrespondence* or *vertical fiscal imbalance.*

In the United States, noncorrespondence has followed its usual form with the central (national) level of government being in a superior position and the state-local (subnational) level being in an inferior position.[4] That is, the federal government enjoys a greater ability to raise revenues to meet its functional expenditure obligations than do state

---

[4] It should be noted, however, that certain other nations, such as Australia, experience a basic noncorrespondence deficit for the lower levels of government greater than that in the United States.

and local governments to meet their obligations. This *vertical imbalance* has resulted largely from the greater income-elasticity of tax revenues in the federal revenue structure as contrasted to the lower income elasticities of state and local government taxes. Relatedly, the income-elasticity of state-local government *expenditures* has tended to be more elastic than that of their revenue sources due to urbanization, industrialization, and population growth. Though noncorrespondence between revenues and expenditures for the two sovereign levels of government would be eliminated by a unitary political structure, certain noneconomic reasons (as noted above) favor a more decentralized government for the United States than the unitary system would provide. Finally, it is interesting to observe that the income elasticities of state tax systems vary considerably among the 50 states.[5]

Horizontal Fiscal Imbalance—The Problem of Equalization

When fiscal imbalance occurs "horizontally" between different units of government at the same level of government in a federation, it is known as the problem of *equalization* or *horizontal fiscal imbalance*. For example, considerable differences in the per capita distribution of income and wealth and in the volume of sales transactions exist among the several economic regions of the nation. Since several states (or parts of states) comprise each economic region, these regional differences in income, wealth, and in sales transactions potential (the three primary "tax bases") take on an interstate dimension and result in horizontal fiscal imbalance between the various states. Furthermore, similar variations may occur among the local units of government within a given state. These differences in the resource endowments of communities, similar to those among the states, cause the per capita revenue collection potentials of the communities to vary sharply.

Admittedly, one advantage of decentralized fiscal decision-making by state and local governments is the fact that a particular revenue structure can be adapted to the unique resource characteristics of a given state or locality. Nonetheless, since resource endowment is the ultimate source of governmental revenue-collection capacity, a given state or community enjoying considerable wealth and income-producing ability and a strong sales base is capable of providing a greater per capita volume of public and quasi-public goods than one which is resource-poor. Moreover, it would be able to provide this greater volume of economic goods with the same per capita "revenue effort" by its citizens as that of the poorer jurisdiction. Or, alternately, a poorer state or community could provide a level of public and quasi-public goods

---

[5] See Table 19–1.

TABLE 19–1
Response of State Tax Structures* to 1 Percent Change in Personal Income, 1970

State	Low Income Elasticity (0.80 to 0.99) Weighted Elasticity	Percent of Taxes Included	State	Medium Income Elasticity (1.00 to 1.19) Weighted Elasticity	Percent of Taxes Included	State	High Income Elasticity (1.20 to 1.47) Weighted Elasticity	Percent of Taxes Included
Ohio	0.80	77.5	Nevada	1.00†	86.2	Massachusetts	1.20	74.9
New Jersey	0.83	60.8	Delaware	1.01	56.9	New York	1.22	76.7
Texas	0.83	66.5	Indiana	1.01	87.2	Virginia	1.22	81.1
Connecticut	0.85	69.7	Nebraska	1.01‡	82.5	Arkansas	1.25	78.4
South Dakota	0.85	84.3	North Dakota	1.01	75.9	Montana	1.28	67.6
Pennsylvania	0.86	63.5	Alabama	1.02	83.9	Oregon	1.29	70.4
Florida	0.87	80.8	Arizona	1.03	74.2	Idaho	1.31†	75.3
Wyoming	0.88	62.8	Mississippi	1.04	85.2	Wisconsin	1.41	62.3
Maryland	0.89	83.5	Oklahoma	1.05†	65.3	Alaska	1.47†‡	61.5
New Hampshire	0.90	66.2	South Carolina	1.05	85.0			
Tennessee	0.90	69.0	Missouri	1.06	82.0			
West Virginia	0.90	88.4	Colorado	1.08	80.5			
Maine	0.92‡	80.8	Michigan	1.08‡	73.8			
Washington	0.93	79.2	North Carolina	1.09	77.2			
Kansas	0.95	80.6	Illinois	1.10†‡	83.0			
New Mexico	0.95	70.1	California	1.11	75.7			
Rhode Island	0.95	68.8	Georgia	1.11	84.5			
Louisiana	0.96	53.5	Kentucky	1.12	82.3			
			Iowa	1.13	78.4			
			Vermont	1.14	81.1			
			Hawaii	1.17	93.7			
			Minnesota	1.17	79.2			
			Utah	1.19	81.1			

* Includes broadbased individual income, general sales and selective sales taxes.
† Elasticity may be slightly overstated since rate increases were not totally excluded from selective sales tax elasticity estimate.
‡ Individual income tax elasticity assumed to be 1.7.
Source: Advisory Commission on Intergovernmental Relations, *Federal-State-Local Finances: Significant Features of Fiscal Federalism* (Washington, D.C., U.S. Government Printing Office, 1974), p. 52.

equal to that of a wealthier state or community, but this could be accomplished by the poorer state or community only through a greater per capita "revenue effort," and a resulting lower level of private sector consumption in that state or community. Most likely, "the worst of all worlds" will be the result, that is, an intermediate position will occur whereby the residents of the poorer jurisdiction will experience both a higher per capita revenue effort burden and a lower per capita consumption of public and quasi-public goods than in the wealthier jurisdiction.

Revenue effort, of course, consists of both the "tax" and "nontax" payments made to government by the residents of a jurisdiction though, in most jurisdictions, tax revenues are by far the more important source of governmental revenues. Thus, revenue effort is primarily an indicator of the "tax burdens" of the members of a political jurisdiction. However, it is possible for some taxes to be ultimately paid to a jurisdiction by taxpayers who are not residents of that jurisdiction. This is known as the phenomenon of *tax exporting.*[6] The ability to transfer or export a tax to the residents of another political jurisdiction will vary depending, among other things, upon the nature of the tax itself. Hence, a state severance tax on the extraction of natural resources is highly conducive to "exporting" because it is a tax on transactions at an early stage of the productive process, and thus it is virtually certain to be followed by a number of further productive transactions which may well involve the residents of other states or nations.

The interstate variation in both *revenue effort* and *tax effort* (exclusive of user charges) is demonstrated in Table 19–2. Since states with "lower" per capita personal incomes tend to have either "higher" *revenue efforts,* with a resulting higher *tax* and *nontax* burden on their taxpayers, or lower per capita public goods consumption, or both, the relevant question thus becomes: Should deliberate federal budgetary policy be undertaken to "equalize" the consumption of public and quasi-public goods and revenue burdens between the various states? Such policy, if adopted, may be termed *equalization* policy.

A "yes" answer to the above question could be based on allocational, distributional, or stabilization-growth grounds. It is argued that a group of states which choose *federation* over *balkanization* necessarily accepts a *common interest* in the living standards of all of the citizens of the federal nation. Each citizen, as it were, has "dual citizenship." That is, he is simultaneously a resident both of a sovereign nation and of a sovereign state. Moreover, the higher the degree of economic inter-

---

[6] For two excellent articles which deal in depth with the issue of "tax exporting," see Charles E. McLure, Jr., "Tax Exporting in the United States: Estimates for 1962," *National Tax Journal,* March 1967, pp. 49–77, and also his "The Inter-regional Incidence of General Regional Taxes," *Public Finance,* No. 3, 1969, pp. 457–83.

TABLE 19-2

Measures of State-Local Revenue Effort and Tax Effort, by State, 1971

State	Taxes and Charges as a Percent of State Personal Income* (Revenue Effort)		Taxes as a Percent of State Personal Income (Tax Effort)	
	Percent of Income	State Percent Related to U.S. Average	Percent of Income	State Percent Related to U.S. Average
UNITED STATES	14.9	100	11.9	100
Alabama......................	14.3	96	9.8	82
Alaska.......................	23.5	158	10.4	87
Arizona......................	16.9	113	13.3	112
Arkansas.....................	13.1	88	9.7	82
California	16.8	113	13.7	115
Colorado.....................	15.8	106	12.1	102
Connecticut..................	12.9	87	11.1	93
Delaware	16.0	107	11.7	98
Dist. of Columbia.............	12.6	85	10.7	90
Florida	14.0	94	10.6	89
Georgia......................	13.9	93	10.1	85
Hawaii.......................	17.6	118	14.1	118
Idaho........................	16.2	109	12.6	106
Illinois......................	13.5	91	11.5	97
Indiana......................	13.9	93	10.8	91
Iowa	15.8	106	12.3	103
Kansas.......................	14.1	95	10.9	92
Kentucky	14.0	94	10.5	88
Louisiana	17.1	115	12.5	105
Maine	15.0	101	12.7	107
Maryland	15.0	101	12.1	102
Massachusetts	14.5	97	12.7	107
Michigan	15.5	104	12.2	103
Minnesota....................	17.2	115	13.2	110
Mississippi	17.0	114	12.3	103
Missouri	12.4	83	9.9	83
Montana......................	16.1	108	12.7	107
Nebraska	15.6	105	11.7	98
Nevada.......................	17.5	117	13.0	109
New Hampshire................	13.2	89	10.7	90
New Jersey	13.0	87	11.0	92
New Mexico	18.0	121	12.7	107
New York.....................	17.3	116	14.5	122
North Carolina	13.4	90	10.6	89
North Dakota	19.9	134	14.2	119
Ohio	12.1	81	9.3	78
Oklahoma....................	14.0	94	9.9	83
Oregon.......................	15.2	102	11.6	97
Pennsylvania.................	13.5	91	11.4	96
Rhode Island.................	14.0	94	12.1	102
South Carolina	13.3	89	10.3	87
South Dakota	18.1	121	13.8	116
Tennessee	13.2	89	9.9	83
Texas........................	13.1	88	9.9	83
Utah	16.2	109	12.5	105
Vermont......................	17.7	119	14.7	124
Virginia......................	13.1	88	10.4	87
Washington	16.4	110	12.3	103
West Virginia	13.9	93	11.1	93
Wisconsin....................	17.9	120	14.6	123
Wyoming.....................	20.4	137	13.9	117

Note: Revenue effort presents only one side of the fiscal equation—the variations in the quality of public services, while not directly measurable, are at least partially responsible for the range in effort. It should also be noted that while certain communities make a heavier use of fees and charges, others place greater emphasis on taxes to finance local public services.

* Total State and local tax collections plus all charges and miscellaneous general revenue, which conforms to the U.S. Bureau of the Census definition of "General Revenue From Own Sources."

Source: Advisory Commission on Intergovernmental Relations, *Federal-State-Local Finances: Significant Features of Fiscal Federalism* (Washington, D.C.: U.S. Government Printing Office, 1974), p. 56.

dependence in the nation, as brought about through advanced technology, specialized production, and trade, the more important this "common interest" becomes in terms of the allocational, distributional, and stabilization-growth goals of society. In terms of *distribution,* the problem takes the form of the variations in the fiscal capacities of the states and localities. Since these jurisdictions possess differential fiscal capacities to supply public and quasi-public goods, the citizens of poorer jurisdictions are likely to either consume fewer such goods, or bear higher revenue-effort burdens, or experience some "intermediate" position of both undesirable effects. The collective consensus of a democratic society thus might well oppose significant inequality in the interstate and interlocality consumption of public and quasi-public goods. Relatedly, society might oppose considerable unevenness in the interstate and interlocality distribution of revenue effort burdens among the taxpayers residing in the respective jurisdictions. Hence, the adoption of budgetary policies to reduce such differentials may be supported on distributional grounds. Moreover, this reasoning often is extended to include a governmental responsibility to alleviate "private sector poverty," as well as poverty in the consumption of "public-type good," since the *dual citizenship* argument applies to both private and to public consumption.

Society may also wish to exert positive equalization nonneutralities due to *allocational* considerations focusing on the concept of "intergovernmental externalities."[7] In an advanced industrial society, for example, high-quality communications and transportation systems allow the conditions imposed by the public sector of one state or locality to "diffuse" into the consumptive and productive activities of other jurisdictions. In other words, a poor state or community through its budget policy cannot help but influence the allocational patterns of production and consumption in wealthier states or localities in an interdependent specialized society in which intergovernmental externalities are common. Thus, fiscal policy of an equalization nature may again be called for.

Finally, the quality of productive resources in a poor state or community is likely to be lower than in an area capable of providing a higher level of public consumption. Labor, for example, is likely to be less educated and health standards lower in a poor as opposed to a wealthy state or community. The aggregate *stabilization-growth* implications of this situation suggest that lower volumes of short-run output and slower long-run rates of economic growth will result for the economy

---

[7] The concept of "intergovernmental externalities" constitutes a major fiscal issue in a federation—one far beyond the scope of only equalization considerations. Hence, this concept is treated below, in greater detail, as a separate intergovernmental fiscal problem.

as a whole. Thus, horizontal intergovernmental inequalities in resource quality, as imposed by the lower public consumption standards of some jurisdictions, may serve as an argument for the institution of intergovernmental equalization programs in order to promote stabilization and economic growth goals.

The alternative techniques for achieving *interstate equalization,* which are described later in this chapter, may exert their "primary" impact on either the *fiscal capacities* of the states to allocate public and quasi-public goods or on the *actual allocation* of such goods. The former refers to the fisc of the state government as represented in "revenue" terms. The latter refers to the ability of the federal fisc to "directly influence interstate allocational patterns" and hence the distribution of real income among the residents of the respective states.

Vertical and Horizontal Intergovernmental Externalities

It was observed in Part One of this book that economic effects initiated in the private sector sometimes "escape the price mechanism." That is, consumers or producers may receive benefits or costs initiated by other private consumers or producers over which there is no direct market control. This phenomenon is known, of course, as the concept of *externality.*

An analogous situation may occur in the "public sector" of the economy since government-initiated benefits and costs sometimes "escape the internal budgetary control" of the unit of government which either initiates or receives these economic effects. This concept in the public sector may be referred to as that of *intergovernmental externality.* It means that the fiscal action of one unit of government can exert either "beneficial" or "harmful" effects on the residents of another governmental jurisdiction in a manner which escapes the fiscal control of the one or the other jurisdiction. Thus, mosquito spraying financed by one city may bring "benefits" to the residents of a nearby city (*positive* intergovernmental externality), or the dumping of poorly-treated sewage into a river by one city may "harm" the drinking water of the residents of a downstream city (*negative* intergovernmental externality). Moreover, an intergovernmental externality may involve governments at different levels (*vertical* intergovernmental externality) or at the same level (*horizontal* intergovernmental externality).

The *public goods* concept developed in Part One of this book may be adopted for analytical purposes so as to include the concepts of *joint consumption* and *intergovernmental externalities* as they exist in a federation. Thus, intergovernmental externalities and economic goods (bads) may be classified as "national," "quasi-national," and "nonnational" public goods (bads). A *national* public good may be defined as one which is consumed equally by all residents of a nation. Moreover, the central fisc is likely to be able to allocate such a good in a more efficient manner than lower-level governments. In this instance, the conditions of "joint and equal consumption" in the whole economy and "publicness of supply" allow the good to be viewed as "national" in scope. Thus, an economic good such as national defense is normally provided through significant central government influence—though such influence does not require outright production of the good, in all aspects, by the central fisc.[8] The requirement for vertical and horizontal intergovernmental fiscal coordination is "minimal" in the case of national public goods.

Quasi-national and *nonnational* public goods (bads), on the other hand, are consumed on a less comprehensive basis throughout the nation and suggest a greater need for intergovernmental fiscal coordination. They are not as likely to be both "jointly" and "equally" consumed throughout the entire nation. Moreover, the central fisc is less likely to hold an efficiency advantage within the public sector for "exclusively" allocating these goods. However, an important additional distinction needs to be made between *quasi-national* and *nonnational* public goods. This distinction relates to the significance of the "intergovernmental externalities" which characterize the respective goods. In the case of *quasi-national* public goods (bads), important intergovernmental externalities exist while in the case of *nonnational* public goods (bads), they do not. In a federation, either the state or local level of government, or both, may play a major role in the allocation of quasi-national and nonnational public goods, though central and/or state government coordination will often be required in the case of the former.

"Education" serves as a good example of a *quasi-national* public good. It is allocated largely by the public sector and part of its benefits are consumed nationally due to important spillover effects. Yet, it can be produced at any level of government. Yet, the presence of "intergovernmental externalities" necessitates *coordination* of the supply of education among various supplying-units of government in order to prevent an "undersupply" of the good. This is so because a government financing educational benefits in a greater volume than consumed by its residents, as some benefits pass to other jurisdictions in the form of "intergovernmental externalities," would tend to reduce the supply of such benefits. In the United States, the state level of government provides the primary coordinative effort for locally-produced public school education.

"Police services" provide an example of an essentially *nonnational*

---

[8] See Chapter 3 for a discussion of the alternative techniques whereby government may influence resource allocation.

public good. The good can be allocated by state or local governments and its primary benefits, being largely "nonnational" in scope, tend to reside primarily within the state or locality which supplies the benefits. Thus, there are "state" troopers or highway patrolmen, "county" sheriff deputies, and "city" policemen.

Finally, it should be useful at this point to compare the complexity of intergovernmental allocational actions with those of the private sector. In the market sector, for example, firms and consumers are able to conduct economic exchange and related market activities on an "interstate basis" with minimal constraint being imposed by the respective state governments. The "interstate commerce clause" of the Constitution assures this result. On the other hand, no such provision exists to effectively minimize "conflict" between the fiscal actions of the 50 states and more than 78,000 units of local government. This phenomenon helps to explain the complexities of intergovernmental fiscal relations in the American federation, as discussed in this chapter. These complexities take the form of such specific problems as noncorrespondence, equalization, and intergovernmental externalities—all discussed above—and tax overlapping, fiscal competition, urban economic problems, and intergoal conflicts—to be discussed below.

Tax Overlapping—Vertical and Horizontal Multiple Taxation

Various situations arise in a federation whereby the same tax base is taxed more than once. This multiple or overlapping taxation may be imposed (1) by different levels of government (*vertical* multiple taxation), (2) by different units of government at the same level (*horizontal* multiple taxation) or (3) by the same unit of government (*intraunit* multiple taxation).[9] Examples of *vertical* multiple taxation by different levels of government include federal, state, and local government imposition of a personal income tax.[10] Another prime example of multiple taxation by different levels of government occurs when both state and local governments apply property tax rates on the same property base. *Horizontal* multiple taxation by different government units at the same level is exemplified by the imposition of property taxes by several units of local government such as counties, municipalities, and school districts. *Intraunit* multiple taxation, with the same tax base being taxed more than once by the same unit of government, also exists within the American public sector. The best example occurs in the dual imposition

---

[9] "Multiple taxation" ("tax overlapping") is often referred to as "*double* taxation," though clearly the latter term is inferior because the same tax base may be taxed more than twice.

[10] Residents of St. Louis and Kansas City, Missouri, for example, are subject to federal, state, and local government personal income taxes.

of federal income taxes—both corporation and personal—on corporate dividend income with only a slight offset provided by law.[11] Another example of intraunit multiple taxation involves the dual imposition by some states of a selective excise tax and a general sales tax on motor fuel.

The fact that multiple taxation or tax overlapping is not undesirable per se must be emphasized. Multiple taxation becomes irrational only when it is practiced by one unit or level of government without concern for its aggregate effects within the public sector and between the public and private sectors. This includes the interacting effects of multiple taxation upon allocation, distribution, stabilization, and economic growth goals.[12] The "cumulative" tax burden created by multiple taxation, for example, may distort the society's concept of equitable distribution.

Regarding the extent of multiple taxation in the American public sector, the Advisory Commission on Intergovernmental Relations observes:[13]

> While tax overlapping [multiple taxation] is widespread in the sense that often a tax category providing the major part of the tax revenues at one level—Federal, State, or local—is used also, if only to a minor degree, at another level, the system is characterized by a substantial degree of revenue separation. Most of the tax overlapping is minimal and could be largely eliminated by foregoing about 20 percent of collections. If by some magic, for example, all three levels of government could turn back the clock just three years (in terms of their latest tax collections), and each could rearrange its tax take of three years ago, they could utilize such a 20 percent reduction in their tax take, in terms of averages, to eliminate tax overlapping. They would accomplish this by leaving the Federal Government with only income taxes, local governments with only property taxes, and the States largely with consumer taxes.

Some reduction in multiple taxation by different levels of government has occurred during recent decades. Most states, for example, are reducing emphasis on the property tax which is now used almost exclusively by local government. In addition, the federal government has abandoned the tax on electrical energy and most of its admissions taxes thus leaving these taxes to lower levels of government.

---

[11] However, as was observed in Chapter 11, the magnitude of such multiple taxation may be significantly reduced through the process of tax shifting.

[12] The problem of *intergoal nonneutrality* resulting from intergovernmental fiscal behavior is treated below as a "separate" intergovernmental fiscal problem.

[13] The Advisory Commission on Intergovernmental Relations, *Tax Overlapping in the United States—1964* (Washington, D.C.: U.S. Government Printing Office, July 1964), p. 18.

Vertical and Horizontal Intergovernmental Fiscal Competition

State and local governments frequently engage in vertical and horizontal *intergovernmental fiscal competition* in an effort to attract *business firms* and, relatedly, residents to their respective political jurisdictions. Tax concessions, and the provision of economic resources such as land and manufacturing plants through "industrial development bond" financing, are among the important fiscal subsidies used for this purpose.[14] Given a present condition of "optimal" resource allocation, such *supply* subsidies would negatively distort the allocation of business operations among various geographical areas since the market mechanism would not be allowed to allocate resources among the alternative locations on the basis of the most efficient resource combinations. However, if the prevailing allocational pattern is "suboptimal," the fiscal subsidies could yield either positive or negative results.

It is sometimes argued that "community differences" in revenue and expenditure patterns can increase the efficiency of meeting *consumer demand* for governmentally-supplied economic goods since an individual may select his residential location from among various communities, each with a different budgetary base, in a manner similar to the free selection of private economic goods in the market.[15] Hence, the greater the diversity of governmental levels and units, as under a federal system, the greater is the motivation for "fiscal competition" for *industry* on the supply side, and for the spatial mobility of *consumers* between different political jurisdictions on the demand side.

Urban Economic Problems

There has been no more significant trend in American history than the movement whereby the nation has been transformed from a basically rural to a basically urban society. In 1790, only 5 percent of the American population resided in urban areas. With the urban growth trend becoming very pronounced after 1880, this percentage increased to 40 percent by 1900. In 1920, for the first time, more Americans lived in the city than in rural areas. The transition toward urban living has continued since that date and is expected to continue well into the future. In 1970, two out of every three Americans resided in metropolitan areas. The ratio increases to nine out of every ten Americans if those persons living in communities with less than 2,500 inhabitants, and in unincorporated suburban areas, are included in the urban total.

---

[14] See the relevant discussion in Chapter 12 regarding the property tax and "industrial development bond" financing.

[15] Relatedly, see Charles M. Tiebout, "A Pure Theory of Local Expenditures," *Journal of Political Economy,* October 1956, pp. 416–24.

The growth of urban areas in the United States, for the most part, has been a function of industrialization. More specifically, the growth has been a product of innovation and technological advancements in the fields of manufacturing, commerce, transportation, and agriculture. The growth of cities, moreover, has been supported by the population decline in rural areas made possible by the income-inelastic demand for most farm products and the fact that improving technology allows much greater farm output per unit of labor input. The social, political, and economic complexities of urbanization are substantial. Indeed, the economic benefits which derive from industrialization, and from the urbanization which it sponsors, are to some extent neutralized by the problems which also result from these phenomena. These problems, many of which are "intergovernmental" in nature, are not insoluble. The failure to meet some of them adequately in recent decades, however, has been alarming.

The Bureau of the Census classifies *local governments* into several categories: (1) standard metropolitan statistical areas (SMSA),[16] (2) counties, (3) municipalities, (4) townships, and (5) special districts. The multiplicity of local government decision-making units on fiscal matters is evident. *The Census of Governments for 1967,* for example, reported that 227 standard metropolitan statistical areas existed in the United States during that year. These metropolitan areas encompassed a multitude of local government units, namely, 404 counties, 4,977 municipalities, 3,255 townships, 5,018 school districts, and 7,049 special districts such as those for sewage disposal, water supply, road and street improvement, and fire protection. In all, 20,703 units of local government —all with budgetary power and 85 percent with the authority to collect property taxes—exist within the 227 SMSAs. Burkhead describes the proliferation of local governments as follows:[17] "This is grass-roots government with a vengeance: it is one of the oddities of American democracy that little government finds such generous representation in the standard metropolitan areas." Indeed, many of the significant contemporary fiscal problems of urban areas derive from the decentralized nature of local government structure in the urban areas of the United States.

The concentration of people in cities is not the sole dimension of the complex socio-politico-economic problems of an urban-industrial society. Equally important is the shift of population and industry away

---

[16] Essentially, an SMSA is defined as a county or group of contiguous counties (except in New England) which contains at least one central city of 50,000 inhabitants or more, or "twin cities" with a combined population of at least 50,000. In New England, towns and cities rather than counties are used in defining an SMSA.

[17] Jesse Burkhead, *Public School Finance* (Syracuse, N.Y.: Syracuse University Press, 1964), p. 133.

from the heart of the city into the suburbs. New and complex problems arise with this latter dimension of urban living. Though 64 percent of the American population presently resides in metropolitan areas, only one half of this population lives in the central city, the remainder living in the surrounding area. Moreover, it is estimated that the suburban population of metropolitan areas will continue to experience both absolute and relative growth in the years ahead.

Thus, a central city must provide governmental services for a population greater than that which resides within its political boundaries while, at the same time, suburban political jurisdictions are faced with the pressing needs of a growing area including such requirements as new schools, water systems, sewage disposal systems, streets, fire protection, and police protection. Each new house in the suburbs requires, on the average, several thousand dollars of incremental governmental services. Meanwhile, the movement of people and industry from the central city to the suburbs tends to decrease the property and income tax bases of the central city while the suburban governments often are inadequate for the performance of the complex functions required of them. The tax burden on those remaining in the central city, moreover, will tend to increase as the tax base declines, thus stimulating an additional exodus to the suburbs. Since many people who live in the suburbs work in the central city, an extreme demand for transportation facilities, particularly roads for highway transportation, often faces the central city.

Substantial intergovernmental externalities—both benefits and costs —exist among the multitude of political jurisdictions comprising urban areas in the United States. Yet, the decentralization of decision-making causes a divergence between the revenue sources and the expenditure decisions of these various political jurisdictions. This divergence exists despite the fact that the problems to be solved and the governmental economic goods to be provided are common to the entire urban area because of externalities. There is an inability to pool financial resources and to coordinate decision-making to meet the problems which face the entire urban complex.

It seems incongruous that urban governments operate under crisis conditions when a disproportionately large proportion of the nation's wealth is concentrated in these areas. Margolis asks: What are the sources of these crises? Are they becoming more critical?[18] He observes that the basic core of metropolitan financial problems lies in *spatial differentiation.* Differentiation and specialization in economic functions make increasing efficiency possible, but they also give rise to costs

---

[18] Julius Margolis, "Metropolitan Finance Problems: Territories, Functions, and Growth," National Bureau of Economic Research, in *Public Finances: Needs, Sources, and Utilization* (Princeton, N.J.: Princeton University Press, 1961), pp. 229–93.

of organization. The possible chaos which might arise because of "functional differentiation" can be overcome by the organization of markets. Likewise, spatial differentiation requires organization, but the role of the market as a spatial organizing force is quite different. *Spatial differentiation*, in this context, refers to the fact that every activity must occupy a unique site within the city. In this instance, the market is of minor significance and governments must perform the vital organizing role. Yet, can government establish a framework for economic and social activity within the city? Does the structure of local government —its limited territorial jurisdiction, functional specialization, and restricted fiscal tools—inhibit it as an efficient organizer?

Margolis observes that locational sites within cities are highly substitutable.[19] Continuous spatial shifting of residential and commercial activities thus occurs, with this shifting causing conflicts of interest among individuals since taxes are not assessed in proportion to the benefits received. The larger the number of government units in a metropolitan area, the greater the frustration of local governments from the vetoes of those whose gains do not compensate for their losses. Hence, the fiscal crisis worsens, not because of overall inadequacy in revenue sources but because of the inability to organize. Indeed, the propensity for self-interest to frustrate political decision making is reinforced by the functional and territorial balkanization of the metropolitan areas. Yet, an effective intergovernmental coordinative effort is very difficult to accomplish.

Vertical and Horizontal Intergovernmental Fiscal Relations and Intergoal Nonneutrality

The aggregate public sector of the United States, consisting of three *levels* and more than 78,000 *units* of government, will inevitably exert "composite" allocational, distributional, stabilization, and growth effects on the economy. Moreover, the revenue-gathering and spending activities of these multitudinous governments may either "complement" or "contradict" each other in the pursuit of any particular societal economic goal. This fact is well demonstrated by both the pattern of "tax sources" used by American governments and by the pattern of "economic effects" which these tax sources exert.

Thus, Table 19–3 is presented in order to focus attention on *intergoal tax nonneutralities* within the American public sector. In this table, each of the major tax sources employed by federal, state, and local governments is evaluated in terms of its ability to serve four major economic objectives—allocational neutrality, distributional equity, ag-

---

[19] Ibid., p. 233.

gregate stabilization performance, and long-run revenue elasticity. The tax sources considered at the *federal* level of government are the personal income tax, corporation income tax, and OASDHI payroll tax. In fiscal 1971, these three taxes yielded 85 percent of all federal tax revenues. The *state-local* tax sources evaluated in the table are the general retail sales, (various) selective sales, personal income, corporation income, and property taxes as well as the *state* unemployment insurance payroll tax. These taxes yielded 82 percent of all state-local government tax revenues in fiscal 1971.

The evaluations in Table 19–3 are based on various principles and empirical studies brought to the attention of the reader (mainly) in Chapters 9–15, which deal with particular types of taxes and their economic effects. Each tax is evaluated in relationship to its actual "rate" and "base" characteristics as it exists in the American public

TABLE 19–3
Estimated Intergoal Effects of Major American Taxes*

	Performance Pertaining to Economic Goal			
Type of Tax	*Allocational Neutrality†*	*Distributional Equity‡*	*Stabilization§*	*"Long-Run" Revenue Elasticity‖*
Federal *Personal Income* Tax.....................	Fair to good	Excellent	Excellent	Excellent
Federal *Corporation Income* Tax	Fair to good	Excellent	Excellent	Excellent
Federal *OASDHI Payroll* Tax.....................	Fair to good	Poor	Fair to good	Fair to good
State-Local *General Retail Sales* Taxes..............	Good	Poor	Poor	Fair to good
State-Local *Selective Sales (excise)* Taxes#	Poor	Poor	Poor	Poor
State-Local *Personal Income* Taxes.............	Fair to good	Fair to good	Fair to good	Fair to good
State-Local *Corporation Income* Taxes...........	Fair to good	Fair to good	Fair to good	Fair to good
State-Local *Property* Taxes**.................	Fair to good	Poor	Poor	Fair to good
State *Unemployment Insurance Payroll* Tax.....................	Fair to good	Poor	Excellent	Fair to good

* The taxes are appraised on the basis of their actual base and rate structures as used in the American public sector, including the relevant consideration of the "level of government" at which each tax is imposed.
† It is assumed that the "pretax" allocational equilibrium approaches optimality. Hence, all nonneutral allocational effects are assumed to be "negative" in character.
‡ Distributional equity is appraised in accordance with the "ability-to-pay" principle with "income" as the indicator of taxpaying ability.
§ This involves an overall appraisal of the effectiveness of each tax as an aggregate economic stabilizer in both "automatic" and "discretionary" fiscal policy terms.
‖ Each tax is evaluated here on the basis of its estimated long-run "income elasticity" (Y_e).
Includes excise taxes on motor fuel.
** Follows the traditional viewpoint that the property tax is shifted forward to renters and consumers.

sector and *not* as it might appear in some pure, conceptual form. In addition, the level of government imposing a tax will, in itself, tend to bear upon the results of a tax. Thus, a national government might be able to achieve significant stabilization policy results from a general sales tax while a subnational government would achieve inferior results. The performance of each tax in relationship to a particular goal is rated as either *excellent, good, fair to good,* or *poor.* Admittedly, these are broad categories and it should not be concluded, for example, that an "excellent" rating precludes any defects in the tax nor that a "poor" rating precludes any merits.

The *allocational* performance of a given tax source is appraised in terms of the degree to which it introduces nonneutral substitution effects into the decision-making processes of producers and consumers. That is, the "greater the nonneutralities introduced," the "poorer the performance" of the tax. The strict assumption of an "optimal pretax equilibrium" is made here out of respect to the traditional public finance interpretation of "nonneutrality." It should be remembered from Chapter 6, however, that a "suboptimal pretax position" would allow tax-induced allocational nonneutralities to be either "positive" or "negative" in nature. It may be observed from Table 19–3 that the public sector as a whole performs in only a "fair to good" fashion in relationship to allocational nonneutrality, strictly defined. This is largely true whether one looks at the federal or at the state-local component of the public sector. The only exceptions to a "fair to good" performance are at the state-local level where general retail sales taxes receive a "good" rating and selective sales (excise) taxes a "poor" rating.

The *distributional* equity goal, in light of the "ability-to-pay" benchmark, is best served at the federal level of government through federal income taxation. However, the federal OASDHI payroll tax offers a "regressive" contrast to the federal income taxes. State and local taxes range from "poor" to "fair to good" in reference to the ability-to-pay principle. The most progressive state-local taxes are the income taxes. These taxes, however, are generally "less progressive" than their federal counterparts.

Economic *stabilization* policy, just as distributional policy, is best served by the federal level of the American public sector. The income-elastic federal personal and corporation income taxes provide the basis for effective "automatic" fiscal stabilization results. Moreover, these same taxes are adaptible to a myriad of "tax rate" and "tax base" changes which can be used as techniques of "discretionary" stabilization policy. Furthermore, the high revenue yield of federal income taxation assures a potentially "very responsive" basis for the application of discretionary fiscal policy. However, the state "unemployment insurance" payroll tax, which is part of a federally-coordinated unemployment compensation program, also performs admirably as a fiscal stabilizer.

The *long-run revenue elasticity* performance of a tax is judged in Table 19–3 on the basis of the "income elasticity" (*Ye*) of a particular tax source. Viewed in this perspective, the federal income taxes, once again, score a high rating with their ability to yield tax revenues over time at a considerably more rapid rate of growth than the growth of per capita national income (Ye > 1).

However, the difference between intertemporal "revenue growth" and "revenue reliability" should be understood. State-local selective sales (excise) taxes, for example, display poor "revenue growth," in *income elasticity* terms, but nonetheless they provide reliable (dependable) sources of tax revenue over a period of time. Thus, it should be noted that even though state-local excise taxes render a poor showing in the table on all counts, other justifications for their existence may exist outside the scope of the present table. Moreover, an "earmarked" state-local motor fuel tax, while violating the allocational neutrality principle in the traditional sense, may yield a "positive" allocational nonneutrality by increasing the consumption of "welfare-increasing" streets and highways if one drops the assumption of pretax allocational optimality.

In conclusion, the "balanced performance" of the federal personal and corporation income taxes in relationship to the four economic goals of Table 19–3 stands out as a primary feature of the table. Also, the table clearly suggests that the goals are influenced, either positively or negatively, to varying degrees by the different taxes imposed by the different levels and units of government. Thus, an aggregate public sector consisting of three levels and some 78,000 units of government will yield, in its "intergovernmental interaction," a composite of "intergoal economic effects" from its varied tax structure. Although the present discussion has focused on *taxation*, it is obvious that similar intergovernmental economic effects will follow from the "*nontax* fiscal decisions" of the federal, state, and local governments which comprise the American public sector.

20

Alternative Techniques for Solving the Intergovernmental Fiscal Problems of the American Federation

TECHNIQUES FOR SOLVING INTERGOVERNMENTAL FISCAL PROBLEMS

Separation of Revenue Sources

One instrument for reducing or eliminating the problem of vertical fiscal imbalance (noncorrespondence), as described in Chapter 19, would be to "reallocate the functions of the various levels of government" so as to diminish the functional expenditure obligations for the lower levels of government by transferring some functional areas to the central government. However, this will not be discussed as a relevant alternative for the American federation because of the deep-seated American cultural preference for substantial state and local government economic activity. Among the remaining "relevant" intergovernmental fiscal techniques, the first to be discussed is the *separation of revenue sources* between the various levels of government. The basic notion here is to increase the revenue sources available to the lower levels of government which bear the brunt of vertical fiscal imbalance between revenues and expenditures. To a limited extent, of course, the Constitution already provides a basis for separation of revenues. Customs duties (tariffs), for example, may be collected only by the federal government. Furthermore, the Constitution in effect prohibits the imposition of a federal property tax since the tax would have to be apportioned in accordance with the population of each state—a task which would involve severe conceptual and administrative obstacles.

In practice, the revenue structure of the U.S. public sector bears considerable resemblance to a separated revenue system. The vast majority of federal revenues are collected from income, payroll, death, and gift taxes. The vast majority of general sales tax receipts and motor vehicle and operator license revenues are collected by state governments. Meanwhile, local government absorbs an extremely high proportion of property tax receipts.

The complete *separation of revenue sources* between the federal, state, and local components of the public sector may appear on the surface to be a utopian arrangement. Closer analysis, however, demonstrates that such is not the case. Admittedly, the complete separation technique would eliminate vertical multiple taxation with its attendant problems. In addition, it would preserve state-local autonomy more than would certain other fiscal techniques which would allow instead a greater role for the central fisc in revenue-source determination. Nevertheless, several important qualifications offer opposition to the technique of completely separated tax revenue sources.

First, there is not an unlimited number of potentially good tax sources to adequately serve the three levels and some 78,000 government units which comprise the American public sector. An overriding constraint of "revenue scarcity" is thus imposed. This constraint cannot be alleviated merely by "separating" tax revenue sources between the three levels of government. In addition, considerable economic differentiation exists within the state and local levels of government. Consequently, a "rational" tax structure for one state or local government might be "irrational" for another. For example, the resource base of one state or locality, which largely generates its income base (from which ultimately all taxpaying ability derives), may differ greatly from the resource combinations of another state or locality. Fiscal irrationality surely would result if two highly differentiated states or communities had identical tax structures.

Another defect in the separations approach concerns its lack of symmetry in considering only the tax side of the aggregate public sector budget. The spending side of the budget, which can influence allocation, distribution, stabilization, and economic growth with force equal to that of the revenue side, is ignored by the separations approach. Thus, it exerts no direct effect on intergovernmental externalities. However, this same criticism may be directed at most of the other relevant intergovernmental fiscal techniques to be discussed below with one notable exception, namely, "earmarked" taxes when they are used to finance specific "conditional" grant programs.[1] Moreover, the separations technique does not provide the complete horizontal intergovernmental uniformity in tax rates, exemptions, and the like that would be necessary to eliminate intergovernmental competition for industrial location—a practice with significant connotation regarding efficient resource usage. Furthermore, the separations approach may frustrate the collective consensus of the society regarding minimal living standards of the population. Such a consensus suggests that a minimum acceptable real income level be attainable for the residents of *all* states and communities. Federal grants-in-aid to states and their subdivisions for such things as highways, public assistance, and unemployment compensation programs exemplify this attitude. Yet, the asymmetrical nature of the separations approach prevents it from working toward the "equalization" of minimal consumption of certain basic economic goods between states and localities. Moreover, it does not promote an "equalization" of tax burdens among taxpayers in the various governmental jurisdictions. In addition, the separations technique would likely distort any distributional objective based upon the desirability of a progressive tax rate system for the public sector as a whole. For example, "complete tax separation" in the United States would likely consist of the exclusive use of income taxes by the federal government, the general sales tax by state governments, and the property tax by local governments. Complete revenue separation along these lines would thus result in a public sector revenue structure containing significant "regressive" elements in the form of general sales and property taxes.[2] Under such conditions, the distribution goal in question would not be attained.

Another qualification concerning use of the revenue separation technique involves the pattern of "intertemporal" performance of revenues and expenditures. Changing tastes, population growth, business cycle conditions, and economic growth rates may be expected to influence both the revenue yields of the "separated taxes" as well as the functional expenditure needs of the various levels and units of government. In fact, it is likely that the income elasticity of state-local government expenditures would be greater than that of tax revenues in a growing economy in which state governments relied mostly on their own sales taxes and local governments on their own property tax revenues. As a result, problems of noncorrespondence would eventually reappear.

Thus, it is concluded from the above discussion that the complete

---

[1] The best example of this in the American federation is the federal excise tax on motor fuel and the subsequent federal grants to states for highway purposes.

[2] This result excludes consideration of the distributional effects of federal grants-in-aid to lower levels of government.

separation of revenue sources between levels of government is not an ideal fiscal technique for solving the intergovernmental fiscal problems of the American federation. For example, it would provide no alleviation of horizontal equalization nor economic competition problems. Though the main thrust of revenue source separation would be toward the reduction of vertical fiscal imbalance or noncorrespondence problems, its performance on this issue is "mixed" in quality. The only positive attribute of the technique—the elimination of vertical multiple taxation—does not seem to be enough to warrant adoption of the technique.

Conditional Revenue Sharing

Revenue (tax) sharing, broadly defined, involves a government unit at a higher level collecting its own tax revenues prior to the disbursement of some part of these revenues to a lower-level government. These disbursements fall mainly into *conditional* (categorical, strings-attached), and *unconditional* (noncategorical no-strings-attached) classifications.

Historically, *conditional* grant-in-aid (revenue sharing) programs have been much more important than unconditional grants in the American public sector.[3] The federal government, for example, is presently involved in many conditional grant-in-aid programs to state and local governments.[4] State governments, in addition, conduct certain conditional grant-in-aid programs for which local units of government are the recipients. In all cases of conditional grants, specific regulations are applied by the "grantor" to the "grantee" government concerning use of the funds.

Federal aid to state and local governments, which amounted to only $1.8 billion in 1949 and to $6.8 billion in 1959, totalled more than $43 billion in 1973. Table 20–1 presents all forms of federal financial assistance to state and local governments, inclusive of both conditional and unconditional grants-in-aid and loans, for fiscal years 1971, 1972, and 1973. However, the table does not reflect the "grant decentralization" effects in the manpower area of the Comprehensive Employment and Training Act of 1973. It may be observed that during fiscal 1973, the two major forms of *conditional revenue sharing* constituted more than $38 billion of the total aid figure of $43.8 billion during that year. Most of the remaining financial aid ($5 billion) was of the *unconditional*

---

[3] "Unconditional" federal revenue sharing with the states, prior to Congressional legislation in 1972, had been used once before in American history—during the late 1830s in the Presidential Administration of Andrew Jackson.

[4] "Trust fund-type" conditional grants, which are financed through "earmarked" taxes, are discussed in detail in Chapter 15. Hence, their discussion in this chapter will be reduced accordingly.

TABLE 20–1

Federal Revenue-Sharing with State and Local Governments, Including Loans, by Form of Aid and Function, Fiscal Years 1971–1973* (millions)

Form of Aid and Function	1971	1972	1973
Total aid to state and local governments...................	$30,021.2	$39,412.6	$43,788.2
Conditional grants-in-aid, general			
Federal funds accounts†............................	24,181.6	30,989.4	32,262.0
Veterans services and benefits	19.0	21.2	24.4
Health...	4,467.0	5,672.0	4,926.3
Education and manpower	4,962.9	5,965.8	6,650.8
Agriculture and rural development....................	659.7	972.0	1,060.9
Natural resources.................................	739.4	1,273.7	1,514.8
Commerce and transportation	675.0	878.3	1,015.3
Community development and housing..................	2,853.8	3,228.9	4,158.4
Income security	9,270.3	12,143.7	11,822.0
General government................................	487.4	787.1	1,031.0
National defense. :................................	41.7	40.9	50.3
International affairs and finance......................	5.4	5.7	7.8
Conditional grants-in-aid, trust			
funds†......................................	5,383.3	5,558.2	5,888.3
Airport and airways trust fund......................	61.5	131.0	200.0
Highway trust fund...............................	4,562.8	4,595.5	4,801.3
Unemployment trust fund..........................	759.0	831.7	887.0
Shared revenues†......................	279.1	282.3	328.6
Natural resources (Federal funds accounts)	181.0	176.7	216.9
General government	98.1	105.6	111.7
Loans and repayable advances (net of			
collections)‡..................................	177.2	332.8	309.3
Natural resources................................	5.0	14.0	15.2
Commerce and transportation	45.9	66.5	67.1
Community development and housing.................	11.5	48.0	37.9
Education and manpower	63.8	32.0	20.4
General government...............................	51.0	172.3	168.7
Unconditional *revenue sharing* funds.....................	—	2,250.0	5,000.0

* Data for 1972 and 1973 are estimated.
† Includes direct Federal loans (either expenditure account or loan account) to state and local governments for purposes similar to those for which conditional grants are made.
‡ Not included in grant-in-aid and shared revenue categories.
Source: Office of Management and Budget.

revenue sharing variety. The "conditional" grants consisted of those from *general* treasury revenue sources ($32.3 billion) and those from *earmarked* trust funds ($5.9 billion). The largest item for which general treasury conditional grants are rendered is "income security," which includes public assistance grants such as aid for dependent children, the needy-aged, and the blind. Other major items in the general treasury category are "education and manpower," "health," and "community development and housing." Meanwhile, conditional grants-in-aid channeled through trust fund financing consisted mainly of the highway and unemployment insurance trust funds.

Conditional revenue sharing by the federal government ordinarily follows formulas for allocation which have been provided by the controlling statutes. Specifically, the formulas are based on such criteria as the income per capita, geographical area, and population of the recipient jurisdiction. In addition, the sharing formulas are usually guided by either the actual amount of revenue collected in each state, or for the purpose of returning relatively greater amounts of revenue to the poorer states. The latter approach, which incorporates the *variable matching grant* concept, recognizes "need" and the desirability of "supplementing deficient revenue-gathering capacity" at the state and local levels of government. Obviously, the "recognition-of-need" approach can yield substantial effects on the distribution of income and wealth in the society. Typically, the conditional grant must be *matched* to some specified percentage from the funds of the lower-level government.

State governments often provide *shared taxes* to local units of government. Some of these are provided on a "strings-attached" basis and others on an "unconditional" basis. State general retail sales, gasoline, and excise taxes are the most commonly shared state taxes, though in a few states income and death taxes are shared with local governments. Such tax sharing reduces "vertical multiple taxation" and contributes to administrative efficiency by avoiding duplicate enforcement machinery. Moreover, the enforcement responsibility is placed at the higher of the two levels of government which normally has an efficiency advantage in such matters.[5]

The "conditional revenue sharing" technique performs well in relationship to the problems of *intergovernmental externalities* and *horizontal fiscal imbalance*. Regarding the former problem, conditional grants are effective in their influence on the allocation of quasi-national public goods (bads) since they provide a "control mechanism" which, though imperfect, allocates part of the financial responsibility for providing a public good (or for removing a public bad) to the various units of government which consume (or supply) the externalities, respectively. That is, the "control mechanism" may increase the supply of desirable quasi-national public goods and reduce the supply of undesirable quasi-national public bads. On another point, favorable equalization results which reduce horizontal fiscal imbalance can be achieved, as observed above, through the use of "variable matching" conditional grants. Under this arrangement, the state or local government matching the federal grant will do so at a ratio or percentage in "direct" relationship to the position of its per capita personal income. Thus, wealthier states would match the conditional grants at a higher ratio

---

[5] In some instances, however, shared state-local death and automotive license taxes are administered by local government.

than would poorer states. This approach is used presently in a number of federal conditional grant programs.

While the strongest arguments for conditional revenue-sharing center upon the "coordination of intergovernmental externalities" and the "equalization" objective, the conditional grant technique also scores favorably on certain other criteria. For example, even though it does not directly alleviate noncorrespondence by increasing the revenue "collected" by lower-level governments from their "own sources," it does enhance indirectly the fiscal abilities of these governments through the specific matching grants which they receive for influencing the allocation of quasi-national public goods and bads. Moreover, in contrast to an alternative technique such as the tax credit which tends to induce lower-level governments to adopt a certain tax or taxes, conditional grants do *not* stimulate an expansion of tax sources. In turn, this tends to reduce the opportunity for horizontal intergovernmental economic competition as well as to reduce the extent of tax overlapping in the public sector.

Unconditional Revenue Sharing and Bloc Grants

Unconditional grants in aid are a fiscal instrument whereby a higher-level government provides some of its tax revenues to a lower level government *"without* stipulating conditions" concerning the usage of the funds. In 1964, a special economic task force suggested to President Johnson that an elaborate extension of the federal revenue-sharing system should be made so as to include the *unconditional revenue-sharing* technique.[6] This proposal was consistent with earlier studies by Walter Heller, who was Chairman of the President's Council of Economic Advisers at the time of the task force report. Subsequently, a number of other unconditional revenue-sharing proposals were offered including a recommendation to Congress in 1969 by President Nixon that such a program be adopted.[7] Most of the proposed programs were basically similar. Finally, *unconditional revenue-sharing,* along with a form of *bloc grants,* became a part of federal law on October 20, 1972, following several years of extensive discussion of the issue. This legislation is known as the *State and Local Fiscal Assistance Act of 1972.*[8] A summary of the primary arguments for and against the

---

[6] The task force was headed by economist, Joseph Pechman.

[7] The Nixon Administration proposal recommended both "unconditional grants," which it termed *general revenue-sharing,* and "bloc grants," which it termed *special revenue-sharing.*

[8] Public Law 92–512, 92nd Congress, H. R. 14,370, October 20, 1972.

adoption of *unconditional* revenue-sharing will now be presented.[9] The following contentions were used in support of the technique:

1. The unconditional sharing of a portion of federal tax revenue is a desirable compromise, since the federal government does not expand relatively within the public sector (thus satisfying political "conservatives"), whereas
2. The public sector still continues to operate at the same absolute level and position relative to the private sector (thus satisfying political "liberals"),
3. Many critical functional expenditure needs can be met more effectively by the lower-level governments,
4. The long-term "fiscal drag" on the economy resulting from the progressive federal income taxes can be lessened,[10]
5. "Horizontal fiscal imbalance" can be alleviated through a reduction of the per capita "tax burden" and "revenue capacity" gaps which unevenly affect the residents of various states and localities,
6. Some of the pressure to meet future social needs can be removed from existing federal conditional grant programs, which have greatly increased in number during recent decades and which have become increasingly complex and difficult to administer.

Opposition to unconditional revenue sharing took the form of arguments such as the following:

1. State and local governments will suffer a decrease in political autonomy as they become more dependent upon the federal government for revenues,
2. State and local governments may be motivated to reduce their own revenue effort as they receive the additional federal revenues,[11]
3. Most of the shared revenues are likely to be retained by the states even though many of the major expenditure needs, such as those in urban areas, exist at the local government level,[12]
4. Many state and local governments are not "forward looking" and, in addition, are full of inefficiency and graft so that nothing in terms

---

[9] Bernard P. Herber, "Unconditional Revenue Sharing as a Solution to Fiscal Imbalance," *Quarterly Review of Economics and Business,* Autumn 1968, pp. 43–54.

[10] *Fiscal drag* will be more thoroughly discussed in Part Four of this book. At this point, it will merely be noted that the federal tax system has a tendency over time to become increasingly "restrictive" in its effect on aggregate economic performance since federal tax revenues tend to increase at a more rapid rate than national income. This phenomenon is primarily a result of the progressive rate structures, and hence the high "income elasticities," of the federal personal and corporation income taxes.

[11] The legislation of 1972 was designed so as to discourage diminished tax effort by the lower-level governments.

[12] The legislation of 1972 was designed so as to require a substantial "flow through" of funds to local governments.

of public sector economic efficiency is likely "to be gained," and something is likely "to be lost," by a relative shift in governmental expenditure decisions to the lower levels of government.

5. A long-term "fiscal drag" problem can best be met by federal tax reductions, such as those enacted in 1964 and 1965, rather than by the unconditional revenue-sharing approach, and

6. State and local governments are less likely than the federal government to impose satisfactory labor practices including wage, overtime, and fair employment standards as enforced under federal conditional grant programs.[13]

Unquestionably, *unconditional revenue-sharing* does possess merit as an intergovernmental fiscal technique. It can be used, for example, to alleviate both vertical and horizontal fiscal imbalance in a federation. Moreover, the unconditional grant approach also performs well in its ability to diminish intergovernmental fiscal competition and tax overlapping. This is accomplished in each instance due to the fact that fewer individual state tax sources tend to exist, along with less intensive use of existing taxes, when the lower-level governments derive unconditional grants from the federal personal income tax. The effects of unconditional revenue-sharing on vertical fiscal imbalance (noncorrespondence) tend to be indirect since the lower-level governments do not derive the additional revenues "from their own sources." Moreover, this constitutes a divorcement between "revenue-raising" and "expenditure" decisions—each being made by a different level and unit of government. Nonetheless, the spending potential of the lower-level governments is enhanced by the revenues received from the federal government.

Yet, the "primary advantage" of the unconditional grant approach rests in its ability to reduce *horizontal fiscal imbalance*. For example, even a straight "per capita grant," without a specific equalization formula being attached for the preferential treatment of poorer states, would redistribute income from the wealthier to the poorer states. This is explained by the progressive nature of the federal personal income tax which causes per capita federal personal income tax collections to be greater in the wealthier states than in the poorer states. Thus, when part of these "unevenly" collected funds are returned to states on an "equal" per capita basis, an automatic redistributional effect occurs.[14] However, use of a "specific equalization formula" to attain a still greater "equalization effect" is very feasible. Furthermore, formula adjustments can be made to reward those states which undertake a greater

---

[13] The legislation of 1972 was designed to minimize this problem.

[14] This phenomenon will be elaborated upon as part of the discussion of a separate intergovernmental fiscal technique—*built-in-equalization*—later in this chapter.

revenue effort from their own revenue sources. Both of these features were included, in principle, in the federal revenue-sharing legislation of 1972.

Next, it should be observed that a "compromise" between conditional and unconditional revenue-sharing is possible. The resulting "hybrid" may be termed a *bloc grant.* Such a grant allows a lower-level (grantee) government "discretion" to spend the revenues shared with it by a higher-level (grantor) government as long as the spending is undertaken within the broad functional expenditure category (such as education) prescribed by the higher-level government. Relatedly, a bloc grant can take the form of "several" functional expenditure categories rather than a "single" functional spending category being designated as an acceptable area for use of the funds by the recipient lower-level government. The *State and Local Fiscal Assistance Act of 1972,* in fact, set up a system of *bloc grants* which follows this pattern of "multiple" designated spending areas.

The landmark revenue sharing legislation of October 1972 established a separate revenue sharing *trust fund* to be financed by federal personal income tax revenues. The legislation, in a sense, is experimental since its coverage is limited initially to a five-year period of time. It applies retroactively to January 1, 1972, and carries through 1976. The total funds appropriated for expenditure during this period are $30.2 billion. As observed earlier, the legislation sets up a program of federal *unconditional* and *bloc* grants for state and local governments—the latter inclusive of county, municipality, township, or other units of "general purpose" local governments. Both state and local governments are prohibited from using any of the shared revenues as "matching funds" for federal conditional grants.

In essence, those federal revenues shared with the states under the new program are *unconditional grants,* since they are not tied to particular functional areas of expenditure, while those shared with local governments are *bloc* grants which contain such designations. The local government grants, for example, must be spent within one of the following areas of functional expenditure activity if they are of a "noncapital" nature:

A.   Ordinary and necessary "maintenance" and "operating" expenses for:

   1.   *Public safety* inclusive of law enforcement, fire protection, and building code enforcement.
   2.   *Environmental protection* inclusive of sewage disposal, sanitation, and pollution abatement.
   3.   *Public transportation* inclusive of transit systems, streets, and roads.
   4.   *Health.*

5. *Recreation.*
6. *Libraries.*
7. *Social services for the poor or aged.*
8. *Financial administration,* or for
B. Ordinary and necessary "capital" expenditures authorized by law.

It is clear that the *bloc grant form* of the 1972 legislation, which applies to all noncapital expenditure of the funds, is "quite broadly defined." That is, the bloc grants are "multiple" over a wide range of functional expenditure options. Nonetheless, they do appear to properly qualify as *bloc grants* and not as either the conditional or unconditional forms of revenue sharing.

A state may choose either the "Senate" or "House" *formula* for determining its share of the overall revenue sharing appropriation. The *Senate formula* weighs population by both the "inverse of per capita income" and by "tax effort," the latter consisting of total state and local government taxes divided by state personal income. The "per capita income" factor tends to favor rural governments while the "tax effort" factor tends to favor *urban* governments. The *House formula* adds to these factors an additional "urbanized population" factor plus an incentive for the usage of "state personal income taxation." The "two thirds" pass through of state revenue sharing funds to local governments are apportioned among the local governments on the basis of population, per capita income, and tax effort, but in a manner favoring the *lower-income urban areas* of a state.[15]

Tax Credits and Deductions[16]

The *tax credit* technique of intergovernmental fiscal coordination in a federation allows a taxpayer to meet his tax liabilities to one unit of

---

[15] A persistent effort was undertaken by the Nixon Administration, especially during its second term of office, to increasingly decentralize expenditure decisions in the direction of state and local governments. This effort was characterized by its support of bloc grant legislation (which it initially termed "special revenue sharing") and, more recently, by the impoundment of funds already appropriated by Congress for various programs. The overall *objective* has been, in effect, to reduce the number of conditional grant programs by merger into bloc grant programs and, in general, toward an expansion of unconditional grants. The *economic rationality* of this approach will be analyzed at an appropriate point later in this chapter.

[16] *Tax credits* and *tax deductions,* as discussed in this chapter, relate primarily to "intergovernmental fiscal coordination." Hence, they differ from individual or business tax credits and deductions for "private sector activities." For example, the deduction of medical expenses or the application of a retirement credit to an individual's federal personal income tax computation reduces the amount of tax which he is required to pay to the government. Moreover, the deduction by a corporate business of advertising expenses or the application of an investment credit in conjunction with its federal corporation income tax obligations would result in a reduction of its tax liability. Yet, these credits do not focus, as such, on intergovernmental fiscal coordination.

government by means of the taxes which he pays to another unit. "Intergovernmental tax credits" may be applied "vertically" between two governments at different levels or "horizontally" between two governments at the same level.

Vertical application usually represents an effort by a higher-level government to encourage a lower-level government to use a "particular tax source or sources." For example, the federal government might allow a credit against federal personal income tax liability for a particular tax or taxes paid to a state and/or local government, or a state government might do likewise on its personal income tax for a certain tax or taxes paid to a local government. Hence, the tax liability, or part thereof, to one unit of government may be met through taxes paid to another unit of government. Thus, if the federal government allowed a credit of 25 percent against federal personal income tax liability for personal income taxes paid to state and local governments, a $1,000 federal tax liability could be reduced to $750 as long as at least $250 of personal income taxes have been paid by the taxpayer to a lower-level government or governments.

This would encourage the state government to utilize personal income taxation, at least up to the limit of the credit. By contrast, *horizontal* tax credits usually represent an effort to improve "distributional equity" among taxpayers rather than the inducement of a greater tax effort by lower-level governments. For example, horizontal multiple taxation in the form of the dual imposition of state or national government income taxes on a person or business may require use of the horizontal tax credit technique in order to avoid the "double taxation" of the income. For example, income tax liabilities paid to one nation would, at least in part, be subtracted from those owed to another nation. The discussion which follows, however, will mainly deal with tax credits in a "vertical" intergovernmental context.

Vertical tax credits may come in a variety of forms.[17] These include:

1. An *unlimited credit subject to a proportional ceiling.* This would be characterized by the 25 percent personal income tax credit example described above whereby a person could fully credit all of the tax paid to a lower-level government(s) up to some percentage limit or ceiling of the tax liability owed to a higher-level government. For example, all personal income taxes paid to state and local governments could be credited up to 25 percent of the taxpayer's federal personal income tax liability.
2. An *unlimited credit subject to a declining ceiling.* For example, personal income taxes paid to state and local governments would

---

[17] For a discussion of "tax credits" as well as "other intergovernmental fiscal instruments," see George F. Break, *Intergovernmental Fiscal Relations in the United States* (Washington, D.C.: Brookings Institution, 1967), Chapter Two.

be fully credited against federal personal income tax liability up to (say) 40 percent of the first $500 of such liability, 20 percent of the next $1,000, and 5 percent of the remainder. This approach, which reduces the value of the credit as taxpaying ability (as measured by income tax liability) increases, introduces an effective "progressivity" into the credit in accordance with the "ability-to-pay" principle of distributional equity.

3. A *limited proportional credit.* Under this form of vertical tax credit, a "specified percentage" of the tax paid to the lower-level government(s), not the "full" amount, may be credited against the tax owed to a higher-level government. For example, a taxpayer may be allowed to subtract 25 percent of whatever personal income taxes which he pays to state and local governments from his federal personal income tax liability.

4. A *limited declining credit.* Under this form of vertical intergovernmental credit, decreasing "specified percentages" of taxes paid to a lower-level government(s) may be subtracted from the tax owed to a higher-level government. For example, 40 percent of state-local personal income taxes might be subtracted from the first $500 of federal personal income tax liability, 20 percent from the next $1000, and 5 percent from all remaining liability. This approach, similar to that of the "unlimited credit subject to a declining ceiling," introduces progressivity into the credit in accordance with the "ability-to-pay" concept.

In the discussion below, the focus will be on the first of these vertical tax credit forms—the "unlimited credit subject to a proportional ceiling"—though the analysis will be largely applicable to the other forms. Also, it will be useful at this point to distinguish between single, bloc, and global tax credits. A *single* tax credit exists when the credit is allowed for only "one" type of tax paid to another unit of government. On the other hand, a *bloc* tax credit exists when the credit is allowed for "several," but not all, types of taxes paid to another government unit. A *global* tax credit, in turn, represents a credit for "all" taxes paid, regardless of type, to another unit of government. In many ways, the "control" over *revenue instruments* exerted by the higher-level government utilizing a "single tax credit" is analogous to the control over *expenditure patterns* exerted by a higher-level government utilizing a "conditional grant." Similarly, a "bloc credit" and "bloc grant" are analogous as are a "global credit" and an "unconditional grant." The unconditional credit and grant, of course, allow the lower-level government to select whatever revenue sources and expenditure patterns that it desires.

In the United States, the federal government used the "horizontal" *tax credit* device as early as 1918 to minimize the multiple international taxation of incomes. In 1926, a "vertical" federal extate tax credit was introduced for the purpose of discouraging interstate competition in attracting wealthy residents based on competitive state death tax structures. The federal government extended its usage of the vertical tax credit device by legislation in 1935 which established a 90 percent unemployment insurance payroll tax credit. In this instance, the states were placed under virtual economic compulsion to adopt state payroll taxes which would be part of the planned federal-state unemployment compensation program. Any state government not imposing such a tax would lose substantial revenues which otherwise could be obtained to support an unemployment insurance program. All states subsequently adopted the tax. It has been suggested recently that an approach similar to that of the vertical federal estate and unemployment tax credits be adopted for the personal income tax in order to encourage all states to use this "income-elastic" and "distributionally progressive" revenue source to a greater extent than at the present time.

A *tax deduction* differs from a tax credit in that it represents a subtraction from the tax base "prior" to the application of the tax rate to that base while the *tax credit* represents a subtraction from the tax itself "following" the application of the tax rate to the tax base. The value of a tax deduction (say against federal personal income tax liability) will vary significantly depending upon the "marginal tax rate bracket" of the taxpayer. For example, assume that Taxpayers *A* and *B* each pay $1,000 in state-local property taxes, but that Taxpayer *A* is in a 50 percent federal personal income tax marginal rate bracket while Taxpayer *B* is in a 25 percent bracket. In this instance, the deduction is worth more in tax saving ($500) to Taxpayer *A* than it is to Taxpayer *B* ($250).

These results would be calculated as follows:

Federal Personal income tax base reduction due to the deductibility of $1,000 in state-local property taxes	= $1,000

Federal personal income tax that would have been owed on this amount of federal personal income tax base without the deduction of the state-local property taxes—hence, the *amount of tax saving* resulting from their deduction	*Taxpayer A:* = $500 with a 50% marginal tax rate (1,000 × .50 = 500) *Taxpayer B:* = $250 with a 25% marginal tax rate (1,000 × .25 = 250)

The *tax deduction* approach to intergovernmental fiscal coordination is used between all levels of the American public sector. The most significant use, however, involves the various deductions from the federal personal income tax for such taxes as personal income, general sales, personal property, real property, and gasoline taxes paid to other governmental jurisdictions. These deductions are subtracted from adjusted gross income. Many state personal income tax structures, moreover, allow a deduction for the federal personal income tax.

The primary contribution to intergovernmental fiscal rationality by the tax credit and tax deduction techniques rests in the alleviation of the vertical fiscal imbalance problem of "noncorrespondence." Moreover, the *tax credit* device contributes more effectively to the solution of this problem than does the *tax deduction* technique. This is demonstrated by the fact that the "total public sector tax liability" of a taxpayer tends, under similar circumstances, to be *less*, and hence the "tax saving" to be *greater*, when the tax credit device is used as compared to use of the tax deduction method. (See Table 20–2). This occurs because the credit is an "off the top" substitution of one tax liability for another. On the other hand, the tax deduction technique reduces the taxable income base prior to tax computation, but does not reduce tax liability on a "dollar-for-dollar" basis. Thus, a tax credit provides the greater *stimulant* for another unit of government to adopt a new tax, or intensify the application of an already existing tax, than does the tax deduction. The practical political reason for this is the fact that a tax credit would be more popular politically than a tax deduction since it tends to result in a "lower total public sector tax burden" and thus, "greater tax saving" for the individual taxpayer.

In effect, a vertical tax credit merely redistributes tax funds within the public sector between levels of government. As an example, a credit for personal income taxes paid offered by a central to a state or provincial government in a federation, if refused by the lower-level government, would amount to a needless sacrifice of funds that the state or provincial government could otherwise possess without increasing the tax burden of its taxpayers. Moreover, the tax credit approach allows a "symmetrical" quid pro quo relationship in the sense that the government which spends the money also has the responsibility for raising the tax revenues. Indeed, the tax credit technique can serve as a significant force in alleviating noncorrespondence in a federation. However, this approach does carry the possibly unpopular facet that the central government is able to influence the "structure" of the tax system of the lower-level government through its influence on the nature of the credit itself.

The tax credit and tax deduction approaches offer modest overall improvement for the problem of "intergovernmental fiscal competition." Here two offsetting forces are at work, namely, the tendency

TABLE 20–2

Hypothetical Example of the Tax Saving Effects for a Given Taxpayer of the Tax Credit and Tax Deduction Fiscal Techniques

	Tax Credit		*Tax Deduction*	
	Federal personal income tax for taxpayer	State personal income tax for taxpayer	Federal personal income tax for taxpayer	State personal income tax for taxpayer
	= $1,000	= $250	= $1,000	= $250
Value of credit / deduction for state personal income taxes paid	= 25% of federal personal income tax liability (unlimited credit) subject to a proportional ceiling) $1,000 × .25 ―――― $250		= Reduction of taxable income base by the amount of the deduction ($250) times (X) the marginal tax rate (25%) (assume a 25% marginal tax rate bracket on the federal tax)	$250 × .25 ―――― $62.50

Federal personal income tax liability following application of credit / deduction	= $1,000
	  −250
	――――
	$ 750
			= $1,000
			  −62.50
			――――
			$937.50	

Tax Credit

Total public sector tax liability without credit
$1,000 (Federal) + $250 (State) = $1,250
Total public sector tax liability with credit
$750 (Federal) + $250 (State) = $1,000

Tax saving = $1,250
             −1,000
             ――――
             $250 (Tax saving)

Tax Deduction

Total public sector tax liability without deduction
$1,000 (Federal) + $250 (State) = $1,250
Total public sector tax liability with deduction
$937.50 (Federal) + $250 (State) = $1,187.50

Tax saving = $1,250.00
             −1,187.50
             ――――――
             $62.50 (Tax saving)

toward greater tax uniformity which would reduce the ability of governments to compete, and the tendency for lower-level governments to adopt additional taxes which, in turn, provides them with a larger tax base for potential fiscal competition with other governments. Also, the tax credit and deduction instruments fail to improve the major intergovernmental fiscal issue of "horizontal fiscal imbalance." The relative fiscal capacities of the respective state and local governments remain unchanged by the two devices. No equalization goal is served since the state and local governments are merely encouraged by the techniques to "more fully utilize" their present fiscal capacities. The relative resource endowments which set the limits to these capacities are not affected, nor is there a transfer of funds among the governments to reduce the negative effects of unequal fiscal capacities and of unequal revenue effort burdens. Furthermore, since tax credits and deductions are asymmetrical in the sense that they deal directly with the revenue side of the budget, they are unable "by themselves" to directly mitigate the problem of "intergovernmental externalities" in the consumption of public-type goods. However, when coordinated with an expenditure program such as under the unemployment compensation trust fund, they indeed can assist in allocating an important economic good (income security) characterized by intergovernmental externalities.

During 1966 the *Advisory Commission on Intergovernmental Relations,* a special intergovernmental fiscal research commission created by Congress in 1959, recommended extensive federal government use of the tax credit device to encourage state government usage of the personal income tax. Ten states, for example, do not use a comprehensive (broadbased) personal income tax. Moreover, most states which do impose the tax apply it with a "modest" rate structure. The Commission suggested the adoption of a federal personal income tax credit (such as 40 percent) for personal income taxes paid to state governments. This amount would then be subtracted from the total federal personal income tax liability of the taxpayer. As observed above, a state would thus be able to collect additional personal income tax revenues up to the limit of the tax credit without increasing the tax liabilities of its taxpayers. In effect, an "implicit" tax credit is present in the *State and Local Fiscal Assistance Act of 1972* which, in one of its alternative formulas for the allocation of revenue sharing funds among the states, includes a factor preferential to those states who more fully utilize personal income taxation.

Tax Supplements

The *tax supplement* technique for improving intergovernmental fiscal relations in a federation involves the application of separate tax rates to an identical (or essentially identical) tax base by different levels of government. A higher-level government normally imposes the basic tax under this arrangement. That is, a state government adopts the base of a federal tax or a local government adopts the base of a state tax. There are two primary variations of this approach: (1) a *pure tax supplement* which occurs when a lower-level government adopts the tax base of a higher-level government, applies its own tax rates to this base, and then collects the tax itself, and (2) the *tax piggybacking* variation which occurs when a lower-level government adopts the tax base of a higher-level government, applies its own tax rates to this base, but allows the higher-level government to collect the tax for it instead of collecting the tax for itself. Moreover, a form of revenue-sharing known as "source revenue-sharing"—which can be either conditional or unconditional in nature—may be discussed for convenience at this point due to the certain similarities to "tax supplements" which it possesses. *Source revenue-sharing* involves the return of some part of the revenues collected by a higher-level government from its own tax(es) to a lower-level government which was the "geographical source" of the funds. However, this form of "revenue-sharing" differs somewhat from the basic "tax supplement" concept in that the two tax bases are "formally merged" into one base, instead of remaining two "formally separate," though similar, tax bases.

The tax supplement approach is used between both the federal and state and the state and local levels of government in the United States. Moreover, both variations of tax supplements described above as well as source revenue-sharing are employed in the American public sector. Primary examples of tax supplements between the federal and state governments include payroll and income taxes. Regarding the former, both federal and state unemployment taxes are levied on the same tax base. Regarding the latter, four states—Alaska, Nebraska, Rhode Island, and Vermont—use a state personal income tax which applies a *fixed* percentage rate to the taxpayer's federal personal income tax liability. In other words, the state personal income tax uses the federal personal income tax base and collects for the state an amount equal to a percentage of the taxpayer's federal tax payment. Moreover, the State-Local Fiscal Assistance Act of 1972 makes it possible for state personal income tax collection to be "piggybacked" on top of the collections of the federal personal income tax by the Internal Revenue Service.

The general sales tax provides an example of the tax supplement device being used between a number of state and local governments in the United States. The receipts of state and local general sales taxes are frequently collected on the same tax base by the state government. Under this "piggyback" form of tax supplement, the revenues derived from the local tax are then returned by the state government to the local government. Local governments, however, usually collect most of their own property tax revenues even though both state and local governments typically use the same property tax base. The main exception to local government collection of property taxes exists in the case of public utility or transportation industry properties which cross county boundaries and are thus administered centrally by a state government.

The "tax piggybacking" and "source revenue-sharing" techniques possess the advantage of providing reduced tax enforcement costs due to the economies of scale inherent in centralized tax collection. Moreover, to the extent that different state or local governments are encouraged to use the same tax base, tax supplements reduce horizontal fiscal competition via the tax structure with its attendant allocational distortions. This does not suggest, however, that interstate or interlocality tax differences would still not remain through the application of "different tax rates" to the uniform tax bases. An additional advantage of tax supplements is their tendency to improve "enforcement equity" to the degree that uniform tax bases reduce the horizontal multiple taxation of taxpayers whose fiscal responsibilities reside in more than one political jurisdiction.

On the negative side, it should be recognized that the tax supplement approach does not represent a strong force for achieving the goal of equalization by reducing horizontal fiscal imbalance. That is, the "relative" fiscal capacities of various states and of various localities are left unchanged by the device. On the other hand, the use of tax supplements may improve the problem of vertical fiscal imbalance (noncorrespondence) through the adoption by the lower-level governments of tax bases with greater revenue potential. However, it is significant to note that tax supplements themselves do not provide a direct "incentive" for encouraging the lower level of government to adopt the new tax base. In this regard, they differ greatly from the *vertical tax credit* fiscal technique. At times, however, a "combination" of the *tax supplement* and *vertical tax credit* devices may yield highly favorable results. The federal-state unemployment compensation tax arrangement, which was developed during the 1930s, is representative of such a "combination" approach.

User Prices and Earmarked Taxes

As observed in Chapters 6 and 15, two basic categories exist for financing the economic goods allocated by government, namely, *general* taxes levied without close attention to the manner in which the taxpayer benefits from public services or to the costs of rendering the services. and *specific* taxes, fees, or prices which attempt to reflect such benefits and costs. Vickrey examines the possibility that the increased usage of "specific charges" may improve intergovernmental economic efficiency in urban areas.[18] Several principles or criteria are suggested to help determine whether a municipal service should be financed by a specific charge. These are:[19] (1) the relative distributional impact of the charge versus that of the general tax which it would displace, (2) the extent to which the proposed charge can be related to the benefits derived from the service, and (3) the consideration of allocative efficiency such as the possibility of extending the concept of marginal cost pricing into the realm of municipal services. The criteria are thus applied to specific governmental services, some of which are more conducive to the pricing technique than others.

A summary of these specific applications follows:[20]

1. *Fire Protection.* From the benefit point of view, the proper way to charge would be on the basis of assessed valuation of property. From the cost point of view, however, the best way to charge would be on the basis of area as characterized by such factors as extent of land occupancy and zoning features.

2. *Transportation Facilities.* All costs of streets would be assigned to vehicular traffic and tolls would vary with the time of day.

3. *Water Supply.* A charge could be made on the basis of use with rates varying according to the cost of the water.

4. *Police and Custodial Services.* It is difficult to find a suitable benefit criterion for this type of service which is not extremely regressive in its distributional effects.

5. *Recreational Facilities.* It is difficult to isolate a marginal cost of recreational services which is rational in nature.

6. *Education.* A sensible approach here would be to turn a portion of federal income tax receipts over to the state in which the taxpayer receives his education. This would compensate for exports of educational capital.

7. *Health and Hospital Services.* This problem is so diverse that about all that can be done is to list the area as one in which there is a possibility of some financing by fees.

8. *Public Utility Services.* Rates can be charged on a marginal cost basis with a supplemental charge in the form of a "front-footage tax" to cover the basic cost of the distribution system.

Built-In Equalization—Interstate Redistribution through the Federal Budget

Figure 20–1 demonstrates the "automatic" ability of the federal fisc (budget) to redistribute income among the states. This chart relates the

---

[18] William S. Vickrey, "General and Specific Financing of Urban Services," in *Public Expenditure Decisions in the Urban Community,* ed. by Howard G. Schaller (Washington, D.C.: Resources for the Future, 1963), pp. 62–90.

[19] Ibid., pp. 62–64.

[20] Ibid., pp. 64–86.

FIGURE 20–1

Net Federal Budget Impact by States (federal payments per dollar of revenue, fiscal 1965–67)

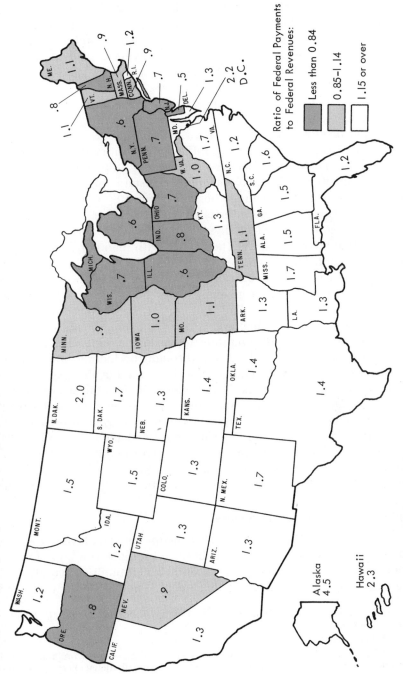

Ratio of Federal Payments to Federal Revenues:

- Less than 0.84
- 0.85–1.14
- 1.15 or over

Source: Library of Congress; The Conference Board.

federal revenues originating in a state to the federal expenditures allocated from the federal budget to that state. The "quotient" which results may be termed the *net impact* of the federal budget on a state.[21] If the ratio (r) of expenditures received to revenues paid exceeds unity ($r > 1$), a net "inflow" of federal funds to a state is indicated. To the contrary, if the ratio is less than unity ($r < 1$), a net "outflow" of funds from the state has taken place through the influence of the federal fisc. During the fiscal period 1965–67, deviation from unity by less than 15 percent" occurred in only 10 states. This demonstrates the fact that most state fiscs received a substantial redistributional effect from the federal fisc. The leading "gainers" consisted mostly of states with fairly small populations while several industrial states (with a few notable exceptions) were the primary "losers" of funds.[22]

A primary cause of this interstate redistribution is the fact that most federal revenues are collected via the *progressive* federal personal and corporation income taxes.[23] Thus, states with high per capita incomes normally contribute revenues to the federal budget above the per capita national average contribution and vice versa. In fact, 13 of the 16 states with per capita incomes under 85 percent of the national average per capita income had "net impact ratios" considerably above unity while 2 of the remaining 3 had "net impact ratios" modestly above unity.[24] The remaining state approximated unity. It is safe to say that such interstate redistribution through the federal budget is due partly to "design," with equalization in mind, but due partly also to "accidental" circumstances. Nonetheless, the federal budget does *in fact* yield an important automatic equalization effect which bears ultimately on the relative fiscal capacities of the state government fiscs. On the other hand, this intergovernmental fiscal technique offers little direct assistance to other primary intergovernmental fiscal problems such as noncorrespondence, economic competition between units of government, intergovernmental externalities, and multiple taxation.

Intergovernmental Tax Immunities

Application of the *tax immunity* concept between levels of governments in a federation may contribute to intergovernmental fiscal rationality.[25] However, intergovernmental tax immunities may also yield negative nonneutral effects. The concept is not spelled out clearly in

---

[21] See the National Industrial Conference Board, *The Federal Budget—Its Impact on the Economy* (New York, 1969), pp. 38–43.

[22] Ibid., p. 43.

[23] This is not to suggest, of course, that conditional grant-in-aid programs and the overall pattern of federal expenditures did not exert redistributional effects of their own.

[24] NICB, *Federal Budget*, p. 43.

[25] See the description of *tax instrumentalities* in Chapter 17 on page 382.

the Constitution. Instead, it has developed over the years through the judiciary process. At times intergovernmental tax immunities have constituted a significant point of controversy between the federal and state levels of governments. The practice of both federal and state governments' exempting certain of each other's "instrumentalities" from taxation was initiated by the famous *McCulloch* v. *Maryland* court case in 1819. The practice expanded throughout the remainder of the nineteenth century, but some narrowing of immunities has occurred during the twentieth century. The principal *immunities* at the present time are: (1) the exemption from federal income taxation of interest earned on state-local government debt obligations, and (2) the exemption of properties of the federal government from certain state and local government property taxes.[26]

Regarding fiscal rationality, immunities granted by the federal government relating to interest income earned on state and local government securities distort "allocational" efficiency by diverting investment funds away from the corporate security market. Moreover, the exemption of such income from federal income taxation opens up a major federal tax preference loophole which is utilized largely by high income taxpayers. This creates a significant "distributional" nonneutrality in violation of the ability-to-pay principle. Furthermore, the growing use of "industrial development bonds" suggests rather serious questions regarding fiscal rationality. Such bonds are typically issued by local governmental units to finance projects aimed at the encouragement of business firms to locate within their political jurisdictions. Such arrangements, of course, are subsidies to the business firms involved. In some cases, a local government issues bonds to finance plant construction, the bonds being sold to the same firm which subsequently purchases or leases the plant. Meanwhile the firm receives tax-exempt interest income. Conventional financing and plant location economics are indeed threatened with distortion by these practices. Yet, on the "positive" side, it should be acknowledged that *intergovernmental tax immunities* do tend to eliminate many needless redundancies of a "fiscal overlapping" nature in a federation.

Intergovernmental Fiscal Cooperation

Congressional and executive endorsement by the federal government of "administrative cooperation" between federal and state tax

---

[26] Some minor exceptions exist regarding the exemption of federal properties from state-local property taxes, namely, (a) a certain small amount of federal property is subject to taxation in the manner of private property, (b) in some cases, payments are made in lieu of property tax payments to state and local governments, and (c) the federal government, on occasion, shares the revenue derived from its property with state and local governments.

administrations has existed for more than a generation. Such cooperation has been rather limited in practice, however, and has consisted
mostly of the exchange of income tax information. In some cases, it has
amounted to a one-way flow of federal information to the states, though
the trend is toward improvement and the Internal Revenue Service
now has formal agreements with most states for the exchange of tax
information.

Among the important considerations in developing a higher degree
of administrative cooperation between levels of government on fiscal
matters is the fact that the basic tax collection technique used within
the American public sector is that of *voluntary taxpayer compliance.*
Administrative efficiency through intergovernmental cooperation is
thus desirable for the encouragement of accuracy in compliance and
for subsequent enforcement equity. Moreover, it is important to recognize that significant *economies of scale* exist in tax administration and
enforcement. Thus, the "piggyback form" of tax supplement stands out
as a desirable fiscal tool—though one underutilized at the present time
in the public sector of the United States. However, the "little publicized," but "potentially very important," provision in the *State and
Local Fiscal Assistance Act of 1972* allowing for federal government
collection of state personal income taxes may possibly accelerate a
movement toward greater tax collection coordination among American
governments.

However, certain other areas of desirable intergovernmental fiscal
cooperation and coordination by American governments demonstrate
a less optimistic outlook. For example, conflicting state requirements
on state income, sales, and use taxes pose a severe problem of distributional equity among taxpayers as well as allocational distortions. A
voluntary state government effort to manage these problems was
proposed by some states in 1965 as an alternative to federal "interstate
tax legislation."[27] This took the form of a "multistate tax compact" and
the related establishment of a *Multistate Tax Commission* in 1967. Yet,
only 21 states have adopted the compact and the plan has largely been
a failure. Indeed, it would seem that only federal coordinative legislation can adequately handle the problem.

Furthermore, it has been frequently recommended that the *state
level of government* play a more decisive role in alleviating urban fiscal
problems. In this regard, Bahl comments that state government alone
seems in a position to provide fiscal coordination and balance among
local governments within SMSA's because:[28]

---

[27] For an evaluation of the interstate tax issue and its solution, see C. R. Cahoon and
William R. Brown, "The Interstate Tax Dilemma—A Proposed Solution," *National Tax
Journal*, June 1973, pp. 187–197.

[28] Roy W. Bahl, "Public Policy and the Urban Fiscal Problem: Piecemeal vs. Aggregate
Solutions," *Land Economics*, February 1970, p. 50.

1. It has a broader tax base than any local government.
2. A state government can institute an aid policy capable of reducing resource-requirements gaps while simultaneously equalizing tax burdens.
3. The state can control the proliferation of local governments within an SMSA and thereby reduce horizontal intergovernmental financial imbalance among local governments.
4. The state can (and already does in many states) administer a planning agency which controls intergovernmental variations in public service levels.
5. Federal aids can be "passed through" the state level to local governments to assure conformity with a comprehensive plan to maintain financial balance among the various units of local government.

Finally, it should be observed that any program directed toward the solution of *urban transportation problems* should encompass "area-wide planning" rather than decentralized decision-making among a multitude of political jurisdictions. Urban transportation problems, moreover, can be solved in the long run only if economic rationality is applied to the issues. Social and private costs must be considered for each alternative mode of urban transportation and the existence of externalities between modes is also a highly relevant consideration. Furthermore, if a given mode of transportation cannot meet all costs (both social and private) on a pricing basis, the degree of governmental subsidization should be approximately equal among the various transportation modes. Otherwise, investment and consumption distortions will result. The degree of automotive subsidization thus should be reduced and that for public transportation facilities increased. Since the entire society, not the urban area alone, receives significant benefits from efficient transportation, the federal government can legitimately bear part of the responsibility for improved urban transportation.

A number of other federal nations have attained a much greater degree of fiscal coordination than has been accomplished in the United States. These include Canada and West Germany.[29] Undoubtedly, a decentralized federation will inherently experience many intergovernmental fiscal conflicts. It is in the interest of such a society to structure a satisfactory level of intergovernmental fiscal cooperation and coordination.

CENTRALIZED VERSUS DECENTRALIZED PUBLIC SECTOR ECONOMIC ACTIVITY IN A FEDERATION

An age-old controversy has existed in the United States, and to a considerable degree in the Western world as a whole, regarding the

---

[29] For a recently-published description and analysis of the intergovernmental fiscal structure of West Germany, see J. S. H. Hunter, *Revenue Sharing in the Federal Republic of Germany* (Canberra: The Australian National University, 1973).

proper relative size and role of central (national) government within the public sector. As observed in Part One of this book, one dimension of a society's *allocation decision* is to determine "which level and unit of government" within the public sector shall allocate public-type economic goods. Historically, American culture has exhibited an attitude giving priority to state and local government in providing such goods. In fact, national defense aside, state and local government expenditures always have exceeded the nonwar (civil) expenditures of the federal government in the United States. There is not one year which serves as an exception to this fact from 1789 to the present time. Yet, despite this cultural preference for decentralization within the American public sector, there remain situations whereby public-type goods may be provided with greater allocative efficiency by the central government. Arguments will be presented below both in favor of a larger relative role by the federal government within the public sector, as well as in behalf of a larger relative role for state and local governments. In part, these arguments will relate to the important matter of determining "which level(s) of government" should apply the particular *intergovernmental fiscal instruments* to the particular *intergovernmental fiscal problems* of the society. Overall, the discussion which follows will demonstrate that sound economic reasons may be found to justify the existence of a *federation*, that is, to justify the coexistence of both *national* and *subnational* governments to perform the economic functions required by the people of the society.

Arguments for Centralized Government

The fact that certain economic goods possess joint consumption benefits or externalities, which are either national or intergovernmental in scope, suggests that the efficient allocation of *national* and *quasi-national* public goods may require substantial central government influence. The benefits of national public goods are consumed collectively on a national basis while those of quasi-national public goods tend to be only partly indivisible to particular state or local governments. National defense, for example, involves a common interest among all individuals in the nation. Because of the nature of national defense, it is not surprising that the central government possesses an efficiency advantage in providing this "national" public good. Part of the joint benefits of a "quasi-national" public good, on the other hand, are diffused among a number of governmental jurisdictions in a federation. When such quasi-national goods are socially important, the public interest becomes involved to the extent that the goods should be allocated in "acceptable" quantities. Thus, a case for *central* government allocational influence may be argued so that the supply of these economic goods may be "coordinated" among the various political jurisdictions which are involved. However, if the primary level of supply of a quasi-national public good is at the local rather than the state level of government, it may be feasible for a state rather than the federal government to provide the appropriate intergovernmental coordination.

Another argument for central government economic activity focuses upon the fact that only a geographically comprehensive central government can work effectively toward the "leveling out" of significant "interstate differences" in fiscal capacities, per capita tax burdens, and real income. Such leveling out, of course, may be desirable from the standpoint of both distributional and allocational objectives. The society, for example, may form a collective consensus for "greater" interstate equality in fiscal capacities and tax burdens and "complete" equality in educational opportunities on a nationwide basis. It would seem that central government would be in the best position to coordinate policy toward the attainment of these goals. Also, central government is in a unique position to implement aggregate economic policy directed toward stabilization and economic growth goals. Fiscal policy aimed at alleviating national unemployment, for example, would be unlikely to come from state and local government initiative since many of its benefits would accrue outside the political boundaries of the initiating jurisdiction.

Another advantage of central government fiscal activity, one referred to earlier in this chapter, is that it possesses a greater ability to collect tax revenues in an efficient manner than does state-local government. In addition, the federal government can impose taxes without considering "tax-cutting competition" such as presently exists between many states and localities in efforts to attract industry. As previously observed, states and communities at times reduce or eliminate property taxes, or otherwise use the budget to subsidize business, in an effort to attract industry to their political jurisdictions. A subsidization type of competition is frequently built up between such jurisdictions which can result in negative market distortions. The comprehensive nature of federal budgeting avoids this intergovernmental competition for industry by which taxes may be escaped or reduced, or expenditure subsidies received, as a reward for the spatial mobility of productive resources from one state or locality to another.

The comparative advantage which higher levels of government possess in gathering tax revenues stems from several factors: First, a level of government with broad political jurisdiction is in a preferred position to discover items relevant to the tax base and to enforce the tax rates which are imposed upon that base. Broad jurisdictional authority, moreover, discourages migration of the tax base to lower-tax locations. If a municipality, for example, levies a comprehensive personal income tax on all types of income and does not receive any enforcement assistance from the state or federal government, it would be at a comparative efficiency disadvantage with the higher levels of government. Some income would be earned outside of the political limits of the city and would be difficult to discover. Moreover, in the long run, economic activity could migrate to other municipalities with lower income tax burdens. Obviously, the discovery of a personal income tax base is easier, and the opportunities to transfer economic activities to lower-tax jurisdictions are fewer, the broader the scope of the political jurisdiction levying the tax.

It is claimed, moreover, that centralized fiscal activity holds an advantage over decentralized fiscal activity in the sense that it is easier to enact rational fiscal legislation at the national level in a society where communications are so efficient that issues can be presented to a complete cross section of the public. On the other hand, decentralized decisions are more susceptible to influence by a biased segment of the community. Some property owners, for example, may be opposed to higher property tax rates to help finance education because they have no children despite a severe need for better educational facilities in the community. In other words, it is argued that a larger sample providing a statistically more reliable cross section of opinion for decision making is provided by central government as opposed to state-local government budgetary action. It is thus concluded from the argument that federal fiscal legislation operates in closer proximity to societal preferences.

In summary, it may be said that the strongest case for centralized governmental economic, including fiscal, activity in a federation rests in the following reasons:[30]

1. Allocating national public goods.
2. Coordinating the *allocation* of certain quasi-national public goods.
3. Seeking national *redistributional* objectives.
4. Directing *stabilization* and *economic growth* policies.

There will be a tendency for economic goods characterized by significant national joint consumption or externalities to be undersupplied in the absence of central government *allocational* influence. Moreover, it would be difficult for state and local governments to carry out income-wealth *redistribution* programs since residential and business mobility would allow an "escape" for those whose economic situations suffer under such programs. Obviously, escape from a national political juris-

---

[30] For a discussion of the performance of the various economic functions by the different levels of government in a federation, see Wallace E. Oates, "The Theory of Public Finance in a Federal System," *Canadian Journal of Economics,* February 1968, pp. 37–54.

diction for this purpose is much less likely. Furthermore, any coordinated effort to achieve an interstate equalization goal must necessarily be directed by a higher level of government. That is, the alleviation of horizontal intergovernmental fiscal imbalance cannot be expected to result from the "voluntary" transfers of funds from wealthier to poorer states.[31] Instead, a societal decision to institute such transfers must be "made at" and "directed from" the central level of government. Finally, the "national nature" of such *aggregate economic goals* as full employment, price stability, and a satisfactory economic growth performance are readily apparent. Hence, a primary central government role in directing fiscal policies toward these goals is entirely rational.

Arguments for Decentralized Government

Next, the arguments favoring state-local (subnational) government economic, including fiscal, activity will be considered. Probably, the strongest point in support of *fiscal decentralization* rests on "quasinational" and "nonnational" public goods (bads). There is little or no economic reason to allocate such goods at the national level of government, though some allocational coordination by the central government may be desirable as states and localities supply certain quasinational public goods. It is reasoned that decentralized governmental decisions approximate those of the market more closely than do those of central government. This argument focuses upon the relationship in the market between the benefits received from the consumption of an economic good and the monetary outlay for the good. In market transactions, a person voluntarily foregoes purchasing power in order to acquire a particular economic good.[32] This correlation between payments and goods received is partially approximated at the state-local level of government, though tax payments (as opposed to user-prices) still retain their "compulsory" feature.

By contrast, members of Congress at the federal level do not usually relate the taxes collected from their particular jurisdictions to the benefits received in these jurisdictions because so many revenues are collected from so many states and districts that a *diffusion effect* exists which makes it easy to say: "Why not give my state or my district a larger portion of the revenue pie since the same amount of taxes will be collected from it in any case?" Federal expenditures thus tend to

---

[31] An alternative technique for achieving interstate fiscal equalization—the levying of a "discriminatory" central government personal income tax whereby those individuals residing in wealthier states would be assessed at higher rates than those individuals residing in poorer states—would be *unconstitutional* in the American federation.

[32] See Chapter 4 for a relevant discussion of the voluntary-exchange theory.

be justified, *not* by a particular tax collection, but by an attempt to obtain more of the "diffused aggregate" of tax revenues. Moreover, since lower-level government decisions are closer to the individual (in terms of political jurisdiction) than are federal government decisions, it is asserted that a representative of the people at the subnational government level will be under greater pressure to establish a meaningful relationship between the benefits received and the tax-cost of a project. In addition, the local government representative will be in a better position to interpret the preferences of the community.

A related argument in behalf of decentralized government asserts that the existence of more than 78,000 units of state and local government in the United States allows an individual a better opportunity to select residence in the particular community whose "fiscal characteristics" best meet his preferences. Such a selection approximates consumer sovereignty and choice in the market since extensive variations exist among these many units of state and local government. As a result, individuals via *spatial mobility* are able to select the state and community which best fits their particular fiscal tastes in tax structure and expenditure patterns. Obviously, there exists no similar choice at the central government level—the only remote comparison being the right of an individual to move from one nation to another national jurisdiction. *Inter*national mobility, however, involves considerably greater constraints than does *intra*national mobility. Tiebout provides the following observation regarding the approximation of market conditions by local government through spatial mobility:[33]

> Policies that promote residential mobility and increase knowledge of the consumer-voter will improve the allocation of government expenditures in the same sense that mobility among jobs and knowledge relevant to the location of industry and labor improve the allocation of private resources.

Another related argument in behalf of decentralized government points out that state and local governments allow the meeting of "regional" and "local" values rather than an "across-the-boards" application of *uniform* standards on a "national" basis. Regional and local fiscal operations will differ as the cultural habits and attitudes of the people vary between regions and communities. On the other hand, a national government policy usually contains considerable uniformity. This uniformity can be partially offset, however, when the federal government uses its tax-collecting power to transfer additional funds to the state-local levels of government without specifying the uses to which these funds are applied.

---

[33] Charles M. Tiebout, "A Pure Theory of Local Expenditures," *Journal of Political Economy*, October 1956, p. 423.

An additional argument favoring decentralized government asserts that individuals attain greater "freedom and responsibility" when public goods are allocated by local government. In this regard, Stigler comments:[34]

> If we give each governmental activity to the smallest governmental unit which can efficiently perform it, there will be a vast resurgence and revitalization of local government in America. A vast reservoir of ability and imagination can be found in the increasing leisure time of the population, and both public functions and private citizens would benefit from the increased participation of citizens in political life. An eminent and powerful structure of local government is a basic ingredient of a society which seeks to give to the individuals the fullest possible freedom and responsibility.

Though Stigler desires a maximum of fiscal decision-making by lower-level governments, he acknowledges that certain fiscal areas require central decision-making. Furthermore, he argues that the great revenue-gathering capabilities of the federal government should be used to a greater extent to help finance state and local government fiscal operations—a goal subsequently accomplished in the unconditional revenue sharing and bloc grant legislation of 1972.

In summary, it may be observed that state and local governments serve an important *allocational* role in a federation. They perform a significant allocational function in supplying certain "quasi-national" public goods possessing significant intergovernmental externalities as well as supplying the vast majority of "nonnational" public goods. Moreover, they more closely approximate the preferences for *market-type decision-making* and *individual responsibility* which have long characterized American culture.

INTERGOVERNMENTAL FISCAL RELATIONS IN THE AMERICAN FEDERATION—THE NEED FOR AN ECLECTIC APPROACH

The fiscal federalism discussion to this point has described the major problems of fiscal federalism and the primary alternative methods of attacking these problems. Moreover, it has provided an economic justification for the establishment of a federation with its co-existing "sovereign" national (central, federal) and subnational (state, provincial) governments. In this final section of the chapter, the desirability of using an *eclectic* policy approach to remedy intergovernmental fiscal

---

[34] George J. Stigler, "The Tenable Range of Functions of Local Government," *Federal Expenditure Policy for Economic Growth and Stability,* Joint Economic Committee, 85th Cong., 1st sess. (Washington, D.C.: U.S. Government Printing Office, 1957), p. 219.

problems will be emphasized.[35] This approach will encompass the simultaneous usage of a variety of intergovernmental fiscal instruments to improve intergovernmental fiscal performance. Importantly, it will be observed that each major fiscal technique serves well in attacking at least one major intergovernmental problem, but that *no single technique* can by itself effectively attack the wide and varied range of major intergovernmental fiscal problems.

In the proposed eclectic approach to intergovernmental fiscal problems in the American federation which follows, it is assumed that the American people do not wish to replace the federal system with a unitary system of democracy. Moreover, it is assumed that there will be no "significant" merger of lower-level government units in the foreseeable future. That is, the number of sovereign state governments will remain at 50, while mergers between local government units will be relatively insignificant. Furthermore, since strong arguments and strong political forces support both centralized and decentralized government within the American public sector, it is assumed that no permanent important "reallocation" of the functional areas of expenditure responsibility will occur between the respective levels of government. Within these parameters, the following set of intergovernmental fiscal tools is proposed:[36]

1. Unconditional Revenue Sharing

This technique should be used for the primary purpose of reducing the *horizontal fiscal imbalance* between states and localities. Of course, the degree to which this distributional decision exists as a goal in a society must be determined by a collective "value-judgment" consensus of the people. Yet, it is likely that the American people desire some intergovernmental fiscal equalization. For example, the very nature of a federation makes it impossible for residents of one state to be totally separated from the economic effects of fiscal actions in other states. Moreover, a citizen of a federation holds "dual citizenship," as it were, in both a sovereign national and a sovereign state or provincial government. In this sense, it can be argued that his residency in a relatively

---

[35] In essence, this approach will apply to the problems of fiscal federalism—the "targets and instruments" method used by economists such as Jan Tinbergen, Bent Hansen, and Leif Johansen. See Jan Tinbergen, *On the Theory of Economic Policy* (Amsterdam: North Holland, 1952); Bent Hansen, *The Economic Theory of Fiscal Policy* (London: Allen and Unwin, 1958); and Leif Johansen, *Public Economics* (Amsterdam: North Holland; Chicago: Rand McNally, 1965).

[36] For a related discussion, see Bernard P. Herber, "Vertical Intergovernmental Fiscal Relations in Australia: A Comparison with Canada and the United States," *Proceedings—National Tax Association—1969*, pp. 269–99, and "The Role of Revenue Sharing in an Intergovernmental Fiscal Reform Program," *MSU Business Topics*, Summer 1972, pp. 19–27.

poor state or province should not deny him an adequate consumption level of quasi-national and nonnational public goods. Moreover, this argument can also be largely extended to the consumption of private-type economic goods. Since the analysis of the previous section demonstrated that *central government* possesses a comparative efficiency advantage in the implementation of redistributional policy, the federal government should utilize unconditional revenue sharing to improve public goods consumption by reducing the degree of inequality among the fiscal capacities of state and local governments. Moreover, it should also employ fiscal techniques such as a *negative income tax* to attack poverty in the private sector.[37]

As observed earlier, the *unconditional revenue sharing* and the related *bloc grant* fiscal instruments were added to the pattern of fiscal relationships between the federal and state-local governments during 1972. However, caution should be used to assure that these instruments be used where they have an efficiency advantage. *Unconditional grants-in-aid*, for example, are unable to coordinate intergovernmental externalities. Yet, the governmental decentralization efforts during the second administration of President Nixon advocated that a number of existing conditional grant programs, some with obvious intergovernmental spillover benefits, be converted into "unconditional" and "bloc" grants. Conversion to the latter, of course, could be fiscally rational, but would not necessarily be so. Rationality, for example, would require that no significant differences exist in benefit spillover ratios between governments for the separate, though related, existing conditional grants programs which would be merged into a bloc grant program.

2. Federal Personal Income Tax Credit

It is recommended that the federal government provide a federal personal income tax credit for personal income taxes paid to state governments. The credit should be substantial enough to encourage all states to use personal income taxation as a major revenue source. The tax credit device would be used as the primary technique to improve conditions of noncorrespondence (*vertical fiscal imbalance*) in the American public sector. In this regard, it is a much better tool than unconditional revenue sharing since it preserves, to a much greater degree, the symmetrical quid pro quo relationship whereby the level (and unit) of government collecting the tax also makes the expenditure decisions. Moreover, it would serve a *distributional equity* goal to the extent that the increased usage of progressive state personal income

---

[37] See Chapter 21.

taxes would reduce the reliance upon regressive state-local sales and property taxes. Meanwhile, unconditional grants would continue to be used as the primary tool for serving the interstate "equalization" goal since tax credits do not exert a direct equalization effect. As noted earlier, an "implicit" tax credit was included in one of the unconditional revenue sharing formulas enacted by Congress during 1972. However, the recommendation here is for an "explicit" and "formal" credit which would provide a much greater incentive for state governments to effectively utilize personal income taxation.

3. Tax Supplement

Furthermore, it is recommended that the states be encouraged to adopt a personal income tax base similar or identical to the one used by the federal government, but that hopefully the federal model would represent a more equitable and comprehensive base than the one in effect at the present time. Ideally, the states would allow the federal government to collect the state personal income taxes in order to take advantage of the *economies of scale* inherent in centralized tax collection. Thus, in effect, the "piggyback" form of *tax supplement* would be incorporated into the system. This was made possible by the State and Local Fiscal Assistance Act of 1972, as noted earlier in the chapter, but it remains to be seen how many, if any, states elect to accept the option to have the federal government collect their personal income taxes. Quite likely, the twofold adoption of both a "formal" tax credit and a "piggybacking option" would provide a greater incentive for the states to elect the latter, since personal income tax revenues would likely increase greatly due to the tax credit incentive. Finally, the increased use of the personal income tax in the public sector would enhance this tax as an "automatic" stabilization tool while the federal government would continue to lead the way on "discretionary" stabilization policy.

4. Conditional Revenue Sharing

The substantial usage of federal conditional revenue-sharing programs should be continued. However, the complexity of the present programs should be reduced, where feasible, and program overlapping eliminated. The primary purpose of conditional grants should be to serve an allocational goal. That is, these grants should be used to improve allocational efficiency under circumstances where important *intergovernmental externalities* are present, as in quasi-national public goods and bads.

Conditional grants, however, may also be used to provide an "indirect" *equalization effect*. To the extent that the equalization goal is desirable in connection with a conditional grant program, the grant should be "variable matching" in nature so that states or localities with greater fiscal capacities would "match" at a higher percentage than low-fiscal capacity states or localities. Moreover, it is desirable at times to finance conditional grants through "earmarked" taxes subject to the symmetrical *quid pro quo* advantage of the benefit principle. Finally, it is suggested that additional efforts be made to apply benefit-cost analysis and the PPBS approach[38] to improve the efficiency of the presently-complex conditional grant programs.

In summary, it may be said that an *eclectic* approach to intergovernmental fiscal issues is advocated. A judicious combination of the unconditional revenue sharing, tax credit, tax supplement, and conditional revenue-sharing techniques should be employed to attain the intergovernmental fiscal goals of the American federation. The primary instrument for attaining the "equalization" goal would be unconditional revenue sharing. The primary tool for alleviating "noncorrespondence" would be a combination use of the tax credit and tax supplement devices. Finally, the conditional revenue-sharing technique can best serve the "allocation" goal when intergovernmental externalities lead to a serious misallocation of important quasi-national public goods and bads. In following an eclectic approach, the American federation would "fall into step" with the current international trend for federations to employ a "package" of intergovernmental fiscal techniques.

---

[38] See Chapter 18.

21

The Public Sector and Poverty in the United States

The living standard of a society is determined, in part, by its patterns of income and wealth distribution. Average figures of income and wealth, of course, are grossly misleading. A nation may enjoy a very high per capita income for its residents. Yet, the distribution of its income may be quite unequal. Although the average would indicate a prosperous nation, the fact may be that the living standard of many residents is low.

Virtually every nation in the world is confronted with a problem of poverty, though to varying degrees. This statement includes the so-called affluent industrial nations of Western Europe as well as the United States. Poverty in a mature industrial nation stems largely from the status of income and wealth *distribution* in that nation. On the other hand, poverty in an underdeveloped nation derives largely from the need for *economic development*. The public sector of a nation, through its fiscal process of taxation and expenditure, may influence both the distribution of income and wealth and the rate of economic development. Hence, the elimination of poverty—whether it be in a mature or in an underdeveloped nation—can be approached through governmental budgetary policy. Moreover, as observed in the federalism discussion of the previous two chapters, national (central) government possesses a comparative advantage in such redistributional policy.

The emphasis in this chapter will be on poverty as a distributional problem, with particular stress on the ability of education to change the real distribution of income and thus alleviate poverty. In turn, the discussion of the next chapter will include the influence of budgetary policy on economic development.

Income Distribution in the United States

Table 21–1 displays the share of money income received by each one fifth (quintile) of "family spending units" as well as by the top 5 percent

TABLE 21–1

Percentage Distribution of U.S. Family Income by Each Quintile (20 Percent) and the Top 5 Percent of Family Spending Units (selected years)

| Family Spending Units | Percentage of Total Family Income Received | | | |
	1950	1960	1967	1970
Lowest Quintile	4.5	4.9	5.4	5.5
Second Quintile	12.0	12.0	12.2	12.0
Third Quintile	17.4	17.6	17.5	17.4
Fourth Quintile	23.5	23.6	23.7	23.5
Highest Quintile	42.6	42.0	41.2	41.6
Total	100.0	100.0	100.0	100.0
Top 5 percent	17.0	16.8	15.3	14.4

Source: U.S. Department of Commerce, December 1972, *Current Population Reports: Consumer Income*, Series P–60, No. 85, p. 38.

of "family spending units" for the years 1950, 1960, 1967, and 1970. A *family spending unit* is defined as a group of two or more persons related by blood, marriage, or adoption who reside together in the same dwelling. It may be observed that the percent of total money income received by the highest quintile declined from 42.6 percent to 41.6 percent between 1950 and 1970. Meanwhile, the percentage received by each of the middle three quintiles remained unchanged. Hence, the one percent decrease in the share of the highest quintile is found as a one percent increase, from a 4.5 percent to a 5.5 percent share, for the lowest quintile. In addition, the share of the top 5 percent declined from 17.0 percent to 14.4 percent during the period. Nonetheless, an income distribution pattern in which 20 percent of the families earn only 5.5 percent of the total family income, while another 20 percent earn 41.6 percent of the total, represents substantial inequality in the distribution of income.

In absolute terms (not shown in the table), the median family income of all families in the United States during 1970 was $9,867. When this figure is disaggregated, it shows the median income of *white* families to be $10,236 and that of *nonwhite* families to be only $6,516.

Table 21–2 and Figure 21–1 further demonstrate the degree of inequality in the distribution of family income in the United States for the year 1970. Both *complete equality* and *complete inequality* of income distribution are shown relative to the *actual distribution* of family income during that year. Figure 21–1 displays the situation by means of the familiar Lorenz curve technique. In Figure 21–1, the diagonal line A represents "complete equality" where each family earns an identical income. The right-angled curve B represents "complete inequality"

TABLE 21–2

Table of *Complete Equality* and *Complete Inequality* in the Distribution of Family Income, and *Actual Distribution* of Family Income, in the United States During 1970

Percentage of Family Spending Units, Cumulated from Poorest to Richest	Percentage of Family Income, Cumulated from Lowest to Highest Income		
	Complete Equality	Complete Inequality	1970 Distribution
0...................	0	0	0
20...................	20	0	5.5
40...................	40	0	17.5
60...................	60	0	34.9
80...................	80	0	58.4
100...................	100	100	100.0

Source: U.S. Department of Commerce data.

where one family earns the entire income of the society. Finally, "actual 1970 distribution" of family income in the United States is demonstrated by curve C which lies between the two curves which represent the two extremes of "complete equality" and "complete inequality" in income distribution.

As observed in Chapters 6, 7, and 8, the *public sector budget* may be utilized to redistribute real income, in the living standard sense, toward either a greater degree of equality or inequality. This can be accomplished through the manner in which it distributes *tax burdens* and *expenditure benefits.* Thus, curve C in Figure 21–1, in effect, may be moved either inward toward curve A, or outward toward curve B, through budgetary policy.

FIGURE 21-1

Graphical Demonstration of *Complete Equality* and *Complete Inequality* in the Distribution of Family Income, and *Actual Distribution* of Family Income, in the United States During 1970

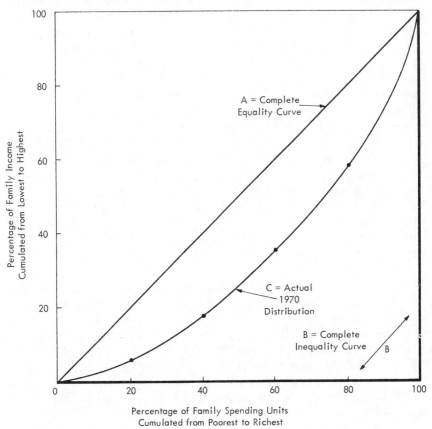

Percentage of Family Spending Units
Cumulated from Poorest to Richest

Source: Based on data in Table 21–2.

Wealth Distribution in the United States

More than 30 percent of the assets and equities held in the personal sector of the economy in 1953 were held by the top wealthholders, who constituted only 1.6 percent of the adult population during that year.[1] The top group owned approximately 80 percent of the corporate stock, virtually all of the state and local government securities, and between 10 and 33 percent of each other type of property owned in the personal

---

[1] Robert J. Lampman, *The Share of Top Wealth-Holders in National Wealth—1922–56,* a National Bureau of Economic Research Study (Princeton, N.J.: Princeton University Press, 1962), p. 23.

sector.[2] The degree of inequality in wealth distribution had increased during the 1920s and then declined during the 1930s and early 1940s. As observed by Smith and Franklin, the redistribution occurred during periods when the market system was either functioning under duress (the Depression of the 1930s), or when it was in administrative abeyance (World War II).[3] The distribution of wealth has remained essentially unchanged since 1945. The considerable inequality in wealthholding which remains is exemplified by data for 1971 showing that 16 percent of the family spending units in the United States owned no "liquid assets."[4] In addition, another 26 percent held liquid assets valued at less than $500 and 66 percent of the spending units held either no liquid assets or liquid assets valued at less than $2,000.

A comparison of recent income and wealth distributions in the United States is provided in Figure 21–2. The Lorenz curves indicate that the degree of wealth inequality is considerably greater than the inequality in the distribution of income. The highest 10 percent of the family spending units, for example, hold 56 percent of the wealth and 29 percent of the income. At the other extreme, the bottom 10 percent of the families receive 1 percent of the income and hold "negative wealth," that is, they owe more than they own.

The reverse extreme from poverty, of course, can be cited in terms of the number of millionaires in the population of the nation. This number is growing rapidly. In 1948, for example, some 13,000 millionaires (families or adult individuals with wealth in excess of $1 million) could be counted, but this figure skyrocketed to a total of 90,000 by the mid-1960s, and to an even larger figure today. Approximately two thirds of the total assets of the millionaire group is held in the form of corporation stock with tax-exempt bonds comprising the next largest segment. It is estimated that in 1962 the top 1 percent of wealthholders owned 62 percent of all publicly-held corporate stock, with the top 5 percent owning 86 percent and the top 20 percent owning 97 percent of the stock.[5] Unquestionably, the ownership of wealth has a direct (positive) relationship with the earning of income, that is, wealth often becomes a source of income. Hence, the existing inequality of income and wealth distribution has a "built-in" basis for its continuance.

---

[2] Ibid., p. 23.

[3] James D. Smith and Stephen D. Franklin, "The Concentration of Personal Wealth, 1922–1969," *American Economic Review,* May 1974, pp. 162–67.

[4] "Liquid assets" refer to such items as checking accounts, savings accounts, and nonmarketable U.S. savings bonds. See U.S. Department of Commerce, *Statistical Abstract of the United States—1972* (Washington, D.C.: U.S. Government Printing Office, 1972), p. 335.

[5] See Nancy Lyons and Letitia Upton, *Basic Facts: Distribution of Personal Income and Wealth in the United States* (Cambridge, Massachusetts: Cambridge Policy Studies Institute, 1972), p. 22.

FIGURE 21-2
Lorenz Curves of Total Income and Wealth Distributions Among Family Spending Units,
1969-70

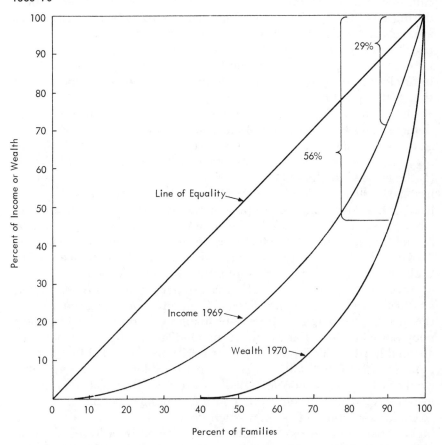

Source: Lewis Mandell, as reprinted from the August 5, 1972 issue of *Business Week* by special permission.
Copyright 1972 by McGraw-Hill, Inc.

POVERTY IN THE UNITED STATES

As noted earlier, poverty in the United States derives largely from
the structure of income and wealth distribution in the nation rather
than from an historic inability to experience satisfactory economic
growth. The federal government provides an official *poverty income
index*, as developed by the Social Security Administration and compiled
by the U.S. Department of Commerce. If one looks at this index for the
year 1970, it reveals that 20.5 million people, or 11 percent of the
population, were officially classified as "poor" in that year since they

resided in families which earned incomes of less than the $3,968 poverty level income for the year.[6] Moreover, the number of poor Americans increases to 25.5 million people, or 12.6 percent of the population, during 1970 if unrelated poor individuals living outside family status are included. Furthermore, if one includes in the total the official "near poor" category, defined as those earning income not exceeding 125 percent of the poverty-line income, the number of Americans living in or close to poverty grows to 35.6 million people or 17.6 percent of the total population.

Data concerning the composition of poverty in the United States demonstrates that 8 percent of all white families and 29.3 percent of all black families were below the poverty-level income in 1970. Moreover, the data reveal that a greater propensity for poverty exists when: (1) the head of the household is over 65, (2) the head of the household has had eight years or less of education, (3) the father is absent, (4) the head of the household is unemployed, that is, he is not classified in the labor force, and (5) the family lives in a rural area. Individuals caught in such circumstances often find themselves in a vicious cycle whereby "poverty begets poverty." Historically, statistics have shown a high probability that the children of the poor will remain poor.

Poverty is a major problem for many elderly Americans. Moreover, a task force of the U.S. Senate Special Committee on Aging reports that the income gap between Americans living in retirement and younger people is widening.[7] For example, the median income of families with an aged head (over 65 years of age) was 51 percent of that for younger families in 1961, but only 46 percent in 1967. Moreover, during 1966, 3 out of 10 people over 65 years of age were officially classified as "living in poverty" while the ratio was 1 in 9 for younger people.

Under conditions of poverty, such diverse circumstances exist as a higher than average risk of illness accompanied by a lower financial ability to obtain medical care, limited geographical and occupational mobility, limited access to education, training, and information, and inadequate housing. Regarding the latter, the Census data of 1960 show that approximately 9.3 million housing units in the United States were seriously deficient at that time. This constituted approximately one sixth of all housing. In metropolitan areas, 7.5 percent of all owner-occupied housing and 21 percent of all renter-occupied housing was classified as unsound. Once more, inadequate housing percentages were even higher for poverty families earning under the then-poverty level income of $3,000 annually. For these people, 34 percent of owner-

---

[6] The *poverty income figure* cited here is for a nonfarm family of four persons. An "adjusted" figure is used for farm families.

[7] U.S. Senate Special Committee on Aging, *Developments in Aging*, 1968.

occupied residences and 60 percent of renter-occupied residences were unsound. Moreover, 4 out of 5 families earning less than $2,000 annual income lived under deficient housing conditions.

Yet, the vicious cycle of poverty is not inevitable! To the contrary, appropriate budgetary policy by the public sector, given an approving value judgment consensus by the society, is capable of eliminating poverty in the United States. Indeed, the nation possesses the productive resources necessary to reach this goal. Table 21–3 shows that American poverty declined rather sharply during the 1960s, but was beginning to increase, once again, during the early 1970s. Despite this overall decline in poverty during the 1960s, a great deal of additional progress is required if poverty within America's overall affluent society is to be

TABLE 21–3
Persons with Below-Poverty Level Incomes, in Absolute Terms and as Percentage of Total Population, 1960–71

Year	*Persons with Below-Poverty Level Income (numbers in millions)*	*Persons with Below-Poverty Level Income (percent of total population)*
1960.	39.9	22.2
1961.	39.6	21.9
1962.	38.6	21.0
1963.	36.4	19.5
1964.	36.1	19.0
1965.	33.2	17.3
1966.	28.5	14.7
1967.	27.8	14.2
1968.	25.4	12.8
1969.	24.1	12.1
1970.	25.5	12.6
1971.	25.6	12.5

Source: Bureau of the Census, U.S. Department of Commerce.

completely eradicated. The remaining sections of this chapter will describe some fiscal approaches which may be directed toward the achievement of this goal.

GOVERNMENTAL PROGRAMS TO ALLEVIATE POVERTY

Public sector programs directed toward the mitigation of poverty fall into two main categories. The programs, for example, may emphasize *exhaustive governmental expenditures* on such basic economic products as "education" and "health services." Or, the programs may concentrate upon the *tax-transfer expenditure* process whereby the initial effect is a redistribution of disposable, posttax and posttransfer income from higher-income to lower-income taxpayers rather than the direct receipt of certain important, public-type, economic goods by the poor. A mix of both program approaches, of course, is a very realistic policy option. Regardless of approach, however, it is important to remember (as determined in the fiscal federalism analysis of the previous chapter) that the national government of a federation holds a "comparative advantage" over subnational governments in the economic capability of directing redistributional programs. Thus, the central government should play a major role in redistributional budgetary policy whether it involves an exhaustive expenditure or a tax-transfer approach. The exhaustive expenditure means of alleviating poverty will be discussed next with an analysis of the tax-transfer approach to follow.

Exhaustive Expenditure Programs for the Alleviation of Poverty

The Relationship of Education to Poverty. Education may serve as a primary means of eliminating or reducing poverty through its ability to increase the earning power of those who are educated. Figure 21–3 demonstrates the direct (positive) functional relationship which exists between "educational training" and "earning power" in the United States. Moreover, this increased earning power represents an increase in the productivity of labor resources in the economy. The total output of the society should thus increase as the quality of its labor force increases. In other words, greater efficiency from productive inputs should expand the aggregate economic product of the society. This, in turn, should raise living standards in the society as a whole and, quite likely, for people at all levels in the income strata. This overall effect, of course, would be in addition to the specific individual monetary benefits accruing to the educated individual.

Similarly, education may contribute toward a higher rate of economic growth in the society. In this regard, a study by Schultz indicates that even though the ratio of physical to human capital in American production remained constant over a 50-year period during this century, the economic potential of the society increased enormously during the period.[8] Denison, moreover, attributes 23 percent of the growth in total real national income and 42 percent of the growth in per capita real income during the period 1929–59 to higher educational attainments.[9] This resulted from increases in productivity, greater adaptability to change, and the "freeing" of productive resources.

---

[8] Theodore W. Schultz, "Capital Formation by Education," *Journal of Political Economy,* December 1960, pp. 571–83.

[9] Edward F. Denison, *The Sources of Economic Growth in the United States and the Alternatives before Us* (New York: Committee for Economic Development, 1962), pp. 67–79.

FIGURE 21-3

Median Income in 1967 of Male Year-Round Full-time Workers 25 Years Old and over, by Years of School Completed, for the United States

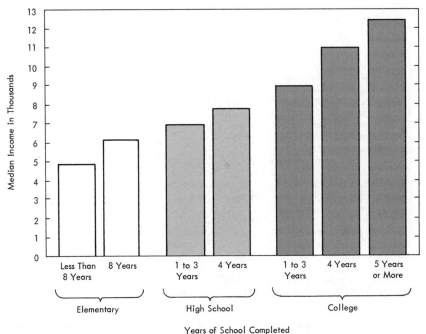

Source: U.S. Department of Commerce.

The positive functional relationship between *human resource development* and the *aggregate economic performance* of a nation is further demonstrated in Table 21–4. In this table, the "human resources index," as constructed by Harbison and Myers, is based on a composite of items such as the proportion of school-age population enrolled at various educational levels, the number of teachers per capita, and the number of doctors per capita.[10] The relationship of the latter to poverty-mitigation is discussed below when governmental exhaustive expenditures for health services are considered. As the table indicates, the nations with the greatest "human resource development" produce the "highest per capita GNP" for their residents, and vice versa.

Also, it should be observed that the benefits associated with economic growth occur over an extended period of time as well as in the short run. Most of the gains, however, accrue to future generations rather than to the present one. Yet, future generations exert no prefer-

---

[10] F. H. Harbison and C. A. Myers, *Education, Manpower and Economic Growth* (New York: McGraw-Hill Book Co., 1964).

TABLE 21–4
Functional Relationship between Human Resource Development and Aggregate Economic
Performance, 75 Nations, 1958–59

Countries (in order from highest to lowest)	National Index of Human Resource Development	Average per Capita GNP ($U.S.)
Advanced countries		
U.S.A., New Zealand, Australia, Netherlands, Belgium, United Kingdom, Japan, France, Canada, U.S.S.R., Finland, West Germany, Israel, Argentina, Sweden, and Denmark......................................	115	1,110
Semiadvanced countries		
Norway, Uruguay, Czechoslovakia, Poland, Yugoslavia, Italy, South Korea, Taiwan, Hungary, Chile, Greece, Venezuela, Costa Rica, Portugal, Egypt, South Africa, Spain, Cuba, India, Thailand, Mexico.....................	50	380
Partially developed countries		
Iraq, Peru, Turkey, Jamaica, Pakistan, Ecuador, Lebanon, Malaya, Ghana, Paraguay, Colombia, Brazil, China, Iran, Tunisia, Bolivia, Dominican Republic, Burma, Libya, Indonesia, Guatemala.....................	21	182
Underdeveloped countries		
Sudan, Uganda, Senegal, Haiti, Nigeria, Kenya, Liberia, Congo, N. Rhodesia, Ivory Coast, Tanganyika, Saudi Arabia, Afghanistan, Somalia, Nyasaland, Ethiopia, Niger...	3.2	84

Source: *Computed* from F. H. Harbison and C. A. Myers, *Education, Manpower and Economic Growth* (New York: McGraw-Hill Book Co., 1964), pp. 23–48, and *published* in Allan M. Cartter, "The Economics of Higher Education," in Neil W. Chamberlain (ed.), *Contemporary Economic Issues* (Homewood, Ill.: Richard D. Irwin, Inc.), p. 157.

ence on the present use of productive resources. Market-determined outlays for education, therefore, will not tend to reflect the value of education to future generations.[11] Thus, total reliance on market-type determination of the supply of education may result in an underinvestment in education.

Education as an Economic Good. The tendency to *undersupply* education stems also from other considerations related to the nature of education as a "public-type" economic good. In the terminology of this book, education may be classified as a *quasi-public* or *impure public good.* Substantial social or community benefits derive from education. These benefits take the form of joint consumption or positive externalities which cannot be easily quantified or priced. However, many other educational benefits accrue directly to the individual who is educated and estimates of the monetary value of some of these private benefits,

---

[11] See Jerry Miner, *Social and Economic Factors in Spending for Public Education* (Syracuse, N.Y.: Syracuse University Press, 1963), p. 29.

and a pricing of these benefits, can be more easily attained. This dual provision of both social and private benefits, and its predominant provision by the public sector in the United States, warrants the classification of education as a *quasi-public good*. Moreover, in the "spatial terminology" of fiscal federalism, education may be regarded as a *quasi-national public good* since it is characterized by significant intergovernmental spillovers between the subnational governments which supply it in the United States.

The fact that education is a "quasi-public good" would suggest a tendency for the private sector to *undersupply* its benefits since some of these benefits escape the price mechanism. It is for this reason that the public sector plays a role in its allocation. Moreover, the fact that education in the United States is a "quasi-national public good," supplied primarily by subnational units of governments, suggests the existence of numerous intergovernmental spillover effects. This characteristic, also, creates a tendency for the good to be *undersupplied*. However, the *redistributional* role of the national government in its efforts to increase the supply of education through an "exhaustive expenditure approach," as contrasted to a "tax-transfer expenditure approach" for the redistribution of income, is intermixed with *allocational* considerations such as the need to coordinate intergovernmental spillovers. Hence, it would be expected that the national government of a federation would play a relatively more direct and comprehensive redistributional role in its "tax-transfer" activities than in its "exhaustive expenditures" for such basic economic goods as education and health services. This is not to suggest, however, that the role of the central government in the latter case should be unimportant.

The planning, financing, and production of *public education* in the United States takes place primarily at the state and local levels of government, though the absolute and relative importance of federal financial support has been increasing in recent decades. State governments are essentially concerned with higher education (college education) while the brunt of responsibility for the provision of elementary and high school education is borne by local units of government. The latter involves considerable decentralization in the production of public school education since many thousands of local governments make decisions regarding the supply, quality, and distribution of the public elementary and high school education received by American children.

Not only is the allocation of resources toward an optimal supply of education important both to the individual who is educated and to the nation as a whole, but it is also important to the local community which produces public school education. As observed above, because of the high degree of "interdependence" in American society, the quantity and quality of education produced by one community will inevitably exert external effects on other communities. That is, a given community produces certain educational effects which it "exports" to other communities. The nonoptimal allocation of resources which may result from such spillover effects, as well as from the other factors mentioned above, justifies a further investigation of the *allocational* characteristics of education. In addition, *distribution* of educational benefits is also a relevant consideration.

Weisbrod has conducted an excellent analysis of the allocation problem as it relates to the external benefits which derive from public education.[12] However, before attempting to isolate these "positive externalities," he discusses the nature of the "total benefits" which accrue from education. He views the *individual student* as receiving:[13] (1) a direct financial return in terms of the incremental earnings which usually accompany additional education;[14] (2) a financial option consisting of the opportunity to obtain still further education, (3) a hedging option consisting of the increased ability to adjust to changing job opportunities caused by such phenomena as automation and changing consumer preferences, and (4) certain nonmarket returns to the individual such as the individual advantages of literacy.

Then, regarding the *social* or *external benefits* of education, Weisbrod separates the persons receiving such benefits into three categories:[15] (1) residence-related beneficiaries, that is, those who benefit by virtue of some relationship between their place of residence and that of the person who is educated; (2) employment-related beneficiaries, that is, those who benefit by virtue of some employment relationship with the person receiving the education, and (3) the society as a whole. These external benefits of education occur at various times and in various places. The benefits do not necessarily accrue to the people who financially support the production of the education, nor do they necessarily reside in the community where it is produced. More specifically, the process of migration provides *spatial shifting* of some of the external effects of education. The phenomenon of migration and spatial shifiting is highly relevant to the questions of allocative and distributive efficiency in education and to the financing of education.

There are various means whereby a community may monetarily benefit from satisfactory education. Since education tends to increase labor productivity and income, for example, it will directly increase aggregate community income as long as the educational capital (those

---

[12] See Burton A. Weisbrod, *External Benefits of Public Education* (Princeton, N.J.: Industrial Relations Section, Department of Economics, Princeton University, 1964).

[13] Ibid. pp. 15–27.

[14] See Figure 21–3 for empirical proof of this fact.

[15] Weisbrod, *Public Education*, pp. 28–39.

educated) remains in the community. Moreover, even if the only incomes which increase are those of the educated people, the rest of the community may indirectly benefit from the additional governmental services which can be financed from the higher taxes paid by the educated people. In addition, the redistribution motive may be present in the sense that improved allocation of education at the present time may reduce the future need for redistributive transfer (welfare) payments to combat poverty. Furthermore, if the productivity and income of some persons in the community are raised by education, there may be secondary effects on the level of income and employment of others in the community.

Weisbrod conducted an empirical study of Clayton, Missouri, a suburb of St. Louis, to supplement his analysis.[16] Estimates are provided for: (1) the educational capital produced by the public school system of Clayton; (2) the portion of that capital which may be expected to remain in Clayton; and (3) the amount of educational capital which may be expected to move into Clayton from other communities. The study reveals a "net migration loss" of educational capital for the community. An estimation of returns in the form of "incremental tax revenue" resulting from the investment in education is also provided. The conclusion is reached that part of the financial return which a student obtains from this education was returned to the community through taxation, but that most of it accrued to fiscal units other than the Clayton School District. Moreover, regarding employers, the higher average educational level of the community (13.3 years as compared to 10 years for the United States) is reflected in a lower unemployment tax on employers. In addition, the community may receive beneficial nonmarket results because of the direct relationship between the level of educational attainment and the degree of political participation.

The study concludes that education is considered, in the political process, as an investment based upon the expectation of returns.[17] Thus, in areas where a substantial outmigration occurs, the level of per capita educational expenditures may often tend to be lower than otherwise. In addition, the spillover effects tend to shift the financing of education increasingly from the local to the state level of government in order to coordinate the spillovers. Education does, indeed, benefit communities other than the ones financing and supplying the education. Yet, no compulsory procedure exists to assure that the educational benefits consumed and provided by any particular community will be equal. The allocation of resources toward education thus tends to be

---

[16] Ibid.
[17] Ibid.

suboptimal in the absence of an intergovernmental coordinative effort. Weisbrod considers two remedies:[18]

1. The widening of the political decisionmaking unit so as to "internalize" more of the external benefits of education.
2. The adoption by all states of educational standards which are high enough to bring educational attainment and quality throughout the nation closer to those of the best state.

He prefers the first solution.

Educational Financing and the Distribution of Educational Benefits. Government involvement in American education is not a recent phenomenon. Educational laws passed by the colonies date back as far as the mid-seventeeth century. It was not until well into the nineteenth century, however, that the public sector began to take a major interest in the financing and production of education. The division of responsibilities between governments for the financing and coordinating of educational activities may be viewed in reference to the concept of a "quasi-national public good," as developed above. To the extent that intergovernmental educational externalities reside within the political jurisdiction of a state, the state government should bear a responsibility with local governments for the financing and coordinating of public educational activities. To the extent that the educational externalities or joint consumption permeate the entire national society, however, financial assistance and coordination directed by the federal government seems appropriate. In all, it may be concluded that the entire public sector should participate in the allocation of education as an economic good, but not necessarily with an equal degree of influence. Since local governments can and do efficiently produce public school elementary and secondary education in the United States, the required coordination of spillover benefits can be largely undertaken by state governments. However, when intergovernmental educational externalities assume more of an "interstate" dimension, as with higher (university, college) education, the coordinative role of the national government may be expected to become more important.[19]

It would appear that an "economically rational" future public sector financial policy toward education should continue the provision of *elementary* and *high school education* on a "free" public school basis without tuition charges in order to attain the societal benefits of a literate and educated population. Furthermore, it would appear ra-

---

[18] Ibid., chap. 10.

[19] The role of government in the allocation of education, however, does not suggest that the public sector must in all cases directly produce education. Instead, it may be more efficient, at times, to have the private sector produce the good subject to governmental quality regulations and financial assistance.

tional to continue to "price" through tuition charges a substantial part of those benefits of *higher education* which truly take on "investment aspects" for the individual. The remaining social benefits, because of the externalities and nonmarket benefits derived by the entire society from an educated population, should continue to be financed from general taxation.

It is important to observe that even though allocational adjustments undertaken to assure the provision of a *satisfactory quantity* of educational services in the society as a whole will make it easier for a society to mitigate poverty, the important matter of the *distribution of educational benefits* among the population will still remain as a critical determinant of ultimate poverty alleviation. Moreover, even if society does provide equal educational availability to its citizens in a "quantitative" sense, it is quite possible that substantial "qualitative" differences may still occur in the educational services received by different members of the population. Indeed, such substantial qualitative differences do exist in the actual distribution of educational services among the American population. This important issue has thrust itself strongly on to the American scene during recent years.

The emergence of the public school educational benefits issue was precipitated in August 1971 when the Supreme Court of the State of California ruled that the public school financing system in that state, which "makes the quality of a child's education a function of the wealth of his parents and neighbors" through its financial reliance on local government property taxes, was unconstitutional.[20] The unconstitutionality was judged to be on the basis of a violation of the "equal protection clause" of the Fourteenth Amendment to the Federal Constitution in the sense that public school education is a "fundamental right" not to be "dependent upon wealth." This significant court decision was quickly followed by similar rulings in Minnesota, Texas, New Jersey, and a number of other states.

The essence of these judicial decisions is the contention that *unequal* local government property tax bases contribute to *unequal* educational opportunities for students attending public elementary and secondary schools since the local property tax is the dominant means of public school financing in the United States.[21] Moreover, existing state "foundation programs" for the purpose of equalizing these educational quality disparities have been unsuccessful. Thus, two local school districts with different wealth endowments can provide equal educational ex-

---

[20] See *Serrano* v. *Priest*, Sup., 96 Cal. Rptr. 604.

[21] In the nation as a whole during 1969–70, revenues raised by local governments financed 52.5 percent of total public school expenditures. Meanwhile, property taxes constitute approximately 87 percent of local government tax revenues and local governments collect some 97 percent of all property tax revenues.

penditures per pupil only if the poorer district levies a higher property tax rate on its lower property tax base. The equally disturbing alternative is for the poorer jurisdiction to provide a lower level of educational spending per pupil while maintaining a property tax rate similar to that imposed by the wealthier district. In practice, some combination of both undesirable results is likely to occur. That is, property tax burdens per student tend to be higher and educational expenditures per student tend to be lower in the poorer school districts. Strong evidence of intrastate school district per capita expenditure disparities, as well as per capita property valuation disparities, in the United States appears in Table 21–5. These data suggest a widespread differentiation in the distribution of public school educational benefits among the populations of the respective states, with few exceptions.

This important issue found its way to a United States Supreme Court decision in the Texas (Rodriguez) counterpart of the California (Serrano) case on March 21, 1973.[22] In a 5–4 vote, the U.S. Supreme Court ruled that the equal protection clause of the Federal Constitution, at least where wealth is involved, does not require "absolute equality or precisely equal advantages."[23] In effect, the Court has said that even though every citizen has a fundamental constitutional right to public school education, he does not have a fundamental constitutional right to "equal" public school education.

Despite this adverse judicial ruling, advocates of public school fiscal reform seem to be achieving some success since a number of states, in response to court action, are now voluntarily and systematically reviewing the role of the local government property tax in reference to its overall distributional equity problems and, in particular, in its relationship to public school financing. A trend seems to be developing toward the assumption of a higher proportion of the financing of local public schools by state governments and a subsequent diminished reliance on the local government property tax for this purpose. Such actions are likely to reduce to some degree the existing extreme variation in the distribution of public school educational benefits. Meanwhile, a recent study suggests that the distribution of the benefits of higher (college) education also favors the more affluent members of the society.[24]

Technical Education for the Poor and Job Discrimination. Education, of course, does not consist exclusively of *formal* public school and college education. It may also take the form of special *technical training*

---

[22] *Rodriguez* v. *San Antonio Independent School District,* U.S. District Court, Western District of Texas, San Antonio Division, December 23, 1971. Ruled on by a U.S. Supreme Court decision, March 21, 1973.

[23] Ibid.

[24] See Robert J. Staaf and Gordon Tullock, "Education and Equality," *Annals,* September 1973, pp. 125–34.

TABLE 21-5

School District per Student Expenditure Disparities and School District per Student Property Valuation Disparities, by State

	Ratio of Max./Min. 1969/70 Expenditures	Ratio of Max./Min. 1968/69 Assessed Valuation
Alabama	2.0/1	4.5/1
Alaska*	3.8/1	3.9/1
Arizona*	7.1/1	22.2/1
Arkansas	3.4/1	10.7/1
California	7.9/1	24.6/1
Colorado*	6.3/1	11.4/1
Connecticut*	6.3/1	5.7/1
Delaware	1.7/1	5.5/1
Florida	1.8/1	9.3/1
Georgia	2.0/1	4.7/1
Hawaii*†	1.3/1	
Idaho*	6.6/1	3.0/1
Illinois*	5.9/1	20.1/1
Indiana	2.6/1	17.4/1
Iowa	2.0/1	5.2/1
Kansas	3.2/1	182.8/1
Kentucky	2.6/1	8.6/1
Louisiana*	1.8/1	13.5/1
Maine	9.1/1	11.2/1
Maryland	1.6/1	2.8/1
Massachusetts	9.3/1	10.4/1
Michigan	3.1/1	30.0/1
Minnesota	4.0/1	5.2/1
Mississippi	2.6/1	5.2/1
Missouri*	9.1/1	29.6/1
Montana	18.2/1	3.1/1
Nebraska	12.4/1	19.0/1
Nevada*	2.2/1	4.0/1
New Hampshire	4.8/1	4.5/1
New Jersey	5.9/1	10.5/1
New Mexico	2.5/1	21.4/1
New York	11.4/1	84.2/1
North Carolina	1.6/1	3.2/1
North Dakota*	24.0/1	1.7/1
Ohio	4.1/1	10.7/1
Oklahoma	29.7/1	22.4/1
Oregon	11.4/1	5.3/1
Pennsylvania	7.9/1	10.5/1
Rhode Island	2.3/1	2.2/1
South Carolina	1.5/1	8.8/1
South Dakota	34.2/1	9.7/1
Tennessee	2.5/1	9.5/1
Texas*	56.2/1	45.1/1
Utah	2.8/1	8.6/1
Vermont	4.2/1	3.3/1
Virginia	2.6/1	6.8/1
Washington	9.2/1	12.5/1
West Virginia	1.4/1	3.6/1
Wisconsin	3.4/1	77.9/1
Wyoming*	26.2/1	6.1/1

* Locally assessed valuation is used for these states. Otherwise, equalized assessed valuation is used.

† Property tax revenues not used to support education.

Source: A Commission Staff Report submitted to the President's Commission on School Finance, *Review of Existing State School Finance Programs, Volume II, Documentation of Disparities in the Financing of Public Elementary and Secondary School Systems—By State* (Washington: U.S. Government Printing Office, 1972).

in various trade skills. In fact, expenditures for such technical education tend to benefit primarily those who are in a lower income status. A concerted effort was made at the federal government level during the Kennedy and Johnson Administrations of the 1960s to promote this type of education for the poor. The first national program to retrain the unemployed took the form of the *Manpower Development and Training Act of 1962*. Moreover, various aspects of the *Economic Opportunity Act of 1964* were also directed toward this purpose.

Indeed, even though the reduction of poverty may be approached in the short run via government tax and transfer payments, as will be described later in this chapter, the *more fundamental* educational approach for the alleviation of poverty involves what is essentially a long-run allocational technique. If the formal and technical education of the poor were increased in quantity and quality, for example, the incomes of the poor would tend to increase during subsequent years. The allocation of additional productive resources to education in the short run would thus contribute to the elimination of poverty in the long run.

Relatedly, the elimination of *job discrimination* would help to eliminate poverty in the United States. As Thurow states:[25]

> No program to raise incomes through raising education will succeed unless other measures are also taken. Raising functional literacy standards to eighth or tenth grade standards may be an important ingredient in raising incomes but the effects will not be apparent unless it is combined with training opportunities and job opportunities. *Eliminating discrimination is necessary if Negro education is to have a significant effect* [italics provided]. As long as there is discrimination, more education produces little payoff.

Job discrimination may be either "educational" or "racial" in nature. Unquestionably, *racial discrimination*, as well as *educational discrimination* in the sense of poor people in general being unable financially to acquire adequate education, are costly to both the individual and to the nation. For example, the Council of Economic Advisors stated that during 1965 "if Negroes also had the same educational attainment as white workers, and earned the same pay, and experienced the same unemployment as whites, their personal income . . . and that of the Nation . . . would be $20.6 billion higher."[26] The significant variation between the unemployment rates of *white* and *nonwhite* Americans is demonstrated in Table 21–6.

Thus, it is concluded that redistributional measures of a tax-transfer

---

[25] Lester C. Thurow, *Poverty and Discrimination* (© 1969 by the Brookings Institution, Washington, D.C.), p. 157.

[26] *Report*, Council of Economic Advisors, March 26, 1965.

TABLE 21-6
Unemployment Rates by Color, 1948–72 (in percentages)

Year	White	Nonwhite
1948.	3.5%	5.9%
1949.	5.6	8.9
1950.	4.9	9.0
1951.	3.1	5.3
1952.	2.8	5.4
1953.	2.7	4.5
1954.	5.0	9.9
1955.	3.9	8.7
1956.	3.6	8.3
1957.	3.8	7.9
1958.	6.1	12.6
1959.	4.8	10.7
1960.	4.9	10.2
1961.	6.0	12.4
1962.	4.9	10.9
1963.	5.0	10.8
1964.	4.6	9.6
1965.	4.1	8.1
1966.	3.4	7.3
1967.	3.4	7.4
1968.	3.2	6.7
1969.	3.1	6.4
1970.	4.5	8.2
1971.	5.4	9.9
1972.	5.0	10.0

Source: Bureau of Labor Statistics, U.S. Department of Labor.

nature to mitigate poverty will not entirely solve the problem. Any rational approach to the subject must also encompass an attack on the basic causes of poverty. Although improved education and job opportunities would be a primary focal point of such an attack, the importance of the availability to the poor of such important consumptive items as *health services* cannot be underestimated. A brief discussion of health services availability, as affected by national government policies, in the United States and certain other Western industrial nations is provided below.

National Health Care Systems—An International Comparison. The public sector of the United States assures the availability of health services for a significantly *lower proportion* of its citizens than most, if not all, other industralized nations in the Western world. Table 21–7 helps to demonstrate this fact. Moreover, that coverage which is available comes essentially under the *medicare* and *medicaid* components of the Social Security Program which dates only from the mid-1960s. Although a *comprehensive* national health care program has been dis-

TABLE 21–7
Coverage of Residents Under National Health
Care Systems, Selected Nations, 1973

Nation	*Percentage*
Australia	100
Austria	92
Canada	99
France	98
Germany (West)	90
Netherlands	70
New Zealand	100
Sweden	100
United Kingdom	100
United States	23

cussed in the United States for several decades, no such program has been enacted. However, a resurgence of interest in the notion of an assured acceptable level of health services for all citizens seems apparent during the first half of the 1970s.

Tax-Transfer Programs for the Alleviation of Poverty

The Redistributional Effects of Existing Tax-Transfer Programs. Income can be redistributed for the purpose of alleviating poverty through the taxation and transfer expenditure activities of the public sector fisc.[27] Such budgetary activities do not directly influence resource allocation as do resource-absorbing exhaustive expenditures. Instead, they directly affect the disposable income of various members of the society through the *pattern* of "tax burdens" and "transfer benefits" which is imposed.[28] Importantly, the ultimate *direct incidence* of these budgetary burdens and benefits must be viewed on a *net basis*, that is, the tax burden of each individual must be weighed against the transfer spending benefits which accrue to that individual in order to judge whether the fiscal redistributional process has increased or decreased the economic welfare of the individual. Moreover, the possibility of tax shifting must be considered in evaluating the ultimate locus of any tax burden. A casual observation of the point of tax impact alone could be very misleading.[29]

The existing *federal* personal income and payroll taxes along with

---

[27] See the relevant discussion of the *symmetrical* character of governmental budgets in Chapters 6 and 8.

[28] However, these *direct* changes in disposable income will *indirectly* affect the pattern of effective demand and thus, also, the pattern of resource-absorbing expenditures in the society.

[29] The concept of tax shifting is analytically developed in Chapter 8.

the major federal transfer expenditure programs exert somewhat modest income redistribution effects among the American people. Table
21–8 demonstrates this fact. It may be observed that the lowest 20
percent of the population which receives 1.7 percent of the total income prior to these federal taxes and transfers receives only 6.3 percent
after the taxes and transfers. Meanwhile, the highest 20 percent of the
population which receives 53.1 percent of the total income before the
federal taxes and transfers still receives 47.1 percent of the total disposable income afterwards.

TABLE 21–8
Combined Effect of Federal Personal Income and Payroll Taxes and Transfer Payments on the Distribution of Income, 1972

	Percentage Distribution			
Income Quintile	*Total Income before Taxes and Transfers* (1)	*Total Individual Income and Pay-roll Taxes Paid* (2)	*Cash Transfers Received** (3)	*Total Income after Taxes and Transfers* (4)
Lowest 20.	1.7	1.1	40.2	6.3
20 to 40	6.6	5.0	26.8	9.1
40 to 60	14.5	13.3	13.1	14.6
60 to 80	24.1	22.8	10.3	22.8
80 to 100	53.1	57.9	9.6	47.1
Total	100.0	100.0	100.0	100.0

* Includes old age, survivors, and disability insurance, unemployment and workmen's compensation,
public and general assistance (welfare), veterans' benefits, and military retired pay.
Source: Based on the Brookings MERGE file of family units with incomes projected to calendar year 1972
levels. Figures may not add to totals because of rounding. These data appear in Edward R. Fried, Alice M.
Rivlin, Charles L. Schultze, and Nancy H. Teeters, *Setting National Priorities: The 1974 Budget* (© 1973 by
the Brookings Institution, Washington, D.C.), Table 3–5, p. 50.

Furthermore, the tax-transfer effects on income distribution of the
entire public sector's budgetary activity, just like that of the federal
government noted above, is modest. Table 21–9, for example, shows
that during 1968 the *"net* tax burden," after adjustment for transfer
benefits received, averaged 25.6 percent of total income for income
groups with up to $2,000 annual income and only 33.6 percent of total
income for those in the $25,000–50,000 annual income range. Thus,
even though those taxpayers with above $50,000 annual incomes are
estimated to bear an average "net tax burden" of 46.6 percent of total
income, the overall public sector redistributional influence on the complete range of income classes would appear to be properly classified as

TABLE 21-9
Net Tax Burden* of the American Public Sector, by
Income Class, 1968

Income Class	Taxes Paid as Percentage of Total Income
under $2,000	25.6
2,000– 4,000	24.7
4,000– 6,000	27.9
6,000– 8,000	30.1
8,000–10,000	29.9
10,000–15,000	30.9
15,000–25,000	31.1
25,000–50,000	33.6
50,000 and over	46.6
Total	31.6

* Taxas as percentage of total income after adjustment for transfer payment benefits.
Source: Roger A. Herriot and Herman P. Miller, "Changes in the Distribution of Taxes Among Income Groups: 1962–1968," *American Statistical Association—1971 Proceedings of the Business and Economic Statistics Section*, Table 3, p. 108.

"modest." The remainder of this chapter will evaluate the widely discussed concept of the *negative income tax* as a possible "tax-transfer" means of further mitigating poverty in the United States.

The Proposed Federal Negative Income Tax as a Poverty-Alleviation Technique

The Negative Income Tax Concept. The decade of the 1960s and the early 1970s have witnessed an active interest in American society for the possible adoption of a *federal government-guaranteed income* device to eliminate poverty in the United States. However, the genesis of this idea in American society is not new. In 1933, for example, a California physician named Francis Townsend received considerable national publicity (and criticism) for his suggestion that the public sector pay $200 per month to all aged persons. Under the *Townsend* plan, each recipient would be required to spend the $200 within 30 days. Hence, the Townsend Plan had both a "distributional" objective—to alleviate poverty for the aged—and also a "stabilization" objective—to increase spending during a period of depression. Though never adopted, historians credit the Townsend proposal with a major "assist" to the passage of the Social Security Act in 1935. This legislation, among other things, resulted in the present pattern of inefficient "public assistance" transfers which center around the Aid for Families with Dependent Children (AFDC) program. More recent recommendations for a new income-maintenance approach to alleviate poverty have taken the form of the *negative income tax* concept. Prominent proposals for a federal negative income tax include those by Milton Friedman, Robert Lampman, Robert Theobald, and James Tobin.[30]

Since the 1960s, comprehensive interest could be detected on a national basis for the use of a federal government "guaranteed income" technique in the form of a *negative income* tax to alleviate poverty. Under this concept, an individual is considered to be capable of making "positive" tax contributions to government if his personal income exceeds poverty-level proportions, but is considered as eligible to receive the "negative" transfer of funds from the government if his personal income is below a designated poverty-level of income. Since both "tax" and "transfer payments" are nonresource-absorbing fiscal activities, a transfer payment may appropriately be considered as a "negative tax," that is, the government transfers funds to an individual rather than exacting them from the individual in the form of a tax.

The reasoning behind the proposed extension of the negative income tax concept to the presently-existing federal personal income tax structure includes the basic fact that an individual with little or no income would be unable to take advantage of otherwise available (to people with greater income) personal exemptions and personal deductions. Thus, it may be viewed that the individual is being doubly penalized by being poor unless monetarily compensated by the government in the form of a negative tax payment.

The negative income tax could be used either as a replacement for various presently-existing federal welfare and educational antipoverty programs or as a supplement to such programs. It should be observed that many of the 25.5 million poor people in the United States today receive little or no assistance under present programs. Those "unassisted" by such programs are primarily the "working poor" who work at very low wages or work irregularly and, in addition, those families who would be eligible under present programs, but who have not taken advantage of them due to either "ignorance" or the "indignity" of being on relief. Certainly, one distinct advantage of the negative in-

---

[30] See Milton Friedman, *Capitalism and Freedom* (Chicago: University of Chicago Press, 1962), chap. 12, and also his "The Case for the Negative Income Tax: A View from the Right," Chamber of Commerce of the United States, *Proceedings of the National Symposium on the Guaranteed Income*, December 1966, pp. 49–55. See also Robert J. Lampman, "Prognosis for Poverty," *Proceedings of the Fifty-Seventh Annual Conference of the National Tax Association*, 1964, pp. 71–81, and his "Approaches to the Reduction of Poverty," *American Economic Review*, May 1965, pp. 521–29, and his "Negative Rates Income Taxation," Office of Economic Opportunity, 1965 (unpublished paper); Robert Theobald, *Free Men and Free Markets* (New York: Clarkson N. Potter, Inc., 1963); James Tobin, "Improving the Economic Status of the Negro," *Daedalus*, Fall 1965, pp. 889–95, and his "The Case for an Income Guarantee," *The Public Interest*, Summer 1966; James Tobin, Joseph Pechman, and Peter Mieszkowski, "Is a Negative Income Tax Practical?" *Yale Law Journal*, November 1967, pp. 1–27.

come tax concept for the alleviation of poverty is that it minimizes the embarrassing "means" test for assistance. An individual or family would receive the negative tax payment on the basis of citizenship within the United States. Moreover, this concept possesses the advantage of compensating for the considerable interstate differences in fiscal capacities among the 50 states which helps to cause vastly unequal welfare programs at the present time. A rational negative income tax program, of course, should not preclude training and other assistance intended to encourage individuals to work and thus obtain greater positive income themselves. However, there are many instances when it is either very difficult, or impossible, for individuals to increase their incomes.

Although a 100 percent negative income tax would tend to cause labor disincentives, the structure of such a tax is exhibited in Figure 21–4 in order to graphically illustrate the *basic notion* of a negative personal income tax. Variations of the basic notion, of course, are feasible and, as the discussion below demonstrates, the negative tax can be designed to better preserve work incentives. In Figure 21–4, the "pov-

FIGURE 21–4

Example of 100 Percent Negative Income Tax below Poverty Level Income of $4,000*

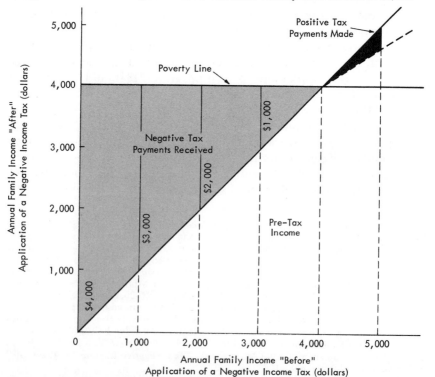

* Based on pretax income for family of four.

erty level of income" for a family of four is assumed to be a $4,000 annual income. Thus, if the pretax annual family income is below the $4,000 poverty line at $1,000, negative income tax payments would amount to $3,000; if the family income before the tax is $2,000, the negative tax payments would be $2,000, and so on. In the event that family income exceeds $4,000 annually, the negative tax payments cease and the taxpaying unit becomes subject to a positive personal income tax obligation by which it will make tax payments rather than receive them.

Poverty Alleviation, Work Effort, and Revenue Yield Aspects of the Negative Income Tax. If the negative income tax example demonstrated in Figure 21–4 is "redesigned" to allow for a protection of *work incentives*, tradeoffs necessarily arise between this goal and two other objectives, namely, the goal of *poverty-alleviation* itself and the degree of *revenue loss* incurred by the governmental treasury.[31] Figure 21–5, which is clearly is more complicated than Figure 21–4, shows these inevitable tradeoffs which occur between the primary objective of a negative income tax, the mitigation of poverty, and the preservation of labor incentives and governmental revenues.

In this graph, the 45-degree angle line *OEA* represents "no income taxation," either positive or negative. Meanwhile, line *OEB*, along its *EB* segment, represents a positive income tax above the $4,000 poverty-income level for a family of four. The main objective of a negative income tax in alleviating poverty is to change the situation to the left of point *E*, that is, to help those families with pretransfer (prenegative income tax) incomes of less than $4,000. This can be accomplished in a number of ways.

For example, line *DEB* could be applied—thus constituting along its *DE* segment a *100 percent* negative income tax, such as was also exemplified in the previous graph (Figure 21–4). However, this would destroy the incentive to earn income below $4,000 since that amount of disposable income is assured to the taxpayer by the 100 percent negative tax rate. Thus, if the taxpayer earns:

Pretransfer Income		Negative Tax Payment		Posttransfer Disposable Income
$4,000	he will receive	$ 0	=	$4,000
3,000		1,000	=	4,000
2,000		2,000	=	4,000
1,000		3,000	=	4,000
0		4,000	=	4,000

---

[31] The discussion of the three-way negative income tax interaction between *work incentives, poverty-alleviation,* and *revenue losses* which follows is based largely on the analysis presented in: Joseph A. Kershaw, with the assistance of Paul N. Courant, *Government Against Poverty* (© 1970 by the Brookings Institution, Washington, D.C.), chapter six.

Figure 21–5

Negative Income Tax Tradeoffs between Poverty-Alleviation, Work Incentives, and Governmental Revenue Losses*

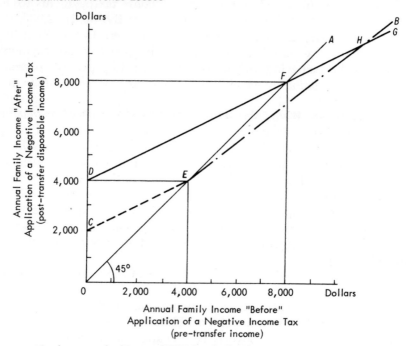

* Based on poverty-level income of $4,000 for a family of four.

Source: Based on Figure 1 in Joseph A. Kershaw, with the assistance of Paul N. Courant, *Government Against Poverty* (© 1970 by the Brookings Institution, Washington, D.C.), p. 114.

Under these conditions, a $4,000 disposable income is assured regardless of the amount of pretransfer income earned by the taxpayer.

If, on the other hand, the negative income tax is applied at a rate below 100 percent, some work incentives can be preserved. In Figure 21–5, this is depicted along the *CE* segment of line *CEB* which represents a *50 percent* negative income tax rate. Importantly, the upward slope of *CE* assures the retention of some work incentives since the more the taxpayer earns himself, the larger will be his posttransfer disposable income. Thus, if the taxpayer earns:

Pretransfer Income		Negative Tax Payment		Posttransfer Disposable Income
$4,000	he will receive	$ 0	=	$4,000
3,000		500	=	3,500
2,000		1,000	=	3,000
1,000		1,500	=	2,500
0		2,000	=	2,000

Hence, the *50 percent* negative income tax has assured the taxpayer of receiving a negative tax payment amounting to *one half* of the deficit between the $4,000 poverty income line and the pretransfer income of the taxpayer. However, the partial preservation of work incentives accomplished by the "less than 100 percent" negative income tax rate is achieved via a tradeoff resulting in a lower degree of poverty-alleviation. For example, the $3,000 pretransfer income taxpayer would possess $3,500 rather than $4,000 in disposable income after the negative income tax payment has been received.

A possible variation of the negative income tax, intended to counteract the above conflict between poverty protection and work incentives, would be to raise the limit for receiving negative tax payments from $4,000 to *$8,000* along with the imposition of a *50 percent* negative income tax rate. This arrangement is represented by line *DFG*. Thus, if the taxpayer earns:

Pretransfer Income		Negative Tax Payment		Posttransfer Disposable Income
$8,000	he will receive	$ 0	=	$8,000
7,000		500	=	7,500
6,000		1,000	=	7,000
5,000		1,500	=	6,500
4,000		2,000	=	6,000
3,000		2,500	=	5,500
2,000		3,000	=	5,000
1,000		3,500	=	4,500
0		4,000	=	4,000

The following observations may be made regarding this form of negative income tax:

1. No taxpayer would have a posttransfer disposable income less than the $4,000 poverty-level income—thus effectively *mitigating poverty.*
2. *Work incentives* would be protected since the greater the income earned by the taxpayer up to $8,000, the receipt of a negative tax payment will leave him with more disposable income than if he had earned less. Graphically, this is depicted by segment *DF* of the *DFG* curve, which is "upward sloping" in contrast to the "horizontal *DE* segment of the pure 100 percent negative income tax which destroys labor incentives.
3. *Revenue Losses* to the government from the operation of the negative income tax program would be significantly increased since
   a. Taxpayers between points *E* and *F* with incomes between $4,000 and $8,000, and who were not previously defined as poor, now receive some negative income tax payments even though they previously had paid some taxes.

b. Those nonpoor taxpayers between points F and H will pay lower positive taxes than before.

c. The poor, those to the left of point E, would receive transfers larger than those required to rise above the $4,000 poverty-level income (except those poor with no income). However, the effect on those with higher incomes would be generally less than those with lower incomes since the DFG and CEB lines converge.

It may be concluded from the above that it is difficult to attain *poverty elimination* through a negative income tax while at the same time fully *avoiding work disincentives* and fully *maintaining adequate revenue yields* for government. There will be substantial revenue loss to government if all taxpayers are assured a $4,000 disposable income while work incentives are protected (line DF). Yet, if revenues are to be preserved along line EB, either work incentives must be harmed as poverty is eliminated along line DE, or poverty will not be eliminated as work incentives are protected along line CE. However, a "compromise" program can be designed which will yield some positive results in terms of each of these three subgoals.

National Government Responsibility in Poverty Alleviation.   As observed in the previous chapters on fiscal federalism, the national (central) government of a federation holds an economic efficiency advantage over subnational governments in performing the *distribution* function of the public sector. However, even though the federal government would thus assume primary responsibility for undertaking redistributional policies in the American federation, a role still can be performed by lower-level American governments (as will be observed below). In the context of federal government responsibility for poverty-alleviation, the late President Johnson appointed a special *Presidential Commission on Income Maintenance* in 1968. In turn, the special Commission filed a highly-publicized report in 1969 (to President Nixon) which, in essence, recommended the adoption of a federal *negative income tax system*.[32] This system would have provided for cash payments to all members of the society with basic income needs. These payments, which would vary by family size, would be available also to single people and childless couples. They would be structured so as to protect some work incentives by providing significantly higher incomes for those who work as opposed to those who do not. The ultimate goal would be to eliminate all presently existing welfare programs of the conditional grant variety based on a "means test." This would include

---

[32] *Poverty amid Plenty: The American Paradox*, Report of the President's Commission on Income Maintenance Programs (Washington, D.C.: U.S. Government Printing Office, 1970).

elimination of the controversial aid for families with dependent children (AFDC) program. Specifically, the Presidential Commission suggested that a minimum annual income of $2,400 be guaranteed to a family of four people. The emphasis would be on cash payments rather than upon income-in-kind. The report opposed differentials in the minimum income based on regional variations in living costs. Moreover, it opposed the use of day-care centers which, by contrast, were included in the income maintenance system proposed, also in 1969, by the Nixon administration.

The proposed Nixon Administration income maintenance program, which was known as the *Family Assistance Plan*, eventually was approved by the House of Representatives, but it never became law due to lack of support in the Senate as well as to an eventual weakened endorsement for the plan by the Nixon Administration itself. The main features of the plan were as follows:

1. Direct payments would be made by the federal government to all families with incomes below a stipulated level who have minor children.
2. The system of payments would include both "working-poor" families, in which the head of the family is a male employed full time, and "dependent" families whose head is either a female or an unemployed father. The former category would be newly included in a major federal support program.
3. The basic federal benefit for a family of four would be $1,600 per year. This would include $500 per person for the first two family members and $300 per person for each subsequent family member. Thus, a family of four with no income would receive $1,600 while a seven-person family with no income would receive $2,500.
4. The system would be devised to protect work incentives by allowing benefits to continue on a diminishing basis as earnings increase. Thus, a family of four would be eligible for some benefits up to an income level of $3,920 under the program and a family of seven would be eligible up to an earnings level of $5,720. That is, benefits are reduced by 50 percent as earnings increase above $720 per year, up to a stipulated cutoff point.
5. The Family Assistance Plan would be coordinated with the Food Stamp Program, so that the benefits under the two programs would be additive.
6. The proposed program would emphasize work since all employable recipients must accept employment or training or lose their portion of the family benefits. This includes mothers except for those with children under six. Training opportunities would be provided for an additional 150,000 mothers, and child-care services would be

provided for an additional 450,000 children in families headed by welfare mothers.

The proposed Family Assistance Plan was neither a pure negative income tax nor, as its name might erroneously suggest, a pure family allowance plan. "Family allowance payments," also known as "children's allowances," consist of regular cash payments from the government to families with minor children.[33] This specialized income-maintenance device is used in more than 60 nations of the world. In fact, all Western industrial nations except the United States have a program of "direct" family allowance payments.[34] These result in a redistribution of income toward the child-rearing portion of a nation's population.

The family allowance (children's allowance) approach to income maintenance differs from the negative income tax (income guarantee) approach in several significant ways. The negative income tax, for example, aims primarily at the reduction of poverty. The "pure" family allowance technique, on the other hand, aims primarily at the improvement of child welfare, though secondary income effects are present. The negative income tax is paid to all impoverished citizens including single persons and married couples without children. Family allowances, however, are paid only to families with minor children. Negative income tax payments are provided only to the poor, but family allowance payments are paid to high-income as well as to poor families— though some plans would later tax these allowances under the income tax structure.

Overall, the Nixon Administration *Family Assistance Plan* appears to have contained more of the basic traits of the "pure" *negative income tax* approach than it does of the "pure" family allowance approach. Indeed, it might be termed a "negative income tax for families." For example, though excluding benefits to impoverished childless couples and unmarried individuals, it does focus upon the income support of those impoverished families with children. Moreover, the benefits under the proposed Family Assistance Plan would have been received only by *poor* families, *not* by *all* families as under the "pure" family allowance (children's allowance) as used in many other nations.

By late 1974, the United States still did not have a comprehensive

---

[33] See the following analyses of family allowance programs including those proposed for use in the United States: Clair Wilcox, *Toward Social Welfare* (Homewood, Ill.: Richard D. Irwin, Inc. 1969), chap. 15; Dorothy S. Projector, "Children's Allowance and Welfare Reform Proposals: Costs and Redistributive Effects," *Proceedings—National Tax Association—1969,* pp. 303–28; and Robert J. Lampman, "Transfer Approaches to Distribution Policy," *American Economic Review,* May 1970, pp. 270–79.

[34] The "Aid for Families with Dependent Children" (AFDC) welfare payments in the United States do not constitute "family allowances" in the present context.

approach which would assure the mitigation of poverty for all of its citizens. The failure in this regard must be placed mainly at the federal level of government where the comparative advantage rests for the direction of redistributional policy. Relatedly, the widely-acknowledged failure of the Aid for Families with Dependent Children (AFDC) program may be largely explained by its excessive decentralization and lack of national government direction. A federal government negative income tax, as discussed above, would not be subject to this problem. Moreover, the existing "positive" income tax machinery could be utilized as the basis for implementing a new "negative" income tax.

Nonetheless, Congress did enact little publicized legislation in late 1972, to be effective in January 1974, for a new federal government program which would subsume into its operation more than 1,000 state-local government programs for assistance to the blind, totally disabled, and needy-aged over 65 years of age. This new federal program will provide guaranteed income payments by the end of 1974 to 6.5 million Americans. The new program, known as the Supplemental Security Income (SSI) program, is not financed out of the Social Security Trust Fund and many Americans will be eligible for both regular social security as well as the new SSI payments. Thus, along with existing social security benefits, the new program will yield a *guaranteed annual income* of $1,752 for a blind, disabled, or needy person over age 65, and $2,592 for a needy couple. Accordingly, this segment of the population will be additionally protected against poverty. However, the main "welfare problem" based on the inefficient "Aid for Families with Dependent Children" program will unfortunately remain. Yet, another new tool for poverty-relief—the *federal food stamp program*—which now helps some 13 million poor Americans to obtain food, will offer some potentially important additional poverty-alleviation effects.

Finally, it should be noted that state governments can also play a useful role in alleviating poverty even though the primary responsibility for such policies rests with the *federal* government. Certainly, states can encourage the flow of resources toward fundamental quasi-national public goods which help to reduce poverty. This is especially true for those goods characterized by substantial intergovernmental spillover effects at the local level of government—such as public elementary and secondary education. Also, state governments can usefully involve themselves in certain "tax-transfer programs" including *personal income tax credits and rebates* for sales and property tax payments made by *low-income* and, in particular, low-income *elderly* taxpayers. This amounts to a limited form of *state negative income tax*, as will be explained below.

State Tax Relief Programs for Low-Income Taxpayers. State governments offer a number of tax policies which reduce the tax burdens of low-income taxpayers. For example, as of July 1, 1973, each of the 50 states offered some form of *property tax relief* for "elderly" taxpayers —a segment of the population containing many poor people due, among other things, to the extreme vulnerability of fixed incomes to inflation. Three and one-half years earlier, on January 1, 1970, only 28 states possessed such property tax relief programs. One of the most attractive fiscal devices used for this purpose is the so-called *circuit-breaker* system used by 21 states.[35] This technique gets its name from the electrical device that cuts off electricity when an electrical circuit is overloaded. Circuit-breaker property tax relief normally "cuts in" when the property tax percentage of family income for the elderly reaches a specified proportion defined by the state government as the "point of overload."

Most of the state-financed property tax circuit-breaker systems allow for *rebate* payments from the state government to homeowners and renters. In effect, a rebate amounts to a tax credit against the state personal income tax liability of the taxpayer which, if the credit exceeds the amount of personal income tax owed, makes the elderly taxpayer eligible to receive a cash payment from the state. This constitutes, in practice, the payment of a *negative income tax* by the state government to the elderly taxpayer. Several states offer similar personal income tax credits for the payment of *sales taxes*, well recognized for their regressivity in ability-to-pay terms, by low-income taxpayers (not necessarily elderly). Finally, a number of states also attack sales tax regressivity by exempting food and-or medicine from the base of the sales tax.[36] In any case, state government tax relief policies such as those described here help to reduce the overall *regressive incidence* of state and local government tax structures. Such regressivity was demonstrated by Tables 8–1 and 8–2 in Chapter Eight.

Concluding Remarks

It is beyond the scope of this book to provide a comprehensive appraisal of the advantages and disadvantages of each possible income-maintenance policy. Moreover, it is beyond the scope of the book to offer an ideal program for the elimination of poverty in the United States. Nonetheless, it does not appear presumptive to conclude that the United States, the would's richest nation, following a societal consensus, should eliminate poverty within its borders. Poverty for any of its citizens seems intolerable in a nation characterized by a gross national product well in excess of $1 trillion. It is in this spirit that the

---

[35] See Advisory Commission on Intergovernmental Relations (ACIR), Information Bulletin No. 73–6, *Circuit-Breaker Updated: Amazing Gains Since January* (Washington, D.C.: ACIR, 1973), p. 2.

[36] See Chapter 14.

following six "guidelines" for poverty elimination are offered. However, these are merely benchmarks and do not constitute in themselves a comprehensive plan for the elimination of American poverty. The six reference points to guide poverty-elimination policies are:

1. Any program for poverty elimination should be "eclectic" in nature. That is, it should be a multiple- or many-faceted program which utilizes a variety of techniques. This approach is necessary because poverty itself has "many sides" and "many causes." An eclectic attack on poverty should thus include both a basic income-maintenance program of the tax-transfer variety, which sets a reasonable minimum "above-poverty-level" income for all citizens, and also specific resource-allocation programs in such functional areas as education, health, and housing.

2. Either of the two primary income-maintenance approaches (negative income tax or family allowances), or a hybrid income-maintenance approach, and any reasonably efficient specific approach for the provision to the poor of such an economic good as education, seem preferable to a policy of "inaction." In other words, the budgetary priority for poverty elimination seems great enough to justify effective action, even though it may not be the most efficient possible action, because time does not permit a thorough comparison of all alternative approaches. Moreover, experience itself can only provide the answer to some important questions. Thus, a rationally implemented initial program may be expected to provide the empirical basis for a subsequently improved, and more efficient, program at a later date.

3. It is necessary that discrimination be eliminated if programs such as those for the improvement of education for poor and minority groups are to be fully effective.

4. All programs directed toward the elimination of poverty, whether of the tax or expenditure variety, should be coordinated with each other in a cohesive overall plan. Also, even though the federal government should bear the primary responsibility for redistributional policy, subnational governments—especially states—can play a useful role.

5. Any set of programs directed toward the elimination of poverty should emphasize the "right" of Americans to live under nonpoverty conditions. The "means" test should be deemphasized in light of the new emphasis on the "right" of all citizens to a basic acceptable living standard.

6. Any set of programs directed toward the elimination of poverty should be designed so as to encourage the incentive to work and to achieve self-betterment.

Finally, it may be observed that the decade of the 1970s finds Americans seriously concerned with a variety of domestic and international problems. It may be safe to predict that the strength of the American

Republic at the end of this decade may well depend largely upon the effectiveness of the policy approaches directed toward the solution of these problems. In this context, it seems reasonable to observe that no single issue is more important to the improvement of American society than the eradication of poverty for all American citizens.

22

The Public Sector in Other Nations

THE PUBLIC SECTOR UNDER CAPITALISM AND SOCIALISM

As observed in Part One of this book, two primary institutions exist for the purpose of performing the basic functions of an economic system. These institutions are the *market* and the *government*. Though no economy in the world follows a purely market nor a purely governmental approach in the solution of its allocational, distributional, stabilization, and economic growth functions, every economy is basically oriented toward one or the other of these polar extremes. Thus, certain economies which depend primarily upon the price system for their functional economic performance are termed *capitalist* economies while others which stress the governmental approach are called *socialist* economies. Though the four basic economic functions which must be performed are common to each system, the means of performing them often varies considerably between capitalist and socialist political economies. Some of the more important similarities and differences between the two systems in their public sector budgetary behavior may now be observed.

Expenditures

As would be expected, *public sector expenditures* as a ratio of some measure of aggregate economic performance, such as *national income,* tend to be larger under socialist than under capitalist politico-economic structures.[1] This fact is demonstrated in Table 22–1 which shows that during 1971 public expenditures were 54 percent of national income in the Soviet Union (USSR) and 38 percent in the United States.[2] One of the major reasons for this differential is the fact that *investment* is largely governmental in character under socialism while it is largely private in nature in capitalist systems. In addition, the composition of governmental expenditures varies between the two systems in the sense that transfer expenditures for *redistributional* purposes are more important to public sector budgets under capitalism than under socialism. This is true because the basic decentralization in decision-making under a capitalist system, and the greater emphasis on private property, combine to yield a more unequal distribution of income and wealth than is the case in a socialist system. Hence, the need for value judgment-determined redistributional policies through the public sector fisc is greater under capitalism.

TABLE 22–1
Public Sector Expenditures, United States and Soviet Union, and Ratio to National Income, 1971

Nation	Expenditures (in billions)	National Income (in billions)	Expenditures as Percent of National Income
United States*	369 dollars	963 dollars	38
Soviet Union†	164 rubles	304 rubles	54

* Includes federal, state, and local government expenditures.
† Includes the expenditures of both the USSR and the Ukrainian SSR.
Source: *United Nations Statistical Yearbook—1972;* U.S. Department of Commerce.

In terms of specific items of expenditure, it is interesting to note the following additional points of comparison in the composition of public sector spending between the United States and the Soviet Union during 1971. First, direct governmental expenditures for *national defense* constituted 7 percent of national income in the United States and 6 percent in the Soviet Union. Secondly, expenditures for *education* by the public sector were 8 percent of national income in the United States and 9

---

[1] The data provided in this chapter for the distinction between the public sector of capitalist and socialist nations will focus upon the United States and the Soviet Union as the respective examples of each system. However, many of the same basic points of comparison would hold if additional national examples of each system were selected. For more comprehensive data, see Richard A. Musgrave, *Fiscal Systems* (New Haven, Conn.: Yale University Press, 1969).

[2] However, these general data probably understate the relative economic influence of government between the two nations since they do not fully account for major structural differences in the economic institutions of the nations. In other words, the true differential of governmental influence probably exceeds the "16 percent differential" indicated in Table 22–1.

percent in the Soviet Union. Thirdly, both the American and Soviet public sectors spent 3 percent of national income for *public health* purposes during 1971.

Revenues

The revenue structures of capitalist and socialist systems reveal several important differences. Again, as with governmental expenditures, public sector revenues comprise a larger percentage of national income under socialism than under capitalism. This is exemplified for the United States and the Soviet Union in Table 22–2. Thus, total governmental revenues comprised 55 percent of national income in the Soviet Union and 36 percent in the United States during 1971. In terms of the composition of public sector revenues, *direct taxes* assume a much more significant role under capitalism than under socialism while the *state's*

TABLE 22–2
Public Sector Revenues, United States and Soviet Union, and Ratio to National Income, 1971

Nation	Public Sector Revenues (in billions)	National Income (in billions)	Revenues as Percent of National Income
United States*	343 dollars	963 dollars	36
Soviet Union†	166 rubles	304 rubles	55

* Includes federal, state, and local government revenues.
† Includes the revenues of both the USSR and the Ukrainian SSR.
Source: *United Nations Statistical Yearbook—1972;* U.S. Department of Commerce.

share in public enterprise profits, a primary governmental revenue source in socialist systems such as the Soviet Union, is not an important source of governmental revenue in capitalist systems such as the United States. These phenomena are demonstrated for the two nations in Tables 22–3 and 22–4, respectively.

In Table 22–3, it may be seen that "direct" taxation, which is defined to include such taxes as income, payroll, property, death, gift, and motor vehicle license taxes, comprises 82 percent of total "tax" revenues in the United States. This leaves only 18 percent of the total for indirect taxes such as sales and gross receipts, excise, and import taxes. On the other hand, an "indirect" tax of the excise variety, known as the *turnover tax,* yields 33 percent of all budget receipts in the Soviet Union.[3]

The above differences in revenue levels as a proportion of national

---

[3] See Table 22–4.

TABLE 22-3
Direct and Indirect Taxes as a Proportion of Total Public Sector
Tax Revenues, United States, 1971

	Billions of Dollars	Percent of Total
All public sector taxes...............	290	100
Direct taxes*.......................	237	82
Indirect taxes†	53	18

* *Direct* taxes are defined to include income, payroll, property, death, gift, and motor vehicle license taxes.
† *Indirect* taxes are defined to include general sales and gross receipts, excise, and import taxes.
Source: U.S. Department of Commerce.

TABLE 22-4
Composition of Total Budget Receipts, Soviet Union, 1971*

Type of Receipt	Billions of Rubles	Percent of Total
Turnover tax..........................	54	33
Share in profits of state enterprises......	56	33
Taxes from population	14	9
Other receipts	42	25
TOTAL RECEIPTS................	166	100

* Includes the revenues of both the USSR and the Ukrainian SSR.
Source: *United Nations Statistical Yearbook—1972.*

income, as well as the composition of revenues between the two systems, reflect the fundamental *conceptual differences* which exist concerning the "purpose of taxation" under capitalism and socialism.[4] In a *capitalist* system where the predominant focus is upon decision-making in the market, the primary claim to income rests with the *individual recipient* of the income. Taxes, in turn, serve the allocational function of helping to finance those public and quasi-public goods which these individual consumers desire, but which are not provided efficiently through the market. Moreover, taxes under capitalism play a major role in achieving the "desired" state of income-wealth distribution, given a value judgment-determined egalitarian consensus in this regard by the society. Hence, it is not surprising that direct progressive taxes on income and wealth serve major roles under capitalism. Importantly, the entire public sector expenditure total for allocational and distributional purposes must be "drawn away" from private individuals,

[4] See Musgrave, *Fiscal Systems,* chaps. 1 and 2 for a thorough discussion of these conceptual differences.

either directly or indirectly, in order to achieve these public sector goals. Indeed, the problems of tax policy must be more complex in a setting in which budgetary revenue must be extracted from taxpayers who are "private agents" rather than being obtained largely from state enterprises, as under socialism, which are under "direct governmental control." Furthermore, production and consumption incentives must be reckoned with in a serious manner in a decentralized market system where consumer sovereignty and the profit motive play an important economic role. Finally, the vagaries of cyclical instability and inconsistent economic growth, which are more likely (especially the former) to be serious problems under capitalism, must be included among the primary goals of taxation, and of the budget in general, in a capitalistic system.

The role of taxation under *socialism*, though not unimportant, is "more limited" than under capitalism. There is less need for distributional adjustments and, moreover, allocation can be controlled by more direct governmental techniques through centralized governmental planning than under capitalism. Table 22–4 above demonstrates the major sources of revenue for the public sector budget in the Soviet Union. The largest revenue shares, 33 percent each, are provided by the turnover tax and by the profits of state enterprises, respectively.

The Soviet *turnover tax* is not a multistage turnover tax of the type defined in this book and used in a number of Western nations. Instead, the turnover tax, as used in the Soviet Union, is a single-stage excise tax applied at differential rates to a large number of economic goods. For the most part, the tax is imposed on the distributor of the goods though, at times, it is levied on the producer. Not only are the rates of the tax differentiated by good (industry), but they vary also among product qualities and by geographical region. The socialist turnover tax serves a number of functions, few of which characterize the functioning of sales or excise taxes in a capitalistic system. Primarily, it serves as a "control" over supply and demand in the "planned" socialist system. Thus, it not only provides the output and sales data required for subsequent planning, but it also helps to adjust demand to the available supplies of economic goods by changing the prices, if necessary, of these goods.

Regarding the other leading Soviet revenue source, *state enterprise profits*, the planning of prices and costs in the Soviet socialist system yields a margin of "planned profit" for each state enterprise. This margin also serves as a benchmark for efficiency in the management of the enterprise. Approximately one third of these "planned profits" of Soviet state enterprises may be retained by the enterprise. The remainder constitutes the contribution of the *profits tax* to the budget. In addition to the turnover tax and the profits derived from state enterprises, the

Soviet budget derives smaller amounts of revenue from several other taxes. These include a *personal income tax,* termed a *tax on population,* which yielded 9 percent of total tax revenues in 1971, an *agricultural land tax* based on the acreage of private farms, and a *tax on bachelors.* The personal income tax is a "class tax" since its rates vary sharply depending upon the "taxpayer's occupation." Thus, workers pay the lowest rates while professional people, tradesmen outside of cooperative enterprises, and landlords pay mugh higher rates. The primary purpose of the tax, of course, is not to produce revenues for the public sector, but instead to control the amount of income earned outside of state enterprises.

Finally, it should be observed that recent changes have occurred in the economic techniques used in a number of socialist nations—including the Soviet Union. These changes point to a trend toward greater decentralization in both productive and consumptive decision-making. That is, the tendency is for the role of the individual to increase. If this trend continues, and it appears likely that it will continue, the relative importance of the turnover tax may be expected to decline since its role as a tool for centralized planning will diminish. Moreover, direct taxes such as the progressive personal income tax, which is so prevalent in capitalist nations, will likely increase in importance as the greater decentralization in the system provides a greater need for redistributional policies to be put into effect.

THE PUBLIC SECTOR IN DEVELOPED AND UNDERDEVELOPED NATIONS

The world today is characterized by sharp contrasts between the stages of economic development in various nations. While countries such as the United States, West Germany, Japan, and the Soviet Union produce impressive per capita outputs (incomes), a large number of lesser-developed nations in Africa, Asia, and Latin America are capable under present conditions of producing only much smaller amounts of economic goods for their citizens. Moreover, "the most basic and alarming feature of the underdevelopment problem is the fact that in the non-Communist area the gap between the developed and the less developed countries is, generally speaking, increasing in terms of real income per head."[5]

The public sector must play a significant role in the process of economic development. It is no coincidence that the public sector of devel-

---

[5] Jan Tinbergen, *Shaping the World Economy* (New York: The Twentieth Century Fund, 1962), p. 8.

oped nations tends to be noticeably larger as a proportion of gross national product or national income than is true in underdeveloped or developing nations. This "positive" relationship between the real per capita output (income) of a nation and the size of its public sector relative to total economic activity is suggestive of the role which the public sector plays in economic development. This phenomenon was examined earlier in the discussion of the Wagner hypothesis.[6] Relatedly, Table 22–5 demonstrates the variation between the relative size of the public sector for a number of developed and underdeveloped nations in terms of their tax revenue/GNP ratios. It may be observed that the average proportion of the public sector to GNP is 31 percent for the developed nations covered in the table. On the other hand, tax revenues constitute only 14 percent of GNP for those underdeveloped nations represented. The Wagner hypothesis may be approached by either an "historical" study, which was the basic approach used by Wagner, or by a "cross-section" comparison of current governmental budget/GNP ratios, as suggested in Table 22–5.[7]

There are a number of reasons for the tendency of developed nations to possess a relatively larger public sector than underdeveloped nations. These include the greater fiscal capacity to finance governmental activities which is possible as an economy develops. In addition, it is more likely for social and egalitarian motives to be prominent in an affluent as opposed to a poor nation in which subsistence itself is of primary concern. Moreover, economic development involves a more complex economy with accompanying demands for governmental services. Yet, every nation at the same stage of economic development cannot be expected to possess an identical governmental budget/GNP ratio. Instead, differences in the relative importance of the public sector for nations at the same stage of economic development will result from

---

[6] See Chapter 16.

[7] Musgrave, *Fiscal Systems* pp. 122–123, observes that taking the *historical* approach, it is evident that the public expenditure/GNP ratio, along with per capita income, has risen over time in the United States, Great Britain, and West Germany. However, he notes that the picture is less conclusive when viewed in *cross-section* terms for a large number of nations at the present time. In using a sample of nations with a wide range of per capita income levels, he finds that even though the share of the public sector as measured by the ratio of total current expenditures to GNP is associated positively with the level of per capita income, with similar results obtained for a tax revenue/GNP ratio, that the relationship disappears and becomes part of a more complex pattern when the sample is divided into "low-" and "high-" income categories. However, this represents more of a breakdown of the "continuous" intertemporal tendency, implied by the Wagner hypothesis, than it does the importance of the public sector relative to aggregate economic activity at a given point in time. In other words, the cross-section data still reflect a positive relationship to GNP for the averages of both the low and high per capita income groups, though they do not confirm a "continuous" historical relationship in the Wagner hypothesis sense.

TABLE 22-5
Public Sector Tax Revenues as a Percent of Gross National Product (selected developed and underdeveloped nations, 1965)

Developed Nations		Underdeveloped Nations	
Nation	*Ratio*	*Nation*	*Ratio*
Canada	31%	Bolivia	13%
France	39	China (Taiwan)	14
West Germany	34	Colombia	12
Italy	30	Ecuador	16
Japan	20	Ghana	16
Sweden	39	Korean Republic	9
United Kingdom	30	Philippines	13
United States	27	Peru	16
Average	31	Average	14

Source: United Nations data.

such factors as the cultural preferences of the nation toward either market or governmental performance of economic functions, the proximity of the nation to open (international) economic transactions, and its involvement with national defense expenditures. Overall, the fisc will reflect the economic, social, and cultural complexity of the society.

In any event, there is no doubt that the public sector, through both expenditure and revenue (especially tax) policies, is in a unique position to influence the economic development process. The fisc, for example, may be used to help break the "vicious circle" of poverty which typically characterizes an underdeveloped nation. That is, governmental expenditure and revenue policies can attack the basic mechanisms which are responsible for the continuing low level of economic performance. These basic mechanisms include the following phenomena:[8]

1. Capital and income are "interdependent." That is, a low capital stock implies a low level of production, and thus a low level of income. However, a low income does not permit large savings and thus the stock of capital cannot easily be increased.

2. Health and income are "interdependent." That is, low incomes depress the level of nutrition and, in addition, do not allow adequate medical services for the maintenance of good health. However, a low quality of human health reduces the qualitative effectiveness of the labor factor of production and its ability to contribute to economic output.

3. Education and income are "interdependent." That is, low incomes restrict the existence of adequate educational facilities for the society. However, inadequate education once again reduces the

[8] Tinbergen, *Shaping World Economy*, pp. 14-15.

qualitative effectiveness of the labor force and its ability to contribute to economic output.

Thus, except for foreign aid, domestic fiscal policy is assigned "the central task of wresting from the pitifully low output of these countries sufficient savings to finance economic development programs and to set the stage for more vigorous private investment activity."[9]

One fundamental budgetary approach to initiate a development process is to promote *social overhead* investment. A primary characteristic of social overhead investment includes the lack of quick and visible profits to investors due to either a very long-term productive process, or because the end product of the investment is not conducive to divisible sale on the market, or both. Investments in health, education, transportation, and natural resource development often fall into the social overhead investment category. Frequently, the public sector is the most efficient institution to influence the allocation of these goods. The governmental role can follow a variety of techniques ranging all the way from comprehensive governmental financing and production of the economic goods to a less-comprehensive approach which encompasses partial governmental subsidization of private production of the goods. The joint consumption benefits and positive externalities exerted by social overhead expenditures tend to increase the quantity and quality of the productive resource base of the underdeveloped nation. The result, with proper management, should be the initiation of an economic development path for the nation.

The revenue side of the budget, especially taxation, can also play a major role in the promotion of social overhead investment as well as to promote the other facets of an economic development process. Though underdeveloped nations cannot expect to immediately expand their tax revenue/GNP ratios to where they are equal to the higher proportions enjoyed by developed nations, they may nonetheless modestly increase the relative importance of their tax collections to help finance the development process. In general terms, the development of the tax and revenue system of a nation will go through several stages as an economy progresses from a state of underdevelopment toward economic maturity. Initially, the lack of a sophisticated commercial sector may cause the nation to concentrate on revenue from *nontax sources* such as tributes or revenues-in-kind in the form of labor services or agricultural crops provided to the government.

At a somewhat higher stage of evolution, the government may collect a direct *personal tax* from the "families" of an underdeveloped

---

[9] Walter Heller, "Fiscal Policies for Underdeveloped Economies," in Bernard Okun and Richard W. Richardson (eds.), *Studies in Economic Development* (New York: Holt, Rinehart & Winston, Inc., 1961), p. 451.

nation. This device has been used successfully by a number of African nations in recent times.[10] A personal tax is directed toward low-income taxpayers. It is characterized by a very low proportional, or modestly graduated, rate structure and by a very simplified base which offers neither exemptions nor deductions to the family taxpaying unit. "Taxpaying ability," especially for the graduated (progressive) version of the tax, may be determined either by money income or by "income-in-kind" such as the number of head of livestock owned by a family. The tax serves the purpose of involving subsistence level families in support of certain necessary public goods which they consume. Moreover, the personal tax helps to provide revenues for economic development which eventually will enhance the income status of these subsistence families. In addition, it provides a foundation for the ultimate application of an orthodox personal income tax as the economy develops to a sufficient level of maturity to allow the practical introduction of such a tax.

At a fairly early stage of economic development, the revenue structure of an underdeveloped nation is likely to show significant use of *import* and *export duties* as a revenue source. The extent to which this is a major revenue source, of course, will depend upon the degree of "openness" in international trade available to the nation. As the underdeveloped economy progresses to an "intermediate" stage of development, the further development of a commercial system makes possible the collection of indirect taxes of the *excise* variety on domestic output and sales. The relative importance of import and export duties, as well as of the personal tax on families, may now be expected to decline. Furthermore, the introduction, or expansion, of an orthodox *income tax* on individual and business income now becomes feasible. Meanwhile, the development of a banking system in relation to the commercial and industrial development of the economy will provide the additional advantage of rendering domestic *governmental borrowing* available as a revenue source.

More specifically, taxes may be designed to render *positive nonneutralities* in the effort to develop the economy. For example, taxes may be utilized to discourage wasteful consumption and thus to increase the domestic savings necessary to assist capital formation. Relatedly, the pattern of taxes may be designed to encourage those types of capital investment deemed most important to economic development. Similarly, import duties may be structured in such a manner that they encourage the importation of those economic goods or resources most essential to the development process. Finally, the tax structure may

---

[10] See the discussion of the personal tax as used in Africa in E. A. Arowolo, "The Taxation of Low Incomes in African Countries," *International Monetary Fund Staff Papers,* July 1968, pp. 322–43.

encourage the flow of foreign money capital to the underdeveloped nation.

Indeed, the public sector budget inevitably influences the aggregate performance, both short run and long run, of an economy. If the economy is underdeveloped, or in an intermediate stage of development, it is critical that the fisc be designed so as to initiate or continue the development process. This will require "budgetary flexibility" since the ideal set of expenditures and revenues at one stage of development will not usually be that required at another stage. For example, social overhead investment in health, education, transportation, and natural resource development may dominate the composition of public sector expenditures in an early stage of development, but these priorities may be replaced by others as the economy approaches an intermediate or higher stage of development. Also, the structure of the tax system may be expected to vary as the development process continues (as described above). Furthermore, changing patterns of income and wealth distribution suggest a reconsideration from time to time of the fiscal structure of a developing nation.

THE PUBLIC SECTOR IN FEDERAL NATIONS—A COMPARISON OF AUSTRALIA, CANADA, AND THE UNITED STATES[11]

Overall Comparisons

Australia, Canada, and the United States, in addition to each being a *federation* with two sovereign levels of government, possess numerous other similarities. Because of the many political, social, and cultural likenesses of the three nations, it will be useful to compare the respective fiscal forms which the governmental structure has taken in each of the federations.[12] Each nation, for example, possesses a large land area endowed with considerable natural resource wealth. In turn, each nation has followed an economic development pattern characterized by a "land-rich" and "labor- and capital-poor" mix of resource combinations during the critical stages of development. Furthermore, each nation is in an "industrial maturity" stage of economic development, in an overall sense, at the present time. Relatedly, population concentrations in each of the three federal nations reflect an urban-industrial pattern for each nation. For example, more than 40 percent of the population of Australia resides in the two cities of Sydney and Mel-

---

[11] See also the related discussion for the United States in Chapters 19 and 20.

[12] No attempt is made here to describe the fiscal patterns of other federations such as those of India and West Germany.

borne. Moreover, Australia, Canada, and the United States each possess a dominant European demographic and cultural heritage as well as the inheritance of an Anglo political tradition.

On the other hand, certain differences between the three nations should also be observed. First, the United States has a much larger population than either Australia or Canada. Hence, the more than 200 million population of the United States is some 10 times greater than the Canadian population and 15 times larger than that of Australia. In addition, the federal political structure of the United States is "more decentralized" in the sense of the number of units of sovereign government at the state (province) level. That is, the 50 American state governments contrast to 10 Canadian provinces and only 6 Australian states. Nonetheless, it would appear that sufficient important similarities exist to outweigh these dissimilarities and thus warrant a comparison of the fiscal patterns used in these three federal nations.

Fiscal Comparisons

In terms of public sector *expenditures* and *revenues* as a proportion of *aggregate economic performance,* Australia, Canada, and the United States each reflect their "developed nation" status by registering significantly high percentages. These data are presented in Table 22–6.[13] Thus, public sector spending inclusive of all levels and units of government constituted 42 percent of national income in Canada, 38 percent in the United States, and 36 percent in Australia during 1971. Public sector revenues as a proportion of national income in the same year were 42 percent in Canada, 36 percent in the United States, and 33 percent in Australia. Hence, the data reveal that the importance of the government sector in the Australian federation is somewhat less than in Canada and the United States while that of the United States, in turn, is somewhat less than that of Canada.

An additional comparison of the fiscal structures of Australia, Canada, and the United States is indicated by Table 22–7. This table reveals that the importance of *direct taxes* is somewhat greater in the public sector of the United States than in the other two nations. Thus, taxes of the income, payroll, property, death, gift, and motor vehicle license varieties constitute 82 percent of the tax revenues collected by federal, state, and local governments in the United States. On the other hand, direct taxes represented 70 percent of public sector tax revenues in Australia and 69 percent in Canada. In Australia, moreover, the sovereign state governments do not even impose an income tax.

---

[13] The percentages would be somewhat lower, of course, if *gross national product* instead of *national income* were used as the indicator of "aggregate economic performance."

TABLE 22–6

Ratio of Public Sector Expenditures and Revenues* to National Income for Australia, Canada, and the United States, 1971 (dollars in billions†)

		Expenditures		Revenues	
Nation	National Income	Total	Ratio to National Income	Total	Ratio to National Income
Australia...............	$ 30	$ 11	36%	$ 10	33%
Canada	82	35	42	35	42
United States...........	963	369	38	343	36

* Expenditures and revenues are exclusive of double counting through intergovernmental transfers.
† Dollar figures are in Australian, Canadian, and U.S. dollars, respectively.
Source: Computed from United Nations, U.S. Department of Commerce, Canadian Tax Foundation, and Commonwealth Treasury (Australia) data.

It is also interesting to briefly compare the Australian, Canadian, and American federations in reference to the three major intergovernmental fiscal problems of *vertical* and *horizontal* fiscal imbalance and *intergovernmental externalities*.[14] Concerning the problem of *vertical fiscal imbalance,* the divorcement between "tax revenues from own sources" and "direct expenditure decisions" is considerably greater in Australia than in Canada and the United States.[15] For example, during 1970–71 the Commonwealth (national) government of Australia collected 83 percent of all public sector tax revenues, but made only 48 percent of the public sector's direct expenditure decisions. If looked at in reverse, this means that subnational governments in Australia collect, under their own authority, only 17 percent of total public sector tax revenues, but make 52 percent of all direct spending decisions. This amounts to a 35 percent spread between governmental taxation and expenditure responsibilities. By contrast, the federal government of Canada derives 56 percent of all public sector tax revenue while making 44 percent of the direct expenditure decisions—a spread of just 12 percent—and the federal government in the United States derives 68 percent of all governmental taxes and makes 57 percent of the direct spending decisions—a spread of 11 percent. Concerning the problem of *horizontal fiscal imbalance,* all three federations possess states (or provinces) which possess relatively poorer economic capacities, and thus relatively poorer fiscal capacities, than others. However, the issue appears to be a more pronounced one in Canada and the United States than in Australia.

The employment of intergovernmental fiscal techniques to deal with

---

[14] As defined in Chapter 19.

[15] A *direct* expenditure decision may be defined as any governmental expenditure "except" the transfer of funds to another level of government.

TABLE 22-7
Direct* and Indirect† Taxes as a Proportion of Total Public Sector Tax
Revenues for Australia, Canada, and the United States

Nation	Direct Taxes as a Percentage of Total Taxes	Indirect Taxes as a Percentage of Total Taxes
Australia‡	70	30
Canada§........................	69	31
United States‖	82	18

* *Direct* taxes are defined to include income, payroll, property, death, gift, and motor vehicle taxes.
† *Indirect* taxes are defined to include general sales and gross receipts taxes, excise taxes, and customs duties (export and import taxes).
‡ Australian data is for the 1970–71 fiscal year.
§ Canadian data is for the 1969–70 fiscal year for the federal and provincial governments and for the 1969 calendar year for municipal governments.
‖ United States data is for the 1970–71 fiscal year.
Source: Computed from U.S. Department of Commerce, Canadian Tax Foundation, and Commonwealth Treasury (Australia) data.

the problems of vertical and horizontal fiscal imbalance differs somewhat among the three federations. For example, the vast majority of revenues shared between the Australian Commonwealth government and lower-level Australian governments are of the unconditional, "no strings-attached," variety. By contrast, the United States did not employ the unconditional revenue sharing device at the federal level of government prior to 1972, except for a single ad hoc usage during the 1830s in the presidential administration of Andrew Jackson. On the other hand, Canada—like Australia—has long used both the unconditional and conditional, "strings-attached," revenue-sharing techniques. The United States, of course, used only the conditional grant-in-aid form of revenue sharing until recently. In addition, the Canadian federal government offers what is, in effect, a partial income tax credit (abatement) against federal personal and corporation income tax liabilities for personal and corporation income taxes paid to provincial governments.[16] This has encouraged the Canadian provinces to make use of "income-elastic" income taxes as revenue sources. In Canada, this tax credit (abatement) technique has been used with the alleviation of vertical fiscal imbalance as its primary objective. On the other hand, the unconditional revenue-sharing technique has been utilized in Canada with the equalization goal as its primary objective. This contrasts with Australia where unconditional revenue-sharing has been directed toward both the vertical and horizontal fiscal imbalance problems. The recent adoption of unconditional revenue-sharing by the

---

[16] Technical changes effective in 1972 render this device a less pure form of "tax credit" than before.

federal government of the United States, along with bloc grants, have been primarily directed toward the "vertical" imbalance issue, but equalization features in the distribution formulas suggest also the consideration of the "horizontal" imbalance issue.

Finally, it is interesting to observe that Canada uses, at the national government level, all three of the basic intergovernmental fiscal techniques discussed above, that is, the *unconditional revenue-sharing*, the *conditional revenue-sharing*, and the *tax credit* techniques. Australia and the United States, on the other hand, utilize only the *conditional* and *unconditional* revenue-sharing devices. Yet, as demonstrated in Chapter 20, each of the three basic techniques has a comparative advantage in serving specific goals. Thus, *unconditional revenue-sharing* can best meet the "horizontal fiscal imbalance" problem, the *tax credit* approach can best meet the problem of "vertical fiscal imbalance," and *conditional revenue-sharing* can most effectively deal with the financing and allocation of economic goods characterized by significant "intergovernmental externalities."

Income Tax Reform in Canada

A comprehensive set of proposals, known as the *White Paper,* was submitted by the government of Canada to the Canadian parliament for consideration during 1969 for the purpose of simplifying the federal income tax structure in Canada.[17] The proposals, if adopted, would provide a more comprehensive income tax base, considerably greater integration between the Canadian personal and corporation income taxes, and a closer adherence to the ability-to-pay principle of taxation. These income tax reform proposals were the outgrowth of the much publicized Report of the Royal Commission on Taxation (*Carter Report*) in 1967. The following is a brief statement of some of the major recommendations submitted in 1969 for income tax reform in Canada, and the ultimate determination of tax law by Parliament.[18]

1. Realized capital gains, in general, would have been taxed at full income tax rates. Parliament rejected the full taxation of such gains, but did introduce limited capital gains taxation.

2. Basic personal exemptions would have been increased by 40 percent, that is, from $1,000 to $1,400 for single taxpayers and from $2,000 to $2,800 for married taxpayers. Parliament, in fact, raised the single exemption to $1,500 and the married taxpayer exemption to $2,850.

---

[17] For a summary of these proposals, see the Canadian Tax Foundation, Tax Memo No. 49, *White Paper on Tax Reform,* November, 1969.

[18] For a detailed analysis of the ultimate determination of Canadian income tax policy by Parliament, see: Meyer Bucovetsky and Richard M. Bird, "Tax Reform in Canada: A Progress Report," *National Tax Journal,* March 1972, pp. 15–41.

3. The combined increased personal exemptions and a new rate schedule were to result in lower personal income taxes for taxpayers in lower-income brackets, but higher taxes initially for all other taxpayers. However, as a result of the proposed capital gains tax increase, after a period of five years the top marginal personal income tax rate of 82.4 percent (inclusive of a 28 percent abatement or credit for provincial personal income taxes) would be lowered to approximately 50 percent. Actual legislation by Parliament resulted in marginal rates, to be effective in 1976, ranging from 7.8 percent on $100 of taxable income (it had been 14.8 percent) to 61.1 percent on a taxable income of $400,000 or above (it had been 82.4 percent).[19] Moreover, the new rate schedule taxes middle bracket "earned income" somewhat less than had been proposed by the *White Paper.*

4. The taxes paid by Canadian corporations and their resident shareholders would have been largely integrated. Thus, a full personal tax credit was proposed for such shareholders for Canadian income taxes paid by "closely-held" corporations and a 50 percent credit for income taxes paid by "widely-held" corporations. Instead of this proposal, the new legislation provided a partial "gross-up" and "credit" for dividends received by individuals from Canadian corporations—the *gross-up* amounting to one third of the dividend received and the *credit* amounting to four fifths of the gross-up.

5. All corporation income would have been taxed at a proportional rate of 50 percent with the existing lower-rate for smaller businesses being eliminated. Parliament rejected this proposal and, as a small business incentive, retained a lower marginal rate (25 percent) on the first $50,000 of business income of Canadian controlled "private" (stock shares not marketed) corporations, up to a maximum of $400,000. Meanwhile, the general corporation income tax rate will drop to 46 percent in 1976.

6. The *White Paper* proposals for inclusion of unemployment insurance benefits in the personal income tax base was accepted by Parliament, with unemployment insurance contributions being deductible from the tax base.

7. Although not proposed, a significant side-effect of the tax reform activities of Parliament was the repeal of the federal estate and gift taxes—a victim of the controversy on how to tax capital gains at death.

In retrospect, the ultimate results of the *Carter Commission* and *White Paper* efforts in behalf of income tax reform in Canada were considerably modified by the final legislation. However, some improvements were made. Moreover, the initial proposals, particularly the initial Royal Commission report, provided a good theoretical approxima-

---

[19] These new rates assume a provincial personal income tax abatement equal to 30 percent of the federal tax.

tion to what a public finance economist would call a "rational income tax structure," that is, one inclusive of a comprehensive income tax base, integration of the personal and corporation income taxes, and recognition of the ability-to-pay principle of taxation.

THE PUBLIC SECTOR IN AN OPEN SYSTEM

The discussion to this point in the chapter has emphasized public sector economic activity "within" a nation instead of "between" nations. Although the analysis has compared the performance of the public sector under conditions of capitalist or socialist resource allocation, in developed or underdeveloped economies, and in different federations, the discussion has been *closed* in the sense that it has focused upon the individual nation. The final section of the chapter will now move to a discussion of an *open* system in which public sector economic activities interact between nations. That is, the issue of "intergovernmental" economic activity on an "international" basis will be the focal point of the analysis.

The peculiar problems which arise in international public finance stem largely from one basic condition, namely, the fact that the economic activity in question transcends the "political boundaries" and hence the "jurisdictional authority" of individual nations. Increasingly, today's "nation-states" are becoming too small in jurisdiction to manage the problems of an international economy.[20] The problems which result tend to fall into two primary, though related, classifications: (1) the taxation of "private" productive resources and economic goods involved in international production and trade, and (2) the financing of "public" and "quasi-public" *goods*, or the control of "public" and "quasi-public" *bads*, which are consumed on an "international basis." These will be discussed in order below.

International Tax Coordination

In a world of continually improving transportation and communications, the potential magnitude of economic activity between nations continually increases. This expansion encompasses both the international flow of productive resources and the exchange of economic goods. In addition, the "earnings" of the owners of the productive resources as well as the economic goods involved in international trade each constitute a significant potential *base for taxation*.[21] In turn, the

---

[20] This point is discussed in Charles P. Kindleberger, *Power and Money* (New York: Basic Books, Inc., Publishers, 1970).

[21] The discussion herein is primarily in the context of market-oriented (capitalist) economies and the unique role of taxation in such economies.

imposition of tax rates on these tax bases may lead to important economic effects. These effects may occur in any or all of the functional areas of economic activity—allocation, distribution, stabilization, and economic growth. Those effects exerted by "income" taxation will generally bear upon the international flow of productive resources. Those effects exerted by "transactions" ("sales") taxation will generally influence the pattern of exchange of economic goods between nations. In either case, the need for *international tax coordination* is apparent. Such coordination may take a variety of institutional forms including tax credits, tax treaties, and tax harmonization.

Many major capital-exporting nations utilize the *tax credit* technique for the coordination of income taxation among nations. That is, they allow a "credit" against domestic income tax liability for income taxes paid to foreign nations by domestic taxpayers. Otherwise, resources applied in production at home would incur less income tax liability than those applied in foreign nations. The subsequent "tax inequity," given an acceptance of the horizontal and vertical tax equity benchmarks, is evident. Moreover, the allocation of productive resources between the two nations may be unduly distorted in violation of the principle of comparative advantage if an international income tax credit, or some other compensating device, does not exist.

The income tax credit and other aspects of international tax coordination are frequently formalized in a *tax treaty*. Bilateral tax treaties now exist between most of the industrialized nations of the world.[22] However, there are only a few treaties in existence between an industrialized nation and an underdeveloped nation and still fewer treaties exist between underdeveloped nations. These bilateral tax treaties render tax administration more efficient. In addition, they contribute to the goal of distributional equity in terms of the horizontal and vertical tax equity benchmarks. A key feature of such treaties is the definition of rules for applying the tax credit in the form of the "territorial principle of taxation." That is, the income tax base must be allocated between the two nations in reference to the "source of the income." For example, a firm may produce an economic good in one nation, but sell the good in the other nation. Thus, even under a tax credit device, either multiple (double) taxation or its opposite, tax escape, may occur if the two nations apply different rules of "income source."

The most sophisticated form of tax coordination is that provided by the adoption of the *tax harmonization* approach which amounts, in effect, to the formation of a *tax union* between nations. Specifically, tax harmonization may be defined as the mutual adjustment of national tax systems to achieve certain objectives which are common to the mem-

---

[22] See the discussion in Carl S. Shoup, *Public Finance* (Chicago: Aldine Publishing Co., 1969), pp. 637–40.

ber nations of the union.[23] Tax harmonization, when fully implemented, provides a common area for economic activity within which productive resources and economic goods flow between the member nations without interference. Obvious advantages of allocational efficiency and of distributional equity will accrue to the member nations. However, less obvious allocational advantages, and very possibly allocational disadvantages, may occur between the nations constituting the tax union and the rest of the world.

The most significant current example of tax harmonization is that provided by the nine nations which comprise the European Economic Community (EEC). These nations, also known as the Common Market nations, are Belgium, Denmark, France, Great Britain, Ireland, Italy, Luxembourg, Netherlands, and West Germany. The EEC adopted a plan in 1967, to be implemented for its then-six members by the early 1970s, which called for a high degree of tax harmonization among the member nations. Specifically, all import duties on goods traded among the nine nations are to be removed. Moreover, all tax rebates are to be eliminated on products traded between the nations. In addition, each nation will adopt a uniform value-added tax at a rate of (approximately) 15 percent. Thus, in effect, all tax obstacles to resource flow and commodity trade between the member nations will be removed under the tax harmonization plan. That is, the tax systems of the nine nations will be "neutral" between each other.

Furthermore, the EEC tax harmonization plan calls for the retention of tax rebates on goods exported by Common Market nations to nations outside of the Common Market area. Also, taxes equal to the 15 percent domestic value-added tax will be imposed on goods imported into the Common Market nations from outside the Common Market. These taxes, though suggestive of ordinary import duties, are more properly referred to as *border taxes* because of their role in the overall tax harmonization plan. Specifically, they provide the equivalent of the domestic value-added tax which is paid on domestically produced goods.

The tax harmonization program adopted by the European Economic Community involves the use of the *country of origin* principle of international taxation. According to this principle, as applied within the EEC, tax jurisdiction rests with the nation in which the value of the good originates, that is, the nation in which the good is produced. This differs from the *country of destination* principle of international taxation which would assign tax jurisdiction to the nation in which the economic good is ultimately consumed. It is the very adoption of the "country of origin" principle, under the design described above, which

---

[23] *Tax Harmonization in Europe and U.S. Business* (New York: Tax Foundation, Inc., 1968), p. 7.

will allow the Common Market member nations to eliminate tax obstacles to free resource mobility and commodity flows within the market. Moreover, such a system does not violate the General Agreement on Tariffs and Trade (GATT) which permits "indirect" taxes such as the value-added tax, which are assumed to be shifted forward to the consumer, to be rebated on exports, and which also permits the application of equalizing border taxes on imported goods to compensate for the application of indirect taxes to domestically produced goods. As observed above, the tax rebate and border tax techniques are used by the EEC nations only in relation to trade with nations outside the Common Market area as part of its tax harmonization plan.

Financing and Regulating International Collective Consumption and Externalities

The collective consumption of economic *goods* and economic *bads* on a multination basis is becoming an increasingly important phenomenon as transportation and communications bring the nations of the world "closer together" in the sense of economic interaction. An analogy may be drawn with the United States of 1870 as compared to the United States of 1970. In the former year, the horizontal intergovernmental fiscal problems of the American federation were less severe than those of today. It was less likely, for example, that the economic actions of one state fisc would exert important interstate economic spillovers on other states than is true today. Similarly, the nations of the world today are less capable of existing in isolation from the actions of each other and thus are more capable of exerting important international spillover effects on each other than they were a century ago.

One of the primary modern-day examples of international collective consumption or externalities is provided by the United Nations Organization (UN). This organization of nations attempts to coordinate the allocation of numerous *economic goods*—such as world peace and the development of underdeveloped economies—and the elimination of numerous *economic bads*—such as world war and poverty—through its varied efforts. The financing of United Nations costs comprises four categories:[24] (1) the financing of the *regular United Nations budget;* (2) the financing of the *special "peace-keeping" operations* of the organization through a combination of assessments and voluntary payments; (3) the financing of *specialized agencies,* each of which has its own membership policy with a decentralized financial system; and (4) the financing of *special voluntary programs.*

The regular budget of the United Nations is financially supported

---

[24] For a relevant discussion, see John G. Stoessinger, *Financing the United Nations System* (Washington, D.C.: Brookings Institution, 1964).

through the assessment of a proportionately rated exaction, which may properly be termed a "tax," on the member nations of the organization. However, the proportional exaction (tax) is rendered "progressive" in effect through a process which allows nations with low per capita incomes (under $1,000) to receive up to 50 percent reductions in their assessment percentages. Overall, the UN considers "total national income" and "per capita income" to be the primary criteria in determining the "ability-to-pay" of a nation. As might be expected, a large percentage of the regular budget of the United Nations is provided by a small minority of the membership.[25] The United States alone contributes almost one third of the regular UN budget and, with four others, almost two thirds of the total.

In early 1970, the United Nations considered a unique proposal for the adoption of an international "good life tax" to alleviate poverty in poor nations. The proposal was submitted by the UN Committee for Development Planning headed by the well-known economist and Nobel Prize winner from the Netherlands, Jan Tinbergen. The proposed tax was a selective sales tax on certain home appliances and luxury items such as automatic dishwashers, refrigerators, television sets, automobiles, and private airplanes. Most of these goods, of course, are consumed in the higher-income nations. The rate would be one half of 1 percent (0.5) of the value of the item. It would be collected by the tax authorities of each nation on its own responsibility. The revenues collected by each nation would then be distributed by that nation for international poverty relief through any international development organization on a list approved by the UN General Assembly. Though early adoption of the proposed tax is unlikely, it may serve as a reference point for future discussion and possible policy action.

Other examples of international collective consumption include the national security efforts of the North Atlantic Treaty Organization (NATO) and the St. Lawrence Seaway. The latter provides water transportation benefits "directly" to Canada and the United States, who are jointly financing the project, and "indirectly" to the other nations of the world.

The "international" economic goods and bads affected by the operation of such organizations as the United Nations and NATO are largely of the "joint consumption" or "externality" variety with numerous *indivisible* economic effects. Those provided by the St. Lawrence Seaway, on the other hand, contain an important segment of *divisible* benefits to the individual shippers *et al.* who utilize the facility, though important joint consumption benefits are also present. Thus, the peace efforts of the United Nations might well be classified as an international

---

[25] *Ibid.*, p. 85.

"pure public good" while the transportation benefits derived from use of the St. Lawrence Seaway may be termed an international "quasi-public good." *Cost sharing* between nations must be employed to help finance either type of international economic good.

While the creation of a bi-nation or multi-nation organization or agreement may be based initially on allocational grounds, the establishment of such an organization or the implementation of an agreement inevitably must carry distributional implications as well. Since the "benefits received" in most instances cannot be aligned on a *quid pro quo* basis with either the *cost shares* of nations or with the *tax* shares of individuals within nations, the "ability-to-pay" principle of tax equity comes forward as an alternative equity bench mark. Once again, the "value judgment" basis of the ability-to-pay doctrine and its attendant problem of "interpersonal utility comparisons"[26] must be recognized in any application of the principle.

Finally, it may be observed that severe problems of international *public bads*, some of which draw very little policy attention, are present in the world. Probably, the strongest case in point is the problem of *environmental pollution*.[27] As a Secretary-General of the United Nations has observed, "For the first time in the history of mankind there is arising a crisis of worldwide proportions involving developed and developing countries alike—the crisis of human environment. . . . It is becoming apparent that if current trends continue, the future of life on earth could be endangered."[28] Air, water, land, and noise pollution, as well as congestion, are not problems which respect national political boundaries. Thus, just as there exists the collective consumption of various *public goods* on an international basis, there exists also a pattern of international consumption of various *public bads*. The geographical scope of these allocational issues, and their related distributional, stabilization, and economic growth effects, transcends the political jurisdictions which might otherwise individually finance or control them. The issues of international collective consumption and externalities are becoming increasingly apparent. Unfortunately, the emergence of international institutional arrangements to effectively deal with these important international economic problems is not similarly apparent at the present time.

---

[26] See Chapter 7.

[27] See the discussion of environmental pollution as an economic problem in Chapter 3.

[28] U Thant, as quoted in George F. Kennan, "To Prevent a World Wasteland—A Proposal," *Foreign Affairs*, April 1970, p. 401.

part four

The Public Sector and Aggregate Economic Performance

23

Aggregate Performance in a Market Economy and the Need for Fiscal Policy

The *great enemy* of the truth is very often not the lie—deliberate, contrived and dishonest but the myth—persistent, persuasive and unrealistic. Too often we hold fast to the clichés of our forebears. We subject all facts to a prefabricated set of interpretations. We enjoy the comfort of opinion without the discomfort of thought.

. . . Let us turn to the problem of our fiscal policy. Here the myths are legion and the truth is hard to find. . . . These are the problems that we should be talking about—that the political parties and the various groups in our country should be discussing. They cannot be solved by incantations from the forgotten past.[1]

In no part of public finance have economic myths and misconceptions been more prevalent than in the basis for macroeconomic fiscal policy. The fact that Americans have been vitally concerned with the stability and growth of the national economy during the last 45 years adds further significance to such fiscal misunderstanding. It is the purpose of this part of the book to review the basic forces (primarily market-directed) which determine both the short-term performance level and the long-term growth rate of the national economy. Then it will be possible to analyze the ability of the public sector to influence these aggregates.

It is inevitable that government exert an important economic influence on the private sector and upon aggregate economic performance

---

[1] Excerpt from an address made by the late President John F. Kennedy at Yale University on June 11, 1962.

in a mixed economic system such as that of the United States. In other words, the public sector cannot act in the budgetary manner of taxing and spending without affecting aggregate production, employment, income, price levels, and economic growth rates. Thus, an aggregate "fiscal policy" exists whether one is desired or not! It is only rational, therefore, to direct this fiscal policy in a deliberate manner toward the achievement of aggregate economic goals. Of course, if the private sector possesses inherent forces which would automatically attain optimal stabilization and growth results, the case for deliberate government fiscal policy would be considerably weakened. The analysis below, however, demonstrates that the private sector does not possess these traits. The pure market economy does *not* automatically achieve a full-employment equilibrium level of performance, reasonably stable price levels, nor a satisfactory rate of economic growth. The following section will consider the basic forces which determine aggregate economic behavior in a pure market economy and will demonstrate the distinct possibility that equilibrium performance levels providing such undesirable phenomena as substantial unemployment, substantial inflation, and lagging growth rates can occur. The model, though a simplification of very complex forces, still validly isolates the main determinants of aggregate economic performance.

THE PERFORMANCE OF A PURE MARKET ECONOMY[2]

The Classical Theory of Aggregate Economic Performance—Say's Law

Classical economics, which originated in the late 1700s, offered an optimistic interpretation of the forces which determine the level of aggregate economic performance in a pure market economy. The names of Smith, Say, Ricardo, Mill, Marshall, and others are associated with this school of economics. Classical production and employment theory, in aggregate terms, dominated the thinking of economists concerning aggregate economic activity until the "Keynesian Revolution" of the 1930s. According to classical theory, the pure market economy through the interaction of impersonal market forces will arrive by itself at an aggregate production level which fully employs *all* units of labor who wish to be employed. A pure market economy is thus said to be automatically a full-employment economy, the only deviations from full employment being occasional short periods of adjustment involving

---

[2] The student may wish to *review* the principles of macroeconomics from a basic *Principles of Economics* textbook before reading this section. The macroeconomic theory presented here will essentially be brief and will assume previous knowledge of macroeconomics by the student.

fluctuation around the full-employment equilibrium level of aggregate performance.

According to Say's Law, this full-employment level of income and output will exist because "supply creates its own demand." In other words, since the end of all economic activity is assumed to be the pleasure derived from consumption, every resource owner who provides resources for the creation of supply does so from the motivation of increasing his consumption of economic goods. Thus, given flexibility in wages and prive levels, the pure market economy will adjust the level of labor employment to the point where involuntary unemployment is absent; that is, aggregate demand equals aggregate supply at full labor employment. In other words, inadequate demand leads to unemployment which causes the *real* wage to fall thus causing a rise in employment. Obviously, governmental fiscal policy, as it is known today, would *not* be required to promote full employment if the economy automatically directed itself toward the full-employment goal in this manner.

Certain premises essential to aggregate economic performance along classical lines, however, are not present in the contemporary market-directed economies of the Western world. While Say's Law may have been a reasonably adequate explanation of aggregate performance for the preindustrial or early industrial market economies of the late seventeenth and early eighteenth centuries, it has become decreasingly applicable to Western nations as they have followed their evolutionary paths toward industrial maturity. This evolutionary industrial development, with its attendant economies of scale, has resulted in a predominance of imperfect market structures accompanied by substantial price and wage rigidities. Hence, the assumptions of perfect competition in product and resource (factor) markets become less useful and the ability of Say's Law to explain the aggregate performance of mature Western economies is subsequently weakened. A better explanation of pure market economy performance is required. Keynesian analysis meets this test.

The Keynesian Theory of Aggregate Economic Performance

The late British economist John Maynard Keynes is primarily responsible for the development of modern macroeconomic theory.[3] This widely accepted explanation of the basic economic forces which determine economic performance in a market-directed economy concentrates upon three primary determinants of aggregate behavior. These

---

[3] His pioneering work in this regard is *The General Theory of Employment, Interest and Money* (London: Macmillan & Co., 1936).

causal forces are Consumption (C), Saving (S), and Investment (I) which operate both as individual forces and in various significant interactions with each other in the determination of aggregate economic performance.

Consumption. In the Keynesian model of the pure market economy, the level of aggregate consumption expenditures is considered to be a function of the level of national income.[4] This functional relationship is known alternately as the "propensity to consume" or the "consumption function." the Equation $C = f(Y)$ symbolizes the consumption function relationship. In Figure 23–1, which is plotted from Table 23–1,

FIGURE 23–1
Consumption and Saving as Functions of Income in the Aggregate Economy

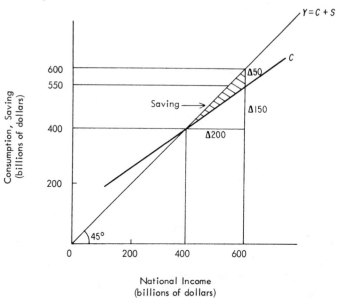

consumption expenditures (along with saving) are measured on the vertical axis and income is measured on the horizontal axis. However, in effect, income is measured along each axis since income by definition is either spent for consumption or not spent for consumption—the latter choice referring to the concept of saving (to be discussed below). Hence, the 45-degree line designated $Y = C + S$ is equidistant from each

---

[4] Technically, "national disposable income" is a source even closer to actual consumption and saving decisions than is "national income." For reasons of simplicity in presentation, however, the disposable income concept is *not* used at this point as the basic source of consumption expenditures and of saving.

axis and represents the aggregate amount of income which can be either consumed or saved.

Consumption expenditures normally change in the same direction as income changes. A *positive* functional relationship thus exists between consumption and income. The level of consumption, of course, will also change in response to certain other causal variables, but income is considered to be the primary determinant. The simplified version of the consumption function based on income as the only causal variable is represented by line *C* in Figure 23–1. As income increases from $400 billion to $600 billion, for example, consumption increases

TABLE 23–1
Consumption and Saving as Functions of Income in the Aggregate Economy (billions of dollars)

Y *National* *Income*	*C* *Con-* *sumption*	*S* *Saving*
$200	$250	$–50
400	400	0
600	550	+50

by $150 billion from $400 billion to $550 billion. The slope of the consumption function is determined by the *marginal propensity to consume* which refers to the ratio between a change in the level of income and the resulting change in consumption expenditure. Thus:

$$\text{Marginal Propensity to Consume} = \frac{\text{Change in Consumption}}{\text{Change in Income}}$$

In the above numerical example, the marginal propensity to consume is 0.75 or 75 percent since:

$$MPC = \frac{\Delta C}{\Delta Y} \text{ and } \frac{\$150 \text{ b.}}{\$200 \text{ b.}} = 0.75$$

The relationship between the level of consumption and the level of income at any *one* point on the consumption function is known as the *average propensity to consume*. Thus:

$$\text{Average Propensity to Consume} = \frac{\text{Consumption}}{\text{Income}}$$

In the above numerical example, the average propensity to consume at the $600 billion income level is 0.91³/₅ or 91³/₅ percent since:

$$APC = \frac{C}{Y} \text{ and } \frac{\$550 \text{ b.}}{\$600 \text{ b.}} = 0.916$$

The student must be careful not to confuse the instantaneous theoretical nature of the consumption function with empirical studies of consumption-income ratios over time. The basic theoretical consumption function holds constant other parameters which influence consumption decisions such as consumer tastes, the introduction of new products, and changes in wealth holdings. It then asks the question: What would aggregate consumption be at various income levels given the constancy of these other forces which influence consumption? Obviously, at any moment of time with these other parameters constant, consumption must rest at some point on the instantaneous short-run consumption function curve.

Duesenberry, in his analysis of the relationship between short-run and long-run consumption functions, concludes that once a consumer achieves a higher income-consumption level, a decrease in income does *not* induce diminished consumption along the same function by which the consumer had reached the higher income-consumption level in the first place.[5] This concept of consumption as a function of "the income to which one is accustomed," however, involves a shift in the consumer tastes parameter which is held constant in the instantaneous short-run consumption function displayed in Figure 23–1.

Saving. That part of income not spent on consumption is said to be saved. Thus, in Figure 23–1 the shaded area above the consumption line (C) and below the income line $(Y = C + S)$ constitutes saving. Saving, like consumption, is a *positive* function of income, that is, saving tends to increase as income increases and to decline as income declines. The *marginal propensity to save* may be defined as the ratio between a change in saving and a change in income while the *average propensity to save* relates saving to income at a given income level. In terms of the example provided in Figure 23–1, the marginal propensity to save is 0.25 (25 percent) as income increases from $400 billion to $600 billion and the average propensity to save is 0.08²/₅ or 8²/₅ percent at the $600 billion income level. These results are determined as follows:

$$\text{Marginal Propensity to Save} = \frac{\text{Change in Saving}}{\text{Change in Income}}$$

$$MPS = \frac{\Delta S}{\Delta Y} \text{ and } \frac{\$50 \text{ b.}}{\$200 \text{ b.}} = 0.25$$

---

[5] James S. Duesenberry, *Income, Saving, and the Theory of Consumer Behavior* (Cambridge, Mass.: Harvard University Press, 1952).

and

$$\text{Average Propensity to Save} = \frac{\text{Saving}}{\text{Income}}$$

$$APS = \frac{S}{Y} \text{ and } \frac{\$50 \text{ b.}}{\$600 \text{ b.}} = 0.084$$

Moreover, for reasons observed above, the summation of the change in consumption (ΔC) and the change in saving (ΔS) equals the total change in income (ΔY). Thus,

$$\Delta C + \Delta S = \Delta Y$$
$$\$150\text{b.} + \$50\text{b.} = \$200\text{b.}$$
$$MPC + MPS = 1$$

Investment. The purchase of new capital goods may be motivated in a variety of ways. Modern macroeconomic theory classifies these various motivating forces into two main categories—autonomous and induced investment. *Autonomous investment* is somewhat of a "catch-all" concept. Any motivation for investment *other than* one resulting from a change in the level of (or rate of change in) aggregate economic performance is said to be autonomous. An improvement in technology, for example, may motivate investment spending regardless of the level of or rate of change in national income. The concept of *induced investment*, on the other hand, refers to changes in business spending for capital goods as influenced by changes in aggregate economic performance. Induced investment may thus be described as a functional relationship between investment and the level (or rate of change in) national income.[6] The relationship between induced investment and national income is normally a positive one. Thus, induced investment increases as national income expands and decreases as national income contracts.

The Determination of Aggregate Economic Performance. Having described the individual forces which determine aggregate economic performance in a market economy (consumption, saving, and investment), it will now be demonstrated how these separately motivated forces determine the aggregate performance level of the economy through their various interactions. The following assumptions allow the analysis to concentrate on those features of the theory which are most fundamental to its operation: (1) the economy possesses a very small government sector, that is, one which is large enough *only* to provide minimal law and order. Thus, taxes and government spending will be omitted from this simplified version of modern macroeconomic theory, (2) the economy is a "closed" economy which means that foreign trade is

---

[6] Induced investment is closely related to the operation of the *acceleration principle* which is highly significant to economic growth theory.

excluded, (3) all corporation profits are paid out as dividends; and (4) all investment is autonomous and thus not influenced by changes in the level of (or rate of change in) national income.

A significant relationship exists between the expected (planned) sales of economic goods by businesses and the production costs incurred in producing these goods. In creating *aggregate supply,* the businesses of a pure market economy incur certain costs in employing the resources necessary to produce the volume of output which they believe will be demanded. Moreover, the aggregate supply costs of businesses comprise, on the receiving end of the flow, the incomes received by consumers. The consumers use the incomes as the purchasing power sources for their decisions regarding consumption expenditure and saving. Thus, aggregate supply may be expressed by the equation:

$$Y = C + S$$

The gross incomes received by businesses in the pure market economy are derived from the sale of consumption goods to consumers and from the sale of investment (capital) goods to other businesses within the economy. The absence of foreign transactions and of governmental purchases of economic goods in the closed, pure market economy means that purchases are made *only* by the domestic private sector and its two components—consumers and businesses. Thus, *aggregate demand* may be expressed by the equation:

$$Y = C + I$$

If the *ex ante* (expected, planned) sales of consumption and investment goods are realized, then the equilibrium performance level is directly attained. If expected sales do not match the *ex post* realities, however, a state of disequilibrium exists which will set forces in motion toward the equilibrium position. Figure 23–2 and Table 23–2 demonstrate this process whereby market forces tend to achieve an equilibrium level of aggregate economic performance.[7] If expected income (column 1 in Table 23–2), which is based upon the creation by businesses of aggregate supply (Column 5 in Table 23–2), is less than $500 billion, planned saving is less than planned investment and aggregate supply is less than aggregate demand. This means that businesses will receive more from the sale of consumer and capital goods than they had expected when they created aggregate supply, and an unexpected reduction in business inventories occurs because sales exceed expectations. At an expected income (aggregate supply) level of $400 billion, for example, investment in capital goods by businesses exceeds the

---

[7] The student should be reminded that the macroeconomic model presented here is a simplified, though valid, description of the basic determinants of aggregate economic performance in a market economy.

FIGURE 23–2
Equilibrium National Income in a Pure Market Economy

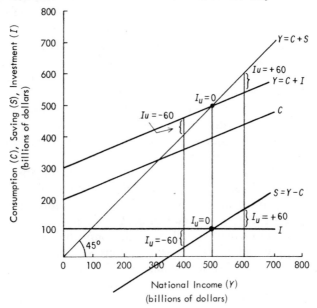

planned saving of consumers by $60 billion and an unexpected inventory reduction takes place. This "unexpected inventory reduction" may be termed a "negative" *unintended investment* or *disinvestment* $(I_u = -60)$. Businesses will thus tend to increase aggregate supply toward the $500 billion equilibrium performance level at which point planned investment and planned saving are equal and no unintended inventory change occurs $(I_u = 0)$.

TABLE 23–2
Equilibrium National Income in a Pure Market Economy (billions of dollars)

(1) Y Expected Income	(2) C Planned Consumption	(3) S Planned Saving		(4) I Planned Investment	(5) C + S Aggregate Supply		(6) C + I Aggregate Demand
$ 0	$200	$−200	<	$100	$ 0	<	$300
100	240	−140	<	100	100	<	340
200	280	− 80	<	100	200	<	380
300	320	− 20	<	100	300	<	420
400	360	+ 40	<	100	400	<	460
500	400	+100	=	100	500	=	500
600	440	+160	>	100	600	>	540
700	480	+220	>	100	700	>	580

If expected income based on the creation of aggregate supply by businesses is greater than the $500 billion equilibrium level, planned saving is greater than planned investment and aggregate supply is greater than aggregate demand. This means that businesses will receive less from the sale of consumer and capital goods than they had expected when they created aggregate supply and an unplanned expansion in business inventories occurs because sales do not meet the expectations upon which the creation of aggregate supply was based. At an expected income (aggregate supply) level of $600 billion, for example, planned saving exceeds the investment purchases of capital goods by $60 billion and unexpected inventory expansion takes place. This "unexpected inventory expansion" may be termed a "positive" *unintended investment* $(I_u = +60)$. Businesses will thus tend to contract aggregate supply toward the $500 billion equilibrium performance level at which point planned saving and planned investment are equal and no unintended inventory change $(I_u = 0)$ occurs. Hence, the equilibrium level of aggregate economic performance will be at the point (income level) where aggregate supply and aggregate demand are equal.

The *investment multiplier,* which may be defined as the ratio between a change in the level of autonomous investment and the resulting change in the level of national income, relates importantly to the equilibrium process described above. Figure 23–3, which is based on the lower part of the diagram in Figure 23–2, will be used to display the multiplier process. Consumption, which is common to both aggregate supply $(Y = C + S)$ and to aggregate demand $(Y = C + I)$, has been excluded from Figure 23–3 so that emphasis may be applied to the critical relationship between saving and investment in the determination of equilibrium.

The multipiler process may be approached from two standpoints: either from the premise of a present state of disequilibrium, or from the premise of a shift upward (increase) or downward (decrease) in the autonomous investment function. For example, a movement from the $400 billion national income level to the equilibrium level of $500 billion may be considered as moving from a disequilibrium position to an equilibrium position if I represents the prevailing level of autonomous investment. Planned saving and planned investment are equal and equilibrium is reestablished at the $500 billion income level. The multiplier in this case represents the ratio between ab and Y^2Y which, in numerical terms, is the relationship between $60 billion ($100 billion −$40 billion) and $100 billion ($500 billion−$400 billion).

The multiplier may also be viewed from the standpoint of an initial equilibrium position existing at $500 billion and a subsequent move from this equilibrium to a new equilibrium position at a different income level. For example, if autonomous investment increases from I

FIGURE 23–3
The Investment Multiplier

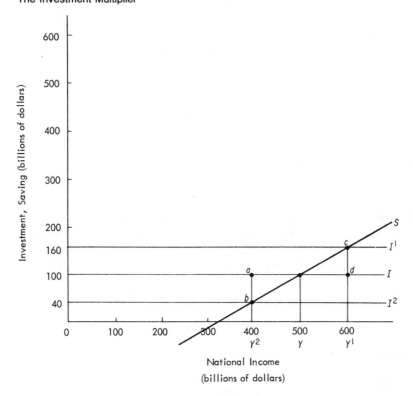

National Income
(billions of dollars)

to I^1 (from \$100 billion to \$160 billion), national income will increase from \$500 billion to \$600 billion. This is represented in Figure 23–3 by the ratio between cd and YY^1. Moreover, since the multiplier may be contractionary as well as expansionary (that is, either negative or positive), a reduction of investment from I to I^2 will cause national income to decline from \$500 billion to \$400 billion. The value of the multiplier ratio is determined by the values of the marginal propensities to consume and to save. The multiplier formula, with K symbolizing the multiplier, may thus be stated as follows:

$$K = \frac{1}{1 - mpc}$$

or, alternately, as

$$K = \frac{1}{mps}$$

where *mpc* indicates the marginal propensity to consume and *mps* indicates the marginal propensity to save.[8]

In terms of the data in Figure 23–3, the multiplier value is 1.66⅔ (assuming a marginal propensity to save of 0.60) since a $60 billion increase in autonomous investment leads to a $100 billion increase in national income. From the formula

$$K = \frac{1}{mps} \text{ or } \frac{1}{0.60} = 1.66\tfrac{2}{3}$$

and $\Delta I(\$60 \text{ billion}) \times K(1.66\tfrac{2}{3}) = \Delta Y(\$100 \text{ billion})$

From the formula, it should be observed that saving is the only leakage from the spending stream in this example of the investment multiplier operating in a closed, pure market economy. Yet, the rather high marginal propensity to save (0.60) used in the example still results in a multiplier value (1.66⅔) which would be a realistic figure for an open, mixed economy where international and public sector economic transactions provide additional leakages from the spending stream.

---

[8] Algebraically, the derivation of the investment multiplier may be stated:

$$\Delta I + \Delta C = \Delta Y \quad \text{(true by definition)}$$

dividing through by Y

$$\therefore \frac{\Delta I}{\Delta Y} + \frac{\Delta C}{\Delta Y} = 1$$

$$\therefore \frac{\Delta I}{\Delta Y} = 1 - \frac{\Delta C}{\Delta Y}$$

$$\therefore \frac{\Delta Y}{\Delta I} = \frac{1}{1 - \frac{\Delta C}{\Delta Y}}$$

but $\frac{\Delta Y}{\Delta I} = K$ (multiplier)

and $\frac{\Delta C}{\Delta Y} = mpc$ (marginal propensity to consume)

$$\therefore \text{ multiplier } (K) = \frac{1}{1 - mpc}$$

or, since $mpc + mps = \Delta Y$ or 1

$$\text{multiplier } (K) = \frac{1}{mps}$$

Deflationary and Inflationary Gaps

It is very significant that the aggregate economic performance level attained through the process described above does *not* necessarily provide full employment of labor and capital and price stability. There is nothing inherent in the Keynesian model, such as wage and price flexibility, to assure these optimal short-run results. The "liquidity trap," moreover, will tend to forestall the ability of changes in the monetary stock to influence aggregate demand through changes in the rate of interest.[9] The pure market economy may, by coincidence, operate at a full-employment noninflationary equilibrium. On the other hand, the economy may attain an undesirable equilibrium level of performance with either substantial labor and capital unemployment or with "monetary" inflation. The former is known as a *deflationary gap* condition and the latter as an *inflationary gap*. These "less than optimal" results are demonstrated in Figure 23–4 and are described in detail below.

"Optimal" results are attained in the graph at a $500 billion national income level because labor and capital resources are fully employed and "monetary" inflation does not exist at this performance level. Full employment, of course, must be defined in some acceptable manner. Typically, *full employment* is said to exist if 4 percent or less of the labor force is involuntarily unemployed and capital capacity in major industries is utilized at approximately 90 percent of capacity. Furthermore, a distinction must be made between *monetary* (demand) inflation and *monopoly* (administered price, sellers') inflation. Although "monetary" inflation does *not* exist at the $500 billion equilibrium level of performance, "monopoly" inflation, as caused by market imperfections in product and factor markets, may well exist.[10] Thus, if optimal performance is defined to include complete price stability, then even the $500 billion level of performance is not optimal when monopoly inflation exists.

Where the intersection of aggregate supply ($Y = C + S$) and aggregate demand ($Y = C + I$) sets the performance level at full employment without monetary inflation, as at the $500 billion national income level in Figure 23–4, the society neither suffers from lost output due to unemployment nor from monetary inflation resulting from resource scarcity. Yet, as observed above, this condition would only be accidentally attained under the operational process of a pure market economy. Aggregate demand may be deficient to aggregate supply at full employment ($Y = C + I^1 < Y = C + S$), thus creating a deflationary gap, or it

---

[9] The student may refer to a *Money and Banking* textbook for a review of the liquidity-preference theory of interest rate determination.

[10] This point will be analyzed further in Chapter 25 with the discussion of the relationship of the Phillips curve and intergoal nonneutrality to fiscal policy.

FIGURE 23–4
Deflationary and Inflationary Gap Conditions

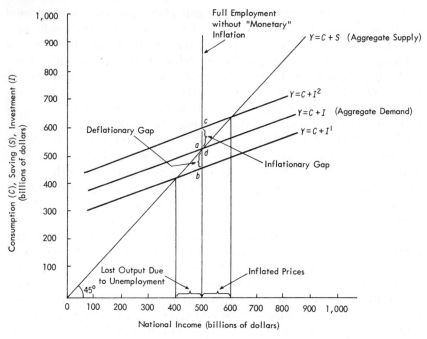

may exceed aggregate supply at full employment ($Y = C + I^2 > Y = C + S$), thus creating an inflationary gap situation. *Any* of these three situations may exist. The pure market economy will not automatically tend toward any one of them. The deflationary gap *ab* will cause reduced output by the amount of $100 billion ($500 billion minus $400 billion). The inflationary gap *cd* will lead to inflated output by the amount of $100 billion ($600 billion minus $500 billion). The ratios between *ab* and the "lost output" and between *cd* and the "inflated output" represent the value of the multiplier as discussed in the previous section. Thus, if an *ab* equal to $60 billion causes reduced output of $100 billion, the multiplier value is 1.66⅔.

The Problem of Economic Growth

Not only does the pure market economy fail to assure full employment without monetary inflation, there is, in addition, no evidence that it will automatically tend to achieve a satisfactory rate of economic growth. The forces which determine economic growth in a market-directed economy are far more complex than those analyzed above for short-run aggregate performance. In addition, they involve significant noneconomic as well as economic variables. No attempt will be made in this book to develop a comprehensive theory of economic growth. Though economic science has contributed many useful theories of economic growth, no single theory is comprehensive enough to be used as a general analytical reference point.[11] Hence, the analysis herein of fiscal procedures to assist economic growth will be based on certain widely accepted general aspects of the growth process rather than on a single definitive theory.

There is no question, for example, that both the quantitative expansion of productive resources, particularly capital, as well as the qualitative improvement of these resources are essential to the maintenance of a satisfactory growth rate. In addition, the importance of noneconomic factors such as political stability, particularly in underdeveloped economies, stands out as a proven fact. There is also no doubt as to the importance of the dual role of investment in the growth process, namely, that investment not only continues its short-run function of utilizing the saving generated at full-employment equilibrium in the economy, but that it also involves the long-run problem of absorbing the incremental output added by net additions to the nation's capital stock.[12] Indeed, if the economy is to grow steadily it must possess a continually rising level of its growing productive capacity.

The fact that the American economy has not always experienced steady growth, not even satisfactory growth rates, is indicated by Figures 23-5 and 23-6 and by Tables 23-3 and 23-4. In Figure 23-5, the cyclically interruped pattern of American economic growth during the 100 years following 1860 is evident. The graph is presented with particular emphasis on the long swing variety of business cycle. Such emphasis is not meant to imply, however, that cycles of shorter duration did not also occur during the period. Figure 23-6 shows the effect of cyclical fluctuations on the employment of nonfarm (industrial) labor. Obviously, growth rates are slowed when involuntary unemployment

---

[11] Some of the more important writings which provide insight into the economic growth process are: Roy F. Harrod, "An Essay in Dynamic Theory," *Economic Journal,* March 1939, pp. 14–33; Evsey Domar, "Expansion and Employment," *American Economic Review,* March 1947, pp. 34–55; James S. Duesenberry, *Business Cycles and Economic Growth* (New York: McGraw-Hill Book Co., 1958); Robert M. Solow, "Technical Change and the Aggregate Production Function," *Review of Economics and Statistics,* August, 1957, pp. 312–20, and "Technical Progress, Capital Formulation, and Economic Growth," *American Economic Review,* May, 1962, pp. 76–86; William Fellner, *Trends and Cycles in Economic Activity* (New York: Holt, 1956), and John R. Hicks, *A Contribution to the Theory of the Trade Cycle* (Oxford: The Clarendon Press, 1950). The Hicksian Model will be summarized in Chapter 25 because of its relevance to intergoal nonneutrality between the stabilization and economic growth goals and the application of fiscal policy to these goals.

[12] This concept is developed in the Harrod-Domar growth models cited in footnote 11.

FIGURE 23-5

Long Swings in United States Aggregate Production, 1860–1961, Annual Estimates and Nine-Year Moving Averages

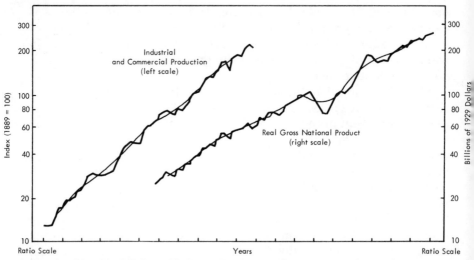

Source: Adapted from Bert G. Hickman, "The Postwar Retardation: Another Long Swing in the Rate of Growth?," *American Economic Review*, May 1963, Chart I, p. 491.

exists in the economy. Tables 23–3 and 23–4 also display the interrupted pattern of American economic growth. The variation in the growth rates of *real net national product* during the period 1889–1968, as shown in Table 23–3, range from 6.2 percent between 1962–68 to a very unsatisfactory 0.2 percent between 1929–37. Moreover, Table 23–4 demonstrates a considerable variability in the growth rates of *real gross national product* during the 1929–72 time span.

Since there is no inherent process in a market-directed economy to assure either noninflationary full employment or a satisfactory rate of economic growth, a case may be built for the deliberate application of governmental economic policy to help achieve these aggregate eco-

FIGURE 23-6

Long Swings in Unemployment in the United States, 1874–1960

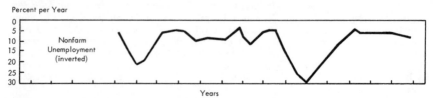

Source: Adapted from Bert G. Hickman, "The Postwar Retardation: Another Long Swing in the Rate of Growth?," *American Economic Review*, May 1963, Chart III, p. 495.

TABLE 23–3
Growth of Real Net National Product in the United States, 1889–1968 (average annual percentage rates of change)

Time Period	Real Net National Product	Time Period	Real Net National Product
1889–99	4.5%	1937–48	4.4%
1899–1909	4.3	1948–53	4.7
1909–19	3.8	1953–57	2.2
1919–29	3.1	1957–62	4.1
1929–37	0.2	1962–68	6.2

Source: John W. Kendrick, *Productivity Trends in the United States,* A National Bureau of Economic Research Study (Princeton, N.J.: Princeton University Press, 1961), Table 6, p. 79. Reprinted by permission of Princeton University Press. Copyright, 1961; *Statistical Abstract of the United States,* 1960, 1964, 1965, 1969; *Federal Reserve Bulletin,* March 1970.

nomic goals. Thus, just as *market failure* of an "allocative" nature (see Part One of this book) helps to establish an economic case for the existence of government in a market-oriented system, so also *market failure* of an "aggregate" variety helps to establish an economic case for the existence of government. Figures 23–7a and 23–7b demonstrate graphically the ability of public sector budgetary policy to promote aggregate *stabilization* and *economic growth* goals. In Figure 23–7a, points *A* and *B* reflect an under-full employment of resources. If fiscal

TABLE 23–4
Growth of Real Gross National Product in the United States, 1929–72 (average annual percentage rates of change)

Time Period	Real Gross National Product	Time Period	Real Gross National Product
1929–33	− 1.9%	1955–56	1.8%
1933–39	8.5	1956–57	1.5
1939–40	8.5	1957–58	−1.1
1940–41	16.1	1958–59	6.4
1941–42	12.9	1959–60	2.5
1942–43	13.2	1960–61	1.9
1943–44	7.2	1961–62	6.6
1944–45	− 1.7	1962–63	4.0
1945–46	−12.0	1963–64	5.4
1946–47	− 0.9	1964–65	6.3
1947–48	4.4	1965–66	6.5
1948–49	0.2	1966–67	2.6
1949–50	9.6	1967–68	4.7
1950–51	7.9	1968–69	2.7
1951–52	3.0	1969–70	−0.5
1952–53	4.5	1970–71	2.7
1953–54	− 1.4	1971–72	6.5
1954–55	7.6		

Source: U.S. Department of Commerce.

FIGURE 23-7
The Use of Government Fiscal Policy to Attain Aggregate Economic Objectives

a. Movement to Full Employment   b. Resource Expansion and Economic Growth

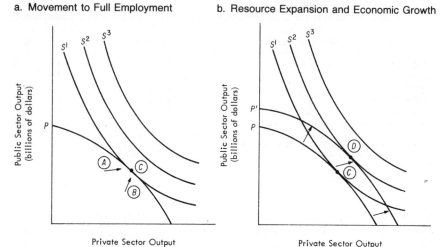

policy can sufficiently stimulate employment of the unemployed resources, production can occur along the societal production-possibility
curve *P,* such as at point *C,* instead of inside the curve.[13] On the other
hand, successful fiscal policy can also stimulate quantitative and qualitative expansion in the economic resource base of the society over time
and, thus, cause the societal production-possibility curve *P* to move to
the right becoming *P¹* (See Figure 23-7b). The result is economic
growth with greater economic output being consumed along social
indifference curve *S²,* as contrasted to curve *S¹.* Importantly, a "fiscal
policy" in the form of "fiscal effects" exists whether one is desired or
not because government cannot act in a budgetary manner without
influencing the various economic goals—including short-run stabilization and long-run growth. Hence, the impact of government might just
as well be "rationalized" in terms of deliberate policy. The primary
responsibility for aggregate economic policy rests with the federal government. It was not until 1946 that Congress formally recognized this
fact and passed legislation providing a mandate for federal fiscal (and
monetary) policy to help improve the aggregate performance of the
economy.

---

[13] Observe once again, as described in Chapter 1, that the full employment of resources is a "necessary," but not a "sufficient," condition for optimal intersector resource
allocation. Thus, a successful stabilization policy may move output from point *A* or point
B to the societal production-possibility curve *P,* but not necessarily to point *C* on that
curve.

THE EMPLOYMENT ACT OF 1946—A LEGISLATIVE MANDATE FOR FISCAL POLICY

Nature of the Employment Act

The year 1946, the first year of the post-World War II economic era, found the nation's economy operating under severe inflationary gap conditions. The enormous federal spending in support of World War II had exerted tremendous inflationary pressures during the previous four years. Aggregate demand was considerably greater than aggregate supply at full-employment output during the period. Once the war was over, the long-postponed demand for consumer goods such as cars, refrigerators, and houses, along with the postponed business demand for peacetime capital goods, provided continued inflationary pressures. Moreover, this high volume of aggregate demand was made "effective" by wartime savings. In addition, World War II had allowed the economy to escape a severe decade-long depression, which had begun with a cyclical downturn just prior to the stock market collapse of late 1929. The lingering fears of depression in the minds of senators and congressmen, businessmen, professional economists, and others, along with the then-existing conditions of inflation, laid the groundwork for the passage of the Employment Act in 1946. The essence of this extremely important legislation reads:[14]

> The Congress hereby declares that it is the continuing policy and responsibility of the Federal Government to use all practicable means consistent with its needs and obligations and other essential considerations of national policy, with the assistance and cooperation of industry, agriculture, labor, and State and local governments, to coordinate and utilize all its plans, functions, and resources for the purpose of creating and maintaining, in a manner calculated to foster and promote free competitive enterprise and the general welfare, conditions under which there will be afforded useful employment opportunities, including self-employment, for those able, willing, and seeking work, and to promote maximum employment, production, and purchasing power.

With the passage of such legislation, the central government of the United States joined the national governments of other mature Western industrial nations in stipulating a governmental responsibility to promote aggregate economic performance through *rational economic policy*. Such policy normally takes the form of *monetary* and *fiscal* tools. The act clearly authorizes federal government economic activity to favorably influence aggregate economic performance. The federal gov-

---

[14] *The Employment Act of 1946,* February 20, 1946, P.L. 304, 79th Cong., 2d sess. (60 Stat. 23).

ernment, however, is given the mandate to conduct such policy only in cooperation with the considerations of the market sector of the economy, as is evident in the part of the above statement which says that the federal government is to act "in a manner calculated to foster and promote free competitive enterprise."

The Employment Act directly specifies the maximum employment goal, but it is somewhat less direct, though by no means unclear, in its mandate for maintaining reasonable price level stability. The latter goal is implicit in the phrase which authorizes efforts to promote "maximum purchasing power" and was also evident in the congressional debate prior to the passage of the bill. Less precise is the mandate for federal fiscal policy to promote satisfactory rates of economic growth. Increasing emphasis on the growth objective, however, has been present in the fiscal policy of recent years and the interpretation of the Employment Act has clearly been broadened to include the economic growth objective. Similarly, it has also been broadened in interpretation in recent years to include the stabilization goal of improvement in the nation's balance of international payments.

The Employment Act requires that a report regarding the state of the American economy be submitted to Congress by the executive branch no later than January 20 of each year. The first report under the act was submitted in January of 1947. The *Economic Report of the President* describes such matters as the employment, output, and price level conditions and trends of the economy, a review of federal fiscal and monetary policies, and other relevant economic considerations.

The legislation also established a Council of Economic Advisers (CEA) to assist and advise the President on economic matters. The *Economic Report of the President,* referred to above, is based in part upon analytical work provided by the CEA. The Council of Economic Advisers consists of three members. The act also established the Joint Committee on the Economic Report. This group was first created for the purpose of conducting economic studies pertinent only to the *Economic Report of the President.* The analysis conducted by the Committee, however, has been gradually extended over a wide range of economic issues and is no longer solely for the *Economic Report.* Furthermore, the name of the Committee has been subsequently changed to Joint Economic Committee (JEC). The JEC consists of eight members each from the Senate and House and is supplemented by a highly competent professional staff. To a large extent, the Joint Economic Committee provides broad economic analysis for the direct benefit of Congress and indirectly for the benefit of academicians, businessmen, labor unions, and others interested in the performance of the aggregate economy. It does so in a manner analagous to the role performed by the Council of Economic Advisers whose studies directly benefit the executive branch of the federal government and indirectly benefit many other interested parties.

Defining and Measuring Employment Act Goals

The Stabilization Objective. Effective administration of the Employment Act requires workable definitions of the important aggregate economic goals and, in addition, relies upon the ability to measure these aggregates in an adequate manner. The discussion at this point will classify the "full-employment," "price stability," and "international balance-of-payments" goals as subparts of the more comprehensive *stabilization* goal, and will consider a satisfactory rate of *economic growth* as the other major aggregate objective. For each goal, definitions will be discussed first and then measurement devices will be considered.

The *full-employment goal* could be approached, in a strict sense, by defining *full employment of labor* as a situation in which there is a complete absence of involuntary labor unemployment in the economy. Thus, full labor employment would be said to exist when all workers are willing to work at the prevailing wages of their occupation and, in addition, are able to obtain employment. On the other hand, *unemployment* would be present if some workers who are willing to work at the prevailing wages of their occupation are unable to find employment after a reasonable time. In a "broader" and more practical sense, however, full labor employment could be defined to include a certain minimal amount of involuntary unemployment. An allowance for "frictional unemployment," for example, should be made in any reasonable definition of full employment. A worker is frictionally unemployed if he is out of work due to labor market imperfections such as the time lost in changing occupations, temporary seasonal layoffs, and unemployment resulting from material shortages. Another variety of involuntary unemployment is known as "structural unemployment." This refers to persistent unemployment caused by technological change (including automation), by changes in the composition of product demand, and by the competition provided to domestic products by the importation of foreign economic goods.

The "definition" of full labor employment to be used in this book, given the above considerations, is similar to the workable definition used by a majority of policymakers. *Full labor employment* will be said to exist when 4 percent or less of the labor force is involuntarily unemployed.[15] An allowance thus is made for a modest amount of involuntary

---

[15] There are a growing number of experts who advocate a higher "full employment percentage," such as 4.5 percent, due to the changing composition of the labor force. For a discussion of the "unemployment rate" implications of the "changing composition of the labor force," see *Economic Report of the President—1974* (Washington: U.S. Government Printing Office, 1974), pp. 58–62.

labor unemployment resulting from frictional and structural causes. In terms of capital capacity, *full capital employment* will be defined along the generally accepted lines of 90 percent utilization.[16]

Labor force data for "measuring" employment and unemployment are provided by four federal agencies. These include the Bureau of Employment Security and the Bureau of Labor Statistics in the U.S. Department of Labor, the Bureau of the Census in the U.S. Department of Commerce, and the Bureau of Agricultural Economics in the U.S. Department of Agriculture. Statistics on the "employment status" of the population, that is, the personal, occupational, and other characteristics of those who are employed, the number of unemployed, and persons not in the labor force, and related data, are compiled by the Bureau of the Census on a monthly basis for the Bureau of Labor Statistics. These monthly surveys use a scientifically selected sample designed to represent the civilian noninstitutional population 16 years of age and over. *Unemployed persons* are classified as those persons who did not work for pay during the week preceding the survey, who made specific efforts to find a job within the previous four weeks, and who were available for work during the survey week. Moreover, the classification includes as "unemployed" those who did not work at all, who were available for work, and who were awaiting a call back to a job from which they had been laid off, who were waiting to report to a new wage or salary job within 30 days, or who would have been looking for work except for temporary illness.

The "unemployment rate" compiled through the above approach is widely used as an indicator of aggregate economic activity. Specifically, this unemployment rate represents the number unemployed, as defined above, as a percentage of the civilian labor force. Moreover, the data also reveal unemployment rates according to groups "within the labor force," as classified by sex, age, marital status, color, and the like. Although some disaggregation of the data thus does exist, it is generally agreed that further disaggregation of the data would be desirable so as to better ascertain the "composition of unemployment" in the United States. This issue, it might be added, is particularly pertinent to the social problem of poverty.

The stabilization goal of full employment, of course, is intrinsically related to the aggregate output of the nation, and to the income earned by productive resources in producing this output. Hence, the social statistics provided by the U.S. Department of Commerce in the form of its "National Income and Product Accounts" play a major role in measuring the aggregate performance of the economy. These accounts

---

[16] It is *not* rational to expect, of course, that all or even most units of the land factor of production (natural resources) be utilized in a given year.

are built on a premise similar to the income statements used by business enterprises in the sense that they are constructed in a double-entry manner. They emphasize the related flows of income and output in the economy during a particular time period. One calendar year divided into four quarters constitutes the time period. Money is used as the common denominator of value for the aggregates. On the one side, the accounts measure the "value of output" ("product") as it is constituted by the major categories of purchasers of national output. Total American production of new goods and services in a given year is purchased by consumers, businesses, and governments within the nation and by foreign purchasers. The output referred to is *final* output, thus eliminating double counting in the various value-added stages of production. In addition, output refers only to currently produced items. "Claims" against the value of national output are measured on the other side of the national income and product accounts. Income for the productive resources which produced the output, indirect business taxes, and capital depreciation allowances are important items on this "claims side" of national income and product accounting.

The Department of Commerce provides four subclassifications which comprise the composite national income and product accounting system. These are: (1) the *personal* income and outlay account which demonstrates the income and expenditure totals for households (consumers); (2) the gross saving and investment account of *business* operations which shows the nation's saving, and the disposition thereof, during the time period involved; (3) the *government* receipts and expenditures account which shows the public sector's resource-allocating activities during the time period; and (4) the *foreign* account which shows purchases by the United States from foreign nations (imports) and purchases by foreign nations from the United States (exports) during the time period. Thus, a *personal* sector, a *business* sector, a *government* sector, and a *foreign* sector comprise the comprehensive national income and product accounts which reveal the value of total current production, and claims against that production, for the entire economy during a specified time period.

Among the aggregate concepts derived from these accounts, which may be useful for information and policy-making purposes, are gross national product, net national product, national income, personal income, and disposable income. *Gross National Product* refers to the money value of all final goods produced by the nation's economy in a certain time period, usually one year. *Net National Product* relates to the money value of all final goods production, as defined above, minus estimated business capital depreciation allowances during the period. *National Income,* which derives from the claims side of the accounts, refers to the factor earnings which accrue to the owners of the resources used to produce national output (gross national product) during the period under consideration. *Personal Income* measures the spending power which individuals and families actually receive as opposed to what they have earned (national income). For example, some earned income such as social security deductions, corporation income taxes, and undistributed corporation profits are not actually received by households. Moreover, some purchasing power is received—transfer payments—though it does not represent current earnings. Finally, *Disposable Income* represents what remains of personal income after various personal taxes such as personal income taxes have been paid. The selection of any one of the five aggregate economic indicators cited above will depend, of course, on the purpose in mind.

The *price stability goal* relates importantly to the control of "inflation." The term *inflation* refers generally to an increase in a level or index of various relevant prices. *Deflation*, of course, is the opposite of inflation as price levels decline. Recent decades have witnessed far more reasons to be concerned with rising than with declining prices. The analysis of various types of inflation is importantly related to rational economic policy. There are two basic types of inflation, namely, *monetary* (demand) and *monopoly* (administered price, sellers') inflation. The former is identified with inflationary gap conditions (as described above). World War II and the immediate postwar era provide an excellent example of monetary inflation whereby aggregate demand, as made effective by adequate purchasing power, exceeds aggregate supply at full resource employment, Monetary and fiscal policy, especially the former, are reasonably adept at combating this type of inflation. However, monopoly inflation, which derives essentially from market imperfections in product and factor markets, is less ably treated by conventional stabilization policy. Though monopoly inflation is obviously interrelated with the overall relationship between aggregate demand and aggregate supply, particularly as a full-employment equilibrium is approached, empirical evidence and conceptual reasoning indicate that it remains to a large extent independent in its mode of behavior.[17] Oligopoly firms, in particular, have been known to increase prices while operating at considerably less than full capital capacity and while national labor unemployment rates were above any acceptable level.

The United States does not possess a "completely adequate measure" of general price level behavior, though the techniques in use do possess overall favorable qualities. The three primary price measurement devices are the Consumer Price Index (CPI), Wholesale Price Index (WPI), and the GNP-deflator. The *Consumer Price Index* is referred to as a

---

[17] See the relevant discussion of the "Phillips curve" in Chapter 25.

cost-of-living index. This index, which is provided monthly by the Bureau of Labor Statistics of the U.S. Department of Labor, serves as a measure of the average change in the prices of goods and services purchased by urban wage earner and clerical worker families as compared to the average level in selected base years. It is limited in scope, however, since it just pertains to consumer purchases, not to business and government purchases. In addition, it measures only *certain* consumer purchases, namely, those by urban wage earner and clerical worker families. These people only comprise around 50 percent of the total urban population of the nation. The CPI, nonetheless, is the most prominently used indicator of price level behavior for the American economy.

Some 400 items are included in the typical "market basket" of purchases in the CPI. These items are differently weighted in the index as based upon estimates of their relative importance to the average urban wage and clerical worker family. A major review of the market basket of items is undertaken every decade or so. Partial revisions of the index and its market basket composition are made on more frequent occasions. This "relatively infrequent" review of purchase patterns may lead to an inflationary bias in the index if people substitute lower-priced for higher-priced items, and the CPI weighting of items does not pick up the change. For example, many consumers may substitute chicken for pork if the price of the latter increases the more rapidly of the two. If the CPI does not account for this change, pork with its more rapidly increasing prices will be a "disproportionately high" proportion of total consumer spending.

The most serious weakness of the CPI is the inability of the index to adequately account for changes in the *quality* of the 400 economic goods included in the index. The CPI could show stable prices over a five-year period, for example, but a 10 percent increase in the quality of the goods consumed during the period would mean that actual deflation had taken place. The purchasing power of the dollar would have increased in this instance, though it would statistically appear that the value of the dollar had not changed. Alternately, this "upward bias" in the index could register a statistical rate of inflation greater than the real or actual amount of inflation which may have occurred. Thus, a 10 percent increase in the CPI over a five-year period, if accompanied by a 5 percent increase in product quality, would "overstate" the rate of inflation. Thus, "undue emphasis" placed on the Consumer Price Index for stabilization policy decisions could, at times, be misleading and lead to undesirable consequences.

The *Wholesale Price Index* is also provided on a monthly basis by the Bureau of Labor Statistics. It is a measure of the average change in the prices of 2,200 goods and resources at the primary market level (the level at which the goods and resources are first commercially sold in substantial volume) as compared to the average prices in selected base years. The WPI is weighted heavily in terms of raw materials and capital goods. Goods and resources sold directly to consumers and to the public sector are excluded from the index. The WPI suffers from many of the same problems as the CPI. It is not comprehensive and, importantly, does not allow for quality changes.

A third indicator of price level performance in the American economy is the implicit price deflator for gross national product which is known as the *GNP-deflator*. It is provided on a quarterly basis by the U.S. Department of Commerce. This is a measure of average changes in the market prices of those goods and services represented in the national income and product accounts, as compared to average price levels in selected base years. That is, it adjusts GNP for price changes and gives the data in constant dollars. This is a more comprehensive measurement of national price level performance than are the CPI and WPI. The public sector, for example, is included in this indicator. Yet, the GNP-deflator also fails to adequately consider changes in the quality of the items which it measures. For example, it does not adjust for changes in the productivity of government workers. In this regard, it shares an important weakness with the CPI and WPI. An improved indicator of price trends would need to account adequately for this deficiency. In addition, better data are required for the service industries, state and local government economic activities, and in the area of fringe benefits. Indeed, much room lies in the direction of improvement in the ability of the nation to measure the price level trends of the economy, though the CPI, WPI, and GNP-deflator techniques do possess many favorable features.

The most recently added Employment Act goal, though not explicitly stated in the act, is that of attaining a satisfactory equilibrium for the nation in its *balance of international payments.* Net gold outflow from the American economy to the rest of the world has persisted during much of the period since the late 1950s. "Monetary" and "fiscal" policy have been applied, with some degree of effectiveness, to rectify this situation. It is easy to understand that monetary policy, by affecting interest rates, will influence the flow of American investment dollars into the international economic arena. Fiscal policy, moreover, can influence the nation's balance of international payments through the overall structure and magnitude of federal revenue-expenditure patterns in the budget. Though a definition of an ideal balance in international payments involves complex considerations beyond the scope of discussion in this book, it is safe to conclude, nonetheless, that a persistent gold outflow is undesirable. Thus, deliberate public sector economic policy can be justifiably directed toward improvement of such a situation.

One measurement approach for international balance of payments performance is "international balance-of-payments accounting." This approach measures the income, product, and financial transactions which occur between the United States and the rest of the world. International balance-of-payments accounting is more comprehensive than the foreign sector account of the national income and product accounting system since it includes financial transactions as well as measurement of the value of goods and services output and the various claims against this output.

"Current-account" transactions in international balance-of-payments accounting measure the total of goods and services available for consumption by Americans and "capital-account" transactions are concerned with dealings in real property or debt instruments. Both current and capital account transactions are reflected normally by changes in the "cash account." Transactions which increase American cash holdings of foreign currency appear in the current and capital accounts preceded by a plus (+) sign. Those transactions which decrease American cash holdings are preceded in each account by a minus (−) sign. In the cash account itself, however, double-entry bookkeeping requires that increases in American cash holdings of foreign currency be preceded by a minus (−) sign while increases in foreign holdings of American currency are preceded by a plus (+) sign. The Department of Commerce collects the data and formulates the international balance-of-payments accounts. This social accounting technique is clearly important to governmental economic policies which seek to improve the balance of international payments.

The Economic Growth Objective. *Economic growth,* in a broad sense, has been the subject of economic discussion for many centuries. Adam Smith and the early classical economists were concerned with the long-term development of a market economy. Later, Karl Marx predicated his theory of socialism on certain predictions involving long-term economic changes under a capitalistic system. Meanwhile, patterns of economic change in this century, including the industrialization of the Soviet Union and the chronic depressions experienced by mature Western market economies during the 1930s, have focused attention on the differences which exist between the process of economic growth in nations where industrialization is in early stages of development as opposed to the growth process in those nations which have already achieved industrial maturity. Thus, for purposes of clarity in discussion, the variant growth processes in "underdeveloped" or "developing" as opposed to "developed" economies should be defined as separate categories.[18]

---

[18] See Chapter 22 entitled "The Public Sector in Other Nations" for relevant discussion of the "fiscal differences" of developed versus underdeveloped nations.

Hence, the term *economic growth* will be used, strictly speaking, to refer to the continuing expansion of an already mature economy while the term *economic development* will be used, in a strict sense, to mean economic progress in an "underdeveloped" or "developing" nation. The former stresses specific economic problems, such as the maintenance of sufficient aggregate demand to fully utilize growing capital capacity in an industralized economy, while the latter involves a broader approach inclusive of such considerations as the need to acquire social overhead capital as a forerunner of the growth process as well as numerous noneconomic considerations.

However, the above classification of *economic progress* into "growth" and "development" segments, though helpful, cannot be applied on a mutually exclusive basis. In other words, the problems of a nation relevant to economic progress are not necessarily *all* growth nor *all* development problems. A mature industrial nation, for example, may possess regions or localities within its aggregate structure which are relatively underdeveloped. An underdeveloped nation, moreover, may have certain isolated sectors or industries which have already achieved industrial maturity. Thus, it is difficult to attain an aggregate distinction between economic growth and economic development which is *precise* enough to place a given nation completely within a single category. The difference between such a "precise aggregate classification" and the still useful *disaggregate* distinction between "economic growth" and "economic development" should be recognized. The economic progress objective of the United States, though primarily one of economic growth in a mature industrial society, still cannot ignore regional and local underdevelopment problems.

Thus, a national economy (in a sense) grows as a "set of regions." Differential resource endowments designate the economic boundaries between these economic regions. Clearly, if each economic region within a national economy produces according to its comparative advantage, that is, produces those economic goods which it has the best relative efficiencies in producing, the total output of the national economy will be maximized and a higher living standard can be attained. Regional specialization, and subsequent trade or exchange, thus is beneficial not only to the regions, but also to the entire national economy in that it furthers the attainment of maximum output by the whole economy. Obviously, the same economic principles apply to regional specialization in production and trade *within* nations as apply to national specialization in production and international trade *between* nations. Indeed, rational fiscal policy should reflect these facts.

Finally, it should be noted that recent years have witnessed a growing number of people who question the advisability of pursuing the economic growth goal in mature industrial societies to the extent this has been done in the past. These people reason that continuing rapid growth leads to an unacceptable level of *negative externalities* such as air and water pollution and urban congestion. Furthermore, they argue that traditional social accounting techniques which attempt to measure economic growth do not account for the "dis-welfare" to society resulting from these growth-induced negative externalities.

The definitions of economic growth and economic development are not easily translated into "measurement" terms. As classified above, both the economic growth of industrial societies and the economic development of nonindustrial societies involve the attainment of "economic progress." Yet, what is economic progress? How is it measured?

Economic progress, as a term inclusive of both economic growth and economic development, derives from the "economic" resource base of a society. Yet, economic progress may also entail significant "noneconomic" activities. Social changes to provide political stability, for example, may be prerequisite to economic progress in an underdeveloped nation. Yet, the economic progress itself derives from the base of economic resources, known as *productive capacity,* which is available to the society.

The productive capacity of an economy thus derives from the land, labor, and capital resources available for the production of economic goods. Yet, the national product or output of the society will be determined not only by the quantity of such resources but also by their quality. In this book, the *level of technology* is used in a broad sense to refer to the ability of the society through a variety of techniques to improve the quality of its productive resources. Economic growth and development may thus be said to consist of absolute growth in the productive capacity of the economy over a period of time as determined by increases in the quantity and/or quality of its productive resources.

Though attractive in many ways, the above definition of economic progress is not completely satisfactory. The expansion of productive capacity over time, for example, does not necessarily mean that the capacity is fully used in producing economic goods. Some of the productive capacity, due to depressions or to natural disasters, may be involuntarily idle during the period in question. Thus, it is not the *potential* production of economic goods, but instead their *actual* production which satisfies human wants. The satisfaction of human wants, of course, is the ultimate objective of all economic activity. *Human welfare* thus becomes the common denominator of economic progress since it is the primary reason for economic production. Generally speaking, if human welfare has been increased in the society over a period of time, economic progress has occurred.

Welfare, as observed in Part One of this book, is *not* a simple proposition conducive to analysis and measurement. In fact, no precise economic definition of "human welfare" exists because the allocation of the economic goods which satisfy material wants is subject to the prerequisite of the society's state of distribution.[19] The "proper" distribution of income, wealth, and political voting power in a society is dependent, in turn, upon a noneconomic value judgment. Since distribution is a prerequisite to allocation decisions and to their resulting welfare effects, an aggregate measurement of economic progress such as the growth of aggregate output is not a completely satisfactory indicator. This is true because distribution, by its very nature, is a disaggregate concept. Human welfare from the consumption of economic goods cannot be viewed merely as a total without consideration of the individual composition of that total. Distribution determines such composition. A step in the right direction toward the attainment of the best possible measure of economic progress is found in the conversion of aggregate output (or aggregate income) to *per capita output.* This can be achieved by adjusting the increase in output between two points of time by any population change which may have occurred during the period. If per capita output has increased, there is good indication that economic growth (or development) has taken place.

Increases in per capita output over time, however, may *not* indicate economic progress if significant price level changes have taken place during the period. If per capita output doubles over a 20-year period while the price level also doubles, for example, real per capita output is unchanged and economic growth, in human welfare terms, seemingly would not have occurred. Thus, *real per capita output* is superior to any of the other indicators of economic progress which have been discussed to this point.

Real per capita output figures, however, include *both* consumption and capital goods. Since capital goods do not directly satisfy human wants, shifts in the proportions of consumption and capital goods production over time may result in a misleading indicator of changes in human welfare. A strong argument may thus be offered that *real per capita consumption* is a better indicator of economic progress than is real per capita output. Theoretically, this argument appears valid. A significant portion of consumption goods in a mixed private sector-public sector economy, however, are not subject to convenient measurement. Consumption goods of a pure public or quasi-public nature provided by government, for example, are normally excluded from per capita consumption figures in social accounts since they are purchased through tax payments rather than from income flows.

---

[19] However, given a value-judgment-selected state of *distribution,* optimal intersector resource *allocation* reflective of "Pareto optimality" can be conceptually determined.

Though such asymmetry in the measurement of consumption is theoretically unjustifiable, the difficulty of measuring the consumptive value of governmental activities is recognizable. Hence, the ideal indicator of economic progress—real per capita consumption inclusive of consumption goods acquired from both the private and public sectors —is not effectively attained in practice. Consequently, real per capita output (or its closely related counterpart, real per capita income) is typically selected as the "best available" indicator for the measurement of economic growth and development over time.[20]

The acceptance of *real per capita output* as the best practical device for measuring economic progress does not mean that alert observers should ignore its imperfections as a measurement device. Some of the more important of these imperfections are summarized below:

1. Expenditures for capital goods, whether by the private sector or by the public sector, are misleading in terms of measuring the increases in the consumption activity which directly provide material welfare to consumers. Yet, these expenditures are included in real per capita output.

2. Real per capita output measurements may not provide a satisfactory means of measuring changes in product quality over time. A 1975 Buick automobile, for example, is generally conceded to be better in overall quality than a 1941 Buick, but real per capita output figures may not show this.

3. The real per capita output device may not adequately differentiate between changes in the composition of consumer purchases over time. In 1900, wagons and wood stoves were important items of purchase, for example, while in today's market basket they are replaced by such items as automobiles and gas furnaces.

4. Economic goods do not provide *all* human happiness since economics is not a universal jurisdiction comprehending all of mankind's activities. Leisure and other aspects of nonmaterial consumption also provide happiness. A reduced workweek, for example, can indicate an increase in welfare. Yet, it does not show up as economic progress under the real per capita output concept. An aesthetically oriented individual such as a monk, moreover, may derive pleasure from the very act of "not consuming" material economic goods. This, again, would not be included as part of welfare by the real per capita output approach.

5. Real per capita output does not directly consider the pattern of income distribution preferred by the society.

6. The social accounts which provide the gross national product and

---

[20] Ideally, this concept should also consider the state of income distribution preferred by the society. An increase in real per capita output (income), for example, does not necessarily improve the overall welfare of the society if income distribution is *very unequal* and the society's values state a preference for fairly equal income distribution.

related data used to construct a "real per capita output" figure do not account for the "dis-welfare" effects of *negative externalities* such as air and water pollution and traffic congestion.

7. Though *average* concepts for measuring economic progress are conceptually superior to the *absolute* concepts of total productive capacity and total output, the latter hold an advantage in the sense that measurements of the real growth of aggregate resources and output indicate growth in the "absolute" economic power of a nation. This was important to militaristic societies such as Hilter's Germany and Mussolini's Italy during the 1930s and early 1940s. These societies stressed national power rather than individual welfare in a consumption sense.

In conclusion, it has been observed in this chapter that the public sector will inevitably influence aggregate economic performance in a mixed economy. Since a pure market economy possesses no inherent mechanism to assure optimal employment, price, international payments, and economic growth performances, it is only rational in light of this "market failure" to deliberately structure the economic actions of the public sector in such a manner that they promote the achievement of these goals. Congress recognized such a responsibility for the federal government by passing the Employment Act of 1946. Effective administration of the act acquires sound definitions and measurements of the aggregate goals.

24

Techniques of Fiscal Policy

The inability of a pure market economy to attain automatically the goals of full employment and price stability provides the basis for governmental stabilization policy. Such policy was enacted into law by the Employment Act of 1946 which, in its present interpretation, broadens the responsibility of the federal government in aggregate economic matters to also include the promotion of economic growth and the achievement of a satisfactory international payments balance. Governmental *economic policy* directed toward the Employment Act goals takes "monetary" and "fiscal" forms. As would be expected, the latter will be emphasized in this study of public sector economics.

The discussion of fiscal policy techniques requires a more elaborate *multiplier* concept than the one described in the simplified model of the preceding chapter. The earlier treatment was primarily concerned with the functioning of a pure market economy operating in a closed environment devoid of international economic transactions. Yet, a more realistic analysis of the functioning of the American economy requires the introduction of both a "government sector" and "international economic transactions" to the model. Importantly, when the aggregate public sector budget and international transactions are added to the analysis, significant new leakages from the private sector spending stream arise. Thus, *saving* leakages alone do not limit the value of the multiplier, but *tax* and *import* leakages, in addition, must be considered. Saving, tax revenue collections, and importation expenditures *all* take on a functional relationship with the level of income. Although the relevance of the foreign trade leakage, which may be termed the *marginal propensity to import*, will not be ignored, "tax leakages" will receive the greater emphasis in the discussion which follows.

AUTOMATIC FISCAL STABILIZERS

The important functional relationship which exists between changes in income and resulting changes in tax revenues may be used as the basis for an analysis of *automatic fiscal stabilizers*. Even though "tax rates" and the "tax base" do not vary, the tax yield (tax collections, the level of tax revenues) may be expected to vary as changes occur in income. This relationship has been termed the *income elasticity* (*Ye*) of a tax (or tax system) earlier in the book (Chapter 6) and was applied mainly to the "revenue productivity" of a tax. The same concept also contains considerable relevance for "aggregate stabilization policy" and is now utilized in the latter context. In this context, the functional relationship between "tax revenues" and "income" may be referred to as the *marginal propensity to tax* (*MPT*). It is represented by the following formula:

$$MPT\,(Ye) = \frac{\dfrac{\Delta RY}{RY_0}}{\dfrac{\Delta Y}{Y_0}}$$

where *RY* refers to the tax revenue or yield, *Y* to national income and *o* to the base year. Thus, similar to the consideration of consumption and saving as functions of income in the "marginal propensity to consume" and "save" concepts, *tax revenues* are treated as a function of income in the "marginal propensity to tax" (or "income elasticity of a tax") concept. The marginal propensity to consume (*MPC*), the marginal propensity to save (*MPS*), and the marginal propensity to tax (*MPT*) *all* represent *positive* functional relationships with income. That is, the dependent variables of consumption, saving, and tax revenues move in the same direction as do changes in the level of income.[1] However, *MPC* tends to increase at a "decreasing" rate as income increases, *MPS* tends to increase at an increasing rate as income increases, while *MPT* may increase either at an increasing, constant, or

---

[1] For purposes of later analysis, it is significant to observe that the tax yield from a federal tax is a function of *national income* while consumption, in the consumption function, is more appropriately considered to be a function of *disposable income*.

decreasing rate depending upon the nature of the tax or tax system.[2]

Figure 24–1 helps to explain the "marginal propensity to tax" and its relationship to the "automatic fiscal stabilizer" approach to aggregate fiscal policy. The unitary function on the graph represents a RY/Y ratio which has a constant numerical value as national income increases. In other words, as national income becomes greater, tax revenues expand by the same percentage rate of increase as national income. Thus, whether the level of national income is $75 billion or $900 billion, the

FIGURE 24–1
Elastic, Unitary, and Inelastic Marginal Propensities to Tax

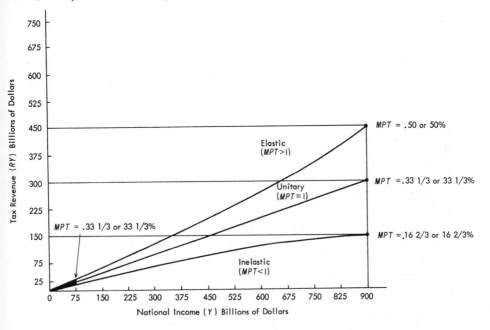

tax revenue/national income ratio remains at 0.33⅓ along the unitary function. If a nation collected all of its public sector tax revenues from a *proportional income tax*, this "unitary" ($MPT = 1$) relationship would tend to reflect the behavior of the marginal propensity to tax.

On the other hand, if tax collections grow at a more rapid rate than the growth of national income, the tax revenue/national income ratios are represented by the elastic function ($MPT > 1$) in Figure 24–1. The marginal propensity to tax, which is 0.33⅓ at a national income level of $75 billion, thus increases to 0.50 at the $900 billion level. A public

---

[2] Described in Chapter 6.

sector in which all tax revenues are derived from *progressive income taxation* would tend to provide this type of result.

However, if tax revenues increase at a slower rate than the increase in national income, the tax revenue/national income ratios are represented by the inelastic function ($MPT < 1$) in Figure 24–1. MPT decreases from $0.33^{1/3}$ at a \$75 billion national income level to $0.16^{2/3}$ at the \$900 billion level. Due to the tendency for the marginal propensity to save to become greater and the marginal propensity to consume (with its effects on retail sales) to become smaller as income increases, the exclusive application of a *regressive* general retail sales tax by the public sector would tend to provide this result. Alternately, a regressive income tax (very uncommon) would provide such an effect. Interestingly, it might be noted that only a lump-sum (head, poll) tax would tend to have a marginal propensity to tax of *zero*. This would be true because a lump-sum tax is a "per capita" tax on a "person as a person," and not upon his income, wealth, or commodity purchases. Such a tax is neither "directly" nor "indirectly" a significant function of the level of national income.

The progressive federal personal income tax and, to a lesser extent, the federal corporation income tax and unemployment compensation trust fund serve as the primary *automatic fiscal stabilizers* in the American public sector. A recent "cross section" study by Snowbarger and Kirk for the period of 1965 to 1969 estimates that the federal personal income tax yielded a 1.4 percent change in federal tax revenues for every 1 percent change in income during the period.[3] This is slightly higher than the 1.3 percent estimate for the period 1954 to 1963.[4] In either case, an "elastic" marginal propensity to tax (income elasticity) coefficient is demonstrated for the federal personal income tax. When revenue yields respond to national income changes in an "elastic" fashion, the potential for anticyclical stabilization policy becomes significant. For example, if the tax revenues extracted from the private sector increase more rapidly than national income, the proportion of tax revenues paid by the private sector (the tax revenue/national income ratio) becomes greater. As a result, a "dampening" effect on private sector purchasing power occurs when full employment and a possible threat of inflation is approached. To the contrary, when national income declines in a depression, an "elastic" tax would allow tax revenues to decline more rapidly than the decline in national income and the resulting net increase in private sector spending power would tend to provide a "cushion" for the cyclical downturn of the economy. The progressive federal personal and corporation income taxes, and the

---

[3] Marvin Snowbarger and John Kirk, "A Cross-sectional Model of Built-in Flexibility, 1954–1969," *National Tax Journal*, June 1973, pp. 241–49.

[4] Ibid.

federal unemployment compensation trust fund, work in the above sense as "automatic fiscal stabilizers."[5]

DISCRETIONARY FISCAL STABILIZERS

The tools or techniques of fiscal policy are essentially implemented through the budgetary procedures of taxation and expenditure. In the case of automatic stabilization tools, as discussed in the previous section, the taxes and expenditures, or both, are of such a nature that counter-cyclical results will occur without an additional policy adjustment. For example, the present federal personal income tax structure will yield tax revenues at a more rapid rate than national income growth and will diminish such collections more rapidly than a decline in national income. This will occur "automatically" without a deliberate change in the structure of the tax (either rate or base). On the other hand, stabilization policy may also involve the "deliberate" ad hoc alteration of taxes and/or expenditures so as to achieve aggregate economic goals. When fiscal policy is approached in this manner, it is termed *discretionary fiscal policy*.

Thus, deliberate changes in either tax rates or tax bases, or the adoption or deletion of a tax, or deliberate changes in governmental spending, or changes in both taxes and spending, can be rationally directed toward the improvement of the aggregate performance level of the economy in terms of such important objectives as full-employment and price stability. The *government fiscal multipliers* which are set into operation under "discretionary" stabilization policy, just as those which are implemented through "automatic" stabilization policy, relate importantly to the marginal propensity to tax concept. For example, as the federal income tax rate reductions of 1964 demonstrated, an initial increase in the size of a budgetary deficit through a tax rate reduction does not necessarily mean that the ultimate deficit will be "equal" to the amount of the tax reduction. This is true because the increased purchasing power in the private sector made possible by the tax reduction allows national income to increase. A higher national income, of course, yields a greater volume of tax collections. The deficit in the federal administrative budget for the 1962 fiscal year, for example, was $6.4 billion but was reduced following the subsequent federal income and excise tax reductions to $2.3 billion in fiscal 1966. This occurred, moreover, despite a substantial increase in federal spending of nearly $20 billion during the four-year period.

The same conclusion could generally be reached for an expansion

---

[5] *Automatic fiscal stabilizers* are discussed also in Chapter 26 in terms of their relationship to *fiscal policy norms*.

in the size of a deficit budget brought about through increases in government exhaustive or transfer expenditures. In addition, this analysis suggests that efforts to balance the budget through increases in tax rates may be partly self-defeating since the higher tax rates reduce the level of disposable income and thus cause a lower tax yield. Hence, a deficit budget may be the ultimate result of efforts to achieve a balanced budget through an initial increase in tax rates.

The following algebraic example demonstrates this interaction between the marginal propensities to consume and save and the marginal propensity to tax with a resulting influence through the multiplier effect on aggregate economic performance. Observe that changes in consumption and saving depend upon changes in disposable income which, in turn, does not change at as fast a rate as national income because of the automatic dampening influence of the increasing level of tax collections.

$$K = \text{Multiplier}$$
$$\Delta I = \$10 \text{ billion} \qquad K = \frac{1}{1 - b + b(d)}$$

$$mpc \ (b) = 0.80 \qquad K = \frac{1}{1 - 0.80 + 0.80(0.20)}$$

$$mpt \ (d) = 0.20 \qquad K = \frac{1}{0.20 + 0.16} = \frac{1}{0.36} = 2.77$$

Thus, an increase in business investment expenditures of $10 billion would exert an increase in national income of $10 billion times the multiplier of 2.77. The result would be an ultimate growth in national income of $27.7 billion. The restraining influence of the marginal propensity to tax is obvious since the multiplier value is 5 instead of 2.77 when only the saving leakage is considered. With a multiplier of 5, a $10 billion increase in governmental spending will lead to a $50 billion increase in national income as compared to the much lower figure of $27.7 billion when the tax leakage is also considered. This differential exists because the $10 billion increase in investment expenditure does not represent a $10 billion increase in disposable income when the tax leakage enters the picture. This leakage, plus the saving leakage of one out of every five dollars of income change, reduces the value of the multiplier effect. Thus, just as the marginal propensities to consume and save help to determine the potential impact of a governmental budget multiplier, so also will the value of the marginal propensity to tax importantly influence the result. With this in mind, the various *discretionary* government budget (fiscal) multipliers will now be discussed.

The Tax Multiplier

A change in the tax rates, and/or the tax base, and/or the adoption or deletion of a tax—and the resulting change in the level of tax revenues—will create a "multiple" change in national income (aggregate economic performance). This phenomenon is known as the *tax multiplier*. In Figure 24–2, *S* refers to saving, *T* to tax revenues, *I* to business investment, and *G* to governmental exhaustive expenditures. A change in tax revenues from such "discretionary" actions as a change in tax rates must be distinguished, of course, from the marginal propensity to tax. This difference may be observed in Figure 24–2. A change in tax rates, for example, and the resulting change in tax revenues, will cause the *S + T* curve to shift while the marginal propensity to tax merely refers to a movement along the *S + T* curve since, even with a given set of tax rates in effect, tax collections will continue to vary as a function of the level of income.

The graph has "netted out" *consumption* from both the aggregate supply (*Y = C + S + T*) and the aggregate demand (*Y = C + I + G*) flows in order to simplify the presentation and allow greater emphasis on the rudiments of the tax multiplier itself. A similar procedure will be followed in the other graphs which follow in this section. Also, for purposes

FIGURE 24–2
The Tax Multiplier

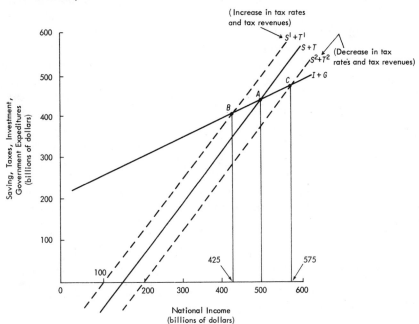

of simplification in presentation, the initial increase or decrease in tax revenues resulting from a discretionary fiscal action is assumed to be by the same amount at all income levels.

The initial equilibrium level of aggregate economic performance in Figure 24–2 is at a national income level of $500 billion. This is determined by the intersection at point A of the $S+T$ and $I+G$ curves. If tax rates are increased, with both government transfer and exhaustive expenditures constant, the $S+T$ curve will shift to the left, as from $S+T$ to S^1+T^1, and the new equilibrium performance level will be at point B. Importantly, national income has decreased from $500 billion at point A to $425 billion at point B after tax rates are increased. If the increase in tax rates causes tax collections to increase by $25 billion, and this leads to the contraction in national income of $75 billion (from $500 billion to $425 billion), the tax multiplier has a value of 3.

On the other hand, a reduction in tax rates, with government transfer and exhaustive expenditures constant, will cause the $S+T$ curve to shift to the right, as from $S+T$ to S^2+T^2, and the new equilibrium performance level will be at point C. The reduction in tax rates in this case has led to a new higher national income level at $575 billion. If the decrease in tax rates causes tax collections to decline by $25 billion, and this leads to an expansion in national income of $75 billion (from $500 billion to $575 billion), the value of the tax multiplier again is 3.

Thus, a variation in tax rates may be either *contractionary* or *expansionary* in its influence on the economy depending upon the direction of the tax rate change.[6] Moreover, the tax multiplier is *negative* in the direction of its relationship between a discretionary change in tax revenues and the resulting change in aggregate economic performance. In other words, changes in aggregate economic performance (national income) move inversely with the direction of changes in tax revenues. For example, an increase in tax rates would increase tax revenues and thus tend to cause economic contraction while a decrease in tax rates would decrease tax revenues and thus tend to create economic expansion. This is true, of course, because higher tax rates reduce the purchasing power of the private sector by causing more tax revenues to be collected, thus reducing aggregate demand, while lower tax rates provide a net increase in private sector purchasing power by causing fewer tax revenues to be collected, which leads to a higher level of aggregate demand.

---

[6] If the tax change is in terms of the "base" instead of the "rate" of the tax, it may be said that a more comprehensive tax base leads to increased tax collections and thus to a lower level of national income, and vice versa. Similarly, the "adoption" of a new tax is contractionary while the "deletion" of an already existing tax is expansionary in aggregate performance terms.

The Transfer Expenditures Multiplier

The spending as well as the tax side of the budget is capable of exerting a multiplier effect. In this regard, government expenditures may be either transfer or exhaustive (resource-absorbing) in nature. A change in the level of transfer payments by government to the private sector, and the resulting multiple change in national income (aggregate economic performance), is known as the *transfer expenditures multiplier*. This is demonstrated in Figure 24–3. The initial equilibrium level of aggregate economic performance is at a $500 billion level of national income (point *A*). If transfer expenditures are decreased, with tax rates and exhaustive expenditures remaining constant, the $S + T$ curve will shift to the left, as from $S + T$ to $S^1 + T^1$, and the new equilibrium performance level will be at point *B* which represents a decrease in national income from $500 billion to $425 billion. On the other hand, an increase in transfer expenditures, with tax rates and exhaustive expenditures remaining constant, will cause the $S + T$ curve to shift to the right, as from $S + T$ to $S^2 + T^2$, and national income expands from $500 to $575 billion at point *C*. The multiplier has a value of 3 in either case if the transfer spending change is $25 billion. Moreover, the transfer expenditures multiplier is *positive* in the direction of its relationship

FIGURE 24–3
The Transfer Expenditures Multiplier

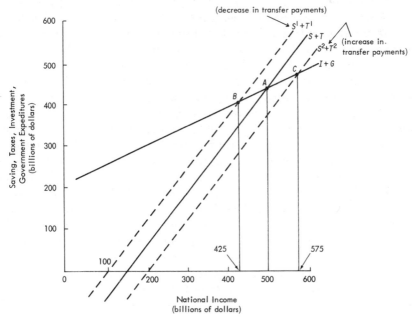

between a change in transfer spending and the resulting multiplier change in aggregate economic performance. In other words, an increase in transfer payments is expansionary and a decrease is contractionary.

An important observation may be made at this point, namely, the fact that both *tax* and *transfer expenditure* changes exert their multiplier effects in an "indirect" manner since they represent the type of governmental budgetary behavior that does not directly absorb resources but, which instead, merely changes private sector purchasing power. Subsequent resource-using and saving decisions are then made by the private sector. This is not true of the government exhaustive expenditures multiplier, however, which directly absorbs resources instead of influencing spending indirectly by altering private sector purchasing power. Graphically, this is why the $S + T$ curve shifts to depict the *tax* and *transfer expenditures* multipliers while the $I + G$ curve shifts to depict the operation of the *exhaustive expenditures* multiplier (as demonstrated below). Relatedly, it is appropriate to term a "transfer payment" a *negative tax* whereby the government transfers money to the taxpayer instead of collecting money from the taxpayer.[7]

The Exhaustive Expenditures Multiplier

Federal exhaustive (resource-absorbing) expenditures may also serve as the basis for aggregate fiscal policy. The *exhaustive expenditures multiplier* thus represents a relationship between a change in the level of governmental resource-absorbing expenditures and the resulting multiple change in the level of national income. This multiplier approach is demonstrated in Figure 24–4. A decrease in exhaustive expenditures, with tax rates and transfer expenditures constant, will cause the $I + G$ curve to shift downward, as from $I + G$ to $I^2 + G^2$, and national income will decline from $500 billion at point A to $400 billion at point B because aggregate demand has been "directly" diminished. On the other hand, an increase in exhaustive expenditures will cause the $I + G$ curve to move upward, as from $I + G$ to $I^1 + G^1$, and national income will increase from $500 billion at point A to $600 billion at point C because aggregate demand has been directly increased by the incremental exhaustive spending of government. The exhaustive expenditures multiplier, just as the transfer expenditures multiplier, represents a *positive* relationship between the direction of a change in spending and the resulting change in national income since the variables move upward and downward together. In other words, an increase in exhaus-

---

[7] This is consistent with the current societal discussion of "negative income taxation."

FIGURE 24-4
The Exhaustive Expenditures Multiplier

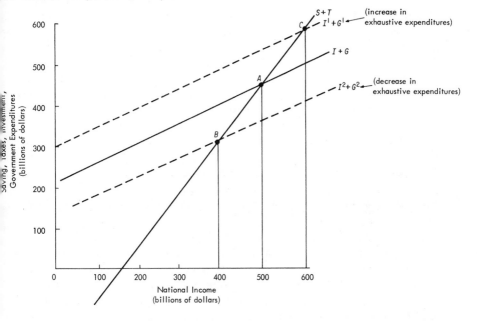

tive spending exerts an expansionary influence and a decrease in exhaustive spending exerts a contractionary influence on aggregate economic performance.

It is significant that the size of the multiplier effect will tend to be
greater in the case of the exhaustive expenditures multiplier than for
the tax and transfer expenditures multipliers. This is demonstrated by
comparing Figures 24-2, 24-3, and 24-4. These graphs show that a $25
billion increase in tax revenues caused by higher tax rates, or a $25
billion decrease in transfer expenditures, will cause national income to
decline from $500 billion to $425 billion, while a $25 billion decrease
in exhaustive expenditures will cause national income to decline from
$500 billion to $400 billion. Furthermore, a $25 billion reduction in tax
revenues caused by a decrease in tax rates, or a $25 billion increase in
transfer expenditures, will cause national income to increase from $500
billion to $575 billion, while a $25 billion increase in exhaustive expenditures will cause national income to increase from $500 billion to
$600 billion. Why does the exhaustive expenditures multiplier tend to
have a greater multiplier value than the tax and transfer expenditures
multipliers?

The exhaustive expenditures multiplier tends to have a larger multiplier effect than the tax and transfer expenditures multipliers because

a change in exhaustive government spending involves no initial (first-round) change in saving (the marginal propensity to consume of government equals one), while a change in private sector spending resulting from either a tax or transfer payment change is subject to the marginal propensity to save behavior of individuals. An increase of $25 billion in exhaustive governmental expenditures, for example, will directly increase national money income by this same amount (and output if resource unemployment permits it), and none of the $25 billion is initially saved. On the other hand, a tax reduction of $25 billion, or a transfer expenditure increase of $25 billion, will lead to a less than $25 billion increase in consumption because some of the incremental purchasing power will be *saved* by the private sector. Private sector purchasing power, of course, and *not* resource-absorbing activities is directly affected by the tax and transfer spending changes. Hence, the amount of additional aggregate demand upon which the ultimate multiplier expansion depends will be less with the decrease in taxes or the increase in transfer payments than it will be with the increase in exhaustive expenditures. In other words, the initial round of exhaustive government expenditures is a total direct component of gross national product, while the initial round of the tax reduction or transfer spending increment is merely a transfer of purchasing power, some of which will be saved before it enters the spending stream.

The phenomenon described in the above paragraph may be enlightened by the following example:

If the federal government cuts Taxpayer *A's* taxes by $1,000, the operation of the *tax multiplier* is indicated.

If the federal government makes $1,000 in welfare payments to Taxpayer *A,* the *transfer expenditures multiplier* is indicated.

If the federal government purchases $1,000 of labor input from Taxpayer *A,* the *exhaustive expenditures multiplier* is indicated.

Assume that Taxpayer *A* has a marginal propensity to consume of 0.80 and a marginal propensity to save of 0.20. The tax and transfer multipliers are thus subject to an initial 20 percent, or $200, saving leakage out of the expanded purchasing power ($1,000 − $200 = $800). However, the exhaustive expenditures multiplier possesses no such initial leakage. Instead, resources (labor input) are directly absorbed by the full value of the exhaustive expenditure ($1,000 − 0 = $1,000).

The Balanced Budget Multiplier

Each of the governmental fiscal multipliers discussed above emphasizes either the tax or the spending side of the budget. Furthermore, it was demonstrated that both a tax rate increase and an expenditure reduction are contractionary, and that both a tax rate reduction and a spending increase are expansionary, in their influence on aggregate economic performance. Thus, it would appear, for example, that an increase in taxes matched by an equal increase in exhaustive spending, and vice versa for a decrease in each, would be "neutral" in its influence on national income. In other words, it would seem that the change in taxes would neutralize the change in exhaustive spending. Surprisingly, this is *not* the case. The explanation for this significant phenomenon is found in the *balanced budget multiplier* concept which is concerned with the aggregate economic effects that derive from changes in tax collections and in governmental exhaustive expenditures in the same direction and by the same amount. For reasons which will become obvious in the analysis below, the balanced budget multiplier concept is concerned only with exhaustive and not with transfer expenditures.

The classical economists had assumed that a balanced budget change, in the above sense, is neutral. Moreover, even in the early Keynesian era economists ordinarily did not conceptualize that aggregate demand could be significantly influenced by such fiscal action. As often has occurred in the development of economic theory, a new concept is developed simultaneously by several persons working in an independent fashion on the subject. In the early 1940s, the balanced budget multiplier doctrine was promulgated in one form or another by Samuelson, Wallich, and Hansen and Perloff.[8] The Wallich article, in particular, initiated an intense discussion of the balanced budget multiplier concept. Wallich, using a simple arithmetic model, demonstrated that a balanced (proportionate) increase in the tax and exhaustive expenditure levels of government, though not directly affecting consumption and investment spending in the private sector, would increase aggregate output by the amount of the increase in governmental revenues and expenditures. In other words, the multiplier would have a value of *unity* (one) since national income would increase by the amount of the incremental budgetary change. In 1945, Haavelmo further refined the concept and concluded similarly that a balanced budget change has a direct multiplier effect with the multiplier value equal to one.[9]

The balanced budget multiplier provides this unit multiplier result,

---

[8] Paul A. Samuelson, "Full Employment after the War," in Seymour Harris (ed.), *Postwar Economic Problems*, (New York: McGraw-Hill Book Co., 1943); Alvin H. Hansen and Harvey S. Perloff, *State and Local Finance in the National Economy* (New York: W. W. Norton & Co., Inc., 1943); Henry C. Wallich, "Income Generating Effects of a Balanced Budget," *Quarterly Journal of Economics,* November 1944, pp. 78–91.

[9] Trygve Haavelmo, "Multiplier Effects of a Balanced Budget," *Econometrica,* October 1945, pp. 311–18.

however, only under the presence of certain strict assumptions.[10] Opposition to the validity of the concept has at times concentrated upon the likelihood that some or all of these assumptions would not hold in the real world. The concept, nevertheless, contains considerable general validity even though its assumptions may not hold to the precise point of providing an exact unit multiplier. This point will be further clarified later in the discussion. Meanwhile, the example presented in Table 24–1 will demonstrate the balanced budget multiplier process in operation with all pertinent assumptions holding, thus providing a multiplier result of unity or one. In other words, the change in the size of the balanced budget leads to an equivalent change in the level of national income.

TABLE 24–1
Balanced Budget Multiplier Example

Fiscal Year	Tax Revenues	Exhaustive Expenditures	National Income
1	$100 billion	$100 billion	$500 billion
2	101	101	501

In Table 24–1, the budget is assumed to be financed in fiscal year 1 with both taxes and exhaustive expenditures at the $100 billion level and with equilibrium national income at $500 billion. Then, an increase in the size of the balanced budget from $100 billion to $101 billion takes place during fiscal year 2, with both taxes and exhaustive spending increasing by $1 billion. National income thus increases by the amount of the balanced budget increase, namely, from $500 billion to $501 billion.

In this example, assume that the marginal propensity to consume is 90 percent (0.90) and the marginal propensity to save is 10 percent (0.10). The investment multiplier thus is 10, as derived from the formula:[11]

---

[10] These assumptions include: (1) the *significant* requirement that government exhaustive spending be used to acquire goods newly produced by the domestic economy; (2) that the marginal propensities to consume and save of the community not shift during the balanced budget multiplier operation; (3) that the change in the size of the budget not alter the incentives for private investment; (4) that the marginal propensity to consume and save be equal throughout the economy for both those who pay the taxes and those who receive the benefits of government spending, that is, in instances where a differentiation can be made between these two groups: (5) that work-leisure habits must not be altered by the governmental budgetary action; and, *very importantly*, (6) that the tax(es) involved not possess a functional relationship with national income. That is, the marginal propensity to tax (*MPT*) must equal zero.

[11] For simplification in presentation, saving is considered in the example as the only leakage from the spending stream.

$$K = \frac{1}{mps} \quad \text{or} \quad \frac{1}{0.10} = 10$$

Significantly, the government spends *all* of the additional $1 billion extracted from the private sector in the form of taxes. If the incremental tax amount had been allowed to remain in the private sector, however, *only* 90 percent of it would have immediately reentered the spending stream as consumption expenditures. Importantly, the fact that the government spends the entire amount of the additional tax collections, while the private sector would save 10 percent of the $1 billion incremental tax dollars, means that the balanced budget increase in government expenditure is expansionary. This expansion takes place because the $900 million which would have been spent by the private sector is less than the $1 billion spent by the public sector, the $100 million difference providing a *net* increment to aggregate demand and a resulting multiplier effect.

In numerical terms, the multiplier of 10 times the $100 million in differential expenditure between the two sectors yields the $1 billion increase in national income. Thus, a $1 billion increase in governmental exhaustive spending, matched by an equivalent increase in tax collections, causes a $1 billion increase in national income. The relationship between the change in government spending balanced by an equal change in tax collections, and the change in national income which results, is *unity*.[12] Oppositely, a decrease in the size of a balanced budget will cause a decline in national income equal to *unity*. Although an exact unity result may be difficult to attain given the strict assumptions,[13] the "direction" of a balanced budget effect on national income can be more readily predicted. That is, a higher magnitude balanced budget should yield a greater national income than a lesser-sized balanced budget.

The balanced budget multiplier, however, would not operate for *transfer* as opposed to exhaustive expenditures by government. In other words, if all governmental spending were of a transfer variety, a balanced budget change would be "neutral" because government would merely be transferring purchasing power from taxpayers to

---

[12] The same unity value results regardless of the values of the marginal propensities to consume and save. If the marginal propensity to consume is 80 percent (0.80) and the marginal propensity to save is 20 percent (0.20), for example, the multiplier value is 5. Under this situation, though the government would again spend the entire $1 billion of additional tax collections, the private sector would have withheld $200 million instead of $100 million from the spending stream. The $200 million (20 percent) of leakages to private saving times the multiplier of 5, however, just as $100 million times a multiplier of 10, results in a $1 billion increment in national income.

[13] Cited in footnote 10.

transfer recipients.[14] The balanced budget multiplier would *not* exist because there would be no net increment to aggregate demand in the private sector. Government in the case of transfer expenditures does not make direct resource-absorbing expenditure decisions. *All* spending decisions are still made by the private sector. Only a transfer of purchasing power has taken place which results merely in a distributive change in the decision-making power of various individuals over aggregate demand *within* the private sector.

THE APPLICATION OF DISCRETIONARY FISCAL STABILIZERS TO ECONOMIC STABILIZATION GOALS

The four *discretionary fiscal multipliers* examined above provide the basis for governmental fiscal policy directed toward macroeconomic goals. Historically, the primary goals of such federal fiscal policy have been centered within the stabilization branch of public finance. Specifically, they have been directed toward the attainment of a high level of labor and capital employment and price stability. The *former* was the primary goal of the 1930s and has intermittently been the main objective since that time while the *latter* has been the primary consideration during wartime (World War II, Korean War, Vietnam War). Other aggregate goals, of course, have assumed importance from time to time. This was especially true during the 1960s with the increased concern for the ability of federal fiscal policy to promote a satisfactory rate of economic growth and an improved balance of international payments. Nevertheless, stabilization in the full-employment and price stability sense remains the primary focal point of policy. Admittedly, the various goals of aggregate fiscal policy are interrelated. One goal, however, usually retains priority in any given set of decisions.

Unemployment, as a stabilization problem, is best demonstrated in terms of the *deflationary gap* conditions and inflation in terms of the *inflationary gap* conditions demonstrated in the previous chapter.[15] The latter, of course, is an especially close fit to monetary inflation, but is less indicative of the conditions which lead to monopoly (administered price) inflation. In Figures 24–5a and 24–5b, the ability of fiscal policy to alleviate the conditions of involuntary labor and capital unemployment is shown. In Figures 24–6a and 24–6b, the ability of fiscal policy to combat monetary inflation is demonstrated.

---

[14] However, "complete neutrality" would require the restrictive assumption that the marginal propensities to consume and save between the taxpaying group and the transfer recipients be the same.

[15] For reasons of simplication in presentation, the deflationary gap and inflationary gap graphs used in this section will "net" consumption (*C*) out of the spending flows. However, the phenomena described will be identical to those presented in Figure 23–4 of the previous chapter.

FIGURE 24–5
Fiscal Policy and a Deflationary Gap

a. Alleviation of a Deflationary Gap Through Measures which Decrease Tax Revenues, such as a Reduction in Tax Rates, or Through an Increase in Government Transfer Expenditures

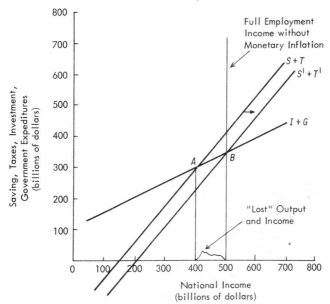

b. Alleviation of a Deflationary Gap Through an Increase in Government Exhaustive Expenditures

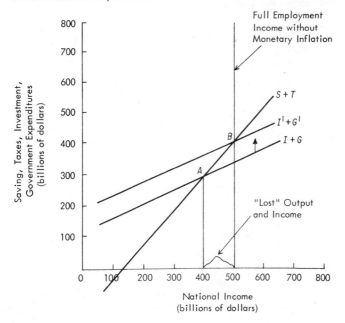

FIGURE 24–6

Fiscal Policy and an Inflationary Gap

a. Alleviation of an Inflationary Gap Through Measures which Increase Tax Revenues, such as an Increase in Tax Rates, or Through a Decrease in Government Transfer Expenditures

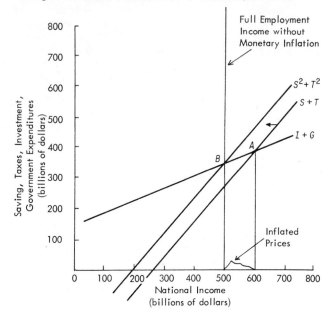

b. Alleviation of an Inflationary Gap Through a Decrease in Government Exhaustive Expenditures

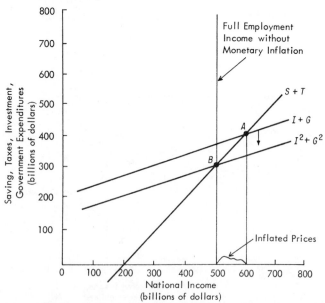

Fiscal Policy Applied to Deflationary Gap Conditions

The excess of aggregate supply $(S + T)$ over aggregate demand $(I + G)$ at noninflationary full employment characterizes the deflationary gap conditions of Figures 24–5a and 24–5b. If the national income performance level of the economy were $500 billion, labor and capital would be fully employed (within reasonable definitions of each term) and the price level would be stable. Under such conditions, federal fiscal policy directed toward stabilization would not be required. The economy, however, is not operating at this full-employment noninflationary level of performance in the graphs. Instead, equilibrium is at a $400 billion level of national income which, it will be assumed, provides under-full-employment conditions whereby 8 percent of the labor force is involuntarily unemployed and 25 percent of the capital capacity (plant and equipment) of the nation is not being utilized. In this instance, deliberate fiscal policy directed toward the improvement of both labor and capital employment is warranted.

The techniques of discretionary fiscal policy for the alleviation of deflationary gap conditions derive primarily from the four government fiscal multipliers. The potentially most effective tool would involve use of the *exhaustive expenditures multiplier* because the government, under this multiplier, has a marginal propensity to consume equal to one. Thus, in Figure 24–5b, an increase in exhaustive expenditures by government would shift the $I + G$ curve upward as in curve $I^1 + G^1$ and, if the increase in spending is sufficiently large—given the limitation imposed by the value of the multiplier as dependent upon the marginal propensities to consume and save of the community and the marginal propensity to tax—a new full-employment equilibrium at the $500 billion level will be attained.

The problem of involuntary labor and capital unemployment can also be attacked by either the *transfer expenditures multiplier* or by the *tax multiplier.* An increase in transfer payments, for example, will shift the $S + T$ curve to the right, as in curve $S^1 + T^1$,[16] thus expanding the equilibrium level of aggregate economic activity. Alternately, a decrease in tax rates, and/or the narrowing of a tax base, and/or the deletion of an existing tax would diminish tax revenue collections and thus cause the $S + T$ curve to shift to the right to become $S^1 + T^1$ with a similar result of expanded national income. In either case, disposable income within the private sector has been increased.

However, the government transfer expenditures and tax multipliers, as observed above, tend to provide a *smaller* multiplier expansion in national income than the exhaustive expenditures multiplier since the "direct" impact of these multipliers is on private sector purchasing

---

[16] See Figure 24–5a.

power (disposable income), which is subject to a *saving leakage*.[17] On the other hand, a disadvantage of the exhaustive expenditures multiplier in a market-oriented economy is that it is less conducive to private sector economic activty since the government directly determines the pattern of additional resource usage when exhaustive expenditures are increased. Moreover, an increase in governmental exhaustive spending may undergo a considerable *time lag* before the actual economic impact of the expenditures takes place. In other words, many delays can occur between the time when exhaustive expenditures are appropriated by Congress and the time when the actual resource-using activity occurs. On the other hand, the tax withholding method of collection allows tax rate changes to be put into effect quickly. This was demonstrated by the federal income tax rate reductions of 1964.

In summary, though "maximum expansion" will occur through the operation of the exhaustive expenditures multiplier, the tax and transfer expenditures multipliers are more attractive from the motive of favoring the private sector, in intersector resource allocation terms, and the tax multiplier is the best of the three in terms of "timing."

A final approach to alleviation of deflationary gap conditions utilizes the balanced budget multiplier whereby an increase in tax rates matched by an equal increase in exhaustive governmental expenditures will provide an expansion in national income, the increase in income being equal to the size of the tax-expenditure increase if certain rigorous assumptions hold. The relevance of the balanced budget multiplier concept to effective fiscal policy will be further analyzed in a later section of the chapter.

Fiscal Policy Applied to Inflationary Gap Conditions

The excess of aggregate demand $(I + G)$ over aggregate supply $(S + T)$ at noninflationary full employment characterizes the inflationary gap conditions as displayed in Figures 24–6a and 24–6b. The $600 billion equilibrium aggregate performance level shown in the graphs represents inflated prices to the extent of $100 billion of national in-

---

[17] In comparing the ultimate multiplier potential of the *tax* versus the *transfer expenditures* multipliers, it should be observed that by the extent to which the taxes collected to make the transfer payments come from higher-income spending units than those who receive the payments, the transfer expenditures multiplier would possess the greater multiplier potential. This would be true because higher-income groups tend to have a higher marginal propensity to save, and thus a lower marginal propensity to consume, than lower-income groups. Hence, the *saving leakage* would be smaller for the "transfer expenditures multiplier" as opposed to the saving that would result from a comparable tax rate reduction for the higher-income group as brought about through a "tax multiplier." Nonetheless, the fact remains that neither the tax nor the transfer expenditures multiplier would possess the multiplier potential of the exhaustive expenditures multiplier which has no initial saving leakage whatsoever.

come because a $500 billion performance level would be sufficient to employ fully all labor and capital resources without monetary inflation. A case for deliberate fiscal policy directed toward the alleviation of monetary inflation is thus established.

The tools of *discretionary fiscal policy* for the alleviation of inflationary gap conditions also derive primarily from the four government fiscal multipliers. Again, the potentially most effective technique involves the use of the exhaustive expenditures multiplier. Hence, in Figure 24–6b, a decrease in exhaustive spending by government will cause the $I + G$ curve to shift downward to $I^2 + G^2$, thus decreasing national income through a reduction in inflated prices. A reduction in exhaustive expenditures of adequate size, given the constraint of the relevant leakages from the spending stream, will lower national income back from $600 billion to the optimal, noninflationary, full-employment equilibrium of $500 billion. In addition, monetary inflation can be alleviated by a decrease in transfer spending (Figure 24–6a), or by a measure increasing tax revenues such as an increase in tax rates (Figure 24–6a). Thus, the $S + T$ curve will shift to the left becoming $S^2 + T^2$. In either case, however, the multiplier contraction in national income will be less than that provided by the exhaustive expenditures multiplier since, as described above, the "direct" impact of these multipliers is on private sector purchasing power which is subject to an initial saving leakage.

In addition to providing maximum contraction, the reduction in exhaustive governmental expenditures for the purpose of attaining a contractionary fiscal policy also increases the relative position of private sector resource allocation and thus, unlike its behavior in the expansionary fiscal policy case, favors the market in intersector resource allocation terms. The achievement of economic contraction through a reduction in exhaustive government expenditures, however, is slower to put into effect than would be an increase in taxes. Yet, an increase in taxes would lead to a relative expansion in public sector economic activity. A unique form of the tax multiplier, based on changes in the "timing of collections" rather than on a change in tax rates, was enacted by Congress during 1966 in the form of a *graduated tax withholding schedule*. At the present time, on the personal income tax the payroll-withholding rate ranges between 14 and 35 percent for individuals (between 14 and 36 percent for married taxpayers) depending upon earnings. In addition, the rate of payment of corporation income taxes was accelerated by the 1966 legislation. Such action, of course, drains purchasing power from the private sector at an earlier time and thus helps to restrain inflationary pressures. Finally, a decrease in tax rates matched by an equal decrease in governmental exhaustive spending (the balanced budget multiplier), under certain conditions, may also initiate contractionary results to help alleviate inflation.

In summarizing both the deflationary and inflationary gap situations, the exhaustive expenditures multiplier provides the maximum expansion and contraction as compared to the tax and transfer expenditures multipliers. Regarding intersector resource allocation, a decrease in tax rates favors the market sector, while higher taxes tend to favor the public sector. The tax multiplier holds the "time implementation" advantage over the other two multipliers, primarily due to the technique of "tax withholding" at the source of income. Finally, it should be observed that several, or all, of the government budget multipliers may be used at one time to help achieve an economic stabilization objective.

The Balanced Budget Multiplier and Fiscal Policy

The validity of the balanced budget multiplier concept as a basis for fiscal policy has been challenged on occasion. Baumol and Peston, for example, argue that the balanced budget multiplier concept assumes away those variables which would almost certainly make the value of the multiplier greater or less than unity.[18] It is suggested that the theorem holds in a unity sense only under the assumption that the change in tax yield does not alter the marginal propensities to consume and save, as well as the fact that only taxes of the lump-sum (poll) tax variety would yield this result because only they are completely "neutral" in their influence on consumption behavior.[19] In addition, they assert that much of the additional spending from the balanced budget increase will not be for newly produced economic goods.[20]

Gurley also analyzes the relationship of the balanced budget multiplier concept to full-employment fiscal policy.[21] Reasoning from the premise that a *higher level balanced budget* is "expansionary" and a *lower level balanced budget* is "contractionary," it may be observed that a government effort to stimulate the economy by a deficit, which is followed by a subsequent decrease in both taxes and exhaustive spending by equal amounts, can have ultimate "contractionary" results. That is, a decrease of sufficient size in the exhaustive spending level *matched* by a decrease in taxes, though the deficit condition continues, can lower the level of national income below what it originally was

---

[18] William J. Baumol and Maurice H. Peston, "More on the Multiplier Effects of a Balanced Budget," *American Economic Review*, March 1955, pp. 140–47. Also, see footnote 10 above.

[19] In addition, only lump-sum (poll) taxes would be "neutral" in terms of the marginal propensity to tax (*MPT*) concept. That is, only lump-sum tax collections lack a functional relationship with national income (*MPT* = 0).

[20] Ibid., pp. 144–47.

[21] See John G. Gurley, "Deficits, Surpluses, and National Income," *Southern Economic Journal*, July 1954, pp. 12–25.

before the initial deficit was incurred. Table 24–2 demonstrates this phenomenon. Thus, it follows that a government deficit budget can ultimately be either expansionary, contractionary, or neutral *depending upon the level at which the budget stands.* The opposite of this is also true, namely, that a surplus budget policy may be either contractionary, expansionary, or neutral depending upon its level. It then may be concluded that only one balanced budget level is consistent with full employment.

The balanced budget multiplier concept thus appears to be a significant dimension of rational fiscal policy. An undue concern with the "precise unity" result, however, endangers the retention of this useful fiscal concept. The importance of the balanced budget multiplier concept for fiscal purposes does not depend primarily on a proportionate (unity) relationship between a change in balanced budget size and a change in national income, but instead on the *direction* of the relation-

---

TABLE 24–2
Example of "Contractionary" Deficit Budget through the Influence of the Balanced Budget Multiplier

---

Deficit Multiplier Value = 2   Balanced Budget Multiplier Value = 1

Stage 1
    Conditions Prior to Deficit Budget Change:
      National Income = $500 billion
      Federal Government Tax Revenues = $100 billion
      Federal Government Exhaustive Expenditures = $100 billion

Stage 2
    Conditions Following Deficit Budget Change:
      National Income = $510 billion
      Federal Government Tax Revenues = $100 billion
      Federal Government Exhaustive Expenditures = $105 billion
      Explanation: Federal Deficit of $5 billion X 2 (multiplier)
                = $10 billion increase in national income
                $500 billion National Income (Stage 1)
                +10 billion
                $510 billion National Income (Stage 2)

Stage 3
    Conditions Following Balanced Budget Multiplier Reduction of $15
    billion—with Deficit Budget Continuing
      National Income = $495 billion
      Federal Government Tax Revenues = $85 billion
      Federal Government Exhaustive Expenditures = $90 billion
      Explanation: $510 billion National Income (Stage 2)
                −15 billion Balanced Budget Reduction in Tax
                          Revenues and Exhaustive Expenditures
                          ($15 billion X multiplier of 1)
                $495 billion National Income (Stage 3)

ship, that is, the tendency for a larger balanced budget to result in a higher national income level than a smaller balanced budget.

Thus, as observed above, the balanced budget multiplier concept can be logically extended to the effects deriving from various budget sizes (levels), whether balanced or unbalanced. This points out to the policy-maker that he must not look to the "simple prescription" of a deficit during depression and a surplus during inflation to solve all problems. Though the deficit or surplus and their respective results are important considerations, it must not be forgotten that the *level* or *size* of the budget itself—regardless of whether it is a deficit, surplus, or balanced budget—is also important to fiscal decision-making. In addition, certain intersector resource allocation considerations are raised by the balanced budget multiplier theorem since, assuming full employment, an upward balanced budget change will tend to increase the relative proportion of *public sector* allocation in the economy and a downward balanced budget change will tend to increase the relative proportion of *private sector* allocation.

The Balance of International Payments and Fiscal Techniques

In addition to the influence exerted on the nation's "balance of international payments" performance through general stabilization policy, certain "specific" fiscal techniques are at times employed to help improve performance relative to this goal. Thus, Congress enacted an *Interest Equalization Tax (IET)* in 1964, retroactive to 1963, to serve this objective. The Interest Equalization Tax is designed to moderate the "outflow" of American investment capital to foreign nations. The tax was enacted as a temporary two-year measure, but has been extended by Congress on several occasions—the most recent being in 1973. The Interest Equalization Tax adds 0.75 percent to the interest cost of foreign securities with the President being given the authority to increase this to 1.5 percent or to lower it to zero. On stocks, the tax is 11.25 percent of the purchase price. Capital transactions involving Canada are excluded under the tax.

In 1966, Congress adopted another fiscal technique to help improve the balance of international payments in the form of the *Foreign Investors Tax Act*. This legislation reduced the tax rates of foreign investors who derive income from portfolio investment in U.S. corporate securities. The objective was to encourage the "inflow" of foreign capital to the United States and thus to improve the balance of payments. During 1968, President Johnson asked Congress for additional fiscal legislation with the balance-of-payments goal in mind. The proposed legislation

would have taxed *foreign travel* through the application of two complementary taxes, namely (1) a temporary 5 percent excise tax on international *travel fares* (which would be permanent in the case of air fares),
and (2) a temporary *expenditure* tax on spending by Americans while
traveling outside the Western hemisphere. The latter expenditure tax
was to have a two-step "graduated rate" ranging from 15 percent on
spending between $7 and $15 per diem to 30 percent on spending in
excess of $15 per day. Neither tax was enacted as such by Congress,
though Congress did subsequently enact a tax on international air tickets. In summary, it may be said that the federal government has employed a limited number of specific fiscal techniques, under the implicit
mandate of the Employment Act of 1946, to help improve the balance
of international payments performance.

25

Techniques of Fiscal Policy
(Continued)

FISCAL TECHNIQUES FOR ECONOMIC GROWTH

The preceding chapter on "fiscal techniques" dealt primarily with automatic and discretionary fiscal stabilizers as applied to problems of economic stabilization. This section of the present chapter will discuss several of the more important tax and expenditure techniques which may be employed by the public sector, especially the federal government, to promote economic growth.[1]

First, *tax policies* will be considered in terms of their ability to assist in the achievement of a satisfactory economic growth rate. A tax structure designed to encourage *research* and *development* efforts, for example, will tend to promote economic growth. The present federal tax law contains certain tax preference provisions which encourage patents. Moreover, the ability of businesses to write off research expenditures as costs in the calculation of net profits and taxable income is significant. The allowance of *accelerated depreciation* for tax purposes can also encourage investment spending and thus promote economic growth.[2] Though the use of accelerated depreciation does not eliminate the eventual tax liability of the business, it does postpone the day of tax

---

[1] For an excellent summary of tax and expenditure techniques directed toward the achievement of economic growth, see Paul A. Samuelson, "Fiscal and Financial Policies for Growth," *Proceedings, A Symposium on Economic Growth* (New York: American Bankers Association, 1963), pp. 78–101, especially pp. 90–96.

[2] See the discussion of accelerated depreciation in Chapter 11.

payment and amounts to an interest-free loan by the government to the business. Unless the business is already highly liquid in its asset portfolio, the effect of accelerated depreciation should be to make the acquisition of capital goods more attractive.

The *investment credit* against tax liabilities, when in effect, represents an effort by the federal government to promote economic growth through the direct subsidization of investment in new capital equipment.[3] The credit, which became part of the Internal Revenue Code in 1962, was repealed by the *Tax Reform Act of 1969* but was reenacted during 1971. Though the credit device provides significant nonneutralities, these nonneutral effects tend to be positive in terms of the economic growth goal. Under the plan, up to 7 percent of the cost of domestically-employed capital equipment can be used directly to offset income tax liabilities. The credit taken in any one year is limited to the first $25,000 of tax liability plus one half of any remaining tax liability. Unused credits may be carried back three years and forward seven years. The investment credit appears to be an effective fiscal tool for the overall encouragement of economic growth. However, its application toward this objective may run counter to its performance in terms of the stabilization objective. Thus, it was temporarily suspended by Congress in October 1966, when inflation pressures predominated, and was reinstated again by Congress in 1967 when a recession appeared to be threatening. Then, it was repealed in 1969 for inflationary reasons, but was reenacted in 1971 for expansionary reasons. This use of the investment credit as a short-run discretionary fiscal stabilizer may result in an undesirable distortion of business investment decisions. Though use of the investment credit as a short-run fiscal stabilizer may be somewhat questionable, its effectiveness as a stimulant to economic growth requires that it be retained as a fiscal tool for possible use when economic growth is a primary fiscal policy goal.

Special treatment for *capital gains* income, as discussed in Chapter 9, comprises another fiscal technique capable of encouraging economic growth. In this instance, the encouragement would apply primarily to "venturesome" investment, though to an extent it would apply to all investments since it allows an individual to pay a lower tax rate on income earned on the purchase and sale of any capital assets held over six months. Asset prices are increased, in effect, by the provision. Moreover, special treatment of capital gains income encourages investment in those industries which tend to reinvest earnings instead of paying them out in dividends. It is hoped that the income will show up in the form of high share values for stock, and thus capital gains when sold, instead of being regular dividend income subject to the higher regular

---

[3] See also the discussion of the *investment credit* tool in Chapter 11.

tax rate. Unquestionably, considerable nonneutrality is introduced into investment decisions by the preferential treatment of capital gains under the Internal Revenue Code. It may be argued, however, that the encouragement of economic growth by such a procedure justifies the classification of this fiscal technique in the positive nonneutrality category.

Various other fiscal tools deriving from the tax side of the budget will now be briefly discussed in terms of their influence upon economic growth. Recent improvements in *income averaging* through the carry-back and carry-forward of profits and losses, for example, have reduced the penalty against risk-taking in the economy. In addition, a further *corporation income tax rate reduction* (other than the 1964 reduction), if not the actual elimination of the corporation income tax, would be expected to encourage private investment and thus promote economic growth. Slitor suggests that the corporate income tax rate reductions of 1964 proved to be an important contributor to economic growth.[4]

The goal of economic growth can also be affected by the "pattern" of public sector *expenditures.* Government, especially the federal government, encourages *research* endeavors through both direct expenditures and subsidization grants. This approach is used in the fields of nuclear development, space, and medicine—to mention only a few. The investment of government funds in *education,* in addition, provides a growth in literacy and knowledge which increases economic productivity and ultimately should lead to a higher rate of economic growth.[5] Furthermore, *social overhead investment* in durable capital such as dams, highways, harbors, communications facilities, airports, and other goods with significant traits of publicness provides economic goods which are important to the attainment of economic growth.

Government spending can also be significant as a growth-promotion factor through its ability to increase knowledge and reduce risk in private investment by information promotion programs, government insurance programs, expenditure subsidies, and by joint participation with private enterprise in an industry. In 1965, for example, Congress enacted the Technical Services Act which provided federal assistance for making scientific information available to private business. Such legislation is particularly beneficial to those industries in which the typical firm is small, that is, too small to do much (if any) of its own research or to be fully apprised of advances in technology. Moreover, several European nations, including France and Sweden, have adopted a policy of combined *business-government planning* whereby business

---

[4] Richard E. Slitor, "The Corporate Tax Cut: What Business Did with the 'Windfall,' " *Challenge,* March–April 1966, p. 38.

[5] Chapter 21 considers in greater detail the economic relationship between the public sector and education as an economic (quasi-public) good.

investment plans and government fiscal plans are revealed in advance and then made consistent with each other. A more rational aggregate economic policy would likely be the result of such consultation between business and government.

Boulding suggested in 1966 that an excessive amount of "knowledge industry" efforts were being devoted to the space-military complex, with very little contribution resulting to the civilian economy.[6] He observed that "outside of agriculture and the military . . . American civilian industry is exhibiting a relatively slow rate of technological development" with an increase in labor productivity during the last two decades averaging *not* more than 2.8 percent annually.[7] Thus, a mere increase in the "quantity" of knowledge industry expenditures is not necessarily enough to stimulate a higher rate of economic growth. The proper "quality" allocation is also required.

Finally, an indirect, though genuine, approach to the promotion of economic growth through governmental fiscal action is to improve the organization of governmental *statistical activities* so that better analysis and policy decisions can be made. Several years ago, the federal government undertook a special study for improving economic growth statistics.[8] It has been recommended in this study that action be taken in a number of areas to improve the organization and coordination of federal statistical collections.[9]

---

[6] Kenneth E. Boulding, "The Knowledge Boom," *Challenge*, July–August 1966, p. 7.

[7] *Ibid.*

[8] Joint Economic Committee, Congress of the the United States, *Improved Statistics for Economic Growth*, Comments by Government Agencies on Views submitted to the Subcommittee on Economic Statistics (Washington, D.C.: U.S. Government Printing Office, 1966), comments by Raymond T. Bowman on the recommendations of governmental agencies for improved statistics.

[9] The recommendations include:

1. A national statistical data center should be established. There is a need for greatly improved accessibility to and coordinated use of federal government statistics. Better coordination, for example, is required in the use of computer facilities. The proper filing, collating, and accessibility of data will make possible considerable improvement in the analytical use of existing data for economic growth and other policy purposes.

2. A coordinated system of federal, state, and local government statistics should be established. Part of this problem is to encourage the more detailed and more frequent collection of pertinent statistical data by state and local governments which, as part of the aggregate public sector budget, cannot avoid influencing economic growth through their budgetary actions.

3. A coordinated program of social statistics is required including the growing need to provide basic data and techniques for appraising the effectiveness of the various social programs.

4. A federal directory of business establishments should be available. The absence of such a master file at the disposal of all official data gathering agencies creates lack of communication between varied requests for information and places unnecessary burdens on respondents, producers, and users of information.

5. Improved industrial, occupational, and geographic classification is desirable. New products and new occupations, for example, need to be taken into account. Improve-

In conclusion, it may be observed that numerous tax and expenditure policies of the federal government may be used to favorably influence the rate of economic growth. For the most part, these fiscal techniques attain their results through the creation of nonneutral effects in the economy. Fortunately, *rational policy* based upon *economic principles* allows these nonneutralities to be "positive" rather than "negative" with the promotion of economic growth being the desirable result of such policy.

INTERACTION BETWEEN FISCAL POLICY GOALS

Full Employment versus Inflation

Significant nonneutral effects occur between the various economic goals which the Employment Act seeks to attain through monetary and fiscal policy. The present dilemma between the full employment and price stability goals of the stabilization function provides an excellent example of such intergoal nonneutrality. Figure 25–1 exhibits this problem by means of the so-called "Phillips curve."[10] In this graph, the annual percentage rate of *price inflation* is measured along the vertical axis and the annual percentage rate of *labor unemployment* is measured along the horizontal axis. The "short-run" *tradeoff* between price stability and labor unemployment along curve *IU* is apparent.[11] Importantly, the labor unemployment rate of 4 percent, which is the arbitrarily designated "full employment" goal of most policy makers in the United States, cannot be achieved on the graph without a 4 percent

---

ments in geographic classifications are required by the recent proliferation of interest in states, countries, and municipalities.

6. Finally, improved coordination based on the national economic accounts and the major models of the behavior of the economy, the educational system, and so on, is desirable. These economic accounts include the national-income-and-product accounts, the input-output tables, and the flow-of-funds accounts. Improvements could follow such lines as the integration of the national-income-and-product accounts to include wealth estimates of the value of tangible capital equipment. All of these improvements would tend to make fiscal decision-making directed toward the economic growth goal, as well as toward the other fiscal goals, more rational.

[10] See A. W. Phillips, "The Relation between Unemployment and the Rate of Change of Money Wage Rates in the United Kingdom, 1862–1957," *Economica*, November 1958, pp. 283–99.

[11] Some economists take the position that an "inflation-labor unemployment tradeoff" does not exist in the *long-run*. For a statement of this position, see Milton Friedman, "The Role of Monetary Policy," *American Economic Review*, March 1968, pp. 1–17. Still other economists suggest that an "inflationary-labor unemployment tradeoff" exists in the long run at *high* labor unemployment levels, but vanishes at some critical level approaching the full employment point. For a statement of this position, see James Tobin, "Inflation and Unemployment," *American Economic Review*, March 1972, pp. 1–18.

FIGURE 25–1
Short-Run Intergoal Nonneutrality Between Inflation and Labor
Unemployment

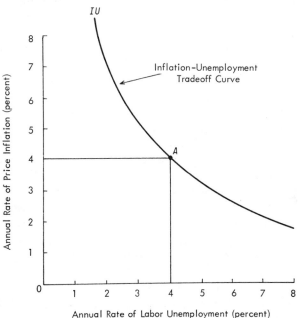

Annual Rate of Labor Unemployment (percent)

rate of inflation (point A).[12] The institutional nature of the economy
itself helps to make difficult the achievement of the ideal combination
of a 4 percent labor unemployment rate and price stability even though
"monetary inflation" caused by excessive aggregate demand may be
absent. The "monopoly power" present in many resource (factor) markets, including labor markets, and in many product markets constitutes
one of the institutional contraints upon the economy in this regard. In
other words, imperfect market structures lead to *monopoly* (*administered price*) inflation of both the "cost-push" and "profit-pull" varieties.

Unfortunately, orthodox *fiscal* and *monetary* policies are unable to
"directly" attack the root causes of monopoly inflation. This is so because "monopoly inflation," unlike "monetary inflation," is a *market
structure phenomenon* rather than a phenomenon caused directly by
excessive aggregate demand. Thus, only *regulatory* policies can directly
modify monopoly inflation. In the "short run," these policies, which are
generally termed *incomes policies,* may take the form of required gov-

---

[12] This 4 percent inflation figure may not be the precise tradeoff point with 4 percent
labor unemployment at any one point of time. The substance of the analysis, instead, is
that *at least some inflation* will be present with 4 percent labor unemployment.

ernmental approval of price increases in major product and resource markets. In the "long-run," the regulatory policies may be of a more general variety directed toward the reduction of monopoly power in product and resource markets. Importantly, the direct governmental regulation of prices in product and resource markets interferes with the functioning of the *price system* and, thus, with the basic role which prices play in a market-oriented economy.

During the administrations of Presidents Kennedy and Johnson, the federal government (executive branch) attempted to use "persuasion" as a short-run means of combating monopoly inflation. This technique, known also as "jawboning," primarily took the form of a *wage-price guidelines* (*wage-price guideposts*) policy based on an estimated annual labor productivity increase in the economy of 3.2 percent. It was suggested by the policy than an increase in wages should not exceed the national trend rate of increase in output per man-hour of labor. Moreover, it was suggested that product prices should remain stable in those industries which experience the same productivity growth as the national average, but should rise in those industries with below average productivity growth and should decline in those industries with above average gains in productivity. This guidelines policy, however, was only "semi-regulatory" in nature since it carried no absolute authority to compel compliance. It merely employed persuasion; yet it did appear to attain modest success.

The guidelines approach was terminated by the administration of President Nixon as it took office in 1969 and no short-run incomes policy was subsequently in effect between early 1969 and August 1971. At that time, however, the "twin problems" of recession or economic stagnation and inflation, a phenomenon known as *stagflation*, were of such a magnitude that a much more comprehensive short-run incomes policy was introduced. After a general "wage-price freeze" was put into effect from August to November 1971 (Phase 1), a system requiring the "direct approval of price increases" in major product and resource markets (Phase 2) became operative. After some success in reducing inflation, this regulatory approach was abandoned, in effect, at the beginning of the second Nixon administration in early 1973. In turn, a rapid worsening of price stability ensued during this "deregulated" Phase 3 and, later in 1973, a more comprehensive incomes policy (Phase 4), in many ways similar to Phase 2, was initiated. However, this was abandoned during 1974.

Fluctuating governmental policies such as those practiced between 1971–74, as well as other causes of *changing expectations* concerning prices, can lead to an *inflationary psychology* which only makes worse the efforts to control inflation. That is, the sellers of products and of resources may be induced to form judgments to the effect that pronounced inflation will continue into the forseeable future. Consequently, the "spiral" of higher product prices as well as higher wages and other factor costs will "accentuate" leading to a still higher rate of inflation. Moreover, intensified efforts may be undertaken by business buyers to acquire a larger inventory of nonlabor inputs and by consumers to acquire durable economic goods "now" instead of "later" when their prices will be still higher. Graphically, this would cause the inflation-unemployment tradeoff curve, *IU*, to shift upward with the result being that the "inflation-unemployment tradeoff" becomes even worse. That is, higher rates of inflation would occur at each level (rate) of labor unemployment.

However, certain governmental policies may be instituted to improve the "inflation-unemployment" tradeoff by shifting the "inflation-unemployment tradeoff curve," *IU*, downward—thus yielding lower rates of inflation at each level of labor unemployment. Such long-run policies involve those of both a *manpower* and *incomes* nature. The former would include retraining to improve the employment opportunities of workers as well as other labor market policies. The latter, on the other hand, would include efforts to reduce inflationary expectations as well as to make markets more competitive through improved antitrust policy.

Full Employment versus the Allocation, Distribution, and Balance-of-Payments Goals

Next, the intergoal influence of "full employment stabilization" policy on the allocation, distribution, and balance-of-payments objectives of fiscal policy will be discussed. The effect of stabilization policy on the *allocation* of productive resources, of course, will vary depending upon the type of fiscal policy pursued to attain the stabilization objective. If the stabilization goal of the society is to expand the level of aggregate economic performance, when *unemployed resources* are present in the economy, the change can be achieved through a variety of fiscal techniques, some of which may impose significant allocational effects. If governmental exhaustive spending is increased while taxes are held constant, for example, a relative intersector expansion of governmental allocational activity will tend to occur. Furthermore, a change in the composition of resource allocation within the private sector may occur as the recipients of the new government spending purchase economic goods. On the other hand, if the increase in national income is approached through a reduction in taxes while government exhaustive spending remains constant, there would tend to be a relative expansion in private sector allocation because of the expanded private sector purchasing power. Once again, there would likely be a change in the composition of resource allocation within the private sector as the pattern of effective demand is influenced by the tax reduction. It should thus be concluded that intersector resource allocation, as well as specific resource allocation between private and quasi-private goods, can be importantly influenced by the use of fiscal policy to achieve the full-employment goal.

Alternative stabilization policies may also directly influence the *distribution* of income and wealth in the society. An increase in governmental spending (exhaustive or transfer), for example, while taxes remain constant, may achieve the desired stabilization goal of expanding national income. At the same time, however, income may be redistributed between those who pay the taxes and those who benefit from the incremental government spending. Such redistribution can be either desirable or undesirable depending upon the value judgments of the community regarding the proper state of income distribution. Furthermore, the desired increase in national income may also be achieved through a reduction in taxes, while government spending is held constant, but the tax reduction will change the distribution of income in accordance with the income brackets which receive the greatest effects of the tax reduction. The various policies aimed at stabilization thus may exert an important influence upon the distribution of income and wealth in the society. Since a given state of distribution is a prerequisite to allocational decisions,[13] fiscal policy which alters distribution will also influence effective demand and allocation.

An interesting "tradeoff" between the stabilization and distribution goals occurred in Congress during 1969 as tax reform legislation was being discussed, Specifically, powerful forces argued for the continuance of the anti-inflationary federal income tax surtax while still other influential forces contended that significant income tax reform should be enacted in the interest of tax equity. Eventually, the surtax was extended after a promise of tax reform legislation was received by those emphasizing tax equity from those most concerned with the stabilization objective. This compromise also involved interaction between Congress and the executive branch of the federal government. Subsequently, a "moderate" tax reform bill was enacted (the Tax Reform Act of 1969).

In addition to exerting important allocational and distributional effects, fiscal policy directed toward full employment may also have a significant impact on the nation's *balance of international payments.* An adverse payments effect would result, for example, if the rising economic activity resulting from an expansionary fiscal policy increased the level of prices which, in turn, tended to reduce the competitive

---

[13] See Chapters 1, 4, and 5.

position of American goods in international markets. Moreover, American goods would become less competitive at a time when higher national income is providing Americans with greater purchasing power to acquire imported foreign goods. Fiscal policies which can improve the balance of international payments include those which stimulate U.S. exports by improving the productivity of labor and capital in American industries and by providing price stability. In addition, fiscal policies which encourage foreign investment in the United States, and discourage American investment in foreign nations, will tend to relieve the balance-of-payments problem. The *Foreign Investors Tax Act* of 1966 and the *interest-equalization tax* exemplify such policies.

Government Fiscal Policy and Interrelated Growth-Cycle Objectives

Most fiscal policy has historically stressed short-run stabilization objectives. There have been some exceptions to this fact, however, such as the federal tax reductions of 1964 and 1965 as well as federal policies regarding accelerated depreciation and the investment credit. Seemingly, a policy which expands aggregate short-run performance should also facilitate the long-run economic growth objective and vice versa. Extreme caution, however, must be used in formulating policy on this basis. The investment credit, for example, performs much better in relationship to the economic growth goal than it does in terms of the stabilization goal. Or, a short-run policy which stresses growth in consumption, and not in investment, will reduce the amount of capital formation and likely slow down the rate of economic growth over a period of time. A realistic example of the importance of this fact is offered by the economic history of the Soviet Union between 1928 (the beginning of the first Soviet five-year plan for economic development) and the 1960s. By stressing capital formation at the sacrifice of consumption, the Soviet Union experienced a substantial rate of economic growth during this period. Though American value judgments might condemn the extreme sacrifice of consumption imposed upon the Soviet people during the period, the positive influence of capital formation on economic development cannot be denied.

Thus, although a positive correlation generally exists between expansionary stabilization policies and satisfactory economic growth, many qualifying circumstances must be considered for policy-making purposes. It must be acknowledged that alternative types of stabilization policy may exert differential effects upon the rate of economic growth. These effects often relate importantly to the manner in which the various fiscal policies influence investment decisions. An expansionary fiscal policy, for example, can be based upon budgetary techniques such as accelerated depreciation and the investment credit which directly encourage investment. Furthermore, an increase in government spending for items such as education and health may be expected to increase significantly the rate of economic growth because of the high economic returns derived from improving the productive capabilities of the labor factor of production. If the incremental governmental spending is for national defense rather than for investment in human capital, however, the rate of economic growth may well be less except for that amount of technological change which would be a product of the "fallout" from the research and development expenditures of the defense sector, Moreover, if the increase in national income is brought about by a reduction in the federal corporation income tax, the amount of new investment will tend to increase by a greater amount than it would increase under conditions where the tax reduction takes the form of rate reductions in the lower brackets of the federal personal income tax.

The interaction between stabilization and growth policy, of course, derives from the basic nature of the relationship between the "trend" and the "cycle." The model of John R. Hicks which relates some of the strategic elements of this relationship will be summarized at this time.[14] Then, the Hicksian model will be used as a basis for the application of fiscal policy with positive nonneutral effects toward the interrelated attainment of *both* the stabilization (anticyclical) and economic growth goals of the society.

Figure 25–2 will now be used to demonstrate the basic tenets of the Hicksian model, and later for the application of fiscal policy to the interrelated stabilization and growth goals. Output (real income) is measured on the vertical axis and time is measured on the horizontal axis. Investment is divided into the traditional autonomous and induced categories. It is assumed that autonomous investment will grow at a constant percentage rate along line *AA* due to long-run trend factors such as improvements in technology and population growth. This constant growth in autonomous investment, working through the multiplier process, provides an equilibrium level of national income growth along line *LL*. Growth of national income along *LL*, however, will lead to induced investment resulting from expanding output (real income) and will set the acceleration principle into motion. The combination of the multiplier and the accelerator, which may be referred to as the "supermultiplier," determines a higher equilibrium growth path for national income along line *EE*. The highest line on the graph, line *FF*, represents the ceiling rate of national income growth as set by the

---

[14] John R. Hicks, *A Contribution to the Theory of the Trade Cycle* (Oxford: The Clarendon Press, 1950).

FIGURE 25–2

Hicksian Growth-Cycle Theory and Fiscal Policy Applications

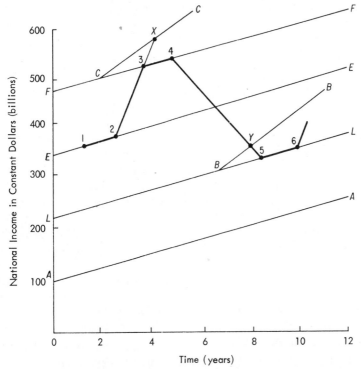

Source: The basic graph, without the fiscal policy applications, is derived from John R. Hicks, *A Contribution to the Theory of the Trade Cycle* (Oxford: The Clarendon Press, 1950), p. 97.

productive capacity of the economy. In other words, line *FF* represents the equilibrium path of the full-employment growth of national income. This ceiling rate of growth is assumed to be the same rate as the growth of antonomous investment since both depend upon improvements in technology and upon population growth.

At points 1 and 2, national income grows at the rate set by the interaction of the multiplier and accelerator. An outside disturbance, such as a "sudden burst" in autonomous investment, then causes the rate of national income growth to depart in an upward direction from growth path *EE*. If only the multiplier were involved, the upward movement would not be "explosive" and national income would soon return to the growth path *EE*. The accelerator working with the multiplier, however, will provide explosive growth which will terminate only when the full-employment growth path *FF* is reached at point 3. The scarcity of productive resources will cause the accelerator to lose its explosive character and, at best, the growth in national income can only continue in the pattern along line *FF* as determined by autonomous investment alone with its multiplier effect.

National income can grow along line *FF*, however, as between points 3 and 4, for only a limited period of time because the equilibrium growth path becomes *LL*, not *EE* or *FF*, when only autonomous investment (through the multiplier) is exerting an expansionary influence. National income thus turns downward, which explains the "upper turning point" of the cycle. The downward movement in national income between points 4 and 5 will be more gradual than the upward movement between points 2 and 3 had been since only the multiplier is at work in the downswing, *not* both the multiplier and accelerator as is true during the upswing. Eventually, the downswing will end at a "lower turning point" and a new upswing will begin as an increase in replacement demand resulting from the physical depreciation of capital goods occurs. Thus, new acceleration activity becomes integrated with the expansionary multiplier and a new surge of explosive growth begins. The turning point upward, which begins a new cycle, occurs at point 6 on growth path *LL*. The downswing had not carried national income below line *LL* where the growth path of national income reflects the continuous expansion created by the multiplier effects of the rate of growth in autonomous investment.

In summary, a full-employment ceiling caused by productive capacity limitations sets the upper turning point of the business cycle, according to Hicks, while the lower turning point is set by autonomous investment working through the investment multiplier. Business cycle fluctuations will occur between these maximum and minimum growth paths. The fact that both the full-employment trend line (line *FF*) and the slump trend line (line *LL*) slope upward, reflecting economic growth, is assured by the continued rate of growth in autonomous investment (line *AA*). Thus, Hicks skillfully integrates the secular trend and the cycle into a meaningful theory. Both the upswing (boom) and the downswing (bust) of the business cycle, moreover, are shown as inevitable results of the operation of a dynamic market economy through the interacting operation of the multiplier and the accelerator.

Next, the ability of federal *fiscal policy* to directly influence growth-cycle patterns is also exhibited in Figure 25–2. Certain fiscal policy alternatives which are capable of either reducing cyclical instability or promoting economic growth, or both, are adapted to the Hick's model in this graph. Line *CC* indicates how fiscal policy may increase the resource ceiling over time and thus delay or avoid the cyclical downturn. The resource ceiling of the economy can be expanded by those fiscal policies which increase the *quantity* and/or *quality* of productive resources. In this regard, "capital formation"—the net additions of private and social capital to the nation's capital stock—is of particular importance. Hence, the cyclical downturn need not occur at point 4. Instead, the appropriate "resource-expanding" fiscal policy can cause it to occur at a higher point such as point X, as shown on the higher growth line CC.

A second fiscal policy alternative would be to stop the downward swing between points 4 and 5, somewhere above point 5. At point 5, it should be remembered, the influence of the multiplier as derived from the rate of growth in autonomous investment sets the pattern for the eventual cyclical upturn. Fiscal policy may set a higher minimum trough and eventual upturn point for the cycle. Thus, an increase in the level of private investment, or in its rate of growth, resulting from such fiscal devices as *accelerated depreciation* and the *investment credit*, can cause national income to follow line BB instead of continuing between points 5 and 6. Line BB, of course, constitutes a higher cyclical trough than line LL. The eventual upturn thus may occur at point Y instead of at point 6.

Other fiscal alternatives such as an increase in tax rates, a reduction in transfer and/or exhaustive expenditures, or both, or a balanced reduction in budget size could be applied between points 3 and 4 to prevent possible monetary inflation. Moreover, a reduction in tax rates, an increase in government spending, or a higher overall budget level can be applied at point 4 to "prevent" the downturn, or somewhere below point 4 to "cushion" the downturn. This policy would result in the operation of a government multiplier capable of reducing the depth of the cyclical downturn without, as in the accelerated depreciation-investment credit approach, directly increasing private autonomous investment. Hence, this should be classified as a separate fiscal approach directed toward the same ultimate goal of cushioning the downturn by raising the eventual trough level of the cycle.

Fiscal Policy and Regional Economic Activity

The *composition* of governmental budgetary activity will inevitably influence both short-run regional economic performance and long-run regional economic growth. Some regions and the states which comprise them, for example, are net importers of federal budgetary benefits both of an expenditure and tax subsidy variety.[15] These two aspects of budgeting, of course, need to be symmetrically considered for purposes of attaining a complete and rational analysis. National defense expenditures provide a good example of how some regions and states benefit more from certain types of federal spending them do others. National fiscal policy, it should be observed, may be frustrated also by the choice

---

[15] See Figure 20–1.

between attainment of the distributional goal of equalization or equity, in the sense of achieving a pattern of balanced growth between the various economic regions within a nation, and the national growth objective. In other words, the distributive goal of making real per capita income and living standards *more equal* between regions may conceivably lessen the rate of national economic growth. This could occur because specialized economic production based upon the economic principle of comparative advantage, and the subsequent exchange of goods produced under specialization, may create substantial per capita income differences between the various regions of a society at a time when it is attaining maximum aggregate output as a result of its regional specialization.

The United States, of course, has never completely followed a laissez-faire policy for resource allocation among economic regions. Historically, federal policies toward land disposal, tariffs, the development of agricultural technology, the development of transportation sectors, and the like have had significant influence upon the patterns of regional economic development as well as national economic development. Federal policies continue to influence regional economic growth though some transitional changes in the type of policy have occurred. Technological change and population growth, for example, have added emphasis to policies of natural resource conservation, the development of recreational areas, public power projects (such as TVA), interstate highway development, and the support of housing. However, Borts and Stein comment that regional economic policies of the federal government have *not* historically been formulated in terms of "an overall view of an efficient free market economy."[16] Encouragingly, Borts and Stein observe that, in terms of efficiency, the interregional and interindustrial growth pattern of the United States appears now to be moving toward an intertemporal competitive equilibrium and thus in the direction of intertemporal efficiency.[17]

TECHNIQUES OF DEFICIT FINANCING AND SURPLUS DISPOSAL

The Deficit Budget

The use of tax and spending (both transfer and exhaustive) changes to promote economic goals, as discussed throughout this chapter, will frequently result in either a deficit or a surplus budget. There are

---

[16] George H. Borts and Jerome L. Stein, *Economic Growth in a Free Market* (New York: Columbia University Press, 1964), p. 189.

[17] Ibid., p. 214.

various means, moreover, by which the federal government may finance a *deficit* budget (when expenditures have exceeded tax and other revenue collections) and dispose of a *surplus* (when tax and other revenue collections have exceeded expenditures). Depending upon the particular deficit financing and surplus disposal technique that is selected, however, substantially different *secondary effects* may be exerted on aggregate economic activity. Importantly, these secondary effects may either "reinforce" or "neutralize" the initial multiplier expansion or contraction resulting from the deficit or surplus. Of course, a *deficit* budget resulting from lower tax rates and/or higher government spending, or both, tends to be "expansionary" and a *surplus* budget resulting from higher tax rates and/or reduced government spending, or both, tends to be "contractionary." The expansionary and contractionary results involve the multiplier effect which the public sector exerts on the private sector when government provides *either* a "net increment" in private sector purchasing power through a deficit budget *or* a "net decrement" in private sector purchasing power through a surplus budget.[18] Yet, once these *direct* multiplier effects are set in motion, the particular means of financing a deficit or disposing of a surplus take on considerable importance because of their ability to exert *secondary* economic effects.

The present discussion will consider five alternative methods of financing a federal deficit budget. These are:

1. The Treasury Department sells securities to the private sector (excluding commercial banks and the Federal Reserve System).
2. The Treasury Department sells securities to commercial banks at a time when they do *not* have excess loanable reserves.
3. The Treasury Department sells securities to commercial banks at a time when they do possess substantial excess reserves.
4. The Treasury Department sells securities to the nation's central bank—the Federal Reserve System.
5. The government creates or prints *fiat* money.

The least expansionary means of financing a federal deficit is listed first above and, as the numbering approaches five, the means of financing the deficit become increasingly expansionary. A sale of Treasury securities (debt instruments) to private individuals and businesses in the market sector of the economy equal in volume to the amount of the deficit, for example, would withdraw purchasing power from the private sector equal to the amount introduced into the private sector by

---

[18] The "net increment" and "net decrement" in private sector purchasing power, as observed earlier, may vary in size and be either "direct" or "indirect" depending upon whether the exhaustive expenditures multiplier, the transfer expenditures multiplier, or the tax multiplier is being considered.

the deficit budget itself. This, indeed, must be classified as a restrictive means of financing a deficit budget since the secondary effects of the financing technique selected tend to neutralize the primary effects of the initial multiplier.

Another highly restrictive means of financing a deficit budget occurs when the Treasury Department sells securities to the commercial banking system at a time when the banks do *not* possess excess loanable reserves. Under such conditions, commercial banks would necessarily restrict their loans to the private sector and/or to state and local levels of government in order to finance the purchase of the securities. This would cause a reduction in aggregate demand which would also tend to neutralize or offset the primary expansionary effects of the initial multiplier.

On the other hand, if Treasury securities equal to the amount of the deficit are sold to the commercial banking system at a time when the banks possess substantial excess reserves, the initial multiplier expansion need not be severely neutralized, if neutralized at all, by restrictive secondary effects because the banks can purchase the securities from their excess reserves without reducing their volume of loans to the private sector and/or to state-local government. Moreover, an expansion of the money supply, as the excess reserves are put to work through the operation of a fractional reserve banking system, will allow the greater magnitude of economic activity made possible by the expansionary multiplier to take place. The expanding money supply will reinforce, not neutralize or offset, the multiplier-caused expansion. A form of "debt monetization" has occurred.

An additional expansionary means of financing a deficit budget is to sell treasury securities to the Federal Reserve System. This process involves an even purer version of the concept of *debt monetization.* The effect in this case is at least as expansionary as that of the sale of securities to commercial banks at a time when they have substantial excess reserves. The following paragraph provides a description of the "debt monetization process" derived from the sale of Treasury securities to the Federal Reserve System.

The Treasury Department sells government securities (debt instruments) to the Federal Reserve banks. The Federal Reserve banks then create new Treasury deposit accounts, or expand present Treasury deposit accounts, at the banks. These deposit accounts are liabilities to the Federal Reserve System, but the securities purchased by the Federal Reserve System are classified as assets. The government then spends the funds for purchasing economic goods and productive resources from the private sector or as transfer payments. Subsequently, checks are drawn by the Treasury Department on its deposit accounts in the Federal Reserve System as the money is spent. Individuals and business firms in the private sector who sell productive resources and economic goods to the federal government and individuals who receive transfer payments receive these checks. Ordinarily, the checks will be deposited in the commercial banking system and the commercial banks, upon receiving the checks as deposits, will credit the deposit accounts of the private individuals and business firms. The commercial banks, in turn, send the checks to the Federal Reserve banks and the commercial bank reserve accounts within the Federal Reserve System are subsequently increased by the full amount of the checks. The commercial banking system thus possesses new excess reserves over and above the reserve amount required legally behind the new demand deposits. This monetary expansion (debt monetization) will reinforce the expansionary influence of the original multiplier.

The federal government, of course, need not resort to ordinary debt creation to finance a budget. It could simply print *fiat* money equal to the amount of the excess of government spending over revenue collections. Historically, such unrestricted monetary creation by government has caused considerable consternation and fear of governmental waste and hyperinflation. Such results, however, would not necessarily occur in a well-controlled, monetary exchange economy which answers to the dictates of the people through a democratic political process. This technique of financing a deficit, which is a unique form of "debt creation," is extremely expansionary and in no way neutralizes the primary multiplier expansion through the imposition of offsetting secondary effects.

The Surplus Budget

When the federal government collects more in taxes and other revenues than it spends, the resulting surplus may be utilized in a variety of ways. An increase in tax rates and/or a reduction in government spending, for example, may lead to a surplus budget. Depending upon the particular surplus disposal technique selected, the contractionary effect of the surplus budget working through a negative multiplier may be either reinforced or neutralized. If maximum economic contraction is desired, the surplus funds should be held idle and not allowed to reenter the private sector. Under such conditions, no neutralization to the negative multiplier occurs since a net decrease in private sector purchasing power has taken place. On the other hand, if some degree of neutralization is desired, the surplus can be (1) distributed among groups who will spend most of it immediately, which would yield a substantial offset to the contractionary effects of the surplus, or (2) the surplus can be used to retire already existing government debt. In the latter case, depending upon who holds the debt that is to be retired, varying degrees of partial neutralization will result. The disposal of a surplus, in addition to influencing the degree of multiplier-caused contraction, may also exert significant "allocational" and "distributional" effects depending upon the pattern of surplus disposal which is selected. The allocational effects, for example, may consist of resource pattern changes both *between* the public and private sectors and *within* each sector.

Thus it is observed that not only do unbalanced budgets provide *primary* multiplier effects through tax rate and spending changes, but also that important *secondary* economic effects may result depending upon the particular technique used to finance a deficit or to dispose of a surplus. The specific technique selected, however, will necessarily depend upon policy objectives and upon the overall conditions of the economy. The huge federal deficits of World War II were inevitable, for example, and the proper fiscal policy under these conditions—a surplus budget—could not be used despite the inflationary gap conditions which prevailed. The next best approach was to finance the deficit in the most restrictive way possible in terms of secondary effects. Consequently, an enormous effort was made to sell war bonds to the private sector of the economy as well as to the banking system, while at the same time monetary policy attempted generally to restrict private credit. It is seen in this example that fiscal and monetary policy cannot be totally divorced from each other. Instead, they require coordination to achieve mutual economic objectives. It is perhaps noteworthy, in terms of improving future policy, to observe that the institutional arrangement for monetary policy working through the quasi-independent Federal Reserve System is considerably different from the institutional arrangement for fiscal policy. The latter often works much more slowly since the federal government budget-making process requires the action of both the executive branch of the federal government and of Congress. The important relationship between fiscal and monetary policy will be explored further in the following chapter as it discusses various fiscal policy norms or benchmarks.

26

Fiscal Policy Norms

RULES OR NORMS OF FISCAL POLICY

It is customary to relate the techniques of fiscal policy discussed in the previous chapters to specific fiscal norms (guidelines, benchmarks) when policy decisions are made. The array of possible fiscal policy norms extends over a wide range between the two extremes of a continuum. Figure 26–1 displays such a continuum, including the approximate relative positions of certain important fiscal norms. On one end, for example, is the *annually balanced budget* norm while the *functional finance* benchmark is at the other extreme. Various intermediate positions include the general concept of the *cyclically balanced budget*

FIGURE 26–1
Continuum of Various Fiscal Policy Norms

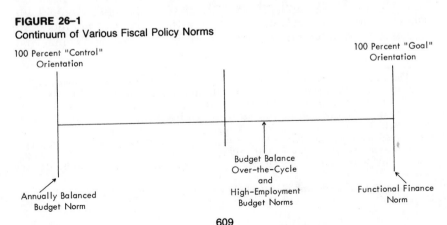

100 Percent "Control"
Orientation

100 Percent "Goal"
Orientation

Annually Balanced
Budget Norm

Budget Balance
Over-the-Cycle
and
High-Employment
Budget Norms

Functional Finance
Norm

and the *high-employment budget* rule.[1] For reasons to be discussed below, these two intermediate norms are *not* placed in the exact middle of the continuum.

The Annually Balanced Budget Fiscal Norm

Since the early days of the sovereign history of the United States, a strong preference has existed for an annually balanced federal government budget. In fact, the philosophy favoring an *annually balanced budget* has also been extended to the public sector as a whole as is indicated by the various restrictions on unbalanced budgets as well as the various spending limitations imposed by state government constitutions on the fiscal operations of state and local governments. The belief that an annually balanced budget is desirable per se is apparently based upon the cultural notion that government budgetary behavior should be "thrifty" since a balanced budget supposedly indicates fiscal responsibility and efficiency for government just as it does for the household and business segments of the private sector. Yet, households and businesses are increasingly carrying debt and apparently are doing so with a wide degree of safety. Hence, the long-established feeling that only a balanced budget is efficient applies, it would seem, on a declining basis to the private sector. Moreover, the analogy between private and public debt is highly tenuous.[2]

The annually balanced budget principle was developed by the classical economists (with a few dissenters) and has been perpetuated for well over a century as a guideline for governmental fiscal behavior. Government debt had not existed on a wide-scale basis until the establishment of the monetary-exchange type of economy under capitalism. To be sure, some debt creation had occurred during the age of feudalism, but this practice was not extensive. The development of public debt and credit on a widespread basis first occurred during the eighteenth century. Hume, Smith, and others expressed strong opposition to unbalanced (deficit) government budgets at that time. Certain moderate positions were to be found, however, including those of Thomas Mal-

---

[1] The discussion of fiscal policy norms in this chapter necessarily includes frequent reference to *government debt* since each of the important norms bears at least indirect implications for public sector debt. Government debt creation, for example, is a necessary corollary to a discussion of the annually balanced budget rule because the failure to maintain budget balance by allowing expenditures to exceed revenue collections creates a condition of deficit spending which is likely to be financed through debt creation. However, since government debt is the subject of Chapter 27, it will be discussed in this chapter only to the extent necessary for a proper evaluation of the various fiscal policy norms.

[2] This point will be described in the following chapter on the subject of "Public Sector Debt."

thus in England and the first Secretary of the Treasury, Alexander Hamilton, in the United States.

The classical case for the annually balanced budget was based upon the following arguments: (1) private sector economic development is retarded by the sale of government debt to the private sector since fewer capital funds are then available for the acquisition of private capital goods, (2) government deficit spending allows a relative expansion of the public sector as opposed to the private sector, in intersector resource allocation terms, and (3) deficit spending necessarily leads to inflation.

Smith defended the annually balanced budget as part of his basic opposition to central government debt.[3] The Smith position on debt, though partly economic, also displays considerable political interpretation as a result of his strong "antimercantilist" feelings. Smith believed that government was fundamentally wasteful in terms of its financial operations. He felt that the money capital needed by the private sector for economic development would be diverted unnecessarily from the private to the public sector if governmental debt creation were allowed. Thus, an insufficient growth in capital goods would take place which, in turn, would retard economic development. He also believed that the financing of wars through borrowing rather than through taxation encouraged the government to wage needless wars. Smith was not particularly concerned with the burden of an *already existing* debt, but instead was concerned mainly with the burden created *at the time that debt is created*, though the burden of existing debt still bore some importance in his evaluation.

Other classical economists such as Say, Ricardo, and Mill opposed government deficit spending to varying degrees and thus, at least implicitly, approved the annually balanced budget concept. Malthus, however, did not believe the national debt to be evil per se. He observed that the individuals who receive interest earnings from public debt spend such earnings, at least in part, for economic goods. Hence, debt contributes to the demand for economic goods. Malthus, at certain other places in his writings, takes a stronger position against government debt, but he never completely condemns it. Mill also took a less firm position against deficit spending than did many other classical economists and noted that government borrowing does not always lead to undesirable results. Following Mill, the classical economists paid less attention to the public debt issue. In fact, Alfred Marshall's *Principles* ignores the subject. Late in the nineteenth century, Bastable observed that one characteristic of a mature economic society is the ability to

---

[3] For an excellent discussion of the classical and neoclassical position on government debt, see Jesse Burkhead, "The Balanced Budget," *Quarterly Journal of Economics*, May 1954, pp. 191–216.

create public debt. Thus, considerable moderation of the "antidebt" and "probalanced budget" position occurred between the early days of classical economics and the early twentieth century. Yet, significant opposition in economics to the annually balanced budget principle did not arrive until the era of Keynesian economics in the 1930s.

Franklin D. Roosevelt was elected President during the Great Depression in 1932 on a political platform which included an annually balanced budget plank. The effects of Keynesian economic analysis were beginning to be felt in the political and economic circles of the Western world, however, by the beginning of Roosevelt's second term of office in 1937, and the first deliberate uses of fiscal policy to promote the economic stabilization objective in the United States came into being. Since the advent of modern macroeconomics, most economists have accepted the legitimacy of the use of the federal government budget to promote economic stabilization and growth objectives. Politicians, however, have accepted such legitimacy to a lesser extent. Nevertheless, a pronounced trend toward greater political acceptance of these fiscal tools has occured during the recent decades. This was indicated by President Kennedy's request to Congress in 1963 for tax reductions to achieve the macroeconomic goals of full employment and satisfactory economic growth. This suggestion reached fruition under President Johnson in the form of the income tax (personal and corporate) reductions of 1964 and the excise tax reductions of 1965.[4]

The annually balanced budget fiscal rule seems seriously deficient and unnecessarily restrictive in a rational, mature, democratic political economy. The fact that it represents an unacceptable extreme on a continuum of fiscal benchmarks, however, does not suggest that it possesses no merit whatsoever. In a society which holds preference for the market allocation of resources, the notion that the annually balanced budget norm exerts "control" over excesses by government, and thus over the relative expansion of the public sector, contains definite merit. Hence, some of the compromise benchmarks discussed below accept certain aspects of the "control function" of the annually balanced budget, though such acceptance remains secondary to the acceptance of deliberate budget manipulation as a fiscal tool.

Finally, even if the annually balanced budget rule were a totally acceptable fiscal norm, certain institutional impediments exist which would tend to prevent its realization. For example, the lobbying influence of pressure groups, which is encouraged by the American political structure, leads to a bias in favor of deficit budgets. This occurs because lobbies attempt to improve the economic status of those whom they

---

[4] For an excellent description and analysis of the evolutionary acceptance of stabilization policy (both fiscal and monetary) in the United States, see Herbert Stein, *The Fiscal Revolution in America* (Chicago: University of Chicago Press, 1969).

represent by either increasing the receipt of government expenditures or decreasing the tax payments of their constituents, or both. Obviously, higher governmental spending and lower taxes add up to a movement toward deficit financing. The individual pressure groups may separately decry deficit spending, but their collective actions frequently add up to this result. Moreover, politicians campaigning for office often contribute to deficit budgeting by promising benefits from government while "holding the line" on taxes.

The Functional Finance Fiscal Norm

The complete antithesis to the annually balanced budget norm is the *functional finance* fiscal rule. While the balanced budget norm stresses the importance of "control" over governmental fiscal activities, the functional finance norm advocates that the government budget be used to promote macroeconomic "goals" without regard to budget balance. Relatedly, it is less concerned than the annually balanced budget with allocational and distributional considerations and more concerned with aggregate economic performance and economic growth objectives.

The functional finance concept was developed rather early in the Keynesian era and is built upon Keynesian economic theory. The early statements of the principle primarily considered stabilization, with emphasis on the relief of unemployment as it existed during the 1930s, and did not stress economic growth as such. Emphasis on economic growth, however, occurred during the latter part of the 1950s and the early 1960s. The most famous statement of the functional finance norm was provided by Abba Lerner in 1943.[5] Lerner observed that World War II had proven the ability of government fiscal action to maintain full employment. The chronic depression conditions that preceded World War II had been relieved as defense-supported aggregate demand expanded. Yet, Lerner asserted that many well-intentioned individuals, who recognize that deficit spending actually works, still oppose it because of a less-than-complete understanding of its operation and because of a misinformed fear regarding its consequences.

Lerner argued that the essential idea of government economic policy—which involves governmental spending, taxing, borrowing, the repayment of loans, the issue of new money, and the withdrawal of money from circulation—should be undertaken with the effects of these actions on the national economy in mind. Attachment to any established fiscal doctrine such as the annually balanced budget rule should not receive priority consideration. "The principle of judging fiscal

---

[5] Abba P. Lerner, "Functional Finance and the Federal Debt," *Social Research*, February 1943, pp. 38–51.

measures by the way they work or function in the economy we may call *Functional Finance.*"[6]

The *first* law (governmental responsibility) of functional finance, according to Lerner, is that the government budget should be directed toward the achievement of full employment and stable prices. It should *not* concern itself with whether tax receipts and governmental expenditures are balanced or unbalanced. In other words, tax collections need not equal the level of government spending, as advocated by the annually balanced budget norm, and taxes need to be imposed only to prevent inflation. The *second* law of functional finance states that the government should incur debt by borrowing money from the private sector *only* if it is desirable that the private sector have less money to spend and more government bonds to hold. This would be a desirable goal if, in the absence of debt, the rate of interest were too low thus inducing an inflationary excess of private investment. *Third,* functional finance would prescribe that any excess of governmental money outlays over the money revenues accruing to government, which cannot be met out of private money hoards for the purchase of the government debt, should be met by the printing of new money. Conversely, any excess of governmental revenues over outlays can be either destroyed or used to replenish private sector money hoards. In effect, the printing, hoarding, or destruction of money should be conducted as required for the achievement of full employment and price stability.

Lerner observed that functional finance is not related to any particular type of political-economic system, but instead only to the existence of a mature money exchange economy. Hence, the functional finance approach may be summarized as follows:

> Functional Finance is not especially related to democracy or to private enterprise. It is applicable to a communist society just as well as to a fascist society or a democratic society. It is applicable to any society in which money is used as an important element in the economic mechanism. It consists of the simple principle of giving up our preconceptions of what is proper or sound or traditional, of what "is done," and instead considering the *functions* performed in the economy by government taxing and spending and borrowing and lending. It means using these instruments simply as instruments, and not as magic charms that will cause mysterious hurt if they are manipulated by the wrong people or without due reverence for tradition. Like any other mechanism, Functional Finance will work no matter who pulls the levers. Its relationship to democracy and free enterprise consists simply in the fact that if the people who believe in these things will not use Functional Finance, they will stand no chance in the long run against others who will.[7]

---

[6] Ibid., p. 39.

[7] Ibid., pp. 50–51.

A Comparison of the Annually Balanced Budget and Functional Finance Norms

Though the functional finance fiscal norm is extreme in its complete noncommitment to budgetary "control," thus placing intersector resource allocation considerations in a secondary position, it contributes importantly to the recognition of the fact that government budgetary action is capable of promoting "macroeconomic goals" in a market-oriented economy. Hence, just as "control" generally must be recognized as a desirable element of the *annually balanced budget rule,* so must the ability of fiscal policy to attain "employment, price level, economic growth, and balance-of-payments goals" be recognized as an advantage of the *functional finance norm.* A rational fiscal norm, of course, should contain some reference to both "control" and "macroeconomic objectives." Nevertheless, the control objective—as long as at least some constraint on governmental size is present—seems secondary in importance to the fact that governmental budgetary actions can be deliberately used to improve aggregate economic performance.

Undoubtedly, undue emphasis on the intersector allocational goal can seriously impede the attainment of stabilization and economic growth objectives. The annually balanced budget rule, for example, would require such policies as a "reduction in government spending" or an "increase in tax rates" when national income declines, and an "increase in government spending" or a "decrease in tax rates" when national income expands. This is so because tax revenues (except for a lump-sum tax) are a positive function of the level of income. Thus, assume a federal government budget "balanced" with $200 billion in both expenditures and tax revenues. A decline in national income would cause tax revenues to decline, say by $20 billion, with the result being a *deficit* budget of $20 billion ($200 billion expenditures minus $180 billion in taxes). This deficit would tend to be "expansionary"—a desirable effect in times of recession and declining national income. However, adherence to a balanced budget rule would necessitate the elimination of the "expansionary deficit" by means of either reduced spending or increased tax revenues, each of which would tend to neutralize the expansion. Moreover, "destabilizing effects" of an opposite nature would occur at times of expanding national income. For example, an increase in national income might convert a previously-existing $200 billion balanced budget into a surplus, say of $20 billion ($220 billion in taxes minus $200 billion of expenditures), as tax revenues increase along with national income. Even though the "contractionary" effects of such a surplus may be desirable in terms of the stabilization goal, an effort to "balance the budget" via an expenditure increase or tax reduction would tend to neutralize these "contractionary" effects.

Thus, no fiscal norm can be expected to attain perfectly all fiscal goals.[8] Instead, it is a "give-and-take" arrangement. The complete attainment of the stabilization goal, for example, would likely cause less than optimal attainment of the allocation objective, and vice versa as discussed above. Musgrave observes that "at the normative level, no conflict exists between the allocation and stabilization functions of budget policy" since the allocation budget is planned ideally to meet individual preferences on the basis of a full-employment income.[9] "Fiscal politics," however, can create a conflict between the allocation and stabilization objectives.[10] If a deficit budget is called for by the stabilization objective, for example, in order to promote the expansion of employment and income, some people may erroneously conclude that the extension of additional public (and quasi-public) goods is virtually costless which, in turn, can lead to an overallocation of public (and quasi-public) goods and a resulting intersector allocation distortion. Taxes thus would not be serving their function as an index of opportunity cost.[11] Oppositely, if a surplus budget is required for stabilization purposes to combat monetary inflation, some of the population may erroneously conclude that public economic goods are more costly (in terms of resource usage) than they actually are—the result being that the supply of public and quasi-public goods will be less than called for by community preferences in reference to the allocation goal. Thus, budget policy directed toward the stabilization objective may significantly distort the allocation objective. Indeed, fiscal norms alone cannot provide comprehensive guidelines to decision-making between interrelated goals.

An adequate fiscal norm should thus attempt to meet all fiscal objectives in an attainable second-best manner. It should not totally ignore one goal for the attainment of another unless the preferences of the community clearly dictate such action. Relatedly, a sound fiscal norm should contain some recognition of both the control and functional finance approaches. Yet, no norm is comprehensive in its ability to provide precise guidelines to fiscal decisions on interrelated goals such as stabilization and allocation.

The remaining fiscal rules[12] represent compromise positions between the annually balanced budget and the functional finance extremes. Each "intermediate" norm recognizes both the importance of budgetary control for allocation purposes and the ability of governmen-

---

[8] This discussion is related to the "interacting fiscal policy goals" discussion in the previous chapter.

[9] Richard A. Musgrave, *The Theory of Public Finance* (New York: McGraw-Hill Book Co., 1959), p. 522.

[10] Ibid.

[11] Ibid.

[12] See below.

tal budgetary behavior to improve aggregate economic performance through rational fiscal policy, though emphasis is placed on the latter objective by the intermediate norms. Yet, these rules, just as the "extreme" rules, also fail to provide precise guidelines to fiscal policy directed toward the complete attainment of both the control and aggregate performance objectives and toward the various interrelated societal goals in the allocation, distribution, stabilization, and economic growth branches of public sector economics.

The Cyclically Balanced Budget Fiscal Norm

One "intermediate" approach to fiscal rationality—the *cyclically balanced budget* fiscal norm—advocates budget balance over the course of a complete business cycle rather than in a particular fiscal or calendar year period. Thus, tax receipts and expenditures would be equal over the course of the cycle—whether measured from "peak-to-peak" or from "trough-to-trough." Figure 26–2 displays the cyclically balanced budget fiscal rule. The policy prescription under this norm calls for the central government to apply a "surplus budget" at the time of a cyclical

FIGURE 26–2
Cyclically Balanced Budget Fiscal Norm

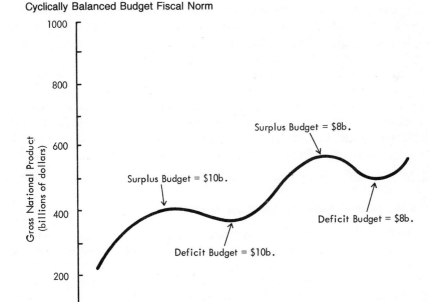

peak or prosperity in order to restrain the pressures of monetary inflation, and to establish a "deficit budget" under conditions of cyclical
recession or depression. Ideally, the surpluses and deficits would offset
each other in equal magnitude over the period of the cycle, thus providing budget balance over the cycle rather than for an annual fiscal or
calendar year. It is argued that both the aggregate performance and
control goals would be well served by this compromise rule.

Many practical difficulties, however, arise in the application of the
cyclically balanced budget norm. These obstacles include, first, the
unlikelihood that a given cycle will be symmetrical in the sense that
the size of the surplus necessary to restrain monetary inflation will be
equal to the size of the deficit necessary to reverse a downturn and
stimulate expansion. Only by great coincidence would an exact cyclical
balance occur. There is no built-in mechanism to assure a symmetrical
cycle. In addition, the peak of a cycle need not be inflationary. In fact,
the peak may not even provide full-employment output, in which case
a surplus budget would constitute an extremely irrational stabilization
policy.

A further drawback of the cyclically balanced budget norm rests on
the institutional fact that in a democratic political structure, such as that
of the United States, lobby groups exert considerable influence over
legislation. As a result, there exists a built-in bias in favor of deficit and
opposed to surplus budgets since the various lobbies ordinarily support
higher spending and lower taxation policies for those whom they represent. Thus, even if the cycle were symmetrical, the institutional impedi-
ment to surplus budgets would make it very difficult to precisely apply
the norm. In general terms, however, the cyclically balanced budget
benchmark contains some merit in that it accepts the best element of
functional finance, namely, the recognition of the fact that deliberate
fiscal policy can favorably affect *macroeconomic goals* and, yet, it still
retains some consideration of *budgetary control* in reference to the
allocation goal.

The High-Employment Budget Fiscal Norm

The compromise fiscal norm represented by the cyclically balanced
budget has received only modest general acceptance. A much more
specific and more widely accepted "intermediate" approach exists in
the form of the *high-employment budget* fiscal benchmark, which is
also known as the *full-employment balanced budget* (or slight surplus)
fiscal rule. Primary initial support for this fiscal norm came from the
Committee for Economic Development (CED) in 1947.[13] The CED

---

[13] See Committee for Economic Development, *Taxes and the Budget: A Program for
Prosperity in a Free Society*, New York, November, 1947.

proposal, which was conceptually structured in terms of the former consolidated-cash budget concept, recommended that tax rates be set to not only balance the budget, but also to provide a surplus budget for debt retirement at agreed high-employment and national income levels.[14] Once these rates are set, they should be left alone unless there is some major change in national policy or condition of national life.

The above norm thus does not require "specific balance" at full employment and stable prices, but willingly accepts a "modest surplus" for debt retirement purposes. Ideally, the CED advocated a full-employment budget surplus of approximately $3 billion (in 1947) at a time when approximately 96 percent or more of the labor force was employed. Most unemployment is of the "between-jobs" variety when the acceptable unemployment rate is set at 4 percent.

The high-employment budget rule is based upon the use of *automatic fiscal stabilizers* and thus avoids discretionary changes in tax rates except under conditions of major national emergency.[15] In this regard, the high-employment budget norm is significantly different from the functional finance and the cyclically balanced budgets rule which allow the use of discretionary fiscal actions. Since the major components of the federal tax base (income, excise, and payroll taxes) are closely related to the level of national income, tax collections tend to rise and fall in positive relationship to changes in the level of national income. This occurs automatically and does not depend upon discretionary changes in tax rates. Thus, rising national income will be accompanied by increasing income tax, payroll tax, and excise tax collections and by a declining volume of unemployment compensation payments. Conversely, declining national income will be accompanied by declining income tax, payroll tax, and excise tax collections and by an increased volume of unemployment compensation payments. Moreover, the federal personal and corporation income taxes are characterized by significantly "elastic" *income elasticities* which means that revenue yields change at a more rapid rate than do changes in the level of national income. Thus, built-in features in the budget work in a rational anticyclical manner because aggregate demand is automatically "restrained" during expansion and "reinforced" during a state of contraction in the economy.

The stabilizing budget principle of the CED emphasizes automatic

---

[14] The former federal *consolidated-cash budget* included *all* federal revenues and expenditures inclusive of both "general" and "earmarked" (trust fund) transactions, and in this manner was similar to the federal *unified budget* which is in current use.

[15] It is strongly argued by some economists that automatic stabilizers are a misnomer and that only discretionary action can be a basic stabilizer. This point will be considered in the discussion which follows. See also the discussion of automatic fiscal stabilizers in Chapter 24.

tax and expenditure responses because, it is argued, such devices do not depend heavily upon an "impossible accuracy" in forecasting economic fluctuations. Moreover, it is argued that automatic stabilizers do not require an "impossible speed" in making tax and expenditure decisions in the legislature and then implementing them into meaningful fiscal action through the executive branch. The CED enumerates three exceptions to its nondiscretionary approach, that is, three conditions requiring discretionary fiscal actions. These are:[16]

1. When a growing population and increasing productivity cause national income and labor employment levels, and relatedly—*tax capacity*, to increase. However, the discretionary readjustments of tax rates made necessary by such long-term growth in the tax base would need to be made only at reasonable intervals, say, five years apart.

2. Occasionally, an urgent need may arise, such as in a *war*, for extraordinary types of expenditure, large in amount but temporary in nature. Often, it would be undesirable under such circumstances to raise tax rates sharply in order to finance the expenditures on a current basis and then reduce tax rates sharply when the expenditure ceases. Under such circumstances, the expenditures can be met through incremental taxes collected over a period of time longer than one year instead of marginally balancing the additional tax collections and expenditures in a single fiscal year.

3. If the recommendations of the CED are combined with appropriate measures in other fields, it is believed that economic fluctuations can be confined to "moderate departures" from a high performance level. Yet, in the case of *severe depression* or *inflation*, discretionary fiscal action should be undertaken. Under such extreme emergencies, the best approach apparently is to change tax rates.

Heller doubts that a genuinely automatic fiscal mechanism can exist because any such mechanism would require that its very establishment, continuance, modification, and abolishment, be accomplished through "discretionary decisions."[17] Under the CED proposal, human discretion *is* allowed to determine when a recession or inflation is sufficiently moderate to ignore deliberate tax rate or expenditure changes as well as when a recession or inflation is severe enough to merit deliberate budgetary action. While a case can be established for the use of automatic fiscal stabilizers as part of a comprehensive set of fiscal tools, it would be foolish to conclude that "non-automatic policy is uncertainly managed by fallible men while an automatic fiscal policy is divinely guided by infallible rules."[18]

---

[16] Committee for Economic Development, *Taxes and the Budget.*

[17] Walter W. Heller, "CED's Stabilizing Budget Policy after 10 Years," *American Economic Review,* September 1957, pp. 634–51.

[18] Ibid., p. 640.

In addition, the operation of a completely automatic fiscal policy would involve a considerable number of both explicit and implicit economic assumptions and forecasts. Revenues and expenditures under existing programs must be calculated in terms of full-employment output and income, for example, and this requires assumptions regarding such relevant considerations as price levels, labor force, and productivity. Yet, it is highly probable that better data are available for economic forecasting now than were available at the time of the initial CED proposal is 1947.

Musgrave, in discussing the high-employment budget norm, observes that the rule helps to provide a certain "disciplinary" effect by requiring that any new expenditure program be met by an increase in tax rates sufficient to provide an *equal amount* of increased tax yield at a full-employment level of income and output.[19] This allocation (disciplinary) effect results in public and quasi-public goods being somewhat underpriced in recessions and somewhat overpriced in prosperities, but the differential with true cost is considerably less than in the cases of an outright deficit or surplus budget with no long-term balance concept attached. Hence, the discipline objective of preserving intersector resource allocation efficiency is served reasonably well by this approach. The stabilization and economic growth objectives, however, are served much less adequately. Automatic stabilization efforts, for example, do not assure that full-employment income and output at stable prices will be maintained or even reached. Thus, in the event of a deep, long-term depression, the automatic stabilizers may provide a peak aggregate performance level for the economy which is below a full-employment level. Oppositely, a secular movement upward may well yield inflationary results from the use of automatic stabilizers. The performance in terms of the stabilization objective may be improved, however, by amending the rule to stipulate that tax rates should be set so as to provide whatever *total budget deficit or surplus* is necessary, on the average, to secure full-employment income and output, at stable prices.

Thus, a deficit or surplus for the *total budget* would be allowed, but a *marginal balance* would be required for a change in expenditures. Nonetheless, an over-reliance on automatic fiscal stabilization devices may still result in only a partial modification of cyclical changes.

THE FULL-EMPLOYMENT BUDGET SURPLUS CONCEPT
AND FISCAL DRAG

The norm described above, which recommends a balanced budget or modest surplus at full employment through the operation of "auto-

---

[19] Musgrave, *Public Finance*, p. 523.

matic fiscal stabilizers," was used as a basis for explaining the fiscal stagnation (slow economic growth) of the American economy between the mid-1950s and the early 1960s. This retarded growth rate alarmed many policy makers, economists, and businessmen, who were interested in the performance of the economy and an explanation was sought. Some experts suggested that the answer lay in the fact that the "automatic stabilizers," which are based upon *constant* tax rates, would collect too great an excess of taxes over expenditures if the economy were performing at an acceptably defined full-employment level (no more than 4 percent of the labor force unemployed). Beginning in 1961, the Council of Economic Advisors (CEA) under President Kennedy supported this explanation. The CEA suggested that budget surpluses tend to occur "too early" in an economic expansion thus preventing the achievement of full employment through a "fiscal drag" effect.

The *Annual Report*[20] of the Council of Economic Advisors in 1962 divided the "full-employment surplus" discussion into three components, namely:

1. The GNP Gap[21]
2. The national-income accounts budget
3. The full-employment budget surplus concept itself.

The *GNP Gap* is the difference between *actual* and *potential* gross national product. "Potential" GNP refers to the volume of economic goods which the nation's economy can produce at reasonably stable prices using the best available technologies, least cost combinations of inputs, and rates of utilization of both capital and labor consistent with the prevailing full-employment norms of the economy. "Actual" GNP, on the other hand, refers to the existing level of GNP. Actual and potential GNP are synonymous, of course, if the full-employment goal has been attained. The gap itself suggests that resources are being under-utilized and that fiscal stagnation is present. The *national-income-accounts-budget* concept, which is based on the national income and product accounts of the U.S. Department of Commerce, initially provided the basic analytical framework for the full-employment budget surplus explanation of fiscal stagnation. Importantly, this budget represents actual "resource-absorbing" activities by the federal component of the public sector. The *full-employment budget surplus* may be defined as that federal budget surplus which would be gener-

---

[20] Council of Economic Advisors, *Annual Report—1962*, chap. 5–7.

[21] Relatedly, see the discussion of the *full employment budget* concept in Chapter 17. Also, for a good discussion of the full-employment budget surplus concept, see Michael E. Levy, *Fiscal Policy, Cycles* and *Growth* (New York: National Industrial Conference Board, 1963).

ated by an established budgetary program under excessively high tax rates if the economy were operating at full employment (no more than 4 percent of the labor force involuntarily unemployed) and stable prices throughout an entire fiscal year. The full-employment budget surplus, in other words, depicts the "restrictive influence" of the federal budget.

More recently, the *full employment budget* concept has been used to justify expansionary federal deficit budgets of the "discretionary" variety at times of underfull employment in the economy. This line of reasoning implies that the expansionary effects resulting from the excess of federal spending over revenue-gathering activities will help to achieve a full-employment production and national income level which, in turn, will generate sufficient revenues, along with a reduction in unemployment compensation payments, to convert the "underfull employment deficit" to a "full employment balanced budget." Hence, the goal of "economic expansion" would have been served by the budget deficit and that of "control" by the full employment budget balance. For example, assume that:

> Full resource employment, as reflected in a labor unemployment rate of 4 percent and a 90 percent rate of capital utilization, would yield a *potential GNP* of $1.4 trillion along with a *balanced federal budget*.

> Yet, *Actual GNP*, with a 6 percent labor unemployment rate and a 70 percent rate of capital utilization, is $1.2 trillion yielding a *federal deficit budget*.

> As production and national income reach full employment levels due to the expansionary budget, federal income and unemployment tax collections will increase and federal unemployment compensation payments will decrease—thus converting the deficit to a *full employment balanced budget* at a $1.4 trillion level of GNP.

Figure 26–3 demonstrates the *GNP Gap* measured as a percentage of potential full-employment GNP for the years 1952 to 1971. Figure 26–4, on the other hand, distinguishes *automatic* from *discretionary* fiscal policy and demonstrates, in addition, how alternative automatic fiscal policies, depending upon the pattern of tax rates and expenditures, can yield differential effects on the level of aggregate economic performance.

The full-employment budget surplus concept itself, of course, is based upon the operation of "automatic" ("nondiscretionary") tax rates and expenditure patterns. Whenever "discretionary" changes in taxes and expenditures are made in the budgetary items which operate as automatic fiscal stabilizers, different economic results tend to occur. Thus, a stabilizer is automatic only so long as its pattern is not changed by discretionary budgetary actions. In Figure 26–4, for example, either

FIGURE 26–3
Actual and Potential Gross National Product, 1952 to 1971 (GNP In 1971 dollars, annual rate)

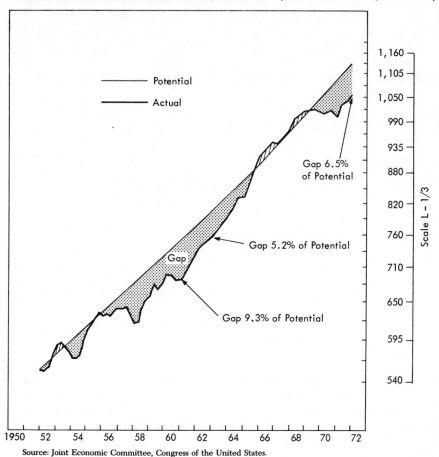

Source: Joint Economic Committee, Congress of the United States.

line *AA, BB, CC,* or *DD* represents "by itself" a *given* set of federal tax rates and expenditures. Each line is drawn *curvilinear* upward in order to express the "elastic" income elasticity of federal taxation as caused by the predominance of progressive income taxes in the federal revenue structure. As national income changes along the horizontal axis, the automatic budgetary relationship moves increasingly from a deficit toward a surplus budget position. However, "discretionary" budgetary changes can shift the budgetary behavior of the "automatic" stabilizers as, for example, from line *AA, BB,* or *DD* to the optimal "full-employment without monetary inflation" line *CC.* This can be accomplished by various discretionary tax and/or expenditure changes.

The full-employment budget surplus explanation of *fiscal stagnation*

FIGURE 26–4

A Comparison of Automatic and Discretionary Fiscal Stabilizers and Their Aggregate Economic Effects

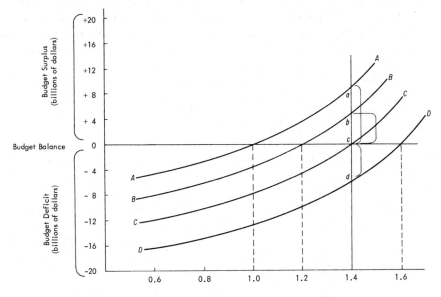

National Income (trillions of dollars)

AA = Most restrictive budget policy.
BB = Moderately restrictive (intermediate) budget policy.
CC = Optimal budget policy.
DD = Overly expansionary budget policy.

Note: $1.4 trillion National Income represents a 4 percent labor unemployment rate and a 90 percent capital utilization rate without monetary inflation.

or *fiscal drag* now becomes evident since the "most restrictive" budgetary structure represented by line *AA,* as compared to optimal line *CC,* provides the budget surplus *ac* at the full-employment income of $1.4 trillion instead of a balanced budget at that income level. Moreover, the budget surplus *ac* at the $1.4 trillion income level is greater than the full-employment budget surplus *bc* resulting from the "moderately restrictive" budgetary structure along curve *BB.* The greater the potential surplus, of course, the more difficult it is for the economy to actually attain the full-employment income and output level of $1.4 trillion. Instead, the economy is likely to stagnate at an "underfull-employment" level of (say) $1.0 trillion or $1.2 trillion, depending upon whether the most restrictive budget policy *AA,* or the moderately restrictive budget policy *BB,* is in effect. On the other hand, if an overly expansionary budget policy such as *DD* is in effect, conditions of monetary inflation will prevail and the deficit *cd* will exist.

Ideally, "fiscal drag" should be combatted via lower taxes and/or higher federal spending while monetary inflation should be met via higher taxes and/or reduced federal spending. The ultimate goal would be to achieve a federal budget represented by line *CC* which is characterized by a balanced federal budget at the $1.4 billion, full employment without monetary inflation, level of national income. The "fiscal drag" problem resulting from a "full employment budget surplus" situation has essentially disappeared during recent years in the United States due to a variety of factors including (1) increased military spending in Southeast Asia, (2) federal tax reductions such as those related to the economic recovery efforts of August 1971, and (3) the federal revenue-sharing legislation of 1972.

There can be little doubt that the full employment budget surplus concept played an important role in the accomplishment of the federal income tax reductions of 1964 and the excise tax reductions of 1965, both of which contributed heavily toward the improvement of the performance level and growth rate of the American economy by alleviating the *fiscal drag* effect of the federal budget. In fact, the full-employment American economy at the conclusion of the 1966 fiscal year (June 30, 1966) provided a federal administrative budget deficit of $2.3 billion. This represented $104.6 billion in revenues and $106.9 billion in expenditures. The "potential" full-employment surplus had been converted to an "actual" deficit by tax rate reductions and, very importantly, the economy was fully employing its resources.

A FURTHER DISCUSSION OF AUTOMATIC FISCAL STABILIZERS

As discussed above, *fiscal stabilizers* may be built into the budgetary structure as automatic responses or they may consist of separate and deliberate budgetary changes. The former are known as *automatic stabilizers* and the latter as *discretionary stabilizers*. Lewis, in his comprehensive study of federal fiscal policy in the post–World War II era, concludes that automatic stabilizers limited both the duration and the severity of economic contractions during the period.[22] Automatic fiscal stabilizers may be classified into those which *directly* affect disposable income and those which *indirectly* affect it.[23] Direct built-in stabilizers have become relatively more important in recent times than those which exert indirect influence. The "direct" automatic stabilizers include the personal income tax, employment (payroll) taxes, and unemployment compensation payments. Although the "indirect" automatic stabilizers—the corporation income tax and the various excise taxes—

---

[22] Wilfred Lewis, Jr., *Federal Fiscal Policy in the Postwar Recessions* (Washington, D.C.: Brookings Institution, 1962).

[23] Ibid., pp. 16–17.

account for sizable portions of any change in a federal surplus or deficit, they tend to be rather ineffective in minor recessions because they add substantially less to private spending than they subtract from federal budget receipts.[24]

The corporation income tax is the largest automatic stabilizer in terms of dollar impact on the federal budget. In percentage terms, corporate income tax receipts decrease significantly more in recession than does GNP, and the volatility of the tax accounts for at least one half of the automatic decrease in federal tax receipts during the postwar recessions.[25] The volatility of the corporation income tax yield results from changes in the level of corporate profits over the cycle and *not* from a high rate of tax rate progressivity. Though the corporation income tax is reasonably important as an automatic stabilizer because the volume of its collections decrease in recession, thus pushing the federal budget toward a deficit, and increase during prosperity, thus reducing the danger of monetary inflation, it is not as important an automatic stabilizer as the personal income tax since its effect (as observed above) on disposable income is less direct and less complete.

The personal income taxes, unemployment taxes, and unemployment compensation payments serve as the primary built-in fiscal stabilizers.[26] In fact, some 45 percent of federal tax receipts are accounted for by the personal income tax. The personal income tax, in addition, possesses the advantage that it provides prompt response of individual tax liabilities to changes in aggregate economic activity. This result is essentially implemented through the withholding means of payment. The progressive rate structure of the tax, moreover, increases it dampening effects against monetary inflation and its cushioning effects against economic downturns. This is made even more effective with a progressive withholding system, as now exists.

Employment (payroll) tax collections increase and unemployment compensation payments decline as labor employment expands toward full employment, thus creating restraint against monetary inflation through a "net reduction" in private sector purchasing power. Oppositely, employment tax collections decline and unemployment compensation payments increase as a greater number of workers are involuntarily unemployed, which provides a cushioning effect against recession through a "net increase" in private sector purchasing power. The "net changes" in private sector purchasing power exert either a contractionary or an expansionary multiplier effect on the economy. Employment taxes thus serve as an important automatic fiscal stabilizer on the reve-

---

[24] Ibid., p. 17.

[25] Ibid., p. 31.

[26] As observed in Chapter 15, the *unemployment compensation payroll tax* consists largely of "state-imposed" taxes as part of a federally-coordinated program.

nue side of the budget while unemployment compensation payments constitute an important built-in fiscal stabilizer on the expenditure side of the federal budget.

Federal excise taxes also demonstrate sensitivity to cyclical changes in aggregate economic performance. The direction of the volume of excise tax collections varies directly with changes in aggregate economic activity, that is, federal excise tax collections increase as national income increases since higher disposable income provides greater purchases of those economic goods subject to excise taxes. Meanwhile, the declining purchasing power during a recession reduces the volume of expenditures for the taxed items and the volume of federal excise tax collections declines.

A study by Eilbott lends strong support to the anticyclical effectiveness of automatic fiscal stabilizers.[27] It is estimated, on the basis of a multiplier model, that the percentage by which the stabilizers "reduced" the potential change in income in each of the three expansions and recessions during the period 1948 to 1960 was significant. The analysis, which stresses the anticyclical and not the growth impact of the stabilizers, selects personal and corporation income taxes, federal excise taxes, OASDI payroll taxes, and OASDI benefit payments as the basic automatic fiscal stabilizers. The findings indicate that, even if one assumes fairly low values for the marginal propensity to consume out of disposable income and for the marginal propensity to invest out of retained corporate earnings, the automatic stabilizers prevented an average of over *one third* of the potential "income declines" during the first three postwar recessions. The effectiveness of the automatic stabilizers in restraining the three "expansions" between 1948 and 1960 was also sizable, though slightly less effective than for the "contractions."

In conclusion, there appears to be no doubt that the *automatic fiscal stabilizers* have provided favorable stabilization and economic growth results since 1945. It should be observed, however, that fiscal stabilizers (both automatic and discretionary) are not the only forces at work.[28] In recessions, for example, corporate saving absorbs part of the income decline and thus cushions the fall or decline of personal income. In addition, residential construction tends to provide a significant semi-automatic stimulus to the economy in periods of recovery though its timing is far from perfect. Furthermore, capital outlays by state and local units of government tend to provide a stabilizing response to easy credit conditions in recession years. They are less volatile in this regard, however, than is residential construction. Finally, the reader should not

---

[27] Peter Eilbott, "The Effectiveness of Automatic Stabilizers," *American Economic Review*, June 1966, pp. 450–65.

[28] See the discussion in Lewis, *Federal Fiscal Policy*, p. 90.

conclude that federal, state, and local government budgetary devices, along with private sector stabilization forces, provide a *complete* explanation of the relative economic stability in terms of "high-level employment" during the postwar era. Importantly, the efforts of monetary policy have also been significant in this regard, especially since the Treasury—Federal Reserve System "Accord of 1951."[29] However, many experts believe that monetary policy, as well as fiscal policy, erred seriously in the "anti-inflation" efforts of the late 1960s.

MONETARY POLICY AS A NORM FOR RATIONAL ECONOMIC POLICY

An interesting stabilization approach suggested a number of years ago by Milton Friedman would create major changes in the *monetary* system of the nation. The approach, in addition, contains significant *fiscal* implications.[30] The Friedman proposal involves the following conditions:

1. A reform of the money and banking system so as to eliminate both the private creation and destruction of money by commercial banks as well as discretionary control over the quantity of money exerted by the Federal Reserve System. The former could be attained, it was suggested, by adopting a 100 percent reserve requirement for commercial banks while the latter could be accomplished by the same approach plus the elimination of existing central bank authority to engage in open-market operations, the setting of stock margins, and the use of consumer credit controls (as during World War II). The remaining obligations of the private banking system would thus consist of the provision of depository facilities, check clearing, and the like, while the central bank would exist primarily for the purpose of creating money to meet governmental fiscal deficits or retiring money when the government shows a surplus.

2. A policy should be established to determine the level of exhaustive government spending on economic goods and resources—excluding transfer expenditures—totally on the basis of the community's preferences for public goods. No discretionary expenditure changes should be undertaken, according to Friedman, for *stabilization* reasons, but

---

[29] During the 1940s and early 1950s, the Federal Reserve System preferred high interest rates to combat inflation while the Treasury Department desired low interest rates in order to reduce the cost of financing the debt. Until March 1951, the Treasury prevailed and stabilization policy was subsequently frustrated.

[30] See Milton Friedman, "A Monetary and Fiscal Framework for Economic Stability," *American Economic Review,* June 1948, pp. 245–64.

only when *allocational* preferences for public goods by the community change over time. Such changes would tend to be gradual.

3. A predetermined program of transfer expenditures, consisting of a statement of the conditions and terms under which relief and assistance and other transfer expenditures will be provided, should be established. This program should be changed only when the community indicates that a change in the *distribution* of income is desirable and that it should be accomplished through this approach. The transfer expenditures would not be changed for stabilization purposes. Absolute outlays and tax collections will, of course, vary automatically over the cycle, but discretionary changes would not be undertaken.

4. A progressive tax rate structure placing primary reliance on the personal income tax should be used. This tax structure should *not* be varied in response to cyclical fluctuations though actual receipts will vary. Again, a "discretionary" change in the tax structure, just as changes in the expenditure structure of the budget, should reflect the community's preferences for either changes in the level of public goods, in an allocation sense, or for transfer expenditure changes to serve a distribution goal. The increased public expenditures should be accompanied by increased taxes. Calculations of both the cost of additional public goods or transfer payments and the yield of additional taxes should be made at a hypothetical (ideal) level of income rather than at the actual level of income. Thus, the government would keep two budgets, namely, a "stabilization budget" in which all figures refer to an ideal national income level, and the "actual budget." The principle of balancing expenditures and receipts at a *hypothetical* income level would be substituted for the principle of balancing *actual* outlays and receipts. In this sense, the Friedman proposal is similar to the CED approach discussed above.[31] It is obvious that the above proposal places heavy emphasis on "automatic" as opposed to "discretionary" economic policy.

Under the proposal, government spending would be financed by *either* tax revenues *or* by the creation of money (the issuance of noninterest-bearing securities). Thus, government debt creation in the form of the sale of securities is avoided under the proposal. Deficits or surpluses in the government budget, as a result, reflect dollar changes in the quantity of money and, oppositely, the quantity of money will change only as a result of deficit or surplus budgets. A deficit budget thus means an increase and a surplus budget means a decrease in the stock of money. Importantly, the deficits or surpluses themselves are the "automatic consequences" of changes in the level of aggregate

---

[31] Ibid., pp. 247–50.

economic performance. An essential element of the proposal is that the level and composition of fiscal activities undertaken by government is to be determined on allocation grounds and not for the achievement of the stabilization goal.

Friedman admits that rigidities in prices could impede the attainment of the cyclical objectives of his proposal.[32] Yet, given a general environment of price flexibility for both products and productive resources and a minimum of lags in other significant responses, he believes that the monetary-fiscal system resulting from his proposal would be capable of moving the economy toward a full-employment equilibrium. In accomplishing this, it is argued that the system would provide a stable framework which eliminates uncertainty and the undesirable political implications which may result from discretionary stabilization action by governmental authorities. In addition, it is claimed that the system would provide a minimal reliance on the uncertain and untested knowledge which tends to make discretionary actions inadequate.

Writing later (1960), Friedman reviewed this earlier proposal (1948) linking changes in the money supply to the state of the budget as a stabilization approach.[33] At the later date, he continued to believe that his earlier proposal would work well in providing a stable monetary background which would render major fluctuations virtually impossible and which would not reinforce, but possibly alleviate, minor fluctuations.[34] He suggests, however, that the original proposal was more sophisticated and complex than was necessary and that a much simpler rule could be applied which would have two important advantages, namely, (1) its simplicity would facilitate public understanding and backing and, (2) it would largely separate the monetary problem from the fiscal problem in terms of the stabilization goal, and thus would require less far-reaching reform.[35]

The simpler rule, an *automatic monetary pilot*, would provide for a constant rate of growth in the stock of money.[36] The stock of money is defined as inclusive of currency outside of commercial banks plus all deposits in commercial banks. Under the plan, the Federal Reserve System would see to it that the total stock of money (as defined above)

---

[32] Ibid., p. 263.

[33] Milton Friedman, *A Program for Monetary Stability* (New York: Fordham University Press, 1960).

[34] Ibid., p. 90.

[35] Ibid., pp. 89–90.

[36] For additional discussion of the proposal, see Milton Friedman, *Capitalism and Freedom* (Chicago: University of Chicago Press, 1962), and Milton Friedman, *The Optimum Quantity of Money and Other Essays* (Chicago: Aldine Publishing Co., 1969). In the latter, Friedman's advocacy of an "automatic monetary pilot" is stated less strongly than in earlier versions.

increases monthly and, if possible, daily at an annual rate of x percent where x is some number between 3 and 5. For fiscal policy, Friedman continued to suggest that the appropriate counterpart to the monetary rule would be to plan expenditure programs entirely in terms of what the community wishes to achieve through governmental allocation and without regard to the problems of economic stability. Moreover, tax rates would be planned for the purpose of providing sufficient revenues to cover planned expenditures on the average of one year with another —again without regard to yearly changes in economic stability. In addition, erratic changes in either governmental spending or taxation should be minimized, though some substantial changes may be unavoidable due to national emergencies.

Shaw also presents a case for an "automatic monetary pilot."[37] He observes that the nation takes pride in its built-in *fiscal* stabilizers and that it is not a radical proposal to suggest that *monetary* control should also be added to the list of self-activating countermeasures against disturbances in the aggregate performance and economic growth processes. The proposed action is defined further on the basis that discretionary control of the money supply has not performed well, and stable growth in money would contribute to efficiency in other economic dimensions such as an improved payments mechanism. In addition, it is claimed that stable growth in the money supply would reduce one important hazard of both private and governmental economic planning, namely, uncertainty concerning the value of the dollar over time as used to measure potential costs and revenues.

Samuelson takes strong opposition to the above automatic monetary rule proposals.[38] He observes that, in principle, the choice has *never* been one between "discretionary" and "nondiscretionary" (automatic) action since, when men set up a definitive mechanism which is to run indefinitely by itself, an act of discretion of considerable magnitude has already been made. The *single* act of discretion which sets up an automatic stabilizer, in this case an automatic monetary pilot ". . . transcends both in its arrogance and its capacity for potential harm any repeated acts of foolish discretion that can be imagined."[39] Thus, since all stabilization action must be discretionary action, the *relevant choices* are those made between the "good" and "bad" effects of the various forms of discretionary action. In addition, for an automatic monetary pilot to work effectively, the quantity theory of money—with its invariant causal relationship between money income and spending and the

---

[37] Edward S. Shaw, "The Case for an Automatic Monetary Pilot," a paper presented to the American Assembly during 1958.

[38] From testimony presented by Paul A. Samuelson to the Canadian Royal Commission on Banking and Finance in 1962.

[39] Ibid.

supply of money—must fully operate. Samuelson argues that little evidence exists in this regard.[40]

THE NEED FOR COMPREHENSIVE AND FLEXIBLE
ECONOMIC POLICY

The most effective and rational economic policy approach for the attainment of the macroeconomic objectives of stabilization and growth, as well as for achieving the microeconomic goals of allocation and distribution, is that which incorporates an *eclectic* combination of the best elements of the various specific norms and types of economic policy.[41] Thus, elements of both the annually balanced budget and functional finance norms must be included in such an approach with the result that one of the "intermediate norms" is to be preferred. In addition, the combination of both discretionary and automatic economic stabilizers along with the coordinated use of both fiscal and monetary policy is desirable. The discussion below will demonstrate the contributions to economic rationality which are made by such a comprehensive and flexible policy approach.

One extreme position on the continuum of fiscal benchmark possibilities—the *annually balanced budget* rule—contributes something of general importance to the eclectic norm in the form of fiscal (budgetary) "constraint," or "control." This is particularly important to a society which voices a preference for the market allocation of resources. An overemphasis on this discipline function of the budget, however, may lead to severe sacrifices in terms of the other legitimate public finance goals, especially those of economic stabilization and growth. Since governmental budgetary actions cannot avoid influencing the macroeconomic variables of stabilization and growth, the *functional finance* extreme on the continuum contains the considerable merit of "rationalizing" the "inevitable" ability of the budget to influence macroeconomic performance. Moreover, an overemphasis of allocation, resulting from the annually balanced budget rule, leads to several fundamental inconsistencies.

First, as developed in Part One of this book, it should be remembered that "market failure" leads to the provision of rather substantial quantities of public and quasi-public goods by the public sector. This may be difficult to finance, however, under an annually balanced budget rule. Moreover, the annually balanced budget norm is based

---

[40] Ibid.

[41] See the arguments in behalf of an "eclectic" approach for macroeconomic policy in: Jan Tinbergen, *On the Theory of Economic Policy* (Amsterdam: North Holland, 1952); Bent Hansen, *The Economic Theory of Fiscal Policy* (London: Allen and Unwin, 1958); and Leif Johansen, *Public Economics* (Amsterdam: North Holland; Chicago: Rand McNally, 1965).

partly on an "irrational" fear of government debt (especially federal debt). This fear, however, is not consistent with the nature of public sector debt in the United States. The federal debt, for example, has been a declining proportion of gross national product during recent decades and it is held internally by Americans to a very large degree.[42] Furthermore, as has been demonstrated earlier, the American economy (like any market-oriented economy) does not automatically arrive at a noninflationary full-employment equilibrium. Thus, an underfull-employment equilibrium of aggregate economic performance will result in a lower national output, and thus will lower the living standard of the society. In this instance, the importance of full resource employment would tend to overshadow the importance of an annually balanced budget.

The best elements of the "functional finance" and "annually balanced budget" norms should thus be *combined* to form an acceptable "intermediate" norm. An effort is made in this regard by the *cyclically balanced budget* benchmark. This rule recognizes the control (discipline) function of the budget while at the same time acknowledging the ability of the budget to promote macroeconomic goals. Nevertheless, it is not a refined approach and is subject to the rather severe limitations discussed earlier in the chapter. A superior hybrid approach is represented by the *high-employment budget* rule which, though it overemphasizes the relative importance of automatic stabilizers, importantly stresses the obvious need to rationalize the impact of the public sector on aggregate economic performance. Moreover, it is not subject to the inherent weaknesses of the cyclically balanced budget approach such as the unlikelihood of matching upswing and downswing phases of the business cycle with resulting matching surpluses and deficits over the period of a cycle. By contrast, the high-employment budget possesses a workable ability to achieve budget balance at a time when "near-optimal" employment and price level conditions are present in the economy.[43]

The high-employment budget approach, in the form proposed by the Committee for Economic Development, suggests that automatic rather than discretionary fiscal stabilizers be used to achieve stabilization objectives. *Automatic* stabilization efforts alone, however, though extremely valuable, do not constitute a complete fiscal policy approach. There is no reason, given adequate sophistication in data collection and in forecasting and the evident success of the discretionary tax reductions of 1964 and 1965, why *discretionary* fiscal efforts should not be

---

[42] The next chapter will elaborate on these points.

[43] "Near-optimal" instead of "optimal" conditions are actually attainable. See the relevant discussion in the previous chapter concerning the *full-employment-inflation paradox*.

used in an intelligent and rational manner along with the automatic stabilizers. Moreover, the apparent validity of the *fiscal drag* explanation of retarded growth rates in the economy during the late 1950s and early 1960s suggests a further modification in the CED approach, namely, the selection of *budget balance* instead of a *modest surplus* at full employment as an objective of automatic stabilization policy.

Perhaps one significant institutional contribution can be made in the foreseeable future to improve the effectiveness of the discretionary stabilizers. This consists of the proposal, made first by President Kennedy, that Congress give authority to the President, within limits prescribed by Congress, to alter federal income tax rates for the purpose of counter-cyclical fiscal policy. This would greatly improve the timing of discretionary fiscal action since the policy could be made effective without involvement in the time-consuming legislative process for each separate tax change. Furthermore, the tax effects would be quickly implemented through the withholding technique of tax collection. Opponents of this proposal argue that it would upset the fiscal "balance of power" between the legislative and executive branches of the federal government.

Finally, a comprehensive and rational economic policy approach should include the coordinated use of both *fiscal* and *monetary* tools. The inevitable interaction between fiscal and monetary policy, whether rationalized or not, is demonstrated by the *IS-LM* model which describes the process whereby equilibrium conditions are simultaneously reached in both the money and product markets[44] In Figures 26–5a and 26–5b, the rate of interest is measured on the vertical axis and national income is measured on the horizontal axis. The *IS* curve displays a series of points at which investment and saving are equal at various interest rate and income levels. The *LM* curve, on the other hand, represents a series of points at which the demand for and supply of money are equal at various interest rate and income levels. In each graph, at the intersection of the two curves (*IS, LM*) at point *A*, the rate of interest (*i*) in the money market and the level of national income (*Y*) in the product market are determined.

Figure 26–5a shows that monetary neutrality does not necessarily result when fiscal policy is applied.[45] The *IS* curve may be shifted to

---

[44] For a more detailed discussion of the determination of simultaneous equilibrium conditions in both the money and product markets, see Thomas F. Dernberg and Duncan M. McDougall, *Macro-Economics* (New York: McGraw-Hill Book Co., 1963), chap. 9; and Norman F. Keiser, *Macroeconomics, Fiscal Policy, and Economic Growth* (New York: John Wiley & Sons, Inc., 1964), chap. 7, or other basic macroeconomic textbooks.

[45] The presentation here will be kept in simple form. However, it should be observed that the *elasticity* of the *IS* and *LM* curves can have important bearing upon policy decisions. Nevertheless, space does not permit an elaborate discussion of the various elasticity implications in this book.

FIGURE 26–5
Fiscal Policy and Monetary Policy as Demonstrated by the *IS-LM* Model

a. The Fiscal Policy Case   b. The Monetary Policy Case

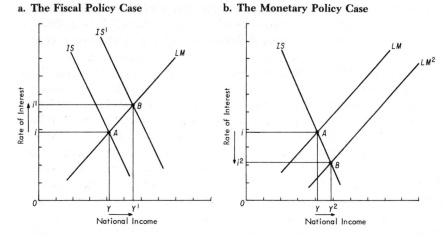

either the right or to the left from its original equilibrium position through *governmental budgetary policy*.[46] The example shown considers only an expansionary fiscal policy which can be brought about by such budgetary policies as a decrease in tax rates and/or an increase in governmental spending. The resulting government multiplier causes the *IS* curve to shift from its initial equilibrium with *LM* at national income level (Y) and interest rate level (i) establishing a new equilibrium (point B) at the higher income level (Y^1) and, very importantly, at the higher interest rate level (i^1). Monetary neutrality thus is *not* maintained and the interest rate increase may offset some or all of the potential national income growth deriving from the expansionary fiscal policy.

In contrast to Figure 26–5a which displays the interest rate results of fiscal policy, Figure 26–5b demonstrates the results of monetary policy. In this instance, the *LM* curve shifts to the right indicating an increase in the stock of money. National income is thus expanded from (Y) to (Y^2) through monetary policy and, quite significantly, the interest rate decreases from (i) to (i^2). Hence, it is argued that monetary policy is superior to fiscal policy when expansion is desired because it does not create the neutralizing influence of higher interest rates which occurs in the fiscal policy case (Figure 26–5a).

No definite conclusion, however, can be made with regard to whether monetary or fiscal policy is a superior tool for aggregate economic expansion. Each case will differ depending upon many relevant

---

[46] Changes in the level of autonomous private investment can also cause the *IS* curve to shift.

variables such as private sector economic incentives and the elasticity of the *IS* and *LM* curves. Moreover, it must be acknowledged that fiscal policy holds an advantage over monetary policy in the sense that exhaustive governmental expenditures directly compel resource absorption, and thus directly expand aggregate demand, while lower interest rates merely make additional consumption and investment spending possible. That is, monetary policy does not lead necessarily to an expansion in aggregate demand by lowering interest rates if investment incentives are low, as was demonstrated during the depression of the 1930s in the United States.

The *IS-LM* model makes an additional contribution to rational fiscal policy since the discussion to this point in the book has concentrated upon multipliers which implicitly assumed monetary neutrality. In other words, changes in the level of private (autonomous) investment and in governmental budgetary behavior regarding taxes and expenditures were assumed *not* to influence the rate of interest. Yet, such influence is possible and an expansionary fiscal policy could be partly or totally neutralized, though complete neutralization is very unlikely, by an increase in the rate of interest. In the absence of an interest rate change, of course, the full multiplier effect on aggregate economic activity could take place.

The need for a *coordinated fiscal and monetary approach* is also indicated by the various stabilization policy *lags.* The *recognition lag,* which relates to the detection of undesirable unemployment and inflationary trends, depends upon the quality of data and the analytical quality of its interpretation for forecasting. Since both fiscal and monetary policy equally face the economic forecasting problem, no preference between fiscal and monetary policy may be detected on this point. However, when we consider the *administrative lag,* which refers to the time taken to make policy decisions after the need for action is detected, discretionary monetary policy carries the advantage over discretionary fiscal policy with its ability to make decisions more quickly due to the semiautonomous nature of the Federal Reserve System. Yet, fiscal policy holds the advantage when the *operation lag* is considered, that is, in terms of the length of time between policy decisions and their actual impact on the economy. This is true because fiscal policy deals directly with resource usage and income flows while monetary policy affects these flows through the indirect manner of influencing the structure of liquidity and assets in the economy. In the latter case, the operational impact on the economy tends to occur over a longer period of time.

In conclusion, the desirability of a *comprehensive and flexible economic policy* directed toward the attainment of the macroeconomic goals of full employment, price stability, a sound balance of international payments performance, and satisfactory economic growth is apparent. Hence, both *monetary* and *fiscal* tools, *discretionary* as well as *automatic,* should be cooperatively employed to promote these objectives. Moreover, a further requirement consists of a hybrid fiscal norm inclusive of some recognition of both the importance of *control* for allocation efficiency purposes, and also of the need to rationalize budgetary procedure so that the inevitable impact of fiscal behavior on *aggregate performance* will be a desirable one.

A "modified" *high-employment budget* rule best meets the above criteria. Hence, tax rates and spending programs should be set in such a manner that a reasonably defined level of full employment, with minimal inflation, would be automatically achieved when the budget is balanced.[47] Moreover, discretionary fiscal actions, which change the tax and expenditure parameters of the budget, should also be utilized as required. In addition, the modified high-employment budget rule, inclusive of both automatic and discretionary techniques, should be implemented in coordination with the goals and techniques of monetary policy. Furthermore, limited discretionary income tax rate authority for the President is desirable. Also, an incomes policy directed toward the undesirable inflationary effects which derive from market structure imperfections in product and factor markets at times may be required. Indeed, a rational democratic political economy should be capable of achieving, to an acceptable level of attainment, both the *macroeconomic* and *microeconomic* goals of the society by means of an eclectic set of economic policy instruments.

---

[47] As observed previously, a commonly accepted definition of *full employment* is when 4 percent or less of the labor force is involuntarily unemployed and at least 90 percent of the capital capacity of manufacturing industries is being utilized.

27

Public Sector Debt

Public sector debt is interrelated with the basic governmental fiscal flows of taxation and spending. If the volume of governmental expenditures exceeds the volume of tax and other (nontax) revenues, a deficit budget exists. This deficit budget provides the fundamental "precondition" for debt creation. Yet, it is not synonymous with debt creation. Instead, debt creation should be viewed as one of several alternative financial arrangements for the provision of public and quasi-public goods by government. In place of the deficit being created, for example, these economic goods could have been financed through other techniques.[1] That is, taxes, whether general or earmarked, user charges, or administrative revenues could have been collected in lieu of the sale of debt. Having once been created, debt requires interest payments to maintain the debt and refinancing operations if the debt is to be continued beyond the maturities of existing securities.

HISTORY OF PUBLIC SECTOR DEBT IN THE UNITED STATES

Federal Government Debt

The first federal government debt arose out of the assumption of the state government debts which had been incurred in winning the Revo-

---

[1] See Chapter 6 for a more detailed discussion of alternative sources of public sector revenues.

lutionary War. Alexander Hamilton favored, while Thomas Jefferson opposed, assumption of the state debts. The view of the former prevailed and the gross federal debt reached a peak of $84 million in 1795. The next debt peak was reached in 1803 at a level of $86 million. The federal debt then declined, reaching a low point in 1811, and rose once again during the War of 1812. A new peak of $127 million occurred in 1815. Following this, the general trend was downward with the debt reaching a level of less than $100,000 in 1834. During the next 17 years, the trend was upward with a peak of $68 million in 1851. By 1865, the last year of the Civil War, the federal debt was in excess of $2 billion. Then, a general decline in federal debt began and by 1888 the debt was less than $1 billion. It next reached the billion-dollar range during the Spanish-American War period, but dropped below $1 billion and remained below until World War I pushed it to over $25 billion in 1919. The decade of the 1920s witnessed debt retirement, the total federal debt dropping to below $17 billion in 1929. It increased again during the 1930s, due to antidepression spending, and was $43 billion by 1940. World War II caused the federal debt to skyrocket to $269 billion in 1946. Since that time, though bolstered by Korean War, cold war, and Vietnam War defense expenditures, the federal debt has followed a more gradual upward trend. It stood near $427 billion in 1972.

State Government Debt

During the ninteenth century, combined state-local debt at times exceeded federal debt. Moreover, local debt frequently exceeded state government debt. In fact, during certain years, such as 1860, local debt was much greater than federal government debt. State debt, which totaled only $25 million in 1829, ascended to $170 million in 1839, to $185 million in 1849, and to $251 million in 1859. During the next 10 years, state debt grew by more than $100 million and reached a level of $357 million in 1869. Despite a rapidly growing population, the trend in state government debt was downward during the next two decades and by 1889 it had dropped to a level of $208 million. During the early twentieth century the downward trend was reversed, and by the early 1920s state debt exceeded $1 billion for the first time. From 1930 to post–World War II, state debt stayed generally within the $2–$3 billion range. Then, it began to increase rapidly following World War II and by 1972 was in excess of $50 billion.

Local Government Debt

Local government debt, which in 1839 was only about one seventh the level of state debt, grew rapidly during the next three decades and was substantially greater than state debt by 1869. At that time, state debt was $357 million while local debt totaled $523 million. The gap between local and state debt widened during the decade of the 1870s and by 1879 local debt was $805 million while state debt was only $222 million. This trend continued during the next few decades. In 1902, local debt of $1.9 billion greatly exceeded the state debt of $270 million. As the twentieth century progressed, local debt continued to exceed state debt, but by a gradually narrowing ratio. The absolute growth of local debt has been substantial during the twentieth century. It has expanded from $1.9 billion in 1902, to $4 billion in 1913, to $9 billion in 1922, to nearly $13 billion in 1927, to nearly $17 billion in 1940, to over $20 billion in the early 1950s, and to the vicinity of $120 billion by 1972. The tremendous absolute growth of local debt since 1950 should be noted with significance.

Intergovernmental Debt Data and Trends

In Table 27–1, twentieth-century debt trends are presented on an intergovernmental basis. For selected years, absolute debt as well as per capita debt are presented in current dollars for each level of government. Then, the percentage distribution of debt between the federal, state, and local components of the public sector is provided. The table clearly demonstrates the enormous growth of public sector debt, in absolute dollar terms, for all levels of government during this century. Interestingly, the fact that federal debt has been increasing much more slowly than state and local debt since World War II is often overlooked. While federal debt in 1972 was only 158 percent of what it had been in 1946, state debt was 2,150 percent and local debt was 871 percent of 1946 levels.

Though the per capita government debt burden has risen during this century, it has not risen as rapidly as absolute government debt because of population growth during the century. Public sector per capita debt (the sum of columns 5, 6, and 7) was $42 in 1902 and $2,869 per person in 1972. During the same period, public sector debt in absolute terms (the sum of columns 2, 3, and 4) increased from $3.3 billion to $597.4 billion. Moreover, though the figures are not shown in Table 27–1, the ability to carry the greater debt burden per capita has increased enormously during the century as the nation's productive power and wealth have grown on a per capita basis. Furthermore, it may be observed that the per capita government debt of $2,869 in 1972 is only modestly more than it was at the close of World War II, as indicated by the 1946 figure of $2,038 per person (the sum of columns 5, 6, and 7).

Table 27–1 reveals some additional significant debt trends. Intergovernmental trends are particularly discernible in the data showing

TABLE 27-1

Gross Debt,* per Capita Debt, and Percentage Distribution of Debt for Federal, State, and Local Government, Selected Years, 1902–1972

Year (1)	Absolute Amount of Debt (current dollars in millions)			Per Capita Debt (current dollars)			Percentage Distribution of Debt		
	Federal (2)	State (3)	Local (4)	Federal (5)	State (6)	Local (7)	Federal (8)	State (9)	Local (10)
1902	$ 1,178	$ 230	$ 1,877	$ 15	$ 3	$ 24	35.9%	7.0%	57.1%
1913	1,193	379	4,035	13	4	42	21.3	6.7	72.0
1922	22,963	1,131	8,978	209	10	82	69.4	3.5	27.1
1932	19,487	2,832	16,373	156	23	131	50.4	7.3	42.3
1940	42,968	3,590	16,693	326	27	127	67.9	5.7	26.4
1946	269,422	2,353	13,564	1,924	17	97	94.4	0.8	4.8
1950	257,357	5,285	18,830	1,702	35	125	91.4	1.9	6.7
1955	274,374	11,198	33,069	1,670	68	201	86.1	3.5	10.4
1960	286,331	18,543	51,412	1,591	103	286	80.4	5.2	14.4
1962	298,201	22,023	58,779	1,604	118	319	78.6	5.8	15.6
1964	311,713	25,041	67,181	1,629	131	351	77.2	6.2	16.6
1968	347,578	35,663	85,492	1,739	178	428	74.2	7.6	18.2
1972	427,260	51,623	118,496	2,052	248	569	71.5	8.6	19.8

* Gross debt includes both "interest-bearing" and "noninterest-bearing" debt including debt held by federal government agencies and trust funds.

Source: U.S. Department of Commerce, U.S. Treasury Department; adapted from Tables 10 and 11, pages 22–23, *Facts and Figures on Government Finance, 1973* (New York: Tax Foundation, 1973).

changes in the percentage distribution of public sector debt between the three levels of American government. A cursory glance at this part of the table, comparing 1902 and 1972, shows that *federal* debt has doubled as a percentage of total public sector debt. During the same 70-year period, the relative importance of *local* debt has decreased sharply to a ratio of one third what it had been at the beginning of the century. *State* debt, however, increased slightly in relative importance during the same period. Thus, while combined *state-local* debt was 64.1 percent of total government debt in 1902, it was only 28.4 percent of the public sector debt in 1972. The present *state-local* share, however, is several times greater than the 5.6 percent state-local distribution in 1946 and the 8.6 percent distribution in 1950. In other words, since the close of World War II there has been a downward trend in federal debt as a percentage of total public sector debt and an upward trend in state and local government debt. This is true whether the two subnational levels of government are combined or considered separately. However, the early 1970's show some signs of a reversal in this trend.

The primary cause of growth in *federal* government debt has been national defense and war. This is evident from Table 27–1. The large increases in federal debt from 1913 to 1922, and again between 1940 and 1946, reflect World War I and World War II expenditures, respectively. Also, much of the post-World War II growth in federal debt may be attributed to defense-related activities. On the other hand, growing population and the derived demand for education, roads, and the like represent the major source of growth in *state* and *local* government debt.[2]

ANALYSIS OF PUBLIC SECTOR DEBT

Debt Misconceptions

Probably no economic concept is subject to more misunderstanding regarding its true nature than *government debt.* There are many sources of such confusion. *One* of the most important of these sources is the false parallel often drawn between "government debt" and "private debt."[3] Important dissimilarities exist between public sector and private sector debt. These differences reach their greatest extreme when federal government debt is compared to private consumer debt.

---

[2] The functional causes of growth in governmental expenditures and debt are discussed in Chapter 16.

[3] *Public* and *private* debt, of course, are similar in the "generic" sense that each involves a creditor-debtor relationship with corresponding debt instruments such as securities and promissory notes.

A *second* area of debt misconception is the confusion between the fiscal flows of taxing and spending and the separate, though related, phenomenon of government debt. As suggested earlier in this chapter, taxing and spending involve the nucleus of the fiscal or budgetary process. On the other hand, debt is merely a means of meeting a particular budgetary situation, namely, a deficit budget caused by the excess of government spending over receipts. Both the fiscal flows of taxation and spending, as well as debt creation and retirement, may exert effects upon the objectives of allocation, distribution, stabilization, and economic growth. Yet, it is important to remember the fact that fiscal flows on the one hand, and debt on the other, may exert such influences in somewhat different ways because they are essentially different phenomena.

A *third* source of confusion regarding public sector debt is the attempt by some people to solve the "optimal" intersector resource allocation (social balance) issue by means of a debt-oriented analogy. Government debt, whether large or small or nonexistent, provides no *direct* implication about the proper size of the public sector relative to the size of the private sector. Conceivably, government could allocate 90 or even 100 percent of society's resources and possess no interest-bearing debt. On the other hand, the public sector could allocate only a small percentage of total productive resources, yet build up a sizable debt over time. In the latter case, however, the mere existence of public sector debt may exert an *indirect* influence upon the allocation, distribution, stabilization, and growth branches of economics. The effects of government debt on these functional areas of economic activity will be discussed later in the chapter.

Internal versus External Debt

The need to distinguish between public and private debt, as discussed above, leads also to a necessary distinction between "internally"- and "externally"-held debt. *Internal debt* may be defined as a situation where the borrowing unit acquires the money from itself (lends to itself). *External debt* is a condition where the borrowing unit acquires money from some lending unit or units other than itself. The borrowing unit may be a unit of government, a business, or a consumer. Political jurisdiction essentially determines the "internal borrowing limit" of government debt while market conditions determine the "internal borrowing limit" of private debt. Government borrowing may be termed "public borrowing" while business and consumer borrowing may be termed "private borrowing."

The only possible case of "purely internal debt" within a nation exists under the category of public borrowing and then only for a sovereign *central* (*national, federal*) unit of government. However, this is a necessary, but not a sufficient, condition of purely internal debt. In other words, only a central government debt can be purely internal. However, even it need not be an internal debt. Our entire federal debt, or part thereof, could be owed to foreigners. In fact, a relatively small portion of it is owed to foreigners. Yet, if the gross federal debt of the United States were financed totally by the sale of securities to *American* governmental agencies, financial institutions, businesses, and individuals, the debt would be a "pure internal debt." No claims against the borrowing unit would arise from outside the borrowing unit. The United States as a sovereign nation, and composed of the people within the nation, would be "borrowing money from itself." The lenders are part of the borrowing unit. There is no outside or external claim against American productive resources nor against the income and output which these resources can create. In reality, as noted above, most federal debt in the United States is held internally. By legislation, the nation could have forbidden the sale of *any* debt outside the political boundaries of the United States. Hence, the debt could have been 100 percent internal.

Since only the federal government possesses the power to issue money, it holds a unique ability to maintain or repay debt. State and local governments do not possess the power of money issuance. They do, however, share with the federal government the power to compel taxation for purposes of maintaining or repaying debt. In addition, all three levels of government tend to acquire offsetting productive assets when they incur debt. Hence, the public sector holds important fiscal advantages as compared to private borrowing. The private sector cannot issue money nor collect taxes. Moroever, private borrowing of a consumptive sort does not ordinarily result in offsetting assets of a real productive nature. Thus, public borrowing, particularly that of the federal government, tends to create a debt which is not only more internal in nature than that resulting from private borrowing, but which also is "easier to carry" since additional financing devices and offsetting productive assets are more readily available. Table 27–2 summarizes the above points.

Despite the fact that a central government is in the best relative position to carry a debt burden, as described above, it cannot be argued that an "externally-held" *central government debt* is more burdensome per se on the people of the society than one which is "internally-held."[4] Yet, this would outwardly seem to be true since the taxes which pay interest to the foreign holders of the debt must be withdrawn from the

---

[4] See James M. Buchanan, *Public Principles of Public Debt* (Homewood, Ill.: Richard D. Irwin, Inc., 1958) for the genesis of this argument.

TABLE 27–2
Continuum of Internal and External Debt Categories and Offsets
to Debt Burdens

Type of Debt	Categories of Borrowing	Offsets to Debt Burdens
Pure internal ↑	Public: by federal, state, and/or local governments	1. Money issuance power 2. Tax power 3. Many expenditures provide offsetting productive assets
Pure external	Private: by business and/or consumer	1. No money issuance power 2. No tax power 3. Expenditures may be for consumptive goods

Note: Direction of arrow indicates increasing offsets to debt burdens.

private sector of the domestic economy. However, the fact is that the tax payments collected to make interest payments on central government debt held by foreigners do *not* constitute a greater burden than those collected for payments on debt held by domestic citizens. The reason is that the national income of the society tends to be larger in the external debt case since resources do *not* need to be withdrawn from the private sector of the "domestic" economy when the debt is initially issued, but instead can be acquired in "international" markets. Hence, the greater amount of resources available to the society when the debt is externally financed will yield a greater national income. From this greater national income, the taxes will be collected which provide the source of the interest payments made to the foreign holders of the debt. Thus, the debt burden is no greater when the debt is externally held than it would be if the debt is internally held. This does not suggest, of course, that an external central government debt does not incur greater "institutional" difficulties than one which is internally held. These greater institutional difficulties for external debt arise from the fact that the prevailing system for processing international payments is more complex and less perfect than the typical domestic payments mechanism, especially in mature economies.

Real versus Financial Debt Burdens and Symmetrical versus Asymmetrical Debt Distribution

While "overall budgetary incidence" was discussed earlier, the distributional implications of "public sector debt" as such are considered in this chapter. Thus, further discussion is desirable regarding the distinction between *real* and *financial* debt burdens and, in addition, the distinction between *symmetrical* and *asymmetrical* debt distribution. The burden of debt may be viewed in *real* terms when the usage of "productive resources" is emphasized. On the other hand, the burden may be viewed in *financial* terms when the monetary flows of "interest payments" and the "taxes" to finance these payments are considered. Furthermore, both the "real" and "financial" aspects of debt burden are concerned with the distinction between "symmetrical" and "asymmetrical" debt distribution.

A "financial" debt burden is *symmetrical* when the debt instruments are held equally by the various spending units of the population who likewise pay equal amounts of taxes to finance the debt. In this instance, no redistribution of money income results from the existence of the debt. The symmetrical distribution of the debt burden takes on a "real" burden connotation, however, when the actual economic goods financed with the debt are divided among the population in proportion to the payment of taxes to service the debt. Under these circumstances, no real income redistribution occurs. On the other hand, an *asymmetrical* debt burden is characterized either by a disproportionate distribution between tax and interest payments, in "financial burden" terms, or by a lack of proportionality between the consumption of debt-financed economic goods and the payment of taxes to finance the debt which paid for these goods, in the "real burden" sense. In either case, a redistribution of income would take place. Thus, it may be said that debt burden "symmetry" is a case of *distributional neutrality* and that debt burden "asymmetry" involves *distributional nonneutrality* due to its "income redistribution effects" among the population.

Some of the distinctions between "real" and "financial" burdens and between "symmetrical" and "asymmetrical" debt distribution are indicated in the following example:

Suppose that the present federal debt is $300 billion. Suppose also that the securities held against this debt are divided equally among some 100 million family (or unmarried adult) spending units in the United States. Thus, every spending unit would possess $3,000 in treasury securities. If the annual interest paid on the securities is 5 percent, each spending unit will receive $150 ($3,000 × 0.05) in annual interest payments. The federal government could tax every spending unit $150 and then turn around and pay each spending unit $150 in interest. Since the debt is held and tax-financed in a *symmetrical* manner, no income redistribution effects of the *financial burden* variety occur. The only possible redistributive effects would result, in a *real burden sense*, from a disproportionate (unequal) relationship between the payment of taxes to service the debt and the receipt of the goods provided with the debt-created funds. Of course, if the goods financed with the expenditures are "pure public goods," such as national defense, no redistributional effect occurs in *real resource* terms since pure public goods are essentially consumed on an "equal consumption for all" basis. On the other hand, if the goods are of the "quasi-public good" variety, individuals may not benefit equally from their consumption and in this event redistribution in *real terms* could occur.[5]

INTERGENERATION TRANSFER OF DEBT BURDENS

The question arises as to whether a debt burden is borne by the *present generation* which creates a debt, or whether the burden is passed on, instead, to *future generations.* The classical economic viewpoint regarding the *intergeneration transfer of debt burdens,* which was later adapted to Keynesian economic theory, has been challenged in recent years by Buchanan, Bowen, Davis, Kopf, Musgrave, Modigliani, and others.[6] The orthodox position holds that a debt burden *may* be shifted to future generations *only* if the present generation reduces its rate of saving as a result of the debt-creation activity. This argument, which descends from Ricardo, was stated brilliantly by Pigou and later adapted to Keynesian terms by economists such as Lerner and Samuelson.[7]

The traditional argument thus suggests that the present generation bears the burden of debt, except in the following "reduced saving" case: Reduced saving by the present debt-creating generation would cause future generations to inherit a smaller amount of real productive capital (that is, plant and equipment) with consequent reduced income for the future generations. Once more, present saving is more likely to be reduced when debt instead of tax financing is used because tax obligations are seen *clearly* by the present generation while debt obligations involve future rather than present tax payments (as the debt is financed and repaid) which are *less certain* in the eyes of the present generation taxpayer. Hence, it is likely that the purchasers of bonds will pay for

---

[5] See the relevant discussion of public and quasi-public goods in Part One.

[6] Buchanan, *Public Principles of Public Debt;* William G. Bowen, Richard G. Davis, and David H. Kopf, "The Public Debt: A Burden on Future Generations?" *American Economic Review,* Septemter 1960, pp. 701–6; Richard A. Musgrave, *The Theory of Public Finance* (New York: McGraw-Hill Book Co., 1959), chap. 23; Franco Modigliani, "Long-Run Implications of Alternative Fiscal Policies and the Burden of the National Debt," *Economic Journal,* December 1961, pp. 730–55.

[7] Abba P. Lerner, "The Burden of the National Debt," in *Income, Employment and Public Policy* (New York: W. W. Norton & Co., Inc., 1948), pp. 255–75; Abba P. Lerner, review of James A. Buchanan's book, *Public Principles of Public Debt,* in the *Journal of Political Economy,* April 1959, pp. 203–06; Abba P. Lerner, "The Burden of Debt," *Review of Economics and Statistics,* May 1961, pp. 139–41; Paul A. Samuelson, *Economics* (New York: McGraw-Hill Book Co., 1964), chap. 18.

them more out of saving than out of consumption because they consider their "net wealth position" better under loan finance than under tax finance. As a result, the reduced level of saving causes less *real* productive capital to be inherited by future generations and, thus, a *real* burden in the form of a "reduced output potential" is passed along through this "indirect" means to future generations.

Note that the orthodox approach interprets "intergenerational debt burden" in terms of the *real resources* that are unavailable to the future generation due to debt-financing by the present generation.

Much of the current controversy over the *intergeneration transfer of debt burdens* centers upon semantics, special assumptions, and the need to distinguish between "direct" and "indirect," and "real" and "financial," "burdens" and "effects." This should be kept in mind by the reader as the various arguments challenging the orthodox viewpoint are described below. After the individual arguments are presented, a synthesis and summary of the current state of public debt theory will be provided.

James M. Buchanan supplied the opening volley against the traditional position in 1958 in his book *Public Principles of Public Debt.*[8] Buchanan denies that the present generation bears the burden of public debt since those individuals who purchase the government securities do so on a "voluntary" basis. These individuals acquire present assets in lieu of present consumption—with future earnings from and repayment of these assets in mind. In other words, they do not realize a *present burden* because they are merely postponing present consumption to the future when they redeem their securities. Meanwhile, these individuals will also earn interest compensation on their bonds.

Since the government securities are purchased "voluntarily," those in the present generation who purchase them do not consider themselves to be undergoing a sacrifice whereas those in future generations who pay the interest and redeem the bonds do experience a sacrifice through "compulsory" tax payments. It is contended that the taxes are an actual "net burden" to future generations since they would not have been collected from the future generations if the present generation had met its expenditures through taxation while, on the other hand, the bondholders of the present generation would have received income anyway from whatever other assets in which they might have invested their savings.

Though the Buchanan argument carries a certain real burden connotation, its primary emphasis is upon burden in a *financial* sense. It is asserted, for example, that the "monetary" contributions of taxes by subsequent generations to maintain or retire the debt created by an

---

[8] Buchanan, *Public Principles of Public Debt.*

earlier generation constitutes an intertemporal burden due to the fact that the generation which created the debt voluntarily purchased "financial" assets (securities). Thus, in a market or exclusion principle sense, these purchases were freely chosen and were based on a time preference financial decision for present earnings and for future consumption.

Moreover, in evaluating the Buchanan argument on intergeneration debt burden transfers, it should be observed that the argument rests upon an *individualistic theory of the state* since it uses freedom of choice as an integral part of intergeneration debt burden determination. Relatedly, the Buchanan approach focuses upon the *disaggregation* of the burden among individuals instead of the aggregate or total debt burden of the society.

Another volley was directed toward the orthodox debt position by William G. Bowen, Richard G. Davis, and David H. Kopf.[9] They attack the traditional viewpoint by posing a case in which *present saving* (saving by Generation 1) is not reduced—present saving being the locus whereby the only "intergeneration burden transfer" can occur under the orthodox argument. If an intergeneration burden transfer can occur when present saving is not reduced, an effective challenge will have been presented to the orthodox position since no reduction in capital formation would seemingly occur. The Bowen-Davis-Kopf case is one in which the first generation incurs debt to carry out a public project within its lifetime. As Generation 1 purchases the bonds (securities) to carry out the public project, "saving" *initially* does take place by this generation. However, Generation 1 then "sells the bonds" to Generation 2 in order to finance the purchase of additional consumer goods during retirement. Importantly, it is assumed that *all* of the bonds are sold and that all of the funds are spent on present consumption by Generation 1. In other words, there is *no inheritance* passed on to Generation 2. The sale of all of the bonds to the next generation constitutes a "dissaving" for Generation 1, which *offsets* its "initial saving." Thus, in effect, the first generation does not reduce saving and capital formation, according to the argument. Now, as the argument continues, if during the lifetime of Generation 2 the government decides to retire the debt by taxing that generation to pay for the bonds which it has purchased from the first generation, the result is a *reduction in the lifetime consumption* of Generation 2. In other words, the second generation bears the burden of the debt even though the saving of the first generation was not ultimately reduced.

Carl S. Shoup, however, argues that the Bowen-Davis-Kopf argu-

---

[9] Bowen, Davis, Kopf, "Public Debt."

ment fails to disprove the traditional analysis.[10] He contends that the generation initiating the debt *does*, indeed, pass a reduced amount of real productive capital to the next generation, that is, the future generation *does not* inherit the same amount of capital stock that it would have inherited had the debt not been incurred. Thus, if the first generation "spends the proceeds" from the sale of its bonds to the second generation on *consumption*, "it must later bequeath a smaller real capital stock than would be the case if it had not so sold its bonds (securities) and spent the proceeds, and this reduction in real bequest is a burden on the second generation."[11] Moreover, if one drops the Bowen-Davis-Kopf "no *legal* inheritance" assumption, part of the bonds as well as part of the funds acquired from the sale of the remaining bonds by Generation 1 may be willed to second-generation survivors, thus reducing the actual intergenerational burden transfer that would occur under the Bowen-Davis-Kopf argument. Furthermore, even if the generation creating the debt sells all of its earlier-acquired government bonds to an overlapping second generation which, in turn, reduces its consumption in order to purchase the securities, the reduction in consumption by the second generation is "voluntary." Thus, in an "individualistic" sense, it may be argued that no burden has been incurred by the later generation. Hence, the orthodox position on the intergenerational transfer of debt burdens would appear to remain largely intact.

Richard A. Musgrave argues that loan (debt) finance *necessarily* spreads the burden among different generations while tax finance causes the present generation to bear the burden.[12] The Musgrave approach is based upon the "benefit principle" of equity as applied to the financing of durable capital items which will last through several generations of taxpayers. The following example is provided by Musgrave:[13]

> . . . consider a project whose services become available in equal installments over three periods. Also, suppose that the life (or residency) span of each generation covers three periods, and that the population is stable. Finally, assume that loans advanced by any one generation must be repaid within its life span. In each period the benefits accrue to three generations, including generations 1, 2, 3 in the first period; 2, 3, 4 in the second; and 3, 4, 5 in the third period. To contribute their proper share, Generations 1 and 5 should pay 1/9 of the cost; Generations 2 and 4 should

[10] See Carl S. Shoup, "Debt Financing and Future Generations," *Economic Journal*, December 1962, pp. 889–92, and also his *Public Finance* (Chicago: Aldine Publishing Co., 1969), pp. 443–44.

[11] Shoup, *Public Finance*, p. 444.

[12] Musgrave, *Theory of Public Finance*, chap. 23.

[13] Ibid., p. 563.

each pay 2/9; and Generation 3 should pay 3/9. Let us now suppose that the total cost is $100 and that it is to be allocated accordingly. To simplify matters, the allocation of interest cost will be disregarded.

The entire outlay of $100 must be raised and spent in the first period. Of this, $33.3 is obtained by taxation, divided equally between Generations 1, 2, and 3. The remainder is obtained by loans from Generations 2 and 3. There can be no loans from Generation 1 owing to our rule that each generation must be repaid during its life span. In the second period, tax revenue is again $33.3, contributed now by Generations 2, 3, and 4; the debt held by Generation 2 is retired in full, and loans of $16.6 are advanced by Generation 4 to retire part of the debt held by Generation 3. In the third period, the tax revenue of $33.3 is contributed by Generations 3, 4, and 5. It is used to retire the remainder of the debt held by Generations 3 and 4. In retrospect, the total cost has been divided between the five generations in accordance with benefits received. Loan finance in this case not only provided credit to taxpayers but resulted in a bona fide division of the cost between generations—a result impossible to secure through tax finance.

The above example thus allows an intergeneration transfer of costs, including debt costs, among the five generations so that an equality is achieved between "cost burdens" and "benefits received" for each generation. Thus, a form of "intergenerational symmetry" would have been achieved.

Yet, in order for the Musgrave case to serve as a valid challenge to the orthodox debt position, the consumption-saving reaction of Generation 1 to loan financing must be "irrelevant" because such reaction is the only means through which intergeneration burden transfer may occur under the traditional analysis. However, the irrelevancy of the consumption-saving reaction of Generation 1 is accomplished in the analysis only upon the basis of the somewhat unrealistic (and implicit rather than explicit) assumption that "inheritance does not take place." Hence, the Musgrave approach does not appear to invalidate the orthodox position.

Franco Modigliani suggests that intergeneration burden analysis should concentrate upon *stock* as well as *flow* variables and *long-run* as well as *impact* effects.[14] Modigliani contends that a debt-financed government expenditure *must* place a gross burden on future generations through a reduction in the stock of private capital, which tends to reduce future income and the future flow of economic goods. The traditional approach had contended merely that debt financing *may* place a burden on future generations by reducing the supply of capital. The Modigliani argument, which is presented in a Keynesian macroeco-

---

[14] Modigliani, "Long-Run Implications of Alternative Fiscal Policies . . . ," p. 731.

nomic framework, is asserted to hold (but to different degrees) for both full-employment and less than full-employment conditions.

According to Modigliani, though a full-employment economy cannot increase governmental expenditures without reducing private capital (investment) spending, *debt financing* reduces investment spending by a "greater amount" than does *tax financing*. This occurs because government borrowing obtains funds which mostly come out of savings while taxes bear more heavily upon consumption. This is true, according to Modigliani, because debt financing—which does not lower the net worth of an individual—does not induce the individual to reduce his level of consumption. On the other hand, the payment of taxes lowers the net worth of an individual and, consequently, induces him to lower his level of consumption. Hence, the higher volume of consumption which occurs under debt financing as opposed to tax financing means a lower level of saving and investment in a full-employment economy. Thus, with a reduced amount of capital stock passed on to future generations, the future flows of income and economic goods must be less than they would have been if the present generation had used tax financing.

As E. J. Mishan points out, a "basic weakness" in the Modigliani approach, as well as in the related approaches of the other dissenters referred to by Mishan as "burden mongers," is the failure to consider that the gross burden may be offset by secondary effects in the form of the future returns derived from the present public expenditures.[15] The failure of intergeneration debt burden analysis to consider as important the aggregate of both public and private sector investment and their returns is a defect which could mislead the general public and government policy makers.[16] This matter may be looked upon as the failure of intergeneration debt burden discussants to distinguish adequately between "primary" and "secondary" burdens and, indeed, to define debt "burden" as distinct from debt "effect."

Earlier in this chapter, "real" burden was distinguished from "financial" burden. The former was said to relate to the real productive resources used in the provision of consumer and capital goods, and the latter was said to refer to the monetary arrangement whereby government debt is financed through tax revenues which flow to those who hold the debt. In either context, it was observed that "redistributional effects" may occur. Significantly, "many effects" of debt financing, as contrasted to tax financing, bear upon the nature of the real and finan-

---

[15] E. J. Mishan, "How to Make a Burden of the Public Debt," *Journal of Political Economy*, December 1963, pp. 537–42.

[16] Ibid., pp. 540–42.

cial burdens of debt. For example, changes in consumption-saving patterns, capital formation, inheritance patterns, net worth positions, the types of governmental expenditures which are financed with the debt, and the like, essentially are "effects" which help through market adjustments to determine the ultimate real and financial "burdens."

Closely related to the desirability of some distinction (though possibly rough) between the terms "burden" and "effect" is the need to distinguish "primary" from "secondary" results. Essentially, *primary results* refer to *burdens*—real and financial—and *secondary results* refer to the *effects* of debt financing which will influence the nature of the burdens. Although the literature on debt does not make this precise distinction, the terms "primary burden" and "secondary effect" will be applied here for the reasons stated above.

In conclusion, it should be observed that the "orthodox" debt position regarding intergeneration transfers has essentially withstood the attacks made on it by the so-called "burden mongers." The dissenting arguments essentially consist of special cases involving specialized assumptions and definitions. Buchanan, for example, stresses freedom of choice for the individual and, in so doing, tends to define burden as an individual burden instead of an aggregate societal burden. The Bowen-Davis-Kopf and Musgrave approaches involve special, somewhat unrealistic, assumptions regarding inheritance. Modigliani underemphasizes (as do some others) the importance of "secondary effects" and their ability to influence debt burdens.

All of the dissenting arguments mentioned above are "logically consistent." However, in an overall sense, they do not appear to be comprehensive enough, nor realistic enough in terms of their assumptions, to repudiate the traditional analysis. In retrospect, the present generation does tend to bear the *direct, real* resource burden of debt-financed expenditures, but the "secondary" effects may well allow some *indirect* transference of the real burden through reduced capital stock, inefficient government investment, and the like. However, it is unlikely that any "significant" *net real burden* will be transferred under these circumstances because many government expenditures are for public and quasi-public goods which contain important positive externalities—some of which may be expected to accrue to future generations. Also, even though the intergenerational transfer of the *financial* burden of debt may occur, it must be similarly recognized that the later generations may be consuming some of the real benefits from earlier, debt-financed governmental investments. The failure to use a comprehensive approach to intergenerational debt equity, that is, the failure to consider fully important "secondary effects" including the social returns from public and quasi-public goods to later generations, has been a major weakness in contemporary debt analysis. The dissenters to the orthodox approach, though forcing the orthodoxy to state its position more precisely, have not themselves contributed a comprehensive approach. Moreover, Mishan's concern over the implications of this upon policy makers perhaps should not be taken lightly.[17]

FEDERAL DEBT AND INTEREST PAYMENTS IN RELATION TO NATIONAL ECONOMIC AGGREGATES

The ability to carry *private debt* is determined largely by the "wealth" and "earning power" of the consumer or business debtor. These considerations are less crucial, however, for *public debt* owed by a sovereign national government possessing the fiscal powers of taxation and money issuance. Nevertheless, the resource base of a nation, and the aggregate level of economic performance which results from that base, do reflect something about the ability of a nation to carry debt. Clearly, a nation with 200 million people can make interest payments and refinance a $400 billion national debt more safely if its productive resources allow it to produce a national output of $1.2 trillion as opposed, say, to one of $300 billion. It should be kept in mind, however, that the ability to carry central government debt may depend also upon such considerations as whether the debt is internally or externally held and the way that the debt is managed.

Table 27–3 displays the historical relationship of *gross federal debt*[18] to *national income.* Early in American history (1799), the (gross) federal debt was only 11 percent of national income but it increased to 32 percent by 1869, mostly because of the Civil War. This ratio had not changed appreciably by 1920, following World War I, at which time the federal debt was 31 percent of national income. Debt retirement during the 1920s, and a rising national income, caused the percentage to drop to 19 percent at the end of the decade in 1929. Then, the astounding drop in national income, production, and employment during the Great Depression (national income dropped from $87.8 billion in 1929 to $40.2 billion in 1933) caused the federal debt to skyrocket to 48 percent of national income in 1932. After the partial economic recovery achieved under Franklin D. Roosevelt's "New Deal" administration during the remainder of the decade, the federal debt still was 47 percent of national income in 1941, though it related to a considerably higher national income figure than in 1932. Then, following the tremendous wartime spending of World War II, the federal debt zoomed to 149 percent of national income by 1946.

Since 1946, the trend of the federal debt in relation to national

---

[17] Ibid., p. 542.
[18] See definition below.

TABLE 27-3
Gross Federal Debt* as a Percentage of National Income, Selected Years,
1799–1973 (current dollars)

Year	Gross Federal Debt (billions)	National Income (billions)	Federal Debt as a Percentage of National Income
1799	$ 0.08	$ 0.7	11%
1869	2.2	6.8	32
1920	24.1	79.1	31
1929	16.6	87.4	19
1932	19.2	39.6	48
1941	48.4	103.9	47
1946	268.1	180.3	149
1950	255.2	239.0	107
1960	286.3	414.5	69
1970	389.2	798.6	49
1973 (July)	459.0	934.9	49

* Includes both interest-bearing and noninterest-bearing debt including debt held by federal government agencies and trust funds.
Source: U.S. Treasury Department; U.S. Department of Commerce; earlier figures adapted from Paul Studenski and Herman E. Krooss, *Financial History of the United States* (New York: McGraw-Hill Book Co., 1963), Table 1 and Appendix.

income has been a declining percentage. From the 1946 ratio of 149 percent of national income, the federal debt ratio declined steadily to 107 percent of national income in 1950, to 69 percent in 1960, and still further to 49 percent in both 1970 and 1973. Indeed, the federal debt is not an increasing relative burden to the American people.

Table 27-4 relates *net federal debt* to *gross national product* for selected years during the twentieth century. *Net federal debt* refers to that debt which is held "outside" of the federal government—with debt held by the Federal Reserve System being placed in the "outside" category.[19] Hence, the difference between *gross* federal debt and *net* federal debt is the amount of debt held "inside" the federal government by federal agencies and by federal trust funds, which debt is included in the "gross" figure, but excluded from the "net" figure.

Since "GNP" by nature tends to be a higher figure than "national income," and "gross debt" a higher figure than "net debt," the "gross debt/national income" ratios in Table 27-3 tend to "overstate" the impact of federal debt on the economy while the "net debt/GNP" ratios in Table 27-4 tend to "understate" the impact. The "general trends" noted in the previous paragraphs, as indicated by Table 27-3, are verified again in Table 27-4. For example: (1) the effects of war, (2) the effects of the income decline of the Great Depression, and (3) the

---

[19] An alternative definition of *net debt*, not used in this book, would classify federal debt held by the Federal Reserve system as debt held "inside" the federal government.

TABLE 27-4
Net Federal Debt as a Percentage of Gross National Product, Selected
Years, 1902–1973 (current dollars)

Year	Net Federal Debt (billions)	Gross National Product (billions)	Net Federal Debt as a Percentage of GNP
1902	$ 1.2	$ 24.2*	5.0%
1913	1.2	40.3*	3.0
1922	22.5	74.0	30.4
1927	17.8	96.3	18.4
1932	18.9	58.0	32.6
1936	31.8	82.5	38.6
1940	36.2	99.7	36.3
1944	182.1	210.1	86.7
1946	240.3	208.5	115.3
1950	219.5	284.8	77.1
1955	223.8	398.0	56.2
1960	235.3	503.8	46.7
1965	261.2	749.9	34.8
1970	292.1	977.1	30
1973 (June)	334.7	1,271.0	26

* Estimates based upon data compiled by Simon Kuznets.
Source: *Historical Statistics of the United States—Colonial Times to 1957,* Department of
Commerce, p. 724; *Federal Reserve Bulletin,* August 1973, p. A–42.

declining ratio of federal debt to national economic performance data
since 1946 are evident in each table. However, Table 27–4 suggests,
in addition, that an increasing proportion of the federal debt is being
internally held by the federal government during 1973 as compared
to 1970 (the net debt/GNP ratio drops from 30 percent to 26 percent).
In fact, if a combination of the data in Tables 27–3 and 27–4 is selected
so as to relate "gross federal debt" to "GNP," the same 4 percent
increase in "internally-held" federal debt would be indicated.

In Table 27–5, it may be observed that the federal government's
interest payments on its debt have ranged from a high of 2.3 percent
to a low of 1.6 percent of gross national product for the years shown
since the end of World War II. Indeed, these ratios indicate no alarming
trend concerning the ability of the federal government, and the productive resource base of the nation, to carry the federal debt. In fact,
the trend is an improving one because the ratio of 2.3 percent was
realized in 1946 as opposed to a 1.7 percent figure in 1972.

However, the post–World War II ratios are higher than those for the
decade preceding the war. Federal interest payments rose from less
than 1 percent of gross national product at the beginning of the Great
Depression in 1930 to 1.1 percent in 1940, and then to 2.3 percent in
1946. The growth between 1930 and 1940 is due primarily to antidepression spending and that between 1940 and 1946 to World War

TABLE 27–5
Federal Interest Payments as a Percentage of Gross National Product,
Selected Years, 1930–1972 (current dollars)

Year	Federal Interest Payments (billions)	Gross National Product (billions)	Federal Interest Payments as a Percentage of GNP
1930	$ 0.7	$ 90.4	0.8%
1940	1.1	99.7	1.1
1946	4.8	208.5	2.3
1950	5.8	284.8	2.0
1960	9.3	503.8	1.8
1964	10.8	628.7	1.7
1968	13.7	865.7	1.6
1972	20.1	1,155.2	1.7

Source: U.S. Treasury Department; U.S. Department of Commerce.

II. The fact that the growth in interest payments in relation to gross national product is modest between 1940 and 1946, while the growth in federal debt was considerable, is explained by the rapid growth in GNP during the war as the economy's productive resources became fully employed for the first time in more than a decade.

DOES PUBLIC DEBT EVENTUALLY HAVE TO BE RETIRED?

This highly relevant question is related closely to the above discussion. The answer generally is "no," especially if the debt is an internal debt of the central government, Indeed, the public sector, like businesses and individuals, should honor and "repay" *specific* obligations at maturity. However, just as businesses under proper conditions can refinance and thus maintain or raise their total outstanding debt, so also can units of government refinance and continue to carry or expand debt. In fact, a sovereign national government such as the federal government can carry and expand debt much more safely than can either private business or state-local government. This is true because the federal government alone possesses the important financial power of issuing money. The power of the federal government (and the public sector) to tax, moreover, gives it a considerable debt-carrying advantage over business, including highly successful corporate giants such as the American Telephone and Telegraph Co. (A.T.&T.).

Although A.T.&T.'s total outstanding debt has increased many times over during recent decades, no one is suggesting that the company is threatened with bankruptcy and that part of its debt should now be retired. The company has much greater earning power today than it did several decades ago because it possesses a much larger stock of more technically efficient capital. In addition, A.T.&T.'s markets are more lucrative in terms of potential demand due to the high level of aggregate economic activity in the nation at the present time, and population growth. Yet, the debt of A.T.&T. is an external debt—it is owed to lenders outside the company. Consequently, if A.T.&T. need not retire its debt to prevent bankruptcy—and indeed it need not—why should the federal government retire its debt, particularly when it is largely an internal rather than an external debt and when the nation's economic ability to carry it in the form of productive resources and income-creating power is expanding more rapidly than the debt itself?

Despite the considerable ability of the federal government of the United States to carry and maintain its debt, Congress has long imposed a maximum limit on the size of the federal debt. This debt limit, known as the federal debt ceiling, was first established in 1917 at a maximum of $11.5 billion.[20] The ceiling has been changed on numerous occasions since that time with the direction of change, of course, being generally upward. It is argued by proponents of the debt ceiling device that it effectively constrains potentially excessive spending by the federal government. On the other hand, it may be argued that policymakers should be free to select the best alternative means, given the economic circumstances of the time, to finance incremental governmental expenditures. It might well be that the best financing alternative under prevailing economic conditions is "debt financing" rather than "tax" or "user price" financing. In this event, fiscal rationality would be distorted by the operation of a rigid debt ceiling.

STATISTICAL COMPARISON OF PRIVATE DEBT AND PUBLIC DEBT

Table 27–6 reflects, in absolute terms, the growth of total debt, both public and private, in the United States between 1930 and 1971. It may be observed that total debt at the end of the depression of the 1930s actually stood at a lower level than it had at the beginning of the Great Depression. This was caused by a decline in both the corporate and noncorporate individual components of private debt during the period. Then, an enormous rise in debt occurred during the first half of the 1940s due to World War II, almost all of the increase coming in the form of public debt owed by the federal component of the public sector. Since World War II, debt in the United States has continued to grow rapidly, but most of the debt growth during this recent era has been

---

[20] See the survey of federal debt ceiling history in *Federal Economic Policy* (4th ed.; Washington, D.C.: Congressional Quarterly Service, 1969).

TABLE 27–6
Public and Private Debt in the United States, Selected Years, 1930–1971 (billions of current dollars)

Year	Public Debt Federal Gross	Public Debt State and Local	Public Debt Total	Private Debt Corporate	Private Debt Individuals and Noncorporate Business	Private Debt Total	Total Public and Private
1930	$ 16.2	$ 18.5	$ 34.7	$107.4	$ 71.1	$ 178.5	$ 213.2
1935	28.7	19.3	48.0	89.8	49.3	139.1	187.1
1940	43.0	20.2	63.2	88.9	53.0	141.9	205.1
1945	258.7	16.6	275.3	97.5	54.7	152.2	427.5
1950	257.4	24.2	281.6	167.1	108.9	276.0	557.6
1960	286.3	67.1	353.4	361.7	286.7	648.4	1.001.8
1968	358.0	132.0	490.0	605.0	522.2	1,127.2	1,617.2
1971	424.1	168.0	592.1	827.0	636.0	1,463.0	2,055.1

Source: *Statistical Abstract of the United States*, 1965, 1969, 1972 (Washington, D.C.: U.S. Government Printing Office); U.S. Treasury Department.

in the form of private debt. By 1971, total U.S. debt (both public and private) stood at a figure in excess of $2 trillion.

Indeed, the years since World War II have thus witnessed some astonishing trends in the composition of total debt in the United States between the public and private sectors. Furthermore, significant changes have occurred within each sector. Table 27–7 presents the relevant data in percentage terms. While *total public debt* represented 64 percent of total U.S. debt in 1945, it declined to 50 percent in 1950 and to only 29 percent of total U.S. debt in 1971. Public debt thus declined in a short space of 26 years from approximately two thirds to approximately one third of total U.S. debt.

The considerable relative and absolute growth of private debt since World War II is explained by rapid growth both in corporate debt and in noncorporate business and individual debt. *Corporate debt,* for example, was 23 percent of total U.S. debt in 1945 but was 40 percent of the total debt in the nation in 1971. *Individual and noncorporate business debt* rose from 13 percent to 31 percent of total U.S. debt during the same period.

A trend even more surprising than the strong trend toward relatively greater private debt is revealed in a disaggregation of the total public sector debt for these years. While *gross federal debt* was 60 percent of total U.S. debt and 94 percent of total public debt in 1945, it constituted only 21 percent of total U.S. debt and 72 percent of total public debt in 1971. In the meantime, *state and local government debt* was rising from 4 percent of total U.S. debt to 8 percent of total U.S. debt between

TABLE 27-7
Distribution of Public and Private Debt by Categories (as a percent of total U.S. debt, selected years, 1945–71)

Year	Public Debt			Private Debt			Total Public and Private
	Federal Gross	State and Local	Total	Corpo-rate	Individ-uals and Noncor-porate Business	Total	
1945	60%	4%	64%	23%	13%	36%	100%
1950	46	4	50	30	20	50	100
1968	22	8	30	38	32	70	100
1971	21	8	29	40	31	71	100

Source: Computations based on data presented in Table 27–6.

1945 and 1971 and from 6 percent to 28 percent of total public debt during the same period.

The significant growth in private debt relative to public debt since World War II, and the sharply declining relative importance of federal government debt during this period, raises a question regarding present debt "misconceptions" and "mythology" in the United States. Why is the absolute growth in federal debt stressed as being "danger-ous" by so many people while the much more rapidly growing private debt and state-local debt are virtually ignored?[21] The answer lies appar-ently in the failure of many people to acquaint themselves with the facts.

COMPOSITION AND INSTITUTIONAL USES OF THE FEDERAL DEBT

In order to evaluate the influence of the federal debt upon the econ-omy, it is important to consider the "composition" of the debt with respect to "ownership" categories. In other words, who holds the fed-eral debt? Table 27–8 provides the basic data. First, it may be noted that only 13 percent of the debt is owed to foreign investors. Thus, 87 percent of the federal debt is *internal* debt. This fact is highly relevant to the earlier discussion concerning the ability of a nation to carry a large central government debt. Clearly, the fact that most of the federal debt in the United States is held internally helps to validate the ability of the nation to carry the debt.

An institutional breakdown of the composition of the federal debt,

---

[21] The author does not wish to suggest that the large private and state-local debts are necessarily undesirable.

TABLE 27–8
Ownership of Federal Debt, June 1973 (current dollars)

	Absolute Value ($ billions)	Percent of Total Federal Debt
Gross Debt	$458.2	100
Federal securities held by U.S. government agencies and trust funds (federal-held debt.)	123.4	27
Net Debt		
Federal securities held by:		
Federal Reserve Banks.	75.0	16
Commercial banks.	57.9	13
Mutual savings banks	2.4	1*
Insurance companies	5.7	1
Other corporations	12.0	3
State and local governments.	28.3	6
Individuals.	75.9	17
Foreign investors.	60.2	13
Miscellaneous	17.4	4
Total debt held outside Federal government (Net Debt).	334.8	73

* Less than one.

moreover, reveals that nearly 43 percent of the debt is held within the federal government if the Federal Reserve System is classified as "federal government." Furthermore, even if the strict definitions of "gross" and "net" debt are followed and the Federal Reserve System is excluded, the percentage held within the federal government is still a substantial 27 percent. Thus, of the federal gross debt of $458 billion as of June 1973, $123 billion or 27 percent is held by U.S. government agencies and trust funds such as the social security and interstate highway trust funds. The remaining 73 percent of the debt, including that part held by the Federal Reserve System, is held "outside of the federal government," in strict definitional terms.

Many important uses are rendered by the federal debt to the federal government. Treasury securities, for example, serve as an ideal investment source for federal trust funds. They allow no "conflict of interest" such as would inevitably occur if the federal trust funds were invested in the securities of private businesses. In addition, they are safe, relatively stable in value, and easily convertible to cash (highly liquid). Moreover, these securities serve the federal government importantly in their usage by the *Federal Reserve System,* the nation's central bank, since they are used as backing for Federal Reserve Notes, the nation's principal currency. Treasury securities, in addition, are used by the Federal Reserve System as the vehicle for conducting open-market operations, the primary technique used to affect the volume of money and credit in the economy. By buying and selling Treasury securities on the open market, the Federal Reserve System can affect purchasing power and interest rate levels in the economy in a manner consistent with the *Employment Act* objectives of full employment and stable prices. Since the federal debt became large during World War II, open-market operations have emerged as the most important monetary policy tool of the Federal Reserve System.

Individual investors, foreign investors, and *commercial banks* head the institutional list of federal debt holders outside the federal government (except for the Federal Reserve System). *Individual* investors hold 17 percent of the gross federal debt while foreign investors and commercial banks each hold 13 percent. As may be noted in the table, lesser amounts, in order of relative importance (except for "miscellaneous investors"), are held by state and local governments, business corporations (other than financial institutions), insurance companies, and mutual savings banks. Treasury securities serve the private sector as ideal investment assets, particularly for financial institutions, because of their tendency to be relatively stable in value, low in risk, and highly liquid.[22] Clearly, if the federal debt did not exist in something approaching its present size, many investors, both private and public, would have to undergo a painful transition to the acquistiton of other suitable assets for investment. In fact, in many instances it appears that equally suitable assets would not be available.

DEBT MANAGEMENT AND THE ECONOMIC EFFECTS OF FEDERAL DEBT

The existence of a large federal debt places considerable responsibility upon the U.S. Treasury Department to maintain the debt in an economically rational fashion. That is, a continual problem of refinancing maturing issues and of making interest payments on current issues must be faced. Moreover, net additions to total federal debt caused by deficit federal budgets require the sale of additional new securities. Furthermore, the maturities on the various outstanding issues must be staggered so as not to create excessive pressure for refunding at any one time. Obviously, in this regard it is in the interest of the Treasury to have a debt structure with the maturities as long-term in nature as possible. Importantly, the various debt-management activities will inevitably exert economic effects on the functional areas of economic

---

[22] Their liquidity falters, of course, in the event of a liquidity crisis.

activity. It is desirable that such activities be "rationalized" so as to promote, rather than retard, the economic goals of the society.

The most direct influence of debt-management policy is exerted on the *distributional* and *stabilization-growth* branches of economic activity. As observed earlier in the chapter, the pattern of "debt ownership" and its relationship to the "taxes" collected to maintain and repay the debt will be capable of yielding *redistributional* effects within the society. Debt management, of course, will participate in such influence primarily through the former technique since it is not directly related to the tax structure of the federal budget. Such redistribution may yield either a more equitable or a less equitable distribution of income and wealth in the society.

Although the potential distributional effects of debt management are worthy of attention, the primary influence of debt-management policy appears to be exerted in the realm of *aggregate economic performance.* In terms of its own primary function, it is only logical that debt-management policy attempt to fund the federal debt at the lowest possible interest cost. Moreover, it is equally logical to attempt to lengthen the maturities of the securities composing the debt structure. Yet, such policies may influence the employment, price level, balance of payments, and economic growth goals of the society in either a "favorable" or "unfavorable" manner. Furthermore, as discussed in the previous chapter, the manner in which securities are sold, that is, whether they are sold primarily to the Federal Reserve System, to commercial banks with or without excess loanable reserves, or to the general public, can result in "secondary" economic forces which may either neutralize or reinforce the expansionary multiplier effects of a deficit budget.

Moreover, regarding economic stabilization, the assertion is often made that the creation of debt by the central government is per se *inflationary.* Although this is not a necessary consequence, under certain conditions the full effect of the issuance of the securities may tend to produce upward price movements. It should be pointed out, however, that alternative arrangements such as printing money are even more likely to produce price increases. The conditions required for price inflation to occur under debt creation are complex. There are *two general cases* against which the alleged inflationary effects of debt creation must be examined—the case in which there is *unemployment* and the case in which *full employment* (or a reasonably close approximation) exists.

In the case of *unemployment,* the issuance of new debt by the government generally will not tend to produce inflation. However, the issuance of the new securities will tend to produce interest rate changes which, given highly elastic supply elasticities in a number of important industries, could cause the general level of prices to rise. The price rise, however, would likely be slight and the probability of the requisite conditions existing is slight. When the proceeds of the debt creation are spent, however, there are likely to be price changes, though a major portion of the adjustment will be in the direction of increased output and increased employment. In the case of approximate *full employment*, the issuance of the debt instruments generally will tend to cause a rise in interest rates and, unless the decrease in spending is equal to the increase in expenditure from the proceeds of the loan, the likely result will be a general price increase. Even in the full-employment case, however, it should be noted that price inflation does not necessarily follow as a consequence of debt creation.

An already-existing debt, as contrasted to a newly-issued debt, could be inflationary through a redistribution effect, under full-employment conditions, if the government obtains the funds for debt service by taxing those with a lower marginal propensity to consume than those who receive the interest payments.[23] This redistribution effect, however, is unlikely in practice to serve as a substantial cause of inflation, particularly since the evidence presented earlier on ownership of the debt suggests that relatively high-income (and hence relatively low-marginal propensity to consume) units are the primary recipients of the debt interest payments. A complete answer to this question demands an empirical investigation which requires knowledge of the income-wealth status of interest-receiving units as well as a knowledge of the structure of the tax system. In any event, it is extremely unlikely that this effect is of any great consequence in the United States.

Management of the federal debt, at times, is at "policy odds" with the monetary policy of the Federal Reserve System. An important objective in the Treasury Department's management of the federal debt is to finance and refinance it at the *lowest possible interest rates*. On the other hand, the economic stabilization objective of Federal Reserve monetary policy dicates *high interest rates* in times of "monetary inflation."[24] The conflict was resolved in favor of low Treasury interest costs from the end of World War II until March 1951. Since that time the Federal Reserve System has had greater, but not complete, discretion in conducting its monetary policy along proper stabilization lines. Meanwhile, debt-management policy was performed rather poorly during the 1950s by the Treasury. The low-interest goal was emphasized and the lengthening of maturities in debt structure was largely ignored.

Ideally, the Treasury would like to sell long-term securities at cyclical troughs or depressions, when interest rates are low, and it would like

---

[23] Even if full employment does not exist, given appropriate elasticities of supply in the industries in which the two groups spend their incomes, inflation could occur.

[24] Monetary policy tends to be less effective against "monopoly inflation."

to sell short-term securities at peak periods of the cycle, when interest rates are high, in order to minimize interest costs over a period of time.[25] This conflicts once again with Federal Reserve monetary policy because extensive Treasury borrowing during a depression would make money capital more scarce, thus raising interest rates and making private investment—which lags during a depression—even less attractive. In a period of monetary inflation, moreover, the Treasury would prefer to minimize long-term borrowing because of high interest rates. Yet, proper stabilization policy would require the Treasury to do considerable long-term borrowing in order to reduce the capital funds available to the private sector and thus reduce aggregate demand. At times, this dilemma has been resolved in favor of low interest costs to the Treasury rather than optimal stabilization policy.

A development in debt-management policy which has assisted the Treasury in its ever-present problem of debt refinancing is the technique of "advance refunding." By this approach, security holders are given the opportunity to exchange intermediate or long-term securities for newly issued securities at higher rates of interest several years before the present securities would mature. This helps to reduce the likelihood of shifts from Treasury debt to other assets at the time when the Treasury securities become due. In addition, advanced refunding helps to lengthen the maturity structure of the federal debt. However, these favorable effects have been largely offset in recent years by a federal statute which places an interest rate ceiling on new federal securities issued with maturities of more than seven years. Thus, the average length of the debt has been reduced. For example, in 1965 less than 69 percent of the federal debt represented by "marketable" securities was set to fall due within five years. By 1972, this percentage had increased to 81 percent with the average maturity being 3 years and 1 month as compared to 5 years and 4 months in 1965.

A much more radical change for the United States than "advanced refunding" would be to convert the debt structure of the federal government to "nonmaturing" debt. Such a debt instrument, known as a *consol,* may be defined as an obligation to pay a certain annual rate of interest on a debt instrument into perpetuity, that is, with no maturity date at all. A number of nations, including Great Britain, prominently use this technique. If the central government wishes to redeem a consol, it merely enters the security market and purchases it. Or it could sell additional consols in the face of continuing deficit budgets. However, if the debt were to remain at a fixed aggregate level, the only action necessary for the Treasury to undertake would be to maintain

---

[25] Treasury security offerings vary in maturities from 91-day *bills,* to one-year *certificates,* to *notes* ranging between 2- and 5-year maturities, to long-term *bonds* with durations up to 35 years.

the interest payments on the outstanding consols. It would have no necessity to redeem maturing debt or to sell new debt.

In general, it may be said that *debt-management policy* in the United States has been "unsatisfactory" in its relationship to aggregate economic goals. In other words, it has tended to exert negative nonneutral effects on the stabilization and economic growth goals of the society. "Minimally," debt-management policy should be neutral in its influence on these goals. "Ideally," it would promote these goals by exerting positive nonneutral effects.

Index

Index